Soviet Evangelicals
Since
World War II

Soviet Evangelicals Since World War II

Walter Sawatsky

Foreword by Gerhard Claas

HERALD PRESS
Kitchener, Ontario
Scottdale, Pennsylvania
1981

Canadian Cataloguing in Publication Data

Sawatsky, Walter, 1945-
    Soviet evangelicals since World War II

Bibliography: p.
Includes index.
ISBN 0-8361-1238-5 (bound). - ISBN 0-8361-1239-3 (pbk.)

1. Evangelicalism - Russia - History - 20th century.
2. Russia - Church history - 1917-   3. Church
and state - Russia - 1917-   I. Title.

BR1642.R87S28   269'.2'0947   C81-094121-X

SOVIET EVANGELICALS SINCE WORLD WAR II
Copyright © 1981 by Herald Press, Kitchener, Ont. N2G 4M5
    Published simultaneously in the United States by
    Herald Press, Scottdale, Pa. 15683
Library of Congress Catalog Card Number: 80-84856
International Standard Book Numbers:
    0-8361-1238-5 (hardcover)
    0-8361-1239-3 (paperback)
Printed in the United States of America
Design: Alice B. Shetler

81 82 83 84 85 86 10 9 8 7 6 5 4 3 2 1

Dedicated
to those believers
in the Soviet Union
whose faith and spirit
dominate this story
but whose names
are recorded in
a more permanent book.

Contents

Foreword

Soviet Evangelicals Since World War II gives an excellent view into the developments and present situation of evangelical churches in a socialist country.

Walter Sawatsky writes as one who is intimately acquainted with the material. He not only has studied the relevant literature and available information, but he knows the relationships from firsthand and personal experiences.

He knows very well the various and necessary attempts of the evangelicals in the USSR to unite not only spiritually but also organizationally, and he knows about the bitter experiences of splits and identity crises within the evangelical spectrum.

He makes clear that the law in the USSR guarantees religious freedom, but that Christians in carrying out their local church work have often been limited and circumscribed. This is particularly true regarding children's and youth work, and mission and evangelism. But at the same time he demonstrates how the evangelicals have zealously and with great sacrifice used their worship services and other avenues of witness for missionary activity.

Walter Sawatsky also acquaints the reader with the present differences of opinion and areas of conflict within the evangelical camp. These include the relationship between church and state and various related issues concerning a Christian's activity in the social and political realm, the question of conscientious objectors, the matter of the relationship to other non-Protestant churches and the World Council of Churches. He portrays how evangelicals for conscience' sake and out of religious conviction sacrifice and even endure persecution. But at the same time he convinces the reader that the church of Christ is not only possible in a socialist country like the USSR, but that the evangelicals in the Soviet Union have become in many ways a genuine model for Christians in the West!

In this sense *Soviet Evangelicals Since World War II* is more than a study of church history. It is in many parts actually a study book for questions of practical theology, forcing one to question one's own position and traditional forms. In doing this the book is a source of inspiration and food for thought.

Although the evangelicals in the USSR do not have the variety of church activities enjoyed elsewhere in the world and must limit their church life completely to the worship service, and although the majority of church members have received no theological training, and although every form of new member recruitment is prohibited, witness to Jesus Christ is always being carried out and the churches are continually growing.

The reason for this is certainly to be found in the personal decision of all evangelicals to follow Jesus and to commit their lives completely to the things of the Lord! Every individual member is a witness to Jesus Christ and committed to lead others to the Lord and His fellowship. Every individual is a "priest of God" pledged to walk with God and, by reading of the Bible and prayer, to make progress in personal sanctification and to become a model for others. Believers see themselves as members of the body of Christ, endeavoring by love, care, and prayer "to be there for the other."

Those who read this study book will be personally enriched and will thank God for the evangelicals in the Soviet Union, "for their work of faith, and labor of love, and patience of hope in our Lord Jesus Christ" (1 Thess. 1:3).

Gerhard Claas, General Secretary
Baptist World Alliance

> We need complete, truthful information.
> And the truth should not depend on whom it is to serve.
> —*V. I. Lenin*

Introduction: Who Are the Soviet Evangelicals?

The popular notion about religion in the Soviet Union follows one of two simple arguments. One is that there is a battle going on in the Soviet Union—a life-and-death struggle between the forces of evil and the forces of good. The evil forces are personified in the communist leadership which is capable of the most perfidious action to attain its ends. The good is personified in a church of heroic martyrs who refuse to submit to state demands. "Since it is a life-and-death struggle," as one proponent of this line of argument once told me, "there are no grey areas. The struggle must be viewed in sharp, clear, black and white terms." That has meant that the good Christians are sorted out from the bad Christians and the latter are linked with the forces of evil as being either weaklings, compromised Christians, apostates, or outright state agents.

Books presenting the alternative thesis are usually written to counter the first. Where the first thesis argues that there is no freedom, the second claims there is adequate freedom. Proponents will list the publication of Bibles, open churches in Moscow, and the claims of Soviet propaganda as evidence. Many religious leaders have been given official tours of the Soviet Union and have returned highly impressed with what they saw. The crowded churches, the overpowering piety of the believers, the fervent preaching of their hosts, all convinced them they had seen a strong church.

The evidence of a life-and-death struggle for faith in the Soviet Union is overpowering. The evidence for state persecution of religion is indisputable. At the same time, the evangelical church in the Soviet Union is a strong one. At present a large section of it is enjoying considerable freedoms. These believers provide clear evidence of growth and progress and they are convinced that they have a legitimate place in Soviet society. Even the Soviet state has demonstrated that it is not purely an agent for evil, but must be credited with major positive achievements. There has been impressive progress in efforts to feed, clothe, shelter and educate all Soviet citizens. The standard of living may not be comparable to America, but the problems were greater in 1917, while the national recovery was delayed by an expensive war in which 10 percent of the population (20 million people) perished. Not the least of the state's worries in attempting a positive transformation of the Russian empire was the possibility that the church represented an evil opposition against these reforms.

One must surely conclude that both theses are dangerously simplistic, of inadequate integrity. I have tried instead to present the Soviet evangelicals and their opponents in their complexity, including the contradictions. Because a serious struggle for the faith of people is going on, it is the responsibility of fellow believers elsewhere to take Soviet evangelicals seriously. To dismiss large numbers of them as hypocrites or phonies is to judge where we have received no mandate to do so. To worship them as super-heroes of the faith in effect denies them a part in common sinful humanity which is looking with hope to a God who came to save sinners. They are part of the same single body of Jesus Christ which has not always maintained a reputation as a healthy body. But this body, the church, has never lost its hope in Jesus, the head of the body.

It is time for a much more reflective, deliberate, and nuanced response to the Soviet evangelicals. This applies equally well to those wishing to help and to those wishing to learn from Soviet evangelicals. This book seeks to provide a reference base for such responses.

The Christian-Communist encounter is one of the basic events of the 20th century. It now seems apparent that increasing areas of the world will be attracted to socialism-communism in the future. Western Christians, especially evangelicals, find themselves ill-equipped intellectually, experientially, and practically to deal with such a situation creatively and redemptively.

Perhaps the reader will experience the story of the Soviet evangelicals as parable. It raises many issues for reflection—perhaps the most thought-provoking are the contradictions, the paradoxes, the ironies. In the 1920s their leaders persuaded the members to abandon pacifism in order to gain credibility with the Soviet government, in order to keep their evangelization program functioning. Here they badly misjudged Soviet intentions. When church life was resumed after World War II, the leaders stressed how patriotically they had fought in the war and how patriotically they were now supporting the peaceful intentions of Soviet foreign policy. Yet in doing so they found it difficult to regain their credibility among fellow believers abroad. There is also a deeper pacifist question which remains puzzling. Why should the state authorities regard pacifism or nonresistance as a dreaded form of dissent?

Repeatedly the story raises the issue of the relationship between the church and the state. What role is possible for a church under an authoritarian regime, a *Weltanschauungsstadt* where ideology is unfriendly to religion? What is the extent of the Christian's obligation to the state? What are the limits? What is the relationship between being faithful to the faith (in theology and practice) and seeking to survive? What is the church's responsibility in speaking truth to power in such a context? Is it worth repeated imprisonment as experienced by Georgi Vins and his associates? What does it cost the church if it opts for a selective conscience?

The Soviet evangelical experience sets one thinking about the way a church reflects its theology. Like evangelicals everywhere, they regard biblical authority and proclamation of a gospel of reconciliation as cardinal tenets. How does one transmit the faith in a context of societal hostility? Soviet evangelicals have devised contextually appropriate methods. They are growing numerically but some of their accommodations to the context make one wonder. How strong is their professed biblicism if the registered Baptists regularly stress Romans 13 and studiously ignore Acts 5?[1] That question is unfair, given our comfortable context, but is it not selective biblicism to insist on baptism by immersion but to reject foot washing? Is it not selective biblicism to insist on evangelism but to refuse members the right to speak in tongues? Perhaps the most uncomfortable aspect of this questioning is to observe how this selective biblicism was imported from evangelical America.

Pondering the story of the Soviet evangelicals inevitably leads us to compare faith in the Soviet Union with faith, or the loss of it, in the West. What kind of persecution most effectively destroys a religious movement? Do all-out antireligious campaigns achieve their goal? Does sustained pressure weaken, or does it really strengthen the church? Or is the desire for social approval the most debilitating? In the Soviet Union it costs something to be a Christian—that is clear to all. Perhaps Western churches might be more self-disciplined if we saw with greater clarity what Christian discipleship costs.

In contrast to the earlier Russian *Corpus Christianum*, many people have come to think of the Soviet Union (or even all of Eastern Europe) as the *Corpus Marxianum*. By that they mean the domain of godless communism where religion can no longer exist, neither by definition nor in fact. Well-informed observers, however, are wont to underline the degree to which the Soviet Union has struggled in vain to liberate itself from *Holy Rus*. Sir John Lawrence, who knows the Soviet Union intimately, affirmed unequivocally that "the number of believing Christians is now far higher than the number of believing Marxists, and many secret Christians are found in the ranks of the Communist Party."[2] Weekly church attendance is estimated to be at least four to five times higher than in Great Britain—that is, at least 20 percent of the Soviet population remains actively Christian.

That Old Russia lived in a perpetual aura of holy incense has been acknowledged by numerous writers. "To be Russian is to be Orthodox" is an oft-repeated way of acknowledging the power of Christian faith on Russian culture and society. But religious dissent is also a part of the long tradition of Holy Rus. The evangelical movement described in this book had its direct beginnings in the nineteenth century through foreign Pietist influences but the ground had been "prepared for them by the deep spirituality of the Russian Orthodox God-seekers."[3] Were the evangelical movement a mere foreign importation, it would have been eliminated as easily as the churches of the foreign colonists were. Today the evangelicals are "the most rapidly growing section of Russian Christianity,"[4] although they will probably continue to remain a minority church.

This growth is due to at least two factors. Soviet evangelicals continue to be part of an international evangelical movement which has shown itself remarkably adaptable to fitting the local context while maintaining uniformity on essential issues of faith and witness. Even in the Soviet Union the evangelicals are a multinational movement, a quality that Orthodoxy lacks. In this multinational aspect, the evangelicals are similar to the Communist Party. Perhaps even more significant, in the eyes of one seasoned scholar, is the fact that the type of people who are attracted to Soviet evangelical churches are the sort of people "who would be attracted to the Communist Party itself."[5] This factor goes far in explaining why "the hostility of the regime towards the Baptists is out of all proportion to a movement whose adherents, according to official figures, number one-quarter of one percent of the total population."[6]

This book is both a history and a descriptive analysis. After summarizing the early history in the first chapter, I have tried to communicate the deeply emotional character of the renewal movements through a composite of individual stories. Because church growth patterns were established then, it seemed fitting to describe present methods of evangelism in the second chapter. In 1944 a unique evangelical church union was formed, thanks to state assistance. Since unity, or rather the struggle for it, runs like a golden thread through the entire story, I have analyzed the little known 1944 unity congress in some detail. Another little known characteristic of the Soviet evangelicals was their pacifism. To understand their present, officially encouraged peace activity, a careful look at the way they've changed from pacifists to militarists to peace people (but not pacifists) seems vital.

The Khrushchev-initiated campaign against religion (1959-64) left shock waves that have not yet disappeared. In Chapter 5 I have sought to summarize the state's policy shifts toward religion during the past 20 years—the chapter can also serve as one of the most recent attempts to analyze overall Soviet policy toward religion. Chapters 6-10 treat the Khrushchev impact on the evangelicals: the beginning of a major split in the All-Union Council of Evangelical Christians-Baptists, and the subsequent, less than successful attempts at reunification. Part of the *Initsiativniki* story has been told in earlier publications. I have brought it up-to-date and revised it in light of more recent information that has become available. A thorough discussion of the registered Baptist response to the *Initsiativniki* challenge has not been attempted before.

The final third of the book is again more thematic. The intense competition between preacher and atheist for the loyalty of the young people deserves its own chapter as do also the principles on which evangelicals base their theology. The Soviet evangelicals are quite unique in their character, but they also have strong ties to fellow evangelicals abroad. These strong ties are both encouraged and discouraged by the state. Since these ties may be of personal interest to many readers, I have sought to evaluate registered Baptist relations with the World Council of Churches, the Baptist World Alliance, and other bodies. Similarly, since many missions to Eastern Europe claim to be helping Soviet evangelicals, their policies and practices merit scrutiny. In fact there is so much controversy about these missionary societies, that a critical assessment seems long overdue. Hopefully, my assessment will not lead to further controversy. Chapter 15 on the new frontiers includes details of the latest Baptist All-Union Congress held in Moscow in December 1979.

Some readers will wish for a more detailed prehistory. That would have exceeded space limitations, however, and would also have drawn attention away from the postwar period which is the least understood. Two recent studies adequately cover the history of the Baptists and of the Evangelical Christians for the prewar period. Hopefully, these will both be published in English.[7] John B. Toews's recent Menno Simons lectures on "The Mennonite Experience in Russia—the Twentieth Century"[8] may fill that gap in the story on the Mennonites. I plan to devote more attention to the Russian Mennonite experience after World War I in a sequel to this book.

The limited attention to the period before 1945 was very deliberate in order to stress a point. By the late thirties, the churches had virtually ceased to exist as institutions. When the evangelical union was born in 1944, it sought to stress its continuity with the past, but it was very much a new creation. The new evangelical church reflected a concern for the basic essentials of the gospel. If an individual was born again, if he accepted the authority of the Bible, then he was accepted as a fellow believer. The more detailed practical theology that developed as the years passed emerged in a Soviet context. Although evangelicals were variously labeled Baptists, Pentecostal, or Mennonite, it is deceptive to immediately assume they are like their counterparts in the West. It is a major assumption of this study that these believers must first be understood in their commonality as Soviet evangelicals and only secondarily according to their denominational labels. Denominational labels (apart from the Baptists) soon came to have the function of a loyalty declaration with little specific denominational content. I have also consciously used the adjective "Soviet" because, with minor exceptions, they consider their home and their future to be in the Soviet Union, which is more inclusive than to be Russian, Ukrainian, Latvian, or one of the many other national subgroupings.

My use of the word "evangelical" also needs an explanation. I sought an inclusive term that would embrace more than "Baptists" or "Pentecostals" and that lacks the pejorative character which is still attached to the word "sect." The sociological designation "sect" can also refer to numerous religious organizations not included in this study. There was also a very conscious attempt not to restrict the treatment to a history of the All-Union

Council of Evangelical Christians-Baptists even though their story looms large in the following pages. Rather, I sought to acknowledge that some evangelicals had joined one of the two competing Evangelical Christian-Baptist unions, while others remained institutionally autonomous though still affirming a common confession of faith. Some attained registration, others have still not attained it, or lost it, or reject registration in principle. These various attitudes are found without distinction among Baptists, Pentecostals, or Mennonites.

The Soviet Evangelicals have their counterparts in the American evangelical experience. As in America, the term "evangelicals" refers more to a movement than to a denomination.[9] Both had their more immediate birth after World War II. Both were heavily influenced by such antecedents as fundamentalism and dispensationalism and even earlier by the revivalism of Methodism and other free churches. The revivalism of Charles Finney, who so strongly influenced the subsequent history of American revivalism, represented a coalition of two theological traditions: "American Puritanism, which was the bearer of orthodox Calvinism, and Wesleyan holiness, which was Arminian in its theology."[10] Russian Baptists and Evangelical Christians were strongly influenced by the holiness movement as it crystallized in annual conventions in Keswick, England, beginning in 1875. American Keswick teachers like D. L. Moody, R. A. Torrey, and A. B. Simpson were the direct and indirect teachers of Russian evangelicals.[11]

The reader will find little about the Adventists, Jehovah's Witnesses, about the Molokany and Dukhobory, or even about the German Lutherans or Catholics. All deserve their due attention which proved impossible here. In any case only the Adventists and German-speaking Lutherans and Catholics have enough in common with the groups treated to be labeled evangelicals. Regrettably, information on them is extremely limited. The Adventists experienced a split in 1924 when they, too, were forced to issue a loyalty statement. Those who refused, the so-called Reform Adventists, still exist today under the able leadership of Vladimir Sholkov. Since 1976 Adventist *Samizdat* has become available in the West. In 1979 state authorities tried to crush them with special severity by sentencing 83-year-old Sholkov to five years. He died in a prison camp in Yakutia on January 27, 1980.[12] The registered Adventists are in the process of forming an officially approved union of their churches.

Trained as a historian, I have sought to apply accepted rules of objectivity in my research. It is of course impossible to write without bias, but it may help the reader if the author's values are stated explicitly. Our understanding of the Soviet religious situation suffers from ignorance. There is a language barrier, true, but a greater barrier has been the withholding of information from each other for fear the other would not understand, would condemn, or would put one in danger. This book is written in the first place for Christians who will not forget their fraternal responsibilities. When the Apostle Paul described his own work he declared that "we put aside all secret and shameful deeds; we do not act with deceit, nor do we falsify the word of God. In the full light of truth we live in God's sight and try to commend ourselves to everyone's good conscience" (2 Corinthians 4:2, GNB). Applied to Soviet evangelical history, this meant for me that by simply laying out the facts for all to see, I might in the long run contribute to strengthening the Soviet evangelical movement and to enabling Western believers to identify with their fellows in the Soviet Union. That has meant discussing many painful issues, yet never feeling completely certain that my treatment was fair in every case. Because the amount of information was often massive, it proved to be difficult to make a fair selection. Perhaps the book will stimulate discussion that can eventually also lead to a better book.

I have also introduced my own Anabaptist-Mennonite viewpoints rather specifically along the way. These viewpoints differ from "established evangelicalism" in emphasis—noticeable in such areas as discipleship, concept of the church and nonviolence.[13] I feel close kinship with the "New Evangelicals," one of whom in particular has helped me see the potential value of applying an Anabaptist theological grid to the Soviet evangelicals.[14]

This book is based on a broad spectrum of primary printed materials, personal information and experience, and unprinted materials. I have combed through the official Baptist journal *Bratskii Vestnik* (Fraternal Messenger) carefully for informational tidbits that gradually assumed a more composite character. The uncensored writings of Soviet Reform Baptists and others, which are now widely referred to as *Samizdat*, provided different and detailed information. Both *Bratskii Vestnik* and the *Samizdat* writers tend to stick to the facts but they perceive them differently.

I have also utilized collections of newspaper clippings at Keston College and elsewhere for supplementary information. Keston College, where I began this study, also has a good collection of literature from the Soviet atheist press, which proved helpful in corroborating facts and in reflecting official state attitudes. Although it was not always deemed prudent to cite chapter and verse, information and understanding gained from examining the files of the Baptist World Alliance and the Mennonite

Central Committee were of great importance. Even more valuable was the information obtained through systematic interviews which I have been conducting since 1974 with Soviet Germans who have immigrated to West Germany in recent years. Often this material could not be quoted in order not to betray a confidence. The usual secondary literature has been listed in the bibliography.

The Soviet evangelical story will evoke many emotions in the sympathetic reader. Often the story is sad. There is conflict. Sometimes there are heroes, other individuals (including Christians) could be designated villains, but the majority are "the meek" whom Jesus promised the earth. That promise seems to have suffered a long-delayed fulfillment in the Soviet Union. But if I were to highlight one emotion dominating this story, it is that of a triumphalism because the church (of which the evangelicals are a part) is God's movement. Negatively stated, one notes a growing exasperation and *de facto* surrender by atheist leaders to this reality.

> *Walter Sawatsky*
> East/West Research Office
> Neuwied, West Germany

Notes to Introduction

1. Similarly, in Reform Baptist literature, references about the nature of obedience to state authority according to Romans 13 seldom appear, while Acts 5—"We ought to obey God rather than men"—has become their slogan.

2. John Lawrence, Reviewing *Christianity and the World Order* by Edward Norman in *Religion in Communist Lands*, VII, 3 (Autumn), 1979, p. 181.

3. Walter Kolarz, *Religion in the Soviet Union* (London: Macmillan & Co., 1961), p. 283.

4. John Lawrence, "Observations on Religion and Atheism in Soviet Society," *RCL*, I, 4-5 (July-Oct. 1973), p. 23.

5. William C. Fletcher, "Protestant Influences on the Outlook of the Soviet Citizen Today," in Fletcher & Strover, Eds. *Religion and the Search for New Ideals in the USSR* (New York: Frederick A. Praeger, 1967), p. 81.

6. *Ibid.*, p. 64.

7. Wilhelm Kahle, *Evangelische Christen in Russland und der Sowjetunion* (Wuppertal: Oncken-Verlag, 1978) and Paul Steeves, "The Russian Baptist Union, 1917-1935: Evangelical Awakening in Russia," unpublished PhD dissertation, University of Kansas, 1976.

8. Lectures delivered October 1979 in Bethel College, Kansas.

9. A good introduction to the evangelicals, who represent approximately 34 percent of the American public, is David F. Wells and John D. Woodbridge, eds.,

The Evangelicals (Grand Rapids, Mich.: Baker Book House, Revised Edition, 1977).

10. C. Norman Kraus, "Evangelicalism: The Great Coalition," in Kraus, ed., *Evangelicalism and Anabaptism* (Scottdale, Pa.: Herald Press, 1979), p. 43.

11. Vinson Synan, "Theological Boundaries: The Arminian Tradition," in Wells & Woodbridge, p. 46. This article provides an excellent introduction to the Holiness and Pentecostal traditions.

12. *Keston News Service*, March 29, 1979. For background see Katharine Murray, "Soviet Seventh-Day Adventists," *Religion in Communist Lands*, V, 2 (Summer, 1977), pp. 88-93; Marite Sapiets, "V. A. Shelkov and the True and Free Seventh-Day Adventists of the USSR." *RCL* VIII, 3, 1980, pp. 201-217.

13. For an excellent summary of various subgroupings of evangelicals, as well as a brief history and critique, see Richard Quebedeaux, *The Young Evangelicals* (New York: Harper & Row, 1974). See especially pp. 28-41 for a description of "Establishment Evangelicalism" and "New Evangelicalism." Quebedeaux states that all evangelicals affirm three major theological principles: "1. The complete reliability and final authority of Scripture in matters of faith and practice; 2. The necessity of a *personal* faith in Jesus Christ as Savior from sin and consequent commitment to him as Lord; 3. The urgency of seeking actively the conversion of sinners to Christ." P. 4.

14. Ronald J. Sider, "Evangelicalism and the Mennonite Tradition," in C. Norman Kraus, ed., *Evangelicalism and Anabaptism*, pp. 149-168.

Acknowledgments

My first acknowledgment must be to the many people who lived through the story of this book personally and who graciously shared their intimate spiritual memories with me. Their words appear on many pages even though I was not at liberty to name the source specifically. I acknowledge also those persons who have written and transported the vast amounts of *Samizdat* materials which are indispensable to a full story. On numerous trips to the Soviet Union believers have been incomparably hospitable and I am grateful as well to friendly authorities who were persuaded to accede to some of my requests.

The strongest encouragement and unfailing support at every stage came from Peter J. Dyck, longtime European Secretary for Mennonite Central Committee with deep ties to the Soviet Union. This association I will always treasure. In addition to Peter Dyck's solicitous attention to the text, I had the pleasure of working with an editorial committee consisting of Robert Kreider, Cornelius Krahn, Frank H. Epp, Cornelius J. Dyck, and Lawrence Klippenstein. Their careful criticisms and suggestions helped me to think deeper and write better. I also received helpful detailed criticism of the text from Michael Rowe of Keston College and on chapter 12 from Keith Parker of the Baptist Theological Seminary in Rüschlikon. I also thank Michael Bourdeaux of Keston College for granting free access to the wealth of materials at Keston College; in fact, this book began during my three-year stay there. Many others, too numerous to mention, stimulated my thinking and provided helpful information. That some mistakes and bad judgments persisted must be attributed to the failings of the author alone.

For the many hours of typing, preparation of card files, and other technical assistance I am heavily indebted to the voluntary labors of Dorothy Wiens, Rosie Yoder, and Lydia Penner, the latter typing the bulk of the manuscript in several drafts. The skilled editorial aid of Paul M. Schrock and his colleagues at Herald Press is acknowledged gratefully.

The creation of a book invariably becomes a major painful process deeply affecting the writer's family. Were it not for the way Natasha and Alexander humanized me and above all that my wife, Margaret, continued to believe in the project, this book might not have been born. I thank Margaret not only for this support but also for the personal labor she contributed and the experiences we were privileged to share together in the Soviet Union.

Neuwied, West Germany
September 8, 1980

List of Abbreviations

To provide appropriate English equivalents for many Russian names, words, and phrases is virtually impossible. Not only do the Russians employ a different alphabet (the Cyrillic), the decades of socialistic-communist government have produced a wealth of Soviet bureaucratic jargon for which no Western equivalents exist because such social arrangements do not exist. The acronym, for example, is so endemic that it takes an effort to recall that a *Kolkhoznik* is an abbreviation for a person living on *kollektivnyi khoziastvo* (collective management or farm).

I have followed the transliteration rules of the American Library of Congress with minor exceptions. Names well known in the West such as Jacob (instead of Iakov) Zhidkov and Alexander (instead of Aleksandr) Karev are anglicized. Where deemed appropriate, German names are given in the original spelling. An exception is Georgi Vins, whose transliterized spelling has become widely accepted, instead of the Germanic, Wiens.

Church polity differs by denomination and by country. It would seem more American to speak of "Pastor" Michael Zhidkov and "Superintendent" or "Bishop" Jacob Dukhonchenko, but that would lead the reader to assume unwarranted similarity with Western organizational models. I have therefore retained the literal translations of "presbyter" (for an ordained leading minister) and "senior presbyter" (for an administrator of a regional grouping of churches). These are derived, in any case, from the original Greek and perhaps closer to New Testament Christianity. Another difficult term is *upolnomochnyi* (plenipotentiary), the official title of the local official for the Council of Religious Affairs. Here I have tried to use the cumbersome "plenipotentiary" as infrequently as possible, using the more vague "state official" which lacks the tone of power that "plenipotentiary" does. For purposes of clarity I have retained *orgkomitet* (organizing committee) to designate the official leadership of the Reformers during the transitional period 1962-65.

I have tried to avoid calling the two major unions the "Russian Baptist Union" and the "Reform Baptist Union." The latter is acceptable and often used but not their own term. They prefer "Council of Churches," which for a Westerner, however, means the World Council of Churches and its national equivalents. The larger union is neither only Russian nor only Baptist, hence to call them "Russian Baptists" as has become common, simply reinforces the elements of power in that union. I therefore chose the letter abbreviations AUCECB and CCECB which have also become common and are indeed widespread Russian acronyms. The following is a list of abbreviations, including the most frequently cited journals that have been used.

AUCECB—All-Union Council of Evangelical Christians-Baptists
BWA—Baptist World Alliance
CCECB—Council of Churches of Evangelical Christians-Baptists
CRA—Council for Religious Affairs
CPC—Christian Peace Conference (Prague)
ECB—Evangelical Christian Baptists
EBF—European Baptist Federation
KGB—Committee of State Security (Soviet secret police)
USSR—Union of Soviet Socialist Republics
RSFSR—Russian Soviet Federated Socialist Republic
BL—*Bratskii Listok* (Fraternal Leaflet), official CCECB journal
BV—*Bratskii Vestnik* (Fraternal Messenger), official AUCECB journal
EBPS—European Baptist Press Service
EPS—Ecumenical Press Service
G2W—Glaube in der 2ten Welt
G2W ID—Glaube in der 2ten Welt Informations Dienst
GNB—Good News Bible
KNS—Keston News Service
MCC—Mennonite Central Committee
MQR—*Mennonite Quarterly Review*
NiR—*Nauka i religiia* (Science and Religion), largest Soviet atheist journal
RCDA—Religion in Communist Dominated Areas
RCL—Religion in Communist Lands
VNA—Voprosy nauchnogo ateizma (Questions of Scientific Atheism)
WCC—World Council of Churches

Soviet Evangelicals
Since
World War II

It would be ridiculous . . . if the Party did not take into account that the history of the sectarians is a history of uninterrupted persecution.

—*Mikhail Kalinin*
President of the Soviet Union at
the 1924 Party Congress

1 Beginnings and Patterns: Persecution Has Become Hereditary

Under cover of darkness on August 20, 1867, Martin Kalweit, a German from Lithuania only recently baptized himself, immersed Nikita Isaevich Voronin in a small stream not far from Tbilissi in the Caucasus. This marks the official date for the beginning of the evangelical movement in the Russian Empire. By 1905 there were 86,538 Baptists and 20,804 Evangelical Christians. By the end of the Civil War membership had increased to 100,000 Baptists and 250,000 Evangelical Christians. At the height of the movement in 1929 the movement had grown to approximately 500,000 baptized evangelicals, representing together with family members over four million people. The growth rate had been phenomenal. The evangelicals had taken seriously the motto: "Every Baptist a missionary!"

Yet in 1930, the Baptist Union reported that its churches had only 50,124 members, and another source indicates that the total number of evangelicals was down to 250,000 by the mid-thirties.[1] By the autumn of 1929, over 100 Baptist preachers were known to have been arrested; all of the regional Baptist unions had been closed because of the arrest of their officials. Some of them, including the central offices in Moscow, were reopened temporarily but the Russian Baptist Union officially came to an end in 1935. Those few ministers who were not arrested or did not go underground managed to join forces with the competing Evangelical Christian Union which continued to maintain a tenuous existence.[2]

The "Mistakes" Factor

For many evangelicals, the Great October Revolution of 1917 had meant hope. As one of the first decrees of the new Soviet state, Lenin signed a decree separating the churches from the state. It sounded like a charter of liberties for all the religious groups that had seen discrimination and persecution under the old partnership of tsar and Orthodoxy. As a result, the evangelicals embarked on a decade of intense activity that produced the amazing growth statistics just cited. It was their golden decade.

They grew so rapidly that the new rulers of Russia, the Bolshevik leaders of the Communist Party, became alarmed. The major party newspaper, *Pravda*, complained that "the clergy and sectarians are developing a frenzied propaganda, and we should be deceiving ourselves if we asserted that only old men and women go to church."[3] The reason for their alarm was reiterated in the other major government newspaper, *Izvestiia*, on April 24, 1929. "Religious ideology," it stated, "is one of the chief obstacles in the path of the socialist reconstruction of the country." That was party conviction, proved by the experience of trying to subdue the Russian Orthodox Church during the first years of Soviet power. Was the doctrine to be expanded to apply with equal vigor to all religious groups?

The irony of Soviet evangelical history is that the first decade of Soviet power, the evangelicals' golden decade, was followed by a decade of such severe persecution that it remains their red or bloody decade without peer. Where this first decade was associated with the tactical tolerance of Lenin, the second was Stalin's decade. The contrast was in no way sweetened by discovering that Joseph Vissarion Dzhugashvili (Stalin) also traced his personal origins to a little town near Tiflis. Did the fact that he had attended a church school and had been expelled from a theological seminary help account for his antireligiosity? Evidence is too limited for even Stalin's biographers to venture a thorough answer, but the personal stamp of Stalin rests heavily on the terror and the purges of the 1930s which included thousands, if not millions, of believers among its estimated eight million victims.[4] The purges came in waves, focusing on various strata of society, decimating the party and the army so that at the outbreak of World War II the latter had only a battered remnant with which to meet the Nazi invaders. Many others were included in these purges since the greatest number of victims came from the non-party people, many of them denounced without cause as the atmosphere of terror took over. Always there were religious persons among those liquidated but there were also little wavelets focusing on the clergy. For evangelicals the major arrest waves came in 1929-30, 1933-35, and 1937-38.

These purges refer primarily to arrests, imprisonments, deportations, and executions, but the antireligious campaign was multidimensional. It coincided with Stalin's accession to full power by 1928 and the decision to abandon the New Economic Policy (which encouraged the small entrepreneur) in favor of an all-out collectivization drive. Religious people represented organizations expected to resist collectivization and must therefore be eliminated. This had been attempted through reeducation including the creation of a League of Militant Godless in 1925,[5] but until tougher administrative measures were added, there was little success. The result of this major assault on the churches was that official religious life had virtually ceased to exist by 1938.

Then came another shift during the war when the antireligious campaign was terminated and churches could be reopened. Stalin permitted the creation of a new centralized church structure for evangelicals as well as for the Orthodox Church.[6] Essentially Soviet evangelicals now began a new history under new conditions which also brought new problems. But the continuing conflict with the state and its attendant varieties of persecution remained. As recently as 1979, Soviet officials denied that there had been or is persecution of believers. They prefer a more neutral nomenclature, Lenin telling the Comintern Congress in 1922 that "it is certain that we have done and will do a lot of stupid things." And he went on:

Why do we do "stupid things"? In the first place, because we are a backward country. Secondly, education in our country is minimal. Thirdly, we are getting no help. Not one civilized country is helping us. On the contrary, they are all working against us. Fourthly, our state *apparat* is to blame. We took over the old state *apparat* and that was our misfortune.[7]

Lenin's reasons for the "stupid things" or "mistakes" are all significant factors to remember in seeking to understand the Soviet evangelicals. But that still leaves many "mistakes" that were unnecessary but which have left their mark on church-state relationships, nevertheless.

This persistent problem of state persecution makes it difficult to gain a proper perspective on the present situation of Soviet evangelicals. Some Soviet evangelicals regularly provide documentary evidence that state persecution of believers is continuing to the present moment. Official spokesmen for the All-Union Council of Evangelical Christians-Baptists are regularly optimistic and emphasize that only during the Soviet period were they able to produce Bibles and songbooks and conduct theological courses.[8] At present they emphasize: "We have never had it so good."[9] Both claimants are truthful in what they say; it is the intended general interpretation that is problematic.

Various Beginnings

To choose 1867 as starting date for the Russian evangelicals is to start late. If Nikita Voronin was the first Russian fruit of evangelical teaching, there surely was a seeding and germination period before. Even if there are no direct links, certain emphases in the long history of the Russian sectarians provide the progenitors of the evangelicals. For example, when the writings of the 18th-century freethinker Grigorii Skovoroda were published recently,[10] one leading Russian Baptist called him an evangelical because of his emphasis on biblicism. To explain the beginnings in the 1860s, we must note three specific influences: Pietism, the Russian Bible, and the Molokan sect. Yet these influences were appealing because the decay within Russian Orthodoxy had become so apparent.

Generally speaking, the Russian Orthodox Church was in a sorry condition by the middle of the nineteenth century. Since the church reform of Peter the Great in 1721 the state had managed to convert the church administration into a sub-department of the state. The Orthodox Church could claim very impressive achievements in education, in the piety of the individual monks and in the liturgy, but the spiritual voice of the church had become muted. A modern translation of the Bible was not completed till 1876. The church had not managed to raise its voice against the institution of serfdom, which was finally abolished in 1861, although the lot of the peasant did not improve significantly through emancipation. And at the parish level where a word from the church was most needed, the clergy were generally in disrepute. Prince S. P. Gagarin, governor of Astrakhan in the 1860s, declared that "our clergy are uncultured, uncouth and needy,"[11] most of them forced to earn a living from the soil like their parishioners, yet overburdened with innumerable bureaucratic tasks imposed on them by various governmental offices. The governor of Perm province declared that the Old Believer schism and the sectarians drew their strength

from the fact that the Orthodox clergymen exercise no moral influence over the people, that they are prejudiced, dull, and too strictly scholastic in their attitudes. . . . In private life the motives of the clergy are mercenary and selfish, of which the masses are well aware, whereas in the Schism the success of the leaders depends largely on the high standards of their life and character.[12]

There was further the simple fact that Orthodoxy had not kept pace with population growth and movements. Where there were 31,333 churches in 1840 with 116,728 clergy, by 1890 the number of churches had increased to 40,205, but the number of clergy had dropped to 96,892. That meant that whereas there were 71 churches per 100,000 inhabitants of Orthodox faith in 1840, by 1890 there were only 56. The ratio of clergy to 100,000 parishioners had dropped more drastically from 265 in 1840 to 137 in 1890.[13]

What brought new life to Russian Orthodoxy in the early nineteenth century and also triggered the birth of evangelicalism was Protestant Pietism. The post-Reformation period in Western Europe is sometimes described as a time of cold confessionalism. As a reaction to it, Christians in various Protestant confessions turned to devotionally and practically oriented writers such as Jakob Böhme and later Jung Stilling. This Pietist movement preceded and partly coincided with the birth of evangelicalism in Germany and England.[14]

Pietism came to Russia at the beginning of the nineteenth century and made a major impact because it was vigorously fostered by the tsar and his leading minister, Alexander Golitsyn.[15] Dynamic preachers from Württemberg (a Pietist center in South Germany) came to Russia, proclaiming the reality of a personal conversion and a sense of devotional nearness to God. Russian high society flocked to hear the preachers, met in each other's salons for Bible study and prayer, some even experiencing ecstasies.[16] Pietist literature was translated into Russian and widely distributed. Increasingly it became accessible to the lower classes, for the Pietists became active proponents of literacy training, for example, through the Lancastrian school movement. Other upper-class Russian Pietists started visiting prisons and trying to reform the prisoners, sometimes also the prison system.

Above all, the Pietist leaders organized the Russian Bible Society, which by 1819 had translated the New Testament into modern Russian. The Bible Society was closed by tsarist order in 1826 when Orthodox reaction set in, but Bible translation and distribution never ceased entirely. A translation of the entire Bible was finally completed in 1876 and circulated by the British and Foreign Bible Society even though the official translation approved by the Orthodox Church did not appear till 1882. The Bible Society was reopened in 1831 to serve the non-Russian peoples of the Russian Empire.[17]

Bible colporteurs again traveled about the countryside and, as a more liberal climate returned in the 1860s, they also began selling books to Russian-speaking peasants. One such Bible colporteur was Martin Kalweit, the man who baptized the first Russian Baptist. This was a life for heroes. The colporteur would arrive in a village, locate the individuals who could read to sell them some books, or he would read to a small group of curious people. Often he had to leave quickly to escape the local constable trying to arrest him for proselytizing among Orthodox believers, which was forbidden. Jacob Zhidkov recalled his own youth spent with his grandparents while his own father traveled the countryside with a rucksack full of books. As a small child he had met two-year-old Polia Kapustinskaia, whose family needed temporary lodging before joining their father S. E. Kapustinskii, who had been exiled to the Trans-Caucasus region because of his work for the Bible Society in Orel Oblast. Years later Jacob and Polia were reunited again, this time in marriage.[18]

The seedbed having been prepared by Pietism and by Bible colporteurs, evangelicalism at first had its greatest success among the Molokans, a purely Russian sect which began in the mid-eighteenth century. One of their leading preachers was Simeon Uklein of Tambov, who emphasized the primacy of Holy Scripture, opposed the sacramentalism of the state church, rejected all militarism, and stressed the equality of all men.[19] The Molokans differed from Russian Baptists primarily in that they rejected baptism. Baptists therefore won converts among them by persuading Molokans about the scriptural admonition to baptism. Major leaders in the evangelical-Baptist movement, such as Nikita J. Voronin, Dei I. Mazaev, Vasili G. Pavlov, Il'ia A. Goliaev, and Ivan S. Prokhanov, as well as Jacob Zhidkov and Alexander Karev, had Molokan backgrounds.

Since the war, official Russian Baptist historians have frequently compared the evangelical movement in the Soviet Union to an ever-widening stream fed initially by three tributaries with several tributary streams joining subsequently. The way such tributaries fused with each other in the central stream and became indistinguishable from each other is precisely the way the AUCECB (All-Union Council of Evangelical Christians-Baptists) leadership likes to regard its union. If we take into consideration that the AUCECB eventually became a multinational union, not only Russian or Slavic, then earlier tributaries must be added. The first Baptists appeared in Poland in 1858 and many of the Polish Baptists were sub-sequently absorbed into the Russian Empire.[20] As early as 1861 the Baptist movement came to the Baltic, to Latvia.[21] But the three most important tributary streams are the Baptists in the Caucasus, *Stundism* in the Ukraine, and the upper-class Pashkovite movement in the capital.

The baptism of Nikita Voronin in 1867 near Tbilissi soon resulted in the organization of a small, specifically Baptist fellowship. Several key leaders joined the group here and later became prominent in the national activity of the Baptist union. Ivan Kargel joined in 1869; he later became fa-mous as the theological teacher and Bible commentator of the Baptists. In 1871 Vasili G. Pavlov joined—he subsequently became, in the words of Paul Steeves, the "patriarch" of the Russian Baptist Union. Also in 1871 Vo-ronin baptized Vasili V. Ivanov-Klyshnikov, who then organized the second Russian Baptist fellowship in Novo-Ivanovka (Elizavetpol' province) and later became secretary of the Russian Baptist Union.[22] The movement in the Caucasus was specifically Baptist from the start because that is what Martin Kalweit said they were. A simultaneous movement in the Ukraine was less specifically Baptist and was able to develop more specifically Russian or Ukrainian coloration.

The movement in the Ukraine came to be known as *Stundism* because it originated through the influence of German Mennonite and Lutheran colonists who held weekly hours (*Stunde*) of Bible study.[23] These colonists were not permitted to proselytize but some of their peasant workers or neighbors were influenced by them to initiate their own Bible studies. These Bible studies were prompted by a deep desire for a greater knowledge of the Scripture than the local Orthodox priest was able to offer and by the desire of literate peasants to read these truths for themselves.

Some years ago the present Ukrainian senior presbyter, Jacob K. Dukhonchenko, stumbled upon a small train station named "Stunde." Sus-pecting a story, he asked the local inhabitants why this strange name had been given to the station. Some of the older residents remembered that people called *Stundists* had formerly lived there. All they could remember about them was that they loved each other.[24]

When they celebrated their seventieth anniversary in 1955, Dukhon-chenko's predecessor had sketched the beginnings of the *Stundist* history for the same region along the Dnieper River. Peter I. Lysenko lived in the village of Sofievka, three kilometers away from the Mennonite village of Friedensfeld. Lysenko was impressed by the life and faith of the Men-nonites, noting that they often read the Bible and prayed. Without any direct aid from the Mennonites, he began reading the gospel himself, even though he was only semiliterate. Soon he was converted. Many times he asked the Mennonites to baptize him, but they refused because it was forbidden by law. Finally, about five years later in 1875, a well-known Mennonite minister who had come to visit agreed to perform the baptism. Peter Lysenko's father then threw Peter and his wife out of the parental home. But the Mennonites from Friedensfeld helped Lysenko build his own small house. Regularly, Lysenko would walk along his village street shouting, "Repent and turn to the gospel." A few curious ones followed him to his house, where he would preach to them. Gradually more were converted, a church was organized, and a better-educated new convert was elected the leader. Seventy years later there were sixty congregations in the oblast.[25]

At first the *Stundists* attempted to remain within the fold of Orthodoxy. But as the number of distrustful and worried priests increased, the persecution of these sectarians labeled *Stundists* intensified, causing them to develop a self-identity outside of Orthodoxy. Then in 1869 the aggressive and self-confident German Baptist leader Johann Gerhard Oncken visited these communities and eventually persuaded them to accept believer's baptism. Some of them accepted an ordained clergy as well.[26]

Oncken had also persuaded key leaders of the newly emerging Mennonite Brethren movement of the rightness of baptism by total immersion. One of these Mennonite Brethren leaders, Abraham Unger, baptized the first *Stundist*, Efim Tsymbal, in 1869. Another of the early Mennonite Brethren evangelists, Johann Wieler, called meetings of *Stundists* and Caucasian Baptists in 1882 and 1884. In 1884 he was elected president of the first short-lived attempt to form a Russian Baptist union.[27]

The third major tributary stream, that of the Pashkovites, was even less structurally precise than were the *Stundists*. A British nobleman, Lord Radstock, had experienced a personal conversion during the stress of the Crimean war and had joined the Plymouth Brethren.[28] In 1874 he visited St. Petersburg to hold a series of evangelistic meetings among the Russian aristocracy. These were primarily Bible studies followed by prayer and intense discussion led by the very persuasive Radstock. As a result, numerous prominent persons, such as Princess Lieven, Baron M. M. Korf and Colonel V. A. Pashkov, were converted. Radstock soon returned home and Colonel Pashkov became such a zealous activist for the movement that it came to be called Pashkovism.[29]

Due to the influence of the Plymouth Brethren, the Pashkovites did not ordain leaders, baptize, or maintain membership rolls. Pashkov became very active in literature publication and used his influence and wealth to this end. Through this activity, Pashkov came in contact with Bible colporteur Deliakov and his stepson Ivan Zhidkov, and they launched joint publication ventures.[30] Also as a result of Pashkov's irenic style, it became possible to call the first meeting of the proposed Russian Baptist Union, which met in his house in 1884. When a full-fledged union was finally organized in 1909, it was called the Union of Evangelical Christians in deference to the Pashkovites, who took a looser attitude toward standardization of doctrine and liturgy.

As long as the evangelical movement was restricted to the foreign colonists living in the empire, it had little to fear. In 1879 the Baptist "sect" had been legalized, but, according to the Ober-Prokuror of the Orthodox Holy Synod, this toleration did not extend to the Russian *Stundists* or Baptists. Ober-Prokuror Pobedonostsev and the local Orthodox leaders feared the evangelicals because they were launching aggressive missionary activity and gained the bulk of their converts from Orthodox ranks.[31] Due to Orthodox opposition, most of the evangelical leaders before 1917 received extended sentences of prison and exile but persisted in their endeavors in spite of this. The Orthodox formed a missionary society which had as a major goal the attempt to stamp out *Stundism*. The authorities forbade the meeting of *Stundists*, confiscated their buildings, and even went so far as to take their children away. Later, one Baptist leader summarized his early memories this way:

This was a time of horrible persecutions. Exiles, arrests, fines, and beatings of believers rained down abundantly upon the audacious followers of the Gospel. Under continual fear of being caught by the police, the brothers nevertheless did not cease their meetings, holding them in basements, across the Dnieper, in the woods, in the cemetery, in ravines, and in the apartments of the more well-to-do brothers.[32]

After 1894 when the Ministry of Internal Affairs proscribed all activities of the *Stundists*, the passports of the most active sectarians were marked *Stundist* "so that no person will accept them for work or lodging, until life in Russia becomes too costly for them."[33]

Revolution Brings Relief

A measure of relief came with a series of acts of toleration between 1903 and 1905. It now became possible to leave the Orthodox Church and join the confession of one's preference. The so-called Revolution of 1905 helped the liberal forces in Russia, including in the Orthodox Church, to argue successfully on behalf of religious toleration. Tolerance, they felt, would benefit Orthodoxy in the long run. But it was to be only a temporary toleration.[34]

The evangelicals were quick to capitalize on the new situation and organized systematic expansion. At a congress of the Evangelical Christians in 1910, Prokhanov set as a goal the organization of one congregation in each of 70 regions of the empire. From this one congregation five more were to be started. These would then form a local union which would continue to multiply itself.[35] Some Baptist leaders encouraged their members to note the locations of evangelical churches on a map of Russia. They were then to head for places where there was no evangelical witness, and begin one.

By 1909 the political climate of 1905 had changed and reactionaries gradually gained the upper hand. This was also apparent in the religious sphere. Additional regulating laws were introduced which were clearly intended to protect Orthodox believers from proselytizing and to restrict the activity of the evangelicals as much as possible. On October 4, 1910, the Ministry of Internal Affairs issued a circular "On the Order for Sectarian Meetings." The circular went into considerable detail in regulating sectarian activity and reminds one of Article 17 of the later Soviet Law on Cults of 1929. Regular meetings of the sect could be held without special permission but all additional meetings outside of the registered building required two weeks' advance notice to the police with a request for permission. The evangelization and teaching of minors was prohibited as were also various special gatherings for reading and discussion. A representative of the police was to attend every prayer meeting. The situation for the evangelicals—or sectarians, as the state regarded them—worsened. During the war they were harassed as potential traitors because their faith was of foreign Protestant origin.[36]

The Revolution of 1917 brought unprecedented relief to Russian sectarians, including evangelicals. When the Bolsheviks took over in the fall and issued the famed Separation Decree in January 1918, the evangelicals welcomed it. Finally the Orthodox Church, which had so long enjoyed a special position, had been reduced to a level of equality with all other religions. Not all the clauses of the decree separating church from state were to be acceptable to them, but most important initially was Article 3 which stated:

Every citizen may confess any religion or profess none at all. Every legal restriction connected with the profession of certain faiths or with the profession of no faith is now revoked.[37]

Initially the Soviet government, due largely to the influence of the sectarian expert Bonch-Bruevich (who was also Lenin's secretary), took a friendly attitude toward the evangelical sectarians and even hoped to cooperate with them in the building of socialism. In addition, because the evangelicals drew the bulk of their converts from Orthodoxy, their success should help the government in breaking the back of Orthodoxy. Both the Evangelical Christian and the Baptist Unions now met in regular congresses where they were able to report dramatic growth. Attempts at a union of the two bodies in 1920 failed so that their development was also characterized by undesirable rivalry. Both unions participated in congresses of the Baptist World Alliance and were particularly prominent at the 1923 congress.

Beginning in 1923, however, there were increasing signs of a parting of the ways between the evangelicals and the Soviet government. Many evangelicals, including the dominant leaders in both the Evangelical Christian and Baptist unions, were pacifists and made use of the 1919 decree permitting alternative service.[38] In 1923 the Soviet authorities began putting on pressure so that both unions would abandon their antimilitarist stand. The evangelicals appealed for aid at the Stockholm Congress and were refused. Leaders were imprisoned. During 1923, Prokhanov, for example, was imprisoned till he agreed to reverse himself and wrote a letter to the congregations urging them to do their military duty. But the issue of military service remained a point of conflict inside both unions.[39]

According to one expert, the Russian evangelicals were most Russian in their social and economic emphasis. A good number of the leaders, of which I. S. Prokhanov was perhaps the most outstanding, were advocates of Christian socialism. Not only did they approve of socialism, but during the twenties they established a number of communes in all parts of the Soviet Union and experienced remarkable success. When the Soviet authorities began to clamp down on this activity, it was obviously due to a growing fear that the Christian communes might be more successful than the Soviet ones and would embarrass them. Prokhanov also had a vision for building a "City in the Sun" to be named "Evangelsk." It was to be a model city for brotherly love. The plans were approved and local Soviet officials even promised the necessary financial aid and participated in the initial tree-planting ceremony. A year later in 1928 they were overruled and Evangelsk never became more than an ambitious promise.[40]

A Growth Decade

During those first twelve years of Soviet rule the Russian evangelicals had experienced truly phenomenal growth. Exiled leaders had returned and new freedoms had permitted increased activity. In addition, the evangelicals benefited from a corps of newly trained missionaries. Several alert evangelical leaders, particularly Jakob Kroeker and Walter Jack, seized the opportunities provided by World War I to engage in evangelistic work among Russian prisoners of war. They formed a mission named Light in the East (*Licht im Osten*) and set about distributing Russian New Testaments and other literature in the camps. When they noted the warm response as well as the concern of prisoners returning to a land of Bible scarcity, they organized a Bible school and correspondence classes. There were about 2,000 such converts among the POWs returning to the Soviet Union.[41] Vasili G. Pavlov, who became the leading Baptist during the twenties, dated the great religious awakening in Russia from the return of the Russian POWs. They held religious meetings in tents, under the open sky, or in large rented halls.

The boldness of the Russian evangelicals was due in part to their attitude to the law. In local areas they experienced "excesses" or mistreatment by local authorities but they were not defeated by this because they believed that the 1918 decree had provided them with religious toleration. "The Baptists took the laws at face value. Since the legal documents declared religious freedom, the Baptists assumed that there existed in Russia the kind of freedom that they had advocated for years."[42] Vasili Pavlov, writing during the early twenties, observed that millions of their fellow believers abroad "are interested in how we breathe under Soviet power. And since religious freedom is most important to us and we turn little attention to material (concerns), we have hitherto consistently answered: 'Well.' "[43]

Their single-minded concern for the religious task is illustrated by the way they submitted to the Soviet authorities. First, they believed that it was God's will to submit to the established government. Second, however, they were convinced that "God's will was for them to preach the Baptist Gospel in the Soviet Union."[44] They hoped to maintain the freedom to evangelize by submitting to the Soviet regime. This was also the logic behind those Baptists such as V. V. Ivanov-Klyshnikov who was prepared to reject pacifism because, as he reported to the 1926 congress, "in the interest of retaining for the Baptist Union its freedom of activity it was necessary for the congress to reject pacifism forthrightly."[45] Later they were to discover that they had misjudged Soviet promises and had been too naive, but to the present day this has been the approach of the AUCECB.

Entirely accurate statistics do not exist, but by 1917 the evangelical movement had grown to about 150,000. During the next seven years both Evangelical Christians and Baptists increased their number almost five-fold.[46] It was reported in 1924 that in Siberia they were maintaining a growth rate of 10 percent annually. In the Ukraine the rate was up to 15 percent. Some local congregations were especially active. The seven Evangelical Christian congregations in Leningrad in 1926 had a combined membership of 392, of which only 165 had been members before the Revolution. By 1930 the membership numbered 900. The Baptist congregation in Leningrad in 1924 had 372 members of which only 92 had joined before 1917. This too was the period of greatest increase in the Far East in the Amur, Primore', and Zabaikal oblasts, where between 1921 and 1927 the number of believers increased 2.5 times.

Jakob Wiens, earlier a key leader in the Siberian Union, had arrived in Blagoveshchensk in 1919 following a seven-year stay in the USA and became president of the Far Eastern Baptist Union. This union had been organized only six years earlier when V. G. Pavlov was exiled there.[47] In the oldest congregations in the Ukrainian union, whose histories went back to the seventies and eighties of the previous century, the growth was dramatic. In the village of Novo-Vasil'evka, for example, membership increased from 130 in 1922 to 315 in 1926. In the village of Astrakhanka membership increased from 100 in 1924 to 189 in 1926.

One of the primary reasons for this rapid growth was surely the role of the evangelists. The central Baptist and Evangelical Christian unions sent out evangelists to start new churches. The regional unions often maintained a staff of full-time evangelists. By 1927 this evangelization ministry was so well organized in the Ukraine that there were no less than 56 evangelists supported by the Ukrainian Baptist Union. At that time there were approximately 1,000 congregations of Baptists and 2,000 congregations or groups of Evangelical Christians in the Ukraine.[48] As early as 1921 the All-Russian Baptist Union had an expense budget of 45 million rubles, most of this for support of evangelists. The importance of literature in their ministry is also illustrated by the 35-million-ruble income from the sale of literature published by the Baptists. In 1926 the council of the Baptist Union was so enthusiastic as to adopt as motto: "Christ for the pagans and Moslems living in the USSR."[49] In April 1927 a mission society named "Friends of Mission to Heathen and Moslems" was founded in Moscow; by September

1928 Ivanov-Klyshnikov reported some success with seven trained workers in Moslem areas. Apparently Baptists also set up a five-year plan of mission to Kirgizia.

Evangelical Christian missionary and expansion activity relied heavily on a literature program. Ivan Prokhanov and his associate Jacob Zhidkov devoted much time to writing, publication, importation, and distribution of periodicals, Bibles, songbooks, and tracts. Using money raised in America, they completed the printing of 25,000 copies of the complete Bible in 1926, printed 10,000 copies of a concordance in 1928 and numerous songbooks. Prokhanov was particularly prolific as a songwriter. Ten thousand copies of an incomplete Bible were printed in Kiev in 1927, and 25,000 copies of the New Testament were printed.[50] This was the last time Bibles were printed in the Soviet Union till 1956.

The Baptist Union's range of activity was also extensive. In 1922 it organized ten commissions to facilitate its work. These were: evangelism, literature and publishing, music, material aid, care of preachers, preparation of workers and evangelists, moral education, finance, judicial affairs, and church order.[51] Bible schools for ministers were organized by the Evangelical Christians in Leningrad and by the Baptists in Moscow and Kiev. Local leaders such as M. A. Orlov in Orel Oblast personally conducted a school for ministers where 90 persons participated. According to Prokhanov, 422 preachers were trained at the St. Petersburg school.[52] None of these theological institutions were highly developed academically but they were the only schools the evangelicals had till a small correspondence course was started 40 years later.

In some areas Evangelical Christians and Baptists competed. During the famine of 1920-22 both bodies distributed aid from abroad. Baptists limited their aid to fellow Baptists, while Evangelical Christians were more open. As a result the Baptists accused them of distributing aid "in order to win adherents to their union."[53]

But in many local areas the rapid growth was a joint effort. For example, in 1920, at a regional congress in Ekaterinoslav in the Ukraine, representatives of both unions met together, approved a merger, and jointly employed four evangelists. In the central Volga region the two unions joined in the same year with Mennonites to coordinate evangelistic activity and form union congregations. In the Don region both unions jointly commissioned eight evangelists. Prokhanov of the Evangelical Christians also cooperated with Mennonites in the Ukraine to form the Raduga publishing house.

The evangelicals were enthusiastic about their growth. Ivan Prokhanov had visions of bringing all of Russia to evangelical Christianity. But such rapid growth also produced problems of its own. Already in 1907, when several churches in the Far East had baptized more than 100 members in one year, the longtime Baptist president Dei Mazaev had urged caution: "In our view, such a massive reception is hardly useful and desirable, because new members who have not been sufficiently trained in our teaching can by their numbers in sessions, make decisions that are immature or even alien to our church structure."[54]

When Pavel Ivanov-Klyshnikov reported to the Baptist World Alliance Congress in Toronto in 1928, he estimated that they had 4,000 congregations and stated: "We have around 900 presbyters and 3,100 societies and groups without prepared leaders."[55] This shortage of strong trained leadership must be regarded as a key factor in why the churches lost ground during the heavy pressure of the 1930s. Ivanov-Klyshnikov went on to identify another problem, the shortage of buildings. He noted that out of the 5,000 preaching places, "we have only about 400 of our own prayer buildings and around 800 rented buildings; the remaining 3,800 places of preaching are in private quarters."[56]

Perhaps the major significance of the rapid increase was not so much that now there were many more evangelicals, but, in the words of the most recent Soviet scholarly treatment, "there was a process of *change of the composition, a renewal of the cadres in Evangelical Christian and Baptist churches.*"[57] Based on the extensive statistical data submitted to the Conference of Anti-Religious Workers in 1926, Soviet sociologist Lialina noted that after 1917 the growth took place primarily in the village population. From 1918 to 1926, 906 new congregations with a total membership of 36,537 were established in the cities. Most of those who joined were peasants primarily of Orthodox background. According to Soviet classification, both Evangelical Christians and Baptists were predominantly poor peasants. Sixty percent were classified as poor peasants (*bedniaki*), 30 percent as middle peasants (*seredniaki*), and 10 percent were well-to-do peasants (*kulaki*).[58]

Other Tributary Streams

Important for the post-World War II era was the growth of evangelicals in two other areas. In 1921 a former Russian Baptist who had become a Pentecostal in New York returned as missionary to Odessa. Ivan Voronaev was an aggressive preacher and organizer and had considerable success.

Part of the reason for his success was that initially at least half of the converts, according to his own admission, came from persons leaving Baptist and Evangelical Christian churches.[59] In 1924 the Union of Christians of Evangelical Faith (Pentecostal) was organized in the Odessa Oblast. Two years later, the union had been extended to the entire Ukraine. In 1928, Voronaev, in his own newspaper *The Evangelist*, listed 350 assemblies with a membership of over 17,000.[60]

Another important factor to remember is that not all Soviet evangelicals are Russian. Walter Kolarz estimated in 1960 that 50 percent of the membership was non-Russian and pointed out also that nearly 10 percent of all Evangelical Christians and Baptists in the USSR were located in those areas along the borders of Poland, Czechoslovakia, and Romania, which only entered the union after World War II.[61] Due to the peace treaty of Brest-Litovsk, which Lenin agreed to in 1918 to extricate Russia from the war quickly, large areas formerly part of the Russian Empire, such as Latvia, Estonia, and Lithuania, as well as the western parts of the Ukraine, became independent. Other parts were under Polish sovereignty. By the beginning of World War II Soviet nationality policy which had at first encouraged national self-determination had changed into a Soviet patriotism.[62] The Baltic countries were incorporated into the new Soviet Empire as republics with very limited rights of self-determination while other areas were simply annexed. This meant that the inter-war period was a period of unprecedented personal freedom for the population in this region. Therefore, in all these areas, the evangelical movement, including that of the Pentecostals, experienced rapid growth during the 1920s.

In the Volhynia and Brest regions, a separate denomination known as the Church of Christ was organized in 1921. By 1928 there were 35 such churches. Since they did not experience the Stalinist persecution, they continued to grow. By 1939 there were 85 churches. Seventy-one of these churches found themselves inside Soviet borders after the war and were joined to the new evangelical union.[63]

Unity Struggles
The search for unity had dominated the evangelical movement from the beginning. It seemed obvious to those leaders with vision that if the evangelicals who had the true message of salvation for Russia (as they believed) were to make any significant impact in Russia, then they could not afford the factionalism usually characteristic of sectarianism. In North America evangelicals had had the advantage of equal treatment with the

older confessions and Protestants were in any case in the majority. If the Protestant West could account for a 400-year history, these new Protestants of Russia needed to rush through all the developments in the much shorter space of a few decades. One observer remarked that the resultant tensions that developed were due largely to the absence of history and tradition.[64]

The first official attempt to unite Russian evangelicals occurred at two conferences held in 1884. Colonel Pashkov and Baron Modest Korf invited believers from the Stundists, Baptists, Mennonite Brethren, Molokans, and Dukhobors to discuss unity. Seventy representatives met on April 1 in St. Petersburg, but the projected eight-day conference was broken up by the authorities on the fourth day. The sought-for unity would in all likelihood not have been achieved, since during the first four days numerous differences became evident. For example, some of the Pashkovites still adhered to paedobaptism and the Baptists from the south refused to begin the conference with a communion service once they discovered that not everyone present had undergone believer's baptism. Baron Korf tried to get the participants to recognize that "unity is not uniformity. It can also exist in diversity, similar to our body."[65]

A unity conference with more restricted representation met in the village of Novo-Vasil'evka in the Ukraine a few weeks later. Participants at this conference of 1884 at least managed to agree on the embryo for the subsequent Russian Baptist Union. At its second meeting in 1886, the first president, Johann Wieler, who had been forced to flee to Romania, was replaced by Dei Mazaev, who became the dominant Baptist figure for the next thirty years.

These events illustrate the nature of the problem preventing unity. For the entire pre-Revolutionary period the organizational structure of the evangelicals remained fluid and the unity conferences that did occur were made to seem more significant and representative by the later AUCECB officials than they were at the time. One of the primary points of difference was that the Baptists under Mazaev's leadership were a strict lot who had emphasized full adherence to Baptist ordinances, whereas other groups who eventually found themselves in the Evangelical Christian Union took an open attitude toward points of disagreement. Thus the Baptists determined the specific agenda for unity discussions.

Theological differences, or more accurately differences in dogmatic practice, were: (1) whether the ceremony of laying on of hands on the newly baptized should be performed; (2) whether presbyters and deacons must be ordained; and (3) whether only an ordained presbyter was entitled to conduct communion. The Evangelical Christians regarded all these practices as unnecessary. Baptists internationally also were not entirely agreed, since German Baptists emphasized the laying on of hands whereas the Evangelical Christians discovered that British Baptists did not follow this practice.[66]

The leadership of the evangelicals was divided on organizational questions. Ivan Prokhanov of the Evangelical Christians worked hard to unite Baptists and Evangelical Christians into one single union. Others felt that Prokhanov wanted to lead and dominate such a union and resisted. Baptist leaders, on the other hand, could not agree among themselves whether to have a centralized union or a federal structure which would allow much greater autonomy to the regional unions. In 1920 at the Baptist congress whose validity was challenged soon after, a reorganization of the Baptist Union was approved which introduced a centralized collegial leadership similar to that employed by the Communist Party. But the last Baptist congress in 1926 introduced a new constitution whereby the Baptists adopted a federated structure consisting of ten unions linked by a federal council.[67]

Although a unity agreement was reached in 1920 and signed by spokesmen from both sides, relations degenerated soon thereafter. By 1923 the Baptists decided to shelve further unity negotiations. In 1925 came the final break. In December the Baptist plenum listed 80 instances in the past six months alone, of local conflict with Evangelical Christians and decided to issue a formal statement severing relations with the Evangelical Christians.[68] This statement contained particularly harsh accusations against Ivan Prokhanov. It advised local churches to avoid all links with the Evangelical Christians, even refusing to allow their ministers access to Baptist pulpits. The Baptist Union now gained the support of the Baptist World Alliance which did not reelect Prokhanov as a vice-president in 1928.

The Stalinist Persecutions

An evaluation of the postwar situation and its development to the present day must always include the consideration that evangelicals experienced unprecedented persecutions during the 1930s. Beginning approximately in 1929 (somewhat earlier or later in different regions), state officials together with so-called voluntary organizations of militant godless launched an all-out attack on religion, utilizing mammoth amounts of propaganda and liberally applying "administrative measures." Virtually everyone was affected somehow. The war on the churches was related to the general purges and one can speak of similar waves of arrests.[69] Evangelical leaders who survived to resume their posts later often listed in their published biographies their activities and positions before this period, as well as the period after 1944, and either omitted the 1930s or spoke obliquely about hard times in their lives or a "severe illness."

Already in 1928 there were increasing signs of new pressures on the evangelicals. Prokhanov was advised not to return to the Soviet Union after attending the World Baptist Congress in Toronto, lest he be arrested. The issues of their denominational newspapers got thinner and there were more articles warning obliquely about dark days ahead. The Bible school in Moscow had to shut down after only four years of operation. The official indication that the situation had changed came with the promulgation of the law on religious cults of April 1929.

This law introduced detailed regulations for controlling the activities of all religious bodies.[70] But the list of activities forbidden to the religious bodies appears to be a list of the techniques evangelicals had introduced for expanding and strengthening their movement. Participation of minors was again severely restricted, clergymen and preachers had to limit their activities to the area of residence of their members, and elaborate registration procedures were introduced. All nonregistered activity was forbidden. Article 17 of the law forbade creation of any mutual credit societies or cooperative commercial undertakings; giving material aid to members; and all auxiliary activities such as special meetings for children, youth, and women, excursions, children's playgrounds, libraries, and so forth. This law and the official instruction for its execution which followed shortly thereafter[71] served as the pretext for closing most of the churches, arresting the ministers, and bringing evangelical church life to a standstill. A corresponding change in the constitution in 1930 still granted believers the right to practice religious ritual but withdrew the right to religious propaganda.

The changed situation became evident in numerous ways. Both unions were temporarily liquidated in 1929. They received no permission to publish and it became increasingly difficult to obtain permission to hold national conferences. The Baptists, for example, were forced to remove P. V. Pavlov and M. D. Timoshenko, both pacifists, as leaders, and a more traditional Baptist, Nikolai Odintsov, took over the leadership.[72] N. V. Odintsov, president since 1926, was himself arrested November 5, 1933, and received a three-year sentence. Subsequently, Odintsov was exiled to Eastern Siberia. Rearrested in 1938, he died shortly thereafter.[73] The secretary of the

Baptist Union, P. V. Ivanov-Klyshnikov, was given a 10-year sentence in 1932 and did not live to complete it. Another board member, P. V. Datsko, was home briefly in 1938 after exile, was rearrested in 1939, and served only two years of his 10-year sentence before he died. Vasili Stepanov, alternate member of the Federal Council, had been exiled following a camp experience that broke his spirit so that he would not go to church. Nevertheless, he was arrested again in 1937 and died in prison.[74] Il'ia Goliaev succeeded to Odintsov's post as president in 1933, but apparently went into hiding in 1935 and eventually died in Tashkent in 1942.

The authorities had managed to exert their influence on the union by officially sponsoring two candidates for membership: I. I. Bondarenko and V. I. Kolesnikov. The reasons for their treachery are unclear, but they apparently gave evidence for the state at Odintsov's trial and in other ways cooperated.[75] Both of them, however, also fell victim to the wave of arrests following the assassination of Kirov and both received five-year sentences. The date of their arrest, March 1935, can be regarded as the date when the Baptist Union ceased to exist.

Although temporarily closed in 1930, the Evangelical Christian Union never ceased to exist entirely. Prokhanov failed to return to the Soviet Union in 1928 and the leadership passed to Jacob Zhidkov. At a meeting of the council plenum in 1931 Prokhanov was elected honorary president (he died in 1935 in Berlin) and Zhidkov, the previous vice-chairman, was elected chairman. Since 1929 the central office had been forced to move to Moscow. In mid-1935 the Evangelical Christian Council consisted of J. I. Zhidkov (chairman), A. L. Andreev (vice-chairman), A. V. Karev (treasurer), I. S. Kapalygin (secretary), and M. A. Orlov. Following Zhidkov's arrest in 1937, only Andreev and Orlov remained at liberty, Orlov assuming chairmanship of the union in January 1938. Orlov managed to maintain church services in the one remaining Moscow church throughout the war. For the short period 1938-40 at least, the Evangelical Christian Union also did not function.[76]

The Stalinist persecution was much more pervasive than merely to decimate the leadership. Local presbyters were arrested and charged with violating the law of cults, or for being kulaks, or for having maintained friendships abroad regarded as traitorous and were given prison sentences. With the presbyters gone, it was easy to close the church buildings. In 1929 the six-day week was introduced, which meant that every day five sixths of the working population worked while one sixth rested. It was only in 1940 that the seven-day week with Sunday free was reintroduced.[77] Even then, although many of the recently converted capitulated and left the church, religious activity did not cease entirely. In the midst of this some bold evangelicals told the antireligious propagandists: "We start our work where you stop. You work in clubs and meetings, but we work in the streets outside the clubs and after the meetings."[78] Some leaders escaped arrest by going into hiding, and these managed to conduct secret services.

Generally speaking, however, closure was the order of the day. In the spring of 1930, 12 Baptist ministers in Leningrad were arrested and all but one of the churches were confiscated. Five of six Baptist churches in Moscow were confiscated. One minister fleeing via Harbin in 1930 estimated that 40 percent of the full-time workers had been arrested or had fled, and that 60 percent of the churches had been closed. In 1936 the remaining Baptist building was confiscated; that left only one functioning Evangelical Christian congregation in Moscow. Believers who dared began attending here, a phenomenon characteristic of other parts of the country where either only a Baptist or an Evangelical Christian meetinghouse still remained open. By now it meant everything simply to be able to pray and read the Word together with other Christians; their denominational affiliation had no significance any longer.[79]

Wartime Activity

Fortunately for all religions, ironic as it may sound, the war preserved them from total extinction. It provided them with the possibility of demonstrating their loyalty and value to the defense of the Soviet Union and Stalin rewarded them by granting them new freedoms but without the corresponding legal protection. The two leaders not in prison, Orlov and Andreev, visited churches during the war and helped them become reestablished as conditions improved. Most of the Baptist leaders were by then either dead or in prison.

Michael Orlov and Alexei Andreev were able to visit the Baltic countries in 1940. As a result of the Soviet-German pact of 1939, the Soviet Union had annexed these independent countries. Immediately thereupon there seemed to follow a pattern whereby the absorption of the local civil administration was followed by the absorption of the local religious administration.[80] Considering general wartime travel restrictions, only state sponsorship could account for the trip undertaken by Orlov and Andreev.

With the invasion of the Soviet Union by Hitler in 1941, wartime propaganda began to include identification with old Russian heroes, including religious ones.[81] The Orthodox leader Sergei appealed to fellow believers to sacrifice everything in defense of the motherland. The Orthodox raised large funds for the war effort.

Michael Orlov on behalf of the Evangelical Christians became equally active in the patriotic war effort. He conducted a large patriotic meeting in Moscow immediately following the invasion and as a result many of the members expressed their willingness publicly to volunteer for the Red Army. In his report to the 1944 congress, Orlov freely stated that his union had written letters to church members in occupied territory urging them to support the Soviet side. After May 1942 when the Baptists had joined the Evangelical Christians, joint appeals were sent out announcing days of prayer for victory over the enemy. These were held on June 14, 1942, February 7, 1943, and February 6, 1944. They were also able to raise 80,000 rubles for the war effort in order to purchase an ambulance plane.[82]

In the middle of the war in May 1942 two spokesmen for the Baptists, one a former secretary of the union, N. A. Levindanto, and M. Ia. Goliaev, son of the last president of the union, sent a formal request to the Evangelical Christian Union asking it to assume pastoral responsibilities for the Baptist churches, as well as for Evangelical Christians.[83] Two years later the formal fusion of Evangelical Christians and Baptists was approved at a hastily called unity congress. Whereas earlier the Evangelical Christians were actively seeking unity, now it was the Baptists who had to come to the Evangelical Christians. For the surviving remnant from other evangelical groups such as Pentecostals and Mennonites, their only chance for official survival after the war appeared to be in joining the new evangelical union.

The new union became a point of controversy with its legal validity doubtful and the cooperative role of the state authorities disconcerting. Some joined and later left disappointed; at first primarily Pentecostals, later many Baptists left. Others praised God that a church was open again where God's Word could be preached, and dramatic revivals swept the nation. Pessimists thought the new union would never last but in spite of its weaknesses it is still a reality and constitutes an admonition to separatist evangelicals in the West to get together.

Patterns

Before the virtual demise of the Soviet evangelicals during the Stalinist purges, their movement had developed a size and character that deserved to be taken seriously. At the 1924 Communist Party Congress, Soviet Union President Kalinin pointed out that the sectarians had known only persecution during the tsarist years and warned against such a policy for the future.

By then it was apparent that the persecution of one generation of evangelicals did not frighten the next generation. Baptist secretary Vasili Ivanov-Klyshnikov was not that unique with his record of 31 imprisonments.[84] The movement had grown despite persecution, perhaps because of it. Yet the facts of nearly uncontrolled growth during the decade of Soviet tolerance cannot have escaped the notice of state officials.

With eased restrictions, the evangelicals had deliberately organized for expansion through evangelism. They employed a large corps of full-time evangelists. There were tent missions. Others debated with atheists in large assembly halls with considerable success. Bible schools and an intensified literature program sought to provide guidance and depth to the movement. It was apparent that the evangelicals could not be used by the communists as had been hoped and so the policy of toleration was abandoned. Most of the evangelicals' techniques for growth were explicitly forbidden by law in 1929. In their resurrected form after the war, the new Soviet evangelicals therefore could not rely on these patterns, although their memory served as motivation for fashioning substitutes.

Renewed attempts to eliminate the evangelicals after the war have made persecution into a hereditary pattern. The Vins family which has known "three generations of suffering" is in essence not unique. There were also several other problem patterns that would persist. Trained leaders remained rare. Trusted leaders were regularly threatened with prison. The lack of buildings remained a problem. And after a short euphoric period of unity in adversity, the inter-evangelical bickering was resumed.

Which side, whether the state authorities or the evangelicals, would learn from their mistakes the quickest remained to be seen.

Notes to Chapter 1

1. Walter Kolarz, *Religion in the Soviet Union* (London: Macmillan & Co., Ltd., 1961), p. 286. Kolarz's solid book has retained its value as a basic reference work. Paul D. Steeves, "The Russian Baptist Union, 1917-1935: Evangelical Awakening in Russia" (unpublished PhD dissertation, University of Kansas, 1976), see pp. iii & 267; Wilhelm Kahle, *Evangelische Christen in Russland und der Sowjetunion: Ivan Stepanovich Prochanov (1869-1935) und der Weg der Evangeliums-christen und Baptisten* (Wuppertal: Oncken Verlag, 1978), pp. 229-32. Steeves's dissertation is without question the most thorough and reliable treatment of the Baptist Union before World War II, whereas the Kahle book is the definitive study of the Evangelical Christians for the same period and reflects admirable breadth and maturity. Kahle and Steeves have strongly influenced this introductory chapter.

2. Steeves, p. 250f.; Kahle, pp. 260-74.

3. Paul Miliukov, *Outlines of Russian Culture*, Vol. I: *Religion and the Church in Russia* (New York: A. S. Barnes & Co. 1, 1942), p. 200.

4. Robert Conquest, *The Great Terror* (Pelican Book, 1968), is the best history of Stalin's purges. See pp. 699-713 on casualty figures.

5. John Shelton Curtiss, *Die Kirche in der Sowjetunion (1917-1956)* (Munich: Isar Verlag, 1957), p. 236. This slightly revised German translation of the English edition (1953) devotes considerable space to the League of Militant Godless.

6. Good treatments of the Orthodox experience are in William C. Fletcher, *A Study in Survival: The Church in Russia, 1927-1943* (London: S.P.C.K., 1965); Nikita Struve, *Christians in Contemporary Russia* (London: Harvill Press 1967); Lev Regel'son, *Tragediia russkoi tserkvi, 1917-1944* (Paris: YMCA Press, 1977).

7. Quoted in Roy Medvedev, *Let History Judge: The Origins and Consequences of Stalinism* (New York: Alfred A. Knopf, 1971), p. 71.

8. *Bratskii Vestnik*, 5/1947, p. 19.

9. Walter Sawatsky, "Baptist Claims About Dramatic Improvement Assessed," *Keston News Service*, May 21, 1976.

10. Grigorii Skovorda, *Sochineniia v dvukh tomakh* (Moscow: "Mysl'," 1973). On Skovoroda, see James M. Edie *et al.* (ed.), *Russian Philosophy* (Chicago: Quadrangle Books, 1965), I, 8-62 and James H. Billington, *The Icon and the Axe* (New York: Alfred A. Knopf, 1968), pp. 328-42. Skovoroda was one of the few religious thinkers read and admired by Lenin.

11. Quoted in Miliukov, p. 126.

12. *Ibid.*

13. *Ibid.*, p. 147; cf. John S. Curtiss, *Church and State in Russia 1900-1917* (New York: Columbia University Press, 1940; reprinted by Octagon Books, 1972), *passim*.

14. F. Ernest Stoeffler, *The Rise of Evangelical Pietism* (Leiden: E. J. Brill, 1965), and his *German Pietism During the Eighteenth Century* (Leiden, 1973). For a thorough treatment of the role of Jung-Stilling, see Max Geiger, *Aufklärung und Erweckung* (Zurich: EVZ Verlag, 1963).

15. The author has dealt with this subject at length in his "Prince Alexander N. Golitsyn (1773-1844): Tsarist Minister of Piety" (unpublished PhD dissertation, University of Minnesota, 1976).

16. Hans Brandenburg, *The Meek and the Mighty* (London & Oxford: Mowbrays, 1976; original German appeared in 1974). One of the best books on the pre-Soviet history of the evangelicals.

17. *Historical Catalogue of British Bibles* (London: Bible House, 1911), pp. 1299-1314. The Russian Bible Society is thoroughly treated in an unpublished dissertation by Judith Cohen Zacek (Columbia, 1964), aspects of which were covered in several published articles. The most helpful here is: "The Russian Bible Society and the Russian Orthodox Church," *Church History*, 1966, No. 4, pp. 411-37. The history of the later Bible Societies has still to be written.

18. *BV*, 5-6/54, p. 24.

19. Serge Bolshakoff, *Russian Nonconformity* (Philadelphia: Westminster Press, 1950), pp. 105-109.

20. Robert L. Kluttig, *Geschichte der deutschen Baptisten in Polen von 1858-1945* (Winnipeg, 1973), p. 25.

21. *BV*, 2/48, p. 61.

22. Steeves, pp. 4-5. Steeves's opening chapter provides short biographies of a large number of the early leaders.

23. The Brandenburg book is conceived as a study of *Stundism*. Other basic sources are: Waldemar Gutsche, *Westliche Quellen des russischen Stundismus*

(Kassel: Oncken, 1959), and Herman Dalton, *Der Stundismus in Russland* (Gütersloh, 1896).

24. From remarks made at 1979 All-Union congress in Moscow, based on author's notes.

25. *BV*, 5/55, pp. 61-67.

26. For an overall treatment of origins see Samuel J. Nesdoly, "Evangelical Sectarianism in Russia: A Study of the Stundists, Baptists, Pashkovites, and Evangelical Christians 1855-1917" (unpublished PhD dissertation, Queen's University, 1972).

27. Kahle, pp. 39-42, 51-64, 332f.; Steeves, pp. 22-30. By 1886 Wieler had fled to Romania, where he led the newly founded church in Tulcea and died in 1889 (*Mennonitische Rundschau*, December 20, 1978).

28. A movement originating in the early 19th century, a key leader being John Nelson Darby (1800-1882), striving to renew the church along New Testament patterns. The emphasis on simplicity included avoidance of institutionalization—that is, no ordained clergy with sacraments or a central board. They were active missionaries, including among their adherents George Muller (of Bristol orphanage fame) and Watchman Nee.

29. Edmund Heier, *Religious Schism in the Russian Aristocracy, 1860-1900: Radstockism and Pashkovism* (The Hague: Martinus Nijhoff, 1970).

30. Iakov D. Deliakov (1829-1898) was the Bible colporteur who had first introduced Voronin to Kalweit. Deliakov had been evangelizing among Molokans, preaching justification by faith, but, due to Presbyterian influence, he advocated infant baptism. His Molokan followers had adopted the label "Evangelical Christians." Deliakov married a widow, the grandmother of the later president of the AU-CECB, Jacob Zhidkov. Deliakov and his stepson Ivan Zhidkov's literature ministry was financed from 1882 to 1887 by Pashkov, and it was Pashkov also who managed to persuade Deliakov in favor of believer's baptism (Steeves, pp. 2-3, 15-18, 21, 32).

31. Cf. Gerhard Simon, *Konstantin Petrovič Pobedonoscev und die Kirchenpolitik des Heiligen Sinod 1880-1905* ("Kirche im Osten," Band 7; Göttingen: Vandenhoeck and Ruprecht, 1969), pp. 188-99.

32. Quoted by Steeves, p. 37.

33. Andrew Blane, "The Relations Between the Russian Protestant Sects and the State, 1900-1921" (unpublished PhD dissertation, Duke University, 1964), p. 31. Blane's work covering the first 50 years is of high caliber and especially good on legal relationships.

34. For a good survey see Curtiss, *Church and State*, Chap. 5. A recent Soviet Orthodox study is Vladimir Rozhkov, *Tserkovnye voprosy v gosudarstvennoi dume* (Rome: Opere Religiose Russe, 1975).

35. Blane, pp. 46-47. A slogan printed on the cover of the union's magazine *The Christian* was: "From City to City, from Town to Town, from Village to Village, from Man to Man."

36. *Ibid.*, pp. 80-82.

37. V. A. Kuroedov and A. S. Pankratov (eds.), *Zakonodatel'stvo o religioznykh kul'takh* (Moscow: Iuridicheskaia literatura, 1971), p. 53. "This paragraph of the January Decree became the Magna Carta of all those religious communions which hitherto had not possessed full religious liberty." (Matthew Spinka, *The Church and the Russian Revolution* [New York, 1927], p. 108.)

38. Steeves, pp. 57-60. (Forty thousand of all sectarians received exemptions.)

39. Steeves, 510f.; Kahl, pp. 382-421, (See below, p. 115.)

40. Kahle, pp. 442-62; Steeves, pp. 510f., 533; Blane, pp. 184f., 241.

41. *Steeves, pp. 117-23.*

42. *Ibid.*, p. 541.

43. *Ibid.*, pp. 540-41.

44. *Ibid.*, p. 595.

45. *Ibid.*, p. 587.

46. G. S. Lialina, *Baptizm: Illiuzii i real'nost'* (Moscow: Politizdat, 1977), pp. 58-60.

47. Steeves, pp. 127-28.

48. *Ibid.*, pp. 231-32; Kahle, p. 252.

49. Steeves, p. 208; Kolarz, pp. 309-10.

50. Kahle, pp. 483-500.

51. Steeves, p. 187.

52. *BV*, 5/47, pp. 66-70; Kahle, p. 477. Cf. pp. 463-82 for a detailed survey of schools abroad where Russians studied, as well as the short-lived Bible schools in the provinces.

53. Steeves, pp. 175-78. By September 1922 they had received 68 million rubles (about $160,000) from abroad plus clothing and farm machinery. Nonmembers who attended Baptist congregations received one third of the rations given to full members!

54. Quoted by Steeves, p. 59.

55. *Ibid.*, p. 239.

56. *Ibid.*

57. Lialina, p. 60; her italics.

58. *Ibid.*, pp. 60, 62-72. Many other studies could be cited, but this is the most recent convenient collection of this sociological data. Most of the new converts during the Soviet period came from the *seredniaki* except in Siberia where the *bedniaki* were the greatest majority, the reason being (according to Lialina) that during the Civil War poverty had increased there. The three Soviet class categories served political purposes and are notably inaccurate designations. The term "kulak" is by now part of the English language, hence the English plural "kulaks."

59. Steve Durasoff, *The Russian Protestants: Evangelicals in the Soviet Union: 1944-1964* (Rutherford, Madison, Teaneck, Tenn.: Fairleigh Dickinson University Press, 1969), p. 73. The strength of the Durasoff book lies in its special attention to the Pentecostals.

60. *Ibid.*

61. Kolarz, p. 303.

62. Richard Pipes, *The Formation of the Soviet Union* (Boston: Harvard University Press, rev. ed. 1964 by Atheneum).

63. Interview with early leader Jerzy Sacewicz, now Warsaw, May 4, 1977.

64. Kahle, p. 103.

65. *BV*, 2/46, p. 25; cf. Steeves, p. 25f. and Kahle, p. 39f.

66. *BV*, 3/57, pp. 52-64; also cited in Kahle, p. 210; cf. Steeves, p. 72.

67. Steeves, pp. 217-23.

68. Kahle, pp. 194-95. In 1924 Prokhanov requested that Russian Baptists in their dealing with the Baptist World Alliance should keep him as vice-president for Russia informed. His concern appeared to be to better coordinate receipt of relief and distribution in the Soviet Union so that the Evangelical Christians would also get a fair share. This violated World Alliance practices and the Russian Baptists perceived the action as an unscrupulous takeover bid. Following this the Baptists published details of the discussions in Stockholm in 1923, including Prokhanov's remark that he would not die before he had stepped over the corpse of the Russian

Baptist Union. In their paper the Baptists even referred to the Evangelical Christian
Union as a bordello (Kahle, pp. 109-91). Steeves passes over this nasty exchange in
1925 in silence.

69. Alexander Solzhenitsyn uses this imagery of waves, especially in Part I,
Chapter 2: "The History of Our Sewage Disposal System" of *The Gulag Archipelago* (London: Collins, 1974). See especially pp. 24, 37, 50-51, and 58-59.

70. N. Orleanskii, *Zakon o religioznykh obedineniiakh. RSFSR* (Moscow,
1930). English trans. in W. B. Stroyen, *Communist Russia and the Russian Orthodox Church 1943-1962* (Washington, D.C.: The Catholic University of America
Press, 1967), pp. 121-27.

71. Detailed in Orleanskii, English trans. in Stroyen, pp. 128-35. The number
of churches closed jumped from 499 in 1928 to 1,379 in 1929; in Otto Luchterhandt,
Der Sowjetstaat und die Russisch-Orthodoxe Kirche (Cologne: Verlag Wissenschaft
und Politik, 1976), footnote 111, p. 272.

72. Steeves, pp. 581-85.

73. Georgi Vins, *Three Generations of Suffering* (London: Hodder &
Stoughton, 1976), pp. 105-11.

74. Steeves, pp. 277-78.

75. *Ibid.*, pp. 258-60, 268-71.

76. Kahle, pp. 260-74, 222-23.

77. Kolarz, p. 31. Cf. Solzhenitsyn, *Gulag* I, p. 59.

78. Kolarz, p. 299.

79. Karev claimed that only four churches had remained open (*Sobranie
Arkhiva Samisdata*, Tom 14, AS 770, p. 221). Cf. William C. Fletcher, *The Russian
Orthodox Church Underground 1917-1970* (London: Oxford University Press,
1971), p. 80ff. Even after churches were closed, believers met secretly and were
aided by clergy in hiding. But the atmosphere of fear that descended on the country
generally was such that devout believers often did not dare say a table prayer or read
the Bible within the intimate family circle for fear that the walls would hear.

80. For a summary of the Orthodox role in the absorption and subjugation of
the new territories see Harvey Fireside, *Icon and Swastika* (Cambridge, Mass.: Harvard University Press, 1971), p. 178f.; William C. Fletcher, *Nikolai, Portrait of a Dilemma* (New York: Macmillan, 1968), p. 33f.; and most of Wassilij Alexeev & Theofanis Stavrou, *The Great Revival* (Minneapolis: Burgess Press, 1976). The Catholic
population proved more difficult to absorb, hence the heavy campaign against the
papacy as described in Dennis Dunn, *The Catholic Church and the Soviet Government 1939-1949* (New York: Columbia University Press, 1977) and Michael
Bourdeaux, *Land of Crosses* (Devon: Augustine Publishing House, Keston Book 12,
1979), Chap. 1.

81. Georg von Rauch, *A History of Soviet Russia* (5th ed.; New York: Praeger
Publishers, 1967), pp. 328-32.

82. *BV*, 1/45, pp. 15-18; 6/57, pp. 47-51; cf. Fletcher, *Nikolai*, pp. 45-46 on
the role of Metropolitan Nikolai in writing church propaganda for distribution behind German lines.

83. *BV*, 1/45, pp. 17.

84. Brandenburg, p. 130.

"What brought you here?" I asked. "What did you read?"
They answered: "We don't know what brought us here. We
just felt that something was missing." "Have you read
anything?" "Nothing in particular." "The Gospels?" I
asked. "How could we have done that, since they're
impossible to obtain?" . . . "We don't doubt any of this. It's
all we can believe in, otherwise life would be meaningless."
—*Dmitrii Dudko*
Our Hope, p. 147

2 The Leap Forward: Revival and Church Growth, 1944-1957

At the end of the Napoleonic War in 1815 when a religious revival swept through Russia, a leading Orthodox hierarch tried to explain the phenomenon to a representative of the Russian Bible Society. "We have a proverb," he said, "that when the thunder rolls, the peasant crosses himself."[1] War, with its thunder and lightning, has often led to increased religiosity. That was true after the Second World War, or "The Great Fatherland War," as it is known in the Soviet Union, which was responsible for extreme social disorientation. Twenty million Russians perished and untold numbers suffered lesser injuries. Every family was affected by the war in some way.

The war became the scapegoat for all the suffering that had been experienced. It had caused hunger, loss of loved ones, and homelessness. The hated fascists who started the war had also engaged in religious persecution. *Bratskii Vestnik,* the official evangelical periodical, has never dared describe the brutal treatments its members received from Soviet authorities but it has given some details about fascist treatment. Ilia Ivanov, who later became president, claimed that the fascists "completely closed the Evangelical Christian-Baptist churches, beat and tormented the presbyters and preachers, and demanded that they renounce their faith."[2]

Revival Begins
In most areas, however, churches had been closed for at least twelve

years—that is, much longer than the duration of the war. The local presbyters had disappeared, many of them forever. But after the war the state showed itself tolerant toward religion, and the search for spiritual faith took on major proportions. *Bratskii Vestnik* began reporting many and large baptismal services. In several of the larger cities as many as 100 persons were baptized in one year alone.[3] AUCECB President Zhidkov reported at the end of the first year that their central office had been flooded with 5,000 letters containing appeals for help.

The dominant request was for Bibles.

> From many brothers and sisters locally came persistent requests to send various spiritual literature and especially Bibles, New Testaments and hymnbooks. We understand this need and the AUCECB is very concerned that these needs are met but it will take time. For the time being, brothers and sisters, one must be patient and earnestly ask the Lord to fulfill this urgent necessity.[4]

This early, surprisingly frank acknowledgement of the Bible hunger resurfaced in *Bratskii Vestnik* only infrequently thereafter, but for believers it became the major desire. Correspondence abroad, where Bibles were more plentiful, was extremely difficult during the first decade, but when this became somewhat easier in the middle fifties, the hunger for Bibles seemed as painful as a decade earlier. One correspondent for a mission reported he was receiving daily an average of twenty letters containing heart-rending appeals for Bibles. He reported there were ministers in the Soviet Union preaching without benefit of a Bible.[5]

The second major need was for ordained presbyters. The war and the earlier purges had severely decimated the experienced and able leaders. Now churches were opening in many locations but there were no presbyters available. In many places women led the services but without the right to perform ordinances. As late as 1953, one fifth of the congregations in the Ukraine still lacked an ordained presbyter.[6] President Zhidkov reported they had received many letters in Moscow with the appeal: "Give us workers even if they are old or invalids—we would be happy for all."[7]

This was the context for a major revival among Soviet evangelicals. Communication was difficult and religious propaganda was prohibited, yet word of a revival spread rapidly. One participant recalled how news reached his village that in the neighboring village there was a Bible and that a person there had dared to read it in public. Late at night the Bible owner's house was crowded with expectant persons. Only one candle was lit to facilitate reading of the Bible, and everyone spoke in hushed tones in order not to draw neighbors' attention. After those persons who could still remember them had sung several hymns, someone stood up to read from the precious Bible. In the prayer that followed, the kneeling assembly implored God to forgive their sins. Hardened persons found themselves weeping like a baby.[8]

The unique context clearly shaped the nature of this religious revival. In most localities it was a movement without visible leadership. Traveling evangelists and AUCECB leaders often served as catalysts for the revival fires to break out but it remained above all a grass-roots phenomenon. In many areas evangelists or other ministers never appeared until years later. One story from the village of Waldheim in Western Siberia is typical:

A young man had spent the winter working in Vorkuta on the Arctic Circle in order to collect the extra salary paid for working under severe climatic conditions. In Vorkuta he encountered believers who had just experienced a dramatic awakening. The young man heard the preaching and was converted. Before returning to his home in the spring, he managed to obtain a Bible. Although no announcement was made on the day he returned to the village of Waldheim, that evening curious neighbors gathered in his home until all three rooms were packed to overflowing. Young Jacob rose to his feet, opened his Bible, and laboriously read a few verses. Closing the book, he managed another two or three halting sentences that scarcely hinted at a sermon. Then, his thoughts exhausted, he suddenly fell to his knees and uttered a simple but staggering prayer: "Lord, I pray to you that each person gathered here will be converted tonight. Amen."

In the silence that followed, a woman from the adjoining room pushed her way through to young Jacob and asked him tearfully, "Help me to pray." Without further ado, he dropped onto his knees again and she began calling out to God to be merciful to her, a terrible sinner. Within a few seconds all in the house were on their knees and screaming to God for mercy. Jacob found himself calming the people and telling them that God could hear them without their screams.

Jacob's prayer was answered literally. In fact, herdsmen in the pasture heard the shouting, came to see, and stayed to experience their personal conversion. Others ran home to awaken relatives with the words, "Come quickly, the entire village is getting converted tonight."

Elsewhere, the awakening followed the journey of some courageous evangelist. Few of these heroic people are known by name. To guard against betrayal to the authorities, the visitor simply introduced himself as Brother Alexei, preached his sermon, baptized the converts, and was already underway to an unknown destination before the authorities had sufficient information to get on his trail. Some of these traveling evangelists were persons who had been converted only a few weeks or months earlier. Filled with the joy of their new experience, they used their weekends and other free time to preach in nearby villages. In many areas the newly converted met regularly for services but had to wait years till a visiting ordained minister could conduct baptism and communion. Communion and baptism were seen as important, but a primary concern was to tell people that there is a gracious God, Someone who forgives their sins, Someone who can give them peace of heart and a purpose for living.

There was little need to counter the so-called scientific arguments of atheism. Young Peter Engbrecht, for example, had studied at an institute for scientific atheism and had been chagrined to discover that the atheists were unable to prove convincingly that God does not exist. After serving a term in concentration camps (because of his German origins), he was finally released in the early 1950s, a physical wreck. Deeply depressed, he amused himself by ridiculing the old minister in the village. The minister ignored his tricky scientific questions and responded to him with a quiet grace. Finally one evening Peter came to announce that he wished to be converted. His excitement was so great that he could not wait till morning to be baptized. Soon he became one of the key evangelists in the area and conducted services where he baptized more than seventy persons.[9]

The AUCECB leadership also played a role in the revival. Most of the members of the All-Union Council spent much time on the road during the first few years visiting churches. In these administrative trips they shared information about activities in Moscow, gave advice on how to organize and register the church, and ordained local presbyters. The reports in the *Bratskii Vestnik* journal are restrained but indicate that wherever they visited, there was always a worship service in which they delivered the major sermons. When Mikhail Orlov traveled to communities in the Volga region, services were held on successive evenings and people were converted.

These leaders, with years of experience in evangelism and Bible teaching, now used their accumulated skills to guide the growth. President Zhidkov reported that in 1947 growth had been significantly less than from 1945 to 1946 because congregations were becoming more cautious in accepting members—they tested them first and gave them solid teaching. He reported that the AUCECB had sent a directive to local congregations warning them not to receive strangers into their pulpits but only such persons who carried identification and endorsement by the AUCECB. This was an attempt to restrain the activities of independent preachers who were sowing disorder among believers. Zhidkov also discouraged presbyters from switching congregations or moving about from place to place, emphasizing that "their task is not to be a missionary, but a pastor."[10] This was strong language that might come back to haunt him. It was an emphasis preferred by the state authorities, but it also reflected concern for stability and validity.

General Secretary Alexander Karev reported in October 1948 that the first task of their union had been to bring the congregations into order again and to register them with the local organs of power. The second task was to put in order the family of presbyters. The AUCECB had collected a list of all the presbyters in the country including their place of service, physical and spiritual age, time spent as presbyter, and their spiritual level. This attempt to husband their resources extended also to senior presbyters who were carefully chosen in order to provide leadership to the presbyters under them.[11]

The State Rewards Loyal Churches

Stalin rewarded Orthodox patriotism by permitting the reestablishment of the patriarchate in 1943 and soon thereafter the Soviet news agency TASS announced the formation of a Council for Russian Orthodox Church Affairs (CROCA), attached to the Council of Ministers, to handle all liaison functions between the Orthodox Church and the Soviet state. In July 1944 a second council, called the Council for the Affairs of Religious Cults (CARC), attached to the Soviet Council of Ministers, was announced. Ivan Vasilevich Polianskii was appointed the chairman with local representatives or plenipotentiaries of the council under him.[12] Clearly this indicated a shift in Soviet state religious policy in favor of the loyal churches. Only a few months later the unity congress of Evangelical Christians and Baptists took place.

Although the creation of the two councils was announced almost immediately, their powers remained shrouded in mystery for decades. The councils did not fit into the 1929 legislation on cults which, when revised in 1932, referred to local commissions to oversee church affairs but otherwise left registration procedures to local state authorities. One eminent scholar has suggested that these two councils "represented an institutional extension of the long-established secret police department for 'churchmen and sectarians.' "[13]

In the *Soviet Encyclopedia* published in 1947 a lengthy article by A. Kolosov describes the councils' functions as follows:[14] (1) To examine all questions put to the government by religious societies which require a state decision, such as obtaining prayer houses, issuing of materials, making printing presses available; (2) reviewing legislative proposals dealing with questions of religious societies, as well as other instructions and orders; (3) overseeing the proper execution throughout the territory of the USSR of all laws based on the strict separation of church from state with the council taking necessary measures to guarantee religious freedom for Soviet citizens as provided by the constitution; (4) cooperating with religious societies in settling those questions which require involvement with Soviet ministries. In a statute issued in 1966 (although first made public in the West in 1976)[15] these duties were spelled out more clearly but till then there appeared to be no clear legislative foundation for the councils.

No changes in the law were announced, although a legally binding letter from G. G. Karpov, head of the Council for Russian Orthodox Church Affairs, to Patriarch Alexei soon became known. This letter permitted the patriarchate to own property and otherwise function as a legal entity even though the legislation forbade this.[16] The emphasis that Karpov and his colleague Polianskii tried to give was that their councils were serving largely a liaisonary function.

It was immediately apparent that churches registered by the Council for the Affairs of Religious Cults were left relatively undisturbed in their conduct of worship services, whereas the unregistered groups experienced considerable harshness from local authorities. The legislation of 1929 stated that a minimum of twenty persons was required before a congregation or "society," to use the Soviet terminology, could be registered.[17] All had to be over eighteen years of age. Twenty persons therefore had to sign the request for initial registration and a list of all the members was maintained by the local state authorities. The law specified that a three-member executive body elected by the society should represent it. The law further specified that the state registration agencies were entitled to remove individual members from the executive council of a local religious society. All meetings additional to regular worship services required special permission.

No criteria for registration were established but the law did list a good number of activities which were violations of the law—any violation of the law was sufficient ground for removal of registration. According to the law, the congregation could not meet for its regular activities until after the registration approval had been given but there was no time limit within which the state authorities were required to respond to the registration request. Once registration had been approved, the congregation needed to negotiate the use of a prayer building.

Obtaining a building for worship was itself a major problem. Unofficial restrictions specified that a prayer house must not be located too close to a school or public building. (The public must be protected from harmful influences!) Sometimes the building had to be purchased and usually it had to be remodeled. If the previous owner discovered the potential purpose of the building, he might decide not to sell, buckling to pressure from unfriendly authorities. The risk of sudden revocation of registration was always present.

The second issue of *Bratskii Vestnik* requested the churches to send all registration materials to Moscow, where the work of registering the churches was being conducted. That soon changed, and it became the task of the senior presbyter to assist local congregations with the registration process. In the Baltic states, especially in Latvia and Estonia, this was a relatively simple process of reconfirming the registration of existing church communities, although many forcible closures also occurred. Registration appears to have moved smoothly in White Russia and the Ukraine, where the bulk of the membership was located. Registration was slower in the central areas of the Russian Federation (RSFSR), as well as further east in Siberia and the Far East, probably because the state administrative machinery for carrying this through was undeveloped.[18]

No statistics exist to indicate exactly how many received registration and how many were refused. The scattered sources available suggest that initially registration was granted with little difficulty to urban churches but it was more difficult for village churches. Often several village congregations were combined in order to produce a larger membership.

The AUCECB promised to announce the number of registered churches once the process was completed.[19] This never materialized and the statistics that were given have only relative value. Moscow Baptist officials claimed 3,000 congregations in 1946, 3,500 congregations in 1947, and 4,000 congregations in 1948.[20] That would indicate a phenomenal increase of 33 percent in two years. However, the apparent growth in congregations was due primarily to the delay in establishing contact with the congregations that were slowly achieving registration and the status of legality. By 1947 President Zhidkov claimed a baptized membership of 350,000.

Detailed statistics have never been shared but the partial information published in *Bratskii Vestnik* during the first decade suggests that there were probably fewer, rather than more than 350,000 members in 1947.[21] The statistical breakdown tends to confirm that without the western border areas which had formerly been outside the Soviet Union the total figure would have been significantly less. Forty-eight percent of the membership was in the Ukraine and three fourths of the believers in the Ukraine came from the Western Ukraine, especially from Volhynia, Rovno, and L'vov provinces. Scattered across the vast regions of the RSFSR from Leningrad in the Northeast to Vladivostok in the Far East were another 21 percent of the membership. More than half of these were located in the central provinces around Moscow. Very likely many more unregistered congregations existed in Siberia and the Far East, since these had been centers of strength before the war and it was to these areas that many believers had been sent to serve their prison sentences and terms of exile. These believers, however, experienced greater difficulties in communicating with the Moscow headquarters. A further 20 percent of the total membership was found in the Baltic republics, White Russia, and Moldavia. The remaining 10 percent was scattered in the Caucasus and Central Asia.

It is not possible to obtain a fully accurate statistical picture but it is sufficiently clear that the Soviet evangelical movement was still alive and that its growth rate would probably not peak very quickly. State authorities were watching events with considerable care and by 1949 there were unmistakable signs that they were worried. As renewed pressure was put on the fledgling congregations and ministers were arrested, many congregations drew back in fear.

The State Becomes Worried

The Soviet state has never been able to demonstrate its conviction that religion is a thing of the past bound to disappear with the advance of scientific progress. Rather, the Soviet state has regularly responded to religious organizations with fear. Therefore, even though the main body of evangelicals and the Orthodox had convincingly demonstrated their patriotic love for the fatherland, when the growing Cold War threatened Soviet security, renewed restrictions on the churches followed.

We have insufficient evidence to permit a detailed analysis of what happened to the AUCECB. By 1948 there were increasing complaints in *Bratskii Vestnik* about violations of the August Agreement by Pentecostals. Zhidkov and Karev issued several instructions intended to suppress the emotional aspects of Pentecostalism. Whether this reflected purely Baptist distaste of Pentecostal emotionalism, as seems plausible, or whether the state wished additional pressures put on the Pentecostals, is a matter of speculation. It was at this period that Pentecostal spokesman Pan'ko was imprisoned and received a 25-year sentence. Only Ponomarchuk of the Pentecostal leaders retained his position.

In the fall of 1948 the AUCECB approved a new, detailed statute. Since this statute was never published, it is difficult to assess its contents. It focused on the organizational aspects of church life, but it was apparent that President Zhidkov anticipated considerable resistance locally. Zhidkov claimed that the statute was worked out on the basis of the Word of God "and contemporary conditions of life."[22] The phrase "contemporary conditions of life" obviously referred to politically imposed limitations, quite possibly to increased restrictions on church activity. These restrictions may have been reflected in the new church statute.

Only two issues of *Bratskii Vestnik* appeared in 1949. The last issue was almost entirely devoted to articles dealing with the subject of Easter—the specific theme of suffering receiving more than adequate treatment. How much physical suffering was experienced by the Moscow leadership is unknown. *Bratskii Vestnik* ceased publication for three years; when it resumed publication in 1953, no explanation for the interval was given. Immediately after the war, letter contact had been established with leaders of the Baptist World Alliance and an official exchange of delegations seemed imminent. All contact with foreign coreligionists was broken off in 1948 and world Baptist leaders could not reestablish contact until 1954.[23]

During the last three or four years of the Stalinist period, numerous restrictive measures against religion were taken by local officials. The Central Church in Kiev (located on Lenin Street) was confiscated by the authorities and three of the four Kiev churches were forced to amalgamate.[24] It was several years later before the senior presbyter for the Ukraine regained use of part of the building as an administrative office. Other churches that had been registered were temporarily or permanently closed. But the severest measures were reserved for that large amorphous group of evangelicals who had not registered formally and did not belong to the AUCECB. Persons who had dared to preach were arrested and usually charged under Article 58 of the Criminal Code for anti-Soviet activities.[25] During that period, 25-year sentences were common, although some "fortunate" persons got only eight or ten years. One story illustrates the procedures.

Heinrich Wiens and Dietrich Klassen had both been prisoners of war,

Klassen having been sent to America. After the war, the Americans, using deception and force, turned them over to the Russians. Upon their return to the Soviet Union, Wiens and Klassen were sent to Kirgizia in Central Asia for forced labor in a uranium mine. Soon they and several others began meeting for fellowship and eventually an evangelical church was formed. Wiens and Klassen were among seven men arrested in 1951 and charged as spies. They were accused of having received training in America in order to organize a fifth-column movement in the Soviet Union by means of religion. Heinrich Wiens received the death sentence and was executed a year later. Although seven of the leadership were in prison, the small congregation continued to meet. Finally it decided to submit a list of its members to the authorities in Moscow with the request to have the congregation registered. In response, nine of the laymen were arrested in April 1952. They were charged under Article 58 and sentenced to 25 years in prison with five years' exile.[26]

The severity of this treatment had the desired effect. Leaderless congregations drew back in terror and ceased meeting. The revival movement had been stopped.

A Second Revival—The Mid-Fifties

A second revival in the mid-fifties had a greater impact on the central and eastern regions of the Soviet Union than on the western border areas where churches grew so rapidly after the war. This movement was also grass roots in character but perhaps more directly affected by preachers recently released from prison. The Russian Germans were to play a major part in it.

On March 5, 1953, Joseph Stalin died. With him died the Stalinist terrors. Some people dared to hope that a better world, a freer world was dawning. Some hoped that in honor of his death an amnesty for prisoners would be declared.

From 1953 to 1956 the struggle for Stalin's succession also affected the religious situation. A violent assault on religion was begun in the press.[27] In late July 1954 a major article urging the "expansion of scientific-atheist propaganda" appeared in *Pravda*. In August Radio Moscow announced that a new periodical to be named *Science and Religion* was about to be published. This journal would specialize in the struggle against God, renewing the atheistic propaganda campaign of the 1930s. But in November 1954 Nikita Khrushchev personally signed a resolution from the Central Committee of the Communist Party which, though it emphasized a need for an increase in the ideological struggle with religion, condemned administrative interference with religious organizations. As a result the antireligious propaganda was relaxed and the promised journal did not begin publication till 1959. During the next several years antireligious articles and pamphlets continued to decrease.

Events would show that it had been futile to hope for the release of all prisoners, but many were released. Many prisoners who had been arrested immediately after the war and sentenced to eight or ten years for so-called anti-Soviet activities (Article 58 of the Criminal Code) completed their terms between 1952 and 1955. These included many preachers, especially of German-Russian background. These sought out their families and tried to settle down for a normal life. Some immediately set about conducting church services; others were finally prevailed upon by former parishioners to risk reading the Bible to them in the secrecy of the home.

Other prisoners, arrested several years later, benefited from Stalin's death in either of two ways. The 25-year sentence was reduced or replaced with an eight-year sentence. Some of these preachers were able to leave prison between 1955 and 1957. Others received amnesty, either as a result of Stalin's death or, as was more common, their sentences were subjected to judicial review and they were rehabilitated. Without question, state authorities were not consciously releasing imprisoned *religiozniks* but rather releasing large numbers of prisoners who had suffered Stalinist injustice.[28] To some extent the Stalinist concentration camp system was being dismantled. For Soviet evangelicals the cumulative effect was significant.

In this second revival wave Soviet Germans, who had officially disappeared from the Soviet Union during World War II, were notably prominent. An Autonomous Volga Republic had been created on February 20, 1924. It had had a population of 500,000, two thirds of it German. In addition there had been large colonies of Soviet Germans in the southern Ukraine along both sides of the Dnieper River. These colonies had been severely uprooted before the war. Many Soviet Germans had immigrated to North America but this was no longer possible after 1930. Many had then been forcibly exiled eastward, having been charged justly or unjustly as kulaks. Many others, especially the men, had disappeared during the purges of the 1930s.[29]

Worried about a potential fifth column aiding the rapidly advancing German invaders, the Soviet Presidium on August 28, 1941, ordered the resettlement of the entire German population in the Volga area eastward to Novosibirsk and Omsk provinces, to the Altai territory and to northern Kazakhstan. Although not officially so reported, the order applied to all

Germans, including those in the Ukraine. In total, about 650,000 Russian Germans were transported to the east in 1941 and 1942. Because of the rapid advance of the German army, most of the Soviet Germans on the west bank of the Dnieper were still awaiting resettlement when the Germans came. These made the trek to the German Reich with the retreating army in 1943. Many died. Perhaps 100,000 managed to stay in the West; the remainder were forcibly repatriated to the Soviet Union. Those not shot immediately joined their brothers in the prisons and concentration camps of Northern and Eastern Russia and Central Asia.[30]

All these Germans were placed under a special command which required them to report to the local command either weekly or monthly. They received no identity papers and it was therefore impossible to move. After Konrad Adenauer's visit to the Soviet Union in 1955, a decree affecting all German citizens in the special settlements was issued.[31] According to this decree, dated December 13, 1955, the special command administration was dismantled. The Germans now received identity cards and were free to move to places of their choice. They had to sign a promise, however, never to move back to their former places of settlement, nor were they given compensation for losses incurred. A fuller rehabilitation did not come till 1964.

The Germans, like other members of the camp system, provided involuntary labor for the great industrial recovery that followed the war.[32] Many were sent to the forests of Northern Russia and Western Siberia. Others found themselves in the Ural Mountains region and in Kazakhstan working in the mines. Usually they were housed in barracks with extremely limited facilities. Untold numbers fell victim to hunger, disease, and frost. Those who managed to survive would never forget how, in their hopelessness, they had cried to God. Some of these groups formed clusters for fellowship in their barracks communities as early as 1948 only to see the authorities come to break up their meetings and arrest their leaders.

With the receipt of internal passports in 1956, these Germans began to seek their immediate relatives and friends throughout the Soviet Union. Wherever they came they sought out fellow believers and shared with them their experiences. Among this group of travelers were experienced ministers whose suffering in prison had increased their spiritual depth. A significant number of the German preachers had attended Bible schools in the 1920s which had been conducted by Mennonites and German Baptists.[33] The revival that they now encountered could therefore be guided toward the systematic organization of churches. Many of these traveling Germans managed to obtain German-language Bibles in the Baltic republics which they then distributed among the scattered Germans in the eastern part of the Soviet Union. Reflecting on the past greatness of the Germans in tsarist Russia, one Volga German told a visitor: "Before the First World War we were like fat tame ducks that had forgotten to fly. Now the Lord has allowed us to be transformed through long periods of suffering and hunger into wild geese, who are able to fly all over Russia for him."[34] That was her picturesque reference to the Bibles she had helped to distribute.

The emotional quality of this revival can be illustrated by various examples but its extent is difficult to quantify. Persons interviewed from as diverse places as Arkhangelsk on the White Sea, Vologda, Western and Eastern Siberia, and Kazakhstan recall this revival of the mid-fifties as something unforgettable. No doubt it affected churches belonging to the AUCECB, but it probably had a much greater impact on the unaffiliated evangelicals. It was also in the mid-fifties that there was a major growth among the Pentecostals in Western Siberia. Four hundred Pentecostals then decided to move to the Far East, resulting in church growth there as well.[35]

AUCECB statistics record considerable growth by 1954. According to Jacob Zhidkov, they baptized 12,000 people in 1954 alone. They now claimed 5,400 congregations with a total membership of 512,000. This claim was also confirmed by a state official.[36] Detailed reports from local regions suggest a more conservative figure but the fact of growth is undeniable. In the Ukraine there was total growth even though in the three largest provinces of the Western Ukraine, 53 congregations representing 3,500 Pentecostals left the Union. By 1954 the member churches in the RSFSR which had consisted of 21 percent of the total membership, now represented 26 percent and showed growth in all major regions of the Russian Federation. Similarly, percentage growth was apparent in Kazakhstan and Central Asia.[37]

The second spurt of growth probably helped to ensure that the church would survive the next major wave of persecution. The rapid growth, however, was also one reason for the launching of a major antireligious campaign. In some places, persecution of religion resumed as early as 1957. By 1959 it had become a generalized campaign with a major propaganda assault. By 1960 the church leadership was forced to institute drastic restrictions of its own activities, and finally in 1961 secret legislation was enforced against the churches. Massive church closures were a major characteristic. Planned as early as 1954, it reached its height during the last five years in which Khrushchev was the unquestioned leader and the policies must be clearly identified with his regime.[38]

Church Growth Techniques Soviet-Style

The Khrushchev antireligious campaign of 1959 to 1964 was second only to the Stalinist persecutions of the 1930s and did major damage to the religious bodies. Many churches were closed; those remaining open had to walk circumspectly. The Evangelical Christian-Baptist Union experienced a major split in its ranks. But the evangelicals were not annihilated as had been hoped; rather, their movement continued to grow in spite of significant losses. Their growth was due to methods of expansion which they had learned during the heady days of the revival era.

Religious education of children was forbidden by law. Only religious education in the home was not explicitly forbidden. Russian evangelicals, especially Mennonites and to a slightly lesser extent the Baptists, placed heavy emphasis on religious education in the home.[39] As historic believers' churches, they had always emphasized that each believer is a priest and above all a priest in his own home. Children learned Bible stories, memorized Scripture verses, and sang the songs of the faith. This accounts for the fact that most new members came from the immediate families of believers.

From its first issue, *Bratskii Vestnik* took great pains to encourage believers to be good examples in their work. Local authorities who included believers on the honor roll at a factory were often ordered by superiors to take down the pictures of Christian work heroes because this was an embarrassment for Soviet propaganda. But through the years the work reliability of Soviet Baptists became proverbial, in spite of numerous propaganda claims to the contrary. This writer once chanced to overhear a conversation between two medium-level officials in a Soviet restaurant. The one remarked that he had a number of believers in his factory and was coming under pressure to dismiss them, but as far as he was concerned, they were good workers and he didn't see why religious persuasion should make a difference in his factory. Those sentiments are becoming widespread except at the party leadership level.

Workmates are a rather significant source for gaining converts. Outright witnessing in the Western sense of introducing the subject of Christianity to some unsuspecting person is not permitted in the Soviet Union. But when the workmates ask questions about the believer's lifestyle and beliefs, he will reply and probably invite the workmate to attend the worship service for himself. The sermon or the music or other aspects of the service may attract his attention and trigger the desire to be converted, but the basic credit belongs to the quiet diligent believer at his place of work.

A great many conversions take place during the week following the beginning of the new year. Most evangelical churches in the Soviet Union conduct a prayer week consisting of nightly services devoted to preaching and congregational prayer. In contrast to worship services during the rest of the year, which are usually unplanned, the prayer week is usually given a special theme so that each sermon, even if delivered by various laymen present, speaks to a common theme. During the revivals of the 1950s, these had been the special occasions where individuals stood up in the service, confessed their sins publicly, broke down in tears, and prayed to God for forgiveness. One man, for example, came to the realization that he had been a prisoner of smoking and therefore wanted to make an end of this sin. Having been converted the night before, he gave his beautiful leather tobacco pouch to a close friend. The friend was converted that night and passed the lovely tobacco pouch on to a third friend. The third friend was converted on the subsequent evening. When he tried to give the tobacco pouch to a fourth friend, the latter protested, fearing that if he accepted the tobacco pouch, he too would have to become converted. This sense of the inevitability of people getting right with God during the first week of the new year because of the concentrated preaching and concentrated praying produced a tradition which has made the new year week of prayer a major tool of evangelism to the present.

Soviet legislation requires that not only the church but also the clergymen must be registered. The clergyman or presbyter is registered with a given congregation and he is not permitted to preach in the neighboring parish.[40] With this stipulation the 1929 legislators tried to restrain the activities of the Baptist evangelists who systematically traveled about trying to gain converts and start new church fellowships. Many evangelists arrested by authorities during the 1950s were punished for violating this legislation. In order to avoid this charge, Soviet evangelicals quickly developed a terminology suited to the occasion. At the end of the service the presiding minister invited visitors from other churches to share greetings. The congregation then stood in formal acceptance of the greetings and asked the visitors to take greetings back in return.

If the person bringing the greeting is a minister, the local leader will invite the guest to step forward to the pulpit to share the greetings with the entire congregation. The visitor then begins giving greetings from his family and his church, describing some of their activities and concerns. As he continues with his greetings he also adds greetings from Paul or Peter or Jesus. Naturally, to share specific greetings from Jesus involves reading a passage of Scripture and explaining what it means and what significance it has for this greeting. In short, the visitor will have used up the equivalent of a twenty-minute sermon for his greeting. The initiated foreign visitor will not be offended if he is simply invited to give a greeting and will know what to do.

Several rather creative techniques have developed to suit the Soviet context for evangelism. Whereas many American churches attribute their high growth rate to a strong emphasis on the Sunday school, the Sunday school is forbidden in the Soviet Union and is in any case not a part of the historical tradition. But in an average church, twelve children ages six to nine will have twelve birthdays, probably one a month on an average. Birthday parties are very important in the Soviet Union. In a believing family friends of the believing child will gather for a party. They will play games which may include Bible quizzes, treasure hunts where the treasure is a Bible verse beautifully printed on a piece of paper, or similar religious didactic games. Mother or Father will surely be present and may read a Scripture passage or lead in prayer, although very often the children will wish to do this themselves. In short, a carefully planned system of birthday parties has provided an excellent Sunday school substitute.

Special youth meetings are also forbidden by law. Every evangelical congregation has a choir consisting of volunteers. Obviously the choir needs to practice regularly in order to sing well. In many congregations the choir practice is carefully planned to serve as a substitute for the youth meetings. Many unconverted young people enjoy singing and the local church choir provides an opportunity for this as well as an opportunity to meet members of the opposite sex. Choir practice begins with a short Scripture meditation and prayer. Often during the middle of the rehearsal, time will be taken for another "sermon," often devoted to a topic of special interest to young people. Not only does this make the choir an important teaching vehicle for the young people, it also means that the choir leader must be a person of special capabilities. His ability to relate to young people and to expound the Word may be as important as his musical skills.

There are two human phenomena that will always continue and which are uniquely suited to reflecting on questions of life and death. For the human race to procreate, men and women must marry. Marriages in the Soviet Union are formalized in a simple civil procedure but a growing number of young people demand the addititional romance of a religious marriage ceremony.[41] Christian weddings are special occasions for evangelism. Both bride and groom will invite unconverted friends and relatives, as well as work colleagues. Often the wedding is conducted outdoors with several preachers present who will address their sermons not only to the young Christian couple before them but also to the guests present, who may be total strangers to a sermon. Persons converted through a wedding often report that the biggest impact made upon them was the way the wedding was conducted without excessive drinking, and also the attractiveness of the Christian young people whom they encountered.

Visitors to the Soviet Union report attending funerals at gravesides that could best be described as an evangelistic rally. Immediate family members had paid their respects to the dear departed in the privacy of the home. At the graveside a religious service, which is legally permitted, was held. Many unbelieving friends, relatives, and neighbors were present to honor the deceased. The service itself, however, made minimal reference to the deceased and focused much more on the needs of those living. Many congregations make certain that their most able preacher is present to deliver an attractive, persuasive gospel sermon. Music sung for the service is also more concerned to communicate the gospel than to speak consolingly to the mourners. After all, as Soviet evangelicals love to repeat, the dear deceased has gone to a place of joy and those who remain rejoice with him, but they weep for those whose eternal destiny is still unsure.

When AUCECB leaders first traveled abroad in 1954, they regularly encountered amazement that a church still existed in the Soviet Union. Westerners had expected that the church would have capitulated many years earlier and if any Christians remained, they would be a mere remnant living in secret. It was clear by 1955 that the evangelicals were thriving in spite of the difficulties. President Zhidkov liked to emphasize their freedoms in comparison with the difficulties they had experienced under the tsars.[42] However, it would be more accurate to say they had enough freedom to continue to exist, yet enough difficulties to ensure that the emerging church was a church of the highly committed only.

A Costly Faith

In one of his famous discussions, Father Dmitrii Dudko read a letter from a young husband who described how he had begun searching for God.[43] Life had become meaningless for him and he had finally decided that perhaps he should explore the ideas contained in religion. He went to a bookstore but found only atheist literature. One book entitled *The Bible for Believers and Unbelievers* turned out to be a satire on Christianity. Finally he asked an old neighbor lady whether she knew a priest and the frightened little *babushka* promised to ask around. The priest that he did meet was quite different from the stereotypes he had read about and he discovered it was interesting to talk to the priest. In fact the priest had a more rounded education than he had himself. The priest gave him a New Testament which he started to read with great interest but was obliged to hide it so that his wife who was teaching in an institute of Marxism-Leninism would not find out about it. After a while he discovered that his wife was reading the Bible secretly but was hiding it from him the way he had hidden it from her. Then he discovered she had been baptized and had baptized their child. Since he also believed the words of the Book, he decided all that remained to be done was for him to be baptized. When he requested baptism, they asked to see his passport. Soon people at work called him in and informed him that if they had known he was a believer they would not have given him the apartment he had received recently. The letter ended with the plucky young man asserting that he would continue with his newfound faith, no matter what.

This story illustrates the numerous disadvantages in joining Christianity, especially for young career-oriented persons. In spite of that, many determined to join as did this young man. Many new converts were baptized into the new evangelical churches after the war. Soon the AUCECB leadership began urging greater restraint. In 1953, 125 persons were baptized in the Moscow church.[44] According to the rules of the AUCECB, no one could be baptized until he had reached the age of 18 years. But Orlov, the presbyter in Moscow at the time, emphasized that baptismal candidates between the ages of eighteen and twenty-five formed an insignificant number of the total baptismal candidates because they were still so young and had not had opportunity to demonstrate their faith in practice.

Perhaps the state was interfering because numerous lay people complained that the minimum age of baptism appeared to be 25 or sometimes even 30 years of age. Before being baptized, the baptismal candidate submitted to the presbyter a written statement requesting baptism. After a year of testing, several members of the church who knew the candidate personally were asked to give a character reference. If the indications were still positive, the congregation would vote to accept the candidate for baptism. What *Bratskii Vestnik* failed to mention was that each baptismal candidate had to be approved by the state authorities before the baptism could take place. This often produced long delays while the candidate's colleagues at work, for example, were putting on pressure to dissuade him from his attempts.

The Moscow leadership repeatedly urged local congregations to install a baptistry in the church building, if possible.[45] Where this was not possible, the baptism could be performed in a lake, river, or sea. If this was the case, the presbyter was urged to conduct the service very early in the morning with only the necessary number of persons present. These would include the presbyter, the baptismal candidates, and sufficient brothers and sisters to assist in the changing room. There should be no big parade to the place of baptism and the worship service itself should be conducted in the prayer house. Nonregistered congregations often held secret baptismal services at night and sometimes accommodating presbyters from registered congregations secretly baptized a young person without submitting his name to the state authorities. But even then the disadvantages of being a Christian in Soviet society were felt.

By the later 1960s another factor made it problematic to join the Soviet evangelicals. Evangelicals placed a strong emphasis on personal ethics and expected their believers to be honest in their dealings. This meant that someone contemplating joining an evangelical church would have to be prepared to forego numerous comforts and even necessities of life because he could not in good conscience purchase items on the black market. Living *na levo* had become widespread; many citizens regarded life as impossible if one did not cheat along the way.[46] Sometimes it even meant that the Christian trying to build a house would have to wait for years or else rely on his own ingenuity because the doors for his house had not been obtainable except on the black market. Often local officials were simply waiting for a Christian to give in to temptation to buy the doors anyway and then would pounce on him. That also helped to guarantee that church discipline would be swift for anyone trying to serve God and mammon at the same time.

In short, deciding to become a Christian, to risk a baptism, and to continue to live and identify with Christians made life difficult. But that is precisely why it is possible to say that the evangelical church in the Soviet Union is a strong church. As Zhidkov remarked, "Better a small group but true followers of Christ, than a large congregation, but such on whom we cannot depend."[47]

Believers still recall with fond memories the early period before the Khrushchev persecution set in. For many believers, that was the period of "first love." It was a time when revival swept the countryside, when the simple joy of hearing God's Word read and preached produced indescribable emotions. Then people rejoiced if a companion was also a believer without caring to know his denominational affiliation. Personally many remembered the bitter tears of repentance at their own conversion and the tears of joy at forgiveness experienced.[48] The physical accommodations for worship were extremely primitive but never was the fellowship as warm as then. Many participants recall miraculous experiences and include among these the discovery of a courage not their own, sometimes even the discovery of a preaching gift not their own. In spite of everything, there had been the unconquerable conviction that God would triumph. That was when they had realized that God had not forgotten them after all, that He still spoke to them with love and forgiveness. That was when hope was renewed that someday Russia would be won for Christ.

The revivals had come in waves because their character and essence was emotional. The state authorities responded emotionally because their own atheism was really anti-theism. That meant a stable church must maintain a momentum of growth or else lose ground to atheist activists. It required new techniques for church growth. The flashy, hard-sell techniques for evangelism so common in North America were inappropriate. Each member and each potential church member knew that it would cost something to espouse the faith.

Notes to Chapter 2

1. John Paterson, *The Book for Every Land* (London, 2d ed., 1858), p. 192.
2. *BV*, 3/47, p. 32.
3. *BV*, 1/48, p. 60. *BV*, 1/47, p. 15, states that baptisms took place in almost all churches; in some churches the newly baptized constituted 30% or more of the membership.
4. *BV*, 1/46, pp. 35-36. In the 70th-anniversary report on Evangelical-Baptist publications Zhidkov stated: "Now we have the necessary quantity of Bibles and when these are used up we can again publish the quantity of Bibles, New Testaments and hymnbooks needed by us" (*BV*, 5/47, p. 19). That statement is incomprehensible and must be regarded as less than candid.
5. *Dein Reich Komme* (May-June 1947), p. 40. A letter in *Der Bote*, September 1957, from the Soviet Union complained that no Bibles had yet arrived. "If it would help, I would cry my heart out (ich weinte mich satt)." Even in 1960 a Mennonite delegation reported that "Bibles, Bibles and Bibles again is the heart cry of the believers" (MCC files, Akron, Pa., USA).
6. *BV*, 2-3/53, p. 110; cf. *BV*, 1/48, where Zhidkov noted that "in certain congregations the leaders are sisters, especially wise and experienced and developed in spiritual relations" (p. 7).
7. *BV*, 1/46, p. 34.
8. This story and the ones following are based on systematic interviews with recent Soviet German emigrants to West Germany which I have conducted since 1974.
9. Virginia Classen, Peter Neufeld, & Vern Q. Preheim, "Glimpses of the Mennonites in Russia, 1848-1947," unpublished research paper based on analysis of

letters in *Der Bote*, Bethel College, February 1957, p. B8.

10. *BV*, 1/48, p. 7.

11. *BV*, 5/48, pp. 32-37.

12. *Pravda*, July 1, 1944. For an extended history and analysis see this writer's "Religious Administration and Modernization," in Dennis Dunn, ed., *Religion and Modernization in the Soviet Union* (Boulder, Colo.: Westview Press, 1978), pp. 60-104; cf. Luchterhandt, *Der Sowjetstaat*, pp. 212-232.

13. Bohdan R. Bociurkiw, "Church-State Relations in the USSR," *Survey* (January 1968), p. 21.

14. A. Kolosov, "Religiia i tserkov v SSSR," *Bolshaia Sovetskaia Entsiklopediia* (Moscow, 1947), p. 1788. Luchterhandt (pp. 102-104) cites an article by Bonch-Bruevich printed 1959 which he believes to be a verbatim rendering of the council's statute. It differs from Kolosov only in that the latter summarizes the work of both councils whereas the statute cited refers to the Council for Russian Orthodox Church Affairs.

15. Walter Sawatsky, "Secret Soviet Lawbook on Religion," *RCL*, IV, 4 (Winter 1976), pp. 24-34. This includes an English translation of the statute. An abridged copy of the lawbook in German translation with commentary by Luchterhandt is: *Die Religionsgesetzgebung der Sowjetunion* (Berlin Verlag, 1978).

16. For the text of the letter and an up-to-date analysis of its significance, see Luchterhandt, *Der Sowjetstaat*, pp. 108-111.

17. An English translation of the Law on Religious Associations of April 8, 1929, and the official Instructions (or interpretation) of October 1, 1929, is available, for example, in William B. Stroyen, *Communist Russia and the Russian Orthodox Church* (Washington, D.C., 1967), pp. 121-35.

18. The Council for the Affairs of Religious Cults (CARC), which had been created in 1944, had to be staffed by regional and local plenipotentiaries. Given the shortage in manpower and the obvious low priority assigned to religion, CARC must have taken some years to develop its authority and efficiency.

19. *BV*, 2/45, p. 43.

20. *BV*, 1/47, p. 13; 5/47, p. 12; 1/48, p. 7.

21. A detailed comparison of all partial statistical data (e.g., actual figures given for congregations and membership in a few oblasts or the number of presbyters under a specific senior presbyter) resulted in the following general estimates: RSFSR—24,471 (390 congregations); Ukraine—54,171 (1,081 cong.); Belorussia—9,934 (116 cong.); Moldavia—3,788 (88 cong.); Baltic Republics—8,720 (163 cong.); Caucasus—3,500 (14 cong.); Kazakh SSR—4,000 (25 cong.); Central Asia—3,800 (23 cong.). A corrected total using additional data suggested a membership of 148,213 in 2,600 congregations in 1948.

22. *BV*, 1/49, p. 21; cf. *BV*, 5/48, p. 37, stated that the statute "consists of 44 points regularizing the work of the AUCECB, senior presbyters, presbyters, deacons, brotherhood councils, revision commissions, choirs, etc."; the next issue announced that congregations were receiving copies of the organizational structure, as well as certain guidelines (6/48, p. 67).

23. When *Bratskii Vestnik* renewed publication in 1953 a list of all the foreign visitors to the AUCECB from 1950 to 1953 was published (1/53, pp. 63-64). Visitors were limited almost exclusively to persons traveling privately or as part of some nonreligious delegation and did include Baptist laymen from Britain, USA and Denmark and a Baptist pastor from Philadelphia.

24. *BV*, 5-6/54, p. 114.

25. Article 58 of the Criminal Code of the RSFSR, established in 1926 and repealed in December 1958, is printed in English in Conquest, *The Great Terror*,

pp. 741-46. It permitted charges against anyone who might represent a threat to the regime; that is, all political prisoners and prisoners of conscience.

26. Interview data including court sentence. For certain details I am indebted to Dr. Cornelius Krahn.

27. Bernard Feron, *Gott in Sowjetrussland* (Essen, 1963), pp. 56-60. Cf. Struve, p. 269; Robert C. Tucker, "Party and Church in the Soviet Union—Travel Notes," *The Russian Review*, 1959, p. 285.

28. But a decade later a Soviet writer publicly acknowledged this when, in connection with the Mennonites, he remarked that "a new wave of activity began in the sect in 1956-57, when active preachers began to return from prison" (F. Fedorenko, *Sekty ikh vera i dela* [Moscow, 1965], p. 153).

29. Major research on this subject is in progress but a useful survey is Adam Giesinger, *From Catharine to Khrushchev: The Story of Russia's Germans* (Winnipeg, 1974), chaps. 16 and 17.

30. On the politics of repatriation see Nikolai Tolstoy, *Victims of Yalta* (London, 1978), and Nicholas Bethell, *The Last Secret* (London, 1974). What happened to those who returned is a story told in semiautobiographical form in Walter Wedel, *Nur zwanzig Kilometer* (Wuppertal: Brockhaus, 1979).

31. Quoted in Giesinger, p. 317.

32. For a general survey see Conquest, *The Great Terror*, Chap. 10, especially p. 481f.

33. Due to a more tolerant treatment under the tsars, German Mennonites and Baptists had a more developed church organization including seminaries. Many of them also attended German theological schools in Lodz (Poland), Dorpat University, or even St. Chrischona seminary in Basel.

34. Licht im Osten, Korntal files.

35. Interview with Evgenii Bresenden, Pasadena, Calif., November 1977.

36. *BV*, 3-4/54, p. 91; 2/54, pp. 61-62. (The text of a program by Radio Moscow in reply to listeners' questions from Brazil about freedom of religion in the Soviet Union.)

37. An estimate based on extrapolations from local detailed statistics suggests a total of 181,889 members in 2,515 congregations.

38. See below, Chap. 5, for an extended treatment.

39. V. F. Krest'ianinov, *Mennonity* (Moscow, 1967), p. 177f.

40. Registration of clergy was introduced by instruction of the Council of Religious Affairs in 1968 (cf. Kuroedov & Pankratov, ed., *Zakonodatel'stvo o religioznykh kul' takh*, pp.133-50), although a licensing of clergy was in effect earlier. Article 19 of the 1929 Law on Religious Associations restricts clergy activity to the local parish; cf. Michael Rowe, "Soviet Policy Towards Evangelicals," *RCL*, VII, 1 (Spring 1979), 6.

41. To counter this trend, state officials in the late fifties introduced a patriotic marriage ritual in special wedding palaces (cf. Feron, pp. 14-15).

42. See for example *BV*, 5/47, celebrating the 80th anniversary of the Evangelical Baptist movement and 6/47 celebrating the 30th anniversary of the Great October Revolution.

43. *Our Hope* (New York, 1978), pp. 31-33.

44. *BV*, 1/53, p. 40. In Moscow 350 persons were baptized during the first six months of 1951 (p. 14).

45. *Ibid.*, p. 40; cf. 5/48, pp. 25-28; 5/48, p. 4.

46. On living *na levo* see Chap. 3 in Hedrick Smith, *The Russians* (New York: Times Books, 1976); cf. Gregory Grossman, "The 'Second Economy' of the USSR," *Problems of Communism*, XXVI (September-October, 1977), 25-41. The "second

economy" refers to all financial transactions of an unofficial or illegal character and may represent nearly half of the GNP.

47. *BV*, 5/48, p. 4.

48. Soviet evangelicals appear to have been influenced by the Orthodox Theology of Tears. Wilhelm Kahle, "Die Tränen der Frommen in der Gottesbegegnung: Ein Beitrag zur oekumenischer Spiritualität," in Andrew Blane, ed., *The Ecumenical World of Orthodox Civilization*, Vol. III of *Russia and Orthodoxy* (The Hague: Mouton, 1974).

The "marriage" did not take place because both partners
wanted to be the man . . .

—*Kahle, p. 208*

3 A New Evangelical Union: The Tangled Unity Thread

In wartime conditions 45 delegates (seven of them women) met on October 26, 1944, in the Moscow Evangelical Christian Church to hold a unity congress. Congress delegates had traveled to Moscow in military transports, hotel accommodation and food was provided by the state, and without question the state ensured that the congress would make the proper decisions. Nevertheless, participants later recalled the moment with exultation. When the crucial vote was taken and the chairman announced that unification was a unanimous decision, leading Baptists and Evangelical Christians embraced. Many wept openly with joy and broke forth into songs and prayers of thanksgiving. What God working through stubborn Christians had been unable to do, God working through Stalin had finally achieved—the wonder of unity.

The Long Search for Unity

Significant unification efforts began only after the revolution of 1905. Several new edicts began to permit the evangelical groupings a legal existence. Both Baptists and Evangelical Christians introduced statements of faith for submission to the authorities.[1] Concerned that a unified front be presented to the government, Ivan Prokhanov and the alliance-oriented congregation in Petersburg invited fellow evangelicals to meet to work out a joint declaration to the government. This congress, meeting January 15-19, 1906, at Princess Lieven's house in St. Petersburg, involved the participation of Evangelical Christians, Baptists, and New Molokans.

The conference had been fairly amicable until the Baptists vehemently rejected a clause which declared that children had the same confession and church membership as their parents. All compromise amendments failed and the New Molokans who could not regard their children as heathen, as did the Baptists, left the meeting.

A foreign observer, greatly disappointed by the results of the meeting, described the participants as sitting in blocs very similar to the left, right, and center groupings in the state *Duma*.[2] On the right sat Dei Mazaev at the head of a forty-man Baptist delegation; on the left were five representatives from the New Molokans; and in the middle were the Evangelical Christians. Although Ivan Kargel was the chairman, Mazaev very quickly proceeded to dominate the meeting in a style that reminded a foreign observer of an Eastern despot. Mazaev announced the Baptist proposals, called for a vote, and all the Baptist representatives shot their hands up into the air, often raising both hands to make a stronger impression.[3]

Swedish missionary Johannes Svensson, who attended this meeting, described Mazaev as follows:

> He is tall and stately, the head is bald, the graying beard covers both his chest as well as the bottom part of his face. He is a good speaker, adroit and clever, and he is Baptist from head to foot.[4]

Once the New Molokans had walked out, the character of the conference was no longer that of an *Allianzkonferenz*, according to Svensson, but purely a Baptist conference, since anyone having a different opinion from Mazaev did not say a word. Svensson went on:

> You felt you were in Russia, where despotism had placed its stamp on everyone and everything. He who has the power rules and pays no heed to what others feel and think.[5]

The historian of the Russian Baptists, Paul Steeves, took a more friendly attitude to Mazaev. He described Mazaev as a skillful administrator who, due to his wealth, appeared better able to avoid imprisonment. He was busy organizing illegal congresses during the decades when Pobedonostsev was harassing the sectarians severely. Steeves also repeated a rumor to the effect that in 1905 Dei Mazaev was elected as a delegate to the new state *Duma* (parliament), but the election was stopped by the authorities because "with his mind, Mazaev will also very likely achieve the chair of president of the

Duma, and then he will become a minister, and we certainly must not be under the influence of the Baptists."[6] Mazaev, born into a poor Molokan family, was baptized in 1885, and in 1887 took over leadership from Johannes Wieler. He remained president of this gradually developing Baptist Union till 1920, except for 1909-11. He died on May 20, 1922, in Siberia, though he had lived most of his life in Rostov-on-Don.[7]

The other major figure in the unity struggle was Ivan S. Prokhanov (1869-1935).[8] He was baptized in 1887 and worked with Baptist groups initially. Within two years he was in St. Petersburg (Leningrad), where he completed an engineering course. After 1901 he worked as engineer for Westinghouse and spent evenings and weekends in the many and varied church activities which another person would have found possible only as a full-time activity. From 1895 to 1898 Prokhanov was abroad studying theology at the Baptist Stokes Croft College and the New Congregational College in Bristol. However, he graduated from the theological faculty of the University of Berlin. He also took in theological lectures at the University of Paris, as well as in Hamburg. This not only meant that Prokhanov became fluent in the major world languages but this heterogeneous education turned him into a supporter of the Evangelical Alliance. After 1901 his activities in St. Petersburg were devoted to fostering the development of small evangelical groups, the founding of the Russian Christian Youth Movement (where Jacob Zhidkov and Alexander Karev began their church careers), involvement in the Raduga press, publication of the journal *Khristianin*, and finally in 1909 the founding of the Evangelical Christian Union.

If Dei Mazaev was the unquestioned leader of the Baptists, Ivan Prokhanov was by 1909 the unchallenged leader of the Evangelical Christians. Especially during the period 1906-1909 Prokhanov had great visions of a union embracing all Russian Protestants through which he hoped to effect a Reformation in Russia. In his repeated calls for union during this period he ignored dogmatic differences by leaving them to the jurisdiction of local congregations and instead called for unity on essentials and freedom on secondary issues. This was the approach of the Evangelical Alliance movement in Western Europe also.[9]

But the New Molokans walked out of the 1907 conference due to irreconcilable differences with the Baptists on the baptism question. They were a small group of several hundred living on the Lower Volga who had been spiritually renewed through the preaching of Jacob Deliakov. Deliakov, of Presbyterian origin, emphasized child baptism. The New Molokans had taken the name "Evangelical Christians."[10] Other groupings, including Prokhanov's own Evangelical Christian Union, thereafter failed to gain as broad support nationally as he had hoped so that by 1911 he had to recognize that outside of the Baptists, there remained no realistic possible partners for the Evangelical Christians. Unity must therefore be sought with that union now dominant in Russian Protestantism, namely the Russian Baptists. Gradually, therefore, Prokhanov and his associates were forced to capitulate to Baptist demands in the hope of attaining unity.

Baptists on the other hand played the passive role in the unity attempt. In 1911, one of their leaders, S. P. Stepanov, had stated at a Baptist congress: "The Evangelical Christians have now accepted the Baptist teaching concerning elders, which not long before they had rejected as unacceptable. In any case, it is not necessary for us to go to them."[11] Other Baptists shared this view, regarding themselves as the older union because they claimed 1884 as their official founding date whereas Evangelical Christians had only formalized their union in 1909.[12]

The Baptist viewpoint was that there had been one union but that a split-away group under Prokhanov's leadership later formed a competing union and immediately tried to claim equal rank with the former by proposing a union of the two bodies. Striving toward unity existed from the beginning but unity as expressed through a council structure was a newer phenomenon, where both sides were just beginning to organize. Confessions of faith were approved in 1906 and 1909 for Baptists and Evangelical Christians respectively, and a full constitution was approved only in 1910 for each of the two respective groups.

No progress was made in unity for a decade. From 1909 to 1911 the jockeying for leadership of the Baptist Union between Dei Mazaev representing the "closed communion" Baptists and Vasili Pavlov of the more open wing prevented full participation of the Baptists in unity talks.[13] After 1911 political reaction meant new harassment of the evangelicals so that no national congress by either union was possible till the Revolution of 1917. Hence, neither union could get official endorsement from its membership on the unity issue. Following the February Revolution the Evangelical Christians again took the initiative. At their congress in 1917 they invited Baptist representatives to be present. A unity resolution was adopted in the presence of five Baptists, all of the latter representing the open Baptists. At an Evangelical Christian congress in 1919, with two Baptists present, a unity committee was set up. This unity committee met in January 1920 and named a ten-member All-Union Council consisting of five Evangelical Christians and five Baptists.[14] A joint journal called *Bratskii Soiuz* (Fraternal Union) was actually started. Later in the year both unions held congresses which intended to approve this union and it was hoped that the second half of the Evangelical Christian congress would become a union congress. The Baptists at their congress approved the decisions. But the strong Siberian and Far Eastern departments were not represented and so the congress was subsequently challenged as unrepresentative.[15] The joint congress scheduled for the following year (1921) could not be held due to the imprisonment of Prokhanov and possibly to other state interference.

At the January 1920 meeting of the ten-man committee to plan the unity conference, participants encountered numerous difficulties. The Civil War provided its tensions, the weather was cold, the building was insufficiently heated, it was difficult to obtain transportation to Petrograd, and a number of participants failed to obtain travel permission from the state. Of those who managed to attend, only two were not Petrograd residents, and one of them, Baptist leader P. V. Pavlov, managed to get to Petrograd only on the third day of the meetings. The historian of the Evangelical Christians, Wilhelm Kahle, remarked: "Such working conditions and the absence or late arrival of participants . . . are important factors in answering the question why unity negotiations took so long, and why they had to be begun anew so often, why points which had been settled by a small circle of participants re-emerged as points of discussion for others."[16]

Why Unity Failed

Unity was almost achieved in 1920 but failed for several reasons. In addition to the fact that Prokhanov's imprisonment in Tver hindered the planned unity congress in 1921, the Baptists suffered from internal conflicts since Mazaev supporters had circulated a letter in June 1921 which stated that in the south there were unions of Baptists who wanted nothing to do with the Baptist leadership in Moscow.[17] Prokhanov had made public the details of the union agreement in the new union newspaper that was launched, but some Baptists objected to this because the agreement still lacked official approval from the respective unions. Other Baptists felt that the points of the agreement gave Evangelical Christians the advantages. In any case, both in this agreement and in subsequent contracts regulating a Bible school and the coordination of relief work, the two groups displayed considerable distrust of each other.[18]

The reasons why earlier unity efforts failed helps to explain the nature of the union that emerged in 1944. Three theological issues were regularly discussed and appeared again as separate points in the 1944 act of union. These were the disagreements on baptism, communion, and the ordination and significance of the clerical office. Very early the Evangelical Christians, due especially to Prokhanov's Baptist origins, came to accept believer's baptism. But there was less agreement on the laying on of hands on new church members. Communion must be administered by an ordained presbyter, according to the Baptists, whereas the Evangelical Christians placed little emphasis on the clerical office.[19]

Although the articulated differences were theological, it becomes evident that the greatest worry of the Baptists, an apprehension far more important than the differing viewpoints on the ordinances, was their concern for church discipline. Repeatedly in their discussions they asked for clarifications of the status of those persons who had been excommunicated from their church and who had been accepted as members in the Evangelical Christian Union. Frequently the excommunication or voluntary departure from the Baptist Union reflected a rejection of the strict regulations enforced by the Baptists. From the Baptist point of view it was clear that their Baptist understanding and practice was biblical, and that they had a greater claim to biblical truth than any other church body. A committed Baptist could not conceive of any other reason for rejecting Baptist distinctives than willful disobedience of the commands of Jesus. Therefore, renunciation of Baptist distinctives was apostasy and with apostates no fellowship could be possible.[20] This became the insoluble question since given the fluid nature of evangelicalism in the twenties, there had been considerable membership migration. The Evangelical Christians were prepared from henceforth to recognize each other's disciplinary measures, but did not wish to make the measure retroactive. It was in this area that the greatest distrust between the two bodies became evident, each apparently competing for members.

But the leading participants also made unity difficult. Jacob Zhidkov later remarked that as young believers they had been very embarrassed by the rabid polemics of Dei Mazaev in the *Baptist* newspaper between 1909 and 1912.[21] Others felt that from the very start Ivan Prokhanov, who had had no following, had developed a record by taking over the church in St. Petersburg, then trying to swallow up nearby Baptist churches, and wherever he went inviting the disaffected to make common cause with him. Thereby, they felt, he hoped to achieve a large union which lacked any doctrinal coherence, but which he would lead and direct for his ends. Outside observers regard this as unjust but do recognize that Prokhanov's powerful

personality brought him as many enemies as friends, thus limiting his
suitability as leader of the union.[22] Prokhanov's attempt to compromise with
the Baptists by accepting their emphases was misinterpreted. Even his decision in 1924 to be ordained was understood as evidence of lack of scruples
rather than as a peace offering.[23]

Conflict within Baptist ranks continued and was never really solved.
The conflict between Mazaev and Pavlov flared up again in the 1920s. Not
only was it the difference between practicing open and closed communion
or a personality conflict between two strong personalities, it also became a
conflict on the question of military service. In the early 1920s the so-called
"new" Baptists favoring conscientious objection, an alignment roughly
identical with the more open Baptists, were in the majority. State interference finally enabled the "old" Baptists to gain the upper hand in the
leadership.[24]

The Decision to Unite

Considering the protracted struggle to unite Evangelical Christians
and Baptists, the unity congress that took place in October 1944 appears de-
ceptively placid. That was because all problematic issues had been settled in
advance. By whom they were settled is not entirely clear. According to the
published record, two Baptist spokesmen, N. A. Levindanto and M. I.
Goliaev, had formally requested the Evangelical Christian Union to look
after their Baptist congregations. But Levindanto was in prison. Secret
police officials visited him and another leading Baptist, F. G. Patkovskii, in
the prison and informed them that churches would be reopened and that
Baptist and Evangelical Christian congregations were to be united. Levindanto and Patkovskii were to be released to help lead the unification. These
men were only too glad to hear that churches would be opened again so
they set about their part of the task immediately.[25] Who took the first initiative therefore remains shrouded in mystery. Perhaps Goliaev was following
a suggestion from his father, the last Baptist president who died in Tashkent
in 1942. Clearly there had been no possibility to obtain authorization from
the church membership, but by 1942 war patriotism hinted at a potential
role for the evangelicals.

At least a number of former church officials were quick to respond
positively to the apparent gestures of goodwill. Presumably they were in no
position to bargain for legal protection or to resist measures that in the early
1920s they would have been unwilling to undertake. The state was not only
rewarding good patriots for helping win the war; friendly gestures to the re-

ligious bodies also helped the Soviet state war propaganda. The creation of the patriarchate and the establishment of an evangelical union improved the Soviet image in the Western world. In addition, both the Orthodox Church and the evangelical union now actively engaged in war propaganda through letters to their fellow believers abroad. Without doubt, their most important contribution was to assist in the pacification of the newly annexed border areas.

One of the first acts at the unity congress was to send a telegram to Joseph Stalin, chairman of the Council of People's Commissars, in appreciation for making possible the satisfaction of the religious needs of believers. On the second day of the congress a five-man delegation was sent to Polianskii, chairman of the Council for the Affairs of Religious Cults, to thank him for that council's assistance in making the congress possible. All the reports on the congress maintained a positive tone. Clearly, no one dared to resist even if the official statements might not have been wholeheartedly endorsed by everyone.

The 1944 unity congress remains to the present day somewhat of a mystery and a point of controversy. Summaries of the activities including verbatim rendering of major decisions were printed in the first issue of *Bratskii Vestnik* that began appearing in 1945. The congress itself is openly presented, but it is the preparations for the congress and the decisions which had obviously been taken by a smaller group earlier that have never been discussed openly. The second issue of *Bratskii Vestnik* reads like a concerted attempt to try to prove the authority of the unity congress. An opening article, unsigned, developed six arguments to prove the authority of the congress: (1) The decisions on unity were based on the commands and prayers of the Lord Jesus Christ. (2) The congress simply confirmed what had been agreed upon at earlier congresses. (3) The persons gathered at the congress were the oldest and most experienced workers at present from both denominations. In this connection the writer noted that all 45 members of the congress were already members of churches before 1917 and then listed those persons participating in a succession of unity conferences who were also present in 1944. (4) All the decisions were unanimous. (5) The conference received greetings and expressions of good wishes from Drs. Rushbrooke and Lewis of the Baptist World Alliance and Dr. Johnson from the Evangelical Christians in America. (6) The authority of the conference also rested on the fact that the central state organ, *Izvestiia*, printed a brief report about it on November 10. These arguments, quite obviously, were needed to offset the fundamental weakness of the congress, namely, that the participants were not elected representatives of congregations or regional unions. This violated the fundamental congregational principle of both unions, although it was in keeping with new state policy toward religion which favored negotiations with a centralized leadership.[26]

The 1944 congress simply approved what had been agreed upon in 1942. There exists a curious letter in translation in the Washington office of the Baptist World Alliance that helps both to illuminate and to obscure what happened. Addressed to Dr. J. H. Rushbrooke, president, and signed by Jacob Zhidkov and Alexander Karev, the opening sentence reads: "We are sending you a second answer to your letter of January 24, 1942."[27] This second letter, dated February 12, 1943, finally arrived in London February 16, 1944, fully a year later! The letter informed Rushbrooke about the creation of a union of Evangelical Christians and Baptists and with its executive organ the All-Union Council domiciled in Moscow. Zhidkov reported that five persons from the Evangelical Christians and five from the Baptists had been delegated into the All-Union Council. President of the council was Jacob Zhidkov and the secretary was Alexander V. Karev. "As soon as circumstances permit we intend to call a general All-Union conference of Evangelical Christians and Baptists, where the final fusion of the two organizations into one union is to be accomplished."

Apparently by February 1943, ten persons had agreed on the nature of the union, had identified the president and secretary, and had left the choice of name up to the local congregations. Levindanto's report to the 1944 congress differs slightly by failing to mention the president and secretary and listing only a nine-member council; one of them, I. A. Goliaev, had died in September 1942.[28] The letter to Rushbrooke mentioned Urstein as the fifth Evangelical Christian representative, but this individual was not mentioned in 1944 and is unknown from earlier Evangelical Christian history.

Unity Congress Participants

Without question, the recipients of the *Bratskii Vestnik* report would look closely at the list of congress participants before deciding to consider it a legitimate congress. Such an examination of participants required not only noting who was present, but also asking who was missing and why. A total of 45 persons attended.[29] There were 21 Moscow representatives; seven of these were women. The next largest delegation came from the Ukraine; these numbered 11. In addition there were three from Novosibirsk, one from Kuibyshev (Levindanto), one from Leningrad, two from White

Russia, and several others from the Russian Federation. A subsequent report on the congress [30] claimed that representatives from Arkhangel'sk and from the Caucasus had also been present but these are not listed among the official 45, although it is easily possible that delegates came from prison camps in these areas but were officially listed as representing their former home church.

Out of the 45 delegates, 28 were Evangelical Christians and 19 were Baptists. This imbalance should not necessarily call the competence of the congress into question. If there were 1½ times as many Baptists as Evangelical Christians in 1907, by the 1930s there were three times as many Evangelical Christians as Baptists.[31] In addition, it was the Evangelical Christian Union that had managed to maintain a form of existence including contact with congregations so that it was in a better position to invite its local leaders to the congress. The seven women present were there because they were the ones who had signed appeals to Christian women to help the war effort with bandages and similar necessities. But a further reason was that hereby the wife of the longtime Baptist president Mazaev could lend her prestige to the congress by her presence. Another woman, A. I. Mozgova, had served as secretary for the last Baptist president, Odintsov.[32]

A much more interesting question is to ask who was missing. That is, who were the last members of the councils of the two unions before their dissolution? Had they not been invited or were they no longer living? Of the nine members elected at the last Evangelical Christian congress in 1926, only two, Jacob Zhidkov and Alexander Karev, were present. Three had died (Ivan Prokhanov, Ivan Kargel, and G. N. Piiparinan, but V. I. Bykov, V. A. Dumbrovksii, and P. S. Kapolygin remain unaccounted for. All three had been in the upper echelons of leadership since the Revolution and may have died for reasons of age. The other absentee, Prokhanov's brother-in-law N. A. Kazakov, later resumed his career as musician and composer for the AUCECB.[33]

On the Baptist side, the missing are more difficult to identify. Because of the organizational changes during the 1920s, due to the conflict between old and new Baptists, it is not fair to ask simply where were the persons elected as leaders at the last congress, in 1926. Of these, only Patkovskii was now present and some claim that he therefore provided the tenuous link to the earlier Baptist Union.[34] The last elected president, N. V. Odintsov, had died in prison in 1938 as had also the last elected secretary, Pavel Ivanov-Klyshnikov, who failed to return from a ten-year sentence imposed in 1932.[35] Council member P. V. Datsko died in 1941 as did also alternate V. S.

Stepanov. The old Baptists with state aid had managed to oust the new Baptists, and the latter's two key leaders from 1920 through 1926, P. V. Pavlov and Michael Timoshenko, were also missing. The former had died in prison in 1938; the latter was not yet released in 1944. But of the four Baptists elected to the All-Union Council, three of them (Malin, Levindanto, and Goliaev), had all served at the All-Union level before 1926.[36] That the Soviet prison-death system had swallowed up so many key leaders must have placed a pall on the proceedings, but the claim that the most experienced representative leaders were present appears to be true. Although Michael Orlov and A. L. Andreev, who had remained at liberty through the most difficult years, are not named as members of the 1926 Evangelical Christian council, still they, together with Zhidkov, had long worked with Prokhanov on tasks which indicated Prokhanov's deep trust in them.[37]

There was, however, a major disconcerting factor. Were the participants free agents, or were they forced to consent to policies dictated by the state? Was it possible that these earlier heroes including all the new council members had been broken by their prison experience? Were Orlov and Andreev to be trusted?[38] This watchful distrust of the leaders by the rank and file remains and still plagues the leadership of today.

Nature of Union Achieved

After the usual opening formalities, the congress heard speeches on the work of the union during the war given by Michael Orlov, a speech by Zhidkov on the theological foundations for unity, and the history of unity attempts by N. A. Levindanto. Then came the great moment when secretary Karev read the joint resolution whereby the congress vowed "to put fully into the past all former disagreements, and to create out of two unions, the Union of Evangelical Christians and the Union of Baptists, one union: The Union of Evangelical Christians and Baptists with an All-Union Council of Evangelical Christians and Baptists as its leading organ and domiciled in the city of Moscow."[39] The vote was unanimous and was followed by joyful weeping and embracing. Karev then proceeded to read and explain the statutes of the new union. This was followed by a communion service.

In 1920 the unity committee had proposed two alternative forms of union. One was a unification (soedinenie) of the two bodies, who would probably retain some form of separate identity. The second alternative was a complete fusion (slianie) which would henceforth erase all distinctions between Baptists and Evangelical Christians. In 1944 the word "fusion" predominated. As long as it was to remain a fusion of Baptists and Evangelical Christians only, complete fusion seemed possible.[40]

As always, the statute for the new union was a careful compromise, but in its sections on dogmatic practice it adopted Baptist views with only slight modifications. That meant, for example, that all congregations of the union "as much as possible have ordained presbyters and deacons in accordance with the word of God: Titus 1:5; Acts 6:1-6; and I Tim. 3:1."[41] Point 8 of the statute further specified that baptism, communion, and marriage must be performed by ordained presbyters only. A qualifier, however, allowed that if no ordained presbyters were present, these activities could be performed by unordained members of the congregation, but only if so charged by the congregation. It could not be merely the decision of an individual. On the troublesome point of laying on of hands, the statute declared that baptism and marriage performed with or without laying on of hands had equal validity. But in order to establish a common practice the statute recommended to churches to employ the laying on of hands at baptismal and marriage services but to interpret this action as a form of festive prayer for blessing. A further liberalizing qualifier suggested that for baptismal classes numbering more than two persons, simply raising the hands over the assembled candidates while pronouncing a prayer was equivalent to laying on of hands. The final point of the statute illustrated how petty the disagreements must have been. As a compromise solution, the statute stated that the Lord's Supper could be conducted either by breaking the bread into many little pieces or by breaking it into two or three larger pieces for distribution. It further specified that both the bread and the wine were to be received by the members standing. Once agreement had been achieved on these points of difference, it became easier to assert that whatever theological differences there had been, they concerned merely secondary matters.[42]

Although the word fusion was used heavily, the statute makes clear that above all this was a union of two formerly separate unions and that an All-Union Council was the leading organ of the union.[43] Nothing is said about how the All-Union Council members were to be elected, although it was obvious that the gathered delegates must now elect an All-Union Council. Whether they did so in their capacity as representatives of the former unions, or of local congregations, or as private individuals was not clarified. Local congregations, formerly existing separately, now were absorbed into one union but were given the freedom to select some version of the name Evangelical Christian and Baptists.

The new statute was also quite loose in specifying the organizational structure. The size of the All-Union Council was not indicated, but initially eight were elected, four Evangelical Christians and four Baptists. The statute did specify that the presidium of the council should consist of a chairman, two vice-chairmen (*Tovarishchi Predsedatelyi*), a secretary, and a treasurer.

The following day Goliaev proposed to the assembly that the same persons who had served on the temporary council since 1942 should be elected to the new council. Goliaev explained that it was desirable to have those persons who had already started the work (the majority of whom lived in Moscow and were experienced workers) continue in office. Seven speakers, according to the stenographic report, then spoke in support of the proposed candidates with one of them requesting that all members be ordained. Candidates were then elected unanimously. During a break the council met to organize itself and Orlov announced the presidium members. Whereas Orlov had been elected as chairman of the congress presidium, he informed the members that he had resigned from the post and that the new chairman was Jacob Zhidkov and the two vice-chairmen were M. I. Goliaev and M. A. Orlov. Elected secretary was Alexander V. Karev and treasurer Pavel I. Malin. Although the eight-man council was equally divided between Baptists and Evangelical Christians, the presidium was dominated by Evangelical Christians. In the next several years it became apparent that the two Baptists, Goliaev and Malin, were less important than the other three.[44]

Although not provided for in the statute, one of the first items of business was to resume the system of plenipotentiaries appointed by the council with responsibilities to oversee the work in major regions. Therefore, when the presidium was elected, the council also appointed the first three plenipotentiaries, naming A. L. Andreev as plenipotentiary for the Ukraine, V. N. Chechnev for Belorussia, and N. I. Kornaukhov for the Northern Caucasus.[45] All three were Evangelical Christians. Two remaining council members of Baptist origin were appointed senior presbyters during the following year. F. G. Patkovskii, initially assigned to his home territory, Siberia, later became Andreev's assistant in the Ukraine and then briefly replaced the deceased Malin as treasurer in 1948 before his own death a few months later.[46] Nikolai Levindanto had liked what he saw in the Baltic on an earlier visit and asked to be assigned as plenipotentiary for this region when the Baltic unions joined the following year.[47]

Reactions to the Union

Reactions to the union are hard to assess. How many joined initially is unclear but apparently people rejoiced wherever the news spread either through letters from the Moscow headquarters or through visits by the leaders. Communication was difficult, but by the beginning of 1946 the All-Union Council claimed 50 plenipotentiaries and senior presbyters and about 2,000 presbyters.[48] By the beginning of 1947 President Zhidkov claimed there were more than 3,000 congregations.[49]

It is doubtful that all local congregations were equally conscious of joining the All-Union Council. In some areas local congregations of Evangelical Christians and of Baptists had approved a formal union earlier. In Belorussia, Baptists, Evangelical Christians, and Pentecostals were officially united on September 4, 1942, and received official approval from the German occupation government.[50] Baptist participant and later historian Waldemar Gutsche saw rather striking parallels between Nazi and Soviet religious policy. The Nazi policy included fostering a union of all denominations practicing believer's baptism, holding the leadership responsible for all the churches, and forcing Pentecostals to surrender such practices as choral prayer and speaking in tongues (glossalalia). These were also the policies of the Soviet authorities.

Major church bodies in the newly annexed areas were persuaded to join the union because this was the only realistic way that they could hope to continue to exist in an unfriendly state. But for the remnants of the 4,000 congregations claimed by the Baptists in 1928 and a nearly equivalent number of Evangelical Christian congregations, the union meant above all that registered churches would become possible again. By and large these church members no longer cared about the label; they simply sought places where the Word of God was being preached.

The All-Union leadership made heavy use of the few congratulatory letters that had arrived from abroad. Here the communication problem was even more difficult. A brief telegram from Moscow dated January 2, 1945, was received by Baptist World Alliance president Dr. J. H. Rushbrooke in London.[51] In forwarding a copy to Dr. Walter Lewis, his colleague in Washington, Rushbrooke drew attention to the fact that both signatories, Zhidkov and Karev, were Evangelical Christians and expressed doubts about "gate-crashing" Evangelical Christians taking over the Baptists, noting further that they had heard from no Baptists so far. A few weeks later in another letter to Lewis, Rushbrooke expressed doubt that the Baptists "as a union" had assented to unification. At the end of March 1945 Rushbrooke again shared his doubts with Lewis, since they still had no word directly from anyone connected with the former Baptist Union. He also wondered "if Goliaev really represents his brethren."[52] Walter Lewis was soon to become even more skeptical and remarked in a letter of May 31, 1945, that "I am not sure that the Baptists are getting a fair deal in the new organization."[53] Further, he felt "that the Russian Government is using this organization for propaganda purposes."[54] Both men, however, tried hard to renew contacts with Moscow, with Rushbrooke offering Baptist World Alliance assistance "to help our brothers and sisters through the period of emergency."[55]

The Union Expands: Pentecostals

With the creation of the new Union of Evangelical Christians and Baptists, Soviet evangelicals entered upon a three-year era of growth and unity. Less than a year later, in August 1945, delegations of Pentecostals, Baptists, and Evangelical Christians from Estonia, Latvia, and Belorussia met with the All-Union Council in Moscow. Each delegation met with the council separately while the others toured Moscow. The official report stressed that all decisions were reached unanimously and the end result was that Pentecostals in the entire Soviet Union, plus Baptists and Evangelical Christians in the Baltic countries, joined the All-Union Council. At a reception given by I. V. Polianskii of the Council for Affairs of Religious Cults for the Pentecostal and Latvian Baptist delegations, the delegations thanked Polianskii for enabling the delegation to travel to the conference and for housing and feeding them during the entire period.[56] Without question the union of 1944 was much more a voluntary union when compared with those who found it necessary to join in 1945.

In their relatively short history Pentecostals had grown rapidly, often at the expense of other evangelicals.[57] They too were forced to issue a loyalty declaration to the state in 1927, but that did not prevent the severe decimation of their leadership a few years later. Voronaev, leader of one wing of the Pentecostals with its center in the southern Ukraine, was arrested. Then the authorities released a statement that he had recanted his faith, which was an exaggeration. They finally freed him in 1935 but rearrested him shortly thereafter, and he did not return from prison.[58] One Soviet writer claimed that Pentecostal leaders had waged anti-Soviet propaganda against collectivization during the 1930s, "therefore their council was dissolved."[59] According to this source, after the war Pentecostal leaders began to petition the authorities to reestablish a council and to register congregations but were refused. Therefore they turned to the AUCECB.

Pentecostals differed from Evangelical Christians and Baptists in no way on the essentials of the faith but placed a stronger stress on the Holy Spirit (sometimes referred to as "the second work of grace") which gave them the strength and power to live a victorious Christian life. Following the model in Acts 2, they felt that the proof of the filling with the Holy Spirit was evident through speaking a strange tongue (glossalalia) and through other gifts of the Spirit, such as healing. This emphasis on experiencing the Holy Spirit produced an emotionalism that was particularly attractive among the lower classes. Baptists, in contrast, relied on a more Wesleyan concept of sanctification which involved gradual progress in experiencing the fullness of the Holy Spirit but rejecting ecstasy. Baptists rejected glossalalia, seeing it as an expression of the Holy Spirit's presence which had been limited to the apostolic church. An additional reason for tension between Baptists and Pentecostals on the teaching of the Holy Spirit was that extreme Pentecostals went so far as to claim that only persons baptized by the Holy Spirit (i.e., having spoken in tongues) were truly Christians.

Neither side was eager for the union. Pentecostals had no other legal possibility. This explains why the August Agreement, which spelled out the terms of union, reads like a Baptist ultimatum. The full terms of the August Agreement were not published officially until twelve years later, but the official letter going out to the churches in September 1945 did quote the crucial points of the agreement concerning glossalalia and foot washing.[60]

The agreement stated that congregations of Christians of Evangelical Faith[61] (since no official union existed) were united with congregations of Evangelical Christians and Baptists into one union. The agreement promised that representatives from the Pentecostals would be included on the executive staff. Throughout the subsequent history they were usually also represented on the council itself. Persons ordained formerly by the Pentecostals were recognized in their spiritual calling; the titles "senior presbyter," "presbyter," and "deacon" were specified. But on the theological differences, a number of points in the agreement forced the Pentecostals to agree to abstain from practicing glossalalia in general meetings. Point 9 of the agreement went so far as to have both sides promise to provide an educational program against manifestations of the Holy Spirit that might destroy the decency and decorum of the service. In addition, Pentecostals were asked not to practice foot washing at the communion service and to conduct educational work among its membership to produce a common understanding with the Evangelical Christians and Baptists on this question. In short, the conditions for joining the union were to abandon all practices that would distinguish them as Pentecostals.

For the Pentecostals, however, there were also some gains. Above all, this paved the way for legal recognition and soon large numbers of their churches were registered locally. It also meant that the rivalry among the evangelicals would be considerably reduced.

As with the earlier union, the authority of the union was not based on a decision by the membership but simply the promises of a few spokesmen who now had to try to persuade their followers to join with Evangelical Christians and Baptists locally. Dimitrii Ivanovich Ponomarchuk became the Pentecostal representative coopted onto the All-Union Council. Ponomarchuk, born in 1892, was well suited for this role since he had served as a Baptist preacher before joining the Pentecostals in 1925, advancing rapidly in two years to membership on the All-Ukrainian Council of the union. Besides becoming an AUCECB member, he was immediately appointed assistant senior presbyter for the Ukraine under Andreev, although for a while retaining his local church responsibilities in Dneprodzerzhinsk.[62] Another leading representative was I. K. Pan'ko, who was soon appointed assistant senior presbyter for Belorussia under the experienced Evangelical Christian V. N. Chechnev. S. I. Vashkevich had earlier been a leading figure in the Polish Pentecostal Union and it became his task to bring Polish Pentecostals now in the Soviet Union into the AUCECB. Vashkevich was appointed senior presbyter for Pinskaia Oblast in Belorussia. Both Pan'ko and Vashkevich had been trained in the Danzig Bible Institute before the war. The fourth person in the delegation, A. I. Bidash, soon became dissatisfied with the union agreement and is to the present day a leader of a large, independent, unregistered Pentecostal movement.[63]

It has been estimated that about 25,000 Pentecostals joined the AUCECB in 1945. This included more than 400 congregations. At the end of 1947 Alexander Karev claimed that most of the Pentecostals in the Ukraine plus all Pentecostals in Belorussia had joined.[64]

The disregard of Pentecostal sensitivities in the August Agreement and the treatment of Pentecostals locally soon prompted a significant portion to leave the union again. I. K. Pan'ko was arrested in 1948 and charged with having helped several young preachers to obtain military exemption during World War II, Soviet authorities claiming these men were charlatans.[65] He received a 25-year sentence for treason which was halved in the amnesty program following Stalin's death. His associate, Vashkevich, managed to emigrate to Poland in 1947, where he is still a leading figure in the United Evangelical Church of Poland. That meant that by 1948 only Ponomarchuk of the four still worked for the AUCECB. Obviously his influence did not suffice because in October 1948 a letter approved at an expanded meeting of the council was sent to local churches, urging them to eliminate from their church services all noisy manifestations such as choral prayer.[66] Another instruction from Zhidkov advised the local presbyter to maintain personal control of the entire worship service including assigning who would pray in order to stop noise and disorder.[67]

Shortly before this a brief six-line announcement appeared in *Bratskii Vestnik* stating that on April 2, 1947, an agreement was signed with representatives of another group of Pentecostals who called themselves Evangelical Christians in the Spirit of the Apostles. N. P. Smorodin, the leader of this group, together with N. I. Shishkov and E. M. Prudnikov, signed the agreement.

This agreement had four points. First of all, the three representatives accepted the August Agreement in full and promised to abide by it. But the second and longest point clarified the issue on which the Evangelical Christians in the Spirit of the Apostles (or Smorodintsy) were unique, namely in their rejection of the Trinity in favor of "Jesus only." Point 2 of the agreement affirmed that to baptize in the name of "Father, Son, and Holy Spirit," or to baptize "in the name of the Lord Jesus," were validly based in Scripture and had equal force. But in future the Smorodintsy promised to use the AUCECB formula: "Father, Son, and Holy Spirit." The other two points involved promises not to engage in any activity that would reflect negatively on the teaching and order of the AUCECB but rather to be fully subordinate to it.

Smorodin and many of his followers left the union a short time later. Perhaps that explains why the details of the agreement were not published till 1976. It is doubtful that this brief unification was voluntary in the first place.[68]

The Union Expands: Baltic Evangelicals

From the AUCECB point of view, the incorporation of Baltic evangelicals was a much more desirable achievement of the August 1945 meeting. Doctrinally, they were in fundamental agreement and the Baltic evangelicals were able to enrich the AUCECB because a large number of their leaders had obtained high-quality theological education before the war.

The first believer's baptism in the Baltic took place in 1860.[69] In Latvia the Baptists developed a strong organization with their own publications, seminary, and charitable enterprises. As small countries, both Latvia and Estonia had little chance of survival in the competition between Hitler and Stalin. The countries were again occupied by the Soviet Union in 1939 and initial purges were carried out, including persecution of Baptists.[70] In 1940 A. L. Andreev called on the Latvian Baptists, who greeted him with suspicious questions. They were surprised a short time later to receive a letter from Andreev to the effect that the union in Moscow had considered their application to join the union and had accepted them. The Latvians had made no such request and were doubly puzzled since Andreev had not even talked about the subject during his visit. They simply ignored the letter. After the second Soviet "liberation" of Latvia, the approaches were less crude and once the union had been achieved, leading individuals began to develop an appreciation of each other even if national differences remained.[71]

The AUCECB met with the Estonian and Latvian delegations separately. The official report emphasized that the discussion had focused on points of clarification but that there had been no differences. The result was that Evangelical Christian and Baptist churches in Estonia, Latvia, and Lithuania joined the AUCECB "and were fused with it into one family and one brotherhood."[72] Structurally this meant that the AUCECB was expanded from eight to twelve persons, thereby allowing for one Pentecostal representative, one from Latvia and one from Estonia. The opportunity was also utilized to add Il'ia G. Ivanov, who was simply identified as a permanent co-worker in Moscow, to the council.[73] In addition, the All-Union Council decided to appoint N. A. Levindanto as AUCECB plenipotentiary for the Baltic region with permanent residence in Riga. Levindanto acted as organizer and made sure that churches adhered to the AUCECB statutes.

The Baltic evangelicals had had no choice but to accept the offer of union. Since then they have tried to make the best of it. Since the Latvian and Estonian languages are not spoken in Moscow (even Levindanto was limited to a translator), Baltic evangelicals sought to maintain friendly relations with Moscow and with Levindanto, yet attempted to pursue a path locally which was more to their liking. In Estonia Johannes Lipstok, a highly respected leader, became the senior presbyter and managed to maintain the respect of the AUCECB leadership, as well as Baptists from abroad who met him. Several key Latvian leaders had emigrated during the war but Professor Johannes Ris declared that he was prepared to meet the So-

viets. He refused to accept responsibilities as senior presbyter for the republic, however. Several different persons filled the office in short succession, and it was a decade before stability was established.[74]

Less significant though adding color to the AUCECB was the assimila-
tion of several other groups. Thanks to the efforts of Il'ia Ivanov, 88 evangelical churches in Moldavia numbering 3,086 members were absorbed into
the union.[75] Karev and Andreev undertook a visit to Transcarpathia in the
southwestern Ukraine. When they set out on their trip they had not one
single address of believers in the oblast. Gradually they found various
churches belonging either to the Hungarian- and Ruthenian-speaking
Baptists or to another group not quite as large called Free Christians.

After visiting a large number of congregations, they held a conference
of Free Christians on February 22, 1946, followed by a conference of
Baptists on February 23 and finally a joint conference on February 24. The
Free Christians represented by 48 ministers agreed to unite with the
AUCECB and promised "to conduct baptism of believers in all their con-
gregations as well as communion . . ." and to register their congregations in
accordance with existing Soviet law.[76] Thirty-six preachers representing
Transcarpathian Baptists agreed to unite with the AUCECB and with the
Free Christians and to register their congregations according to the require-
ments of Soviet law.

At the joint conference a senior presbyter for the oblast was elected, as
well as two assistants. The senior presbyter was a Baptist, his assistant
represented the Free Christians, and the second assistant represented the
Ruthenian-speaking Baptists.[77] On their return Karev and Andreev could
report that 81 churches representing about 2,200 members had been added
to the union. Free Christians needed more coaxing on a second visit two
years later but generally speaking they were absorbed into the union.[78]

No separate recognition was made of the Polish Church of Christ, 71
of whose 85 congregations found themselves in Soviet territory after the
war. These were absorbed automatically into the AUCECB in 1944.[79] As
late as the 1920s the German Baptists based in South Russia and Volhynia
had played an influential role and felt themselves distinct from the Russian
and Ukrainian Baptists because their church life was more orderly.[80]
German Baptists had disappeared from the Ukraine, as well as from
Volhynia, and were treated as non-persons till 1956 when the Germans finally received identity papers. German Baptists then joined existing Russian
churches and any separate influence they were to exert on the AUCECB
came in concert with the Mennonites in the 1960s.

Had Unity Been Achieved?

A year after the Moscow unity conference the little connective word "and" was dropped from the title so that the name of the union was the All-Union Council of Evangelical Christians-Baptists to be abbreviated as AUCECB.[81] What had been achieved? Had unity finally taken place? A longtime Evangelical Christian leader, I. I. Motorin, noted that some might feel "that the unity accomplished meant the loss of inner spiritual freedom for the churches."[82] Motorin vigorously denied this, feeling that the churches had not been deprived of spiritual freedom. He stressed that "without spiritual freedom true unity is impossible."[83] Local presbyters were constantly admonished from Moscow to strive to realize the unity that had been proclaimed.

Clearly a *modus vivendi* had been achieved with the government, but quite clearly, too, the state was playing a very dominant role. Registrations of churches were undertaken in large numbers. These churches had to agree to the excessive restrictions of the 1929 law on cults. Fortunately for many, the content of the law was not generally known; the authorities, in fact, deliberately withheld the details so they were not fully conscious of what they might have promised.

Initially there was a wide-scale positive response to the AUCECB. Here was the possibility to obtain legal recognition. Any such possibility following the long years of closed churches seemed welcome. The sermons of the leaders such as Karev, Orlov, and Zhidkov produced trust because of their spiritual content and tone. Leading Baptists were less active, except for Levindanto, who came to be appreciated in the Baltic. Additional men of authority such as I. I. Motorin and M. D. Timoshenko wrote articles for *Bratskii Vestnik*, even if the state appeared not to permit them any major post.

It was in maintaining unity over a longer period that the flaws in the agreement became evident. At a major extended session of the council in October 1948 a new statute for the AUCECB was approved.[84] This had 44 clauses and elaborated the structural organization of the union, specifying the duties of senior presbyter, presbyter, and so forth. Copies were sent out to the churches, but a complete version of the statute was never made public. Zhidkov in his cover letter explaining the new statute stated that the congregations had full liberty and he wished to exercise no coercion. But then he went on to state in unmistakably coercive terms that those who did not accept this new statute approved by the union had no right to remain as Evangelical Christians-Baptists.[85]

The wave of success was ebbing by 1949. There had been many church registrations, many baptisms—almost too many—so that Zhidkov urged that the candidates be given a longer proving period,[86] and the tone of *Bratskii Vestnik* was surprisingly open and optimistic. Yet by 1949 many Pentecostals had left the union and the union itself appeared to be in difficulty with the state. From 1949 to 1952 no issues of the journal appeared. When it reappeared no explanation was given for the gap. All that was evident was that now peace seemed officially to be the major concern of the union.

Notes to Chapter 3

1. Kahle rightly remarks that these confessions of faith should be seen in the context of the need for more precision in dealings with the legislators, p. 47.

2. Though variously interpreted, spokesmen from numerous sides later regarded this meeting as a major conference. Among the foreign missionaries present were Johannes Svensson and Walter Jack (Kahle, p. 119f.); cf. Steeves, p. 64f.

3. Kahle, p. 121.
4. *Ibid.*
5. *Ibid.*
6. Steeves, p. 31.
7. Kahle, p. 120; cf. *BV*, 2-3/53, pp. 95-98.
8. Kahle, p. 20f.
9. *Ibid.*, pp. 107-108.
10. *Ibid.*, p. 94; Steeves, p. 16.
11. Quoted by Kahle, p. 141.
12. Steeves, p. 60f.
13. Steeves, p. 74, notes this problem but argues in a footnote that Soviet sociologist Lialina's categorization between a rightist Mazaev group and a "liberal-bourgeois" Pavlov group are due to Lialina's economic determinism and serves to exaggerate the disagreement. The distinction between "open" and "closed" Baptists employed by Kahle appears more relevant, especially when compared with a second crisis in the early twenties.
14. The 1920 union agreement was signed by P. V. Pavlov, president of the Baptist Union; M. D. Timoshenko, Baptist council member; and by Prokhanov and A. L. Andreev of the Evangelical Christians. Also signing as secretary was N. A. Levindanto, secretary of the Baptist Union. (Kahle, p. 181 and Steeves, pp. 141-142.)
15. Steeves, p. 142. This congress had also restructured the union.
16. *Ibid.*, p. 168.
17. Kahle, p. 177; cf. Steeves, p. 145.
18. Kahle, p. 181.
19. For a thorough discussion of the Baptist belief system see Steeves, p. 452ff.
20. Steeves, p. 481.
21. *BV*, 3/57, pp. 61-62.
22. Cf. Kahle, pp. 558-571, and Steeves, pp. 86-88.

23. Kahle, pp. 204-205. Prokhanov had himself ordained in Prague by Czech Baptists with preachers from the Church of the Czech Brethren present, thereby symbolizing his affinity for Jan Hus and his concerns for unity.

24. Steeves, p. 581f.

25. Interview data, November 1978.

26. Both the separation decree of 1918 and the law on cults of 1929 acknowledged only the local congregation (*obshchina*) which not only reflected the early emphasis on autonomy of local soviets but also served to break the Orthodox hierarchy. The 1929 law directly led to the temporary discontinuation of both the Baptist and Evangelical Christian unions. For a broader discussion of the new centralism, see below, pp. 159, 274.

27. "Rushbrooke, J. H." file, BWA Archives, Washington, D.C.

28. *BV*, 1/45, p. 31.

29. Names of the delegates (with denominational origin in brackets as established by this writer) were as follows: from Moscow: M. A. Orlov (EC), Ia. I. Zhidkov (EC), A. V. Karev (EC), M. I. Goliaev (Bap), P. I. Malin (Bap), F. L. Burenkov, F. S. Savel'ev (EC), V. T. Pelevin (EC), I. G. Ivanov (EC), A. S. Elin, Ia. G. Otrubiannikov, V. G. Lakoshchenkov, I. I. Motorin (Bap), T. E. Davydov, A. G. Mazaeva (Bap), P. S. Zhidkova (EC), A. P. Andreeva (EC), M. F. Orlova (EC), E. I. Kon'kova, A. I. Afanas'eva (EC), A. I. Mozgova (Bap); Kiev: A. L. Andreev (EC), A. T. Tridnadsatko, G. G. Aksenov, G. A. Dobrenko, P. P. Metelitsa, N. M. Korzhov; Kharkov: D. A. Voinov (EC), G. S. Fesenko; Leningrad: I. S. Sokolov; Odessa: S. V. Krapivnitskii (Bap); Zdolbunovo (Rovenskaia Obl.); M. A. Nichiporuk (EC); Novosibirsk: E. P. Starostin, F. G. Patkovskii (Bap), I. F. Lisitskii; Kuibyshev: N. A. Levindanto (Bap); Minsk: V. N. Chechnev (EC), M. K. Voitkun; Maikop: N. I. Kornaukhov (EC); Simferopol': A. F. Avgustinovich, G. P. Kostiukov (Bap); Ural'sk: P. P. Petrov (EC); Ul'ianovsk: M. I. Gus'kov (EC); Gor'k. Obl.: K. E. Matveev (Bap); L'vov: S. M. Brichuk (EC).

30. *BV*, 2/45, p. 18.

31. *BV*, 3/57, p. 64; Lialina, p. 106f.; cf. Kahle, p. 229, containing a statistical comparison of Evangelical Christian and Baptist growth from 1905 to 1928.

32. Biography of her in Georgi Vins, *Testament from Prison* (Wheaton, Ill.: David C. Cook Foundation, 1976), pp. 200-207.

33. On Kazakov, see Katherine Murray, "Death of a Baptist Musician," *RCL*, II, 1 (January-February 1974), 8-10.

34. Steeves, p. 278.

35. See the brief biographical sketches on Odintsov, Datsko, and Ivanov-Klyshnikov in Vins, *Testament from Prison*, pp. 99-181. Vins also wonders why A. Ananin, chairman of the Siberian union, known to be alive in a northern prison camp till 1946, was not released to attend (p. 201). The Russian edition (*Vernyi do kontsa*) contains photos of the men.

36. Malin was elected alternate member of the All-Russian Union in 1920 and one of the Baptist representatives to BWA in Stockholm in 1923 (*BV*, 1/48, pp. 21-22); Levindanto was secretary of the 1920 All-Russian Congress (Steeves, p. 142); Goliaev served as president of the finance commission in 1922 (Steeves, p. 187). Goliaev's father, Il'ia Andreevich Goliaev, was a vital link in attempts to legitimize the new union. Goliaev had been president in 1911 and again in 1925-26. When his successor Odintsov was arrested in November 1933 Goliaev again resumed the presidency but did not return from a trip to Kiev in early 1935, Steeves speculating that he went into hiding. He died in Tashkent in 1942 but shortly before his death telegrammed his agreement to use of his signature on a joint Evangelical Christian

and Baptist letter in support of the war effort and this letter was taken to indicate his approval of the intended union. (Steeves, pp. 198, 268-70; Kahle, p. 223, mistakenly claims that Il'ia Goliaev, rather than Michael his son, signed the 1942 letter with Levindanto requesting union with the Evangelical Christians.)

37. Kahle, pp. 223, 270.

38. Kahle notes (p. 249) that both Orlov and Andreev after 1923 carried extra weight in the union because their election appeared assured since "they held the special trust of the state officials." Andreev was also the person (p. 395) who persuaded Prokhanov when the latter was in prison in 1923 not to resist but follow state orders and issue a loyalty declaration.

39. *BV*, 1/45, p. 33. The ten-point statute was printed pp. 33-34. For a translation see Appendix.

40. Kahle, p. 171.

41. *BV*, 1/45, p. 34.

42. *Ibid.* The problematic excommunication question was ignored as presumably no longer relevant. Also the conflict between Moscow or Leningrad as headquarters had been settled by a forced move to Moscow in 1931.

43. Hans Hebly, *Protestants in Russia* (Belfast: Christian Journals Ltd., 1976), described the union as a federation of congregations but his thinking is colored by the nature of the later union with the Mennonites (pp. 105 and 124); cf. Kahle, "Fragen der Einheit im Bunde der Evangeliumschristen-Baptisten in der Sowjetunion," *Kyrios* (1968, No. 3/4), p. 164.

44. The other three council members were: N. A. Levindanto, F. G. Patkovskii, and A. L. Andreev. Durasoff (p. 106) speculates that the backroom replacement of Orlov with Zhidkov as chairman indicates that the latter was "possibly the Soviet government's choice." Although possible, considering Orlov's demotion in 1954, more likely, considering the general record of both men, is the fact that since 1931 Zhidkov had been the elected president of the Evangelical Christian Union and already earlier was Prokhanov's designated successor. During Zhidkov's imprisonment Orlov had assumed whatever presidential functions were still possible but not the title. Orlov in 1944 was elected president or chairman of the congress sessions, which is technically distinct from chairmanship of the council. In essence the council opted for continuity but had expressed its appreciation for Orlov's lifesaver role during the interim by electing him president of the congress and having him deliver the report on the past decade as the most knowledgeable person present.

45. *Supra*, Chap. 1, p. 42. This confirmation of Andreev's role in the Ukraine appears parallel to that of the Orthodox Metropolitan Nikolai (cf. Fletcher, *Nikolai*, p. 33f.).

46. *BV*, 3/47, pp. 20-22 and obit. 1/49, p. 56.

47. *BV*, 1/46, p. 39.

48. *Ibid.*, p. 5.

49. *BV*, 1/47, pp. 13-18. Fifteen persons worked in the Moscow office and 70 senior workers served as plenipotentiaries or senior presbyters of regions, republics, or oblasts. They had received 12,000 letters in 1946 and dispatched 3,000 pastoral letters.

50. Waldemar Gutsche, *Westliche Quellen des Russischen Stundismus* (Kassel: Oncken Verlag, 1956), p. 120. In Novosibirsk, for example, Patkovskii had achieved a local union by March 1944.

51. "J. H. Rushbrooke, 1945" file, BWA Archives, Washington, D.C.

52. *Ibid.*

53. *Ibid.*

54. *Ibid.* A year later on July 26, 1946, Lewis wrote to Rushbrooke: "I have plenty of evidence that there has been no real change of policy of the USSR as to religious liberty. There has been a little relaxation in some things, but there is still much persecution of religion in many parts of Russia with the full sanction of the Soviet Government. When I refer to such matters I usually hold back about nine-tenths of what I know, simply dropping a hint to those who are intelligent enough to draw inferences from facts. I love the Russian people, and I would like to see them free from their communist rulers. I think it is our duty to help the Russian people to win their freedom, even as it was our duty to help the Germans and Italians to win their freedom from their masters. I have no intention of carrying on any open propaganda against the Soviet Government, but I do not wish to make the impression that I believe whàt they say when they put out their propaganda about freedom of worship in Russia."

55. *Ibid.* Rushbrooke to AUCECB, May 7, 1945.

56. *BV*, 4/45, p. 15.

57. The literature on Soviet Pentecostals is not very satisfactory. Aside from passages in Durasoff's work, see also his *Pentecost Behind the Iron Curtain* (1973), which is partisan. Major Soviet treatments are V. Ie. Soldatenko, *Piatidesiatniki* (Donetsk, 1972); A. T. Moskalenko, *Piatidesiatniki* (Moscow, 1966); and N. V. Koltsov, *Kto takie Piatidesiatniki* (Moscow, Znania, 1965). For the most thorough treatment see Michael Rowe, "The Pentecostal Movement in the USSR—a Historical and Social Survey," PhD dissertation being completed for Glasgow University.

58. Durasoff, *The Russian Protestants*, p. 82, based on interview with son Paul.

59. Koltsov, p. 5, from Cosmos Translations summary.

60. *Ibid.*, pp. 18-19. The text of the agreement was printed in *BV*, 4/57, p. 36. Durasoff argued that in 1954 "Bratskii Vestnik altered part of the Agreement of 1945 by inserting the stipulation that no Pentecostal members could exercise the liberty of personal persuasion upon their fellow members. This was referred to as a major condition of the August Agreement, despite its nonexistence! Rather, it replaced the proviso to abstain from footwashing which was originally stated in 1945" (p. 143). Durasoff's point appears to be overstated, since points 10 and 11 of the published agreement which commit both sides to educational work against Pentecostal phenomena were already quoted in 1945. That amounts to the same thing as prohibition against proselytization. For an English translation of the August Agreement, see Appendix.

61. *Khristiane very evangelskoi* (Christians of Evangelical Faith) was the official name for the Voronaev Pentecostals. Since this was very similar to "Evangelical Christians," Zhidkov suggested that they were already included in the name for the union (*BV*, 2/46, p. 12).

62. Autobiography in *BV*, 1/47, pp. 61-63; cf. 3/45, p. 16; 1/46, p. 56; 2/46, pp. 27 and 53; 3/46, p. 40.

63. Durasoff, pp. 120-123.

64. *BV*, 5/48, p. 33; cf. *BV*, 4/46, pp. 16 and 39. Of the 30 congregations in Dnepropetrovsk Oblast visited by Mel'nikov, 16 were Pentecostal and in each a formal statement of union with the AUCECB was signed. *BV*, 6/47, pp. 50-56, is a report on a trip made by Andreev and Mitskevich to the Western Ukraine to strengthen relations with Pentecostals and to speak with leaders such as P. A. Il'chuk, who were stalling on joining the union. In Rovno Oblast, 102 of 185 congregations were newly joined Pentecostals; in L'vov Oblast it was 32 of 56; in

Ternopol Oblast 60 of 80 congregations.
    65. Durasoff, pp. 122-23.
    66. *BV*, 1/49, pp. 33-46.
    67. Durasoff, pp. 142 and 160.
    68. *BV*, 2/47, p. 62; ECB *Kalendar* 1976, p. 57; the Smorodintsy are still listed at present as an illegal sect; cf. A. Sediulin, *Zadonodatel' stvo o religioznykh kul' takh* (Moscow, 1974), p. 27.
    69. On August 15, 1860, sixteen Latvians were baptized in Memel. During the night of September 9, 1861, their leader, Adam Gertner, baptized 72 newly converted Latvians in a little stream located in Latvia itself (*BV*, 2/48, p. 61).
    70. Boris Meissner, *Die Sowjetunion, die baltischen Staaten und das Völkerrecht* (Cologne, 1956). Lewis and Rushbrooke of the BWA exchanged information about such persecution, which they had obtained from refugees.
    71. I am indebted to Adolphs Klaupiks for some of this information. Karev, in reflecting on a visit, remarked on the differing temperaments caused by nationality and character: "We Russians are ardent and fervent, the Latvians and Estonians more peaceful and sober-minded" (*BV*, 1/46, p. 38).
    72. *BV*, 3/45, p. 18. Representing the Estonians were J. K. Lipstok, O. Tiark, Laks and Nurk; from the Latvians: K. Latseklis, Ia. Ris, Papeliuk, Andreenko and Petrov; Apanasenok from Lithuania. Also present for these union meetings were four men from Belorussia (Chechnev, Shatura, Minailo, and Alemseev) plus the Pentecostals Ponomarchuk and Bidash from the Ukraine.
    73. *BV*, 1/46, p. 56. I. I. Motorin, longtime Ukrainian Evangelical Christian leader but now merely identified as a "longtime Evangelical Christian Baptist worker" was appointed at this time as director for publishing activities of the AUCECB. As of August 1945 the AUCECB members were: Ia. I. Zhidkov, M. I. Goliaev, M. A. Orlov, N. A. Levindanto, A. V. Karev, F. G. Patkovskii, A. L. Andreev, P. I. Malin, I. G. Ivanov, D. I. Ponomarchuk, J. Lipstok, and K. Latseklis. The latter four were "coopted," it was stated.
    74. Lipstok remained senior presbyter of Estonia till his death in 1963. The series of senior presbyters for Latvia were K. Latseklis, 1945-46; A. M. Korp, 1946-48; Redlich, 1948-53; Khuns, 1953-61.
    75. *BV*, 3/46.
    76. *BV*, 2/46, p. 41. The *Svobodnye Khristiane* (Free Christians) were found primarily among the Ruthenians in Transcarpathia and were the second largest sect in the area next to the Baptists. Andreev and Karev noted that their special teaching had been brought to them from the USA by their present leader Petr Semenovich and was heavily influenced by the journal *Light of Prophecy*, founded by the former Swedish Adventist Dr. Lee. According to Karev and Andreev, "This journal preached against water baptism, against communion, against special prayer houses, against salaried presbyters and preachers, against celebrating Christmas, Easter, and other such religious holidays, against pictures and similar depictions, against birthday parties, against musical instruments, against registration of congregations or churches with authorities and so forth" (pp. 32-33).
    77. Evgenii Evgen'evich Stumpf was elected senior presbyter, Petr Semenovich was the assistant senior presbyter with responsibilities for the Free Christians, and Dondor, the assistant senior presbyter for the Ruthenian Baptist congregations. Stumpf, age 43, was a Magyar. His father had started the Baptist movement in Hungarian-speaking Transcarpathia in 1900. Stumpf began his ministry in 1923; 1924-26 he studied at the Baptist seminary in Budapest and in 1928 completed the course at the Baptist seminary in Prague. Stumpf's wife was an American

missionary, a Moody Bible Institute graduate (*ibid.*, p. 32).

78. *BV*, 3/48, pp. 49-56.

79. Interview May 4, 1977 with Jerzy Sacewicz (Warsaw), one of three founders of *Tserkvyi Khristov* (Church of Christ).

80. Kahle, p. 69, noting that German Baptists separated from Russian and Ukrainian Baptists in 1890 cites a Russian named Stefanovich that "The German is a man of strict order, the Russian tends toward disorderliness. Misunderstandings grew out of national character differences." Cf. pp. 114-115.

81. *BV*, 2/46, p. 12.

82. *Ibid.*, p. 22.

83. *Ibid.*

84. *BV*, 5/48, p. 37. The following issue (p. 67) merely stated that the congregations would be receiving a copy of the organizational structure and also certain guidelines for conducting the work of the Lord.

85. *BV*, 1/49, p. 21.

86. *BV*, 1/48, p. 6. Later in the year he stated: "Better a small group, but true followers of Christ, than a large congregation, but such on whom we cannot depend" (5/48, p. 4).

You can pray freely
but just so God alone can hear.
—*Tanya Khodkevich*
(She received a 10-year sentence for these
verses.) *Gulag I*, p. 37

God not only established but also strengthened the Soviet
state. As a result the Soviet land became the chief of all
freedom-loving peoples in its unceasing struggle for peace,
for social and political justice.
—*Jacob Zhidkov* in *BV*, 6/47. p. 6

4 Preaching and Peace: The Christian in a Communist Country

"The Soviet Union is a country that has systematically denied all liberties to its citizens. How can a Christian wish to live there?" Is this not the unspoken assumption of the average Westerner who has heard about Stalin's purges, the persecution of Christians, and the tough treatment of Soviet dissenters today? The average Westerner may not remember the details, but the idea that Soviet citizens are not free seems to have taken root.

Well aware of this attitude, Soviet authorities regularly proclaim that the Soviet Union is a land of freedom. They even insist that it is the freest country in the world. Repeatedly they claim that "our legislation on religious cults is the most humane and democratic in the world."[1]

Official Soviet claims can readily be dismissed as propaganda, but similar assertions by Soviet churchmen are more disconcerting. Jacob Zhidkov, like his Orthodox colleagues, sought to give the impression that they were enjoying full religious liberty. In 1947, for example, he stated that "Evangelical Christian-Baptists have full freedom, not only for their divine services but also to conduct the necessary activities embracing all aspects of our religious life."[2] Persons from abroad who circulated rumors to the contrary, he warned, were saying things about which they knew nothing and God would judge them.

Soviet evangelicals who had no rights or freedoms under tsarism expected great things from the Soviet regime. One of the Soviet government's first decrees separated the churches from the state. No longer would the Orthodox Church receive unfair advantages as the state religion. Now evangelicals could meet for worship freely; the first decade of the Soviet regime proved to be their golden age of expansion.

But after 1929, Soviet evangelicals experienced equally with other religions the state's antireligious attitude. Once the Stalinist terror passed and loyal churches were rewarded with renewed tolerance, the churchmen with their uncritical affirmations exaggerated the extent of the limited freedoms granted. But these limited freedoms may well have meant as much to them as full freedom in a relaxed society.

Separation of church from state had been a concern of the evangelical free churches for centuries. During the Reformation the Anabaptists had emphasized that the state had no business in internal church affairs. By contrast, the Soviet state was more anxious to prevent the church from interfering in state affairs. At first the similarity in the language of "separation" encouraged the evangelicals to anticipate religious freedom. As the difference in emphasis became apparent, evangelicals were compelled to examine the situation more critically.[3]

At its last general conference in 1925, the Mennonite church submitted an eight-point memorandum to the state outlining what it regarded as the minimal requirements for religious freedom.[4] The Mennonites said the state should interfere neither with church meetings nor in discussion groups for adults and children. It should not hinder the acquisition of Bibles and the conduction of Bible courses. Further, they requested the state not to restrict church societies, choirs, the erection of new church buildings, and the operation of orphanages. The Mennonites also argued that the schools should have a non-ideological emphasis where neither religion nor atheism would be fostered. Most serious was their request for exemption from military service and training in order to engage in useful alternative service.

Although the memorandum could be regarded as distinctly Mennonite, it is an accurate summary of what all evangelicals expected in a land of religious freedom; even the pacifist clause reflected broad evangelical sentiments. State officials rejected the memorandum immediately— probably more friendly treatment than that received by the Evangelical Christians and the Baptists. Both of the latter movements were forced to issue declarations of loyalty and officially reject pacifism against the wishes of their membership.

The state followed up these loyalty declarations with unprecedented pressures that produced a more inward-looking, less socially active church leadership. The surviving evangelicals gradually came to accept restricting freedom of religion to the freedom to practice the rituals inside a church. This was the orientation of Jacob Zhidkov, the leading spokesman after the war. When he summarized their history in 1947, he concluded that "our goal must be to use the possibility for freedom of religious confession *as given* [italics mine] to preach the good news of the gospel" and to strive for the prosperity of the motherland.[5] This is still the main orientation. Zhidkov's son Michael has repeatedly claimed freedom of religion and re-jects protests to the contrary in the West; in his view the cause of liberty is better served by making use of every favorable opportunity granted by the state.[6]

Since both state legislation and the inner orientation of Soviet evangel-icals leads to apoliticism and lack of social involvement, a survey of evangel-ical religious practice will help illuminate the role of evangelicals in Soviet society.

Evangelical Religious Practice

Evangelical religious practice revolves around the worship services. Throughout the postwar period visitors have invariably described them with wonder. Especially older worshipers, hoping for a seat, begin to arrive long before the service starts. When the service begins, there isn't even standing room left.

The worship service begins with congregational singing which slowly gathers force, always maintaining a distinctive Slavic melancholy. Then follow three or more sermons, interspersed with singing from the choir and congregation. Services also begin and end with public prayer sessions in which usually three members from the congregation pray audibly while others whisper their prayers. The prayers revolve around personal praise and thankfulness, and there is much weeping.

A worship service lasts two hours but, because of the variety in the program, passes more quickly than one might expect. Few of the sermons last more than 15 minutes, and they are usually delivered with emotional fervor. There is a heavy emphasis on singing. The Moscow choir, for instance, sings five times in a service.[7] Some of the women may participate by reciting poetry, a much-loved cultural expression.

In all evangelical congregations, whether Baptist, Mennonite, or Pentecostal, the sermon is the basic part of the service. AUCECB president

Zhidkov emphasized that the purpose of preaching is to strengthen the believers in faith, hope, and love, and to complete their understanding of the Lord.[8] That is, the sermons should be exegetical, didactic, and exhortative. Although these are the commonly acknowledged goals of preaching, evangelicals are accustomed to emphasizing that the first goal of preaching should be to produce conversions—an evangelistic sermon. No doubt because of the "condition of the times," Zhidkov discouraged evangelistic preaching, arguing that "it is our fundamental task to instruct those already believing."[9] He also criticized preachers who favored the prophets and the Book of Revelation, which involved problematic interpretations. Putting it positively, he stated: "We may preach from the entire Scripture, but the major subject for sermons in our congregations is the New Testament."[10]

A scholarly study of Soviet evangelical preaching is difficult. *Bratskii Vestnik* is replete with printed sermons which are intended as model sermons that other preachers should imitate.[11] Throughout the years heavy emphasis has been put on providing homiletical guidelines for sermon preparation and to provide background information that the presbyters would find useful. Such information included a survey of the Bible, a summary statement of evangelical doctrine, and commentaries on books of the Bible usually printed as sermon outlines. Alexander Karev in particular gained a reputation not only by his outstanding preaching but by reprinting large numbers of his sermon outlines in the journal. This concern for the needs of the preachers also confirms that the average preaching in the congregations was of a different caliber than that fostered in *Bratskii Vestnik*.

One Soviet sociologist, Iarygin, was able to analyze 800 sermons delivered in Baptist churches in the Northern Caucasus in the middle sixties.[12] Since he had read the sermons, presumably he had access to reports submitted by the watchdog assigned to monitor church activity. Although tendentious, this study provides some interesting information. In spite of Zhidkov's cautions and the much more explicit discouragement of evangelistic preaching contained in the 1960 Letter of Instruction to senior presbyters,[13] Iarygin found that more than 70 percent of all sermons were devoted to the theme of salvation. According to his classifications, 60 percent of the sermons were edificatory or exegetical. Another 25 to 30 percent dealt with religious-ethical themes. Approximately 8 percent of the sermons were apologetic in nature, seeking to defend the faith against scientific criticism. Another 5 percent were devoted to the burning questions of the day, such as the problem of war and peace. The obvious conclusion one must draw is that the bulk of the preaching was inward-oriented, seeking to meet spiritual needs of believers and above all to respond to the spiritual needs of the seekers.

On an average, Soviet evangelicals meet for worship at least twice on Sunday and three times during the week. In addition, some of the members are involved in choir and instrumental music practice, the degree of activity depending on how much local officials allow. Unregistered congregations such as the Reform Baptists and Pentecostals are usually more resolute in maintaining these additional church functions, including special children's activity. Members' meetings are held at least annually; in unregistered congregations they can be as frequent as monthly. In addition, there are regular meetings of the preaching corps. In an article on preaching, Zhidkov cited Paragraph 38 of the AUCECB statute of 1948 which stated:

(a) In addition to the presbyters and deacons, also individual brothers and sisters who have the gift and can edify the church are permitted to preach in the congregations;

(b) Those members with preaching ability who are encouraged by the presbyter and church council to serve the congregation constitute the regular contingent of preachers for the given congregation. [14]

Zhidkov also noted that these preachers must be members of the congregation, although it is unclear whether the statute itself clearly specified this provision.

As is traditional in evangelical circles, one midweek meeting is devoted to Bible study. Mennonite congregations in the Soviet Union, as well as Reform Baptists, maintain this practice. AUCECB churches vary in their practice, often substituting a preaching service in order to avoid divisive argumentation. Technically, a Bible study circle is illegal. Usual procedure at a Bible study is to study a book of the Bible systematically—verse by verse. Each participant takes his turn reading one of the verses and is expected to explain its meaning. Other participants may then contribute their ideas. The leader, usually the presbyter, concludes with a corrective summary.

Some churches attempted to conduct Bible study but were robbed of the blessing when too many participants insisted they alone had the right interpretation. This need to agree on a correct interpretation reminds one of the tendency in Soviet society to have a single party line on every issue. In one resourceful church the ministers began meeting the night before Bible study to discuss the Scripture passage. A uniform interpretation was agreed upon, and the following evening the ministers took turns exegeting each verse correctly according to a prearranged plan.[15]

Soviet evangelicals cannot imagine a religious gathering without music and singing. The birth of a baby, a wedding, even a funeral are accompanied by singing. Conferences and congresses are unimaginable without singing. For me, the reverberations of more than 1,000 male voices lifted in praise remains one of the unforgettable experiences of the 1974 AUCECB congress.

Paradoxically, the Soviet evangelical repertoire of songs is both limited and broad. It is limited in a literal sense in that printed music is almost as scarce as are Bibles. Usually the leader of the service "lines out" the text of each verse before the rest of the congregation, lacking hymnbooks, joins in the singing. Many members, however, know great numbers of songs from memory. One of the functions of the choir is to teach new songs to the congregation.

Numerous hymnals were produced for the early Russian evangelical movement. One hymnal, *Gusli*, attained wide popularity as it expanded with each edition until it was finally included in a larger collection of *Spiritual Songs* containing more than 1,200 songs. Approximately half had been composed by Prokhanov and the remainder were translations of German and English gospel songs. As a result, Soviet evangelical hymnody became a mixture of the typical songs produced by 19th-century revivalists and songs having a distinctly Slavic character. By 1947, President Zhidkov acknowledged that all the published collections of hymns were gone and it was necessary to issue a new hymnal. They hoped to provide each congregation with several copies of this new hymnal and anticipated completing the printing in 1948, provided the problem of the paper shortage was resolved. Permission to publish the hymnal finally came in 1955, and the following year the *Sbornik Dukhovnykh Pesni* (Collection of Spiritual Songs) first appeared. This is now the most common hymnal, although most congregations have no more than a few copies.[16]

Prokhanov did not remain the only composer. The AUCECB lays claim to a number of composers such as Sheve, Kazakov, and Viazovski from the inter-war period, as well as others such as N. I. Vysotskii, B. M. Basisty, Kazimirski, I. M. Skirdy, S. I. Voevody, and V. M. Kreiman.[17] Nikolai Alexandrovich Kazakov (1899-1973), Prokhanov's brother-in-law, provided words and music for 65 hymns printed between 1924 and 1928. In the 1950s and 1960s he was again active in Leningrad, providing music for the more demanding choirs that were developing. His Christmas oratorio was performed for the first time in 1969. He had also written a cantata based on Psalm 41.[18]

Another influential musician was Nikolai Ivanovich Vysotskii, who was deliberately transferred from region to region in order to foster music. From 1951 to 1953 he led the choir in the large Kiev church and used it as a laboratory to try out the hymns of the new composers emerging among the Baptist brotherhood. By reporting on this activity in *Bratskii Vestnik*, he sought to stimulate the work of other composers. His article contained a request to all composers to produce melodies in the national church spirit with the national motifs and to send them to the AUCECB.[19] Many songs, including many written by Christians in prison, circulate in manuscript form only.[20]

More recently, the Moscow choir, under the able direction of Leonid Tkachenko, has become well known. Tkachenko has played a significant role by teaching choral conducting to other choir leaders in the Union and has also made known the compositions of the Leningrad choir leader.[21]

Gabriel Pavlenko enlivened the 1974 congress with a dramatic presentation spelling out a detailed program of music education in the church. Music, he said, is the second pulpit in our churches and "the lives of those who serve this second pulpit must be holy and spiritual."[22] Pavlenko called for a section in *Bratskii Vestnik* devoted to music education. This began appearing in 1978. His recommendation that courses on vocal theory and singing be incorporated into the Bible correspondence program was carried out several years later. Pavlenko, whose rolling bass voice and charisma were a significant contribution to the cause of Baptist music, was accidentally killed in a traffic accident in 1977,[23] but there appear to be sufficient persons to carry his vision forward. Vysotskii's latest article on church music reveals great musical breadth. Better than any other statement, it shows how strongly the "second pulpit" advocates are concerned to produce deep feelings of reverence and to avoid the secular.[24]

In evangelical religious practice, fellowship is emphasized next to preaching and singing. The average evangelical knows no social life besides the church. The leadership has regularly tried to encourage local members to become involved in the cultural and social activities of their community but with little success.[25] For the typical Soviet evangelical, church is his life and the fellowship with other believers is his support in a largely unfriendly world. This in part explains the importance attached to the short session of greetings at the end of each service.

"Rodina"—Evangelicals and Society

Personal predilection, state policy toward believers, and the general isolation of Soviet society account for the deep apoliticism of Soviet evangelicals. Believers are encouraged to vote but in the Soviet Union that requires even less personal accountability than in the West. Because of their highly developed sense of conflict between church and state goals, local preachers carefully avoid political subjects lest this occasion closure of the church.[26] Soviet evangelicals have also been influenced by the fatalist, other-worldly social orientation of Russian orthodoxy. The Christian socialism of the early Soviet evangelicals has long ago faded into a dim memory.

Still it must be emphasized that the major reason for the evangelicals' undeveloped social conscience is that the state wishes it so. In his last "Conversation," Father Dudko raised the question:

Why not use the sincere donations of believers for good deeds? Why can't the church create a temperance society, for example, which would do something useful like curing drunks? Or organize a home for the aged or for children abandoned by their parents? Or, finally, she could simply help the sick and the needy, or set up a model school where children would receive a religiously-oriented education.... It's probably not common knowledge, but the atheists have forbidden the church to carry on any charitable activity, and, as a result, she is unable to use her own resources for good deeds.[27]

The prohibition on charitable activity was introduced in Article 17 of the 1929 law on cults. Recently the chairman of the Council of Religious Affairs, V. A. Kuroedov, stated that the reason for this prohibition was that:

Such activity is not directly related to the performance of religious rites. Neither is there any practical need for such activity. Poverty, famine and unemployment have long been done away with in the Soviet Union. The socialist state undertakes responsibility for social security, for providing leisure and recreational facilities for the workers, and for the cultural development of the people.[28]

It is striking that in other socialist countries Christians have persisted in involving themselves in charitable activity and are recognizing a broader responsibility as church. In the Soviet Union, in contrast, the only organized church charities are those conducted by the illegal Reform Baptists and Pentecostals, and this activity is limited primarily to serving its own membership. The one socially responsible role that the Soviet state expects from the churches is patriotism, expressed in military service and peace propaganda.

The first of eight points the editors of *Bratskii Vestnik* listed in 1945 as goals for the new journal was that it was to educate the churches in a feeling of love toward the motherland and its people. Their patriotic goal was listed ahead of the goal to print sermons and spiritual articles. Zhidkov announced in his introduction that the word *Rodina*, or variations thereof, would appear frequently on the pages of the journal. He defined *Rodina* as

> that country where we were born and grew up, where we walked and where our fields are spread out; here are our families and the families of those close to us; here is our people which we must love especially deeply and strongly from the heart and according to the glorious teachings of our Savior, since Jesus himself loved his people Israel. . . . In like fashion we must have a great love for our country, in order to give to it all our strength, our abilities and means, and, if necessary, also our life.[29]

A few pages later he defined patriotism as love for the *Rodina* and argued that good Christians must be fervent patriots. "Each Christian must know," he stated, "that God gave him not only a fatherland in heaven, but also a motherland on earth."[30] In order to counter the other-worldly attitudes of his co-believers, he then expanded on the rather novel argument that Jesus was a fervent patriot because he loved his people the Jews.

As promised, patriotism and *Rodina* appeared frequently in *Bratskii Vestnik*, but one article entitled "Khristianin i Rodina" merits special attention. This article, printed in 1970, had been presented by the general secretary Alexander Karev to the All-Union Congress in 1969. It had elicited considerable debate. Negative attitudes toward this paper were remembered by people from the provinces almost a decade later. Perhaps he was not a free agent in composing it, but he had misjudged the sentiments of the Union membership. As a result of the discussion at the congress, the published version was heavily revised with the patriotic language toned down, offensive sections omitted and others restated to produce a different emphasis.[31]

Karev adopted Zhidkov's argument that Jesus was a fervent patriot and cited Jesus' instructions to the 70 followers to go to the lost of the House of Israel only (Matthew 10:6). The revised version introduced an extended discussion which argued that nationalism and Christianity had nothing in common, and "true Christianity cannot be nationalist." This was followed by an extended argument noting that in Christ there is neither Jew nor Greek, that Jesus liked to be designated Son of Man because he came to be the Savior of all mankind. Christ loved all the people, and "this is also the task of all Christians: like their teacher, Christ, to treasure all people, all races, and all mankind in their hearts."[32]

In 1945 Zhidkov had stressed that one must love one's country, faults and all, and stated specifically that this meant obeying the laws and directives of the government. He based his claims on Romans 13 and Jesus' remark in Matthew 22:21 to give to Caesar what was Caesar's. Restating this rather baldly in his paper to the congress, Karev affirmed that "Rodina is the state and the state powers and laws, and it is also the task of the Christian to have a right relationship to the powers."[33] This straightforward statement was retained in the printed copy but some of the significant supporting argumentation was omitted. In arguing that the Christian must give to Caesar what is Caesar's, Karev had noted that in Christ's time, the cult of the emperor had developed in Rome. But, he added, "in time this cult passed, and now there are no countries in the world where rulers claim divine prerogatives and demand worship."[34] Karev's fellow delegates managed to expunge this remark from the published version because, even if Soviet rulers did not claim to be God, their ideology insisted on worshiping the god of materialism.

Another more critical paragraph also not allowed to stand was one in which Karev had suggested that, at an unspecified time earlier, Soviet Christians had not taken a proper attitude toward the authorities.

In spite of these revisions, the thrust of the published version still focused exclusively on the concern to give to Caesar what was Caesar's, with no recognition that this involved deciding what belonged to God and what to Caesar. In an eloquent statement, the famed Russian writer Solzhenitsyn once remarked that the clear intention behind Jesus' words was to indicate that "Caesar's concern is not with the most important thing in our lives." He went on to warn that "when Caesar, having exacted what is Caesar's, demands still more insistently that we render unto him what is God's—that is a sacrifice we dare not make!"[35]

Karev's paper, in contrast, seemed to indicate entirely uncritical support for the state. Once again, where he listed great Soviet achievements as having been unequaled elsewhere, the revised version was more restrained. By simply inserting or omitting a phrase, AUCECB members affirmed a qualified loyalty to the motherland. The printed article even hinted that the

Pauline injunction to obedience (Romans 13) was obedience to the state in its action for good but that the Evangelical Christian-Baptists did not identify all the state's actions as good. Karev had included the claim that "in our dearly beloved country there are thousands of places where the gospel and the good news of our Lord Jesus Christ is preached unhindered."[36] That claim did not appear in the printed version!

It is quite likely that Karev was forced to present a paper on this theme and it is quite likely that he will have preferred the published version with its more restrained "enlightened" patriotism, to use a word employed in one of the revisions. Even the published version, however, met with extensive criticism, including specific attacks from the Reform Baptist Union. In *Bratskii Listok* (4/1975), their leaders charged that in Karev's article, "all love for the homeland in practice amounted to the necessity of observing the legislation on the cults." For the Reform Baptists, patriotism included recognition and respect of the government, as well as loyalty toward the state but rejection of all its attempts to interfere in church affairs. Georgi Vins, general secretary of the Reform Baptists, was as eloquent as Karev in his patriotism. In February 1968 he wrote from a labor camp that "most of all I love my people—the soul of Russia! Your grim history, so full of suffering, is close to my heart. . . . You need Christ, my homeland, and especially today. . . ."[37] On another evening he wrote,

> All sleeps in peace. Only the sentry
> Stands on the watchtower guarding the camps.
> But I cannot sleep at the midnight hour;
> I am thinking of my beloved Ukraine:[38]

As far as the Soviet government was concerned, Soviet evangelicals would prove how patriotic they were by serving in the armed forces. President Zhidkov had stated the official AUCECB position back in 1945: "Serving the motherland means," he affirmed, "that the Christian honorably bears military service. In this question two opinions are impossible. A Christian who loves his motherland must defend it with weapons in his hands."[39]

Evangelical Pacifism
Pro-military statements like Zhidkov's have succeeded in creating the impression that Soviet evangelicals are not pacifists. Actually in the early 1920s more than 50 percent of the evangelicals were pacifists.

Zhidkov claimed that the influence of the Tolstoyans on some individuals in Evangelical and Baptist ranks had prompted them to protest against the imperialist war and in a few cases against military service in general. The influence and its impact was much broader. In South Russia and the Caucasus one could point to the influence of Mennonites and Molokans who rejected military service. The war-weariness after World War I and the Civil War also accounted for the rise of pacifism, but it is also possible that pacifist convictions developed among evangelicals simply through the influence of the Bible. In any case, by 1920 pacifism appeared to be the dominant position in the Baptist and Evangelical Christian unions.[40] During the war, 837 persons had refused to accept military service; 370 of them were Evangelical Christians and Baptists.[41] At the union congress held in 1920, they passed the following statement:

Considering . . . the participation of Evangelical Christians and Baptists in the shedding of human blood under every state system as a crime against conscience and the exact teaching and spirit of the Holy Scriptures, and likewise recognizing for Evangelical Christians and Baptists as impossible both the bearing of arms, the making of such for military purposes in all forms, and also the study of military affairs which would be equivalent to direct participation in the shedding of blood, . . . to consider it to be our sacred obligation openly to refuse military service in all its forms.[42]

In 1919 the Soviet government issued a decree permitting exemption from military service for conscience reasons. It is estimated that more than 40,000 pacifists made use of this exemption.[43] Jacob Zhidkov, for example, was one of those serving on the review board and advising Evangelical Christian conscientious objectors of their rights.[44] As the Soviet state became more sure of its power, it began to exert every pressure on the sectarians (including the evangelicals) to renounce pacifism. Denunciation of pacifism became the litmus test of loyalty to the Soviet state.

Prokhanov, leader of the Evangelical Christians, published an appeal in 1922 calling upon Christians in the entire world to take concrete steps so that every Christian would refuse all involvement in war. In 1923 he was imprisoned and finally allowed to meet with one of his associates, A. L. Andreev, in the Moscow interrogation prison. Andreev, who was personally not a convinced pacifist, informed him that the other Evangelical Christian leaders had discussed the matter and agreed in principle to recognize the Soviet government and to accept military service in it.[45] Prokhanov capitulated, and a declaration of loyalty was composed and signed by four Evangelical Christian leaders. Before the union had a chance to approve the statement, the letter was published in *Izvestiia*, thereby producing widespread opposition within Evangelical Christian ranks. The resolution passed by the congress meeting in October 1923 accepted military service but did leave the manner of service (with weapons, in the medical, or in working battalions) up to the personal conscience of each Christian.[46]

The Baptist union under the pacifist leadership of Pavel V. Pavlov and Michael D. Timoshenko also came under strong pressure. Both unions appealed to the Baptist World Alliance, meeting in Stockholm in 1923, requesting Alliance support through a resolution which would declare the "refusal by Baptists of all the world to participate in military service in any way."[47] The Baptist World Alliance rejected the proposal, leaving the question of military service to the individual conscience. Upon returning home the Russian Baptists sought in vain to gain permission to hold a congress. Finally, in December, they were able to assure the authorities that the congress would produce the desired result on the military service question. The resolution adopted acknowledged that unanimity had not been obtained but stated:

> Recognizing war as the greatest evil and greeting the peaceful policy of the Soviet state in its call to the peoples of the world for universal disarmament, the congress leaves the determination of its own attitude toward the means of fulfilling his military obligation to the individual conscience of each Baptist.[48]

Even with this compromise, final acceptance was obtained only after 12 delegates had been removed from the congress by the secret police.

During the next three years the military service question was the major issue of conflict in both unions, especially among the Baptists. At congresses in 1926, both unions were forced to condemn pacifism forthrightly. The Baptists split into equal parts and were only able to agree on a resolution following a compromise suggestion which involved reaffirmation of the old Baptist confession of faith which spoke only vaguely to the military service question.[49] At the Evangelical Christian congress the anti-pacifist resolution was approved by a majority of those who registered for this vote but the 224 "yes" votes were less than half of the 507 delegates registered for the congress.[50] Both unions lost some members, and there were attempts in local regions such as Moscow to form separate evangelical unions.[51]

A number of unreconstructed pacifists left the Evangelical Christian and Baptist churches and joined the Pentecostal churches. But Pentecostals were also subjected to heavy pressure and were forced to issue a loyalty statement in 1927 and to declare that Pentecostals objecting to military service were putting a blot on the relations between the Union of Christians of Evangelical Faith (Pentecostals) and the Soviet state. The statement noted further that refusal to serve in the Red Army could be based neither on the confession of faith of the Pentecostals nor on the gospels.[52]

Of all the evangelicals, only the Mennonites did not submit a declaration of loyalty to the Soviet state.[53] Mennonites had had the longest tradition of pacifism, having rejected military service under tsarist and Soviet regimes alike. Their only lapse (which the Soviets have never forgotten) was a 1½-year period during the Civil War when a Self-Defense League was formed and weapons were used against anarchist bands.[54] Soon the error of this decision was recognized and the membership once again listened to those preachers calling for an unequivocal stand in favor of pacifism. Even if no official renunciation of pacifism was forced from the Mennonites, after 1929 it no longer mattered. After 1929 the arrest of ministers, closure of churches, or the direct threat of arrest forced nearly all eligible Mennonites to accept military service.[55]

Forcing Mennonites to serve in the army was the pivotal factor in breaking the Mennonite church, according to one prominent Soviet sociologist. Since pacifism had almost come to be a talisman to distinguish Mennonites from other evangelicals, forcing them into submission on this matter broke the hold that the Mennonite religion had over its people.[56] That claim, however, contained some wishful optimism, since Soviet writings of the 1960s still complained that Mennonite preachers were discouraging young people from doing their duty in the army. Soviet writers complained that their theology of love undermined the class struggle.[57]

Even if anti-pacifist declarations were wrung from the evangelicals, grass-roots sentiment was not as easily eliminated. Following the war, the AUCECB has consciously attempted to rewrite its history by passing over its pacifist period in silence. Zhidkov cited Prokhanov as a supporter of military service and claimed that he had remarked:

> Examine the history of religious movements and you will see that those religious movements which in their time had dynamism, like the Quakers and Mennonites, died out, thanks to the fact that they followed the narrow teaching of nonresistance. But in contrast such mighty re-

ligious movements as the Baptists, Methodists, Presbyterians, and others had a healthy view of the relationship to government; they grew and they have a full potential for growth in the future also.[58]

To further buttress their position, the AUCECB noted that the pacifist position rested on three Scripture passages: Exodus 20:13; Matthew 26:51-52; Matthew 5:39 and 44. But all three passages, the official AUCECB statement claimed, are "concerned exclusively with our personal enemies but by no means with the enemies of society or government."[59] To help their argument, they were able to quote support from Dr. Walter Lewis, general secretary of the Baptist World Alliance. During the war Lewis had sent them a letter lauding the patriotism of American Baptists and had declared that one should take up weapons in the battle with the enemy. Lewis's letter was read into the minutes of the 1944 unity congress and the military sections of the letter were then quoted in a letter sent out to AUCECB churches.

During World War II evangelicals had distinguished themselves at the front as loyal soldiers. How many did serve is not known but it was sufficient to convince the state of their loyalty. Evangelicals, like the Orthodox, were rewarded with official permission to resume work as a national union of churches.

Throughout the years Baptist leaders have proudly drawn attention to the fact that their members served in the war. Zhidkov lost three sons in the war. N. T. Tsunenko, full-time worker for *Bratskii Vestnik* in the 1950s, returned from the front with four medals. Many other specific illustrations can be cited.[60] Michael Orlov, who kept the Evangelical Christian union alive during its most difficult period, held patriotic rallies in the Moscow church during the war, wrote letters to believers in occupied zones, encouraging them to side with the partisans, and helped to raise money for an ambulance plane for the Soviet army.[61]

Compared with the Orthodox Church donating and blessing army tanks, the evangelicals' donation of an ambulance plane suggests a more restrained militarism, implying perhaps that vestiges of pacifism remained.[62] The leaders' loud affirmations in the postwar period, that AUCECB members were fully committed to fighting the enemy with weapons, suggest that the leadership was still trying to convince its membership.

The AUCECB still reacts nervously to this question. In 1970 Assistant General Secretary Mitskevich found it necessary to reject pacifism rather sharply in a six-page article. The article concluded by quoting the 1926 and 1927 loyalty statements of the Baptists, Evangelical Christians, and Pentecostals, and asserting that this was also the viewpoint of the Mennonites who had joined the AUCECB.[63] When North American Mennonites asked about pacifism in 1976, AUCECB spokesmen replied that their union considers nonresistance relevant in person-to-person relationships but it has nothing to do with politics or the nation. Further, the North Americans were advised that "you would be wise not to raise questions that have been forgotten."[64]

Although not easily documented, evidence suggests that there is still considerable pacifist sentiment at the grass-roots level.[65] Individual cases of conscientious objection have occurred. In recent years the state has responded in one of two ways. According to the law, a soldier refusing induction can be punished with a four-year loss of freedom.[66] Beginning in 1976, the Council of Prisoners' Relatives of the Reform Baptist movement officially recognized imprisoned conscientious objectors from its ranks as legitimately suffering for their faith. Thirteen individuals have been included on their prisoner list.[67] Many more young people in the Reform Baptist union are conscientious objectors who have benefited from a second alternative state response. By indicating that they are believers, they immediately become suspicious characters in the eyes of the state and are transferred to working brigades where they do not need to bear weapons. In fact, as numerous individuals have assured this writer, this is also a widespread practice among AUCECB Baptists.

Pacifism is not yet a majority position in the Christian church in general, but in recent years leading theologians have reached broad agreement that the thrust of the New Testament message is unquestionably pacifist in both a personal and a social sense. Most theologians and churchmen, however, argue that the New Testament emphasis is too idealistic and opt for a Niebuhrian ethic.[68] But the Russian Baptist union, with its strong claim to reject all modernism and its assertion of an unquestioning commitment to the Bible as the source of truth, should logically reject the war theology espoused by Zhidkov and Mitskevich.

The Peace Offensive and the Evangelicals

If the Second World War resulted in the emergence of the new Soviet evangelicals, the Cold War significantly influenced the shape of their development. In March 1947 Winston Churchill summed up the Western attitude to postwar Soviet foreign policy by declaring that an Iron Curtain had descended across the continent. Behind that curtain lay the Soviet sphere and all the ancient capitals and states of Central and Eastern Europe were coming under increasing control from Moscow. "This is certainly not the liberated Europe we fought to build up," he declared, "nor is it one which contains the essentials of permanent peace."[69] Simultaneously the counsels of the young George F. Kennan gained attention in the American State Department, and the Americans announced a policy of "containing" the Soviet advance. Similar warlike language from the Cominform spoke of two camps: the "imperialist anti-democratic camp" over against the "anti-imperialist democratic camp." Historians are not yet agreed on assigning appropriate blame, but it is probably accurate to say that the Cold War developed through a chain of actions and reactions reflecting the growing distrust that the two camps had of each other.

The Cold War forced Russian Baptists into isolation inside the Soviet camp. They genuinely shared the fearful distrust of the capitalist world with its "terrible atomic bomb." AUCECB leadership had fully expected to attend the Seventh World Baptist Congress in Copenhagen, Denmark, in early August 1947, but, upon receiving copies of the congress program, refused to attend. In a letter stating their reasons, they argued that it was apparent that the congress would not have a merely spiritual and edifying character but also a political one. Many of the topics, such as "Church and State," "The Social and Cultural Responsibilities of Baptists," and "The United Nations," would likely produce contradictory viewpoints resulting in a purely political discussion and "contribute to unnecessary friction in our whole brotherhood."[70] The congress had included a statement concerning relationships with the USSR in which it spoke about "communism as an obstacle to world evangelization."[71] To this the AUCECB letter replied that "Russian Baptists not only do not consider communism an obstacle to evangelization, but they also share its social-economic principles as not contradicting the teachings of our Lord Jesus Christ."[72] In another issue of *Bratskii Vestnik* for 1947, Zhidkov claimed that "the government of our country adequately and energetically struggles against all war hawks and is conducting a policy of peace."[73] An even more emphatic declaration was the claim that "the Soviet land became the chief of all freedom-loving peoples in its unceasing struggle for peace, for social and political justice."[74]

As noted earlier, the situation of the Russian Baptists was closely related to the vicissitudes of foreign policy, and by 1949 *Bratskii Vestnik* had to cease publication. Only after the death of Stalin did the journal reappear, and its opening salvos revealed that it was to play its role along with the Orthodox and other religions in fostering Soviet peace propaganda.

With suitable bombast the opening issue began with a declaration that nonparticipation in certain movements in history was equivalent to a crime. Examples cited were the struggle for the liberation of Negroes in the United States or the struggle against the opium trade in China. In the present day, "such a movement is the great movement on behalf of peace. Nonparticipation in it is also equivalent to a crime."[75] The opening article then went on to assert that:

> When an armaments race began in the U.S.A. and several other countries, and the danger of a new world war fell on humanity, and when the Soviet Union adopted the holy banner of the struggle for peace, calling on all countries and peoples to stand under this banner, Evangelical Christian-Baptists of the USSR stood as one man under the banner of peace. In this great advance for peace they recognized a truly Christian task; not to participate in it would be a disgrace for a Christian.[76]

Nearly the entire issue was devoted to the peace offensive.

AUCECB involvement in the peace movement began with the creation of a World Peace Council in 1949, an organization controlled and sponsored by the Soviet government. It held several well-publicized conferences in Paris, Prague, Warsaw, Stockholm, and Vienna. The AUCECB sent delegates to these conferences, as well as to a conference called by Patriarch Alexei in Zagorsk. On radio in October 1953 President Zhidkov also addressed Baptists in the whole world. In this radio speech he stated that:

> We know that there are Baptists, especially in the U.S.A. and England, who support the militarists and approve their aggressive actions. We, Baptists in the Soviet Union, consider that these Baptists discredit Christianity and are unworthy of the Baptist name. The Baptists must be completely committed to the great ideals of Christianity: The ideals of human brotherhood and peace among nations.[77]

Also in 1953, Walter O. Lewis of the Baptist World Alliance had written a letter of reply in response to a packet of declarations and speeches from several conferences sent him by the AUCECB. Lewis had stated in his letter that the impression he had received in reading the Zagorsk papers was that the Soviet government was behind the conference. In his published reply Karev asked:

Why do you think that those in our country believing in God who truly crave peace would not be able to take a personal initiative in such a sacred matter and that for such a holy Christian task—to conduct a conference of Christian churches and representatives of other religions in defence of peace—it must have our government behind it?[78]

Karev argued further that the speeches the Baptists had given at the conferences had not required permission from the government. Lewis had also criticized the absence of any criticism of Soviet peace policy in the Baptist statements. To this, Karev replied that:

Our government truly strives for peace and does everything possible to conserve and consolidate peace in the whole world. Why is it necessary to criticize our government, if its actions fully correspond to the most fervent desires of all our people?[79]

The AUCECB public statements on behalf of the peace offensive were uncritically pro-Soviet but at least have the merit of being less vitriolic than those of Metropolitan Nikolai of the Orthodox Church. Nikolai had referred to the U.S.A. as:

... the trans-Atlantic octopus [which] is trying to fasten its greedy tentacles around the whole globe.... The trans-Atlantic sirens sing of "liberties." But only a man with a black conscience and a clouded intellect can say that liberty exists in a country where people are lynched, where children are kidnapped, where tear gas bombs are thrown at workers ... liberty to rob, coerce, and slaughter—such is their liberty![80]

All Soviet believers shared a fervent desire for peace. It is probably fair to assume, given their lack of access to information about the Soviet Union's own staggering rearmament program,[81] that they sincerely believed the Soviet peace movement was seeking peace. It is also fair to assume that the Soviet government deliberately used Soviet churchmen to help give the Soviet Union a better image abroad and to influence their fellow religionists abroad to oppose such activities as the American involvement in Korea. But the initial propaganda campaign under the auspices of the World Peace Council was so transparently pro-Soviet that Western churches and Western public opinion rejected the statements with incredulity.[82]

An incident occurring in 1955 illustrates the degree to which Baptist activities and success in the peace propaganda campaign determined their freedom to act elsewhere. Western Baptists had sought to demonstrate that they too were speaking out on behalf of peace. The first meeting between Townley Lord, president of the Baptist World Alliance, and the Russian Baptists took place in Sweden when Lord and several others attended a small peace conference sponsored by the Quakers. Lord and two British Baptist leaders were then invited to visit the Soviet Union in 1954. One major purpose of the trip was to invite the AUCECB to send delegates to the next world congress to be held in London in 1955. The AUCECB emitted positive signals, but as the time drew near, the BWA leaders were informed that, unless they participated in the World Peace Council meeting in Helsinki, they could expect no Russian Baptists at the London congress. World Baptist leaders found themselves in a dilemma, not simply because of the obvious extortion attempt, but also because attendance at such a peace conference or even a visit to the Soviet Union might mean loss of support from the American constituency. The McCarthy era was not yet history. General Secretary Arnold Ohrn stalled by requesting information about the conference, about which he had heard nothing. It was finally suggested that Dr. Williamson, retired missionary to China, whose reputation was unimpeachable, might attend as an observer.[83] At this World Peace Assembly Alexander Karev was elected a member of the World Peace Council. He had also been elected a member of the All-Union Congress of Peace Supporters which met in Moscow in May 1955.[84]

With the collapse of the Soviet-sponsored World Peace Council in the later fifties, Baptist involvement in the peace movement remained active but more moderate. They were involved from the start with the Christian Peace Movement headquartered in Prague. Because of the reputation and personality of its president, Czech theologian Jozef Hromadka, the Christian Peace Conference (CPC) appeared to have greater integrity, and peace-minded Western churchmen and theologians became actively involved. Throughout its existence, the CPC's theological commission has served as the point where some dialogue between East and West could take place. After the Soviet invasion of Czechoslovakia in 1968 led to the unpleasant ouster of Hromadka and his associates, the CPC fell under the dominance of the Soviet authorities and Western churchmen broke with it.[85] Russian Baptists continue to attend CPC assemblies, have been elected to the working committee and some of the commissions, but their influence has been negligible.

Russian church involvement in the peace offensive, including Russian Baptist involvement, has continued to the present. In the process many words have been said or written, innumerable delegates have been sent abroad to conferences, and unknown sums of money have been donated to the Soviet Peace Fund. This activity has achieved some positive results. In recent years governments from both "camps" have acknowledged the value of the role played by nongovernmental organizations (including churches) to the causes of human rights, peace, and development.[86] The many seminars have also influenced the thinking of the Russian delegates. Through them they were forced to learn about the extent of Soviet defense spending and to consider other evidence that Soviet foreign policy is not always peaceful. They, like Western participants, are now much more sophisticated in recognizing the complexity of achieving world peace with justice. Soviet Baptists earnestly wish for peace and in this sense the leaders represent the concerns of the constituency. Yet the motivation for their involvement remains enigmatic.

In a posthumous article, Alexander Karev, who as general secretary had been the chief activist in the AUCECB peace offensive, identified a nine-point peace program they were pursuing. The program was as follows:

1. All AUCECB churches pray for peace.

2. To preach sermons from time to time to teach believers the importance of peace on earth both for the blessing of the kingdom of God and for the happiness of mankind.

3. To devote a special section to peace in *Bratskii Vestnik* entitled "Christian Voice in Defense of Peace."

4. AUCECB representatives participate in conferences dedicated to peace both in the USSR and abroad.

5. To participate through its representatives in the work of the Soviet committee to defend peace.

6. The AUCECB conducts extensive correspondence with many churches in the world, appealing to them for active participation in building peace and friendship between nations.

7. In personal encounters with Christian workers from various countries to strive to touch upon the peace questions, as well as other questions.

8. AUCECB representatives sometimes give addresses on radio on peace questions.

9. Welcoming the peace program adopted by the 12th Baptist World Alliance congress in Tokyo, 1970, the AUCECB will participate zealously in carrying it out.[87]

This is a broad-scale program involving considerable effort and much money. In international religious circles they have gained in respect and even though they, like the Orthodox, have never raised a prophetic voice of criticism against the policies of their own government, their arguments for peace are acknowledged to have merit.

Although the public image is that of zealous peace activists, the AUCECB leadership has been criticized by its constituency for its heavy peace emphasis. At the 1969 congress, for example, this emerged through complaints about the pages of *Bratskii Vestnik* being wasted on uninteresting communiqués about peace.[88] Church leaders have acknowledged in private conversation that they attended a peace conference because they were ordered to and have often expressed concern about how to explain their presence to the church members back home who want to trust them but wonder. Other evangelicals not in the AUCECB are not involved in the peace movement. They have always regarded the peace movement as an aspect of Soviet foreign policy and feel that the AUCECB has compromised itself by consorting with all manner of religious and state officials at such conferences.

Actually the role of the Russian Baptists in the peace movement has been minimal. It might best be described as passively allowing the Orthodox Church to take the lead, merely demonstrating support with its presence. Russian Baptists have had some success by urging Baptists and other evangelicals abroad to increase their peace emphasis and to secure their attendance at international peace gatherings.[89] In the latest Soviet propaganda assault, Russian Baptists wrote letters to their Baptist brother, President Carter of the United States, urging him in forceful language not to order production of the neutron bomb.[90]

But involvement in the peace movement also has its dangers. Russian Baptist contacts with the historic peace churches have increased, forcing a new confrontation with the unwelcome subject of pacifism. Many peace conferences have also exposed them to a theology of social action that they dare not act upon.

It is unfortunate that the history of Russian evangelicals' witness for peace has been so contradictory. Peace is a major world concern and must be taken seriously. Yet peace without pacifism appears to be a contradiction, at least according to Anabaptist theology to which the Russian Baptists were heavily indebted. Peace without self-criticism of one's own society and government can scarcely be considered genuine. True peace requires action, especially moral action, and a multiplicity of conferences is a poor substitute. Considerations of expediency still play a major role in the Soviet evangelical peace offensive. Will the foreign churchmen with whom they share these concerns have the courage to maintain a stance of moral integrity?

Notes to Chapter 4

1. V. A. Kuroedov, "Soviet Law and Freedom of Conscience," *Izvestiia*, 31 Jan. 1976, p. 5.

2. *BV*, 1/47, p. 16.

3. The best legal study (Luchterhandt, *Der Sowjetstaat und die Russisch-Orthodoxe Kirche*) concludes that the language of "separation" never represented the actual nature of the relationship. Instead he postulates a system of "unfriendly state supremacy over the church" which is a step further than the friendly Josephinism of the 18th century. Bociurkiw, "Church-State Relations . . ." called separation of church and state a "constitutional fiction," since this liberal notion could not be reconciled with a *Weltanschauungstaat* or confessional state (p. 5).

4. John B. Toews (ed.), *Selected Documents: The Mennonites in Russia from 1917 to 1930* (Winnipeg, Man.: Christian Press, 1975), pp. 430-31. Also cited in Trevor Beeson, pp. 106-107.

5. *BV*, 5/47, p. 14.

6. "USSR: AUCECB 1970-76," BWA Archives. For an example of the replies given by Michael Zhidkov on Moscow radio see *RCL*, 4-5/75, pp. 28-30.

7. *BV*, 3/57, pp. 74-77.

8. *BV*, 3-4/55, p. 58.

9. *BV*, 1/49, p. 5.

10. *BV*, 3-4/55, p. 59. Zhidkov also urged the avoidance of all theatrics and gesticulation; rather, preach loudly, clearly, naturally, and simply like John the Baptist, Jesus and his apostles. I. I. Motorin also wrote numerous guidelines for preachers, which included one to persuade preachers to use notes and a plan when preaching (*BV*, 1/54, pp. 43-47).

11. See, for example, 3/46, p. 28; 1/48, pp. 46-50; 2/48, pp. 53-57; 2/55; 3-4/55; and 1/56.

12. A. F. Iarygin, "Kharakter sovremennoi baptistskoi propovedi," *Voprosy nauchnogo ateizma*, No. 12, 1971, pp. 149-63.

13. See below, chaps. 5 and 6.

14. *BV*, 3-4/55, p. 58.

15. Soviet emigrants explain this as due to the more passionate nature of the Russian and Ukrainian evangelical, as well as noting that the Germans had a century of practice with Bible study and were used to the rules of procedure.

16. For a survey see *BV*, 5/47, pp. 21-25; cf. 2/55, p. 72.

17. Cited in Bychkov's congress report (*BV*, 1/75, pp. 50-52). A dozen Latvian and Estonian composers are also acknowledged.

18. Katherine Murray, "Death of a Baptist Musician," *RCL*, 1/74, pp. 3-10. See also *BV*, 1/58, pp. 59-61 on A. G. Kuznetsov.

19. *BV*, 5-6/54, pp. 113-18.

20. Peter and Anita Deyneka, Jr., *A Song in Siberia* (Elgin, Ill.: David C. Cook, 1977), p. 54. Since 1956 *BV* has regularly printed one song (with notation) per issue to disseminate the new compositions.

21. Tkachenko studied in England and benefited from Vysotskii's tutelage in the fifties. Other directors worthy of mention are A. I. Erin (Leningrad) and I. A. Plekhnevich (Kharkov); cf. *BV*, 5-6/54, p. 117.

22. *BV*, 1/75, p. 64. His plea was echoed by the next speaker, N. I. Vysotskii, now choir leader in Odessa.

23. *BV*, 6/77, pp. 59-63.

24. *BV*, 5/78, pp. 57-67; cf. K. V. Somova, "Pesnia v zhizni khristianina," *BV*, 4/64, pp. 29-34.

25. For examples, *BV*, 1/79, pp. 36-40; 2/77, p. 69; 5/77, pp. 60-65, for recent statements.

26. A recent official spokesman, Archpriest G. Razumovsky, drew a distinction between justice as the goal of the state and the truth of God as the goal of the church (Herbert Waddams, "The Church in Soviet Russia," *Soviet Studies*, July 1953, pp. 14-16). To be fair it should be noted that committed Orthodox laymen like Anatoli Levitin or the historian Evgenii Barabanov have heavily criticized their church for restricting itself "to an 'intimate little corner' of piety locked away with seven locks from the life of the world . . ." and hope for the recovery of social responsibility. Alexander Solzhenitsyn, *et al. From Under the Rubble* (London: Collins & Harvill Press, 1975), p. 187.

27. Dmitrii Dudko, *Our Hope* (Crestwood, N.Y.: St. Vladimir's Seminary Press, 1977), p. 247.

28. *Church and Religion in the USSR* (Moscow: Novosti, 1977), p. 43.

29. *BV*, 1/45, p. 4.

30. *Ibid.*, p. 7.

31. *BV*, 3/70, pp. 48-54. I am indebted to Keston College files for a copy of the original manuscript as presented to the 1969 congress. The latter was mailed to all churches.

32. *Ibid.*, p. 52.

33. *Ibid.*, (p. 7 in ms.).

34. P. 8 in ms.

35. "As Breathing and Consciousness Return," in *From Under the Rubble*, pp. 24-25.

36. P. 4 in ms.

37. Vins, *Three Generations of Suffering*, p.79.

38. *Ibid.*, pp. 80-82.

39. *BV*, 1/45, p. 7. The "weapons in his hands" phrase appeared frequently in the early issues.

40. The little-known history of evangelical pacifism has been discussed at length in Steeves's dissertation on the Baptists (pp. 557-592) and in Kahle's book on the Evangelical Christians (pp. 382-419). A recent Soviet study providing helpful archival documentation—though differing from the above interpretations—is Z. V. Kalinicheva, *Sotsial'naia sushchnost' baptizma* (Leningrad, 1972), especially pp. 49-85.

41. P. M. Putintsev, *Politicheskaia rol' i taktika sekt* (Moscow, 1935), pp.96-97.

42. Quoted by Steeves, p. 564.

43. A. I. Klibanov, *Religioznoe sektantstvo: sovremennost'* (Moscow: Nauka, 1969), p. 203.

44. *BV*, 5-6/54, p. 31, which he recalled as unpleasant work and now thanked God that the EC union in 1923 decided in favor of military service.

45. Andreev appeared to be the preferred negotiating partner for the authorities. Andreev apparently underwent no imprisonment and after the war served as plenipotentiary for the Ukraine and became a vice-president of the union in the 1954 shake-up (Kahle, pp. 395, 399).

46. *Ibid.*, pp. 400-402.

47. Steeves, p. 571. The BWA response reflected the traditional view indicat-

ing that pacifism was considered a secondary issue. A statement on Baptist distinctives approved by six North American Baptist conventions in 1967 includes such themes as democracy, liberty, and mission but the word "peace" does not appear once. (See *Watchman Examiner*, January 26, 1956, pp. 38-40.)

48. Steeves, p. 478.

49. *Ibid.*, pp. 488-89. Steeves develops a distinction between "Old" and "New" Baptists, with the latter led by P. V. Pavlov, both pacifist and pro-socialist. State pressure led to the reinstatement of Old Baptist leadership. The leading Old Baptist, I. V. Ivanov-Klyshnikov, argued that by rejecting pacifism they would secure freedom to hold regular congresses, but, ironically, this was the last congress the state permitted (p. 592).

50. Kahle, pp. 406-407. Kahle attempts to explain Prokhanov's actions as the expression of an optimism and faith in Soviet promises that he later recognized to have been unrealistic (p. 377f.).

51. Steeves, p. 589.

52. *BV*, 3/71, p. 71.

53. Krest'ianinov, p. 59, tried to account for this by claiming a higher percentage of kulaks among Mennonites than other evangelicals.

54. John B. Toews, "The Origins and Activities of the Mennonite *Selbstschutz* in the Ukraine (1918-1919)," *Mennonite Quarterly Review*, Jan/72, pp. 4-40.

55. As late as 1936 there were still some Mennonite conscientious objectors, but the conditions of their alternative service scarcely differed from that of a concentration camp. (I am indebted to an unpublished graduate paper by Peter Rempel.)

56. A. I. Klibanov, *Iz mira religioznogo sektantstva* (Moscow, 1974), pp. 110-11.

57. Krest'ianinov, pp. 102-119. The textbook, *Basic Course on Scientific Communism* (Moscow, 1973), declared that "religious morality with its preaching of nonresistance results in the withering away of class consciousness and preparedness among believers." (Cited from *G2W*, Sept/74, p. 14.)

58. *BV*, 2/45, p. 26.

59. *BV*, 3/45, pp. 51-52.

60. *BV*, 2/45, p. 37f.; 3/46, p. 6; 5/47, p. 14.

61. *BV*, 1/45, pp. 14-22.

62. Kolarz, p. 314.

63. *BV*, 3/71, pp. 66-71. See also 4/70, pp. 21-22 for a statement from the well-known Pentecostal G. G. Ponurko affirming that his union had approved military service in 1928.

64. MCC files, 1976.

65. This writer encountered such sentiment in many areas of the USSR, especially the Ukraine and Central Asia.

66. A. Bilinsky in *Religion und Atheismus in der UdSSR*, 7-8/1976, pp. 21-24.

67. *Ibid.*, pp. 18-21. For prisoners' list see: *CPR Bulletin*, No. 43 (1977); 56, 57, 59 (1978); 67/79. Sentences averaged 3.5 years.

68. See, for example, the statement from the WCC unit on Church and Society entitled "Violence, Nonviolence, and the Struggle for Social Justice," August, 1973, reprinted in Donald Durnbaugh (ed.), *On Earth Peace* (Elgin, Ill.: The Brethren Press, 1978), pp. 374-85.

69. Quote in Louis J. Halle, *The Cold War as History* (New York: Harper & Row, 1967), p. 104; cf. pp. 106f., 155.

70. *BV*, 4/47, p. 7.

71. *Ibid.*

72. *Ibid.*
73. *BV*, 6/47, p. 5.
74. *Ibid.*, p. 6.
75. *BV*, 1/53, p. 3.
76. *Ibid.*, p. 4.
77. *Ibid.*, p. 6.
78. *Ibid.*, p. 66.
79. *Ibid.*
80. Quoted in William C. Fletcher, *Religion and Soviet Foreign Policy 1945-1970* (London: Oxford University Press, 1973), p. 31. Fletcher's study is the only attempt to examine the role of Soviet churches in Soviet foreign policy. Replete with stimulating hypotheses, many of which are not contradicted by the data available to me; the problem lies in the proof.
81. The Soviet Union began rearming in 1948. From a high of 137.9 billion rubles in 1944, military expenditures had fallen to 66.1 billion. This now rose to 79 billion rubles in 1949 and to 96.4 billion in 1951 (Georg von Rauch, *A History of Soviet Russia* [New York: Praeger Publishers, 1967], pp. 405-406). High military expenditures continue to the present, the Soviets regularly devoting about 12-13% of GNP to military spending, compared to 5 or 6% by the U.S.A. In 1962 the total Soviet military budget was estimated at 20-25 billion rubles, and in 1978 it was 150 billion (*Newsweek*, 12 June, 1978, p. 15). (The Soviet ruble was devalued in 1958 to 1/10 its former value.)
82. Fletcher (p. 34) credits it with success in connection with the Korean war, but later the churches' contributions declined.
83. "Russia Tour," BWA files. Cf. *BV*, 5/55.
84. *BV*, 5/55, p. 80. The peace portfolio appears to have been included in the general secretary's duties, rather than the president's. Karev's successor Bychkov became the member in subsequent committees.
85. Metropolitan Nikodim took the lead in securing the ouster of Hromadka and Ondra. It is striking that it was primarily Alexei Stoian of the international department who represented the Baptists. No critical history of the CPC has been produced, but the CPC has printed reports after major assemblies as well as numerous communiqués. An invaluable document collection to assess the 1968 Sovietization of the CPC is *Christliche Friedenskonferenz 1968-1971*, Georges Casalis, *et al.* (Wuppertal: Jugenddienst Verlag, 1971).
86. This is well illustrated by the letters of official greeting sent to such gatherings as the Christian Peace Assembly in Prague (1977) and was stated explicitly by a German diplomat at Belgrade (1977) for the follow-up Conference on Security and Cooperation in Europe (*Frankfurter Allgemeine Zeitung*, 14 Oct. 1977).
87. *BV*, 2/72, pp. 6-7. A strange omission is any reference to the Soviet Peace Fund to which Orthodox and Baptists have donated extensively. Begun in April 1961 upon the initiative of "public activists," its funds are said to have been given for nonmilitary purposes in Vietnam, the Middle East, Peru, and Pakistan (*BV*, 5/71, pp. 4-6). No financial statements have been released nor did Karev himself know how much the Baptists had donated (*BV*, 3/73, p. 10). Local churches have complained that the Moscow leaders urged donating as a virtual state requirement.
88. Acknowledged by Karev in his Congress Report (*BV*, 2/70, p. 34).
89. *BV*, 4/78, pp. 39-40.
90. Published in *Izvestiia*, 12 July 1977; an open letter to President Nixon (30 Dec. 1972) urging him to halt the bombing in Vietnam is another example.

The grossest and most widespread administrative measures that have been taken against believers are the closure of prayer houses, refusal to register religious communities . . . breaking up prayer meetings of believers forcibly with police and auxiliary police, arbitrary searches of believers' homes and prayer houses, confiscation of religious literature, illegal arrests of believers . . .

—*Chairman Puzin*
Council for Affairs of Religious Cults
to Party Workers in RSFSR
August 5, 1965, in AS 620

5 Crisis: The Khrushchev Campaign Against Religion

Was it a centenary year? Exactly 100 years earlier, in 1859, a new era in natural science had been ushered in with the publication of Charles Darwin's *The Origin of Species*. Karl Marx's *Critique of Political Economy*, also published in 1859, had resulted in a new political science. The so-called warfare between science and religion had been joined. Put crassly, the conflict consisted of two philosophies (or was it two faiths?) that differed on whether "people eat first and think afterward" or is it the other way around?[1] Was it now time, a century later, to terminate the war of science with religion by dealing the latter a mortal blow? Was that what Nikita Khrushchev had in mind when he announced the schedule for the changeover from socialism to full communism?

Soviet churchmen had just begun to convince a surprised Western public that the Christian church still existed in the Soviet Union, when a state onslaught on religion once again threatened the church's very existence. In the first half of 1961 alone, 300 Baptist churches were closed and worried members expressed concern that, if this rate continued, all their churches would be closed within three years.[2] Leading Soviet churchmen not only continued to travel abroad as Soviet peace ambassadors but in fact increased their visits, loudly proclaiming a freedom of religion that they in fact were in serious danger of losing. Before the major campaign ended following Khrushchev's ouster in 1964, more than half the churches of both the Orthodox and the Baptists had been closed and the number of Orthodox clergy had been reduced by two thirds.

The churches' unofficial concordat with Stalin had never been confirmed by law. The 1929 law that had earlier launched the major Stalinist persecution wave was still in effect; since 1944 state officials had simply ignored its more restrictive features. Church leaders were well aware that this could change at any moment. This accounts for their highly submissive posture, but it damaged their reputation among their own followers, who did not know about the nature of the concessions. The Orthodox hierarchical structure had been reestablished in violation of the law, and the reigning Patriarch Alexei had already recognized in 1927 that Orthodox survival depended on the maintenance of this institutional structure.[3] Evangelical Christian-Baptists, on the other hand, could afford to be more flexible. Once more they were to demonstrate that their church polity was well suited to the Soviet system, and it was above all the Baptists who turned this second big assault on religion into an embarrassing failure for the state.

Motivations

Motivations are often more important than the observable policy, yet in the best of circumstances the identification of real motivations must remain tentative. Russian and subsequently Soviet leaders have earned a reputation for paranoia. One seasoned observer noted rather aptly that "The Soviet state is by nature irritable. Any foreign body sets up in it an intolerable itch which sooner or later must be relieved by a violent scratch."[4] Were we to approach our subject simply from the perspective of the evangelicals, then the major motivation might be to scratch out the Baptist itch. The Baptists, with their readily comprehensible world-view, pragmatic orientation, determinist strain, apocalyptic and messianic tendencies, an emphasis on a highly committed membership and a well-disciplined organization, as well as their historic social consciousness, were demonstrating very similar characteristics to those of the Communist Party member. Since both appealed to a similar psychological type, the Baptists might be considered serious competition to the party. With its rapid growth to a membership of one-half million, it was not that much smaller than the party, which claimed 3.6 percent of the population as members.[5]

The campaign, however, was directed against religion in general, and the evangelicals were not given any special treatment initially. Religious policy was clearly related to the political power struggle that began after Stalin's death. On July 7, 1954, came the first signal. The party Central Committee approved a decision to take measures to improve scientific atheist propaganda which had fallen into decay.[6] Although the decision remained secret till 1962, there was a sudden flourishing of atheist propaganda.[7] But in November 1954 a second Central Committee decision signed by Nikita Khrushchev alone condemned all administrative interference in religious affairs and all propaganda offensive to the feelings of believers. Khrushchev apparently signed this decision personally to demonstrate that this compromise was not a political setback for him. But by 1959, when the real campaign began under the direction of Khrushchev and his protegé, L. F. Il'ichev, he no longer needed to compromise with Bulganin, Zhukov, and Malenkov, the earlier proponents of moderation.[8]

Although Stalin's seventieth birthday celebrations in 1949 had amounted to an unprecedented deification of the leader, Joseph Stalin died like other mortal men on March 5, 1952. Soviet citizens were deeply moved but many were unsure whether to celebrate or to mourn. The leaders in government were also unsure what should happen next. The next few years came to be known as "The Thaw" because in many areas, especially of thought and culture, it seemed as if the freeze was off. Finally at the Twentieth Party Congress in 1956 Nikita Khrushchev read a major speech lasting seven hours in which he catalogued many of Stalin's sins and soundly condemned the cult of personality. This secret speech was leaked to an American official soon after and it was published by the American State Department. The de-Stalinization reached its peak at the Twenty-second Party Congress in October 1961 where the congress resolved to remove Stalin's embalmed body from its place beside Lenin and bury it by the Kremlin wall. By then Khrushchev, the new leading spokesman against Stalin's personality cult, was threatening to begin his own personality cult.[9]

When Stalin died, a collective leadership consisting of Voroshilov, Malenkov, Beria, Molotov, Bulganin, and Kaganovich was announced. Nikita Khrushchev only emerged two weeks later when he took over Malenkov's post as first secretary of the party, Malenkov retaining his post as prime minister. In December 1953, Lavrenti Beria, who had seemed the most likely successor to Stalin, was executed, having been removed from high office in July. Another change followed in February 1955 when Nikolai A. Bulganin became prime minister, Malenkov being consigned to a lesser post. What had seemed to be a triumvirate of Malenkov, Beria, and Khrushchev now became a two-man team with Khrushchev holding more power as head of the party than Bulganin as head of the state administration. Khrushchev finally took over Bulganin's post as well in March 1958. Where Stalin had been taciturn, Khrushchev's ebullient personality assured six years of turbulence before he was put aside by his subordinates, Brezhnev and Kosygin.

Probably even more significant than the power struggle was the role ideology played in providing the motivation. Khrushchev has been heavily criticized for fostering a personality cult and for acting arbitrarily due to personal whim or the dictates of pragmatism. But in the same way that Khrushchev's heavily criticized educational reform and agricultural policy were due to his attempt to put communist ideology into practice, so an ideological commitment explains the politically unwise attack on religion. Beginning in 1958, when Khrushchev was fully in the saddle, there was much talk about the necessity to plan for the changeover from socialism to communism. Since in simplistic communist ideology religion is defined as a remnant of the capitalist past, any full changeover to communism requires a final eradication of past vestiges. There are also striking parallels between this attempt to move from socialism to communism and the attempt by Stalin after 1928 to enforce collectivization and industrialization. In both cases religion served as an unacceptable theological vestige and as a useful scapegoat.[10]

Other motivating factors were probably of lesser importance. Seen in the longer history of modernization, the restoration of two state agencies meant that the Orthodox church was once again receiving preferential treatment. Khrushchev's religious policy was relatively more successful against the Orthodox church, so that finally, by 1965, a single state agency with increased powers could attempt to deal with all religions equally.[11] Still another motivation that has been advanced is that during the 1930s many *Bezbozhniki* (workers in the Godless League) had been trained. These were said to be chafing under enforced unemployment and inability to have a fulfilling career. A new antireligious campaign would give them something to do! This was an insignificant factor, since, by 1964, a major campaign had to be launched to train the necessary atheist cadres and in a real sense Soviet antireligious policy continues to stumble due to inadequate manpower.

Vospitanie vs. Administrirovanie
(Brains vs. Brawn—Very Free Translation)

Communist ideology assumes the unalterable advance of history toward the dictatorship of a proletariat that is attaining ever-greater enlightenment as science progresses. That means that all vestiges of the capitalist and religious past are doomed to disappear. But communists have always argued with each other whether this will happen automatically through proper education *(vospitanie)* or whether the process should not be given a helpful historical push *(administrirovanie)*. The history of Soviet religious policy can be described as a history of vacillation between these two methods. Which method became primary depended on which Bolsheviks were in power.[12] Khrushchev had a natural leaning toward *administrirovanie*, although in the antireligious campaign his spokesmen, as well as he himself, repeatedly condemned *administrirovanie* and urged educational methods. As many as eleven different variations on these two general approaches can be identified for the Khrushchev campaign against religion.

An All-Union conference in 1957 of the *Znanie* society (which had replaced the League of Militant Godless) focused on the subject of scientific atheist propaganda. In 1959 this society finally launched its long-promised monthly, *Nauka i religiia* (Science and Religion). Two years later its Ukrainian branch launched *Voiovnyichyi ateist* (Militant Atheist). Also in 1959, the large-scale publication of antireligious books began. By 1962 this had increased to a production of 355 titles with a total circulation of 5,422,000, twice as much as had been produced in 1930 when antireligious propaganda had reached its previous peak.[13]

Generally speaking, the propaganda tried to demonstrate the incompatibility between religion and science and the opposition between communist and religious morality. But as propaganda, it was characterized much more by slander, scandal-mongering about the clergy, and accusations of collaboration with the Nazis. Crude propaganda soon strained the credulity of the population in general, and, shortly before the end of Khrushchev's term, another major strategy session was held, which resulted in the announcement of intensified *vospitanie* that involved a more systematic and scientific approach to propaganda.

In 1959, the educational system was forced to introduce an atheist world-view into all the subjects taught, and, soon after, all university students were required to take exams in scientific atheism.[14] The intensified program also included carefully planned coordinated pure research on scientific atheism. Probably most significant, a series of specialist schools— one might say seminaries for atheists—were established, so that these could then conduct the increased educational program anticipated. One other educational method introduced more systematically in 1968 was a new law calling upon parents to educate their children in the spirit of communism. It was, in a sense, the ultimate weapon at the level of *vospitanie* since it reached right into the family itself.[15]

Simultaneous with the major propaganda onslaught came the *administrirovanie*. In October 1958 a secret instruction from the Council of Ministers ordered the Council for Russian Orthodox Church Affairs to prepare recommendations within the space of six months on how to reduce the number of monasteries.[16] Before Khrushchev was ousted, over 40 monasteries had been closed, some of them with the use of physical force.[17]

When the campaign itself got underway in 1959, the major administrative theme was "Leninist legality." This meant that from now on state officials would adhere very closely to the restrictions of the legislation on religion, especially the restrictive features of the 1929 law on cults. At a bishops' conference in July 1961, Russian Orthodox Patriarch Alexei reported that in April the Council for Russian Orthodox Church Affairs had informed them that the Council of Ministers of the USSR had again drawn attention to the numerous instances where Soviet legislation on religion was being violated. The council ordered the church to take measures to bring its church statutes in line with state legislation on religion.[18] The AUCECB had apparently been forced to bring its statutes into line with existing law in the summer of 1960. By this means the state was able to use the church leaders in carrying out its antireligious measures.

Soon thereafter the legislation itself was changed. More restrictive measures were introduced but these were kept secret, which had the additional advantage of allowing local officials to demand even greater restrictions than specified in the new law. Already in 1960, Article 142 was introduced into the Criminal Code to provide up to three years' imprisonment for violation of the law on religion. In July 1962 Article 227 was added, which specified up to five years' prison or exile for persons leading others to violate the religious legislation. Once the antireligious course had been resumed by Brezhnev and Kozygin, additional clauses of the criminal code were revised, involving greater restrictions and harsher treatment of the sectarians in particular.[19]

With the secret revision of the fundamental law in 1962, the two councils for religious affairs were given greater discretionary power and soon both Orthodox and Baptist *Samizdat* writers complained that these councils seemed to be the chief agents in the antireligious campaign. In December 1965 these two councils were united and given still greater discretionary powers. Also after 1966 local commissions were introduced which had the task of supervising religious activity in its minute detail. These commissions had the right to submit any violations to the Council for Religious Affairs which recommended appropriate measure to the police or courts.[20]

Although one can identify such a creative variety of *vospitanie* and *administrirovanie*, for those affected, the most striking feature was the intimate cooperation of their persecutors: the Council for Religious Affairs, the Committee for State Security (KGB), the police, the courts, and the local city or county officials. The believers complained about the *vospitanie* method, but they complained much more about the crude administrative measures that were used.

In a major summary of the first decade, the Reform Baptists' Council of Prisoners' Relatives listed 14 different administrative abuses[21]: More than 500 had been put in prison; numerous congregations had experienced physical force from the authorities; hundreds of children had been interrogated; hundreds of children had been refused entrance into secondary and higher education because their families were believers and they went to church; all the leaders and most of the members had been subjected to harassment and terrorization; many had lost their jobs and were then prosecuted under the newly introduced parasite laws; large quantities of literature had been confiscated; houses had been confiscated in Tula, Novosibirsk, etc.; authorities had prevented church services by physically transporting believers elsewhere; the old and the sick were kept in prison, contrary to Soviet legislation; frequent arrests—some persons arrested as often as three times in nine years; preventing marriage and funeral services; fines for attending an unregistered worship service which by 1970 totaled over 100,000 rubles; and finally, they complained that the leaders of the Reform Baptist union were not being permitted to work full time as clergy and had therefore been forced into hiding.

Since the illustrative documentation has become immense, the temptation to go into detail is great. We must restrict ourselves to a brief sketch of the eight phases that can be identified so far.

The Khrushchev Campaign, 1959-1964
Phase I: Leninist Legality, 1959-1961

The campaign began in 1959 with a propaganda barrage and the closure of churches. One scholar has argued that the official decision was probably taken at the party congress meeting from January 29 to February 5, 1959.[22] Baptist dissidents repeatedly claimed that only one third of existing Evangelical Christian-Baptist congregations had attained registration by then. For the Orthodox more so than for Baptists, it was vital that the priest should be able to conduct the liturgy in a registered building, and this therefore became a chief point of attack initially. By 1966 only 7,500 churches were left from the 22,000 that had been registered by the Orthodox before the persecution began.[23]

Many different arguments were used in order to ensure closure of a church. An old law was resurrected, whereby any church which had been given its registration by the Nazi occupying forces was declared illegal. This affected in particular the churches in the West Ukraine where religion was particularly strong.[24] Some churches were closed because they were located too close to a school and therefore posed a threat to the school's freedom from religion. Other churches were declared historical monuments which must therefore be available for the enjoyment of all citizens, not just believers. In other cases, such as the Orthodox Church in Perm, the throngs attending the worship services hindered normal traffic and therefore the church must be closed. Others were demolished to make room for urban renewal while still others were condemned because they were in urgent need of repair. However, the authorities blocked the purchase of the necessary materials to repair the church and therefore the believers could not meet the legal requirements. Another argument used was that the church was not needed any longer because no service had taken place in the past few weeks. This break in the regularity of services had been achieved by detaining the priest or presbyter for questioning or for observation in a mental clinic.

Once again also, countless believers, especially clergymen, were arrested, charged with violating the legislation on religion and given prison sentences which initially averaged five-year periods. Exact statistics are not readily available but the Orthodox clergy had been reduced from 30,000 before 1959 to only 14,500 in early 1962.[25] The Baptists began collecting data in 1961, and by 1964 could produce the names of 197 persons in prison.[26]

When the campaign began, Orthodox leaders attempted a short resistance. One feature of the propaganda attack had included the confession of apostate priests. In February 1960, the *Journal of the Moscow Patriarchate* announced the unprecedented fact that the best-known of these apostates, Professor Osipov, and four others had been excommunicated.[27] Also on February 16, 1960, Patriarch Alexei (or more likely his speech writer Metropolitan Nikolai) attempted a mild protest. Speaking at a peace conference in the Kremlin, he expressed firm support for the Soviet peace program but also drew major attention to the fact that the church had played a vital role in Russian history. Then toward the end of the speech he noted that the church was being attacked and denounced and promised

firmly that "the gates of hell shall not prevail against it."[28] Five days later G.
G. Karpov, chairman of the Council for Russian Orthodox Church Affairs,
was dismissed for having cooperated with the church and was replaced by
V. A. Kuroedov.[29] By June 1960, Metropolitan Nikolai himself was forced to
resign as head of the foreign department, the Moscow vicar Bishop Pimen
(later patriarch) took over administration of the patriarchate and by September Nikolai was under house arrest. On September 13 he died after an
unexplained illness.[30]

The much-less-influential Baptist leaders watched these events and apparently decided that resistance would be futile. During the summer of
1960, they produced a revision of their church statutes which, they later
explained, brought it into line with the 1929 legislation on religion. This
statute was sent to the churches and an accompanying "Letter of Instruction" to senior presbyters clearly indicated that this statute was binding
and advised senior presbyters how it was to be enforced. Until recently only
excerpts of this letter have been published but the most vital part, quoted
already in 1966, by atheist scholars, helps to explain why the Baptist
membership quickly labeled it an "anti-evangelical document." The letter
stated, among other things:

> In the past, due to insufficient knowledge of Soviet legislation on cults,
> certain of our congregations have violated it. There have been occasions
> of baptizing persons younger than 18 years, giving material aid from the
> congregation's treasury, holding biblical and other meetings of a spe-
> cialist character, permitting declamations of poetry, there were excur-
> sions for believing youth, financial accounts for mutual aid were created,
> meetings for preachers and for training choir leaders were held. . . . All
> this must now be eliminated in our congregations and our activities must
> be conducted in agreement with existing legislation.[31]

The directives that were to evoke the greatest concern were the prohibition
against children attending services, and the reference to "unhealthy
missionary tendencies." As the letter explained, "the chief goal of religious
services at the present time is not the attraction of new members but satisfaction of the spiritual needs of believers."[32]

Much of this cautionary advice about caring for the spiritual needs of
existing believers and avoiding aggressive evangelism had appeared numerous times earlier in *Bratskii Vestnik*.[33] This time, a significant part of the
membership refused to submit. In the village of Uzlovaia (Tula Oblast) a

members' meeting was held and an initiative group was formed to protest the anti-evangelical character of the new statutes. The movement quickly spread, and on August 13, 1961, a delegation delivered to the Moscow headquarters a letter which condemned the two documents. This Initiative Group urged the Baptist leadership to repent, and to call a congress at which new statutes and new leadership could be elected. Baptist leaders replied that it was unthinkable that the authorities would permit a congress; they had difficulty enough getting permission to hold council meetings. Karev, the general secretary, emphasized then and subsequently, that the statutes were based on Soviet legislation which therefore made the statute legally binding.[34]

Ten days later the Initiative Group, or *Initsiativniki* as they soon came to be known, addressed a letter to all ECB congregations in the Soviet Union. With primitive hectograph material, they duplicated the letter and succeeded in distributing it broadly. This letter summarized the events and made a major appeal to congregations to examine themselves and, if necessary, to purge and rededicate themselves to a life of holiness. The sanctification theme awakened responsive chords and participants have subsequently estimated that approximately half the AUCECB membership initially supported the reformers.

The action group continued to issue statements to the congregations, to the USSR Ministry of Internal Affairs, and to the Council for the Affairs of Religious Cults. At the end of November, the AUCECB was able to hold a conference with 19 senior presbyters in attendance in which the actions of the *Initsiativniki* were the main agenda item. Regrettably, details of this meeting have never been made available but the apparent decision was to reject the *Initsiativniki* challenge.[35] But by the end of 1961, it was apparent that the sharply restrictive change in the church's constitution would not be accepted by the general membership. In comparison, new Orthodox statutes in 1961 were approved with relative ease.[36]

Phase II: Resistance and Toughened Legislation, 1961-62

Although beginning the campaign by emphasizing literal adherence to the law, subsequent research has shown that the function of new legislation appeared to be to sanction new policies already in force. Thus, for example, in April 1961, the two councils for religious affairs issued an official but secret instruction on applying the 1929 legislation on religion. A year and a half later, in December 1962, the Supreme Soviet of the RSFSR approved revisions in the 1929 legislation which affected more than half of its sixty-four articles. This legislative revision simply confirmed the 1961 instructions.[37]

Hereby it became much more difficult to register congregations. For example, whereas formerly the signature of a representative had sufficed, now all the members of the congregation must sign the registration application. Given the atmosphere of persecution, it should be possible to find one coward in each congregation who would thereby veto the request. The right to appeal rejection of registration was also dropped. It was now stated clearly that registration could be withdrawn for violation of the laws on religion. The laws on religion included not only published laws but also the secret legislation and also the directives including verbal or telephone instructions from the two councils for religious affairs. In order to strengthen the centralized nature of the religious policy, religious affairs agencies were given expanded discretionary powers so that local authorities could act on registration requests only with the agreement of the central councils for religious affairs.

Although the first Orthodox *Samizdat* appeared in 1958,[38] major resistance during the early sixties came from the Reform Baptists. During 1962 the *Samizdat* phenomenon expanded. The action group itself sent a total of seven letters to state officials in which they repeatedly complained about the "terrible illegality" of state religious policy but they received no detailed replies.[39] The only tangible reply appeared to be increased arrests of local Baptist leaders. Thirty persons were arrested in 1961. In 1962 an additional sixty-four arrests brought the total of known prisoners to ninety-four. The key *Initsiativniki* leader, A. F. Prokofiev was himself arrested in May 1962, and at his trial in August was sentenced to five years' imprisonment followed by five years' exile. This effectively removed him from any position of influence for the next ten years.[40] One of his key associates, Boris Zdorovets, was also sent to prison.[41] The reformers remained undaunted, and the key leaders now became Gennadi K. Kriuchkov and Georgi P. Vins.

Realizing that the present AUCECB leadership was in no mood to challenge the state, the initiative group called an expanded conference on February 25, 1962, and instituted procedures (in accordance with the Soviet constitution) to form their own organization. The action group was dissolved and an organizing committee *(Orgkomitet)* elected, which was given the task of organizing an All-Union congress of ECB churches. On April 22, 1962, the *Orgkomitet* dispatched a letter to the churches which again denounced the anti-church activities of the AUCECB. It called upon the AUCECB members to repent within the next two months or else they would be excommunicated. The letter to the churches requested the local congregations to submit names of individuals no longer worthy of their office because of their cooperation with state authorities and to excommunicate them locally. Finally, at an expanded conference of the *Orgkomitet* held on June 23, 1962, the so-called "Protocoll No. 7" was approved, which announced the excommunication from office and from church membership of all AUCECB members as well as individual senior presbyters. The list of names totaled twenty-seven persons and the *Orgkomitet* promised to print supplements as the congregations sent in their decisions.[42] This marks the point at which a schism in the Baptist ranks became irrevocable.

Phase III: A Differentiated Policy Begins, 1963

With so many churches closed, by the fourth year of the campaign it became evident that administrative measures, though readily measurable, had not reduced religiosity. Now the first indication of a differentiated response to the religious groupings appeared. What had been regarded as unthinkable in 1960 actually happened in 1963. The AUCECB received permission to hold an extended conference of presbyters. Over 200 delegates arrived, and on the second day of the sessions, someone found the courage to propose that the conference be converted into a congress, and this was approved. Major business at the congress involved the rejection of the 1960 statute which now in retrospect was labeled "merely a proposal," and the adoption of new statutes which went a long way toward incorporating the changes proposed by the *Orgkomitet*. The *Initsiativniki*, however, could only send observers and they subsequently condemned it as a false congress.[43]

Without doubt, AUCECB leaders had been able to persuade state authorities to permit revision of the 1960 statutes even though such a revision meant that the statute itself would be violating existing law. Obedient Baptists would be given some extra-legal concessions in order to make it easier for the wavering church member to support the AUCECB. Even if the church statute was revised, the fundamental law with its restrictions remained in force, and in local instances, superseded the statutes as also local AUCECB churchmen were to discover.

The major conclusion that Khrushchev and his associate Il'ichev seem to have drawn from the progress of the campaign so far was that the campaign should be intensified but made more sophisticated. L. F. Il'ichev had headed the party Central Committee department for propaganda and agitation for the Union republics from 1958 to 1961. Then he was appointed Central Committee secretary for ideological affairs and from 1962 headed the ideological commission.[44] In November 1963 the ideological commission held an expanded session at which high-ranking officials from the entire propaganda and agitation apparatus attended. Il'ichev delivered the major report in which he called for intensification of religious propaganda.[45]

Although Il'ichev's pep talk seemed to emphasize more *vospitanie* over against *administrirovanie*, local officials appeared to get the message that believers must be treated more roughly. For example, four members from the Kalunda community in Western Siberia were arrested for illegal activities in an unregistered congregation and given prison sentences.[46]

One of the men, Nikolai K. Khmara, had been converted only a few years before after leading a life of drunkenness. His conversion had transformed him into a model husband, father, and active church worker. Two weeks after the trial, his family received word that he had died due to illness. Contrary to instructions, the Kalunda believers insisted on opening the coffin and found a brutally mutilated body. There were chain marks on his arms, scorch marks on his hands and feet, his finger- and toenails had been torn off, and there were gaping wounds in his abdomen made by a hot object. The most revolting part occurred when someone pulled the cotton stuffing out of his mouth and discovered that Khmara's tongue was missing. Other prisoners later informed them that Khmara had talked about Christ till the end and therefore his captors had torn out his tongue. Khmara had also suffered psychological torture, receiving injections to create a personality change. This brought to five the number of persons who had died in prison and exile.[47]

Only six weeks later, relatives of ECB prisoners met in a secret All-Union conference and announced the formation of a temporary Council of Prisoners' Relatives. At the conference they produced a list of 102 prisoners. At their second meeting in July 1964 the list already totaled 197 persons.[48] If the state was going to be tougher, Baptist resistance would be stiffer.

Phase IV: Both Reformers and the State Reevaluate, 1964

The year 1964 opened with an article in the party's journal *Kommunist* written by L. F. Il'ichev, which spelled out a twelve-point program for major atheist education. Il'ichev noted that "we have dealt frequent blows to those who propagate the ideas of religion, but the ideas themselves remain undamaged."[49] In order to attack the ideas themselves, he announced the creation of a new Institute of Scientific Atheism at the

Academy of Sciences which would have powers to supervise and coordinate all indoctrinational activities. A course in fundamentals of scientific atheism became compulsory at all universities, medical schools, agricultural colleges and teachers' colleges starting in the 1964 school year. All party officials, teachers, and doctors were required to attend seminars on atheism. All teachers, professors in higher education, writers, journalists, and advanced students were required to participate actively in the antireligious program.

Not only must a regular program of antireligious films and on television be undertaken, but competitions were to be held for the best works on atheism in the areas of literature, drama, film, and painting. The state press commission was ordered to draw up a comprehensive plan to produce atheistic literature in all languages of the Union. All political and scientific journals were ordered to inaugurate new columns for antireligious propaganda. Lower party committees were told that they must assume responsibility and supervision of "the degree of religiosity existing in every community and collective." Elementary and secondary school curricula would be reviewed in order to intensify the antireligious point of view. Each local party unit was to select a permanent organizer of antireligious work. Another point that hinted more at *administrirovanie* than *vospitanie* was the statement that:

> In order to forestall the illegal activities of the clergy, church groups, and individual church-goers, measures must be taken to fence off children and adolescents from the influence of church-goers and from the efforts of parents to get their children to join them in religious observances.[50]

Obviously, religious ideology had been declared the major enemy of the state and this was perhaps the clearest acknowledgement that atheism had become the state religion.

The *Orgkomitet* was also reevaluating its tactics. Appeals to the AUCECB had been unsuccessful; it was clear that the latter was powerless to act. Since appeals to local state officials and to the Council for the Affairs of Religious Cults also brought no relief, the *Orgkomitet* now began to appeal for a personal interview with Nikita Khrushchev. In the spring of 1964 Georgi Vins and P. S. Zinchenko held a series of telephone discussions with Communist Party Central Committee officer Morozov. Morozov urged them to see Chairman Puzin of the Council for the Affairs of Religious Cults, but the latter informed them that his council was merely executing policy. When the Baptist spokesman asked what were the basic laws they were being called upon to obey, council officials mentioned the 1918 decree, the 1929 legislation, and the 1936 constitution. Even at this point there was no indication by Puzin and his officials that the 1962 revisions had taken place.[51]

The multiplication of local complaints and declarations addressed to leading governmental officials coming independently from scattered areas of the country did have its effect. In June 1964 Chairman Puzin called an All-Union meeting of his plenipotentiaries in order to review events. Puzin's speech, leaked to the *Initsiativniki* later, included detailed lists describing how local officials had abused believers and Puzin punctuated his remarks by stating that state investigatory commissions confirmed the accuracy of the believers' complaints.[52] Following the meeting, local abuses were reduced and it seemed that the ouster of Khrushchev in October 1964 might lead to further easing of the pressure.

The Brezhnev-Kosygin Approach
Phase V: Year of Drift, 1965

The official legal journal, *Sovetskoie Gosudarstvo i Pravo*, in its January 1965 issue called for a more correct interpretation of the laws on religion, officially condemning the crude administrative measures which had been taken during Khrushchev's personality cult. The level of atheist propaganda continued (about 300 titles were published, and 738,188 lectures sponsored), but there was a significant change in tone.[53] The January 1965 issue of *Nauka i religiia* (Science and Religion) received a more colorful format to make it more appealing, and the Ukrainian counterpart changed its name from *The Militant Atheist* to *Man and the World (Liudyna i svit)*. There was also a virtual moratorium on slanderous attacks against believers in the press.

In March 1965 a letter from the editors of *Nauka i religiia* attacked the atheist propagandist Alla Trubnikova for the reprehensible methods she employed in her investigations and also for the substance of her articles, which depicted believers "as scoundrels or vagrants or mental and moral cripples" and had argued that "religious practice is a form of criminal behavior" and that believers were enemies of Soviet society. Instead the editors argued that believers were loyal citizens and that patient dialogue, not slander, would win them away from their foolish ideology. This attack on Trubnikova was supported by other well-known atheist activists such as the former theologian Osipov. Trubnikova herself wrote a sharply defensive reply, which *Nauka i religiia* also printed. In short, during the early part of

1965, there were the beginnings of a debate in the press about religious policy.

Another very significant event was the dismissal in January 1965 of the chief ideologue against religion, N. F. Il'ichev. Not only was he dismissed, but the ideological commission that he had headed was dissolved and its duties divided among a number of other bodies. In August both state councils for religious affairs called meetings of their local officials where they, too, called for a halt in administrative abuse. Chairman Puzin, however, did inform his listeners that their task had been to "isolate the *Orgkomitet* from the basic mass of Baptist congregations, so that the leaders of this committee lose the trust and respect of the believers."[54] Other parts of his speech also warned against administrative abuse but still urged interference in local church affairs.

As far as the Baptists themselves were concerned, there were almost no arrests, Aida Skripnikova being a notable exception.[55] A number of persons were released early or given amnesty in connection with Khrushchev's ouster. Leaders of the *Orgkomitet* also met with Anastas Mikoyan, president of the Soviet Union, on September 22, and presented their concerns, although receiving no promises.[56]

If the authorities did indulge in some criticism of the Khrushchevian religious policy and the beginnings of a high-level debate were apparent, the absence of any clear directives for the future prompted Professor Andrew Blane to describe 1965 as the year of drift, of no policy. The *Orgkomitet,* in contrast, continued to pursue clear goals. At a meeting in September 1965, its name was changed to the Council of Churches of the Evangelical Christian Baptists (CCECB), challenging the AUCECB to leadership of all the ECB churches. A congress of all the churches, they said, should settle the matter.

Phase VI: Pressure Is Resumed, 1966-70

A new policy of resumed administrative pressure on dissidents and of intensive *vospitanie* finally emerged in early 1966. The two councils for religious affairs merged into the single Council for Religious Affairs and the tough-minded chairman of the Council for Russian Orthodox Church Affairs, Vladimir A. Kuroedov, became the chairman of the joint council. Puzin, former chairman of the Council for Religious Cults, disappeared from view. The new council received a constitution which represented increased centralized power and increased discretionary power in the interpretation of the law.[57]

More indicative of the new pressures were several changes in the criminal code which were approved on March 18, 1966. The first was an order by the Supreme Soviet giving the official interpretation of what constituted a violation of the legislation on religion. These were:

Refusal by religious leaders of communities to register them with state organs;

Violating the legally-established rules for organizing and conducting religious gatherings, processions and other cult ceremonies;

The organizing and conducting, by servants of the cult and members of religious communities, of special children and youth meetings, and also of workers, literary and similar circles and groups, not related to cultic activities. . . .[58]

Local administrative commissions could fine violators 50 rubles. At the same time, Article 142 of the Criminal Code was expanded and violations were interpreted as:

. . . requiring compulsory collections and taxes for the use of religious organizations and cult servants;

The preparing for the purpose of mass distribution plus the actual mass distribution of statements, letters, leaflets and similar documents, which call on people not to observe the legislation on religious cults;

Carrying out deceitful acts with the purpose of awakening religious superstition in the population;

Organizing and carrying out religious meetings, processions and other cult ceremonies which violate social order;

Organizing and systematically conducting activities for teaching religion to under-age children in violation of established legislative rules. . . .[59]

For these violations, a sentence of up to three years could be given. It was apparent that this new legislation was directed particularly against the dissenters, especially Baptist dissenters, who were conducting an active program with children and distributing their *Samizdat* widely.

This new pressure should be understood in light of a general state policy against dissenters that was instituted and symbolized in the trial of Sinyavsky and Daniel in 1965 which received wide publicity in the West. The new Soviet leaders feared that Khrushchev's de-Stalinization could lead to unrestrained dissent, therefore they opted for a maintenance of the status quo.[60]

As far as the Baptists are concerned, there were now clearer indications that the state was distinguishing between AUCECB and CCECB. In the June 1966 issue of *Nauka i religiia* came the first official account of the Baptists' split, reporting on the *Initsiativniki* in detail. Shortly thereafter, two other publications quoted at length from *Initsiativniki Samizdat* and generally confirmed its accuracy.[61]

In many localities, after 1966 it once again became possible to apply for registration of local congregations. Beginning in 1967, Mennonite and Pentecostal congregations could register as autonomous churches.

But for the *Initsiativniki*, in spite of the promises to the contrary, local acts of administrative abuse persisted. Without direct coordinated leadership by the CCECB, over 400 persons representing 130 congregations converged on the Kremlin in Moscow and conducted an unprecedented demonstration on May 16, 1966.[62] The demonstrators with their petitions were refused entrance and on the second day they were forcibly dispersed and many of them were arrested. A few days later, when CCECB leaders Georgi Vins and Mikhail Khorev arrived at the Central Committee building to inquire what was happening, they too were arrested. A wave of arrests followed. The year 1966 remains to the present day the peak period with 128 arrests, which also brought the total prisoner list to a high of 202. It continued to climb with additional arrests in 1967 and 1968, to a high of 240. After many of those arrested in 1966 completed their three years, the total number of prisoners remained steady at around 180 till 1975.[63]

But the renewed pressure helped to expand the dissident movement. In 1966 the Orthodox priests Nikolai Eshliman and Gleb Yakunin wrote a series of lengthy documents that appealed to the patriarch to free himself from state domination and accused the Council for Religious Affairs of chief responsibility for persecution of believers. A number of other Orthodox dissidents joined them, including Bishop Hermogen.[64]

Arresting 21 of the key *Initsiativniki* leaders also failed to muzzle Baptist dissent. In 1969 and 1970, the Council of Prisoners' Relatives met to hold All-Union congresses and continued to provide detailed lists of prisoners and their dependents. Beginning in 1970, the *Samizdat* expanded with the CPR launching a *Bulletin* that has been appearing at least four or five times a year. Probably most aggravating to the authorities was an open letter to Prime Minister Kosygin on June 5, 1971 informing him of the existence of the *Khristianin* Publishing House. The CCECB explained that in 1966 they had requested permission for Bibles and other literature. When this was refused them, they had decided to produce it themselves.[65]

Search for Normalcy

Phase VII: Stalemate, 1970-75

During the first half of the seventies, Baptist and Orthodox church life began to return to what might be described as normal for the Soviet Union. Regular and registered church services could be held with the state keeping careful watch through its commissions, which had been established in 1966. If a local congregation began to grow, there might be harassment of believers at their jobs, or atheist workers would attempt to do "personal work" with them. If the local choir presented its Christmas concert in a neighboring church, the local presbyter could anticipate a fifty-ruble fine. Sometimes hooligans were sent to interfere with meetings. Very little of this milder form of persecution has ever been acknowledged officially by the AUCECB but it should be kept in mind so that the treatment of dissidents can be seen in perspective. When the CPR issued a summary statement at the end of 1970, they concluded with an appeal for prayer support from all believers and cited the well-known Russian evangelical V. F. Martsynkovski of the twenties, who had once stated: "We are writing to you from a burning house, in which you also are living, only one storey higher."[66] AUCECB church members in private readily acknowledged this truth.

At the beginning of this phase, there had been some optimism that the CCECB might finally be granted a measure of tolerance. Already in the spring of 1969 official reconciliation talks had taken place with the AUCECB leadership. After Vins and Kriuchkov were released, additional talks were held in Moscow in the autumn. But by now the AUCECB had regained much of its prestige, had repented adequately in the eyes of many, whereas the CCECB demanded abject repentance and refused to treat the leaders as Christian brothers.[67] Then in December 1969 local authorities granted the CCECB permission to hold an All-Union congress in the city of Tula, and it seemed as if it would be possible for two rival unions to maintain a legal existence. The leaders were optimistic enough to send a letter to Prime Minister Kosygin asking him to instruct the relevant authorities to permit their leading workers to devote themselves full time to church work, as was true of AUCECB leaders.[68]

For whatever reason, the optimism was short-lived. Vins was again arrested and ordered by the court to work as an engineer. Several other council members were arrested and received three-year sentences.[69] The key figure in the Council of Prisoners' Relatives, Mrs. Lidia Vins, was arrested in December 1970 and received a three-year sentence. Soon thereafter both Vins and Kriuchkov and two other CCECB members found it advisable to go underground and the authorities began to search for them like hunted criminals. In 1969 a Council of Christian Mothers was formed as resistance to the threat to take children away from believing parents.[70] Appeals and detailed reports were also circulating about the Sloboda family. The two older children and then the two younger children were forcibly placed in orphanages. Finally Mrs. Sloboda herself received a four-year prison sentence.[71] In spite of all these pressures, the CCECB gradually developed its own church structure and highly organized activities.

Orthodox dissenters, on the other hand, were more severely crippled by the pressures. The gifted mathematician and writer Boris V. Talantov died in prison. Anatoli Levitin-Krasnov was imprisoned from 1969 to 1974 and then emigrated in the summer of 1974. Gleb Yakunin and Nikolai Eshliman seemed muzzled till their next major letter to the World Council of Churches in Nairobi in 1975.[72]

The Baptist split was first made public in the West around 1964.[73] Generally speaking, however, till 1970 the existence of religious dissent was relatively unknown. During the seventies, due to the increased activities of Western journalists possible in the new atmosphere of détente, as well as due to the growth of tourism, much more information about Soviet religious life became available. Scholarly studies relying on *Samizdat* proliferated. During the year or so before Solzhenitsyn was forcibly exiled (February 1974), he became known for his Lenten letter to the patriarch which identified him as a believer and for his support of other religious dissidents.[74]

Shortly after Solzhenitsyn's expulsion, Georgi Vins was finally caught and eventually brought to trial in January 1975. During the ten months that Vins was in custody before his trial, he became the symbol in the Western world for all suffering believers in the Soviet Union and an unprecedented campaign calling for his release took place. Soviet authorities, however, had correctly assessed that although sympathy for Soviet dissent had never been as strong in the West as now, in the Soviet Union itself it had no broad base of support and therefore Vins was given a five-year sentence, strict regime.

Phase VIII: "Normalization," 1975-80

A label for this latest phase can be only tentative, but there are numerous signs that the stalemate can now be regarded as "normalization." Normalization in this context might be defined paradoxically both as a relaxing and a toughening of the Soviet stance toward specific religious groups.

In July 1975, major revisions to the 1929 law on cults were officially announced.[75] In one sense they made public what had been established secretly in 1962 but in several instances the changes were in a moderate direction. That is, the 1975 law was more moderate than that of 1962 but was more restrictive than the old 1929 law. Above all, the powers of the Council for Religious Affairs were once again increased. Both central church headquarters, as well as local congregations, were now granted the near equivalent of the right of juridical personhood which therefore allowed them a legal basis for organizing their activity.

Other evidence suggests that there has been a slight return to the pre-1959 situation, with churches granted concessions in practice even though the law forbids such activities. For example, the AUCECB churches have been reporting rapid growth, new registrations, increased publication (though in very small quantities) of the Bible and their journal; children are again evident at services, and the youth choirs and instrumental groups belie an active concern for youth work. CCECB congregations in general pursue their activities with little concern for legislative restrictions. Several congregations, however, were granted state registration even though they refused to acknowledge Soviet legislation on religion.[76]

Basket Three of the Helsinki Agreement has also been widely quoted by the normalized churches who have used it with success to attain small gains. Paradoxically, local watchdog committees to ensure adherence to the Helsinki agreements have been heavily harassed and all the key leaders are in prison.[77] A similar paradox was the continued tough treatment of Vins in prison and the continued hunt for Kriuchkov while at the same time the number of arrests of *Initsiativniki* declined and the total number of prisoners reached record lows.[78] But in only one year following Vins' expulsion from the Soviet Union, the number of prisoners doubled.

Another feature of the Reform Baptist movement is that since approximately 1964 it has gradually but steadily been losing support. With each successive AUCECB congress, additional groups of *Initsiativniki* found their way back into the AUCECB fold. Perhaps the revisions in the statute, or the election of new leadership, or the replacement of the offending local pastor prompted them to reevaluate their attitude toward the old union. For many, especially in recent years, the primary reason has been fatigue. After fifteen or more years of harassment, meetings broken up, fines, and so on, one's stomach ulcers demand some peace and quiet. After all, they say, the Word of God is preached in the registered church, people are converted, and God is blessing there too. This has meant that the CCECB remnant has become more purist and exclusivist. Documents in recent years convey a sense of futility.[79]

Evaluation

What did *Administrirovanie* achieve? As one rather frank atheist pointed out in the pages of *Komsomolskaya Pravda* in 1965, "the closing of a parish does not make atheists of the believers. On the contrary, it attracts people all the more to religion and in addition embitters their hearts."[80] The rapid expansion of a "religious underground" was without question the most unacceptable result for a regime that fears anything it cannot control. The brutality and violation of "socialist legality" not only alienated believers but also produced sympathy for believers from the general public. The administrative measures especially awakened a world opinion that has had at least some impact on the ability of the Soviet Union to conduct foreign relations, at least after the Helsinki Agreement of 1975. The regime itself had obviously not itself anticipated a dissent that would prove to be as creative and persistent as its persecutors.

Even an evaluation of *vospitanie* must be more negative than positive. Standard propaganda campaigns with their slander strained the credulity of even the most gullible. The average Soviet citizen today claims that no one except atheist activists reads Soviet propaganda. Instead, during the past decade, experienced observers have been reporting a growing interest in religion, particularly among the young and the intellectuals. Positively speaking, however, since approximately 1966 there has been steady improvement in the quality of atheist research. Sociological studies actually demonstrated greater religiosity than expected. The sociology of religion can now claim the results of a number of thorough field studies but sociological theory is still rather limited and heavily dependent on the standard dictates of Marxist ideology.

During the past two decades of the antireligious emphasis, instead of observing a transformation from socialism to communism, the reverse has been the case. There has been widespread loss of commitment to communism as ideology and it is quite apparent that communism is further away now than it was in 1959. Closely related to this loss of faith in communism has also been a loss in cohesiveness of the population. In short, for the Soviet leaders, it has been a very costly campaign.

But it was also a very costly campaign for the evangelicals. It produced a major split in a union that has always been threatened with dissension. Some of the AUCECB's most experienced and able leaders were badly compromised in the eyes of the membership. There was also much suffering. Who suffered more and how is hard to measure. But this antireligious policy also had positive effects. We now turn to an examination of how this policy affected major aspects of the life of the evangelicals.

Notes to Chapter 5

1. Jacques Barzun, *Darwin, Marx, Wagner* (New York: Doubleday, 1958), pp. 37, 170.

2. *Bratsky Listok*, 78-8/71 (AS 880). For the next several chapters in particular I will be relying heavily on *Samizdat* sources. Large portions of Baptist *Samizdat* for the period 1961-66 have been printed in English in Michael Bourdeaux, *Religious Ferment in Russia* (London: Macmillan, 1968). The most complete collection of religious *Samizdat* is at Keston College. Since much of the Baptist *Samizdat* was printed in Radio Liberty's *Arkhiv Samizdata* (Vols. 14, 15, 16, and 19), I will cite the relevant archival numbers (AS) because these are readily accessible in major libraries.

3. Fletcher, *A Study in Survival, passim.*

4. Harry Willetts, "De-opiating the Masses," *Problems of Communism*, 6/ 64, p. 33.

5. William C. Fletcher, "Protestant Influences on the Outlook of the Soviet Citizen Today," in Fletcher and A. J. Strover, eds., *Religion and the Search for New Ideals in the USSR* (New York: Praeger, 1967), pp. 75-81. In 1976, Party Chairman Brezhnev reported that 9% of the population (23.5 million) were party members.

6. The opening paragraphs were a detailed complaint about how the churches and sects were using all means possible to expand and strengthen their influence in the population. *O religii i tserkvi. Sbornik dokumentov* (Moscow: Politizdat, 1965), pp. 71-77.

7. One hundred and nineteen titles and 1,944,000 copies. Struve, p. 278.

8. Luchterhandt's closely reasoned arguments *(Der Sowjetstaat*, pp. 120-25) are convincing.

9. Georg van Rauch, pp. 417-50.

10. Luchterhandt, pp. 133-34.

11. I have developed this argument at greater length in my "Religious Administration and Modernization" in Dennis Dunn, ed., *Religion and Modernization.*

12. An excellent analytical survey is Bohdan R. Bociurkiw, "The Shaping of Soviet Religious Policy," *Problems of Communism*, May-June 1973, pp. 37-51.

13. Struve, pp. 267-89.

14. Introduced in the 1964-65 school year. A. Avtorkhanov, "New Assault on Religion," *Problems of the Peoples of the USSR*, No. 21, Spring 1964, pp. 12-15.

15. "Legislative Discrimination Against Believers in the USSR," in Michael Bourdeaux, ed., *et al.*, *Religious Liberty in the Soviet Union* (Keston, Kent: Keston College, 1976), p. 38.

16. First referred to in Shafarevich's *Samizdat* study: *Zakonodatel'stvo o religioznykh kul'takh*, p. 66f.; the text was printed in Kuroedov and Pankratova, eds., *Zakonodatel' stvo o religioznykh kul'takh* (Moscow, 1971), pp. 108-109. Although a restricted publication, a copy was leaked to the West in 1976. (Cf. *RCL*, IV, 4, 1976, 25-34.)

17. Gerhard Simon, *Church State and Opposition in the USSR* (London: C. Hurst & Company, 1974), p. 73; Struve, p. 203, notes that by 1964, fifty-seven had been closed.

18. Quoted in Luchterhandt, p. 143.

19. All were printed in Kuroedov & Pankratova, which was available only to state officials.

20. *Ibid.* for sample statutes for the commissions.

21. AS 441 (dated October 1, 1970); cf. AS 617.

22. Luchterhandt, p. 124.

23. *Ibid.*, p. 131. For a list of church closures see Roland Gaucher, *Opposition in the USSR 1917-1967* (New York: Funk & Wagnalls, 1969), p. 472f.

24. Struve, p. 296f.

25. *Ibid.*, p. 319.

26. AS 779 and 794.

27. For background on Osipov, see Bourdeaux, *Opium of the People*, pp. 109-22; Struve notes that out of about 200 apostates, only thirty have been identified by name, p. 320.

28. Full text in Struve, pp. 368-71.

29. An article in *Sovetskaia Belorussia*, February 18, 1960, complained that officials in charge of controlling the activities of churchmen, "have in some cases become virtually their assistants." V. A. Kuroedov (1906-   ) was born in the Gorki region, graduated from the Gorki Teacher's College in 1930, and taught since 1927. He joined the party in 1936, held leading party and government posts in the Gorki region, then became science editor of the national party newspaper, *Sovetskaia Rossiia* (biographical data given in Kuroedov, *Church and Religion in the USSR* [Moscow, 1979]); Luchterhandt, citing *Kommunist* Nr. 18, 1954, p. 53, identified him as party secretary in Sverdlovsk (p. 281).

30. Struve, p. 313f.; cf. Fletcher, *Nikolai*, p. 188ff.

31. L. N. Mitrokhin, *Baptizm* (2nd ed.; Moscow, 1974), p. 80; cf. *Religion in Communist Dominated Areas (RCDA)*, XIII, 1974, pp. 75-76 for full text in English.

32. RCDA, XIII, 1974, p. 75.

33. *BV*, 1/48, p. 7; 1/99, p. 5.

34. The *Initsiativniki* cited Senior Presbyter Veliseichik to Belorussian churches along similar lines (AS 770, p. 53) and then analyzed the new statutes on the basis of known Soviet legislation, concluding that one does not oppose the law by opposing the statutes. Western scholars, often not aware of the secret legislation, accepted the *Initsiativniki* logic. Luchterhandt as legal specialist, on the other hand, came to the conclusion that the Orthodox Church statute was regarded by state officials as having the force of law—this is certainly what Karev also meant (p. 253).

35. Briefly referred to at the 1963 Congress, *BV*, 6/63, p. 13.

36. Luchterhandt, pp. 125-30.

37. Kuroedov & Pankratova, pp. 150-60; 83-97. For a detailed discussion see my article in *RCL*, IV, 4, 1976, 25-34.

38. The first writings of the Orthodox layman Levitin-Krasnov. *G2W*, 2/75, p. 70; for a good introduction to religious *Samizdat*, see also *G2W* 2Q73, and 2/76.

39. AS 771, which includes a total of thirty-three documents submitted to authorities from 1961 through 1966.

40. AS 771, p. 8. Prokofiev was one of the first prosecuted under the new Article 227 of the Criminal Code.

41. *Bulletin*, 12/73, reporting second arrest on May 2, 1973, after release in 1972 from a ten-year term.

42. AS 770. For details see below, pp. 187-188.

43. Bourdeaux, *Ferment;* Chap. 4 gives the most detailed treatment. See below, Chap. 7.

44. Bohdan Bociurkiw, "Religion in the USSR after Khrushchev," John W. Strong, ed., *The Soviet Union under Brezhnev and Kosygin* (New York: Van Nostrand, 1971), p. 135.

45. Assessed in detail in Andrew Blane, "Church and State in Soviet Russia: The Rise of a New Era," unpublished ms. 1974. This article is one of the best overall discussions of the 1959-1964 period.

46. The impact of this murder on the Kulunda and nearby Barnaul churches is described in detail in Deyneka, *Song in Siberia.*

47. AS 794. The others were N. S. Kucherenko (1962), O. P. Wiebe (1964), M. F. Lopaev (1963), Ryzhenko (1963 in exile).

48. AS 779 & 794. The names of three children taken from parents were also given. Cf. Bourdeaux, *Ferment*, pp. 91-93.

49. Avtorkhanov, p. 13.

50. *Ibid.*

51. AS 770, pp. 152-66.

52. Photostat of section of speech affecting evangelicals at Keston Archive.

53. Blane, "A Year of Drift," *RCL*, II, 3, 1974, 11.

54. Quoted in AS 622, p. 8.

55. Michael Bourdeaux & Xenia Howard-Johnston, *Aida of Leningrad* (London: Mowbrays, 1972), *passim.*

56. AS 771.

57. The CRA statute, which has been kept secret, is printed in English translation in *RCL*, IV, 4, 1976, pp. 31-34.

58. Although published in various sources, translation here is based on Kuroedov & Pankratova, pp. 259-60.

59. *Ibid.*, pp. 271-72.

60. See Rudolf Tőkés, ed., *Dissent in the USSR* (Baltimore: Johns Hopkins University Press, 1975).

61. Mitrokhin, *Baptizm*, pp. 79-89, and A. I. Klibanov & L. N. Mitrokhin, "Raskol v sovremennom baptizme, *Voprosy nauchnogo ateizma*, 3/67, pp. 84-110.

62. See the dramatic description in Bourdeaux, *Faith on Trial in Russia* (London: Hodder and Stoughton, 1971), Chap. 1.

63. Based on CPR data, the totals were: 202 (March/67), 240 (August/68), 176 (November/69), 176 (October/70), 187 (April/71), 181 (March/73), 187 (June/73), 188 (January/74), 110 (June/75).

64. See the major documentary collection and survey, Michael Bourdeaux, *Patriarch and Prophets: Persecution in the Russian Orthodox Church Today* (London: Mowbrays, 1975; 2nd ed.).

65. AS 880, p. 6 Issue No. 81 of the *Bulletin* had appeared by July 1980.

66. AS 565.

67. See below, Chaps. 7 and 8.

68. *BL*, 1/70 in AS 629.

69. They were M. I. Khorev, S. T. Golev, and I. Ia. Antonov. By October 1970 Kriuchkov, Vins, S. G. Dubovoi, P. A. Iakimenko, and V. I. Kozlov were in hiding. (AS 441 & 443). That left only N. G. Baturin (a four-year sentence in 1972) and M. T. Shaptala.

70. AS 256 which contained signatures of 1,453 mothers protesting against the practice. *Nauka i Religiia*, 7/71 printed an article on orphanages, noting that the majority of children were not orphans but had been removed for various other reasons; the example given concerned the True Orthodox Sect.

71. A full account with photos in AS 845, see also AS 90, 270, 615, 616, 816 and 819.

72. Bourdeaux, *Patriarch and Prophets*, pp. 344-45 (1975 reprint).

73. Simon, p. 85.

74. A useful documentary collection is Leopold Labedz, ed., *Solzhenitsyn: A Documentary Record* (2nd ed.; London: Penguin, 1974). The nuclear physicist Andrei Sakharov became the most prominent human rights activist and appealed on behalf of believers, including evangelicals, as well as other dissidents.

75. *Vedomosti verkhovnogo soveta RSFSR*, No. 27 (873), July 3, 1975, pp. 487-91.

76. Vins's own church in Kiev is the best-known example. Seen as an experiment by the local church leadership, Soviet propaganda tried to isolate Vins from his church hereby but failed.

77. Vins's son Peter was given a one-year prison sentence in February 1978 because of his membership in the Ukrainian Human Rights Committee.

78. Total Baptist prisoners were: 110 (June/75); 69 (December/76); 53 (May/77); 40 (September/78); 34 (March/79); 34 (December/79).

79. Bohdan R. Bociurkiw, "Religious Dissent in the Soviet State," in B. R. Bociurkiw & J. W. Strong, ed., *Religion and Atheism in the USSR and Eastern Europe* (London: Macmillan, 197), p. 83.

80. Quoted by Blane in "Year of Drift," p. 12.

> In 1953-1954 after certain older workers returned to the congregations who had for a long time not been participating in the complex and laborious work of uniting three separate denominations, they stuck to their old separatist views . . .
> —*BV,* 6/63, p. 21

> I was released from prison in 1956. It's possible that that peculiar prison smell hasn't worn off yet.
> —*Dudko, Our Hope,* p. 94

6 Dissent Begins, 1960-1965: *Samizdat,* Excommunication, Prison

According to Marxist-Leninist theory every advance in science and social progress in the Soviet Union should automatically mean a further decline in the number of persons still clinging to survivals of the past. The new enlightenment, which the frantic publication of atheist literature was supposed to foster, should also hasten the decline of religiosity. This wishful line of reasoning is behind the official Soviet interpretation for the split that took place in evangelical ranks.

Soviet sociologists speak about a crisis confronting the Russian Baptists in the middle fifties.[1] The evangelicals had capitalized on the psychological disruptions of the war to boost their membership. A large percentage of the new Baptist members came from Orthodoxy—in the Ukraine this was over 50 percent and in Belorussia as much as 76 percent.[2] This later was to result in differences on ritual and, the sociologists argued, these ex-Orthodox Baptists slackened off sooner in teaching religion to their children. The sociologists argued that by the middle fifties, the overall membership was much older, far fewer members came from the educated ranks, and most serious of all were the major inroads on membership through advancing secularization.

The split developed because younger leaders in the Baptist movement panicked and tried to launch a major missionary drive to rejuvenate the membership and preserve it from extinction. The Soviet scholar Lialina noted that the AUCECB leadership agreed with the dissident leaders on these goals but differed on the methods for achieving them. The official leaders emphasized religious education and did not wish to violate the law, whereas the dissident leaders paid no attention to the law and focused their efforts on isolating believers as much as possible from the pernicious influences of society.[3]

The argument is logical and the statistical data sounds impressive but this interpretation has several fundamental weaknesses. All sources convey a sense of crisis. Dissident Baptist sources have been the most explicit in describing the excessive administrative measures employed by state authorities to try to make Baptist membership as unattractive as possible. Lialina is somewhat more forthright than some of her earlier colleagues or even the official Baptist journal has been in acknowledging this factor. Soviet sociology has improved, but the tendency to manipulate statistical data to prove a predetermined point of view still makes the overall conclusions suspect.

What Went Wrong?

Had the Baptist union changed significantly? The key leadership in Moscow and Kiev had changed very little. That of course meant that the small ruling elite was 15 years older than when they began in 1945. President Jacob Zhidkov was now seventy-five, Vice-President A. L. Andreev was seventy-eight, Vice-President N. A. Levindanto was sixty-four and suffering from a heart condition, General Secretary Alexander Karev was sixty-seven. All these men had been aggressive influential workers before the war and continued to work with astounding energy to make the new unity a reality.

From the start, the new union was threatened with splits. One small group of Pentecostals left almost as soon as they had joined and by 1948 it was necessary to issue sharp instructions to Pentecostals to adhere to the agreement. From 1957 to 1959 continued cooperation with the Pentecostals was threatened once again. Almost annually top-level conferences were held between members of the AUCECB Presidium and former key Pentecostal leaders who now agreed to travel through the churches to settle disagreements and to persuade those still keeping aloof of the advantages of joining.[4] *Bratskii Vestnik* printed several appeals to Pentecostals and also urged other members not to be afraid to elect a former Pentecostal as presbyter if he now promised to abide by the agreement.[5] In fact, one gets the distinct impression that this over-concern about keeping the Pentecostals, as well as the rapidly increasing time and energy devoted to international peace conferences, meant that the leadership was caught by surprise when the Baptist dissent movement started.

The fundamental factor which some of the key dissident leaders never fully recognized was that little had changed since 1945. Former evangelical leaders, at least some of them broken in spirit in the Stalinist terror, had been released from prison in order to form a registered union of evangelicals. Stalin had granted some concessions but the evangelical leaders knew that in the negotiations they merely had the rights of a hostage. They were reminded of that fact repeatedly. By the time general registration of the churches ceased in 1948, only about one third of all the congregations had been legalized.[6] Ministers were arrested, including such key persons as the Pentecostal leader Ivan Pan'ko, while many other former leaders remained in prison till the mid-fifties. Each man knew he should carefully watch his tongue and not simply because the Apostle James had advised it. I. I. Motorin, who became a member of the presidium in 1958, once lost his preaching license for six months because he had made a passing reference to the crosses in the Kremlin in a sermon on the cross.

Soviet historian Mitrokhin was quite correct in pointing out that the AUCECB structure fostered centralization which was a Russian Baptist tradition.[7] It was of course a key concern in the new Soviet religious policy. Zhidkov and his associates, especially A. L. Andreev, exercised an authoritarian control over the union. Usually it was paternal in intent but Moscow directives right from the start ensured that local zealots would be restrained or eliminated from leadership positions if state officials required it. A legitimate argument in favor of this authoritarianism was that the bulk of the membership was at best semi-literate and needed to be dependent on a few men of wisdom.

What had actually changed was that Soviet society had become less rigid. Many former preachers were released in the mid-fifties. These were persons who had never bowed the knee to the Caesar God and who intended to resume their preaching activities where they had left off. These had also been more isolated than Soviet society generally, so that the new spirit of ecumenism and disarmament was strange to them. The more they learned about the nature of the AUCECB, the less they liked it. Anybody who received permission to travel abroad they suspected as having made a deal with the secret police. When in early 1960 Alexander Karev and Michael Orlov received state peace medals, their suspicions seemed confirmed.[8]

A major split threatened between 1955 and 1957 as a direct result of the released prisoners. There were attempts to set up free church unions in the North-Central Russian Federation, in Baku, in Novosibirsk, in the Donbass region, in the Northern Caucasus, in the Crimea, and in Central Asia.[9] Mennonites and Pentecostals also made futile efforts to organize their own unions of churches. In the Donetsk region in particular so-called "pure Baptists," who insisted that all ministers must be ordained, managed to split twenty-two churches. Evangelical Christian Perfectionists had initial success in the Sumi Oblast of the Ukraine. Both movements opposed the union with Pentecostals.[10]

The first leader of the Baptist *Initsiativniki* was Aleksei F. Prokofiev, so that initially the atheist press referred to the movement as the *Prokofievtsy*. Born 1915 in Ishim (Western Siberia), Prokofiev's biography is less well known than that of his associates. He only became a believer in 1945 while in prison, where he had been sent in 1941 under Article 58 for anti-Soviet activity. Earlier he had worked as a teacher and in 1940 was studying geology in university. In 1937 he was married but separated soon after. Then he formed a common-law link with Paraskovia Markovna in 1939. A daughter was born to them in 1940. As a Christian in the postwar years he joined the Evangelical Christian-Baptists, but in 1954 was again sent to prison. This time the sentence was for twenty-five years and the charge was missionary activity. The sentence was reduced, however, and he was released in 1958. Soon he went into full-time Christian work as traveling evangelist. Prokofiev was the first leader of the *Initsiativniki* but with his arrest in May 1962 he disappears from the story. Word only filtered through indirectly in the seventies that in September 1969 he had been excommunicated by the CCECB for immoral behavior.[11]

Within two years, Gennadi Konstantinovich Kriuchkov and Georgi Petrovich Vins had become the outstanding leaders.[12] Kriuchkov was from Tula, not far from Tolstoy's Yasnaya Polyana estate. He had been converted in 1951 and was serving as presbyter in an unregistered church in the town of Uzlovaia. Georgi Vins now lived in Kiev. He moved there with his Ukrainian mother after his father, a Siberian Baptist preacher of German Mennonite background, had disappeared in the camps. He was converted in 1945 and became a member of one of the registered churches in Kiev.

Kriuchkov and Vins were only thirty-four and thirty-two years of age respectively when the movement began and a disproportionately high percentage of their supporters were young. Prokofiev, on the other hand, was already forty-five and had been imprisoned previously. Many of the other key *Initsiativniki* leaders such as S. T. Golev (1896-1976), S. Kh.

AUCECB General Secretary Alexander Karev consulting with Jacob I. Zhidkov. (Photo courtesy of Keston College)

TOP LEFT: Current AUCECB President Andrei E. Klimenko at his desk. (Photo courtesy of Keston College)

TOP RIGHT: Arthur I. Mitskevich (assistant general secretary and head of Bible correspondence course) with President Andrei E. Klimenko (1974). (Photo courtesy of Keston College)

BOTTOM: Ukrainian Assistant Senior Presbyter Matthew Mel'nik (left) displaying blueprints at Brighton EBF congress (1979) for anticipated theological seminary in Moscow.

TOP: AUCECB delegation at European Baptist congress in Brighton, England, July 1979. From right to left are: Michael Zhidkov, Alexei M. Bychkov (general secretary), K. S. Sedletski, Peter K. Shatrov, A. I. Klimenko, J. K. Dukhonchenko. Visible behind Bychkov is *Bratskii Vestnik* editor Vitalii Kulikov.

BOTTOM: Ukrainian Senior Presbyter Jacob Dukhonchenko performing baptism in the Dnieper River, spring 1979. (Photo courtesy of Keston College)

TOP: Thirty-three baptismal candidates in Novosibirsk, June 15, 1977.

BOTTOM: Following baptism in the Moscow church in the mid-fifties, new members each received a bouquet of flowers. (Both photos courtesy of Keston College)

164

Longtime Moscow organist and vice-chairman of the international department, Il'ia M. Orlov, at the start of his career. (Photo courtesy of Keston College)

ABOVE: Communion service led by Jacob Dukhonchenko and Arthur Mitskevich in Kiev following a baptism in early spring 1979. (Photo courtesy of Keston College)

BELOW: E. A. Tarasov (left), vice-chairman in the state Council for Religious Affairs, with responsibility for the non-Orthodox sects, conversing with Gerhard Claas (center), BWA associate secretary for Europe, with Jakob Fast translating. (June 1977)

ABOVE: Presbyter council for the Ukraine, newly elected in October 1975. Front, left to right: V. S. Glukhovski (deputy SP, Pentecostal), J. K. Dukhonchenko (senior presbyter), I. S. Gnida (deputy senior presbyter). Present deputy senior presbyter for the RSFSR, V. E. Logvinenko (second from right in third row), was then a member of the Ukrainian council.

BELOW: Ukrainian leader Jacob K. Dukhonchenko consulting with deputy senior presbyter Ivan S. Gnida in their offices in Kiev.

TOP: Jacob K. Dukhonchenko conducting a wedding in the Central Kiev Church, 1979.

BOTTOM: Zaporozh'e Senior Presbyter Brynza (right) baptizing his own son, spring 1979.

Bibles, imported in December 1978, being unloaded at the Moscow church.

TOP: RSFSR Deputy Senior Presbyter V. E. Logvinenko (left), then a presbyter in Odessa, receiving his share of the 25,000 Bibles imported in December 1978.

BOTTOM: *Bratskii Vestnik*, AUCECB biomonthly journal.

TOP: Exterior view of Frunze Baptist Church. The sanctuary floor is below ground level so that the building will not tower above the neighboring houses.

BOTTOM: External view of the central (Iamskaia) church in Kiev. This building belongs to the Adventists, the Baptists only recently receiving permission to build their own suitably large building.

TOP (both pages): All three choirs in the Central Moscow Church combine for the final festive program at the 1979 AUCECB congress.

BOTTOM: A youthful spokesman from Kiev urging delegates at the 1979 congress to take the concerns of young people to heart.

172

BOTTOM: Interior of Tashkent ECB Church, 1974. The signs proclaim: "God is love"; "Christ is risen"; "I am coming soon."

TOP: Preparations for thanksgiving in the newly built church in Frunze, Kirgizia.

BOTTOM: Leaders of the 1,000-member church in Frunze in the offices of the senior presbyter. Seated left to right are: Vasil'ev (presbyter), N. N. Sizov (senior presbyter for Kirgizia), A. A. Warkentin (assistant presbyter).

TOP: Graduating class of the Bible correspondence school in 1974, together with Moscow leaders. In the second row center is AUCECB president Il'ia G. Ivanov. (Photo courtesy of Keston College)

BOTTOM: The new church building in Frunze, built with voluntary labor only. The entrance in foreground reflects the below-ground level sanctuary so that the entire building does not tower above the neighboring houses.

An additional preacher ordained in Moscow by Presbyter Michael Zhidkov (right) and A. I. Mitskevich. (Photo courtesy of Keston College)

Tsurkan, and A. S. Goncherov (1895) were senior people with considerable experience in church leadership.[13] But none of them had led churches belonging to the AUCECB for any length of time. This means that the *Init-siativniki* movement crystallized out of older leaders and younger men who had one thing in common—they were unaccustomed to a church that was not free. The new statute of 1960 really shocked them.

The Issue: Separation of Church and State

All sources agree that the new AUCECB statute dispatched to the churches in the summer of 1960 and the accompanying secret letter of instructions to the senior presbyters precipitated the split. This letter warned about "unhealthy missionary tendencies," asserting that a membership drive "must be decisively terminated." Baptism of young people between eighteen and thirty must be kept "to a complete minimum." Believers should also be encouraged to abandon their negative views on art, literature, radio, movies, and television. The instruction included advice to ensure that children would no longer be present at services.[14]

Those few thousand individuals who regularly received copies of *Bratskii Vestnik* (and this certainly included the senior presbyters) were less shocked. Already in 1948 Jacob Zhidkov noted with approval that the number of baptisms had declined. This signified that congregations were proving and teaching neophytes more thoroughly and would also guarantee that excommunications would be less frequent. Later in the year he again complained about the rush to baptism and urged that the candidate should be a Christian for at least one year. In 1949 he discouraged allowing unconverted people into the choir because this lowered the spiritual standard. In 1955 the AUCECB again expressed concern about rushing to baptize new believers. Early in 1959 Sergei P. Fadiukhin in a major article, "On the Church," declared that the most important issue where the church could work for good was to oppose the new weapons of massive destruction. Then he went on to declare that at the beginning of the third century in the history of Christianity when persecution had ceased, many unreliable types joined the rush to church membership. A church council had therefore decided that baptismal candidates must undergo a probation period of from one to three years.[15]

At the 1963 congress Vice-President N. A. Levindanto made an apologetic attempt to rewrite recent history by asserting that the new statute of 1960 had been introduced as a draft and that the AUCECB had repeatedly requested constituency responses and suggestions. But the letter of instruction had made it clear that the new statute must be enforced rigidly. Already in 1948 when the first statute was issued unilaterally by the All-Union Council, President Zhidkov admitted that "we cannot force anyone to accept and observe the statutes of the union" and went on to eschew all coercion. But in the same breath he added that "those believers who do not wish to subordinate themselves to the statute, naturally cannot have a place among the members of the congregations of the Council of Evangelical Christian Baptists whose statutes they reject."[16] That non-coercive coercion was at least as strong in 1960.

Some local church members never learned of the statute because their presbyter or even senior presbyter gave it a pocket veto. In another congregation the entire issue was discussed at a members' meeting where they decided as a local church to resist. Often this was successful. Other congregations decided to keep their children home from church for a few months and to devote their preaching to the Book of Job until the storm passed and they could gradually resume their usual activities. But in other localities the presbyter or deacon stood in the doorway and prevented children from entering. In Novosibirsk, for example, active evangelists were excommunicated from the church. In many other localities fearful Christians or even phony Christians served as stool pigeons to help authorities ferret out any resisters.[17]

This link with the state was the most damaging feature. Since 1959 there had been a major propaganda attack and administratively churches were closed forcibly with considerable haste. The new statute, even if it may not have differed that significantly from the statute of 1948,[18] suggested that their own leadership seemed to be cooperating with the state authorities to destroy the church.

The *Initsiativniki* resistance officially began on August 13, 1961 when the initiative group presented a statement of protest to the Moscow leadership. The original initiators had met in the village of Uzlovaia in Tula Oblast with Prokofiev and Kriuchkov the prime movers. Tula, where Kriuchkov lived, had for many years been neglected by the AUCECB leadership. Prokofiev was living in the village of Volnovakha in Donetsk Oblast where the "pure Baptist" movement had been centered and where B. A. Rusanov had recently been replaced by Senior Presbyter I. Ia. Tatarchenko.[19]

Twelve days after the initiative group presented their appeal to the Moscow leadership only to meet with rebuffs, Prokofiev and Kriuchkov wrote a letter addressed to all ECB congregations using a very sharp language. "In our day Satan is dictating through the workers of the All-Union Council of Evangelical Christians and Baptists," they declared.[20] They condemned the 1960 statute as an "anti-evangelical document" and appealed for a congress where a new statute would be approved. Not only did they condemn the statute, they demanded that the Moscow leadership repent of its sinful cooperation with the forces of Satan.

From the first the critique was not directed at the Moscow leadership alone but included all the churches which had accepted the anti-evangelical documents. The appeal to the churches was therefore a call for widespread renewal in the church, for sanctification and rededication. The increasing number of circular letters issued by the initiative group were full of calls for "repentance," "sanctification," "church reform," "new leadership," and above all an appeal to convene a "national congress of the churches."[21] All these words refer to internal religious matters but they were all an expression of a fundamental concern that the time had come for the evangelical church to be fully separated from the state. The primary initial emphasis was an appeal to the church to separate itself from the state and return to its historical roots.

The AUCECB Approach

AUCECB officials eventually admitted that they had been forced to issue the new statute.[22] Did that mean they had merely signed a document prepared by a state official or had they composed the statute along guidelines presented by the state? Who drafted the document? No evidence is available to answer this last question. In the AUCECB structure, this would have been the responsibility of the general secretary, Karev, possibly with the aid of his new assistant, Arthur Mitskevich. President Zhidkov necessarily had to assume responsibility but at his age and considering his many trips abroad that summer, his contribution may not have been very major. There had been a shake-up of leadership in 1954 whereby daily leadership was entrusted to three men (Zhidkov, Karev, and Ivanov), and two former vice-presidents (Orlov and Goliaev) were demoted. This particular meeting of the presidium had been conducted under the chairmanship of N. A. Levindanto, who also emerged as first vice-president. It was Levindanto who presented the revised statute to the 1963 congress and secured its approval.[23]

The letter of instruction had explained that revised church statutes were required so that they would correspond to existing Soviet legislation on religion. Such a new statute was necessary because copies of the 1929 law were rare. In April 1959, for the first time since the 1930s, a documentary collection of legislation on religion was published.[24] Two hundred thousand copies were distributed, marking an unusually large edition. This volume included the 1929 law in full and described it as the most important document which at the moment regulated the changing relations between the religious organizations and the state. But a second edition of this collection printed in 1961 omitted the 1929 law. As a matter of fact, the full text of the law has not been published since. An official commentary, also published in April 1961, affirmed that this law was still binding but neglected to mention that only a month previously, the two councils for religious affairs had issued an officially binding instruction which drastically altered the law. This legal trickery by state authorities meant that local churches should consult their new church statute to discover what the law did not permit. Since the new statute was issued nearly a year before the Orthodox Church was forced to revise its statute, it seems likely that the Baptist leaders hoped that with immediate acquiescence they would get favored treatment compared with the Orthodox and therefore stand a better chance to survive the new attack that had obviously begun.[25]

Since the *Initsiativniki* regarded the new statute as the last and worst manifestation of a leadership that had become unfaithful, let us look at this leadership more closely. In general these were men whose actions and statements on behalf of the Soviet state caused suspicion yet whose spiritual and pastoral qualities are equally striking. These contradictory qualities remind one of Metropolitan Nikolai and his successor Metropolitan Nikodim. By 1960 primary leadership was in the hands of three men: Jacob Zhidkov, president; Alexander Karev, general secretary; and Ilia G. Ivanov, treasurer.

Zhidkov had already been acting president of the Evangelical Christian Union since 1928 except for the period from 1938 to 1942 when he was in prison or exiled.[26] Initially he played the dominant role through the editorial pages of *Bratskii Vestnik*. He was also very active initially when the peace campaign began in the 1950s. In 1955 he was elected one of nine vice-presidents of the Baptist World Alliance and was the only one of the nine to be reelected in that important summer of 1960. Whereas initially he had made several trips to visit the churches, this local fence-mending activity soon became the responsibility of senior presbyters, plus infrequent visits were made by other specially appointed Moscow leaders.

Alexander Karev was eight years his junior, had turned sixty-seven in 1960, and by then had assumed a greater leadership role than Zhidkov.

Karev had studied in German Lutheran schools in Leningrad, graduated from a polytechnic institute which had famous professors such as Peter Struve and Bernadskii. He had also been active in the Student Christian Movement which had introduced him to men like John Mott and Sherwood Eddy. During the 1920s he made many preaching missions throughout the Soviet Union, taught pastoral theology at the Leningrad Bible School, and wrote articles for the journal *Khristianin*. After 1930 he worked in Moscow except for an eight-year exile term.

From the new beginning, Karev as general secretary was administratively responsible for the central office and conducted foreign affairs himself. After his first trip abroad in 1953, his involvement in the peace program escalated, necessitating long absences abroad.[27] During the 1950s he reigned unchallenged as the pastor of pastors. Virtually every issue of *Bratskii Vestnik* was filled with his sermon outlines for preachers, extended commentaries on different books of the New Testament, as well as major theological articles. In addition he preached three times a week. He was the best-educated, brightest, and most able of the Moscow leadership. Wherever he went, people loved him because they sensed that his heart overflowed with love for them. His role in the *Initsiativniki* conflict is highly enigmatic.

Ilia G. Ivanov, born 1898, was five years younger than Karev. Converted in the tent mission in Moscow in 1918, he had been active as youth worker and evangelist during the 1920s. No information is available on the subsequent period, but the author of a birthday greeting in 1968 stated that his "earthly path was a thorny one. He experienced much, passing through many trials."[28] In 1944 he suddenly emerged as one of the most influential plenipotentiaries for the AUCECB who was sent to organize the work in Moldavia and Belorussia before being co-opted into the council in 1945 with permanent residence in Moscow. Here he remained as treasurer and gradually assumed overall responsibility for correspondence with the churches. He too was a gifted preacher in the Moscow church. In 1966 he succeeded Zhidkov as president, remaining in office till 1974. It is apparent that Ivanov was one of the few favored by the authorities. Perhaps he had experienced especially severe prison conditions, perhaps he was especially susceptible to pain, perhaps the authorities were able to blackmail him, or perhaps he truly felt that Romans 13 demanded full submission to state authorities. That must remain speculation, but what is more apparent is that as a church leader he was one of the first to tremble before the authorities.

Three other men, also living in Moscow, played a less prominent but dominant role in the central leadership. In the summer of 1956, Arthur I. Mitskevich, the longtime deputy senior presbyter for the Ukraine, was brought to Moscow as assistant general secretary.[29] Since 1948 he had been senior presbyter for the large Kiev Oblast, as well as a member of the powerful All-Union revision or auditing commission. In 1954 he became chairman of the revision commission, retaining this position when he became assistant general secretary. Like Karev, he demonstrated considerable exegetical and didactic abilities (although much more self-taught than was Karev). By 1960 he was traveling abroad more frequently than his superior. In the summer of 1961, just prior to the split in the AUCECB, he attended an executive committee session of the Baptist World Alliance leadership to work for unity in those countries in which the Baptists were divided. He went so far as to propose that some of the authoritative workers from the Baptist world leadership could be utilized for this purpose.[30]

I. I. Motorin had been an Evangelical Christian leader and publisher in the Ukraine till at least 1929. In 1945 he was appointed to head the publishing division of the AUCECB, which meant that he held executive responsibility for *Bratskii Vestnik*. During the late fifties he was dispatched on several troubleshooting missions, for example three visits to Voronezh in 1956, twice again in 1957, and again in 1959. Here a separatist free church union was threatening. In 1958 he was added to the AUCECB council although he had participated in most of the meetings previously. The other appointment at that time was A. N. Karpov, who had switched places with Michael Orlov in 1954 to become the Moscow presbyter when Orlov went to Leningrad. Karpov's role, however, does not appear to have been prominent.[31]

From the beginning there had been a conscious attempt to have as many Baptists as Evangelical Christians in the central leadership. At one point there was also an attempt at parity for the senior presbyters.[32] After the leadership shake-up in 1954, the two former vice-presidents Orlov and Goliaev were sent to Leningrad and Rostov respectively. By 1960 Orlov was fighting a losing battle with cancer and died in 1961.[33] Goliaev was still able to attend the 1963 congress as an honored pensioner of 81 years of age. His leadership role had, however, never been taken very seriously. Two key leaders who emerged in 1954 as the new vice-presidents were N. A. Levindanto and A. L. Andreev.

Levindanto, born 1896 in Saratov, had been a secretary of the Baptist Federation in 1921. Released from prison in 1942 in order to arrange for a Baptist union with the Evangelical Christians, he was appointed AUCECB plenipotentiary for the Baltic region at his own request in 1945. He gained a reputation for toughness in the initial purge of the Latvian Baptist leadership but eventually was accepted as a necessary overlord who allowed Latvian and Estonian leaders considerable latitude on local affairs. When the 1960 statute was issued, he called a meeting of Latvian presbyters and in closed session read the instructions to them. The Latvians responded with silence.[34]

The other vice-president, A. L. Andreev, was much more influential in the church as a whole. Andreev, five years older than Zhidkov, had worked together with him since 1903. Andreev, like Orlov, successfully maintained the good will of the authorities, which guaranteed him a post in the central leadership of the Evangelical Christian Union at the time when that union was forced to abandon pacifism.[35] During the war Andreev and Orlov had remained at liberty and during the period of restriction were able to travel in border areas on church business. Like his opposite number Metropolitan Nikolai, he became the head of the AUCECB movement in the Ukraine which from the start represented half the membership. By the late fifties Karev claimed that 75 percent of the membership was in the Ukraine.[36] Andreev ran the Ukraine with an iron hand. By the late forties, he was relying increasingly on Mitskevich as his assistant to conduct the arduous journeys to the different oblasts, especially to those where there were conflicts. When Mitskevich moved to Moscow, he was replaced by N. N. Mel'nikov, whose leadership style was similar to Andreev's.[37] Andreev was already seventy-eight years of age in 1960 but still very much in charge in Kiev. Senior presbyters were brought to Kiev for consultations or his deputies were sent to carry out his instructions. Had it not been for his authoritarian style, Georgi Vins and his associates in Kiev might not have become so antagonized.[38] On the other hand, were it not for his strictly enforced discipline, the evangelical movement in the Ukraine might have suffered more from state harassment.

The Trouble Spots

AUCECB spokesmen have consistently understated the strength of the *Initsiativniki* movement, whereas spokesmen for the latter went so far as to claim the support of most of the unregistered congregations which represented two thirds of all congregations.[39] Official Soviet statistical estimates gradually increased, and the most recent assessment, which is obviously based on statistical data unavailable to Western scholars, indicates that at its height the *Initsiativniki* movement probably represented about

155,000 members.[40] At their congress in Tula in 1969, the Reform Baptists announced participation from forty-five oblasts. Although widespread throughout the Soviet Union, the *Initsiativniki* movement was particularly strong in a handful of regions.[41] Seventy-two percent of those who joined the *Initsiativniki* did so between 1961 and 1963. Perhaps they joined because they lived in areas where state persecution was most intense. But an examination of the prisoners' list for the period 1961 to 1966 suggests a double explanation for the geographic groupings.[42] Arrests took place in precisely those oblasts where the senior presbyter was included on the list of persons to be excommunicated for cooperating with the government.[43] In several oblasts, persons were arrested, yet the senior presbyter for the region was not included on the excommunication list.[44] Conversely, large numbers of arrests took place in areas where the senior presbyter had traditionally wielded little influence, where there were mainly unregistered congregations.[45]

Out of the first 197 prisoners, ninety-six came from the Russian Federation, fifty from the Ukraine, forty-two from Central Asia, eight from Belorussia and one from Moldavia. One might have expected more than 50 percent to come from the Ukraine. As it was, eleven were arrested in the Kharkov region, where Senior Presbyter Parchevski was finally replaced in 1963. Five other arrests in Cherkassy Oblast and three in Kirovograd Oblast belonged to I. Ia. Kaliuzhnyi's supervision.[46] Five more came from Sumi Oblast, where the senior presbyters were changed numerous times between 1958 and 1962.

From the beginning the *Initsiativniki* in Kiev with Georgi Vins at their head were highly influential in the reform movement, yet the first arrests in Kiev only took place in 1966. What accounts for the strong support in Kiev for the *Initsiativniki*? Here it appears much more to be the negative record of Andreev. In one document, the *Initsiativniki* charged that during the period 1945 to 1960 the most arrests had taken place in the Ukraine, where Andreev was senior presbyter, in Moldavia where Ivanov (later Astakhov) was senior presbyter, and the Baltic under Levindanto.[47] The arrests in Belorussia were relatively few and concentrated in that area which was under the direct administration of senior presbyter for the republic, Konstantin Veliseichik. Veliseichik (born 1910) had risen very rapidly, seeming to be the least likely candidate to succeed the esteemed old Evangelical Christian leader Chechnev, who died in 1958.[48] The *Initsiativniki* were particularly critical of a letter signed by Veliseichik and his new assistant N. N. Germanovich which demanded full adherence to the new statute, declaring that violation of the statute represented violation of Soviet law.[49]

When the newly created *Orgkomitet* reported to the churches in 1962, they complained specifically about several senior presbyters. The most serious charges were advanced against F. R. Astakhov who they said had been excommunicated from the Kishinev congregation in 1957, after which he was transferred to be assistant senior presbyter for the Ukraine but from here too came requests signed by thousands of Ukrainian believers to have him dismissed.[50] Astakhov was indeed removed as leader in Moldavia in 1957, served briefly as senior presbyter for the Caucasus region, and then emerged by 1961 as assistant to Mel'nikov and Andreev in the Ukraine. Astakhov had considerable influence as a member of the revision or auditing commission. The references in *Bratskii Vestnik* to his role in the Ukraine are notably restrained.[51]

The other person specifically attacked was V. I. Ermilov who the *Initsiativniki* claimed had first been excommunicated from Volgograd, then from the Kazan congregation, but then he was appionted senior presbyter for Western Siberia and again declarations of his dismissal had been received. Once again this tended to correspond with Ermilov's career as revealed in *Bratskii Vestnik*. During the period 1958-62 there was a noticeable increase in the replacement of senior presbyters. How many of these were being replaced because congregations excommunicated them and how many were being replaced because state authorities insisted cannot be determined from the evidence available.

Two major trouble areas were Western Siberia, especially the Altai region, and Kazakhstan. *Initsiativniki* doubts about Ermilov's integrity have already been noted. But in Western Siberia a much more serious problem was the fact that the AUCECB had been able to establish only tenuous links with the churches and relatively few had received registration, primarily in the large cities. A number of these, such as Barnaul, Slavgorod, and Omsk had been temporarily closed according to official Baptist sources.[52] Similarly in Kazakhstan there had been major changes in the leadership so that by 1960, M. S. Vashchuk, who had emerged only two years previously, now became the sole senior presbyter for all four Central Asian republics, where formerly there had been three.[53] Vashchuk, born in 1904 and a Belorussian by nationality, had studied in Latvia and England and then worked in Warsaw as publisher of religious literature.[54] After release from prison in the Karaganda region, the Baptist Union wished to utilize his considerable talent in Moscow but he was refused an internal passport. When he did receive one and became senior presbyter, local believers became suspicious in spite of his good sermons and apparent commitment and he was finally excommunicated in 1970.[55] If Vashchuk was not included on the *Initsiativniki* list of senior presbyters to be excommunicated, it may be because the *Initsiativniki* strength was in Tselinograd and Dzhezkazgen in Kazakhstan, which were unregistered.

Several cities stand out as obvious trouble spots. Fourteen out of the fifteen persons arrested in Uzbekistan came from Tashkent and a nearby village. Here there had been several changes in local leadership until in 1962 the experienced S. P. Fadiukhin was transferred here.[56] Soon Fadiukhin became assistant senior presbyter to Vashchuk. One of the key *Initsiativniki* leaders, Nikolai Khrapov, also lived in Tashkent. Khrapov, born 1914, had served twenty-five years in prison for his faith previously and was sentenced to a seven-year term in 1961. Before that he had composed some of the major spiritual articles in the *Samizdat* journal *Herald of Salvation*, as well as a major article giving advice to youth, which was widely distributed in *Initsiativniki* circles.[57]

One congregation in Dedovsk in the Moscow region summarized what had been the experience of many of the unregistered congregations. Since 1949 the congregations had requested registration but had been refused. By 1969 this small congregation of sixty members had had its services in believers' homes disturbed more than 300 times, often some of the windows were broken and people were physically carried out into the street. The believers had been fined thirty times for a total of 1,055 rubles. The writer of the letter, V. I. Kozlov, who was the leading minister, could no longer show himself at home because the police were waiting to arrest him.[58]

Kozlov's story is particularly appealing. Born in 1924, he lost his father when he was nine and together with five siblings found himself out on the street. At age fifteen he received his first four-year prison sentence as a criminal. After serving in the war and being imprisoned, he was again arrested in 1946 and sentenced to five years' imprisonment for armed robbery. The next year he received an additional ten-year sentence for banditry in the prison camp. Finally in 1953 he was moved to a prison camp in Eastern Siberia, where he met N. P. Khrapov, who was then serving a twenty- to twenty-five-year sentence for his faith. Khrapov's witness in the prison impressed him and Kozlov was converted. Released in the amnesty in 1954, he married and became active in the church. Seven years and five children later he was sentenced to five years' exile in Eastern Siberia, but this time for his faith. From 1966 to 1969 he was again imprisoned and at the time of this writing was in hiding from the authorities.[59]

From Orgkomitet to CCECB

The initiative group, which first visited the AUCECB offices on August 13, 1961, claimed that they had been promised a reply but had received none. After they wrote again on August 23 without a reply, they decided to make a public appeal to all the churches. The short time they waited for the AUCECB to reply indicates that they expected no reply and that they expected to take the initiative further. The reformers immediately emphasized that they were not engaging in a power struggle and that if a congress would be called they would rest their labors and abide by the congress decision. Yet the progressive steps that the reformers took clearly demonstrate that they were following constitutionally approved procedures for forming a new society which would replace the AUCECB.[60] In February, at an enlarged conference, a decision was taken to form an organizing committee *(Orgkomitet)* which was entrusted with the preparatory work for an All-Union congress of ECB churches.[61]

The new *Orgkomitet* also made two other major decisions at its meeting on February 25, 1962. It produced a revised draft of the 1960 statute and announced a major decision concerning the antichurch activities of the AUCECB. The *Orgkomitet* accused the AUCECB of putting anti-evangelical documents into effect, of including only one third of the congregations in the union—only the registered ones, and of conducting "hostile activities against the convocation of an All-Union congress."[62] As a result they warned that if the AUCECB members, as well as regional and local presbyters, persisted in their ways, they would be excommunicated from the church. The *Orgkomitet* announced a general day of fasting and prayer for May 6, 1962, and gave the AUCECB time to repent.

Instead of repentance, the AUCECB sent a letter to the churches on June 20, 1962, indicating that the *Initsiativniki* work was inspired by "the enemy of God's work."[63] An enlarged conference of the *Orgkomitet* meeting three days later in Moscow reached the momentous decision to excommunicate the AUCECB leadership. In the official statement subsequently referred to as Protocoll No. 7 they denied the AUCECB and its officials the right to be ministers in the church, the right to represent ECB churches inside the union, and also the right to represent it abroad. Protocoll No. 7 named twenty-seven persons by name and promised supplementary lists. Local presbyters, however, were to be excommunicated by the local churches.[64]

The *Orgkomitet* claimed the right to take this unusual step on the basis of written declarations from churches throughout the country which gave "unanimous testimony to the fact that members of the AUCECB have long deprived themselves of the right to be members of Christ's church."[65] Those letters from churches had also stated that they recognized the *Orgkomitet* as the sole leadership for ECB churches. Therefore Protocoll No. 7 also declared that the *Orgkomitet* would take upon itself the leadership of the ECB churches till a congress was held, that the guiding principle for the churches would be the Word of God. They repeated earlier resolutions that all AUCECB meetings and documents concerning a congress which did not involve the *Orgkomitet* would be considered invalid. Finally, they also declared invalid the excommunication of believers for having supported the movement to sanctify the church. This controversial document was signed by G. K. Kriuchkov, A. A. Shalashov, and N. G. Baturin.[66]

The AUCECB has never considered the excommunication legitimate. In fact, as a result, many churches which had sided with the reformers initially, withdrew their support, becoming neutral or returning to the AUCECB. Baptist teaching on excommunication procedures had always emphasized that this was the prerogative of the local congregation. Levindanto had repeatedly argued in major articles that in the case of excommunicating a presbyter, this should be done only in the presence of a senior presbyter or neighboring presbyters to avoid using excommunication as a weapon of power.[67] Numerous local sources indicate that AUCECB leaders had violated this procedure repeatedly since 1959 by sending its appointed agents to secure the excommunication of presbyters and preachers who refused to accept the new statute. But the *Orgkomitet* action was also an attempt to exercise power which superseded the right of a congregation to excommunicate unfaithful members. Most of the AUCECB members resided in Moscow and the Moscow congregation refused to excommunicate them. This was also true in Kiev, for example. A more logically Baptist approach would have been for those churches rejecting the Moscow leadership to withdraw from the union and form a new union.

There are obvious contradictory strains in the reformers' actions which betray either inexperience or disagreement among the reformers on a proper method to follow.[68] They found themselves in a situation of power politics. In August 1963 they addressed a letter to Premier Khrushchev which began by noting that this was the seventh time that they had dispatched an appeal to the government requesting permission to convene a congress, but since there were no replies, it was becoming a serious problem. The long letter was extremely frank in charging that the church was "completely under the illegal control of various state authorities."[69] The letter accused government authorities of molding local church councils like clay and of appointing senior presbyters "from among their own trusted men, and they subordinated them to the AUCECB." After further details, they stated in summary that such thorough unanimity has been established between the AUCECB and the state authorities that any expression of opinion against the AUCECB is looked upon by both as opposition to the state."[70]

Recognizing that both state authorities and AUCECB officials were exercising their considerable powers against them, they tried to get Khrushchev to see that this exercise of power was illegal. In an earlier document addressed to the churches, they had challenged the AUCECB's claim that the new statutes were based on the Soviet legislation on cults.[71] Analyzing numerous clauses of the 1960 statute on the basis of an official legal commentary of 1961,[72] they argued that religious centers had no right to appoint local church clergy, this was the right of local congregations only; that local executive bodies had no right to make decisions, only to execute decisions taken by the members; and that the law only restricted *membership* to persons over eighteen, whereas the statute went so far as to forbid *baptism* for persons under fifteen.[73] These criticisms involved differing interpretations of the law but that is less important than the fact that the law had changed. Since this was kept secret, the reformers protested in vain about terrible illegality. In fact, according to the new changes, individuals, interested groups, or local congregations no longer had the right to call a congress, only the AUCECB could do that.

In their published statements the AUCECB leaders ignored the excommunications although these may have influenced replacement of some senior presbyters. Without referring to the *Initsiativniki* specifically, a series of articles on the subject of sanctification began appearing in *Bratskii Vestnik* immediately after the first *Initsiativniki* visit to Moscow in 1961. The first article by S. P. Fadiukhin described sanctification as a process and defined it as "knowing the will of God and converting it into life."[74] Sanctification concerned one's personal relationship to God and also the relationship to other people. Fadiukhin declared that our relationship to the people around us could be guided by two laws: "The law of the state and the law of God." He then cited Romans 13:1-4 and Titus 3:1, 2, which urge obedience to the laws of the state. As far as the law of God was concerned, he quoted Psalm 18:8 and James 1:25. Fadiukhin then concluded that for the Apostle Paul the supreme sign of sanctification had been "to strive earnestly to live peaceably." Fadiukhin underlined this emphasis on peace and quiet by quoting Isaiah 30:15: "In quietness and confidence shall be your strength." This tendency toward quietism, toward regarding uncritical obedience to the state as a major sign of sanctification, remained the official position against the reformers' challenge.[75]

One looks in vain in the pages of *Bratskii Vestnik* for the statement by Peter and John, quoted in Acts 5, that "we ought to obey God rather than men." Ironically, precisely during this time Mitskevich was writing a commentary on the Books of Acts. He dwelt at length on the story of Ananias and Sapphira and emphasized that the church could grow only if it was purified.[76] If the church was not purified, then Paul's reference in the letter to the Romans would apply to them: "The name of God is blasphemed among the Gentiles because of you" (Romans 2:24, RSV). Mitskevich then skipped over the section describing the conflict Peter and John had with the authorities and moved to the election of deacons, which is discussed in Acts 6.

The State-Reformers-AUCECB Triad

If it were not for interference by the state authorities in this matter, if the state had not declared a war with new persecution, if it were not backing its planted men, the church itself would quickly, painlessly and without any complication re-establish the necessary internal church order by removing the unrepentant officials. By this it would break the essential link in the criminal chain binding church and state. In this way the illegal relationship would be liquidated without mentioning the state in so much as a word at the congress. All this could be attained painlessly.[77]

This wishful declaration to Premier Khrushchev expressed the essential problem candidly. The state had launched a policy of liquidating the church but church officials were unable to acknowledge it publicly. In fact they were under tremendous pressure to assist in the liquidation and the only hope they saw was to give in so that at least some of the church could survive. But the bold opposition by the initiative group forced the state to show its hand. Those who resisted were threatened with prison and to achieve this, trials had to be held and charges established. *Initsiativniki* supporters managed to produce near verbatim transcripts of court trials and photocopies of the official charges. In numerous cases the primary charge seemed to be that the accused leaders of the local congregation had refused to accept the statutes of the AUCECB.

One of the worst instances occurred immediately after the 1963 congress. During the Christmas holidays, four persons were put on trial in the Altai regional court, where they were declared guilty of reactionary activity harmful to society because "they analyzed various biblical texts, permitted arbitrary incorrect interpretations, criticized and did not accept the new constitution of the AUCECB."[78] The presbyter received a five-year sentence, while the two brothers Nikolai and Vasilii Khmara were sentenced to three years and Mrs. Liubov Khmara received a suspended sentence. Nikolai Khmara's name soon became famous because he died two weeks after the trial after gross torture.[79]

This was the worst case where local zealots had utilized the antireligious propaganda and restrictive instructions from Moscow to engage in bestiality. But this act involved the unregistered Baptist congregation in Barnaul which had been blessed with a large number of younger men with courage and the deep conviction that as long as a congregation maintained solidarity, state authorities would have to give in. The Barnaul congregation had been among the first to begin writing *Samizdat* documents in 1961, after their officially registered church had been closed by the authorities because the congregation refused to accept an immoral man as presbyter. Now they took documentary photographs which were later circulated around the world and dispatched a delegation of twenty-one persons to Moscow to demand an official investigation. The AUCECB at first sent I. I. Motorin to Barnaul in February, who urged the believers to rejoin the newly opened registered congregation. A commission of investigation was finally sent at the end of May and Alexander Karev also visited Barnaul at this time.[80] Local believers remembered that Karev in the presence of the state officials had grilled them with a series of questions asking them why they were not obeying state law. This permanently soured the Barnaul relationship to Moscow. The commission, on the other hand, confirmed the accuracy of the torture and murder charges and the prison superintendent was at least suspended although no one was prosecuted. Nor did the authorities agree to a public acknowledgment of the crime.

Much more widespread were other aspects of state interference. In their letter to Khrushchev, the reformers complained that secret police and other government agents were constantly asking church members the following questions:

> Where is the next church service to be?
> Who will preach?
> Which preachers have come from outside?

> Who made any trips and to where?
> Who preached a call to repentance?
> Who prayed for the imprisoned brethren?[81]

Such questions they regarded as unwarranted interference in internal church affairs. They found particularly offensive the fact that Karev, for example, had advised the Barnaul believers against praying for imprisoned believers. As the split widened, the support for the reformers continued to grow, reaching its high point in 1966.

Local discussions such as those in Barnaul had been undertaken from the start but it was only in 1965 that the first reconciliation talks between leaders from both sides took place. A constant problem in these reconciliation attempts was the uncanny coincidences where the words that a reformer had spoken to a registered believer were repeated to him the next day by a secret police official who came to interrogate him. Some of the registered believers and leaders were aiding the authorities in sending dissenters to prison, in other cases, believers finally broke down under intense pressure and told the authorities what they wished to hear.[82] In either case the result was the same. Harassments continued, and, worst of all, the number of persons in prison continued to rise. At best, the AUCECB leaders were powerless. Most responded with cowardice and servility but some also with vindictiveness.

What finally guaranteed failure of state policy against the Baptists was the courage of the women. Six weeks after Nikolai Khmara's death, the first secret meeting of a council of prisoners' relatives was held and the first detailed lists of prisoners were collected for circulation. The history of this remarkable organization has been intimately connected with the careers of Lidia Vins and Galina Rytikova, but the first three founders were: Lidia K. Govorun of Smolensk, Nina P. Iastrebova from Kharkov, and Rudneva from faraway Semipalatinsk, Kazakhstan. Rudneva's husband, Victor, was serving a five-year sentence and she was left with eight children. N. P. Iastrebova's husband also received a five-year sentence plus five years' internal exile. They had four children. Lidia K. Govorun was herself sentenced to three years' imprisonment in 1966. All were in their thirties.[83]

Impact of Dissent

After 1965 when the CCECB had been organized, the attention of the reformers no longer focused on the AUCECB, but rather on the state. In its proselytizing activities it now turned much more to the unregistered congregations, both unions competing during the next decade for the support of these congregations which had been untouched by the split.[84]

In theory, the state campaign of closing churches affected the AUCECB more because they had the monopoly of registered churches, but in practice there was less discrimination. Where in one place the prayer house was padlocked or bulldozed to the ground, in another location the individual's private house which had been used for meetings was confiscated or destroyed. Seldom did the closure of a church signify the termination of religious activities. Very often fearful believers carefully avoided all groupings of more than three persons but after a few months smaller groups began gathering again in homes. Word soon spread that whereas persecution was quite severe in the Russian Federation and in Kazakhstan, in Kirgizia the semi-Muslim administrators were turning a blind eye to religious activities. As a result, considerable moving ensued although not everyone sought refuge in Kirgizia. Others moved to the Baltic region where there was much less restriction.[85]

Initially there was widespread sympathy for the reformers. Statistical claims were wildly contradictory as one side tried to minimize the threat and the other tried to dramatize its support. The *Initsiativniki* claimed that the AUCECB spoke only for one third of the membership since two thirds of the congregations were unregistered and implied that the latter were in the reformers' camp. According to Soviet sociologists, at its height the reformers were able to claim the support of approximately half of the unregistered congregations.[86] It should be noted, however, that as a rule unregistered congregations were smaller in membership. In 1958 before the Khrushchev campaign, Baptist leaders had claimed a membership of 530,000.[87] By 1966 Karev was saying that 250,000 was more likely. Available data would tend to support the latter figure and suggest that the 500,000 figure was inflated unless it also included the unregistered congregations. The most recent and most reliable official Soviet statistics indicate that by the end of 1965, 13 percent of all believers in registered congregations supported the split with the percentage as high as 19.4 percent in the major cities.[88] This would mean a total of 30,000 to 80,000 supporters from the AUCECB registered churches plus half of the perhaps 250,000 Baptists in unregistered congregations. Therefore at its height in 1966 the reform movement very likely had around 155,000 supporters.

Whatever the precise figures, this constituted a major threat to the AUCECB, especially during the early years, when one state official declared that the reformers had the potential to win over half the membership.[89] After 1966, the hysterical attention paid to the *Initsiativniki* in the Soviet press clearly indicates that the authorities were worried. Some concessions had been granted to the AUCECB by 1963 already, but we will see in the following chapter that those turned out to be only the first of many concessions granted to the AUCECB in the subsequent years in order to win the reformers back.

As the percentage of Christians in the prison population increased, authorities discovered that here, too, new converts were being made. When the leaders were dispatched into exile, it often meant the birth of a new mission outpost. In many places authorities removed the entire church leadership only to return a few weeks later to find other men assuming the leadership. One man who experienced how new replacements were found to replace those arrested recalled that the most unlikely person suddenly discovered a preaching gift no one had suspected. Out of this emergency situation an expanding corps of self-taught preachers was emerging.

The witness of believers such as those in Barnaul impressed the public, which began to wonder why morally upright workers and peaceable neighbors were vilified as monsters, scum, obscurantists, extortionists, parasites, and bloodthirsty people.[90] Some of those neighbors began to take an interest in religion.

Yet the most important impact of the dissent is an emotional one. How does one assess the sufferings of people striving to be true to their Lord at all costs? How does one understand the frustration of state officials upon realizing that religion refused to disappear and their shame in discovering that through their struggle against religion they were debasing themselves rather than attaining new heights of communist morality? How does one do justice to the feelings of the AUCECB leaders and their supporters who were suffering in silence? Some of them were suffering because they hoped that their low-key negotiations for believers would eventually bear fruit even though this made them look bad in the eyes of the reformers. Others were suffering because they knew the reformers' accusations were only too true and they did not have the courage to repent.

Having seldom heard an official word of sympathy for those in prison, Reform Baptist leaders are incapable of discussing the AUCECB's policies objectively. As far as they are concerned, the hands of the Moscow leadership are dripping with blood. AUCECB leaders are less passionate and in recent years have openly acknowledged fraternal sympathy for those they believe to be misguided, but they cannot forget that the reformers were responsible for airing their dirty linen in the world's newspapers. The

AUCECB set about trying to restore their proud unity by means of congresses while the reformers cooled their heels in prison because they had dared to call for such a congress.

Notes to Chapter 6

1. Lialina, Chaps. 1-4; Klibanov & Mitrokhin, "Raskol . . .," p. 100f. See also *Voprosy nauchnogo ateizma*, Vol. XXIV, 1979, which devotes the entire issue to the Christian sects.

2. Lialina, p. 14.

3. *Ibid.*, pp. 26-29.

4. *BV*, 5/56, p. 59; 1/57, p. 79; 5-6/58, p. 37; and August 1959 (as reported in 6/63, p. 13).

5. *BV*, 5-6/58, p. 39.

6. AS 565; AS 772, p. 6; in AS 871 the reformers claimed that between 1945 and 1947 hundreds of presbyters and preachers in the Ukraine, Belorussia, Moldavia, Siberia and elsewhere were sent to prison. The AUCECB has not challenged these claims.

7. Mitrokhin, *Baptizm*, p. 77.

8. *BV*, 1/60, p. 87.

9. Lialina, p. 40. The Voronezh split was the subject of a major sociological study reported in N. S. Zlobina, "Sovremennyi baptizm i ego ideologiia," *Voprosy istorii religii i ateizma*, Vol. IX, 1963, pp. 95-125.

10. *BV*, 6/63, pp. 34 and 39.

11. Biographical data on Prokofiev and other *Initsiativniki* is based on card files at Keston College and my own card file.

12. On Kriuchkov see AS 1039 (*Bulletin* No. 3, 1971), pp. 7-9. For more biographical details see Chap. 8 below.

13. In his autobiography published posthumously, Sergei T. Golev described how upon his release from prison and exile in 1953 Ilia G. Ivanov had invited him to work for the AUCECB. But after discovering that this would involve reporting to the state authorities, he refused. Later he led an unregistered group in Riazan which joined the reformers in 1961 after they received the first copies of *Samizdat* (Jakob Esau, Sergi T. Golev & Johann Steffen, *Unter dem Schirm des Höchsten* [Wuppertal: R. Brockhaus Verlag, 1979], pp. 121-143). S. Kh. Tsurkan was described by Ivanov when visiting him in 1947 as an experienced, leading worker in Moldavia, but subsequently Tsurkan was no longer mentioned in the pages of *Bratskii Vestnik*.

14. Letter quoted from Mitrokhin & Klibanov, p. 86.

15. *BV*, 1/48, p. 6; 5/48, p. 4; 1/49, p. 5; 2/55, p. 69; 1/59, p. 62.

16. *BV*, 1/49, p. 21.

17. Umsiedler interview data.

18. A copy of the 1948 statute has not become available nor is the reaction of the congregations at that time known. Senior presbyters regularly reported that on their visits to congregations they enforced the statute, implying that resistance had been encountered.

19. B. A. Rusanov was one of those excommunicated by the Reformers (AS 770); he became the senior presbyter for the Caucasus and served till 1964. On I. Ia. Tatarchenko (1899-1972) see below, p. 210.

20. AS 770, p. 6.

21. A handy list of the appeals, chronologically arranged, appears as appendix

to Michael Bourdeaux & Albert Boiter, "Baptists in the Soviet Union 1960-71," *Radio Liberty Research Bulletin*, January 31, 1972.

22. At the 1966 and 1969 congresses they spoke about a "mistake." More explicit admissions were made in private talks with foreign churchmen.

23. *BV*, 2/54, pp. 38-41; 6/63, p. 42.

24. *Kommunisticheskaia partiia i sovetskoe pravitel'stvo o religii i tserkvi* (Moscow, 1959).

25. Luchterhandt, *Der Sowjet Staat*, pp. 125-26. The existence of the 1961 legally binding instruction became known through a reference to it at trials in 1966. This was confirmed in Igor Shafarevich's legal study (1971 *Samizdat*) but the full text as printed in Kuroedov & Pankratova became available only when a copy was leaked to the West in 1976. (See my article in *RCL*, IV, 4, 1976, pp. 24-30.)

26. Kahle, p. 269; the following biographical data was taken from my biographical card file.

27. Karev made a total of thirty-nine trips abroad.

28. *BV*, 3/68, p. 75.

29. *BV*, 1/59, p. 75. Why the post was created was not explained; at Karev's death in 1969 Mitskevich did not succeed him; perhaps by then he was too old. A. I. Mitskevich was born 1901 in Lithuania as the son of a Lithuanian Baptist preacher and a Latvian-German mother. Converted at age 10, he and his family joined the Evangelical Christian church in Moscow in 1915. At the 1919 youth congress I. S. Prokhanov nominated him as All-Union evangelist and in 1921 he traveled together with I. G. Ivanov on an evangelistic tour of Kalinin Oblast. In 1926 he headed the Kirov regional department of the AUCECB and in 1929 became the senior presbyter for Gorki Oblast, working there for many years. He spent the war in Novosibirsk, moving to Kiev at Patkovskii's invitation in 1946. In Kiev he was Andreev's office manager, later becoming his deputy. Initially he also led the Kiev church when the three congregations were reduced to one.

30. *BV*, 5-6/61, p. 35. This is most ironic since the Baptist World Alliance has subsequently been unable to interfere in the Soviet Baptist conflict because the AUCECB always insisted that the BWA had no such mandate.

31. Considering the importance of A. N. Karpov's position as leading presbyter of the two largest congregations in the union, the absence of biographical information on him is striking. Part of the reason was that in 1965 he was quietly removed for having committed adultery. He still attends services in Moscow, sometimes being asked to preach in the outlying churches.

32. *BV*, 5-6/54, p. 65. Of the forty-five senior presbyters, twenty-two were Evangelical Christian, twenty-one were Baptist, and two were Pentecostal.

33. *BV*, 6/57, pp. 47-51 in which Orlov summarized his career and his apparently successful bout with cancer.

34. *BV*, 2/59, p. 19, and interview with Adolphs Klaupiks.

35. Kahle, pp. 395, 399.

36. *BV*, 1/58, p. 28.

37. N. N. Mel'nikov (born 1904) had been senior presbyter of Dnepropetrovsk Oblast since 1945.

38. An explanation given by Alexander Karev in private in 1969 (BWA files, December 1969).

39. For a discussion of the contradictory claims see Bourdeaux, *Religious Ferment*, pp. 2-6.

40. Lialina, pp. 42-51. For further details see below, p. 193.

41. These were: Kiev, Tula, Rostov, Krasnodar, W. Siberia and Northern

Kazakhstan, Southern Belorussia and in Moldavia.

42. See the handy compilation in Bourdeaux, pp. 211-29, and in Rosemary Harris & Xenia Howard-Johnston, eds., *Christian Appeals from Russia* (London: Hodder & Stoughton, 1968), pp. 92-143.

43. These were: Kharkov (P. A. Parchevski); Cherkassy & Kirovograd (I. Ia. Kaliuznyi & D. M. Andrikevich); Kiev (A. L. Andreev, N. N. Mel'nikov, F. R. Astakhov but not D. I. Eniukov the SP for Kiev Oblast); Voroshilovgrad (A. V. Gaivoronski); Moldavia (D. I. Ponomarchuk); Middle Volga region (G. M. Buzynin); Rostov (I. A. Evstratenko); Novosibirsk (V. I. Ermolov).

44. For example: Khmel'nitski (E. A. Mazin); Sumi (A. M. Tesliuk); Kursk (M. I. Sorokin); Belgorod (I. D. Shavyrin); Moscow (A. N. Karpov); Kazakhstan & Central Asia (M. S. Vashchuk).

45. That is: the Altai region of Eastern Siberia, Omsk, Perm, and the Northwest region of the RSFSR. Lialina identified major regions of unregistered congregations which gave strong support to the *Initsiativniki* as Tula, Cheliabinsk, Sverdlovsk, Omsk, and the Ural Mountain region which, she remarked, were formerly strong points of the early Baptist and Evangelical Christian movements (p. 50).

46. I. Ia. Kaliuzhnyi first served as Mitskevich's assistant in Kiev, then when this was subdivided in 1956 he became senior presbyter for Cherkassy, temporarily also for Kirovograd. His regularly printed reports indicate close cooperation with Moscow. In spite of the excommunication, he was elected to the AUCECB in 1966, and since 1966 he has been an assistant senior presbyter for the entire Ukraine. He retired in 1979.

47. AS 871, p. 33. They noted that during the entire previous fifteen-year period "not one sympathetic word was said by the AUCECB leadership to those suffering for Christ."

48. I. G. Ivanov came from Moscow and personally traveled around the republic with K. S. Veliseichik to demonstrate Moscow's support for him (*BV*, 3/58, pp. 51-52; 5-6/58, pp. 16-18).

49. AS 770, p. 53.

50. *Ibid.*, p. 55.

51. Jacob Zhidkov called on F. R. Astakhov at his home when visiting Kiev in 1963 but Astakhov did not take part in the deliberations to which Zhidkov had been invited (*BV*, 4/63, pp. 73-74). Astakhov accompanied a Canadian Baptist delegation to Odessa, but the local report ignored him, but raved about the young translator, Matthew Mel'nik (*BV*, 5-6/62, p. 118). Born 1904, Astakhov was converted in 1918 and baptized in 1924 in Orel Oblast. He attended the Leningrad Bible School 1927-28, was sent to Orel in 1928 as evangelist, then was transferred to Novosibirsk in 1929 to assist M. A. Orlov, working there till the start of the war. After the war he became senior presbyter for Western Siberia.

52. *BV*, 2/63, pp. 74-75.

53. In 1957 they were: M. S. Vashchuk (Kazakhstan), N. A. Iadykin (Kirgizia), and L. M. Karakai (Uzbekistan & Tadzhikistan).

54. *BV*, 6/64, pp. 59-61.

55. Umsiedler interview data. Vashchuk then moved to Kazan, where he is still the local presbyter (*BV*, 4/70, p. 77; 2/77, p. 76).

56. They had been: L. M. Karakai (1955-60?), E. M. Rudenko (1961), S. P. Fadiukhin (1962-64), I. S. Semchenko (1957-73, variously chairman of church council and presbyter, died 1973), A. S. Kolganov 1966- ?. B. N. Serin became presbyter in 1977. M. M. Samotugin, who was senior presbyter of Central Asia 1967-

76, had lived in Tashkent since the war and held leading posts. A. T. Pen'kov, who had been the senior presbyter in 1947, reemerged in 1966 as one of three candidates for presbyter, losing to Kolganov; he became a deacon.

57. Klibanov & Mitrokhin, pp. 104-107.

58. AS 443.

59. Subsequently Peter Rumachik became the leader and CCECB member. The Dedovsk congregation was finally registered as an autonomous congregation in 1975 but in May 1978 the church was locked up by the authorities (CPR *Bulletin*, No. 54, pp. 24-36; No. 61, pp. 10-14).

60. Article 126 of the Soviet constitution of 1936, slightly changed in Article 51 of the 1977 constitution.

61. Its members were: A. F. Prokofiev, G. K. Kriuchkov, G. P. Vins, A. A. Shalashov (died 1963), and N. G. Baturin.

62. AS 770, pp. 34-36.

63. AS 785 (*BL*, 2-3/65). The letter itself has not become available.

64. Those excommunicated were (identification [SP=senior presbyter] and spelling corrections by the author): AUCECB council members Jacob Zhidkov, Alexander Karev, Ilia G. Ivanov, I. I. Motorin and A. I. Mitskevich, G. M. Buzynin (SP for Penza and Middle Volga) and the longtime Moscow office official, briefly SP for the Kazan area, S. G. Shchepetov, were incorrectly identified as council members. Others excommunicated were: A. L. Andreev (SP for Ukraine); P. A. Parchevski (SP for Kharkov); N. N. Mel'nikov (Deputy SP for Ukraine); F. R. Astakhov (Assistant SP for Ukraine); K. S. Veliseichik (SP for Belorussia); N. N. Germanovich (Assistant SP for Belorussia); V. I. Ermolov (SP for Volgograd, Saratov and Astrakhan, earlier for Western Siberia); T. S. Kasaev (presbyter in Ordzhonikidze, Caucasus); I. Ia. Tatarchenko (SP for Donets); A. V. Gaivoronski (SP for Voroshilovgrad); I. E. Egorov (SP for Krasnodarskii Krai); I. A. Evstratenko (SP for Rostov); R. R. Podgaiski (SP for Stavropolskii Krai); D. D. Shapovalov (SP for Vinnitsa); B. A. Rusanov (SP for Caucasian Republics and N. Caucasus); K. L. Kalibabchuk (SP for Kherson); D. I. Ponomarchuk (SP for Moldavia); I. Ia. Kaliuzhnyi (SP for Cherkassy); E. N. Raevski (SP for Eastern Siberia and the Far East); and D. M. Andrikevich (Assistant SP for Cherkassy) (AS 770, pp. 38-41).

65. *Ibid.*

66. A. A. Shalashov was presbyter in Cheliabinsk (obituary in AS 770, pp. 126-40). N. G. Baturin was presbyter in Shakhty near Rostov. A. F. Prokofiev, who fully supported this action, did not sign because he had been arrested a month earlier.

67. *BV*, 3-4/55, pp. 10-24; 1/56, pp. 50-52. Cf. 1/64, p. 38; 2/65, pp. 28-34.

68. Disagreement on method began to split the CCECB after 1976. See below, p. 275f.

69. Quoted in Bourdeaux, p. 54.

70. *Ibid.*, pp. 55 and 60.

71. AS 770, p. 58f.

72. F. M. Rudinskii, *Svoboda sovesti v SSSR* (Moscow: Gosiurizdat, 1961).

73. Neither the 1960 statute nor the letter of instruction refer to the age of eighteen.

74. *BV*, 3/61, pp. 36-39. Cf. other articles on sanctification: 4/62, p. 35 and 51 (which includes a warning against false Christians who try to draw suffering upon themselves); 2/64, pp. 44-57; 4/64, pp. 43-53; and 3/65, pp. 38-45.

75. At the 1969 congress Alexander Karev repeated the reference to Isaiah 30:15 calling the observance of "quietness and confidence" a "condition for blessing" (*BV*, 2/70, p. 23).

76. *BV*, 1/61, pp. 43-49.

77. Quoted in Bourdeaux, p. 60. Officials from the Council for Religious Affairs in conversations with the author in May 1979 still referred to such action as legitimate interference in order to maintain decency and order as demanded by the Bible in 1 Cor. 14:40!

78. AS 777.

79. *Supra*, Chap. 5, p. 143.

80. *BV*, 3/64, pp. 78-79; 4/64, p. 76. Deyneka, *Song in Siberia*, focuses on the Barnaul story.

81. Quoted in Bourdeaux, pp. 54-55.

82. Umsiedler interview data.

83. AS 779; AS 794.

84. Lialina, pp. 48-51.

85. Umsiedler interview data.

86. Lialina, p. 51.

87. *BV*, 1/58, p. 29, where Karev claimed 5,400 congregations and 25,000 preachers.

88. Lialina, p. 51.

89. Puzin, quoted in AS 622, p. 5.

90. Some of the terms applied to *Initsiativniki* in the Soviet press (AS 565).

What divides us is not differences of opinion, but distrust of each other.
—*BV*, 6/66, p. 69

There is no openness or trust without suffering. There can be no reconciliation, no peace, no justice in our world unless we are prepared to place ourselves on the line.
—*Philip Potter*
EPS, August 4, 1977

7 The Union Defended, 1963-1969: Congresses

Jacob Zhidkov, president of the AUCECB since 1944, was already old when the *Initsiativniki* challenge came. He had a long illustrious career behind him beginning with youth work before the Revolution. He had led the Evangelical Christian Union till his imprisonment in 1938 and he was the key figure in helping the AUCECB become established in the difficult postwar years. The teamwork with Alexander Karev had worked well. One associate noted that Jacob Zhidkov had been especially endowed with wisdom and Alexander Karev had received an extra measure of love.[1] Yet Zhidkov's last appearance before his union showed him a tragic figure.

At the closing session of the All-Union congress in 1966 Zhidkov left his sickbed to address the delegates. He was thankful, he told the delegates, for one more chance to speak to them. He had begged God to let him live long enough so that once more he could beg the congress members to forgive him for his part in issuing the 1960 statute and letter of instructions. Three weeks later Jacob Zhidkov died, a bad conscience eased.[2] But this sense of wrongdoing had not been readily apparent initially.

Once Aleksei Prokofiev and Gennadi Kriuchkov had personally presented their letter of protest in August 1961, the dissent and subsequent division within local congregations spread rapidly. The Moscow leadership at first acted as if this was an "embarrassment" that one did not talk about. Through the pages of *Bratskii Vestnik* and the speeches of their representatives abroad they tried their best to project an image of normalcy. Just when the state campaign against the churches was at its worst, Russian Baptist visits abroad intensified. The AUCECB leaders even took the trouble to attend provincial Baptist conventions in Canada.[3]

These trips abroad also reflected rapidly expanding official contacts with other national and international religious bodies. In 1958 the AUCECB joined the European Baptist Federation as well as the Christian Peace Conference and also sent its representatives to the Congress of European Churches. After 1960, its representatives began participating more regularly in the executive committee meetings of the Baptist World Alliance. Shortly after the *Orgkomitet* excommunicated the Moscow leadership, Jacob Zhidkov and Alexei Stoian traveled to Paris and officially requested membership in the World Council of Churches. Beginning in 1960, especially after Stoian returned from studies in England, a small coterie of AUCECB-appointed officials began attending an almost innumerable series of international gatherings. The young and unknown Alexei Stoian became one of the most regular AUCECB representatives.[4]

This image of normalcy also extended to the regular reports from local churches. These reports had usually consisted of excerpts from the quarterly reports of senior presbyters, which listed the churches they had visited, the names of presbyters, and often included a brief statement rating the spiritual condition of the congregation and indicating whether it was adhering to Moscow directives. Between 1961 and 1963, these reports gave little indication that a split was taking place and that many congregations had been closed. The careful reader would have noticed that the number of local presbyters who were being replaced without any reason given had increased. Similarly, there were references to several local churches being fused into one or a congregation having succeeded in finding another building after the landlord refused to renew the contract for unknown reasons. Careful readers also noticed that fewer than half of the senior presbyters were reporting regularly. Evidence suggests that those senior presbyters who were most regular in their reporting were most dependent on support from Moscow and that several senior presbyters who seldom reported also had less trouble with splits locally.[5]

Each year the AUCECB sent a New Year's greeting to the churches which offered brief reflections on the past and suggested goals for the future. In 1960 the greeting included the cryptic statement that God's way was often incomprehensible to them but that "All things work for good to them that love Him." The following year, an editorial signed by Jacob Zhidkov was entitled "Our New Year's Tasks." Yet the only task he mentioned was that Christians must raise their voice for peace—a point repeated in four or five additional articles. In 1962, after the split had taken place, the New Year's letter proclaimed as motto Philippians 3:13: "Forgetting the things that are behind and striving forward. . . ." The annual letters to congregations on unity day were slightly more forthcoming in acknowledging that not all was well. In 1960 the letter referred to fissures in the churches and urged all necessary measures to restore unity. The following year the unity letter appealed to the brotherhood "to recognize all our inadequacies and imperfections and . . . forgive each other from a pure heart. . . ." There were also references to "splits in the brotherhood" in the past and present, but, till the report to the congress in October 1963, there had been no official acknowledgment of the existence of the *Initsiativniki*.

Later the AUCECB acknowledged that they had responded to the *Initsiativniki* challenge directly. In November 1961 they had called an expanded meeting of the presidium where an additional nineteen senior presbyters were present to discuss the threat to unity.[6] Following another meeting of the presidium in February 1962, they dispatched a letter to the churches which, according to dissident sources, discouraged local presbyters from signing requests for an All-Union congress.[7] Another letter to the churches dated June 20, 1962, warned about the activities of the *Initsiativniki* as "enemies of the work of the Lord." Yet aside from that initial meeting on August 13, 1961, and possible chance encounters later, there were no formal talks with *Initsiativniki* leaders.

A Congress After All

Instead of dealing with the *Initsiativniki* directly and working out a joint reform program as requested by the *Initsiativniki*, the AUCECB now launched a program for reunification which, step by step, included more and more of the *Initsiativniki* suggestions. The first step was the boldest, because, suddenly in September 1963, local congregations received a letter inviting them to send delegates to a conference in Moscow to be held October 15-17. Soon after the conference opened and the mandate commission could confirm the credentials of the delegates, vice-president A. L. Andreev declared that the conference had the legitimate rights of a congress. During a break delegate tickets were changed—the word "conference" was struck out and replaced by "congress."

The *Orgkomitet* was not present, nor had it received an invitation to attend, but several *Initsiativniki* supporters did attend. The AUCECB printed a forty-eight-page report on the congress which went into extensive detail. The *Orgkomitet* also printed a report on the congress based on the notes taken by a participant and added their own comments. At several points the *Orgkomitet* version includes rather significant data which is helpful for assessing what happened.[8]

The 450 persons attending (compared with forty-seven at the 1944 unity congress) represents a significant improvement in general representation. Two hundred and ten persons were present as official delegates, had been elected by congregations, and represented all oblasts, republics, and regions. I. I. Motorin, credentials or mandate commission chairman, emphasized that the representatives included not only senior presbyters but also presbyters and preachers, including persons from former Pentecostal and Mennonite congregations. An additional forty-five persons had the right to speak but not to vote and the remainder were guests. Not quite half of the delegates (eighty-nine to be exact) represented the Ukraine and an additional fourteen came from Belorussia. The Russian Federation had sixty-six delegates, of whom fourteen came from Eastern and Western Siberia. The remaining delegates were divided as follows: Latvia, six; Estonia, five; Moldavia, five; the Caucasus, seven; and Central Asia, seventeen, of which eight came from Kazakhstan.[9]

In 1969 Karev explained that since detailed statistics had never been given he would also avoid them at that congress. But the reformers in their report quoted Karev as claiming that on July 1, 1963, there were 1,696 registered congregations totaling 175,688 members. This would mean that each delegate represented 840 members or eight congregations. Distribution of delegates by region roughly conforms to the estimated membership distribution, although in Rovno, the oblast in the Western Ukraine with the greatest number of churches, each of the six delegates represented 1,700 members or twenty-seven congregations.[10]

At each congress letters of thanks to the Council for Religious Affairs and even to the head of government were approved, although this was not reported in *Bratskii Vestnik* till 1969. One other fact that has never been acknowledged publicly until 1979 is that representatives of the Council for Religious Affairs attended each congress. Considering this damper on freedom of expression, the relative frankness with which some delegates expressed their feelings is remarkable, but it also makes understandable why many of the printed comments can be dismissed as safe affirmations of the status quo.

The General Secretary Reports

At each of the congresses in 1963, 1966, and 1969, the general secretary Alexander Karev delivered a major report. Its style, comprehensiveness, and length are reminiscent of the reports read by the general secretary at Communist Party congresses. At this first congress, Karev had to compress the data, since he needed to report on activities during the past nineteen years. For most of the conference participants, this was also a first introduction to the AUCECB structure in general.

Karev explained that the three-member presidium usually met several times a week and that AUCECB members I. I. Motorin and A. N. Karpov, who were resident in Moscow, as well as the chairman of the revision commission, A. I. Mitskevich, usually took part in these meetings. Major questions were considered at expanded sessions of the presidium and relevant persons were invited to participate. Most presidium meetings held recently had focused on relationships with the Pentecostals, although there had also been meetings of the AUCECB council to hear annual, or sometimes biannual, reports on activities. It was also apparent that the members of the AUCECB had almost all been co-opted by the council itself, and those few who could claim to have been elected in 1944 had gained or lost in influence without a congress having confirmed this. Karev also reported that there were now forty-two senior presbyters with five assistants, and listed them.[11] Informed listeners may have remembered that at the time of the fortieth jubilee in 1957, there had been fifty-three senior presbyters, which meant there had been a loss of 20 percent.[12] In addition, the 1963 lists included other new faces because of the numerous shifts in senior presbyters that had taken place during the turmoils of the past five years.

Karev also announced that the central office was divided into six departments: (1) correspondence with congregations, (2) foreign relations, (3) typing department, (4) editorial office of *Bratskii Vestnik*, (5) bookkeeping, and (6) administration. Most of these departments had been functioning since the beginning, although, until 1960, foreign relations had been Karev's personal responsibility. In 1963 there were sixteen employees in the office.

A major section of his report then listed the achievements of recent years. One could evaluate these in one of three ways, he said. One could say either that they had done very much, or that they had done very little, or that they had done what was possible to do. Karev left it to the delegates to make their own evaluation but asserted that the presidium supported the third alternative, namely that they claimed to have done what had been possible.

What had they achieved? They had printed 10,000 copies of the Bible in 1957 and 15,000 copies of the songbook, but a new edition of the Bible was not yet possible. The journal *Bratskii Vestnik* had appeared regularly with a few exceptions; it emphasized peace, theological, and spiritual articles for ministers and local church news to foster relationships between churches. They had started to collect data for a thorough history of the union, but Karev complained that there was no qualified historian to write it, a lament he and his successor have regularly repeated. But without question, the major emphasis in his report was on foreign relations. Karev did list the trips that Moscow leaders had made to various regions of the country but he was forced to apologize, that, because of the heavy work pressure in Moscow, including the receiving of 4,958 foreign guests between 1957 and 1963, as well as the numerous trips abroad, the presidium members were prevented from taking sufficient time to visit congregations. He promised to try harder, but it turned out to be a promise that had to be repeated regularly. This listing of achievements also included the statement that seven of their young men had studied abroad and five of them were now working full time for the AUCECB.[13]

The thrust of this heavy attention to foreign relations seemed clear. Local critics should realize that fellow Baptists in Europe and around the world respected the AUCECB leaders and considered them important. They were no longer an insignificant sect but were now being taken seriously as members of the European Conference of Churches, the World Council of Churches, and other international organizations. Foreign representatives had also taken the effort to visit them. This was also a message to the governmental officials to remind them that the number of important friends of the Baptists abroad had increased. This discomfort and feeling of inferiority about being a minority group helps account for their readiness to participate in Soviet ecumenical peace delegations.

This congress set the pattern for subsequent ones where the general secretary's report was always followed by a financial report and a statement from the revision or auditing commission. The official account is almost absurd, since treasurer Ilia G. Ivanov forgot to mention any figures. His published report merely noted that in the early years there had been financial difficulties but the congregations had then begun to send in their contributions regularly. From these funds senior presbyters were paid regularly. Ivanov also acknowledged that in recent years money for travel abroad and for hosting foreign guests had become a significant item in the budget.[14] The remainder of his report involved a didactic explanation about their banking procedures, and he announced that the state financial organs checked the books twice a year in order to determine how much tax was to be collected. According to the reformers' report, Ivanov had also listed total annual income from 1956 to 1963 and had provided a rough breakdown of 1962 expenses.[15] This was not a very promising report because it showed that, from an annual income of 280,000 rubles in 1956, income had declined steadily, so that for 1963 they were anticipating an income of only 124,000 rubles. This reveals a loss of confidence in the leadership and was a significant factor for calling the congress.

The Unity Issue

Everyone knew that the major issue at the congress was unity. What would Karev say to that question? The reformers were disappointed by the brevity of the report and more still by the limited time available to discuss this major question.[16]

Karev's manner of approaching the subject was an obvious attempt to minimize the significance of the *Initsiativniki* challenge. The first half of this section contained complaints about older workers who had recently returned to active church work (that is, they were released from prison) and had immediately begun fostering a spirit of separatism. But the so-called "pure Baptists" and the "Evangelical Christian perfectionists" had both had little success. The bulk of the delegates' discussion (that which was quoted in *Bratskii Vestnik*) focused on the confessions and reconciliations of several persons who had supported the "pure Baptist" movement.[17]

At the end of this paragraph of his report, Karev merely stated that "a new, stronger attempt to divide our brotherhood was undertaken by the so-called initiative group, beginning in August 1961. The reasons for this attempt are known to all our brotherhood and we will not take time to go into detail."[18] It seemed Karev planned to restrict the discussion and to dismiss the *Initsiativniki* as narrow fanatics, just like the "pure Baptists." A second and longer section of Karev's report on unity focused on relations with Pentecostals. Karev's concluding remarks did, however, set a more conciliatory tone. In order to help those who had left their ranks to return, he stated, they were submitting a thorough revision of the 1960 statute, which he hoped would be acceptable to all congregations.[19]

There was actually little time available for a thorough airing of views among delegates on this question. Senior presbyter A. L. Andreev set a precedent later followed by his successors by supplementing the general secretary's report with a description of life in the Ukraine. He was followed by Belorussia senior presbyter K. S. Veliseichik, who gave details about church life under his jurisdiction. Andreev was more blunt than Karev had been and claimed that the *Initsiativniki* movement was centered primarily in Donetsk, Kharkov, and Lugansk (Voroshilovgrad) oblasts. At first many believers saw nothing wrong or bad in the *Initsiativniki* movement, but then many began to understand "that this sanctification to which they were appealing, in itself constitutes a division of the church and is therefore a matter not pleasing to the Lord."[20] Andreev repeated this interpretation by describing the *Initsiativniki* work as "dangerous" because it led to division. If reformers repeatedly charged that unity seemed more important to the Moscow leadership than the purity of the gospel, the oft-repeated official claim that the reformers were simply intent on fostering dissension seems to be an admission that the unity concern was supreme.

In any case, the published discussion concluded with a surprising statement from an unknown German Mennonite representative from Karaganda (Kazakhstan) who asked the AUCECB to accept the Mennonites into membership.[21] The relatively successful relationship to the Mennonite Brethren and the more problematic ties with the Pentecostals regularly received attention at the congresses and helped to shift some of the focus away from the *Initsiativniki* issue.

There were other speakers listed in the official report and the contents of some of these speeches appear in the reformers' version of the congress. AUCECB vice-president and senior presbyter for the Baltic, N. A. Levindanto apparently spoke much more forthrightly than the few lines in *Bratskii Vestnik* indicate. After giving a statistical summary for his region, he declared that he did not consider himself as excommunicated by the *Orgkomitet* because only the local church is entitled to excommunicate. Because the statement which the *Orgkomitet* had sent to the congress was full of pride and insults, the presidium had decided not to read the declaration to the congress. Levindanto added that they agreed with some of the excellent suggestions of the *Orgkomitet* but that these activities had not been permitted earlier. According to Levindanto, the AUCECB operating principle was quite simple: "If we had no sugar, we would drink tea without sugar. But now sugar has appeared, so we will now drink tea with sugar." Levindanto rather favored picturesque language and later explained that the school which they had attended had helped them wise up. For example, "If you cannot go forward, then you can go sideways."[22]

Levindanto, however, was followed by more independent-minded speakers from Latvia and Estonia, who indicated that even AUCECB supporters were not prepared to accept the claim that the leaders had done all that was possible. Latvian presbyter P. K. Egle declared flatly that the situation in Latvia was not satisfactory because they were losing members, and he urged that younger leaders should be brought into the work. They would also like the freedom for their preachers to visit neighboring congregations, especially during holidays. Egle even took the liberty to express a personal assessment of Karev's leadership. Karev, he felt, was a good orator and well suited to be presbyter of a large congregation, but not to be general secretary of the union. He continued the rather sharp needling by adding that the Latvians were a thrifty people, and they felt that the leaders' salaries were rather high. In fact, the Latvians sometimes thought that the union leadership was afraid of suffering and confrontation, and it also seemed to them that the leaders were hanging onto their positions a long time.[23]

Egle was the highly respected historian for the Latvians and would soon be appointed senior presbyter.[24] His sharp remarks, expressed in a soft-spoken manner through a translator, had to be taken seriously. He concluded his speech by asserting that the Latvians had no clear opinion about the *Orgkomitet* because the information was contradictory, but they did know that these men were people of honor. Would it not be necessary, he asked, to elect some of the *Orgkomitet* spokesmen into the new AUCECB presidium? Karev replied briefly by affirming that they were ready to establish contacts with the *Orgkomitet* but not at this conference.

A Revised Statute

It may have sounded as if the *Orgkomitet* was insignificant and that there had been no need to establish contact with the reformers till now, but when N. A. Levindanto presented the revised statutes, it was evident that the AUCECB had taken a very major step forward in meeting the reformers' demands. Levindanto acknowledged that they had received very thorough and excellent suggestions for revising the statutes. He then declared that, "considering all this and the possibilities that are now available," the AUCECB wished to present a new revision for approval.[25] In contrast to the next congress, the atmosphere was still so restrained and the time so limited that Levindanto simply read the statute paragraph by paragraph, and it was accepted without any significant changes.

Perhaps church conventions seem dull to the average person, and often the dullest moments involve the haggling between parliamentarians when a new constitution is to be accepted. But at the AUCECB congress in 1963, this was the electric moment. Even if no discussion was permitted, members had submitted proposed changes in written form, and it soon became apparent that the new constitution contained major concessions. Michael Bourdeaux, in a thorough study of this subject, demonstrated the amazing coincidence between the new changes and those which had been proposed by Prokofiev and Kriuchkov.[26] The average delegate lacked the ability to make a close comparison, but cannot have missed the major thrust of the changes.

The most important change was a shift from a presbyterial or even episcopal form of church polity to a congregational polity. This was achieved simply by replacing the All-Union Council with the All-Union Congress as the supreme organ for ECB churches. From now on, the statute granted the congress decision-making powers and reduced the council to a body that executed the decisions of the congress or, when making its own decisions during the interval between congresses, basing its decisions on congress guidelines. It is not unfair to say that all the rest of the changes concern details. For the first time since 1944, this union of free churches in the Soviet Union had a free church structure. It meant a major step against the centralism still being fostered by Soviet policy on religion.

Many other changes clearly demonstrated how little the 1960 statute had reflected the spirit of the church. For example, the 1960 statute spoke of a "principle of worship," whereby senior presbyters no longer participated in church services but simply acted as observers and judges to make sure the rules were being observed. The 1963 statute, in contrast, stressed that both council and senior presbyter have responsibilities as spiritual leaders, as pastors, not simply as administrators. No longer did the statute restrict membership to registered congregations. By eliminating the two-to-three-year probation period for baptism and by eliminating a stipulation that choir members must be church members, several major restrictions on the involvement of young people in the church had been lifted.

One further half step toward greater democratization was the assertion that senior presbyters must meet with congregational approval, although the latter had no voice in their appointment. A small recognition of the traditional Baptist claim to local church autonomy was the opening statement which now affirmed that this was a voluntary association of *churches* instead of a union of *believers* as had been affirmed earlier.[27]

Elections Bring No Change

Karev claimed that with this new constitution, the former causes for the split had been removed. The wording of the constitution was obviously promising. What remained to be seen was whether this all-powerful council and its senior presbyters would abide by the new rules and whether the state authorities would permit the constitution to function. One doubtful sign was the election that followed.

Former members and candidates left the room, while their candidacies were discussed and a vote taken. The new council had only one new name, that of I. Ia. Tatarchenko, an old Baptist, who now assumed the seat that had been vacant since Michael Orlov's death in 1961.[28] There were, however, also five candidate members, who usually attended council sessions, and some of these could be expected to replace some of the old men who might soon die.[29] The revision commission also remained unchanged.[30] This reelection of the old guard, considering the heavy criticism leveled against it, did not look very promising. In his closing address, General Secretary Karev acknowledged that they needed younger leaders, then went on to argue for the status quo by using the imagery of a ship being piloted carefully into harbor: "We need brothers with white hairs on their heads, who can calmly guide our brotherhood through the many hidden reefs."[31]

This first congress of 1963 turned out to be only the beginning of the concessions that the Soviet state had to permit and which the AUCECB leadership had to offer if it was to defend the unity successfully. The first congress was carefully stage-managed (and that aspect has never disappeared entirely), but it soon became evident that the existence of an alternative *Orgkomitet* meant that local churches and believers must now be wooed rather than dictated to. By the middle of 1964, the AUCECB presidium was already reporting in detail on its activities. Representatives had made eight major visits to congregations, and an additional twenty-seven persons had visited the headquarters office on various questions.

For the first time in many years, senior presbyter appointments were announced and one could tell that two of them involved a shake-up, whereas others involved new appointments in oblasts where the duties had for a while been transferred to the senior presbyter of a nearby province.[32] Even more important was a special expanded session of the AUCECB plenum, meeting in September 1964, which devoted major time to the unity question. Specially invited participants included former *Initsiativniki* supporters or waverers who now confirmed that their return to the AUCECB would be permanent. One young preacher who had supported the *Orgkomitet*, V. F. Vasilenko, was appointed senior presbyter for Vinnitsa Oblast.[33]

The Perfect Congress—1966

Even though the Moscow leaders constantly proclaimed that by replacing the 1960 statute, the reasons for the split had disappeared, support for the *Orgkomitet* continued to grow. Growth peaked in 1966 and is the best confirmation of the fact that the additional concessions offered at the 1966 congress persuaded so many to return to the old union.[34]

One participant in later years remembered this as the perfect congress because it was the most democratic and the most open of the three he attended. As usual, even before the regional conferences met to discuss the congress agenda and to elect the delegates, secret police agents knocked on the doors of influential believers and discussed the candidacy of delegates with them. In spite of the strong pressure to elect "safe" delegates, many regional conferences dared elect enough outspoken persons to ensure that congregational complaints would be heard in faraway Moscow. The 8,127 persons participating in sixty-four such regional conferences elected 478 delegates with full voting rights and an additional 233 delegates who had the right to address the assembly though not to vote. An additional 315 guests produced a total assembly of 1,026, which was more than twice the size of the 450 who gathered in 1963. Regrettably, a list of delegates was not published this time, making it impossible to determine whether it was sufficiently representative geographically.[35]

The eighty-one-year-old President Zhidkov gave a brief welcome and reappeared again for a short sad farewell speech, but this marked the end of his leadership. Three weeks later, he died. Even more so than in 1963, this was Alexander Karev's congress, which he again dominated with his major report, his preaching and spirit. Most of the morning and afternoon was spent listening to his report.

Listening to the report, delegates sensed the broad spiritual concerns Karev communicated. First he spoke about the general makeup of the denomination and stressed that it was both a multinational and a multidenominational union. Another special characteristic was that they were unacquainted with theological discussion and had remained unexposed to modernism. In a brief reference to statistics, he pointed out that the frequently used figure of 500,000 was too high—an estimated 250,000 baptized believers was closer to the truth. He underlined the fact that their statistics were only estimates. He noted that for a long time not all congregations were on their list and that they were still discovering groups of believers about whom they had had no information so far.

Karev then turned to a discussion of the spiritual condition of the churches. The major spiritual illness in the churches was discord among believers. Karev identified seven causes for discord. There was disorder in the churches because believers were dissatisfied. Some argued over secondary questions. Others showed insufficient respect for each other and for the work. Too many demonstrated a love of power. There was conflict because some wanted to baptize new believers immediately the way Philip baptized the eunuch, while others argued for a probation period. Some churches also practiced re-baptism. Additional problem questions were excommunication procedures, with some churches much too hasty in excommunicating. Still another unsolved problem concerned the marriage and divorce of persons who had subsequently become believers.

The two major changes that Karev emphasized in his report dealt directly with his concern for the spiritual condition of the church. The congress debated the brief confession of faith written by I. V. Kargel in 1913, although Karev stressed that this would be provisional until a more detailed confession of faith could be worked out. The second major proposal involved new changes in the AUCECB statute. Karev emphasized that these changes focused primarily on trying to lighten the work of the senior presbyter, to make it more productive and more democratic.

AUCECB foreign relations continued to be a vital activity but at this congress Karev emphasized the goals of this foreign activity rather than trying to show that the AUCECB was widely respected. Karev claimed that the great majority of Christian churches abroad had departed from the ideals and structure of early Christianity and declared that "our Evangelical-Baptist church represents the only example of this apostolic Christianity in the entire world."[36] That meant, therefore, that the AUCECB representatives "must be fulfilments of the ideals of this apostolic Christianity, and their mission must be to witness about the Christianity of apostolic days which has been forgotten in the West."[37] In defense of their involvement with the ecumenical movement, Karev emphasized that the task of the Christian was to be light and salt in the world, including among other Christians.

Initsiativniki Concerns Thoroughly Discussed

Many, of course, came to hear what Karev would say about the Initsiativniki. Karev once again sought to balance his remarks with comments about unity with Pentecostals and with Mennonites. He spoke in particularly friendly fashion about the Pentecostals, whose spiritual ancestors in the second century of Christianity had "saved Christianity from spiritual death and gnosticism."[38] His remarks about the *Initsiativniki* were much more specific, and this, no doubt, helped ensure that the subsequent discussion was much more open. In addition, Riga presbyter A. P. Vasks read a theological paper on unity and S. P. Fadiukhin, recently appointed assistant general secretary, read the official unity report, which dealt with the *Initsiativniki* at length.

Karev stated very generally that they had sent repeated appeals to the CCECB to settle all misunderstandings but the only reply received was increased insults. Karev characterized the many messages, fraternal leaflets, and other documents as instilled with arrogance and self-glorification. This was somewhat unfair because those insults and sharply worded statements were written by persons desperately struggling for survival. State pressure had been resumed in 1966 until finally the sense of outrage was so strong that more than 400 persons took part in a sit-in demonstration at the Kremlin in May 1966. The state responded with massive arrests, and, by the time the congress was held, almost all of the CCECB leadership was in custody. The two leaders, Kriuchkov and Vins, went on trial shortly after this.[39]

Both the official speeches and the discussion period included a thorough airing of the causes for the split. These revealed a considerable difference of opinion among delegates and also among the different leaders. In his speech, S. P. Fadiukhin focused on several major charges of the CCECB which he tried to refute. Fadiukhin claimed that the *Initsiativniki* had argued that in the late twenties the church lost the blessing of the Lord when it began to subordinate itself to human directives. Fadiukhin distorted the chronology of the argument to make the *Initsiativniki* say that the heroes of the *early* twenties had been following purely human directives.[40] Similarly he tried to brand *Initsiativniki* with opportunism by arguing that one day they were against registration and the next they were for it.[41] Finally he dismissed the charge that the AUCECB was conducting work destructive to the ECB churches. But he did acknowledge that earlier it had been possible to appoint senior presbyters without the agreement of churches and that senior presbyters and presbyters who were unworthy had been kept in office. In fact, all Fadiukhin could promise was that with the combined strength of the children of God and the Lord's help these would be eliminated in the future.[42]

At this session, two CCECB spokesmen, G. I. Maiboroda and E. T. Kovalenko were permitted to read a formal statement from the CCECB. This was a stiff restatement of the charges, focusing on the anti-evangelical documents. Both then explained that they were authorized to restrict themselves to reading the statement and therefore rejected a dialogue. Thus the two official sides exchanged accusations, one complaining about anti-evangelical documents and the other about arrogance and pride.

Quite a few of those taking part in the discussion, however, focused the attention on another issue which they thought was more serious. It was the senior presbyters who should ask for forgiveness for splitting the church with their high-handed administrative actions, said several speakers. "These presbyters were not senior presbyters, but strict presbyters.... As long as such presbyters will not be removed, we cannot be reunited."[43] The highly respected N. I. Vysotski from Odessa also observed that some AUCECB supporters were "more Catholic than the pope in Rome because they are ready to call all those who split away servants of the devil, children of Satan and other objectionable names."[44]

At this congress Karev in particular insisted that their actions in 1960 did not deserve to be regarded as a deathly sin because they had submitted to laws which did not forbid worship services and preaching. He was still committed to the principle that one may not ignore the laws, for that only leads to a dead end.[45] A congress resolution gave the AUCECB leadership strong endorsement by formally rejecting the legitimacy of the excommunications announced by the *Orgkomitet*.[46] Other pro-AUCECB spokesmen, however, emphasized that the work of the *Orgkomitet* had been completed with the adoption of the new statute in 1963.[47] That represented an affirmation of the necessity of the *Orgkomitet's* work during those first three years.

An obvious problem within AUCECB ranks was the disagreement on the proper attitude to take toward the dissidents. Some of S. P. Fadiukhin's remarks were unfair misrepresentations of the CCECB, although he, too, did affirm that the AUCECB should respond with love. Alexander Karev had stated openly that "we pray for our suffering brothers and sisters in the Council of Churches ... and hope that the organs of power will show humanity and lenience to those who are at present on trial."[48] After the two *Initsiativniki* spokesmen had finished reading their statement, senior presbyter D. D. Shapovalov called to them: "We are your brothers. We pray for you, your tears are our tears, we suffer about your arrogance. Stop this! Come back to our prayer houses and together we will work and praise the Lord."[49] The Latvian senior presbyter P. K. Egle, who had already spoken his mind freely in 1963, also affirmed that in spite of the mistakes they had made, "they remain our brothers and they need help in finding the right way, not the way of edicts and orders, but of true love and cooperation."[50]

In moving the adoption of Karev's report, A. I. Mitskevich declared that "we fully recognize our mistakes. . . . I think, brothers and sisters, that you also will forgive us all our mistakes." The assembly replied: "We forgive and will not remember."[51] Since individual delegates later remembered that Karev and Mitskevich had personally asked for forgiveness, this may have been the moment they meant. President Zhidkov made his own moving apology at the end of the congress. It was sufficient for most, although others felt that other key individuals in the leadership had refused to repent. But the whole issue had been discussed about as thoroughly as one could expect and many more went home convinced the AUCECB was sincerely striving for unity. Unfortunately, during all these painful exchanges at the congress, no one could afford to accuse the chief culprit, the state with its *administrirovanie*.

A New Free Church Statute

Maybe the *Initsiativniki* would remain unconvinced but this congress finally completed the positive reformation of the AUCECB into a growth-oriented, forward-looking free church union. The constitutional revisions of 1966 were bolder and more thoroughgoing than those of 1963. The new constitution demonstrated that congress delegates had successfully exerted their pressure and the cautious Moscow leadership could only retreat gracefully and with secret pleasure.

A. I. Mitskevich, who introduced the revised statutes, pointed out that the new changes underlined the autonomy of the local church.[52] Karev had already emphasized that the major changes focused on democratizing the leadership so that the senior presbyter would now be elected and would also receive a council to assist him. There were two other, much more fundamental and daring changes, but perhaps the leaders thought that unnecessary publicity might antagonize the state. Whereas the 1963 statute had reaffirmed the spiritual role of the leaders, the 1966 changes restored biblicism in general. In a fashion similar to the CCECB's statute, major sections and subclauses were buttressed with biblical texts. Earlier the statute had stated that Holy Scripture was the basis of their confession of faith. To this they now added that it was also the basis for the life and activities of the union, albeit at one vital point concerning obedience to state laws, the quietist approach was emphasized by citing Romans 13.

As a working church statute, another very significant change was the introduction of clauses spelling out what were the tasks and goals of the union, of the senior presbyters, and of the member churches. The new statute stated that the union had the task of putting into effect the principles and confession of faith, of fostering unity, and of maintaining purity of doctrine. Local congregations had as their primary goals preaching the gospel, teaching believers in holy living, and strengthening love and unity.

Subtle word changes and additions reveal that major progress had been made in restricting state interference in internal church life. The brief declaration in paragraph 13 that head office workers must be church members must be seen as an attempt to oust the state-appointed watchdogs. The introduction of open voting could help make delegates more honest before their peers—how they voted secretly was known to the authorities anyway. The statute also reflected an apparent increase in the legal rights of the church, since central union, senior presbyter, and local congregation were all entitled to their own seal and stamp which usually signifies the right of juridical personhood.[53]

Leadership Changes

Would the 1966 congress also be as radical in electing new leadership? First of all, council membership was expanded from ten persons to twenty-five persons.[54] Instead of five candidate members, eight were elected.[55] Only five of these thirty-three persons were reelected from the previous council, although two more who had been candidate members in 1963 now attained full membership. Seven council members represented the Ukraine, two of them also representing Pentecostals.[56] If one adds Mitskevich and Timchenko as former Ukrainians, then the Ukrainians represented one third of the council, although their membership was more than 50 percent of the total. The Russian Federation was represented by five persons, and there were individual representatives for Central Asia, the Caucasus, Belorussia, but surprisingly, none from Moldavia. For the first time, a Mennonite representative joined the council while another was elected a candidate member.[57] Latvia and Estonia each had one representative and the young Michael Zhidkov, who had been elected their spokesman in Moscow, was also elected to the council.

The council, however, met irregularly, so that practical power was in the hands of the ten-member presidium, which met monthly.[58] Half of these were the old guard and included all of the former presidium members who would now need to be persuaded to make some changes in their management style. The new president, Ilia G. Ivanov, had been usually influential since 1945. He was not likely to start up a new path. In fact, the four major executive positions of chairman, general secretary, assistant general secretary, and treasurer were all held by men whom the reformers held responsible for the 1960 statute and letter of instructions. But the other five members were all untainted by that event. S. T. Timchenko and N. N. Mel'nikov replaced the deceased Baptist leader, N. A. Levindanto, and the Evangelical Christian, A. L. Andreev respectively. Mel'nikov must be regarded as part of the old guard since he had functioned as virtual head of the Ukraine under the aged Andreev since 1956. Sergei T. Timchenko (1902-1971), on the other hand, provided the image of wisdom and age. He could claim distant links to the prewar Baptist leadership, but had not, since his move to Moscow in 1952, played any leadership role till this moment.[59]

The other three presidium members deserve an extra comment. S. P. Fadiukhin was present at this congress in his capacity as assistant general secretary. He was a staunch Baptist, graduate of the Bible school in Leningrad in the twenties, and had reappeared in the mid-fifties. He was advancing rapidly, and it was clear that his theological skills were needed for the *Bratskii Vestnik* journal. Perhaps he was expected to replace the aged Karev, but within a year he had been transferred to take over the large Leningrad parish following the sudden death of its young presbyter. A. N. Kiriukhantsev and Michael Zhidkov were among the first students to study in England. They became full-time AUCECB workers on their return. Since 1960 Kiriukhantsev had replaced Michael Orlov as leader in Leningrad. Michael Zhidkov had recently been elected to replace the deceased N. A. Levindanto as spokesman for the Baltic but retained his Moscow residence and in 1966 also became the leading minister in the Moscow church. The two men were forty and thirty-eight years of age respectively. Zhidkov's rapid rise was only one illustration of a nepotism that was becoming apparent. Both young men were, however, highly gifted, trained, but also acceptable to the authorities.

The congress results showed significant changes for the better and confirmed that reform would be gradual—there would be no outright confrontation with the state. During the election only the longtime senior presbyter for the Far East, E. N. Raevskii, was excluded from the council, although the heavily criticized K. S. Veliseichik barely managed to retain a council seat. In an apparent gesture to the reformers, V. F. Vasilenko, who had formerly supported the *Orgkomitet*, was elected to the council.

The Regular Congress, 1969

The 1969 congress marks the end of the AUCECB defense against the reformers' challenge. After this the task of winning back the dissenters became primarily a local task, and the hope for the reunification with the CCECB was abandoned, even though leaders continued to say that reunification should happen. Only a week earlier CCECB supporters had met in a legally approved all-Union congress in Tula. Here they heard reports, elected members, and sent a letter to Kosygin requesting permission for their leadership to devote full time to the work as was true of the AUCECB leadership. Four meetings between representatives of the two bodies had been held that year. Many saw this as an optimistic sign, but within a few months of the congress, these efforts were confirmed as fruitless.

The AUCECB congress met December 9-11 with 475 delegates and 269 guests. Mandate commission chairman Motorin reported that these delegates had been elected at sixty-three regional conferences and that each delegate represented 500 members.[60]

The atmosphere was more open than previously—for the first time, a Baptist representative from the West attended.[61] It was Karev's last congress, and he betrayed some irritation that it was still necessary to discuss what had happened in 1960. Alexander Karev was suffering from cancer and would die two years later. It was apparent that there would be a struggle for the succession. In this atmosphere, it was the middle generation, people like A. I. Mitskevich and N. N. Mel'nikov, who played the dominant role.

Karev had his usual lengthy report[62] and he also read a major controversial paper on the Christian and his motherland.[63] There was more caution in his speech. Again he stressed that the work must proceed in observance of the laws. "Throughout our entire history," he said, "we never forgot that the condition for blessing is 'quietness and confidence' (Is. 30:15), and when we did not forget this, the work of the Lord always went forward with blessing for us."[64] *Initsiativniki* criticism that they still maintained "ties with the world" were unfair because such "ties with the world by no means contradict the Word of God. Without such ties with the world, we would not have the present congress, would not print our Bibles and hymnbooks, would not print our dear *Bratskii Vestnik*, and so on."[65]

Karev focused on two major problems: unity and leadership. He summarized the abortive reconciliation talks briefly but left most of the discussion on the CCECB to others. The second problem was that too many of the senior presbyters, presbyters, deacons, and preachers were old, very poorly educated and not sufficiently competent. There was need for teaching, and he was proud to report that a correspondence course with 100 students had been introduced the previous year. In 1968 the council had also dealt with the problem of electing presbyters whose children were un-believers and had reached a compromise solution.[66] Above all, Karev em-phasized that "it is necessary for us to rejuvenate the corps of our church workers. It is important for us to have workers with higher cultural and spiritual education, and especially with greater capability."[67]

Karev concluded with a moving summary that also served to sum-marize his own career:

> We had triumphs, and there were defeats; we were strong, and we were weak; we had joys, and we had sorrows; there were roses on our path, and also thorns; we strove to work, expecting to rest only in heaven.[68]

With one-and-one-half days of discussion on the unity question, this subject was covered more thoroughly than heretofore. There were two spe-cial speeches on unity by Vice-President S. T. Timchenko and Leningrad presbyter S. P. Fadiukhin, as well as a report on the work of the unity com-mission established at the 1966 congress.[69]

The major speeches on unity complained about *Initsiativniki* pride, especially their insistence on one-sided repentance by the AUCECB and denounced the latest appeal of the Council of Prisoners' Relatives to all Christians in the world, which opened with the statement that "the condi-tion of the church is worsening."[70] Such false data, Timchenko claimed, was being used by persons like Richard Wurmbrand in order to brand AUCECB leaders as liars.

Discussion participants shared illuminating information, but the most dramatic aspect of the discussion was the seven CCECB supporters who confessed their mistakes and received public forgiveness and acceptance.[71] The most important of these was G. I. Maiboroda, one of the two who had read the CCECB statement to the previous congress. The unity commission claimed that 3,500 had returned during the past three years and Timchenko claimed that a total of 10,000 had returned since 1963.[72]

This time the revisions of the constitution were minor, yet they revealed the resoluteness of the delegates over against the cautious leadership. An attempt to restrict the participation of young people in choirs failed. The revision commission was expanded to five members, and they were given the added task of auditing the financial records of the senior presbyters as had been suggested by the delegates. Another slight addition extended the interval between congresses to five years, which would have the effect of strengthening the power of the council.

More New Faces Elected

The leaders were worried what would happen in the elections. There was an intense power struggle because some of the old leaders were not ready to make room for new ones while there were nonchurch pressures to keep certain individuals in office. Many of the candidate members elected in 1966 had been office staff from Moscow, whose loyalties were distrusted, and this time their reelection proved impossible. Those that *were* elected naturally did not get equal support, but in spite of the external pressures, the negative votes registered against some of the well-established leaders was striking. I. I. Motorin, the longtime treasurer, whose visits in the constituency had often resulted in leadership shake-ups locally, received 108 negative votes. He did, however, retain his seat on the council, but senior presbyter K. S. Veliseichik of Belorussia, who received 102 negative votes, lost his seat. Several others, such as S. P. Fadiukhin and N. N. Mel'nikov, had many critics.[73]

No one was ousted from the presidium, but three new faces appeared. S. P. Fadiukhin replaced the deceased A. N. Kiriukhantsev as the Leningrad representative and the presidium was increased to eleven members in order to make room for a Pentecostal representative, P. K. Shatrov, and for a Moscow insider, A. M. Bychkov. The latter also emerged, to the surprise of many, as one of the vice-presidents. The number of vice-presidents was increased to three. Even greater changes followed two years later when Karev and Timchenko died. Alexei M. Bychkov became the new general secretary with Michael Zhidkov and Andrei E. Klimenko promoted to vice-presidents.

The council itself also experienced a gradual change. Nine of the twenty-five elected were new.[74] Four members from the previous council had died, and these were replaced. Five others lost their seats, so that Belorussia had no representation on the council. The ousted representative for Central Asia was replaced by his three successors, one as full member, another as candidate, and a third on the revision commission.[75] E. N. Raevskii, the much-criticized senior presbyter for Eastern Siberia and the Far East, at least made it as candidate member, since, after all, contact had to be maintained with that vast region. Il'ia Orlov, approved to full council membership in March 1969, lost his seat.

After three congresses, sufficient changes had been achieved in the governing structure and the statute in order to persuade the majority of the evangelicals to support the union. The AUCECB had become more congregational. Most supporters accepted that further change must come gradually. For such change to continue to move in the right direction, the quality of leadership was vital. After everything had been discussed and voted on, tangible results would be heavily dependent on individual leaders at all levels. Without question, the least desired hot spot was the office of senior presbyter.

The Life of a Senior Presbyter

What did a day in the life of a senior presbyter look like? It included going to the local plenipotentiary for the Council for Religious Affairs to negotiate permission for a baptismal service in one of the churches, and for permission to baptize all those persons on the list he had submitted months previously. Then he had to take the bus to another building to clarify a complaint about a fire safety hazard in another church. When he returned home, the presbyter from a nearby town was waiting to pour out his troubles to him. Once that man had been comforted, he sat down to plan the agenda for the next presbyter conference and also wrote a half-dozen letters to churches farther away, announcing that he was coming to visit and asking them to prepare for the ordination service. Before completing this, he had to run about town again in order to reserve hotels, restaurants, and vehicles for the next foreign delegation that was coming to visit. During all this activity, part of his subconcious was groping for an appropriate text and a few ideas for the sermon he was to preach that night. And then after the two-hour service there would be the usual counseling and committee meetings.

The senior presbyter, as the vital link between the churches and the union, and between the churches and the state, fulfilled a multiplicity of roles. He was called upon to be a unifier and troubleshooter. Senior presbyter Ivan S. Gnida complained that the senior presbyter was constantly being called on to make emergency trips to put out fires, and he wished there might be more fire prevention.[76] This latter role, that of a teacher and pastor to presbyters, was also his task. Fortunately the presbyter conferences and councils introduced in 1966 provided significant help in this area.

As chief regional negotiator with the state, the senior presbyter bore the brunt of the state's unfriendly attitude toward religion. This role also involved many temptations. If he would cooperate with the authorities, they would treat him better. Senior presbyters who started off straight gradually became bent, so claimed one presbyter. But even the resolute ones faced constant temptation. For example, it might happen that a senior presbyter and a local presbyter were close friends, cooperated and trusted each other. The presbyter was capable and his church grew. His zealous young people decided to share their successful Christmas program with the church in a nearby city. The next morning the state official for religious affairs complained to the senior presbyter about this legal violation. A few weeks later, the presbyter permitted a visitor to preach without permission, and once again the senior presbyter had to listen to abuse from the state official. Both men understood each other, and both were trying to obtain as much freedom as possible for the church, but after a while the senior presbyter realized that he had become irritable toward his dear friend because, inadvertently, that man's church had become a burden to the senior presbyter.

It was a job filled with responsibility, little praise, and lots of criticism. In fact, the senior presbyter knew he was doing his job correctly if there was moderate criticism from the churches, from Moscow, and from the state officials. Woe to him if one of those three should increase its criticisms. And then there was the potential criticism from his own family. Travel conditions in the Soviet Union are strenuous at best, and he was forced to be on the road constantly. That was not the life for a family man, but also not for an old widower.

Gradually the beneficial results of the reorganized senior presbyter system became apparent. Conferences of presbyters for each oblast soon became annual events. In the pre-congress sessions, the senior presbyter now presented his report before persons who knew how to evaluate it. Usually his work was affirmed, but if there were problems, his superiors from Moscow often attended to help sort things out. Gradually it became possible to force unacceptable persons into early retirement or to dismiss them. Younger and more acceptable men were now elected rather than appointed. State officials and the Moscow leadership often exerted heavy pressure for their candidate, however, so that the successful election of a man of integrity was never automatic. That need not mean that the candidate supported by Moscow lacked integrity. There were also denominational considerations and educational qualifications that might seem less important to local presbyters.

AUCECB Defense Succeeds

After the 1969 congress it finally became clear that the AUCECB had defended its union successfully. But it was also clear that an attempt to return to the *status quo ante* would encounter still more opposition from congress delegates who were gradually becoming accustomed to meeting in congress regularly. Some of the Moscow leadership had repented and been forgiven; at least, an increasing number of delegates felt that issue had been dealt with and belonged to the past. Other Moscow leaders had died while the new leadership after 1969 had attained its authority after the split.

State interference remained a problem; survival remained the major concern; but there were some signals pointing toward normalization. During the 1970s the international world awakened to the fact that a major split had taken place. Although none of the Western church organizations abandoned their support for the AUCECB, a growing number were searching for ways to support the *Initsiativniki* as well.

The dawning of 1970 also marked a watershed for the CCECB. Reconciliation talks had failed. They had held their one and only legal congress and had organized themselves for a wide-ranging sphere of activities. Most of their leaders would soon be behind bars again or hiding from the authorities. Would their full and total obedience to God ever be vindicated, they wondered.

Notes to Chapter 7

1. BV 2/72, p. 74. Remark made by I. Ia. Tatarchenko.
2. As recalled by a participant (Umsiedler interview data).
3. W. C. Fletcher, *Religion and Soviet Foreign Policy 1945-1970* (London: Oxford University Press, 1973), pp. 94-97; BV 1/62, pp. 12-17.
4. See below, chapter 13, p. 365.
5. Between 1959 and 1963 *Bratskii Vestnik* referred directly or indirectly to 21 churches that had to seek new quarters; problems in 22 churches (18 of them in 1962-63). There were 46 leadership changes without reason given or because the presbyter was considered unsatisfactory by the senior presbyter. In a further 22 cases leadership conflicts were reported. The senior presbyters most frequently reporting were: A. P. Miroshnichenko (Crimea), reporting seven times; I. D. Shavyrin (Belgorod), P. A. Parchevskii (Kharkov), and G. G. Ponurko (Dnepropetrovsk), reporting six times; K. L. Kolibabchik (Kherson and Nikolaev), K. S. Sevashko (Grodno), D. I. Ponomarchuk (Moldavia), M. S. Vashchuk (Central Asia), Z. N. Golik (Chernovitsy), R. R. Podgaiskii (Stavropol) and M. I. Sorokin (Kursk), reporting five times. E. N. Raevskii from Eastern Siberia made no report between 1961 and 1963 and G. M. Buzynin of the Middle Volga region had not reported since 1957. Such data can only be indicative since other senior presbyters may have reported quarterly as required but the fact of publishing excerpts from the reports indicated Moscow support. When I. Ia. Kaliuzhnyi (Cherkassy) reported (4 times), it usually involved a list of churches where the context indicates that he had enforced the Moscow line with toughness and had exerted his influence in local leadership changes.
6. BV 6/63, p. 13.
7. AS 770, p. 52.

8. BV 6/63. Unless specifically indicated, the following conference details are based on this official report. *Initsiativniki* supporter M. T. Shaptala, preacher in Khartsyzsk (Donets Oblast), was listed as a guest. The reformer's report is available in AS 770, pp. 121-136.

9. This was the last congress where the names and addresses of all representatives were listed in the official report.

10. AS 770, pp. 123-4. On Rovno statistics see BV 3-4/54, p. 67; 5/56, p. 65.

11. See appendix for list.

12. BV 4/57 provided photographs of each.

13. They were: Michael Zhidkov, A. N. Kiriukhantsev, Ilia M. Orlov, and M. V. Mel'nik in England (1956-58); A. N. Stoian and G. V. Nebesnyi in England (1957-59). Michael Zhidkov studied in Canada (1961-62) and N. I. Iuvanen in Sweden at the same time. Iuvanen and Nebesnyi appear not to have worked for the AUCECB subsequently. (BV 6/63, p. 20.)

14. In 1962, the 30,000 rubles spent on hosting foreign guests accounted for most of the deficit spending. (AS 770, p. 121.)

15. Annual income was: 275,000 rubles (1956); 280,000 (1957); 258,000 (1958); 224,000 (1959); 222,700 (1960); 197,200 (1961); 178,000 (1962); 93,000 (first 9 months of 1963). The 1962 expenses totaled 217,800 rubles, which was 39,800 more than the income for that year. (AS 770, pp. 125-27.)

16. *Ibid.*

17. A key leader, M. E. Ziubanov, who had split 22 congregations, made a speech followed by D. D. Shapovalov, who had persuaded Ziubanov of the error of his separatism. (BV 6/63, p. 39.)

18. *Ibid.*, pp. 21-22.

19. *Ibid.*, p. 36. It had no influence in Chernovitsy, Zakarpathia, Ternopol, Volhynia, Rovno, and other oblasts while in Kherson, Nikolaev, Dnepropetrovsk, L'vov, Poltava, and other oblasts there were only two or three groups.

20. *Ibid.*

21. His name was Heinrich K. Allert. See below, chapter 10, p. 281.

22. AS 770, pp. 130, 132.

23. *Ibid.*, p. 130. Based on financial indicators given by Ivanov, presidium members received 5,000 rubles annually. This was indeed higher than the average Soviet salary of 120 rubles per month but clergymen had to pay an income tax of 40%.

24. P. K. Egle, born 1903, was presbyter of one of the strongest central Latvian churches (Talsen) in the forties and fifties. In 1963 he was presbyter in Iaunelgav. He served as senior presbyter or bishop of Latvia from 1966-1977, when he became bishop emeritus.

25. BV 6/63, p. 47.

26. *Religious Ferment*, Appendix I, pp. 190-210. My approach here is to assume the influence of Kriuchkov and Prokofiev as demonstrated by Bourdeaux and to focus instead on the significance of the changes for a free church polity.

27. This is a corrective to Hans Hebly's assertion (*Protestants in Russia*, pp. 121-24) that the union was a federal union from the beginning.

28. Council members were: Jacob I. Zhidkov, N. A. Levindanto, A. L. Andreev, A. V. Karev, I. G. Ivanov, K. S. Veliseichik, D. I. Ponomarchuk, I. Ia. Tatarchenko, I. I. Motorin, and A. N. Karpov.

29. They were: E. N. Raevskii, A. M. Sil'dos, S. P. Fadiukhin, M. S. Vashchuk, G. G. Ponurko.

30. A. I. Mitsevich, Chmn.; N. N. Mel'nikov; F. R. Astakhov.

31. BV 3/64, p. 65.

32. BV 4/64, p. 76. A. A. Nosarev replaced M. I. Sorokin in Kursk, the latter returning to Leningrad and later became senior presbyter for the North West; N. V. Kuz'menko (Pentecostal) replaced A. G. Kvashenko in Odessa; F. I. Priimenko was appointed to Sumy and F. B. Kislits to Zaporozh'e.

33. BV 6/64, pp. 41-43.

34. Lialina, p. 42. Already at the September 1964 plenum the leadership had decided to devote more effort to establish contact with unregistered congregations through personal visits and letter contact (BV 6/64, p. 41).

35. The official congress report appeared in BV 6/66 *passim* and was also printed in an English-language brochure.

36. BV 6/66, p. 26.

37. *Ibid.*

38. *Ibid.*, p. 30.

39. See below, chapter 8.

40. Vins in *Three Generations of Suffering* stresses the capitulation after 1929.

41. On their views about registration, see below, chapter 8.

42. BV 6/66, p. 67.

43. *Ibid.* p. 70. In Russian there is a word play on *starshyi* (senior) and *strashnyi* (strict). This speaker sharply criticized the senior presbyter for Belgorod Oblast, I. D. Shavyrin, who was removed in 1966.

44. *Ibid.*, p. 68.

45. *Ibid.*, p. 32.

46. *Ibid.*, p. 72.

47. *Ibid.* p. 60. V. F. Vasilenko argued that the AUCECB recognized its mistakes and corrected them while the *Orgkomitet* continued to regard itself as completely sinless.

48. *Ibid.*, p. 32.

49. *Ibid.*, p. 60.

50. *Ibid.*, pp. 46-7.

51. *Ibid.*, N. N. Mel'nikov of the Ukraine also quoted an AUCECB statement dated 15 July 1966: "With deep humility we bow before Him, who alone has power to forgive sins on earth (Mt. 9:6) and before a merciful Lord we confess our mistakes, inadequacies and sins. 'For we have sinned much' (James 3:2). We are striving not only to admit our mistakes and inadequacies, but also to correct them, that is, to bring adequate fruits of repentance" (p. 39). Cf. BV 1/74, pp. 70-71.

52. See appendix. The statutes were reprinted in full in *ibid.*, pp. 50-53.

53. This right was only confirmed in the 1975 revision of the Soviet legislation on cults.

54. They were: A. V. Karev, A. M. Sil'dos (Estonia), P. K. Egle (Latvia), M. Ia. Zhidkov (Moscow), Jacob Fast (Novosibirsk), A. I. Mitskevich (Moscow), I. Ia. Tatarchenko (Donets), A. N. Kiriukhantsev (Leningrad), N. N. Mel'nikov (Kiev), S. T. Timchenko (Moscow), I. G. Ivanov (Moscow), S. P. Fadiukhin (Moscow), I. Ia. Kaliuzhnyi (Kiev), A. E. Klimenko (Kuibyshev), K. P. Borodinov (Novosibirsk), I. I. Motorin (Moscow), M. S. Vashchuk (Alma Ata), N. V. Kuz'menko (Odessa), V. M. Kovalkov (Moscow), M. Ia. Rubanenko (Krasnodar), D. D. Shapovalov (Kharkov), V. F. Vasilenko (Vinnitsa), A. A. Nesteruk (Volhynia), P. A. Dzhaniashvili (Tbilissi), K. S. Veliseichik (Minsk).

55. They were: V. T. Mitin (Voroshilovgrad), Arpad A. Arder (Estonia), V. A. Kriger (Moscow), L. F. Tkachenko (Moscow), G. T. Bulgakov (Kazan), D. M. Andrikevich (Khmel'nitskii), V. F. Semenov (Leningrad), Ilia M. Orlov (Moscow).

56. The Ukrainian representatives were: N. N. Mel'nikov, I. Ia. Tatarchenko,

D. D. Shapovalov, I. Ia. Kaliuzhnyi, V. F. Vasilenko, N. V. Kuz'menko (Pentecostal), A. A. Nesteruk (Pentecostal).

57. Jakob Fast, full member, Viktor Kriger, candidate. Kriger had joined the Moscow staff in 1964 following his military service.

58. Presidium members were: I. G. Ivanov, president; A. V. Karev, general secretary; I. I. Motorin, treasurer; A. I. Mitskevich, ass't general secretary; S. T. Timchenko, vice-president; N. N. Mel'nikov, vice-president; and S. P. Fadiukhin, A. N. Kiriukhantsev, M. Ia. Zhidkov as members.

59. Sergei T. Timchenko was born in Poltava (Ukraine), where he was converted and baptized in 1918. In 1929 he was ordained presbyter in Poltava. The official biography says nothing about the long and very likely difficult interval but from 1947-52 he lived in Alma Ata (Kazakhstan) and then moved to Moscow, where he continued in civilian employ till he was pensioned in 1963, after which he became an active worker in the Moscow congregation. In the last five years of his life as first vice-president of the union he became widely respected, the Estonian presbyters crediting him with persuading the Estonian church to remain on the side of the AUCECB leadership. (BV 4/73, p. 73.)

60. The official report in BV 2/70, *passim*. An English-language brochure was again published.

61. Dr. C. Ronald Goulding (England), then European secretary for the Baptist World Alliance and secretary-treasurer of the European Baptist Federation.

62. This was based very heavily on his report to an extended plenum held in March 1969 (BV 3/69, pp. 61-73).

63. See above, chapter 4, pp. 112-115.

64. BV 2/70, p. 23.

65. *Ibid.*, p. 26.

66. Based on the decision at an Evangelical Christian congress of 1920 the 1969 plenum had decided that if a man's family lives a decent life and there is no disorder in the family, then such a person may be ordained even if his children are not believers. (*Ibid.*, pp. 63-65; 2/70, p. 32.)

67. BV 2/70, p. 45.

68. *Ibid.*, p. 46.

69. Discussed in detail in the following chapter.

70. AS 565 (Dec. 1970).

71. They were: G. I. Maiboroda, P. P. Raka, A. G. Popov, sister Kopylova, Ia. B. Starodubets, F. I. Saprykin (a guest), and G. P. Tsorba.

72. At the plenum in March 1969 A. I. Mitskevich had reported that 960 *Initsiativniki* had returned in 1968, and more than 30 of those returning so far were presbyters and preachers. Some of these were then elected as senior presbyters such as: N. N. Sizov (SP for Kirgizia), M. I. Azarov (ass't SP for Belgorod), V. F. Vasilenko (SP for Vinnitsa), I. D. Laiko (SP for Chernigov), and E. A. Savenok (ass't presbyter in the large Rostov church). BV 3/69, p. 69.

73. Nominees needed to get a majority vote, with each candidate voted on separately. The number of negative votes were revealed to this writer later.

74. New members were: Robert P. Vyzu (Estonia), Viktor A. Kriger (Moscow), Alexei M. Bychkov (Moscow), N. I. Dolmatov (Rostov), Ivan S. Gnida (Kirovograd), A. D. Savin (Krasnodar), V. S. Glukhovskii (L'vov), M. M. Samotugin (Tashkent), P. K. Shatrov (Leningrad, now Moscow).

75. i.e., M. S. Vashchuk. His successors were M. M. Samotugin, N. A. Kolesnikov (candidate), and N. N. Sizov (Revision Commission). During the previous three years the Central Asian administration had been decentralized again.

76. BV 2/70, p. 48.

How to die . . . one must also know this . . .
Not as a crushed, pitiful worm,
Not as a slave, not daring to dare—
But as a fighter against unbelief!
(January 1968)

My persecutors, I do not curse you,
But I am saddened by your fate.
The immortal examples of history
Speak of the futility of persecution . . .
I pray for you and bless you
With the simple humanity of Christ.
—*Georgi Vins*
(December 1968)
Testament from Prison, pp. 77 and 83

8 Reunification Rejected, 1964-1974: The CCECB

What was it that made the reformers appealing? Theirs was both a negative and positive appeal.

Negatively, the *Initsiativniki* were attractive because they had finally verbalized the suspicions of many concerning the AUCECB leaders. Finally someone had come forward who dared to speak out against the state persecution and against state interference in the church. Some were even relieved to face persecution again.

Positively, many welcomed the call for spiritual renewal, for sanctification and dedication. They were attracted to the aggressive missionary spirit which the reformers displayed. And, thankfully, the reformers were going to make children and youth work a high priority. Soon loyal AUCECB parents explained apologetically that their children were bored with worship services in their church but found the youth programs in *Initsiativniki* congregations exciting. After all, the parents explained, their primary concern was to see their children respond to Christianity positively.

Unity Talks Clarify Issues
Between 1963 and 1969 the AUCECB had held three All-Union congresses, at which they claimed that the causes for the split had been

removed. Yet reunification with the CCECB did not take place. What was missing?

Congress delegates in 1963 appeared to be geographically representative while at subsequent congresses, each delegate was representing approximately 500 church members. Yet the key problem was that the *Orgkomitet* was not officially represented at the 1963 congress and was even prevented from reading its statement to the delegates. At the 1966 and 1969 congresses, the CCECB decided to reject an invitation that would grant them only the status of guests without voting rights. The reformers therefore condemned the first congress as a false congress because it had not fully represented the church. In part they also meant by this that the delegates represented a church membership that had not been fully purged of apostates. But a greater complaint was that the delegates represented only the registered congregations—that is, only one third of the membership, according to their estimate.[1]

By 1966, when the AUCECB had approved a statute which included most of the reformers' demands, events had transpired that prevented the reformers from affirming the changes. Although not reported in print, AUCECB leaders had exerted pressure at local conferences to secure condemnation of *Orgkomitet* statements. On trips abroad, they always stressed that believers were imprisoned because they violated the law, not because their religious convictions were severely restricted by the law.[2] Another recurrent problem was that potential moments for reconciliation (such as the 1963 and 1966 congresses) were missed because, at the first one, their leader, Prokofiev, was in prison, while in 1966 Kriuchkov and Vins were on trial. AUCECB leaders might have made a risky conciliatory gesture by postponing the congress till these men were able to attend.[3] They did, however, elect a unity commission that consisted of widely respected persons who made a special effort to restore unity.

The unity commission had held four consultations, had sent out two letters to the churches giving guidelines for attaining unity locally and individual members had made 200 visits to churches. The reporter, V. I. Lebedev, complained that in some registered churches they encountered persons who felt that those who had left local churches to support the CCECB had thereby left Christ and they were unable to forgive them. Another problem had been local presbyters who were too proud to admit their mistakes. An even greater problem had been the outright opposition of the CCECB leadership which had advised local members against speaking with commission members. The Moscow-appointed reporter revealed another weakness when he complained that initially the unity commission had mistakenly considered itself "some sort of neutral organization, independent of the AUCECB and as a result engaged in useless activity...." This inability to be non-partisan was complicated by the fact that the members elected were trusted by both sides but they did not occupy positions of power. In addition, the reporter failed to explain why a commission of twelve elected persons now included fifteen, three of them from Moscow.[4]

With each passing year reunification became more difficult, for two reasons. Each additional arrest, each slanderous article in the press, especially those which made the AUCECB sound like a partner of the state, built up the psychological barrier to unity. When the CCECB supporter, M. I. Azarov, asked Karev at the 1966 congress whether they would help and pray for those in prison, Karev replied that, because he had been in prison, he never forgot and would never forget to pray for them.[5] That helped break the barrier for many, but there was another, deeper barrier.

This was the growing recognition that they differed on fundamental convictions, even though they affirmed verbally that they were agreed on doctrine. This became clearer in the unity talks that were finally held in 1969.

Actually, the first meeting of representatives took place on March 23, 1966, in Moscow. Five CCECB representatives (Gennadi Kriuchkov, S. G. Dubovoi, M. P. Kondrashov, M. G. Baturin, and M. P. Khrapov) met with nine of the Moscow leaders.[6] The meeting lasted four hours, and, according to the stenographic report from the reformers' side,[7] the exchanges were surprisingly frank. The meeting nearly ended before it began because the reformers refused to greet the others with a brotherly kiss. When Karev asked why, Gennadi Kriuchkov said they still recognized the correctness and legality of the excommunication and did not regard them as brothers.

The reformers had planned their discussion and simply went through the major points of their agenda, otherwise refusing to enter into dialogue. Their purpose was to find out whether the AUCECB was now ready to eliminate the causes of the split. That is, would the leaders reject what they had written in 1960 and repent of their cooperation with the state? Karev and the others asserted that the 1960 statute had never been approved, but they defended as necessary their action in issuing the offending documents. Karev declared that it was the Soviet authorities which had split the evangelical brotherhood into registered and unregistered groupings and that the statute for the registered churches was based on the law, in particular the unpublished laws.

Karev went on to say that the Bible refers to doors being opened and closed. During the history of the atheist state, the door was sometimes wide open for Christian work. Then in 1929 the door closed. "We all went to prison. Then Stalin died, and the door again began to open, but only till 1959, when the Twenty-first Party Congress decided to make a swift end to organized religion. Then that door became very small . . . and so, in view of this situation, we in 1960 articulated the 'closed doors' by means of the letter of instruction and the statute."[8] Kriuchkov responded that Christ did not close doors; one should not let circumstances dictate. But Karev replied that Paul's missionary tour, which finally brought him to Europe, was shaped by a series of closed doors.

The remainder of the discussion concerned their differing attitudes toward the state. The reformers repeatedly charged that the leaders were urging cooperation with the state, were united with the state, whereas they affirmed absolute separation. Karev had once sent them a copy of the 1918 declaration on separation which affirmed that the church was separated from the state and had penciled in the remark: "But not the state from the church! That's what all believers should know!"[9] For Karev, this was a statement of political realism, but he also understood this to mean that the church must subordinate itself to the state. That was how he understood Romans 13.

Space does not permit repeating more of this fascinating exchange of views, but it was clear that they were not finding the necessary common language. CCECB member Nikolai Baturin concluded the meeting by reading one of their favorite passages from 2 Corinthians 6: "Separate yourselves from them, have nothing to do with what is unclean, and I will accept you" (GNB). As far as the reformers were concerned, they felt that the meeting confirmed the fact "that the AUCECB workers have departed far from God; all of them justify their sins and continue in them."[10]

AUCECB leaders felt that these talks plus the discussions at the 1966 congress had brought them forward one step toward unity. But these high-level talks were not resumed until 1969, when a series of four meetings were held. At the first two meetings, more moderate spokesmen from both sides tried to establish some points of agreement and each side drafted joint statements that the other side was supposed to sign.

A Final Round of Talks
At the first two meetings, held on April 19 and May 17, the key leaders were missing.[11] Gennadi Kriuchkov and Georgi Vins were still in prison, so

that the key spokesman was M. T. Shaptala, who had led the CCECB while the other leaders were in prison. The AUCECB spokesman proposed that unity discussions proceed from an acceptance of the revised statute at the last two congresses and a mutual admission of error. The reformers, however, saw the meeting as an exploratory discussion and asked four major questions.

First of all they wanted to know whether the AUCECB regarded the offending documents of 1960 as necessary, as a mistake, or as a sin? Several Moscow spokesmen responded, and the reformers reached the conclusion that only a few were prepared to state cautiously that they were a "sinful mistake," but all emphasized that the document simply triggered a split that was already in progress.

Second, the reformers wanted assurance that the activities of the *Orgkomitet* were no longer regarded as "the fire of the devil." The Moscow leaders affirmed that they regarded them as brothers whom they loved and tried to have fellowship with. But in their report the reformers appeared to be asking for more, for they complained that it was unfortunate that the leaders did not recognize the action of the *Initsiativniki* as an expression of the will of God for the good of the brotherhood.

The third question sought to elucidate the AUCECB attitude toward those in prison. The AUCECB was prepared to acknowledge that the majority of prisoners were suffering because of their religious convictions, but they also argued that some were suffering because they were being unreasonable. These persons showed obvious zeal for God's work, but it was not a considered zeal. The reformers rejected that even one person was imprisoned because of conflict with the authorities, all were there simply for their faith.

The final question revealed the distrust which had become deeply rooted. The reformers asked for assurances that, when the AUCECB spokesmen traveled abroad, they would not paint a false picture of the *Initsiativniki*. The AUCECB later refused to produce a document showing what they had said at recent BWA meetings.[12]

At this first meeting the CCECB spokesmen presented a letter that they requested the AUCECB leaders to sign and make public. The thrust of the letter was that the AUCECB leaders acknowledged their guilt, asked forgiveness for having issued the anti-evangelical documents, and also asked forgiveness for maintaining fellowship only with the registered churches.[13] CCECB spokesmen, in fact, asserted that only after a full confession were they prepared to discuss the question of a congress and reunification. The AUCECB spokesmen promised that a document of repentance would be written, and it was decided to meet again at a later date.

At the next meeting on May 17, 1969, the AUCECB spokesmen took the lead by reporting the decisions taken at an AUCECB plenum held ten days earlier.[14] This decision affirmed that the daily life of the ECB churches was to be guided solely by the Word of God and the statutes approved at the 1966 congress, and that the decisions on unity taken at the 1963 and 1966 congress should serve as the basis for unification. The third point was that they intended to preserve the principles of the brotherhood in accordance with the existing legislation on worship. Then they handed the reformers a statement of mutual repentance and asked them to sign it. The reformers refused, protesting that instead of a repentance statement from the AUCECB, they now offered a statement in which both sides repented of their mistakes and asked forgiveness. Actually, had they read their own notes from the previous meeting carefully, they would have seen that the AUCECB participants had thought of a mutual repentance statement from the first.

More significant was the fact that both sides tried to gain support by publishing their versions of the meetings. The *Initsiativniki* had referred to the first meeting in its journal[15] and called upon its members to resist all local efforts to discuss unity, that is, to allow the CCECB to decide the question for all. Shortly after the second meeting, the AUCECB printed what it considered as the prerequisites for unity.[16] The AUCECB claimed that both sides had written harmful things and both sides had excommunicated each other, which meant that, as a first step toward unity, both sides must put an end to the mutual recriminations and must forgive each other. More talks on unity should be held and their contents should be published for the whole brotherhood to evaluate.

Once Georgi Vins was released, Alexander Karev invited him to renew the unity talks, but Vins insisted on a formal invitation to the CCECB, which was his way of demanding recognition of the CCECB as the legitimate negotiating body. President Ilia G. Ivanov then wrote such a letter following which two more discussions were held, on October 29 and December 4, 1969. Only four persons were present at all four unity talks,[17] which helps account for the problems and illustrates the importance of negotiating styles and personal egos. At these last two sessions, there were sharper clashes between the old leadership (Ivanov, Karev, and Motorin) and the reformers Kriuchkov and Vins. But once again both sides handed each other suggested repentance statements which the other refused to sign.[18]

It was apparent that the AUCECB hoped its concessions plus a publicized statement on repentance would now lead to reconciliation, whereas the CCECB leaders viewed the talks primarily as an opportunity to accept a statement of surrender. In addition, the talks were beset with numerous other problems. The reports reveal that on both sides there were moderates and hard-liners whose differences made negotiation difficult.[19] Both sides were also negotiating under duress. Immediately after the first two sessions, S. T. Golev was brought to trial and sentenced.[20] Throughout the discussions the reformers could never forget that some of their key leaders were imprisoned and they dare not leave them in the lurch. On the other side, there was both delegate and state pressure to bring the CCECB back into the fold, but not at the cost of a total surrender. The Moscow head office as a place of meeting was itself a problem because of the listening ears. No one completely trusted anyone because, too often, a Judas had been discovered on both sides.

What Kind of Unity?

The unity talks and subsequent printed exchanges made clear a more fundamental problem, namely, that the two sides were talking about two different concepts of church unity. A year later the CCECB summarized what it meant by declaring that "you cannot be in union with the AUCECB and in union with God at the same time."[21] Already in a letter of September 22, 1962, they had declared that they were for unity in Christ and for unity with all saints, which included unity of all the ECB churches, even unity for the whole church of Christ, but "we are against unity with apostates, we are against unity with sinners."[22] That meant a visible church whose members were prepared to make a judgment on the integrity of their fellows.[23] Kriuchkov also developed the argument that, whereas the individual Christian as citizen must be subordinate to the state, the Bible nowhere declares that the church must subordinate itself to the state.

The AUCECB repeatedly stressed unity as the primary concern but meant by this a structural unity. Soon it became apparent that structural unity must also mean uniformity, official disclaimers notwithstanding.[24] They felt that unity was a predominant emphasis in the New Testament, and they felt it was imperative that the evangelicals should be able to speak with a united voice. A united body would also be stronger in negotiating situations. A further reason why the AUCECB set great store by unity was that the state wished it so. In short, the issue was spiritual unity versus organizational unity.

Behind this difference in emphasis lay a fundamental difference on the concept of the church. Both sides agreed that the church must consist only of members who had made a voluntary commitment, a believers' church, yet they followed divergent tendencies in practice. For example, the reformers stressed holiness above unity, with the result that they were happy to wait for the attainment of full unity in heaven. As they put it, "Our major goal is purity and unity, but above all purity."[25] The AUCECB was more prepared to accept a membership that still showed numerous failings. They hoped that sanctification as a continuing process would gradually produce more holy living. Such differences in emphasis may be insufficient to claim that at its roots the split concerned dogmatic differences, but it is such differences in emphasis that have regularly served to distinguish denominations within the free church movement. The *Initsiativniki* holiness emphasis also explained why their concept of the church did not include Pentecostals and why in general they rejected ecumenism.

From the beginning AUCECB spokesmen repeatedly stressed that the major threat to unity was pride. *Initsiativniki* documents, they claimed, were filled with a spirit of arrogance, revealing persons who considered themselves sinless and saw only the sins of the AUCECB leadership. This may have been a tactical cover-up to draw attention away from their own mistakes but by 1966 it became apparent that blanket condemnation of AUCECB leaders and all its supporters were not followed by humble admission of the reformers' mistakes. Even if it had been possible for *Initsiativniki* leaders to affirm that they had always acted from the highest motives, that all personal, baser motives had been eliminated, a New Testament ethic would have demanded from them that they ought to repent, even if they felt this was going the second mile.[26] Christian reconciliation always seeks the best for the other person. This also meant that, although Karev and others had legitimate grounds for accusing the reformers of pride, their own desperate clinging to office was also an expression of unusual self-esteem. The leaders appeared to believe they were indispensable, that the future of the evangelical union depended on keeping them in office.

We have now touched upon the most common and at the same time the most tragic cause for the failure of an evangelical union. Whereas the Apostle Paul argued that the great mystery which the church must demonstrate to the powers was that oneness is possible,[27] Soviet evangelicals had been forced to acknowledge defeat. That hurt. Throughout the negotiations each side always expected the other to make the bigger concession. Neither side appeared to be influenced by those spiritual heirs of the 1920s, who expressed their faith in nonresistant love.[28] Those early pacifists had been successfully eliminated. Among Pentecostals and Mennonites that nonresistant mentality was still functioning. That explains why those two bodies agreed to subordinate themselves to a union where they were treated as second rank. I. K. Pan'ko, shortly before his death, again urged fellow Pentecostals to join and stay in the union, because the New Testament admonished the Christian to take the attitude of "always considering others better than yourselves."[29]

A Second Union Develops—CCECB

The AUCECB agreed to engage in formal discussions with the *Orgkomitet* leaders only after the reformers announced, in September 1965, that they had formed the Council of Churches of Evangelical Christian-Baptists (CCECB). Once the CCECB had formed, it quickly developed a momentum of its own and from then on there were, in fact, two ECB unions of churches functioning in the Soviet Union.

The reformers' first leader, A. F. Prokofiev, ceased to play a leading role following his arrest in May 1962. This man, about whom relatively little is known, eventually became an embarrassment to the reformers. During his five-year term of exile (1967-72) he had circulated one letter which reemphasized the sanctification theme,[30] but then committed adultery and was excommunicated by the CCECB.[31] Another gifted and much more irenic person, Boris M. Zdorovets, was also eliminated from any influential role. After his first ten years of prison and exile (1962-72) he was rearrested at a youth rally ten months later and received a further four-year sentence.[32]

Gennadi K. Kriuchkov and Georgi P. Vins (beginning in August 1963) very quickly emerged as the two dominant figures in the movement.[33] Both were relatively well educated; Kriuchkov was an electrician, and Vins an electrical engineer. Both were young and aggressive, and both were no strangers to prison. Vins's father had been an active evangelical leader in Siberia and the Far East. He was first arrested in Moscow in 1930 at a conference of Baptists when Georgi was only two. Young Georgi saw his father for short intervals a few years later between two other arrests, but after the final arrest in 1937, he never heard from his father again.

Georgi started attending church in Omsk, Siberia, in 1944 and was converted soon after. Baptism followed on June 5, 1945, when he was only seventeen years old. In 1946 he and his mother moved to Kiev where he soon started to preach in the registered church located on Spassky Street. During these years he continued to study, graduating in 1954 from the Kiev Polytechnical Institute as an electrical engineer. He had married Nadezhda Ivanovna Lazaruk in January 1952. Nadezhda had been baptized when she was fifteen. By October 1961 Georgi Vins, together with other members of the local AUCECB affiliate, had spoken out in favor of the reformers' call for a congress. Then in May 1962 he was present for the first time at an extended meeting of the *Orgkomitet*. The following month the church in Kiev responded by excommunicating him. Vins and others promptly organized a separate unregistered church, where he was elected an evangelist in October 1962. The aged *Initsiativniki* leader A. A. Shalashov came to perform the ordination. Finally in August 1963 Georgi Vins left his job in an institute and began to work full time for the *Orgkomitet*, having been elected secretary in September 1963.[34]

Kriuchkov was the son of a choir leader and evangelist in Moscow. His father, Konstantin Pavlovich, began a three-year prison sentence in 1929 when Gennadi was only three.[35] There were five children in the family, and life from then on became very difficult. In 1933 Konstantin Pavlovich was forbidden to live in Moscow, and they now began moving from place to place. Although in declining health, he was sent to work in the mines in the Donbass region, and then again in the mines at Uzlovaia (Tula Oblast). After 1955, when Gennadi's mother died leaving twelve children, Konstantin Pavlovich moved back to Moscow, remarried, and became active in the church. He too joined the *Initsiativniki* in 1961 and was the presbyter of the Reform Baptist congregation in Moscow until his death in 1976.

Young Gennadi Kriuchkov remembered having lived in such faraway places as Ashkhabad (Turkmenia), Astrakhan, and the Kalmyk Steppes. From 1944 to 1950 he served in the Soviet army. When he returned home to Uzlovaia (Tula Oblast) in 1950 he worked as an electrician in the mines. In 1951 he was converted and baptized in the Tula Evangelical Christian Baptist church and was also married to Lidia Vasilevna. Immediately he started to preach. Soon he was elected choir leader, then deacon, and finally he became presbyter of the unregistered church in Uzlovaia. Severe state pressure on the unregistered churches in Tula Oblast began in 1959 and in 1961 at a members' meeting with visitors from the Ukraine present, Kriuchkov proposed organizing an initiative group. Soon after, he escaped police arrest because he was attending a meeting in Moscow at the time. As a result he left his job, went into hiding, and devoted all his time to the *Init-siativniki* cause.[36]

During the early years of the reform movement, Kriuchkov and Vins remained at liberty while local church leaders who supported them were arrested and given prison sentences. The two leaders, both young and constantly on the move, managed to keep one step ahead of the pursuing authorities. Their supporters staunchly refused to give evidence that might incriminate them. This changed after the mass demonstration in Moscow in May 1966. Within a few months, both Vins and Kriuchkov were behind bars, as well as most of the other leaders. The two men were put on trial together and gave an eloquent defense at a trial whose outcome had been predetermined.[37] For three years they were kept in prisons, which ruined the health of both, especially Vins. Kriuchkov utilized this period of enforced idleness for extensive reading and emerged as the reformers' authority on Soviet law and philosophy. Vins wrote poetry which was later to move the hearts of thousands around the world.

The Council

To become a member of the reformers' leading council (CCECB) was much more dangerous than election to the AUCECB. Perhaps this explains why they have never elected a full fifteen-to-seventeen-member council as provided for in the statute which they issued in November 1965.[38] The membership hovered around eleven, with a discouragingly high percentage serving what could only be an honorary membership while they were languishing in prison. Those that were free spent their time on the road. These persons, plus a small corps of evangelists, traveled throughout the Soviet Union visiting congregations, trying to win more supporters, maintaining the vital communication links, and helping supervise the local leadership.

The CCECB has demonstrated impressive organizational skills by successfully directing a well-developed, nationwide church program; yet this did not appear to be the key quality supporters looked for in the leaders. Most of the CCECB members, especially the older men, are held in honor as spiritual giants.[39] A. A. Shalashov was a key initial leader, who died in December 1963 at age seventy-three.

Born in 1890, he was converted in 1914 and immediately began a ministry as evangelist in the Volgo-Kamsk ECB church. He had spent a total of nineteen years in prison for his faith and at his death was presbyter of the unregistered church in Cheliabinsk. He had made a major contribution to the revivals in the fifties.[40]

Ivan Iakovlevich Antonov was somewhat younger, having been born into a Russian Orthodox family in Kalinin Oblast in 1919. In 1938 Antonov started medical school in Moscow but after the third year the war interfered with his studies. In the summer of 1941 he had gained access to a Bible which he read for a month with the result that he got rid of his icons. But in the army he took to drinking until in June 1944 he met a young woman whose witness led to his decisive conversion. Soon several other soldiers were converted through his work with the result that in November 1944 a military tribunal sentenced him to ten years in the prison camps in the Far North. Soon after his release in August 1954 he was baptized. In December 1955 he married Lina Korol'kova who had been rehabilitated and released in June of that year from a twenty-five-year prison sentence she had received in 1950. They moved to Kirovograd in the Ukraine, joined the AUCECB church and Antonov became secretary to the presbyter. When Antonov objected to state interference in the list of baptismal candidates he lost his post as secretary and began to baptize young people secretly. In spite of this, the congregation elected him presbyter in 1960. From 1962 to 1965 he worked full time for the *Orgkomitet.*

A man with an even stranger story was Dmitri Vasilevich Miniakov (1922-   ). He had met Christian believers for the first time when he began a prison sentence in 1944. He was finally converted in 1949 in the prison camp and baptized there, the prisoners having organized their own congregation. The presbyter of this congregation was transferred to another camp in 1950 so fellow prisoners elected Miniakov presbyter and he was ordained by the departing presbyter prisoner! Miniakov was released in 1952 and moved to the city of Mariinsk (Kemerovo Oblast) where he became the local presbyter. In 1958 he moved his family (he had married in 1953) to Barnaul, Siberia and was again active as a preacher. Here the congregation tried to excommunicate its presbyter Ia. F. Sablin in 1960 because of the latter's close cooperation with the authorities but Sablin went to the authorities and the church was closed. Miniakov then became the presbyter of the unregistered house fellowships that began to meet. When Gennadi Kriuchkov visited them in the fall of 1961 the congregation elected Miniakov as their representative to the *Orgkomitet.* But he missed out personally on much of the subsequent drama in Barnaul since he was in prison from 1962 to 1965 and again from 1967 to 1970.

Still another gifted leader was Kornelius Korneivich Kreker (Kroeker), who was born into a Mennonite Brethren family in the Altai region of Siberia in 1920. Although he had a Christian upbringing (his father was arrested for his faith in 1938 and never returned), Kreker started studies in a pedagogical institute and did not become converted till 1943 in Osinniki (Kemerovo Oblast). He had been sent there in 1942 to work as a teacher in the Workers' Army. In 1944 he was baptized in the local ECB church and almost immediately after was interrogated by the authorities who expressed their usual surprise that an educated man would be religious. Kreker remained with the church group that split away when the authorities began to interfere. He was ordained presbyter in 1958, served a five-year term in exile in the taiga from 1962 to 1967, after which the *Initsiativniki* elected him to work for the CCECB. After a prison term (1968-71) he became a full member of the CCECB.

Another very important leader, although only briefly on the council itself, was young Josef D. Bondarenko, who functioned as the Billy Graham of Russia whenever he wasn't in prison. Bondarenko, born 1947, was first arrested at home in Odessa and sentenced to three years in 1962. After a brief period of freedom he was sentenced to another three years (1966-69) in a strict regime labor camp. Upon his release he was married in a huge outdoor ceremony with 2,000 present, which upset the authorities because it was more like an evangelistic rally. He therefore spent a number of years in hiding but in the three years before his arrest in May 1978 he was leader of the church in Riga. Following highly successful evangelistic campaigns in the spring of 1978 he was arrested and sentenced to another three years. He has four children and suffers from a heart condition since his second arrest.[41]

Soon the responsibilities of the council were eased by the formation of regional unions. A precise organizational structure could never develop satisfactorily because of the need for secrecy. By 1976 an internal dispute had broken out between those who affirmed the necessity of centralized, authoritarian leadership by the CCECB over against others arguing for a federated structure, where the regional unions would have more power.[42] The regional unions were the product of local initiative.

There is insufficient data available to determine how many regional unions there were, but by the mid-sixties there were regional unions in the Caucasus, in Siberia and Northern Kazakhstan, in the Baltic region, in Moldavia, in the Leningrad area, and probably one or several in the Ukraine.[43] The Baltic region represented eighteen or nineteen congregations who elected a seven-member presbyter council which met monthly. The Siberian union (which included Northern Kazakhstan) consisted of nine oblasts, in each of which a senior presbyter had been elected by the local churches. The Siberian union itself met semiannually and usually two

or three CCECB members participated. This was a very secret meeting lasting up to two days (without any pause for sleeping) with forty-five to sixty
people participating. In addition to edificatory preaching, the local regions
reported their literature needs, how many had been sentenced, and the financial needs of the members, especially those with relatives in prison.
They discussed general church life and the CCECB reported on its work.

The entire church program had to be conducted with great secrecy so
that there was the constant danger of an abuse of power. Participants at all
levels have affirmed that their activity was highly organized and that all finances were recorded and reports were given on a need-to-know basis. Re-
gionally, church activity was organized sufficiently so that one person
supervised youth work, another organized transportation, while others were
responsible for communication, choral work, evangelism, and finance. The
CCECB statute declared that the council included a department for evangelism and another for publication, as well as others which remained un-
named. Other clauses of the statute specified additional activity, and it
seems evident that the CCECB tried, where possible, to follow the statute
guidelines. But the major problem was the difficulty of holding a national
congress and establishing a consensus. A year after the creation of the
CCECB, a major event took place that Gennadi Kriuchkov later claimed
had not been organized by the council but was genuinely a grass-roots
phenomenon.

The May Demonstration

On May 16, 1966, onlookers near the Communist Party Central Committee building in Moscow witnessed a mass demonstration that had not
been organized by the authorities.[44] ECB congregations from 130 cities sent
representatives to Moscow with a petition addressed to Communist Party
Chairman Leonid Brezhnev. The leaders of the 500 delegates failed to see
Brezhnev, but did submit the petition. It contained requests for permission
to hold a congress, for recognition of the CCECB, for an end to religious
persecution and state interference in church affairs, and for the right to
receive religious instruction. Initially the authorities did nothing, but on the
second day the demonstration grew to 600 persons, as members of the
Moscow registered church joined them. Finally, soldiers, police, and KGB
officers applied force, physically beating up people and dragging them into
buses for the trip to prison. Most were released the next day; others received
fifteen-day sentences. A week later a similar event occurred in Kiev. On
May 19 Georgi Vins and Mikhail I. Khorev, who had been instructed by the

CCECB to find out what had happened to the believers, presented themselves at the reception desk of the Central Committee. They were told to come back in an hour and a half. When they did so, they were hustled into Black Marias for the trip to prison.

Such mass demonstrations were an embarrassingly public protest against the new wave of religious persecution that had been resumed that winter.[45] The Western world soon learned of the event, although newsmen encountered the same restrictions as at the Sinyevsky-Daniel trial. Aside from the many people who received fifteen-day sentences, the authorities began tracing down the local leaders of the Reform Baptists. Thirty-one were arrested in the month of May alone, but arrests continued throughout the summer—a total of 128 persons were arrested, bringing the total prisoner list to 202. Arrests continued in the following year, until in August 1968 the number of Baptist prisoners peaked at 240.[46]

The Council of Prisoners' Relatives

The CCECB might have been destroyed had it not been for the work of the Council of Prisoners' Relatives (CPR). This remarkable organization held its first meeting in February 1964 and very likely organized the May demonstration. Nothing is known about the first leaders, but after Georgi Vins's arrest, his mother, Lidia, became the dominant personality in the CPR. Not only had Lidia Vins suffered through the agonies of losing her husband in prison, and raising her son alone, but she had also lost a brother and a sister-in-law in the Stalinist persecution.[47] She now demonstrated unshakable courage, an organizing talent, and had a flair for utilizing world public opinion. Under her guidance, letters of protest were sent to numerous high-level state agencies, as well as to leading church organizations abroad. A characteristic letter, composed at the second All-Union Congress of Prisoners' Relatives, gave a historical survey and cited hard evidence to illustrate the complaints.[48] Not only had 524 persons been imprisoned since 1961, of which forty-four were women, there had been an additional 391 receiving fifteen-day prison sentences while they had evidence for a total of 8,648 interrogations of believers, including 390 children who had been interrogated. Church members had now paid a total of 94,300 rubles in fines. In other letters they listed a bibliography of propaganda articles from central, regional, and provincial newspapers which, contrary to the law, abused the feelings of believers by calling them fanatics, barbarians, pigs, dope addicts, hypocrites, or obscurantists.[49]

Between 1965 and 1970 the CPR collected data on prisoners, helped circulate appeals and addressed great numbers of telegrams and letters on behalf of all the believers to higher authorities. Finally, in 1969 the council was able to hold its first All-Union congress, which greatly helped to organize and systematize the information. A second congress met the following year, again in secret, on December 12-13, 1970. All of the leaders were either in prison or had gone underground to escape the authorities. But the CPR appeared to be even more upset by the arrest of its leader Lidia Vins on December 1, 1969. The appeals were to no avail, and Lidia Vins, in spite of her age and ill health, spent three years in prison.[50]

With the arrest of Lidia Vins, CPR leadership was taken over by a younger woman named Galina Rytikova. Rytikova's husband, Peter, was an evangelist and candidate member of the CCECB. With him in prison, she was left to struggle for survival for herself and their six children. Rytikova has remained the leader of the CPR to the present and has put her stamp on the organization by introducing the *Bulletin*.[51]

The *Bulletin* became the regular journal of the CPR; the organizers promised to issue it on a quarterly basis. The reformers had circulated a journal called *Herald of Salvation* from the beginning, but it appeared at highly irregular intervals and suffered extensively when the key leaders who provided its spiritual content were imprisoned. The CCECB published its own newspaper, *Fraternal Leaflet*, beginning in 1965, but it literally remained a leaflet appearing bimonthly. It took awhile for the *Bulletin* to become regular, but by 1974 it was appearing almost bimonthly.

In the early years, the *Bulletin* varied between twenty-five and eighty pages of information, which had been laboriously hand-lettered and then duplicated by hectograph process. This also meant that each issue was hand-lettered numerous times onto stencils in order to attain the necessary circulation. Later most issues were typed but duplication remained a problem. Almost all of the *Bulletiny* (up to No. 72 by the end of 1979) have reached the West and provide a major source for the history of the movement.[52] The *Bulletin* included letters from prisoners, copies of appeals to the state, biographical information and, at regular intervals, an updating of the prisoners' list.

Through its *Bulletin*, therefore, the CPR has emerged as second spokesman for the CCECB and reflects a more intense negativist tone than the CCECB itself. The fact that women dominate it also represents a problem for the reformers. Reform Baptists even more than AUCECB members place a very heavy emphasis on the subordination of women and feel uncomfortable that women are often the *de facto* leaders of their movement.

The Tula Congress

Unity talks failed in 1969 but there was a mood of optimism, especially since many had completed their prison terms. CCECB officials submitted a request to the state authorities in Tula for permission to hold a congress, and, to their surprise, three days before the congress began on December 6, they received notice of official permission. This may have been an ignorant mistake by the Tula city council, although it is possible that the Moscow authorities were hopeful that the last session of joint talks between the two unions, which took place on December 4, might actually lead to reconciliation. Another factor may have been that the state hoped hereby to gain more details of *Initsiativniki* activity. In any case, shortly thereafter permission was withdrawn and the CCECB has been treated as an illegal organization by the Soviet authorities to the present day.

One hundred and twenty persons representing Central Russia, the Urals, Siberia, Northern Caucasus, the Ukraine, Moldavia, Belorussia, the Baltic, Kazakhstan, Central Asia, Azerbaidzhan, and Georgia met in the unregistered prayer house in Tula, which was the personal residence of N. I. Vladykin.[53] Kriuchkov opened the meeting with prayer, and communion followed. The agenda was not very long, and the one-day session lasted from 10:00 a.m. to 10:30 p.m. The CCECB report was presented in two parts. M. T. Shaptala, presbyter in Khartsyzsk (Donetsk Oblast), had been elected to take temporary leadership while Kriuchkov and the others were in prison. He reported that since 1966 they had had only one meeting with the Council of Religious Affairs and had immediately reported to the church on this through the journal, *Bratskii Listok*. Two meetings had been held with the AUCECB in April and May 1969, and Shaptala also noted that the shortcomings of certain local presbyters had been reported to their local congregations for appropriate action.[54]

Gennadi Kriuchkov as elected chairman then reported on the brief period from May to December 1969, which was primarily a report on the latest unity talks. The congress then took a unanimous decision to reject the invitation to attend the AUCECB congress because they were invited without voting rights.

The third point on the agenda concerned relations to the AUCECB, but this was quickly covered by the decision not to attend the congress. Subsequent declarations from the CCECB not only repeated their conviction that the Moscow leadership had not changed, but also warned local churches to avoid all ties with the AUCECB. But the Tula conference tried to clarify the misunderstanding in the general public, which seemed to think that the CCECB was opposed to registration.

Six congregations registered by the state were represented at the conference.[55] The conference body also approved a declaration to the churches which urged all congregations to apply for registration on the basis of a new declaration form prepared by the CCECB leadership.[56] A year later the CCECB issued a position statement which declared that almost all of their congregations had submitted registration requests to the authorities, and the council itself had submitted the minutes of the Tula conference plus a list of the elected members to the state organs. "Is there a lawyer who can, after all this, call the activities of the Council of Churches and the ECB congregations illegal?" they asked.[57] They went on to state that recently they had said little about persecutions even though these were continuing and had taken other practical steps to regulate relations with the authorities, such as notifying them where meetings of the brethren would take place.

The elections also reflected a sense of hope. All members of the previous council were reelected except S. Kh. Tsurkan and A. S. Goncharov, who refused reelection for reasons of age and health. Three of these council members (I. Ia. Antonov, D. V. Miniakov, and S. T. Golev) were still in prison. Following the election, Gennadi Kriuchkov then proposed that two other persons who had been elected temporarily earlier should be elected to the council. The congress then approved the election of M. T. Shaptala and P. V. Rumachik.[58] With great optimism the congress dispatched a letter to Premier Kosygin in which they reported the names of those elected (except the three in prison) and went on:

> On the basis of their election, we ask you to regard the CCECB workers as having the legal right to be freed from work in industry and that you give directives accordingly to the organs not to hinder them in carrying out the work entrusted to them.[59]

As if to emphasize that they were not being provocatory but simply demanding their legal rights, they went on to say:

> The activity of the CCECB is not connected with the violation of social order nor infringing the rights of citizens, and does not concern itself with social-political or similar questions, only inner church religious questions.[60]

The letter also requested similar rights for its evangelists.

Premier Alexei Kosygin did not reply personally. But the answer was soon clear. Kriuchkov and Vins were both ordered to work in industry and Vins's wages were garnished. Only a few days after the conference, M. I. Khorev was arrested, and following a secret trial, was sentenced to three years in prison.[61] Numerous CCECB leaders followed, and by the end of the year both Kriuchkov and Vins went into hiding.[62] Vins successfully eluded the authorities till March 1974. Kriuchkov, on the other hand, is still sought. Kriuchkov's portrait, for example, was included on bulletin boards along with other most-wanted criminals. In 1974 his wife discovered that a listening device had been installed in their apartment, and Kriuchkov has had other narrow escapes.[63]

Major Activity

In spite of the unrelieved pressure since 1969, the CCECB has succeeded in carrying out a remarkable program of activity. Members of the council tried to meet annually, although sometimes the meeting could be completed only after several short interruptions while they fled from one house to another to avoid capture. In 1972, when all were free except P. G. Rumachik, the council membership was expanded.[64] In May 1976 at another secret congress Gennadi Kriuchkov delivered a major report by means of a tape recorder. At a second meeting in December the *de facto* general secretary (Vins was in prison) I. Ia. Antonov reported.[65]

One activity that turned out to be futile was their request to have the legislation on religion revised in order to make it conform to the freedom of conscience promised by Lenin in 1918. Detailed proposals were submitted beginning April 14, 1965, to Brezhnev as president of the commission for drafting a new constitution. More suggestions followed when the Brezhnev constitution was published in the spring of 1977, but to no avail.[66]

A more successful program was evangelization. Some of the evangelists were appointed by the CCECB, which supported them financially and arranged evangelistic tours for them. Gerhard Hamm, a leader in the Baltic, was one such evangelist whose work the authorities tried to hinder.[67] A fellow believer who owned an automobile drove him to a train station in the next city in order to avoid the police who were waiting for him at the train station. When he arrived at his destination and found that others besides believers were expecting him, he traveled onward to the next station, where someone then took him to the evangelistic rally. Exactly where that meeting was to be held was determined only a few hours in advance, and by the time the authorities caught up, Gerhard Hamm had already returned home. Young Peter Peters had a special appeal for young people and often participated in the semiannual regional youth rallies that were held.[68] The authorities knew that on May-day and on November 7 (anniversary of the Revolution) Reform Baptist young people would be meeting somewhere in the hills or woods for a large rally and tried to prevent this happening. Once they sealed off an entire town in Kazakhstan, but the young people who had gathered refused to let the authorities enter the house to arrest the leaders until under cover of darkness they could be spirited away. These youth rallies usually resulted in tens of new converts.[69]

Another major activity upset the authorities even more. One expert has observed that all the court cases concerning *Initsiativniki* in 1966, the year of the greatest arrests, were connected with children's work.[70] Religious educational material was widely circulated in *Samizdat*. In one rather sad incident, two young girls, Maria Braun and Elena Chernetskaia, decided to continue their Sunday school activity even though pressure was increasing. Maria declared that, if it had to be, they would hold Sunday school for the children at five o'clock in the morning. Both girls were arrested, tried and sentenced to five years in prison. Three years later the terrible conditions in a women's prison brought their results. Maria Braun announced she had broken with religion, and she became a prized propagandist for atheism.[71]

A less-publicized activity was the financial aid given to prisoners' families. The families of prisoners, as well as those of persons who were unemployed, received no state aid, and therefore the absence of a breadwinner placed the family under severe financial hardship. Very often, as well, part of the prisoner's punishment was the confiscation of all his movable property. The CPR was vital in organizing relief, much of the money coming from abroad.

Lidia Vins at a recent meeting in West Germany recalled how things had changed since the 1930s when her husband disappeared into the prison camps. Then their home had been confiscated, everyone else was poor and as relatives of prisoners they received no ration cards. But she had relied on Jesus' promise that "I will not leave you fatherless." From time to time, in the evenings, someone would knock on their window and there they would find food. Who was the unseen donor? It was the deputy director of the state bank. Apparently he helped them because his wife was a believer.[72]

Now since the establishment of the Council of Prisoners' Relatives, the whole church knew the details about the prisoners and their families. Soviet legislation prohibits the church from providing aid to prisoners, but the CCECB had informed the government that all their families would be supported. This was a rather bold promise, Lidia Vins acknowledged, but so far they had managed to keep it. Their first task as CPR had been to make certain that no one went hungry even if the breadwinner was in prison or in hiding. Then they made sure that the schoolchildren had adequate clothing for school. Next they arranged for adequate bedding and heating. Once the financial aid from the West reached them, they were finally able to ensure that prisoners' families did not live worse than other families. Yet another major problem was to help returning prisoners find work because many managers were afraid to employ them lest the authorities show displeasure.

Without doubt, state authorities have been most irritated by another activity that they have been unable to stop. In 1971 the CCECB journal *Bratskii Listok* (Fraternal Leaflet) declared that since 1966 they had been appealing to the government printing presses to print 10,000 Bibles and 5, 000 hymnbooks and other literature. Since this was refused, they had started their own press, they announced, which they had named *Khristianin*.[73] After 1971 most copies of *Bratskii Listok* were printed, and soon it became apparent that one of their printing presses was capable of printing on both sides of a sheet of paper. This was no mean achievement. In addition to conducting everything in secret, the reformers were forced to construct their own printing press because all duplicators or presses in the Soviet Union are registered and a careful watch is kept on all paper supplies.

Khristianin was the name of a semi-independent publishing house which was closer to the CCECB than to the CPR but also made its services available to other evangelicals. The authorities soon discovered that once they had confiscated one press, there were others that could continue the work. For example, in 1974, after a careful and prolonged search, a printing press was discovered in Latvia and seven workers were arrested.[74] Two days after the arrests, the *Khristianin* publishing house was already printing photos of those arrested plus the full story. Another printing press was discovered in 1977 but the work of *Khristianin* continues.[75]

Khristianin's ability to survive is not only a dramatic expression of the tremendous hunger for religious literature, it is also an illustration of widespread Christian cooperation under the most severe circumstances. One printing press was run by a small electric motor which used only a small amount of electric current so that a high electric bill would not betray the press location. Usually the press was started by hand in order to overcome the initial inertia, after which the motor could run the machine on its own. It was constructed out of washing machine wringer rollers, bicycle pedals and chains, and other assorted materials. It could be packed into five small suitcases at very short notice and be hand-carried elsewhere. But for this press to function, supporters throughout the country were busy stripping off bark from trees in Northern Siberia, burning tires and finding other scraps of the correct metal, which were melted down and cooked together in order to provide the proper chemical mixture for making ink and other necessities. There was no typesetter, but some of the workers, who spent up to two years literally underground, were engaged in the laborious task of finding perfectly shaped letters in other printed books in order to provide typeset equivalent master sheets which were then photographed. Since no single person could buy more than a ream of paper without attracting suspicion, there were literally hundreds of persons involved in collecting paper and transporting it.

It is difficult to obtain accurate statistics on *Khristianin* production achievements. It has printed a number of books, including *Pilgrim's Progress*, New Testaments, songbooks, and some books by Charles Spurgeon. In 1968 the first copies of the Gospel of John were distributed, and congregations received fifteen copies each. Finally, in the spring of 1978, *Khristianin* printed its first Bibles.[76]

The organizing geniuses behind the publication work were Georgi Vins (until his arrest in 1974) and Gennadi Kriuchkov. Many other key individuals have devoted their lives to this work but their names can become public only when they are arrested. Local AUCECB churches secretly support this work and have also shared in the distribution, but here, too, the less said, the better.

Bleak Prospects for the Seventies

After 1969, the AUCECB gave up on a formal reconciliation, turning its attention to winning *Initsiativniki* back locally. They also became much more aggressive in seeking the support of the unregistered churches so that the decade of the seventies became a period when more churches were registering each year.

A shift in state policy also became apparent. After 1966 many congregations discovered it was again possible to obtain registration. By 1969 state officials were actually offering registration to churches that had requested it in vain for the past several decades. The purpose behind this was clear, and the CCECB issued very sharp warning statements.[77] The latter felt that the authorities were intent on permitting a large number of congregations to obtain autonomous registration. These would then be permitted to form a new, legalized Council of Churches of Evangelical Christian Baptists and thereby the CCECB would be left without a constituency.

That may have been an over-reaction, since most of the autonomous registration was given to Pentecostal and Mennonite congregations.

In the decade of the seventies the reports of the religious situation for ECB churches became increasingly contradictory. AUCECB congregations reported increased freedom, whereas the CPR had negative news to report. In spite of world pressure, Georgi Vins was sentenced to five years' imprisonment plus five years exile. At the end of the prison term he was deported to America in exchange for Soviet spies, effectively terminating his influence on the churches. Kriuchkov is only one of a number of leaders who are hunted like criminals.[78]

Christian mothers became increasingly concerned that the authorities would carry out their threats to take their children away because they were not being raised in a spirit of communism. For the CCECB, this contradiction in conditions seemed evidence enough that the Moscow leadership was still cooperating in the church's destruction. The CCECB no longer desired the unification because it was not possible to join light and darkness. Yet their members locally were becoming tired of the tension that life in a CCECB congregation required and became increasingly uncomfortable with the unbending attitudes of its leaders.

Some Open Questions

The split became permanent after 1969. Living conditions for CCECB churches are now so difficult that their ability to survive is questionable. Not only have the moderates and those who are tired returned to AUCECB churches, in Siberia, Northern Kazakhstan, and the Baltic region many of the key leaders emigrated to West Germany before they realized that state policy had made it easier for leaders to emigrate. Each one promised help from abroad and left only after a replacement was assured, but some loss in quality is apparent.

How realistic are the appeals of the Reform Baptists? Will the laws change to permit freedom of religion in the classic liberal sense? Will their union eventually receive legalization?

There is a deeper and more disturbing question. Was it realistic to expect broad support among fellow Christians for their uncompromising stance that the church must be completely separated from the state? When taken to its full consequences as the *Initsiativniki* have done, how many of the Christians in North America would follow their stance? Or did they expect from the beginning that they would remain a remnant that would be persecuted?

Has the AUCECB really gained by fighting the split? Can their slogan for unity—"On essentials, unity; on secondary matters, freedom; and in everything, love"—ever become more than a defensive statement to preserve unity? Can it provide the basis for an offensive program, or is that possible only as long as a specifically Baptist viewpoint dominates?

Perhaps the much-discussed split among evangelicals soon lost its significance for believers in the provinces because the daily questions of Christian life were more immediate and urgent.

Notes to Chapter 8

1. Their estimate was eventually confirmed by Soviet sociologist Lialina, p. 51.

2. One Mennonite journalist, for example, heard General Secretary Alexei Bychkov say: "Vins is in prison because he violated an existing law. We feel the door is open for witness in our way. Vins says we must change the law by political methods. But we speak to government in our own way." The journalist concluded: "The delegation appeared somewhat unsympathetic to Vins." *Mennonite Reporter*, June 14, 1976.

3. Michael Bourdeaux's argument in *Faith on Trial in Russia* (London: Hodder & Stoughton, 1971), pp. 101-110.

4. *BV*, 2/70, pp. 62-65. Unity commission members were: I. G. Il'in (Ivanova, recently deceased), V. M. Koval'kov, chairman (Moscow), V. I. Lebedev (Moscow), Ia. N. Tolpygin (Gor'ki), S. V. Sevast'ianov (Riga), O. A. Tiark (Tallinn), A. A. Arder (Rakvere), A. D. Bespalov (Dnepropetrovsk), A. M. Ketsko (Minsk), A. A. Bogatyrev (Alma-Ata), D. I. Klassen (Karaganda), N. F. Samsakov (Moscow), A. P. Vasks (Riga), P. G. Kovalev (Omsk), N. I. Vysotski (Odessa).

5. *BV*, 6/66, p. 71. By 1968 Azarov had rejoined the AUCECB and became assistant senior presbyter for Belgorod Oblast.

6. They were: Jacob Zhidkov, Alexander Karev, I. I. Motorin, A. I. Mitskevich, A. N. Karpov, V. M. Koval'kov, M. Ia. Zhidkov. Also present were V. A. Mitskevich and V. L. Fedichkin.

7. The detailed report by the reformers (AS 770, pp. 216-233) gave their own perspective but a careful reading can lead the observer to quite different conclusions.

8. *Ibid.*, p. 221.

9. *Ibid.*, p. 222. The reformers explained that this remark showed that Karev believed "that the church must be *united with* the state" (italics mine). That is reading into Karev's statement what was not there.

10. *Ibid.*, p. 233.

11. Present were from the AUCECB: S. T. Timchenko, N. N. Mel'nikov, A. I. Mitskevich, M. Ia. Zhidkov, S. P. Fadiukhin, M. P. Chernopiatov, V. I. Lebedev. From the CCECB: S. T. Golev, M. T. Shaptala, M. I. Khorev, D. M. Vinogradskii, M. A. Pavlov. Again the most detailed report came from the reformers' side (AS 827) but Alexander Karev also reported to the congress. An AUCECB letter to the congregations dated May 26, 1969, was also circulated by the reformers (AS 828).

12. Bourdeaux, *Faith on Trial*, p. 159.

13. AS 827.

14. *BV*, 4/69, pp. 69-72; AS 827.

15. *BL*, 5/69 (AS 829).

16. *BV*, 4/69, pp. 71-72.

17. I.e. Michael Zhidkov, S. T. Timchenko, V. I. Lebedev of the AUCECB and M. T. Shaptala of the CCECB.

18. *BV*, 2/70, p. 61; *BL*, 10-11/69 (AS 837); AS 629.

19. For example, in the first meetings Jacob Zhidkov saw little need to talk if the reformers did not treat him like a brother. A. I. Mitskevich and Michael Zhidkov were less defensive. According to Timchenko, Kriuchkov and Vins had indicated that recent harshly worded statements by the Council of Prisoners' Relatives were issued without their approval or participation (*BV*, 2/70, p. 61). The reformers called that a lie later.

20. AS 831 is the trial report. Golev died shortly after his release three years later.

21. AS 622, p. 24. In fact they declared frequently: "Your salvation is in danger, if you continue to fellowship with AUCECB workers."

22. AS 770, p. 69f.

23. The reformers concluded their report on the unity talks with the remark, "But for the AUCECB workers their authority and their good income is more important than the salvation of their souls" (AS 827, p. 9).

24. The elimination of the connective "and" between "Evangelical Christian" and "Baptist" said this symbolically.

25. AS 770, p. 70.

26. Peter asked Jesus how often one should forgive and Jesus in his reply suggested forgiveness should be limitless (Mt. 18:21-35).

27. "In order that at the present time, by means of the church, the angelic rulers and powers in the heavenly world might learn of his wisdom in all its different forms" (Eph. 3:10; cf. Eph. 2:14-22; 4:1-6).

28. See above, Chapter 4.

29. *BV*, 1/61, pp. 50-51. He was paraphrasing Phil. 2:4.

30. AS 817. In it he compared the AUCECB with sinful Aachen. Cf. AS 784.

31. A. Belov and A. Shilkin, *Diversiia bez dinamita* (2nd ed.; Moscow, 1976), pp. 88-89 indicate the excommunication occurred on September 13, 1969. The CCECB has remained silent about Prokofiev.

32. Since his release in 1976 little has been heard of him except that he and Prokofiev both signed a letter together with representatives of other confessions (a rarity for CCECB leaders) on behalf of freedom of conscience. *KNS*, July 15, 1976. He parted company with the CCECB recently.

33. I am relying on card files based on scattered information. Since his deportation to America in April 1979, Vins has become more widely known as a person. Cf. Jane Ellis, *Georgi Vins and His Family* (Keston College, 1979), p. 31.

34. *Vestnik Istiny*, 2-3/78, pp. 25-30.

35. Obituary in *Bulletin* No. 38, 1976.

36. AS 1039, pp. 7-10.

37. Bourdeaux, *Faith on Trial*, pp. 110-130 gives a dramatic account.

38. AS 770, pp. 207-15, in English trans. in *RCDA*, 4-6/76, pp. 77-80.

39. The first council consisted of G. K. Kriuchkov, G. P. Vins, S. G. Dubovoi (Dzhezkazgan, Kazakhstan), I. Ia. Antonov (Kirovograd), N. G. Baturin (near Rostov), P. A. Iakimenkov (Moscow), D. V. Miniakov (Barnaul), S. T. Golev (Riazan), A. S. Goncharov (Prokop'evsk, Kemerovo), M. P. Kondrashov (Mozdak, N. Ossetia), S. Kh. Tsurkan (Moldavia). AS 771, p. 60.

40. AS 770, pp. 126-40. The biographical sketches that follow are based on

card files and *Vestnik Istiny*, 2-3/78, pp. 37-47.

41. Due to disagreements with the CCECB in 1976, his name does not appear on the CPR prisoner list.

42. See below, Chap. 10, p. 275f.

43. Based on Umsiedler interview data.

44. Told in detail in Bourdeaux, *Faith on Trial*, Chap. 1.

45. See above, Chap. 5, p. 148.

46. Compiled from various CPR *Bulletins*.

47. They were P. M. Zharikov, arrested in Blagoveshchensk, and his wife, who was arrested in 1939 and sentenced to seventeen years in the tough Magadan region. This woman's father, T. Koz'min, received a five-year sentence that same year (AS 620).

48. AS 565.

49. AS 871, pp. 56-57. The list has been brought up-to-date periodically.

50. Lidia Vins (born 1907) survived the three-year prison sentence, was released in 1973, returned to active work in the CPR until finally in mid-June 1979 she was able to join her son and his family in America.

51. Because of Lidia Vins's departure to America, Alexandra T. Kozorezova was elected acting chairman on June 25, 1979. Galina Rytikova now has nine children and her husband and son are both in prison at the time of this writing.

52 A complete file is available in Keston College. Approximately half of the issues which have appeared so far have been published in Vols. 15, 19, and 27 of *Arkhiv Samizdata*. More recent issues are available through Missionswerk Friedensstimme, Gummersbach, BRD, official representative of the CCECB in the West since 1976.

53. His house was confiscated soon after.

54. Their official report appeared in *BL*, 1/70 (AS 629). One such disciplinary action reported the following year involved a council member. At the end of 1966 when nearly all CCECB members were in prison, I. A. Punk (formerly presbyter of the two AUCECB churches united in Frunze) was brought into the council. He was dropped from the council in 1969 and two years later the church in Zaporozh'e, where he was serving as presbyter, excommunicated him (albeit not unanimously—seventy-seven votes against Punk, seventeen abstentions) because they suspected his reliability (*BL*, 9-10/71 in AS 1098).

55. They were: Slobodzeia (S. Kh. Tsurkan's village in Moldavia), Piriutin (Poltava Oblast), Salykha (village in Kiev Oblast), Khrushchevo (Tula Oblast), Naryshkino, and Dmitrov (Orel Oblast).

56. English trans. in *RCDA*, 4-9/75, p. 119.

57. AS 622, p. 19.

58. Biographical information on M. T. Shaptala is scanty. Senior Presbyter Tatarchenko had stated in 1960 that Shaptala, then presbyter in Khanzhenkovo (Donets Oblast) impressed him as dedicated to God. By 1963 he was leading an unregistered congregation in Khartsyzsk (which has since been registered while maintaining ties to the CCECB). Shaptala attended the AUCECB congress in 1963 as *Initsiativniki* representative. Shaptala has not been imprisoned apparently as most of his colleagues have been, although in 1979 he was imprisoned for fifteen days. His address has often served as point of contact with the CCECB. Renewed dissension within the CCECB in 1980 led to his separation from Kriuchkov. Peter V. Rumachik (1931) is a Belorussian who has been leading the Dedovsk (Moscow Oblast) congregation when not in prison or hiding. After a total of 11½ years in prison and exile he tried to return home in 1977 but has been harassed by the authorities

since (*Vestnik istiny*, 2-3/78, pp. 30-36). After serving a fifteen day sentence in June 1979 together with Shaptala, he was rearrested in August 1980 and sentenced to 3 years of strict regime.

59. AS 629, p. 9.

60. *Ibid.* Attached were thirty-one signatures, none of the CCECB members signing.

61. *BL*, 6-7/70 (AS 864). Khorev's father, Ivan, when arrested during the Stalinist purges (he died after two years in prison) knelt and prayed with his children that all would come to share his faith. The son Mikhail Ivanovich (1931) was educated as a medical doctor but joined the *Initsiativniki* in 1965 in Moldavia. He was arrested together with Georgi Vins in 1966 and during his prison term lost the sight of one eye. Before his latest arrest in 1978 he was fully blind but still impressed everyone with his deep spirituality.

62. AS 565, AS 441. The latter listed G. K. Kriuchkov, G. P. Vins, S. G. Dubovoi, and P. A. Iakimenkov in hiding.

63. *BL*, 2/78 printed the photos from the 1974 incident.

64. *BL*, 4/72 (AS 1306). New additions were M. I. Khorev, K. K. Kreker, and N. P. Khrapov.

65. *BL*, 1/77; 4/77; *Vestnik istiny*, 3-4/76, pp. 3-28.

66. AS 771, pp. 47-55; *BL*, 4/77.

67. Some of his experiences are related in his recent book, Gerhard Hamm, *Du hast uns nie verlassen* (Wuppertal: R. Brockhaus Verlag, 1978).

68. Peter D. Peters (1942) began his fourth prison term in 1978 (released in July 1980). He went on a futile hunger strike in order to get a copy of the Bible.

69. An especially unfortunate incident occurred in 1974 when one of the youths from Minsk, Nikolai Loiko, was severely wounded when a policeman's gun fired (*Bulletin* No. 44, pp. 3-4).

70. Bourdeaux, *Religious Ferment*, p. 126f.

71. For example, *Nauka i religiia*, 7/73, pp. 76-79. Persons who knew her thought they detected unnecessary pride on her part at the trial. Her initial sentence was for three years but Maria stood up and said she wanted as long a sentence as her colleague Elena—five years. These observers noted that she had remained steadfast during the first three years but lost her faith during those two years when she had relied on herself! Conditions in Soviet women's prisons are frightening for Christian or other decent women.

72. Author's notes on meeting in Paderborn, West Germany, September 29, 1979.

73. AS 878, 879. The first printed version of *BL* was 7-8/71 (AS 880).

74. They were: Vitalii I. Pidchenko (1941), Ekaterina I. Gritsenio (1943), Viktor A. Pikalov (1950), Zinaida P. Tarasova (1942), Ida D. Korotun (1938), Tatiana S. Kozhemiakina (1937), and Nadezhda G. L'vova (1946) (*Bulletin* 18).

75. Arrested were: Ivan I. Leven (1928), David I. Koop (1931), Liudmila Zaitseva (1946), Larisa Zaitseva (1950). A printed announcement with photos appeared soon after. Recently one *Khristianin* co-worker developed cancer. Instead of obtaining treatments at a nearby hospital, this co-worker bade farewell, then left for a distant city to die in unknown surroundings in order not to betray the work. She had devoted ten of her 40 years to the secret press. Another press was discovered in Dnepropetrovsk in January 1980. The four arrested received three year prison terms. In June 1980 still another printing press was found in the village of Glivenki, Krasnodarskii Krai. There were four arrests.

76. *Nachrichten von den Feldern der Verfolgung*, Nov.-Dec./78, pp. 9-10.

77. *BL*, 1-3/75; 4/75 reprinted in *RCDA*, 4-9/75, pp. 114-20.

78. For a more detailed recent assessment see my article, "The Reform Baptists Today," *RCL*, 1/80. pp. 28-38.

We want to remind you, brothers, of the troubles we had in the province of Asia. The burdens laid upon us were so heavy that we gave up all hope of being alive. We felt that the death sentence had been passed on us. But this happened so that we should rely not on ourselves, but only on God, who raises the dead.

—*2 Corinthians 1:8-10*

9 Life in the Provinces: Moscow Is Not Asia, Siberia, nor Even Kiev

Moscow is not the Soviet Union. It may be the capital of a highly centralized state and the headquarters of a highly centralized evangelical union, but life in the provinces is often very different. In fact, the word province is inadequate to suggest the differences between the different republics that make up the Soviet Union. A tour of the Baltic, the Ukraine, Russia, Siberia, and Central Asia is like visiting that many different worlds.

Already in 1947 President Zhidkov had claimed that twelve nationality groupings were included in their union.[1] There were Russians, Ukrainians, Belorussians (White Russians), Latvians, Estonians, Lithuanians, Karelo-Finns, Romanians, Hungarians, Moldavians, Georgians, and Armenians. At the All-Union congress in 1974, an additional five nationalities were represented: Germans, Poles, Bulgarians, Mordvinians, and Gagaus.[2] A handy, widely accepted name for this motley group is Russian Baptists. But we do them an injustice if we assume that they are all Russians and that they are all Baptists.

Already in the 1920s, non-Russian evangelicals complained about a russification tendency which they detected in Prokhanov's Evangelical Christian Union.[3] The statute of that union, in fact, stipulated that the World Alliance of Evangelical Christians could become a reality only under Russian leadership. The postwar AUCECB evangelical body disclaims a russification policy. But already in 1948 an article praising the great Russian language appeared in *Bratskii Vestnik*. It urged all ECB members to strive to speak a good Russian. "Love of the Russian language is one of the manifestations of our love to our great motherland."[4] The Russian language is the official language of the Soviet Union, but more than 20 percent of the population is unable to speak Russian. That includes some of the AUCECB leaders. At the 1974 congress, quite a few delegates expressed a wish to read the Bible and even *Bratskii Vestnik* in their mother tongue.

The Ukraine

At least 46 percent (some experts argue it is over 50 percent) of the AUCECB membership is in the Ukraine.[5] When delegates met for the All-Union congress in 1974, the 213 Ukrainian representatives completely filled one side of the church, a visible expression of their influence. In 1960 the Moscow leadership had thought that the only way to survive was for them to issue a church statute dictated by the state. But the survival of Soviet evangelicals was in essence due much more to its great strength in the Ukraine. This was the area where *Stundism* had begun and it was an area of rapid growth during the 1920s. The western parts of present-day Ukraine had been outside Soviet territory during the inter-war period and had been spared Stalinist persecutions. When these territories were incorporated, it meant that well-organized churches, often led by presbyters with Bible school training received in Danzig (Pentecostal) or Lodz (Baptist), could now help their weaker brothers in the east. Between 1952 and 1965 the evangelicals in the Ukraine increased by 47 percent, with over half of these representing converts from Orthodoxy, and possibly also from the Uniate Church that was violently suppressed after the war.[6]

The Soviet state fully recognized the importance of the Ukraine, and its influence is apparent in the appointment of two key church officials to lead the Ukrainian church. Metropolitan Nikolai, often more powerful than the patriarch himself, headed up postwar reconstruction efforts for the Orthodox Church in the Ukraine. A. L. Andreev performed a parallel role as AUCECB senior presbyter for the Ukraine. Andreev was a Russian, an Evangelical Christian, who reigned for twenty-one years over a membership that was more Baptist than Evangelical Christian. From the beginning he usually had several assistants. His first assistant was F. G. Patkovskii, a major Baptist representative in the union. When the Pentecostals joined the union a year later, D. I. Ponomarchuk became a second assistant senior presbyter to represent Pentecostal interests or, more accurately, to persuade Pentecostals to join the union.[7]

Andreev was already sixty years of age in 1945, so that it soon became necessary for his assistants to visit the congregations while Andreev issued directives from Kiev and periodically called provincial senior presbyters to Kiev for consultation. There were usually twenty-three or twenty-five senior presbyters under his jurisdiction who were usually appointed by Moscow, but Andreev made the actual decisions. Sometimes, as, for example, in L'vov, in 1954, he removed the entire leadership and brought in others from elsewhere and enforced their acceptance.[8] The oblasts varied in size; some senior presbyters were responsible for thirty churches, while others had 150 churches. Generally speaking, he maintained the closest ties with the nearby oblasts such as Kiev, Dnepropetrovsk, and Zaporozh'e, and, as a result, it was these senior presbyters who eventually succeeded him.

From 1948 to 1956 A. I. Mitskevich (also of Evangelical Christian stock) served as his deputy, making many visits throughout the Ukraine. Mitskevich was generally appreciated.[9] He then moved to Moscow, and his place was taken by N. N. Mel'nikov, who had provided strong leadership for fifty-seven churches in Dnepropetrovsk Oblast. There were many Pentecostals in this region, and Mel'nikov had been fairly successful in bringing them into the union and maintaining cooperation with Pentecostal leaders in his region. One of these, G. G. Ponurko, succeeded him as oblast senior presbyter.[10] Officially, Mel'nikov served only as senior presbyter for the entire Ukraine from 1966 until 1974, when he was forced into retirement. But he had placed his stamp on the Ukrainian organization for a period of eighteen years. In the end, delegates voted to dismiss him and successfully pushed through the election of a relatively inexperienced but highly admired younger man named Jacob K. Dukhonchenko.

Mel'nikov had come to be disliked for his authoritarian ways and his sharp defense of the AUCECB against the CCECB, but it would be unfair to include him among those church officials whose loyalty to the church was in question. When he finally became senior presbyter in his own right, a presbyter council of six persons was created to assist him. These were I. Ia. Tatarchenko and I. Ia. Kaliuzhnyi, who became his deputies, while F. R. Astakhov, D. D. Shapovalov, and N. V. Kuzmenko (the latter representing Pentecostals) became assistant senior presbyters, and young M. V. Mel'nik served as full-time secretary.[11] These divided the responsibilities, and in the first years Mel'nikov often called all the senior presbyters together for consultation, but by 1969 his new deputy, I. S. Gnida, complained that Mel'nikov had stopped this again.[12]

Another structural strength for the Ukrainian organization was that it had its own treasury for conducting Ukrainian affairs. At the congress in

1974, treasurer Mitskevich complained that some regions were not giving their fair share to Moscow and used the Ukraine as an illustration. Mel'nikov was highly offended and insisted that he was sure they had given three times as much as Mitskevich said, but there have been subsequent in- · dications that Kiev only follows reluctantly when Moscow calls.

If the Ukraine was a revival center during the early years and again in the fifties,[13] there has also been rapid growth in the seventies. Why this should be so remains somewhat of a mystery. The Ukrainians themselves prefer to attribute this to the work of the Holy Spirit in their midst, but they do acknowledge that Ukrainians are often more ardent, emotional, perhaps also more responsive to faith. This feature also characterizes the Pentecostals and the Reform Baptists in the Ukraine.

Yet one constant problem has been the shortage of presbyters. In 1953 N. I. Vysotskii declared that in recent years the number of ordained presbyters had nearly doubled, so that, at the moment, only one fifth of the congregations still had no ordained presbyter.[14] Around this time there were 1,800 congregations. In 1974, even though the number of congregations had decreased through fusing local groups and closing many, still, out of the 1,033 presbyters in the Ukraine, 270 were not ordained.[15] But the new senior presbyter Jacob Dukhonchenko did draw attention to the fact that many new, younger men had been elected to office and they were trying hard to encourage the election of younger, better educated leaders. He wished that the theological correspondence course could take more students. At that time 55 Ukrainians had completed the course.[16]

It is also difficult to explain why there should be large groups of Reform Baptists[17] and independent Pentecostals in the Ukraine. A possible reason for the latter phenomenon is that Pentecostals are particularly strong in those regions of the Western Ukraine, such as Rovno and Volhynia, which had close links to the Pentecostals in Poland before the war. This movement developed a Bible school in Danzig, whose students played a leading role in the Western Ukraine.[18] Perhaps, some might argue, the more ebullient Ukrainian character was especially responsive to the emotionalism of Pentecostalism, but this was also the area most frequently visited by foreign preachers once tourism resumed. Many of these, as well as several radio programs, were Pentecostalist in character.

Belorussia and Moldavia

The Belorussians speak their own language and have their own traditions even though they are dwarfed by their Ukrainian neighbors. The evangelical movement began here relatively late in the early 1920s. Stories about evangelical life in this area are attractive enough to make one want to live there, but there are also stories that one would rather not have experienced. It is indeed strange to hear about a senior presbyter who preached but whom the believers referred to behind his back as comrade rather than brother. Senior Presbyter K. S. Veliseichik, who had Moscow support, became the leader of the republic in 1958 and remained in office till 1976. He was a very energetic leader who also represented the AUCECB on the WCC executive committee, but locally he was heavily criticized for forcing adherence to the 1960 statute.[19]

His predecessor, V. N. Chechnev (1882-1958), had been very different. Chechnev began his service in the Ukraine (Dnepropetrovsk Oblast) and was sent by Ivan Prokhanov to Minsk (Belorussia) in 1924 because an experienced worker was needed there to organize church growth. Chechnev remained at his post till his death, also serving as an AUCECB member after 1948. He was a wise leader who read extensively and was especially respected for his loving manner.[20] The present senior presbyter, Ivan Bukatyi, attended the Swedish Baptist Seminary and is also highly respected.[21]

Belorussia has the second largest concentration of Pentecostals. Until 1949 the senior presbyter was assisted by a Pentecostal. This was I. K. Pan'ko (1901-1964), who bears primary responsibility for successfully bringing the Belorussian Pentecostals into the union. Even a term of imprisonment (1949-55) did not alter his deep commitment to the unity.[22] It was not until 1966 that another Pentecostal, L. S. Vladyko, began to exercise a similar leadership role. Vladyko became a candidate member of the AUCECB in 1969 and a full member a decade later. The Belorussian Republic, with its 10,000 members, also has a structure whereby the senior presbyter is assisted by five oblast senior presbyters.[23]

No doubt the strictness of Veliseichik and his assistant, M. N. Germanovich (Brest Oblast), helped trigger the split in Belorussia, but state officials did their part through severe methods. From 1961 to 1965 only eight persons served prison sentences, but during the next two years an additional twenty-five persons were sentenced to prison. In 1978 the entire prison alumni met for a reunion. The group totaled forty-eight persons, including six women.[24]

Imprisonment of leaders did not stop the work nor reduce the boldness of the believers. The Reform Baptist church in Brest with a membership over 800 was finally offered state registration without conditions several

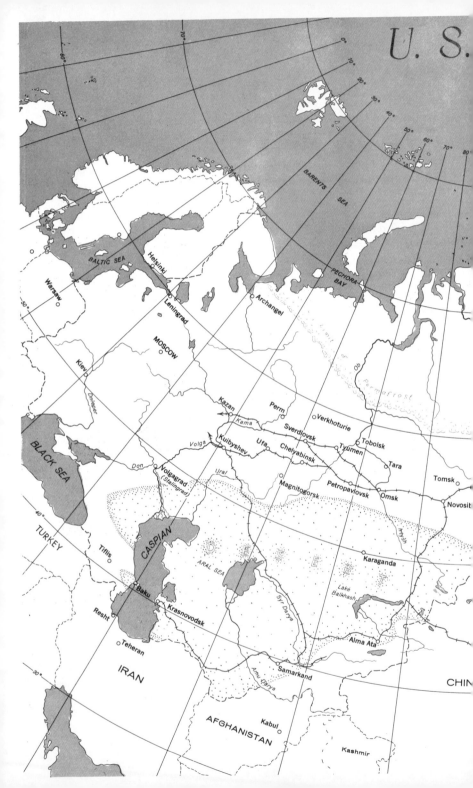

years ago, and then began the negotiations for an adequate church building. When the authorities refused one church building, the believers suggested that they should take over the atheist club since only ten persons attended it anyway. That, too, was refused, as well as an unused Roman Catholic church, so finally the believers told the authorities that, if they did not receive a building, they would divide up into fifteen small groups and meet in houses! This church also had many young people. After the evening service, which had lasted from six to eight o'clock, the youth conducted their own service, which went on till 11:00 p.m. Upon questioning, the presbyter replied that he could do nothing about it because the 300 young people had so much enthusiasm they would simply meet in spite of any cautions he might give.[25]

An AUCECB church demonstrated its own boldness and creativity. Once, when a foreign visitor attended, the local plenipotentiary for the Council for Religious Affairs suddenly arrived to attend the service. The presiding minister called on one of his preachers, who delivered an excellent sermon on the Christian's duty to the state. The next preacher preached about the Bible, emphasizing how important it is that the contents of the Bible should also be in one's heart. But it was not good, the preacher stated, if only one person in a hundred had the possibility of holding a Bible in his hands. It would be much better that each person had a Bible. Then the congregation stood for prayer, and one of the sisters managed to convert her prayer into an appeal to God and the state official. She began with profuse thanksgiving for the many blessings, and for their freedoms, especially the freedom to be able to meet together for prayer. Then she went on to ask God to help Leonid Brezhnev so that Brezhnev could see his way through to granting them a new prayer house. She also prayed for the plenipotentiary, saying he was a good man, and asked God to help him do his work well. The service closed, the state official left, got into his car and drove away. The guest speaker had assumed he would not be invited to preach, but as soon as the state official was gone, the local leader invited everyone back into the church and the guest preached for two more hours!

On the southwestern border of the Soviet Union is Moldavia, which has a very different history, more closely linked to Romania. After the war, Ilia Ivanov was sent there to reorganize and rebuild churches which had been destroyed during the war. I. T. Slobodchikov then became the senior presbyter (1946-49).[26] He had studied four years at Bucharest at a seminary and was obviously well qualified. But in 1949 he was demoted to assistant senior presbyter and F. R. Astakhov replaced him. Astakhov had been moved there from Siberia and now administered the church with authoritarianism. According to the reformers, after the local church had excommunicated him, he was finally moved to the Caucasus and spent the early sixties as an assistant to Andreev in the Ukraine.[27] Astakhov was succeeded by the Pentecostal leader D. I. Ponomarchuk, who helped improve relations with the Pentecostals but that did not prevent the *Initsiativniki* split.[28]

The *Initsiativniki* leader in Moldavia, S. Kh. Tsurkan, was an older, highly respected presbyter in a registered church, who became a member of the *Orgkomitet* in 1962.[29] He and a younger associate, M. I. Khorev, regularly organized large meetings in the forest near Kishinev. An atheist source claims that the reformers established twenty congregations totalling no more than 400 persons, but that appears to be a major understatement considering the attention paid to the movement in Moldavia.[30]

Moldavia had the unhappy distinction of becoming another Barnaul when a young twenty-one-year-old Moldavian soldier was tortured to death in 1970. The story of Ivan Moiseev was circulated in CPR *Bulletin* No. 9 and in other *Samizdat*. The authorities rendered their account absurd by changing the official version several times. Registered churches as far away as Central Asia were fined fifty rubles for mentioning Moiseev in the service. The torture of this soldier appears to have been unusually severe. But the major impact of Moiseev's story is the picture it gives of the remarkable faith and witness of a simple peasant, while the miracles he experienced forced some of the medical doctors to begin to wonder about God.[31]

Baltic Baptists

Whereas Belorussia and the Ukraine are Slavic, Estonia and Latvia have a West European culture. Not only do the medieval city centers appear German, the European culture is evident in the more restrained worship style, the performance of oratorios and also less crowded church services. At the 1963 congress Senior Presbyter P. G. Egle of Latvia complained that they were losing membership and were in sore need of younger ministers.[32]

Till then Latvian membership had actually been growing. By 1954 there were ninety-one churches with 6,600 baptized members and two years later Senior Presbyter Friedrich E. Khuns referred to 100 congregations with 9,000 members. Yet, when they celebrated their hundredth anniversary in 1960, Khuns declared that there were eighty churches, while in 1963 Baltic Senior Presbyter Levindanto reported that Latvia had sixty-seven congregations with 6,488 members. The drop had been sudden and appeared to be directly linked to the antireligious policy under Khrushchev. Since then, Latvians have held their own, and at present they represent about 6,000 members.[33]

Estonia, the neighboring republic, has its own unique history and unique language. Estonian evangelicals celebrated their seventy-fifth anniversary in 1959. At that time Senior Presbyter Johannes Lipstok stated that the gradual decline had been stopped. Whereas there had been 100 congregations in 1949, there were now eighty-eight congregations with 9,000 persons. Their massive church in Tallinn had 1,800 members, but otherwise each local church averaged 100 members. The membership decline did not stop, and there are at present seventy-eight congregations with 7,500 members.[34]

The puzzle behind this decline, which was artificially induced, at least partially, is why no Reform Baptist movement split the Estonian and Latvian churches. In both countries before the war there had been competing unions of Evangelical Christians and Baptists, as well as Pentecostals, but these conflicts were eventually settled through union, although in Latvia this took place only after the war. Because both republics were small and their membership was relatively small, the leaders in both republics settled their differences internally, invariably presenting a united voice in Moscow. Without question, the internal squabbling was also reduced because a greater percentage of the presbyters had formal theological training. In 1955, for example, one third of the Latvian presbyters were trained persons, and they had also been able to conduct a short-course Bible school in 1947.[35] In Estonia, a legally permitted correspondence course with 40 students opened in 1956. It was able to continue for four years.[36]

This rather similar history for Latvia and Estonia also serves to illustrate that the senior presbyter was not the most important factor in its history. Johannes Lipstok became the first Estonian senior presbyter, remaining in office until his death in 1961.[37] After a short interval, during which Baltic Senior Presbyter Levindanto handled affairs himself, A. Sil'dos held this office from 1963 to 1970. Following his retirement, church historian Robert Vyzu became senior presbyter.[38] But in Latvia there were numerous senior presbyter shifts during the first decade, until finally in 1953, with the ouster of A. M. Redlikh, a period of stability set in.[39] The new senior presbyter, Friedrich E. Khuns, was already sixty-nine years old, but he remained in office till 1959, when he retired with pension and Levindanto took over personal control, but Khuns remained a respected leader till his death in 1971.[40] P. G. Egle, Latvian senior presbyter since 1966, was succeeded by Ia. E. Tervits in 1977. From the beginning, the Latvian leaders have always carried the title of bishop.

Latvian and Estonian Baptists might be insignificant in number, but their contribution to the evangelical movement in the Soviet Union has been considerable. They provided the few theologians who were in a position to present doctrinal speeches at national congresses. Oswald Tiark and Arpad Arder were highly appreciated for their contribution to the unity commission, especially through their visits to Central Asia and Siberia.[41] Arpad Arder was one of the delegates' choice for AUCECB council membership, but his local activity in helping the Reform Baptist churches that moved to his area for refuge, as well as the Mennonite groups that began moving to Estonia and Latvia, evoked official displeasure. In at least nine Latvian churches, German-speaking fellowships were able to develop their own structure under the protection of the officially registered Latvian pastor. In short, there are very few critics of the Latvian and Estonian Baptists.

Central Asia and the Germans

There are not many churches in Central Asia, but those that do exist often have a very large membership.[42] One reason for this is that in Kazakhstan, as well as in the other four Central Asian republics, there are large regions of desert. This is a predominantly Muslim area, but there are almost no converts from these peoples to Christianity. The location of Baptist churches is therefore due to Soviet resettlement policy.

One peculiarity of the Central Asian Baptist churches is the high proportion of Germans. Some of these German Mennonites came here at the beginning of the century to form new settlements on the frontier. Many more were brought here forcibly during the war to do forced labor in the mines around Karaganda or to dig canals near Frunze or to grow cotton in Uzbekistan and Tadzhikistan. The high percentage of Ukrainians and Russians in these churches can often also be explained by this involuntary migration, although there were also many people moving to Kazakhstan voluntarily in response to Khrushchev's virgin lands program.[43]

The story of Karaganda illustrates what happened in many of these churches. This church had been registered after the war and consisted primarily of Russians and Ukrainians. By 1956 Germans became influential, with some of their ministers preaching in German. Soon the registered church was closed by the authorities but the believers began meeting in private homes in different parts of the city. When state pressure eased and the church was reopened, the number of believers had grown significantly. The registered church became a large one and included a German wing led by Abram Friesen.[44] Other Mennonites finally managed to secure autonomous registration as a German-speaking Mennonite Brethren church.[45] Since this congregation did not give the Mennonites (Kirchliche) full rights, the latter finally obtained their own registration. Still others led by David D. Klassen, who had had very negative experiences in the registered church in Novosibirsk, remained unregistered and became closely linked with the CCECB.[46] In contrast to one regular-sized church building, such as in Moscow or Leningrad where 3,000 to 5,000 members tried to find room, the Karaganda evangelicals, through diversification, had five large congregations meeting in four buildings.[47]

The conflict with the Reform Baptists was also different in this region.[48] In many areas, church members first became aware of the split after 1966 when the state resumed its pressure, now more specifically focused on the reformers. Registered churches that had closed were reopened, with leadership that had not compromised itself in the interval. Even most of those that remained open managed with minimal state interference. In Kirgizia in particular, the Khrushchev campaign was not very thoroughly enforced.

Consequently, CCECB churches in the region can be characterized by greater radicalism, a confrontationist stance against the state which was rejected by many on theological grounds. One of the ministers in Dushanbe sided temporarily with the reformers but found their radicalism distasteful.[49] N. N. Sizov was a young preacher in Frunze who found Ilia Ivanov's explanations for submitting to state demands unacceptable and joined the CCECB. He, too, returned after about a year and was elected senior presbyter for Kirgizia in 1969 in spite of state resistance. As a result the Kirgizian leadership gained wide respect, which made the CCECB alternative less attractive.

Another change that took place after 1965 was the gradual ouster of senior presbyter for all of Central Asia, M. S. Vashchuk. Local believers distrusted him, whereas his successors now enjoy wide respect.[50] The problem may have been, however, that the well-educated Vashchuk with his wide-ranging interests in theological trends, may have seemed too liberal for the conservative and suspicious membership. The churches in Kirgizia once took a decision to reject AUCECB membership in the WCC and are still showing great reluctance about the Moscow course, which they consider too liberal theologically. They were the ones who helped the Ukrainians elect Andrei Klimenko as the president acceptable to their simple and conservative tastes.

The Caucasus

This is a region rich in romance. It includes the territory between the Black and Caspian seas and includes not only the republics of Georgia, Armenia, and Azerbaidzhan, but also the large region around Stavropol and Krasnodar and the autonomous republics of Dagestan, Checheno-Ingush, Kabardino-Belkar, and Osetia. For the evangelicals this is also a place of romance because their movement began in a little village near Tbilissi.

Key persons such as V. G. Pavlov and V. V. Ivanov-Klyshnikov started here and eventually became national evangelical leaders. I. S. Prokhanov also had his origins in Ordzhonikidze. But after the war this leadership role disappeared. A long-time, much-beloved leader was Pavel G. Ter-Avanesov who was a real father-figure to the members. Once some Moscow representatives had to reprimand local church members who literally kissed his feet.[51] When he died in 1962 there were a number of years of problematic leadership which weakened the church.[52] Reform Baptists found support here, especially in the Northern Caucasus where state treatment was more unfriendly. In recent years the AUCECB has gained senior presbyters who have graduated from the Bible correspondence course and new growth is anticipated.[53]

The North and the East

In Soviet dissident circles, the Northeast sometimes refers to the region which Solzhenitsyn has labeled "The Gulag Archipelago." From Arkhangelsk in the north to Vladivostok in the Far East, there are isolated churches, most of them unregistered. In fact, the existence of many of these congregations is still unknown. In this region there are also churches that began after persons were converted through hearing a religious radio broadcast and the radio speaker remains their presbyter to the present day.

This region is rich in natural resources and represents the frontier for Soviet industrial advance. In the Ural Mountain region and farther east throughout the vast Siberian expanse, new cities have sprung up in recent decades.[54] In very few of these are there churches, although the evangelicals have been more successful than the Orthodox in forming small fellowships. This is the new frontier for growth and expansion, for mission to people who are religious illiterates.

Reform Baptists are well organized in Western Siberia and Northern

Kazakhstan. Unregistered Pentecostals began moving further east after 1956, and estimations of their strength are as high as several hundred thousand.[55] But the AUCECB structure in this region is undeveloped. In 1974 Senior Presbyter E. N. Raevski received an assistant to help him administer a territory that covered over twenty million square kilometers.[56] In Western Siberia, Senior Presbyter Konstantin Borodinov tried to visit the registered churches scattered throughout his vast region. Andrei Klimenko, who had been senior presbyter of nine oblasts on the other side of the Volga, was also overtaxed physically. Not only was there a problem of distance but for years the senior presbyter could not automatically travel where he wished. If he was not permitted to visit the unregistered congregations in Orenburg Oblast, then other men had to try to provide some leadership when they came to visit their relatives. In recent years large numbers of churches have been registered in the Omsk and Tomsk regions and a senior presbyter for Omsk Oblast was finally appointed.[57]

Energetic and creative leadership has the potential to work wonders. In October 1978 Sergei Nikolaev gained the distinction of being elected the youngest senior presbyter in the union. He was only twenty-nine. He was a gifted musician and preacher who had been sponsored by the AUCECB for two years of study in England. With the death of M. I. Sorokin, Nikolaev succeeded him as senior presbyter for the Northwest region of the RSFSR, a region larger than West Germany. There were only twenty-six congregations in his charge but they were widely scattered, travel being especially difficult in winter. Nikolaev set to work with a burst of energy and twelve months later reported that his charge had doubled to fifty-two congregations. Twenty-two of these congregations he had literally discovered—their existence had been unknown or forgotten. Aided by a council of presbyters and local groups of zealous young people, he was anticipating an extensive program of church growth which included systematic teaching.[58]

It will probably be decades before evangelical isolation in this region comes to an end and a network of churches similar to that in the Ukraine becomes established. Already in 1966 senior presbyter Raevski had invited young, energetic presbyters to move to his region because they were badly needed.[59] Few, apparently, have responded so far, for that is nearly equivalent to asking affluent Westerners to accept the rigors of a Third World country.

Soviet or Russian Evangelicals?
At best, these brief comments provide insight into the tremendous

diversity of evangelical life in the Soviet Union. In contrast to the more dominant Russian Orthodox Church, which is almost exclusively Slavic, Soviet evangelicals have become almost as international as the Communist Party itself. That is why they are regarded as a potentially dangerous challenge since the Great Russians will soon lose their status as representing more than 50 percent of the population.

It is apparent that the AUCECB leadership is still dominated by the Great Russians, but the 1974 congress reflected growing sentiments of nationalism. That calls for selfless leadership if the union is to avoid further division. One of the Ukrainian delegates turned to his own, and with the eloquence of poetry urged them to forego their deep desire to read the Bible in their mother tongue but rather support the general effort so that they would at least get more Bibles even if they were Russian.[60] Those local sentiments indicate that as the Moscow leadership continues to gain more concessions for the church, the new freedom may eventually permit the luxury of nationalist division. The restlessness under Great Russian leadership from Moscow is an underlying factor in the movement toward denominational autonomy to which we now turn.

Notes to Chapter 9

1. *BV*, 1/47, p. 14.
2. Author's personal notes as observer based on report from mandate commission.
3. Kahle, pp. 294-95, 306-309.
4. *BV*, 4/48, p. 4.
5. *EBPS*, April 25, 1977. Ray Oppenheim, American chaplain in Moscow who traveled widely in the Ukraine, estimated it to be 60 percent—200,000 members in 1975.
6. Lialina, p. 16. On the Uniate Church, see Bohdan Bociurkiw, "The Uniate Church in the Soviet Ukraine: A Case Study in Soviet Church Policy," *Canadian Slavonic Papers*, VII, 1965, 89-113; and his forthcoming book, *The Ukrainian Greek-Catholic Church and the Soviet State Since World War II*.
7. D. I. Ponomarchuk (1892-1968); converted 1915; Baptist preacher in Dnepropetrovsk Oblast; joined Pentecostals in 1925 and became member of All-Ukrainian Council of Pentecostal Union; leader of Pentecostal Union 1944-45; assistant SP for Ukraine 1947-57; SP for Moldavia 1957-61. Biographical data (true also for others mentioned in this chapter) has been culled from *BV* and other sources. I will cite my "Biographical Card File" as source hereafter.
8. *BV*, 5-6/54, p. 138.
9. Mitskevich's father was Lithuanian, his mother German. He first worked in Evangelical Christian circles, later with Baptists. *Supra* Chap. 6, Note 29.
10. *BV*, 3-4/56, p. 97. Cf. 2-3/53, p. 112.
11. *BV*, 6/66, p. 38.
12. *BV*, 2/70, p. 48.

13. See above, Chap. 3.
14. *BV*, 2-3/53, pp. 110-11; cf. 1/49, p. 71.
15. *BV*, 1/75, p. 44.
16. *Ibid.*, p. 64; *Die Gemeinde*, 23/74.
17. Puzin, Chairman of the Council for the Affairs of Religious Cults, in 1964 stated there were 126 unregistered ECB congregations comprising about 10,000 believers in the Ukraine (partial copy of speech at Keston Archives).
18. Kolarz, p. 332. Cf. A. T. Moskalenko, *Piatidesiatniki* (2nd ed.; Moscow, 1973), pp. 37-74.
19. AS 770, p. 52.
20. *BV*, 5-6/58, pp. 16-20.
21. *BV*, 6/77, pp. 55-58. L. S. Vladyko (Pentecostal) and A. M. Ketsko (1907-1978) were elected as his assistants. Bukatyi was also elected to the AUCECB in 1974, from which Veliseichik had been eliminated in 1969.
22. *BV*, 6/64, pp. 62-66; cf. Durasoff, pp. 122-23, 163.
23. In 1948 there were 116 congregations with 9,934 members (*BV*, 3/48, p. 48). Although in 1963 the leadership had been reduced to Veliseichik (responsible personally for Minsk, Gomel', Mogilev, and Vitebsk Oblasts), M. N. Germanovich (Brest Oblast which had 48 percent of the congregations), and K. I. Sevashko (Grodno), by 1966 this had again increased to five senior presbyters through the addition of A. P. Polovikov (Mogilev) and A. T. Pashkovskii (Gomel'). In 1974 there were six: Veliseichik, A. M. Ketsko, K. I. Sevashko, U. R. Shust, N. D. Snitko, and A. T. Pashkovskii (*BV*, 1/75, p. 46).
24. Prisoners' lists; alumni photo in *Nachrichten von den Feldern der Verfolgung*, November-December, 1978, p. 2.
25. Interview data, Warsaw, May 4, 1977.
26. *BV*, 2/55, p. 54; finally retired as presbyter in Kishinev (*BV*, 6/77, p. 73).
27. *BV*, 4/63, p. 74; 6/63, p. 35. For a short time he was SP for the Caucasus. When Bychkov surveyed Moldavian history at the 1974 congress, he omitted Astakhov from the list of senior presbyters for Moldavia (*BV*, 1/75, p. 36)!
28. Ponomarchuk was succeeded by S. K. Malanchuk (1968-73) and K. S. Sedletskii (1973-).
29. Identified in *BV*, 3/46, p. 38 as a leading worker in Moldavia.
30. A Danilov and D. Tabakaru, "Kto takie 'initsiativniki'?" *Kommunist Moldavii*, 12/67, p. 70. Cf. V. F. Gazhos, *Evoliutsia religioznogo sektantstva v Moldavii* (Kishinev, 1975), pp. 12-35.
31. An English-language dramatization with extensive translation of documents is Myrna Grant, *Vanya* (Wheaton: Creation House, 1974).
32. As quoted in AS 770, p. 130.
33. *BV*, 3/54, p. 62; 2/56, p. 46; 5-6/60, pp. 76-82; AS 770, p. 130. In an *Orgkomitet* letter to the AUCECB (March 23, 1965) they complained that fourteen churches had been closed in 1960-63. They also noted that whereas 1,246 persons were baptized in Latvia and Estonia from 1957 to 1959, only 195 persons were baptized in 1960-62 while 1,099 died; i.e., a loss of 904 in membership (AS 772, p. 16).
34. *BV*, 2/49, pp. 71-80; 3/58, p. 66; 2/59, p. 19; *EBPS*, February 18, 1974; October 20, 1977, p. 4.
35. *BV*, 2/55, p. 6; 4/48, pp. 57-58.
36. *BV*, 2/58, p. 66; 6/66, pp. 21, 46.
37. *BV*, 5/48, pp. 52-53. At first he was assisted by Io. Kh. Laks, an evangelical Christian.

38. Since 1947 Sil'dos had repeatedly acted as assistant senior presbyter; Levindanto relied on him because he spoke Russian. Robert Vyzu was trained at the Baptist seminary and then at the University of Tartu, Estonia.

39. They were: K. Latseklis (1945-47), August Korp (1948), A. M. Redlikh (1949-1953), F. E. Khuns (1953-59), P. K. Egle (1966-77), Ia. E. Tervits (1977-). Redlikh, a dark horse candidate, was ousted for Pentecostal leanings.

40. *BV*, 3/61, p. 79; 1/72, pp. 72-74. Why Levindanto took over without the help of Estonian and Latvian senior presbyters is unclear, but it is apparent that he and the Moscow leadership needed several years before the Latvians accepted Sil'dos as senior presbyter.

41. O. A. Tiark (born 1904) had a master's degree from Columbia University (*BV*, 1/56, p. 26). In large part due to his regular Bible commentary series in *BV*, when he was announced as speaker at the 1974 congress, delegates craned their necks to see him, as if he were a patriarch. Arpad A. Arder, converted 1945; ordained 1955; presbyter in Rakvere 1956-70; elected AUCECB candidate in 1966. Later state pressure forced his transfer to a smaller church. Robert Vyzu read a major doctrinal paper at the 1979 congress.

42. In Kazakhstan there are 17,000 members (162 congregations); in Kirgizia, 6,200 (forty percent German); and in Uzbekistan, Tadzhikistan and Turkmenia, thirty congregations; fifteen of them are not registered (*BV*, 1/75 and 1979 congress notes).

43. See Martin McCauley, *Khrushchev and the Development of Soviet Agriculture: The Virgin Land Programme 1953-1964* (London: Macmillan, 1976), p. 232.

44. In 1976 Emil Baumbach, a German, became presbyter for the entire congregation (*BV*, 2/76, p. 79).

45. Registered in 1967 (*BV*, 4/67, p. 42). H. Woelk and W. Matthies were the leaders; present leader is Heinrich Goertzen. The Church Mennonites who meet in the same building were registered in 1975.

46. An additional factor was that this group was a mixture of Germans and Russians and rejected the ethnic exclusivism of the Mennonite Brethren.

47. There is a registered Pentecostal *(Edinstvenniki)* congregation of 500 members, and a large German Lutheran congregation of 2,800 members. Data supplied by Dr. Paul Hansen of the Lutheran World Federation, the first foreign churchman to receive permission to visit Karaganda.

48. Heavily based on Umsiedler interview data.

49. *BV*, 4/64, p. 75.

50. The successors were: N. A. Kolesnikov (SP for Kazakhstan, 1970-); N. N. Sizov (SP for Kirgizia, 1969-); M. M. Samotugin (SP for Central Asia, 1967-1977); T. F. Kviring, 1977- . Vashchuk was pensioned in 1970 and moved to Kazan, where he is still presbyter. Kolesnikov, elected AUCECB treasurer in 1979, is expected to move to Moscow.

51. *BV*, 1/49.

52. After P. G. Ter-Avanesov (1944-49) and N. I. Kornaukhov (1944-54), who were responsible for the Trans-Caucasus and North Caucasus regions respectively, both regions were combined under M. S. Dushenko (1949-57), F. R. Astakhov (1957-60) and B. A. Rusanov (1961-63), and P. A. Dzhaniashvili (1965-68). Subordinate to them were R. R. Podgaiskii (SP for Stavropol'skii Krai, 1954-65) and for Krasnodarskii Krai there were V. I. Andreenko (1956-60), I. E. Egorov (1960-65), M. Ia. Rubanenko (1965-66). The two North Caucasus regions were united again under A. D. Savin (1968-79).

53. N. Z. Kvirikashvili (SP for Caucasus since 1974), V. D. Erisov (SP for Krasnodarskii Krai, 1977-79, now for Stavropol'skii Krai).

54. For a description see Smith, *The Russians*, p. 326f.

55. See, for example, the testimony of Evgenii Bresenden in *Hearings before the Commission on Security and Cooperation in Europe*, 95th congress, Vol. II, "Religious Liberty and Minority Rights in the Soviet Union," April 27, 28, 1977, pp. 5-42.

56. Iu. A. Maksimchuk, a younger man; Raevski, born 1904, has served continuously since 1948 (*BV*, 1/75, p. 45).

57. He is B. Sipko (*EBPS*, July 18, 1978).

58. Reported at 1979 congress.

59. *BV*, 6/66, p. 41. Six congregations had been registered between 1963 and 1966.

60. Author's personal notes of congress. The official report printed only a few such comments.

Where they love Jesus, there is warmth and life. Why have so many left who formerly belonged to the union and its congregations, like, for example, the Pentecostal brethren? Because it is often too cold in our midst. As a result, these brothers caught a cold and now they are seriously ill, running around feverishly and talking nonsense.

—*Martsinkovski* [1]

Through Jesus there is a place for all men in the family of God. Men may put up their barriers; churches may keep their communion tables for their own members. God never does; it is the tragedy of the church that it is so often more exclusive than God.

—*William Barclay* [2]

10 The Movement Toward Autonomy: Reform Baptists, Mennonites, Pentecostals

If this were simply a history of the AUCECB instead of the Soviet evangelical movement as a whole, this chapter might more appropriately be headed "unity." This was always the motto for the All-Union congresses because unity remains threatened to the present. But from the perspective of free church ideology, autonomy has always seemed more significant than unity.

Public statements by Soviet evangelicals on unity or autonomy have an aspect of artificiality because too often they were not the spontaneous expression of a personal viewpoint. Rather, they reflected the vacillation in state policy toward religion which church leaders then had to clothe with religious language. Soviet policy toward the churches started out by opposing religious centralization in order to break the institutional power of the churches, especially that of the Orthodox Patriarchate. The basic law on cults speaks almost exclusively about a local religious society which organizes and administers itself as an autonomous unit. When church life began again after the war, special dispensations from Stalin permitted the restoration of religious headquarters, and the new church statutes (including that of the AUCECB) reflected the new centralism. The 1960 statute increased the power of the Moscow headquarters at the expense of the local presbyter. The advantage for the state was obvious: control over and domination of the churches through pressure focused on a few leaders would be easier. When this failed, the state resorted once again to the earlier divide and rule tactic by encouraging autonomous registration of churches which were not affiliated with the AUCECB. Although the AUCECB had nearly recovered from the split with the Reform Baptists, this new tactic has kept it on the defensive in its relations not only with the CCECB, but also with the Pentecostals and Mennonites.

The CCECB and the Autonomous Churches

State encouragement of autonomous registration after 1969 was a greater threat to the CCECB than to the AUCECB. The state has remained intransigent in refusing to legalize it as a second ECB union. But in order to prevent evangelicals from meeting in private homes, often in secret, state authorities now began offering registration, sometimes even an unconditional registration.

At its legal congress in 1969, the CCECB had decided to advise its churches to renew their application for registration. They also devised their own application form, which included only that information about church life which they felt the state was entitled to know.[3] Because that meant that these churches thereby refused to promise complete obedience to state legislation on religion, most of such applications were refused. But some CCECB churches, perhaps as many as fifteen, succeeded in obtaining registration that was not conditional upon obeying state law.[4]

Sensing that the registration of the Kiev church in August 1975 was being used by Soviet propaganda to undermine imprisoned Georgi Vins's own position, the CCECB issued a sharply worded warning to its churches.[5] In it they stated that authorities were illegally preventing local registration unless the local church agreed to be autonomous from the CCECB. The CCECB therefore urged that new registration applications be submitted with an "accompanying letter." With this letter the local congregation declared its affiliation with the CCECB. The letter cited recent statements by the chairman of the Council for Religious Affairs, Vladimir Kuroedev himself, which promised that "the Soviet state does not keep any record of citizens according to their religious affiliation."[6] In their warning they quoted extensively some official legal publications to prove that the CRA and its newly established local commissions were maintaining systematic card files of local church activity and demanded detailed reports of local clergy which, they said, "literally turn executives of the congregations and ministers into state informers."[7]

Since detailed information about church activity appeared to be the prerequisite for AUCECB-affiliated congregations to keep their registration, this was positive proof for the reformers that the AUCECB churches were continuing their ties with the world. The CCECB advised its member churches to follow "the principle of open relations and closed membership." That meant that in all negotiations with the state, at least two or three persons representing the congregation must take part and should report fully to the brotherhood. The latter must make all its decisions in a closed session where no state officials or informers could take part. Still further, they advised the congregations not to conduct their services in a prayer house belonging to a registered AUCECB congregation (a phenomenon prevalent in the Baltic) because the CCECB presbyter could be arrested at any time, and then the leaderless congregation might fall prey to the AUCECB, which "may lead them along the path of apostasy from God's commandments."[8]

The relations between the two unions had obviously worsened. One reason was the continuing number of Reform Baptist individuals and even congregations that returned to the AUCECB. The AUCECB claimed that 10,000 had returned between 1963 and 1969, and subsequently they have claimed that on an average 1,000 returned annually. Bychkov did acknowledge at the 1974 congress that during the previous four years the CCECB membership had increased by 1,000 although the number of congregations had declined by six, to make a total of 452. But the reaction of the delegates suggested to this observer that Bychkov's estimate of 18,000 was too low to be credible.[9] There was definite attrition which the CCECB recognized and responded to in 1976. In order to inform their many young people who had been converted and had joined after 1960, they reprinted the letters of August 1961 addressed to the AUCECB and to all ECB congregations which had spelled out the reasons for the split.[10]

In spite of these efforts, a major split within CCECB leadership ranks became public during the summer of 1976. On May 22 an expanded meeting of the CCECB, which included 100 representatives from churches throughout the Soviet Union, met in M. T. Shaptala's church in Khartsyzsk (Rostov Oblast). Gennadi Kriuchkov did not dare attend the meeting but delivered a major report by means of a tape recording which he appeared to have recorded in the forest.[11] He was able to report that the *Khristianin* press had printed 350,000 copies of religious literature since 1971, that a Bible course for young Christians was in preparation and affirmed that finances were strictly supervised with no worker receiving more than 100 rubles a month. But then he moved into a long, personal attack on fellow council members S. G. Dubovoi and the Ukrainian evangelist Josef Bondarenko, who had served on the council temporarily. He accused Dubovoi of having compromised himself with the KGB, reminded him of the suffering they had shared in prison and urged him to repent.[12] Rumors were soon circulating that Bondarenko had absconded with 50,000 rubles and had also compromised with the state. After all, how else was one to understand the fact that his name had been removed from the most-wanted-criminal list and he had been able to return to his home in Riga?

The CCECB at first tried to keep the report from being publicized except to inform mission societies abroad not to trust Dubovoi and Bondarenko, but the Underground Evangelism mission circulated a summary and soon AUCECB leaders were mentioning it in *Bratskii Vestnik*.[13] The financial charges against Josef Bondarenko turned out to be without foundation. Bondarenko agreed to a repentance and reconciliation but some felt his repentance had not been complete. Fortunately for his reputation, after a series of highly successful evangelistic campaigns in various Soviet cities, he was arrested in the summer of 1978 and given another three-year prison sentence.[14]

Although Gennadi Kriuchkov presented the conflict as a case of trusted comrades having been snared by the KGB, other evidence reveals a basic disagreement on issues.[15] Bondarenko, for example, had come to the conclusion that the years of controversy between AUCECB and CCECB churches had led to much heartache and unchristian treatment of persons who were obviously born-again Christians but who did not think alike about their duties to the state. Bondarenko felt that fellowship and cooperation should be possible in those locations where AUCECB churches showed genuine fruits of the Spirit. Kriuchkov was afraid that anything but total loyalty to the CCECB leadership would threaten the existence of what he regarded as the true church, whereas Bondarenko and Dubovoi preferred placing greater emphasis on the regional unions and on the autonomy of the local church. In short, Kriuchkov's broad authority was challenged and some reformers were wondering whether purity should always have first priority, even at the expense of fellowship and blessing.

Recently some observers, partisan to the AUCECB, have been suggesting that the CCECB now has three competing centers. In addition to those supporting Bondarenko and those siding with Kriuchkov, who exerts leadership through the journal *Bratskii Listok*, they identify a more extreme, confrontationist grouping in the CPR organization centered around Galina Rytikova and the church in Rostov, which has experienced very severe persecution recently.[16] Lidia Vins, an influential figure in the CPR till she left in 1979, felt betrayed by her congregation in Kiev which agreed to register. Actually, disagreements on methods were evident from the start. Aida Skrypnikova, for example, was not always in full agreement with the letters appearing in the *Bulletin* if their tone was too confrontationist, and David D. Klassen, for example, did not consider hunger strikes in prison as appropriate for a Christian. But both of them, like many others, supported the basic goals of the movement, namely a church totally dedicated to God and not subordinate to the state.

This bickering at the leadership level is only the most prominent manifestation of a problem that has been afflicting all Soviet evangelicals. That is the inability of one Christian to trust another fully. Among the reformers, this became particularly severe because, in spite of their efforts, informers, often within their own congregation, betrayed them to the authorities. The psychological impact of prolonged imprisonment contributed to distrustfulness and embitterment. Soviet prison conditions virtually guaranteed that the prisoner would return with major physical ailments.[17] Regularly the CCECB reported how KGB officers had offered an early release in exchange for cooperation. When someone was released early it could mean he had capitulated. Because most of the CCECB leadership was imprisoned or in hiding, it was impossible to maintain an adequate overview of developments and this, too, contributed to distrust of each other. The years of state censorship and distortion of all information has produced a situation where all printed news is viewed with distrust and rumors abound. AUCECB and CCECB leaders are less well informed of each other's activities than are observers in the West. Finally, the problem of distrust is intensified for the reformers because their rigid concern for doctrinal purity has stifled creativity.

In recent decades it has become fashionable to speak with great respect about the third wing of the reformation, the Anabaptists.[18] Their emphasis on a radical separation of church and state, on an active priesthood of all believers, on church discipline, on a costly discipleship, on church as community, and on religious liberty, are now recognized as progressive emphases which their Lutheran and Catholic opponents have begun to appreciate and imitate. But the Anabaptists themselves were subjected to fierce persecution during which the best of them were killed, many more fled to America and Russia, and others were beaten into submission. What remained was a martyrology made possible by the "Samizdat" of that time and the attempts by a later generation to recover the Anabaptist vision.[19]

The striking similarity in emphasis makes one wonder whether the Reform Baptists may not represent some of the new Anabaptists of the twentieth century. Very few conscious links are apparent; their most-cited hero from the 1920s is Ivan Kargel, a man deeply imbued with Calvinism, and they never refer to Ivan Prokhanov or Pavel Pavlov who had some admiration for the Anabaptists. But another striking feature of the *Initsiativniki* prisoners' lists is the disproportionately high number of names which betray a Russian-Mennonite background. In the list of thirty-five persons, in January 1979, ten are Mennonite names.[20] Is it possible that the Anabaptist theology, which the Mennonites claim to follow, caused some sons of Menno to make common cause with Reform Baptists? Most of these ex-Mennonites, such as K. K. Kreker, reject their Mennonite roots with a near passion, but what they reject are the traditions and mores of a people that has largely forgotten the vision.

Such observations also make one wonder whether the new Anabaptists of Russia will, like their spiritual forebears, lose their greatest leaders as martyrs, lose others through emigration,[21] and will themselves disappear into the surrounding conformity to await rediscovery in less tempestuous times.

Who Are the Mennonites?

This is the question asked in the title of a recent book about Soviet Mennonites. The author, A. N. Ipatov, thought this question was important because, through their mission and preaching activities, this rather small Protestant church was influencing other confessions. In fact, "many Mennonite forms and methods of religious molding of the population have been adopted by the Baptists—*Initsiativniki* . . ."[22] Although they had sixteenth-century roots in the Anabaptist movement, the exclusivist emphasis had become so strong in the nineteenth century, while during the Soviet period their historical awareness had become so weak that even unbelievers from this ethnic-confessional society call themselves Mennonites.[23] In some Soviet passports these persons had even listed their nationality as Mennonites.[24]

A bibliography of Mennonites, including Russian Mennonites, now fills volumes,[25] and there are multi-volume Mennonite encyclopedias in both German and in English,[26] yet most writing on Soviet religious history betrays surprising ignorance about them. The few Soviet publications which have usually served as source material for Western scholars are characterized by a deliberate mixture of fact and fiction as well as an interpretive scheme determined by Marxist ideology. According to that scheme, for example, the sixteenth-century Anabaptists, especially Thomas Müntzer and the Münsterite rebellion led by Jan van Leyden,[27] are treated as a peasant movement in feudal Europe, which was a precurser of communism. But a Dutch priest named Menno Simons managed to convert the remnant into a quietist religious society, progressive in the sense that it affirmed bourgeois values in a feudal era but therefore also socially and politically backward in the communist era.[28]

Space limitations permit no more than the assertion that the Russian Mennonites trace their historical origins to the Anabaptists in Holland and North Germany who with their fellows in Switzerland and South Germany formed the first modern so-called believers' churches—that is, a church practicing adult baptism and church membership following a conscious voluntary commitment to Christ. Beginning in 1789, Mennonite settlers in Russia began emigrating to Russia in response to the privileged terms of settlement offered by Empress Catherine II and her successors. During the following century they managed to create a most remarkable self-governing commonwealth which became a model for the surrounding society in its agricultural and educational achievements as well as for their highly developed charity program.[29] But this Mennonite commonwealth also fell prey to the temptation of becoming a "church" type rather than a voluntaristic "sect" type, to use Ernst Troeltsch's classic sociological formulations.[30] A major renewal movement, due to the influence of the Moravian Brethren, Württemburg Pietists, German Baptists, and the Bible Society crystallized in 1860 into a separately organized Mennonite denomination bearing the name Mennonite Brethren. The old church that initially resisted religious renewal through a most unchristian exercise of force continued to call itself the Mennonite Church, insisted on keeping the buildings (Kirche) while the new Mennonites spoke about a "prayer house" and preferred the term "Brethren" to "Church." Soviet writings still label them Church and Brethren Mennonites. Spiritual renewal soon became widespread in Mennonite circles as well and eventually, during the 1920s, these two major Mennonite bodies plus smaller, split-away groups met in a general conference and spoke with a united voice to the authorities.[31]

This is all very dim history for present-day Soviet Mennonites because during the past fifty years their church has experienced an upheaval which prompts some to say that all that has remained is the name Mennonite, their characteristic Low German dialect, and traditional cooking. Between 1923 and 1929 approximately 20,000 emigrated to Canada and South America, an immigration that included a disproportionately large number of their most able leaders. Collectivization or dekulakization, as it was experienced by many Mennonites, changed the shape of their large colonies in South Russia and on the Volga.[32]

The Mennonite remnant now had several important features. A high percentage of the families consisted of mothers with children whose fathers had disappeared while they were small. The children, due to the upheavals of the war and the subsequent ten years in the camps, had received almost no education, and an educated Mennonite became a rarity. Mennonites were labeled as Germans and fascists and indeed retained a strong sense of identity as Germans, even though a recent Soviet scholar argues that their roots were more Dutch than German.[33] Mennonites had refused to issue an official declaration of loyalty and therefore became an illegal denomination after the war. This meant there was no central church headquarters to provide leadership. Their chief doctrinal distinctive, pacifism, had been beaten out of them. Individual Mennonites lost contact with each other, and the result was that the religious meaning behind the term Mennonite had been virtually obliterated.

The Mennonite church very slowly began to re-emerge in the mid-fifties. The role of the released prisoners in fostering the revival was described earlier.[34] In 1956 two North American Mennonites, Harold S. Bender and David P. Wiens, reestablished contact on a visit and gained an insight into the seriousness of the problem. A few leaders, such as Heinrich Voth, Philip Cornies, and Franz Pauls managed to meet them at some of the hotels, but these men experienced serious difficulties with the state subsequently. Harold Bender, on his own initiative, urged the Mennonites to try to seek shelter under the Baptist umbrella and did his part to seek out AUCECB leaders and ask their assistance.[35]

Many Mennonites had found their way to a registered Baptist church while many others shared in the fellowship groupings which emerged during the revivals, in which denominational affiliation was initially secondary. When the Baptists finally succeeded in calling a congress in 1963, there were three Mennonites with full voting rights and one with advisory rights among those attending.[36] All represented AUCECB member churches, that is, they represented Russians, Ukrainians, as well as Germans. Heinrich K. Allert, a preacher from Karaganda, was persuaded to ask the delegates to accept the Mennonites into the union. Although 1963 has since been claimed as the year when the union took place, 1966 would be more accurate.

Bratskii Vestnik had mentioned that Harold Bender met the Baptists in London in 1955, but did not mention the first Mennonite visit to the Soviet Union, and it was only in 1958 when the Germans in Novosibirsk organized separately within the Russian church structure that the first references to Mennonites in the Soviet Union began.[37] Allert's statement in 1963 was not only a surprise to the other delegates, who began asking who these Mennonites were, but it was also a surprise to most of the Mennonites he claimed to represent. During the next three years a few regional discussions were held, and at the subsequent congress in 1966, with seventeen Mennonites present, a formal application with conditions was submitted. The new additional denomination was also acknowledged in the new statute.[38]

In the new expanded All-Union council that was elected, Jacob Fast, leader of the German congregation in Novosibirsk, was elected a council member, and Victor Kriger was elected a candidate member. Kriger, who had grown up in Kirgizia, had done his military service in Moscow, married a Russian, and remained in the capital. In 1964 he became a full-time worker for the union and began traveling about to establish ties with the Mennonites.[39] Kriger became a full council member in 1969 but did not stand for reelection in 1974 and also discontinued much of his traveling.

Initially the AUCECB claimed that 16,000 Mennonites had joined; by 1968 Kriger claimed there were 18,500; and, more recently, 30,000 have been claimed for the AUCECB. This growing strength was also reflected structurally, so that in 1974 Fast was elected to the ten-member presidium. Both he and the other Mennonite representatives were also highly popular with the delegates in general. Fast and his associate, Kviring, completed the Bible correspondence course, while Victor Kriger was able to study two years at the Baptist seminary in Hamburg. In 1977 Traugott Kviring became the first German appointed as a senior presbyter—responsible for Central Asia.[40]

Similar to the Pentecostal pattern in 1945, the formal voting procedure for joining was less significant than attempting to get the local Mennonite

Brethren to support the union *post facto*. Mennonite Brethren joined because they no longer had an awareness of theological difference with the Baptists, and both sides acknowledged "a living relationship with Christ and the teachings of Christ on the rebirth as the most important of biblical teachings."[41] The old distinctives of pacifism and refusal to swear the oath had long ago been lost, and local congregations now agreed not to practice footwashing at communion, the same stipulation made for the Pentecostals earlier. What the Mennonites gained were cultural concessions—the possibility to hold services in the German language.[42] An official statement published after a meeting between Mennonite representatives and the presidium in March 1976 declared that the Mennonite entry into the ECB union gave them greater opportunities for preaching the gospel, for proper church order and spiritual education of believers.[43]

Willi Matthies, who had attended the 1966 congress, produced a small bombshell when he announced at a meeting in May 1967, where seventeen Mennonite leaders met with the AUCECB presidium, that the Council for Religious Affairs had granted permission for their 800-member church in Karaganda to register autonomously as a Mennonite Brethren congregation. Matthies assured the Baptists that their congregation would like to maintain fraternal ties with them but also that they did not wish to lose their Mennonite identity. It was a decade before another autonomous Mennonite Brethren congregation achieved registration, but the fact that autonomy was now a theoretical possibility did mean that the AUCECB had to continue to woo the Mennonites. They did so through periodic meetings, where their relationship was regularly affirmed as positive, and through appeals sent out urging the remaining Mennonites to join.[44] For a long time establishing contact with the Mennonites in the Omsk and Orenburg regions was a problem because the state officials refused to register these congregations. When it became possible to register and to visit them in the mid-seventies, many local congregations responded with caution. They could find nothing in the Bible about registration, they said, and they had heard that the AUCECB belonged to the World Council of Churches, which others had told them was the Babylonian whore. But some progress has been made. AUCECB President Andrei Klimenko recently claimed there were fifty-three German-speaking congregations in the union,[45] and another recent announcement referred to ten congregations registered in Kazakhstan.[46]

Nearly as many Mennonites belonged to the Church Mennonites, but union remained a problem for these. According to Soviet sources, in 1957 there was a meeting in Solikamsk (Ural region), where leaders tried to form a Mennonite church union.[47] But the state authorities nipped it in the bud. The AUCECB also made an unsuccessful effort to incorporate them. The problem with the Mennonites was that although all those who had become active again after the war were clearly born-again Christians who spoke the same evangelical language as the Baptists, they practiced believer's baptism with a difference. The difference was that, instead of totally immersing a person, they simply poured water on his head as the Anabaptists in the sixteenth century had done.

The AUCECB' discussed the Church Mennonite problem at an enlarged plenum which met in September 1964 and decided to circulate a letter to the churches.[48] In this letter they urged local churches to permit Church Mennonites to preach (but not to lead), to sing in the choir, and to take communion with AUCECB members. It seems more than coincidental, that the revised statute of 1963 omitted the statement that their union practiced baptism by immersion. But this attempt to open the door for the Church Mennonites failed, and the 1966 statute restored the immersion clause, S. P. Fadiukhin prefacing his speech on unity with a sharp assertion that "one baptism" does not only mean to baptize only once, but it also means that there should be only one form of baptism, namely, immersion.[49] The 1978 appeal to Mennonite Brethren stated explicitly that baptism "must be performed by immersion."[50]

The 1964 circular letter helped in some localities, but in general it remained a dead letter. In Dzhetisai (Uzbekistan), for example, Mennonites and Mennonite Brethren worshiped together till David Regier moved there in 1957. He insisted that Mennonites must first be rebaptized by immersion, denied communion to those who refused, and a split resulted. When the Moscow letter arrived in 1964, he moderated his stance, but two separate churches remained. Elsewhere the letter never arrived, at least the members never heard about it, and the solutions reached were not always pleasant. One man, who had attended Baptist services for twenty years, was never permitted to take communion, and the local leadership even refused his deathbed wish for communion. In another city individual Baptists and Mennonite Brethren were too afraid of possible prison or fines to offer their own house as a place of worship for the unregistered congregation. A Mennonite invited them to meet in his house, but on communion Sunday he was asked to leave his own house so they could conduct communion without him! Generally speaking, however, in those places where large independent congregations of Mennonite Brethren and Mennonites developed, relations gradually improved, so that there are regular pulpit exchanges, but the baptismal question remains insoluble.[51]

The Mennonites benefited from the new state policy that fostered autonomous registration. In 1967, Heinrich Heese and Elder Hans Penner personally traveled to Moscow and obtained permission from the Council for Religious Affairs to register several churches in Kirgizia as autonomous Mennonite congregations. This included the submission of a Mennonite confession of faith, although minus the pacifist clauses. Some of these congregations then received permission (often through state pressure) to share use of the registered Baptist building. In some cases these churches received verbal permission to conduct their activities but without the security of a signed document to prove their registration.[52] But a union of Mennonites has not yet become possible. These registered congregations do maintain informal communication links and managed to consult together to send an official representative to the Mennonite World Conference in 1978.[53]

This recent progress in relationship to the state has strengthened the sense of being Mennonite. Ironically, however, Russian Mennonites are themselves still asking the question—"Who are the Mennonites?"—because it is becoming increasingly difficult to explain this convincingly to their young people. The problem appears to be a lack of vision for the possibility that non-German Mennonites could become Mennonites. Soviet historian A. N. Ipatov's advice to atheist activists was that those who persisted in speaking German were the older, incorrigible ones, but that the younger people were becoming Russianized. Rather than training atheist workers to learn Low German, he urged that they concentrate on winning away those who spoke Russian. This indeed is the Mennonites' greatest fear, yet the lessons of acculturation for Mennonites who came to Canada and Brazil was that those who adopted the new national language were also those most active in revivifying the doctrine and renewing the missionary expansion.[54]

Will Pentecostals Leave?

A Ukrainian atheist journal declared in October 1974 that research had shown that the majority of all Pentecostal leaders had at some time been sentenced for breaking Soviet law.[55] The writers saw this as proof that the Pentecostals were a harmful phenomenon; but from another perspective it is a dramatic demonstration of the problems which have confronted the Pentecostals in their struggle to survive in the Soviet Union. It is not simply a case of a small sect being unwilling to unite with other evangelical sects. Some extreme Pentecostal groups are outrightly banned by law, and their well-known emphasis on glossalalia (speaking in tongues) is freely referred to in the Soviet press as superstitious rituals which are harmful to health.[56] Refusal to bear arms in military service has also been a major cause for imprisonment.

Neither the AUCECB nor the Pentecostals particularly desired the union that was forced on them in 1945. The subsequent history of the relationship has been a history of dissatisfaction from the perspective of the Pentecostals. Baptists regarded it as "a long and still unfinished story of embarrassment."[57] Although Ernest Payne's sensitivity to embarrassment is typically British, it shows the insensitivity many Russian Baptists displayed toward the deeply felt convictions of the Pentecostals.[58]

In 1948 and 1949 increasingly tough measures were taken by the Moscow leadership to stop all aspects of emotionalism in worship services; Pentecostals in the union must now worship just like Baptists. A. N. Bidash, one of the four leaders who had signed the unity agreement, left during these years. Renewed attempts at a separate organization began. About thirty-eight percent of the Pentecostals in Dnepropetrovsk Oblast left the union and were followed by many Pentecostals in the Western Ukraine.[59] In 1948 Bidash and others met in Dneprodzerzhinsk to form the union of Voronaev Pentecostals.[60] This failed because most of the leaders were imprisoned, but when they were released in the amnesty of 1955, they resumed their efforts. In June 1956 a new headquarters was established in Piatikhatki. The following month they issued a new confession of faith for Pentecostals and then conducted an All-Union congress in Kharkov in August 1956.[61] The authorities disliked these developments especially because the congress came a step closer again toward encouraging pacifism. Bidash also attempted to obtain registration for this union, but it was rejected.

The AUCECB now began renewed efforts to win the Pentecostals back. Alexander Karev and Jacob Zhidkov sent a letter to all presbyters in January 1955 which not only repeated the conditions which Pentecostals had agreed to, namely, to restrain themselves from glossalalia in worship services and not to spread their views among other believers, but also stressed the promises made by the AUCECB. The AUCECB had "made a promise to respect their convictions and not to attack their views from the pulpit. . ."[62] Zhidkov and Karev complained that they were receiving information that local presbyters were treating Pentecostals with great intolerance, sometimes excommunicating them as soon as they discovered that they had Pentecostal views.

The following year Zhidkov attended a conference of senior presbyters in the Ukraine which met with five Pentecostal leaders.[63] Officially, they reported that about ninety percent of all Pentecostals had already joined the union, but the major action resulting from this meeting was that these Pentecostal leaders now began tours of Pentecostal regions in order to persuade local Pentecostals to join and also to persuade local presbyters of the serious intent of Pentecostals to have fellowship with other evangelical believers. In January 1957 the AUCECB presidium met with six Pentecostal representatives. Here the Pentecostals secured agreement on a four-point statement of principles whereby the AUCECB recognized the legitimacy of spiritual gifts (and by implication the Pentecostal gifts) but emphasized that believers should not strive for gifts above everything because the deciding factor at the judgment is "our life and walk in the Spirit."[64] In addition, the August Agreement of 1945 was finally published in *Bratskii Vestnik*.[65]

Pentecostal dissatisfaction remained the chief worry for the AUCECB, and in August 1959 they called another meeting with seven Pentecostal leaders.[66] These reported that although 25,000 Pentecostals were in the union, a further 14,000 were outside the union, although they claimed that 4,000 of these had recently expressed willingness to join. The next winter Moscow sent out a letter to all presbyters, including Pentecostal congregations not in the union. The letter included several questions, and the majority of the replies indicated that most of the Pentecostals not in the union did not wish to join, Karev characterizing these as the more fanatical Pentecostals. Therefore, he said, no further initiatives had been taken with the Pentecostals.[67]

A more important reason why no further initiatives were taken was that the AUCECB now became preoccupied with the *Initsiativniki* threat to the union. It soon became apparent that the *Initsiativniki* had an anti-Pentecostal bias which might mean that further concessions to the Pentecostals could mean losing part of its own membership. The Moscow leadership, however, maintained its former stance toward the Pentecostals, so that as the reformers' position became more entrenched, it became easier for Pentecostals to return. Already at the 1963 congress, twenty Pentecostal representatives attended, while Senior Presbyter A. L. Andreev reported that in the Ukraine one fourth of all senior presbyters and one fifth of all local presbyters were Pentecostals.[68] At that first congress considerable attention was paid to the Pentecostals and Mennonites in order to balance off the *Initsiativniki* threat. At the next two congresses, however, Pentecostals began to complain of neglect, and Karev apologized, promising them more attention next time. In fact, already at the 1966 congress he drew attention to the major impact that the Pentecostal movement worldwide was having on the churches. He informed his listeners that in the second century it was the Montanists, the ancient Pentecostals, who "saved Christianity from spiritual death in gnosticism" and with that as background, expressed a hope that the Pentecostals would provide a good ferment in their brotherhood.[69] Both in 1966 and 1969 Karev could report that approximately another 2,500 Pentecostals had joined the union.

From the beginning, D. I. Ponomarchuk and I. K. Pan'ko had worked as assistant senior presbyters in the Ukraine and Belorussia respectively, the chief Pentecostal centers. By the late fifties, this had expanded. When the AUCECB was increased to twenty-five members in 1966, Pentecostal representation increased from one person to two.[70] Shortly thereafter, P. K. Shatrov became a full-time worker in the Moscow headquarters, as had Viktor Kriger for the Mennonites. In 1974 Shaktrov also became the Pentecostal member on the presidium, where a Pentecostal voice had been missing since Ponomarchuk took ill in 1961.[71]

The Pentecostal problem did not disappear. In 1971 eight major Pentecostal leaders sent a letter to all Pentecostals both inside and outside the union in which they once again urged Pentecostals to support the August Agreement in all its points and to follow their personal example by joining the union.[72] The year before, the Pentecostal question had again been discussed at an AUCECB plenum and a decision had been taken to call a meeting in the second half of the year with representatives of the Pentecostals not in the union, but that attempt failed. Local complaints about violations of the August Agreement by both sides continued. There was increasing pressure by the Pentecostal leaders in the union to modify the August Agreement.[73]

Finally, in 1972, the AUCECB agreed to appoint a seven-man commission to analyze and revise the agreement. The commission met several times during the following year and also received various recommendations from local churches. But a year later they reported that the 1945 agreement had by now become a historic document which had been reaffirmed at three All-Union congresses in the sixties,[74] and therefore they came to the conclusion that it should continue to remain unchanged as the basic document for regulating relationships between the Pentecostals and the union. The decision was scarcely surprising, since only two members of the commission were Pentecostals and all the rest were powerful AUCECB leaders, including S. P. Fadiukhin, who is well known for his staunchly Baptist stance against Pentecostals in his own large congregation in Leningrad.[75] The decision was disappointing to Pentecostals and also to many local leaders who had dissatisfied Pentecostals in their membership.

Some delegates came to the 1974 congress hoping that the Pentecostal question would be thoroughly discussed and that perhaps the August Agreement could still be changed.[76] This did not happen. Later at the next major meeting of the AUCECB's plenum, General Secretary Alexei Bychkov spoke with approval of a new development among unaffiliated Pentecostals. These, he said, were now expressing a desire to worship openly, to obey the laws, and up to twenty-five such congregations had been registered without affiliation to the AUCECB.[77] Pentecostal spokesman Peter Shatrov also presented a major paper on the subject of unity with the Pentecostals in which he pointed out that about 33,000 had joined the AUCECB and that relations between Baptists and Pentecostals in the Western Ukraine and the Baltic region were good. He listed seven factors which united them with the ECB and could also report that as a result of increased travel in the congregations, at least seven more Pentecostal congregations had joined the union, not to mention the many individuals who had found their way to an established congregation. But there were still 500 congregations with more than 20,000 members outside the union. There was also continuing discontent because individuals did not recognize the agreement. On one side were persons who felt that only those with the gift of tongues had salvation, while on the other side were those who said that speaking in tongues did not come from God. This intolerance must be eliminated, Shatrov emphasized. He urged the presbyters of united congregations in particular to do their utmost to abide by the agreement.[78]

In 1977, at another expanded plenum with more than seventy persons in attendance, President Andrei Klimenko and General Secretary Alexei Bychkov both dealt with the problem at length, noting that it was complicated and hinting at a new solution. Klimenko reported that the number of Pentecostals joining the union had declined and also complained that the major problem was the partisan attitude toward the August Agreement, where he faulted both sides for partisanship. Both he and Bychkov spoke positively about Pentecostal congregations registering autonomously, Klimenko in fact saying: "We approve such a step also."[79] Klimenko also noted that leading Pentecostal brethren had submitted a declaration to the presidium proposing structural changes in the AUCECB in order to improve the work for union. He reported that the presidium planned to study the proposals further but that they were of the opinion that, rather than structural changes, improved work for unity should be achieved through greater efforts from all church members, senior presbyters, and presbyter council. The council did approve a suggestion made by Klimenko and Bychkov to introduce local evangelists or assistant senior presbyters whose special task would be to deal with the unity issue. In short, they would work harder at unity locally but Pentecostals who wanted to maintain their distinctives were welcome to leave.

Generally speaking, it was the more moderate Pentecostals who were humble enough to accept second-class treatment within AUCECB ranks. Official estimates still tried to minimize the number that remained outside the union. Soviet scholars have also tried to ascribe minority status to the unregistered Pentecostals.[80] Supporters of the unregistered Pentecostals have claimed that they number between 200,000 and 500,000. Precise statistics are impossible, but the best-informed authority in the West feels there must be at least 100,000.[81]

Unregistered Pentecostals Try to Emigrate

These unregistered Pentecostals are located in the Ukraine and Belorussia with Melitopol in Dnepropetrovsk Oblast as unofficial center. Many Pentecostals are scattered throughout the Russian Federation, especially in Siberia and the Far East. One of their representatives has claimed that there are sixty congregations totaling 3,000 persons in Moscow alone. These are loosely divided into two groupings, a larger one led by A. N. Bidash and a smaller grouping led by Grigorii Vashchenko, which practices greater ethical strictness.[82]

In January 1963 North Americans first learned of the plight of these Pentecostals when thirty-nine persons managed to force their way into the American embassy in Moscow to ask help for emigrating from the USSR.[83] The Americans were embarrassed, and these believers were sent back to their home in Chernogorsk in Eastern Siberia. They had come to Moscow after despairing of ever receiving freedom of religion. Thereafter some of their leaders served prison sentences until finally, in 1973, they renewed their attempts to emigrate. First they submitted requests to the Soviet authorities, then expanded their appeal to the United Nations. By January 1978, the Pentecostal emigration movement encompassed 10,000 people, and by July the number of people wishing to emigrate had increased to 20,000 and was still spreading to new congregations and to more members within congregations.[84] In a virtual repeat of the 1963 drama, seven Soviet Pentecostals from Chernogorsk managed to enter the American embassy a second time on June 27, 1978. This time the Americans did not turn them out, nor were they able to act on their request, so they are still in the embassy at the time of this writing.[85] Recently AUCECB Pentecostal spokesman Peter Shatrov urged educational work in the churches against doing something foolish in order to emigrate.[86]

Soviet Jews and Soviet Germans have been able to emigrate in large numbers during the past decade, but so far only two Pentecostal families were able to emigrate after major press campaigns. A major reason why the Pentecostals wish to emigrate is that they feel there is no place for them in Soviet society. At the International Sakharov Hearings in Copenhagen in 1977 recently emigrated Evgenii Bresenden stated:

> In view of the religious intolerance in the USSR, the majority of Christian Pentecostals wait for a chance to leave the country and to emigrate to any non-communist country. They would rather go to Israel than to any other place because according to the Bible and Gospel, when justice and peace will be re-established after the present turmoil, the beginning of everything will be in Israel. Therefore we would be prepared to share all the Israeli People's difficulties and hardships.[87]

Another of the Pentecostal leaders, V. M. Vatulko, addressed a letter to the Conference for European Security meeting in Belgrade in 1977 in which he listed ten requests.[88] They wanted unhindered worship services, buildings for worship, the right of parents to raise children in the faith, freedom to organize Sunday schools and youth groups in the congregations, no restriction on religious congresses, no discrimination in education, permission to print literature, returning children to parents from whom they had been taken, releasing persons from prison, and rehabilitating those persons imprisoned because of religion. It is a familiar litany of the problems that persist. For a short period an organized Pentecostal *Samizdat* journal was begun, but then the leaders stopped it.[89]

An important reason why Mennonites have gained in status within the AUCECB is their intimate link with fellow Mennonites abroad. Foreign support for Soviet Pentecostals leaves something to be desired. The largest wing of the Pentecostals, the Voronaev movement, was initially sponsored by the general council and then the mission society of the Assemblies of God from North America.[90] In recent decades Pentecostal-oriented East European missions have tried to help Soviet Pentecostals, but links with those in the Far East have been difficult to establish. Official Pentecostal ties to the Soviet Union are still weakly developed.

Evangelical Ecumenism—Yes or No?

Alexander Karev wanted to emphasize that the union of four different strands of evangelicals in the AUCECB was an achievement of evangelical ecumenism that should serve as an encouragement to evangelicals elsewhere to unite.[91] Toward the end of his career there was increasing doubt that a real union of evangelicals would survive. In local cities such a union was threatened by anti-Pentecostal sentiments, by anti-Mennonite sentiments, not to mention the anti-Moscow sentiments that have never entirely disappeared. Compared with the separatist feelings locally, the open door stance of the Moscow leadership reveals commendable tolerance. Yet their policy has fostered a development whereby unity means uniformity. In 1969 the statute was changed so that the union consisted of Mennonites, Pentecostals, and Evangelical Christian-Baptists, whereas formerly the latter had been identified as two groupings.[92] At the 1974 congress Fadiukhin reported with pleasure that an increasing number of persons were identifying themselves as ECB, including those from Mennonite and Pentecostal backgrounds.[93]

The movement toward autonomy has prompted a few key leaders to voice their thoughts about the possibility of a different structural arrangement which might be more successful in achieving evangelical unity without uniformity. Perhaps it might be possible to form a federated council of free churches as has been done in Hungary. This council would unite all evangelicals in dealing with the state on matters of concern to all of them; they could cooperate together in peace work and in other international activity, yet allow the freedom of each denomination to emphasize its distinctives. But such thinking has not even reached the formal discussion stage so far.

Many Pentecostals and a significant number of Mennonite Brethren remain outside the union. A growing number of them have obtained autonomous registration. Pentecostals inside the union at present are itching to leave, and it is no secret that many Baptist leaders would be relieved to see them go. If the Pentecostals would choose to leave, then many Mennonite Brethren would do the same. That would represent a loss of at least fifteen percent of the AUCECB membership, not counting the fifteen percent lost earlier to the Reform Baptists. It is also apparent that if the Pentecostals left at their own initiative, fraternal relationships with the AUCECB would be strained. This was barely averted in December 1979 when delegates refused to reelect Peter Shatrov. If, however, the AUCECB took the initiative in proposing a restructuring, the results in cooperation would be greater and the AUCECB would maintain its leadership role.

The movement toward autonomy presents a challenge to the AUCECB to demonstrate church-statesmanship of a quality that might persuade evangelicals in other countries to take their example seriously. Perhaps that is part of the new frontier for Soviet evangelicals.

Notes to Chapter 10

1. Quoted in Kahle, p. 285.

2. *Daily Study Bible: The Letters to the Galatians and Ephesians* (Edinburgh: The Saint Andrew Press, rev. ed., 1976), p. 118.

3. Recently printed in English translation in *RCDA*, 4-9/75, p. 119.

4. Archives, Licht im Osten Mission, Korntal, 1976.

5. *BL*, 1-3/75.

6. *BV*, 4/75.

7. *BL*, 1-3/75. The publications they cited were *Zakonodatel'stvo o religioznykh kultakh* (1969) and *Ateisticheskie chtenie*, Vol. V, Moscow, 1971.

8. *BL*, 4/75; cf. my article, "Who's Making Reconciliation Difficult?" *MCC News Service*, July, 1976.

9. *BV*, 1/75, p. 49. Georgi Vins claims 100,000 members at present, which is plausible in light of Soviet sociological and AUCECB statistics.

10. *BL*, 4-5/76; *Vestnik istiny*, 2/76, pp. 2-4.

11. Copy of tape recording is in the author's possession. An abbreviated report was printed in *Vestnik istiny*, 3-4, 1976, pp. 8-28.

12. Stepan Gerasimovich Dubovoi (born 1913) was the leader in Dzhezkazgan (Kazakhstan) when the reform movement began; later lived in Shevchenko (Odessa Oblast). Had been in hiding since October 1970; was in prison 1966-69 (his second sentence).

13. *Newsline West*, September 1976; *BV*, 2/77, p. 61. The reformers' abbreviated printed report in *Vestnik istiny* omitted all mention of the conflict.

14. *Newsline West*, October 1978.

15. Based on discussions with individuals personally acquainted with Bondarenko, including a few siding with Kriuchkov, who argued that Bondarenko's vanity had been affronted when he was not elected a full CCECB member.

16. In Rostov 117 of the members had experienced arrest and fifteen-day prison sentences. Presbyter Peter D. Peters (age 34), a popular evangelist for the CCECB, was arrested and sentenced for the fourth time in January 1978 to two-and-a-half years. Services in the woods were disrupted. Cf. *Bulletin*, 53/78, pp. 4-6.

17. A good description of prison conditions in *Prisoners of Conscience in the USSR* (London: Amnesty International, 1975).

18. See, for example, Roland Bainton's college text, *The Reformation of the Sixteenth Century* (Boston: Beacon Press, 1952), and George Williams, *The Radical Reformation* (Philadelphia: The Westminster Press, 1962).

19. T. van Braght, *Martyrs Mirror* (9th ed.; Scottdale, Pa.: Herald Press 1972), which has been reprinted repeatedly in German and English translations; Guy F. Hershberger, ed., *Recovery of the Anabaptist Vision* (Scottdale, Pa.: Herald Press, 1957).

20. *Dein Reich Komme*, January 1979. A study of the *Initsiativniki* card file at

Keston College in February 1975 revealed that 147 out of 750 or 12 percent were of Mennonite origin.

21. Approximately 5,000 of the *Initsiativniki* have emigrated to West Germany since 1970 on the basis of a reunification of war-torn families program. The number of church leaders in this number was disproportionately high, some reporting that Soviet authorities encouraged them to leave.

22. A. N. Ipatov, *Kto takie mennonity* (Alma-Ata, 1977), p. 3.

23. A. N. Ipatov, *Mennonity (Voprosy formirovaniia i evoliutsii etnokonfessional'noi obshchnosti)* (Moscow: "Mysl'," 1978), p. 3.

24. *Ibid.*, p. 65.

25. See, for example, A. J. Klassen and Nelson Springer, eds., *Mennonite Bibliography, 1631-1961* (2 vols.; Scottdale, Pa.: Herald Press, 1977); David G. Rempel, "Introduction to Russian Mennonite Historiography," *MQR*, 1974, pp. 409-446.

26. *Mennonite Encyclopedia* (4 vols.; Scottdale, Pa.; Mennonite Publishing House, 1955-59); *Mennonitsiches Lexikon* (4 vols.; Korntal, West Germany: Mennonitischer Geschichtsverein, 1913-67). Both provide some of the fullest source material on Russian Mennonites up to World War II.

27. Müntzer is not usually considered an Anabaptist and most scholars consider the Münsterite rebellion as an atypical phenomenon.

28. V. F. Krest'ianinov, *Mennonity* (Moscow, 1967), p. 14f.

29. The best short survey is David G. Rempel, "The Mennonite Commonwealth in Russia," *MQR*, XLVII, 3, 1973, and XLVII, 1, 1974 (available as separate reprint).

30. Ernst Troeltsch, *The Social Teaching of the Christian Churches* (New York: Harper Torchbook, 1960), Vol. I, pp. 331-43, cf. E. K. Francis, *In Search of Utopia* (Altona, Man.: D. W. Friesen & Sons, 1955).

31. Well illustrated in J. B. Toews, *Lost Fatherland* (Scottdale, Pa.: Herald Press, 1967). I am following the preferred North American nomenclature of Mennonite for Kirchliche Mennonite and Mennonite Brethren. The context indicates when "Mennonite" refers to all Mennonite denominations.

32. For a fuller survey, see my "Mennonite Congregations in the Soviet Union Today," *Mennonite Life*, March 1978, pp. 12-26, and "Union of Soviet Socialist Republics," *Mennonite World Handbook* (Lombard, Ill., 1978), pp. 63-71.

33. Ipatov, *Mennonity*, pp. 44-47.

34. See above, Chap. 2.

35. Trip report, MCC files. His meeting with Baptists is reported in *BV*, 5/55, p. 11; 3-4/56, p. 12. Bender also petitioned the Council for the Affairs of Religious Cults to permit Mennonite registration, although this appeal has long been regarded by other North American Mennonite leaders as a mistake.

36. They were: Jakob J. Fast (Novosibirsk preacher), Johann J. Martens (Kant, Kirgizia presbyter), Heinrich K. Allert (Karaganda preacher), and Traugott F. Kviring (Dushanbe preacher). The latter was a guest. Allert has not played a leading role among Mennonites before or after this occasion (*BV*, 3/63, pp. 25-32, 40).

37. *BV*, 4/58, pp. 74-79; cf. 5-6/58, p. 26.

38. The unification is discussed in greater detail in my article "What Makes Russian Mennonites Mennonite?" *MQR*, January 1979, pp. 5-20.

39. *BV*, 2/65, p. 76. He also became a preacher in the Moscow church at this time but was only ordained in 1970.

40. *BV*, 6/77, p. 73.

41. The basis for unity emphasized by Jakob Fast at a recent meeting of Mennonites with the presidium (*BV*, 3/76, pp. 67-74).

42. The first such German-language service was announced in Novosibirsk in 1958 with the explanation: "This will serve to make meetings of Germans in apartments unnecessary and to prevent violation of the statutes and directives of the AUCECB, to observe discipline in the church, and to relieve the Russian service" (*BV*, 4/58, p. 75).

43. *BV*, 4/76, p. 74.

44. Joint meetings were held in 1967, 1973, 1976, and 1978. The latest appeal (*BV*, 4/78, pp. 65-66) was published in German, which spokesmen referred to hopefully as the beginning of a German-language periodical. Jakob Fast, who had also served as assistant senior presbyter for Western Siberia, resigned that post in August 1976 to devote himself full time to the Novosibirsk church and his work on the presidium. In 1979 he was elected deputy senior presbyter for the RSFSR and at the All-Union congress in December 1979, where he was reelected to the presidium, Mennonite and German delegates requested that he move to Moscow.

45. *BV*, 2/77, p. 61.

46. *BV*, 5/76, p. 66.

47. Krest'ianinov, p. 78.

48. *BV*, 6/66, p. 31; cf. 4/67, p. 42; 4/78, p. 65.

49. *BV*, 6/66, pp. 53, 61.

50. *BV*, 4/78, p. 65. Ipatov, *Mennonity*, p. 162, notes that following the 1964 decision to accommodate the Church Mennonites, some Mennonite Brethren joined the unregistered congregations of Baptists or sought autonomous registration.

51. Umsiedler interview data.

52. For example, in Alma-Ata, which had this status 1973-77, when it obtained full registration.

53. *Mennonitische Rundschau*, June 14, 1978.

54. Ipatov, p. 189f., apparently forgetting this phenomenon which he had stressed on pp. 46-47.

55. *Liudyna i Svit*, 10/74, pp. 37-40.

56. Kuroedov and Pankratov, *Zakonodatel'stvo* . . . , p. 291; A. T. Moskalenko, *Piatidesiatniki* (2nd ed.; Moscow, 1973), p. 5; N. V. Koltsov, *Kto takie piatidesiatniki* (Moscow: Znanie, 1965).

57. Ernest A. Payne, *Out of Great Tribulation: Baptists in the USSR* (London: Baptist Union of Great Britain and Ireland, 1974), p. 25.

58. The most understanding treatment of Soviet Pentecostals is Steve Durasoff, *The Russian Protestants* . . . . Michael Rowe of Keston College is currently completing what promises to be the definitive Western study of Soviet Pentecostals as a doctoral dissertation at Glasgow University. See also the relevant sections in Walter Hollenberger, *The Pentecostals* (London: SCM Press, 1972).

59. Fedorenko, *Sekty, ikh vera i dela* (Moscow, 1965).

60. Moskalenko, p. 72.

61. *Ibid.*, p. 73; cf. "The Pentecostalist Movement," *Radio Liberty Research*, January 31, 1975, a ten-page up-to-date survey written by a well-informed scholar.

62. *BV*, 1/55, p. 5.

63. *BV*, 5/56, p. 59. Senior presbyters from Dnepropetrovskaia, Nikolaevskaia, Vinnitskaia, Stalinskaia (Donetskaia), Poltavskaia, Voroshilovgradskaia, and L'vovskaia Oblasts met with Pentecostal leaders M. I. But, G. G. Ponurko, N. V. Kuz'menko, G. A. Goroshko and D. I. Ponomarchuk. Pentecostal strong points (Rovenskaia and Volynskaia Oblasts) were not represented.

64. *BV*, 1/57, p. 79. Instead of G. A. Goroshko, A. M. Tesliuk (Sumy Oblast) and S. I. Marin attended.

65. *BV*, 4/57, p. 36, as part of the jubilee history. It has been reprinted in 3/70, pp. 59-60 as part of Fadiukhin's unity speech at the 1969 congress; and in *Kalendar' evangel'skikh khristian-baptistov 1976*, pp. 55-56. This calendar also printed for the first time the four-point agreement with Christians in the Spirit of the Apostles—Pentecostals, led by N. P. Smorodin (p. 57). The Smorodintsy (stressing "Jesus only") had been forced to perform baptism henceforth in the name of Father, Son, and Holy Spirit.

66. *BV*, 1/60, p. 87.

67. *BV*, 6/63, p. 22.

68. *Ibid.*, p. 35. Andreev freely admitted that the number of Pentecostals within the union was declining.

69. *BV*, 6/66, p. 30.

70. They were: N. V. Kuz'menko (assistant SP for Ukraine) and A. A. Nesteruk. D. I. Ponomarchuk was ill (died 1968), G. G. Ponurko too old (died 1978), and I. K. Pan'ko had died in 1964.

71. P. K. Shatrov (born 1928); converted in 1946; and baptized as member of Smorodin Pentecostals. Following union in 1956 he worked as preacher in the Leningrad ECB church and moved to Moscow around 1966 to take up full-time duties. At the 1969 congress he and V. S. Glukhovskii were elected to the council (representing a younger generation of Pentecostals) and L. S. Vladyko (Belorussia) became a candidate member. Kuz'menko died in 1970 (*BV*, 1/71, pp. 71-72).

72. *BV*, 3/71, pp. 33-34.

73. *BV*, 5/70, p. 14; 2/71, pp. 72-78.

74. Not really; the congress resolution, which received pro-forma unanimous approval, simply affirmed the union with the Pentecostals. There has never been a discussion of the union conditions at a congress.

75. *BV*, 2/72, p. 65; 2/73, pp. 78-79. The members were I. G. Ivanov (AUCECB president), A. I. Mitskevich, A. M. Bychkov, N. N. Melnikov, S. P. Fadiukhin (all presidium members), plus V. S. Glukhovskii and P. K. Shatrov representing Pentecostals.

76. For example, the remarks by the Leningrad assistant leader which are not reported in the official congress report.

77. *BV*, 6/75, pp. 52-53.

78. *BV*, 1/76, pp. 64-70. Newly registered congregations in the union were Obukhovka and Singai (Zhitomir Oblast), Chernysh and Rozhishche (Volynskaia Oblast), Aleksandriia (Kirovograd), Kazanka (Nikolaev), and Brianka (Voroshilovgrad).

79. *BV*, 2/77, p. 64.

80. The standard works avoid giving an estimate of strength.

81. Durasoff in his book *Pentecost Behind the Iron Curtain* (Plainfield, N.J.: Logos International, 1972) estimated 500,000; Michael Rowe uses 100,000 as a plausible figure.

82. Interview with Evgenii Bresenden, November 23, 1975.

83. J. C. Pollock, *The Christians from Siberia* (London: Hodder and Stoughton, 1964).

84. *KNS*, October 1975; September 1977; January 1978; March 1978; July 1978.

85. A recent dramatic account is John C. Pollock, *The Siberian Seven* (London: Hodder and Stoughton, 1979). Cf. *G2W Informationsdienst*, May 10, 1979; *KNS*, July 1978; "The Vashchenko Chronicle: An Attempt to Emigrate: 1962-1978," *RCDA*, XVII, 4-6, 1978, 84-88; cf. pp. 51-52.

86. *BV*, 3/78, p. 61.

87. Evgenii Bresenden, "The Persecution of Pentecostal Evangelical Christians," in Marta Harasowska and Orest Olhovych, eds., *The International Sakharov Hearing* (Baltimore-Toronto: Smoloskyp Publishers, 1977), p. 163.

88. *G2W*, VI, 11, 1978, p. 20f., especially p. 35.

89. Michael Rowe, "Pentecostal Documents from the USSR," *RCL*, January-June 1975, pp. 16-18.

90. Moskalenko, p. 54.

91. *BV*, 3/68, p. 15. See translation and analysis of Karev's speech by this writer in *MQR*, L, 3, 1976, 230-39.

92. *BV*, 2/70, p. 74.

93. *BV*, 3/75, p. 68.

It is necessary to fight for each young man and woman who comes under the influence of religion. The question of children is a question of the life and death of the church.

—*A. N. Puzin,* Chairman
Council for Affairs of Religious Cults

... After Golgotha, the resurrection begins. Atheism, so to speak, is the manure that has prepared the ground for this resurrection. This is its significance.
—*Dmitrii Dudko*

11 Children and Youth: Competition Between Presbyter and Atheist

In August 1976 twelve-year-old Oleg Korovin sent the following telegram to Prime Minister Kosygin: "I am afraid to go to school because, according to a court ruling, they are going to send me to a boarding school. I would like to live with my aunt Natasha and have her as my parental guardian."[1] Oleg's parents had died and the authorities did not wish his aunt, Natalia Korovina, a Christian, to become the guardian. Oleg stopped going to school and the authorities came to search for him, even opening up the bags of sawdust in the attic. Oleg was virtually in a state of shock. Fortunately in this instance, Natalia Korovina could report that in September the court decision was reversed and Oleg could remain in her home.

To some extent Soviet atheists have given up trying to persuade older believers to become atheists, rather placing increased emphasis on training the children and young people. That includes trying to keep them from coming under systematic religious influence. One of the first acts of the Soviet state was to separate the churches from the schools and to deny the churches the right of religious instruction for children. Officially, parents have the right to communicate their beliefs to their children, although in practice this, too, has been challenged. During the past decade there has been an increasing emphasis on the responsibilities that parents have to raise their children in the spirit of communism. In the past several years there appears to have been some relaxation in this area and the Council for

Religious Affairs chairman, Vladimir Kuroedov, wrote in *Izvestia* on January 28, 1978, that "children may visit church and participate in the worship service." The CPR *Bulletin*, however, printed numerous letters claiming that practical experience still gave them the opposite impression.[2]

In 1968 the fate of the Sloboda family became a matter of widespread concern because the authorities had first sent the children away to orphanages, and when the mother still persisted in teaching religion to the other children, sent the mother to prison.[3] Not long afterward the Reform Baptists circulated a document containing 1,433 signatures collected from forty-two different towns and villages in seven republics. All of the signators were mothers complaining about persecution because of their children.[4] They mentioned sixty-four new arrests which affected about 200 children. When the atheist journal *Nauka i Religiia* published an article on orphanages in 1971, it stated that the great majority of children in orphanages were not orphans but had in fact been removed from their parents for various reasons.[5] The illustration given concerned a member of the True Orthodox sect. Generally speaking, however, most of the Baptist documentation suggests that actual loss of parental rights has been relatively rare, but the threat to remove children has been employed with alarming frequency. In recent issues of the CPR *Bulletin* there is now a special section devoted to the subject of children.

It was the children who were largely responsible for precipitating the split in the Russian Baptist movement. The major criticism against the 1960 statute and letter of instruction was that it advised against teaching religion to children, against permitting them in the worship services. State legislation did not and still does not permit children under eighteen to be members of religious societies. As a result, the primary complaint against the Reform Baptists became that they had such an active program for children. Michael Bourdeaux has pointed out that in 1966 all the court cases emphasized this as the primary charge and it was also the primary complaint in newspaper articles.[6]

Soviet atheists, committed to the theory of social conditioning, have placed tremendous emphasis on atheist education. Soviet society has indeed become much more outrightly atheist than most other societies, yet official complaints about the insufficiency of the atheist propaganda reads like a never-ending litany. An article in *Pravda* (January 22, 1979) complains that many young people were not yet liberated from the religious influence of their parents and did not mind going to church.[7] In spite of improvement in volume and quality of the atheist literature, *Pravda* still found that this literature suffered from a frightening thematic monotony and lack of creativity.

The struggle for the hearts of Soviet children and young people continues. Believers encounter tremendous handicaps in trying to compete with the state-sponsored atheist apparatus and yet the believers appear to be making some gains. During the past decade reports about young people searching for religion have increased steadily.

What the Atheists Offer

Actually, atheist instruction begins at childbirth when the mother is instructed how to protect the new Soviet citizen from the harmful influences of religion.[8] The kindergarten is also supposed to foster a spirit of atheism. But the major program of atheist propaganda begins in school.

With the beginning of the Khrushchev campaign, the Ministry of Education began to introduce stronger guidelines whereby atheist propaganda would be included in the subject matter of all grades beginning with the fifth grade. In the older classes atheist instruction was more systematic and in Belorussia, for example, strudents in the tenth or graduating class were required to write essays giving their views on atheism and religion. In the universitites and other institutes of higher education, courses on the fundamentals of scientific atheism became mandatory with the 1964-65 school year. This included twenty-four hours of course work, examination, and, according to a resolution of the Council of Ministers (December 29, 1975), scientific degrees were awarded to persons who "have mastered Marxist-Leninist theory . . . and who observe the norms of communist morality. . ."[9]

Soviet specialists have emphasized that not only do students study atheism, they are also drawn into atheist work. Under the guidance of experienced teachers, they participate in conducting atheist conversations, disputes, celebrate special atheist days or weeks, and help produce atheist displays.

For the child from a Christian family, one of the major worries is the pressure to join the junior party organizations. Although some believers regard membership in the Young Octobrists, Pioneers, or even Komsomol (Communist Youth League) as harmless—they serve a useful function for teaching children discipline, how to survive in the woods, as North American children would in Boy Scout organizations—there is an initiation ceremony with an oath that includes an affirmation of atheism. For many Baptists, especially the Reform Baptists, this is a serious matter. It means that the young school child must personally take a stand to refuse to join the Octobrists, to refuse to wear the red tie of the Pioneers, in spite of extreme pressure from classmates and teachers. One resourceful Orthodox girl confessed to her priest that she had committed a sin by wearing the red tie of the Young Pioneers. But she explained: "Of course, we're powerless. They make us do it. So this is what we did. First we blessed it with holy water, and then put it on."[10]

The schoolteacher not only has the task of including teaching units on atheism in her curriculum, she also has to play the role of antireligious spy. Regularly, children are asked whether they or their parents go to church. Sometimes teachers are expected to keep watch at the church to note which of their students are attending. Legally, any reference to religious affiliation may not appear in state documents, including school grades, but in practice this is often violated. Rita Goge, tenth-grade student, reported that her literature teacher had indicated to her that if they would receive one more report from the authorities that she was attending church, then she would get the grade "unsatisfactory" for the next exam.[11] In school No. 31 in Simferopol lecturer Moskivitin had spoken so viciously about believers, especially the Dubrovik family, whose son attended the school, that the listeners responded by shouting, "They should be hanged." Some of the older students thereupon beat up young Dubrovik so severely that he suffered a concussion and was admitted to hospital. Later the mother discovered that Dubrovik's teacher and the deputy director of the school had stood by while the beating was taking place without interfering.[12]

It is no secret that many schoolteachers do not enjoy teaching atheism and authorities regularly complain that the teachers are not presenting the material with sufficient conviction or even omitting it altogether. School curriculum planners were also criticized by the recent *Pravda* article. Not only did it complain about the lack of antireligious content in children's literature, it was discovered that only four books containing antireligious material were included in the publication plans for children's literature until 1980. None of the books recently published by the youth publishing house, *Molodaia Gvardia*, were worth mentioning, for here, too, *Pravda* complained that they were "boring and superficial."[13]

Particularly since 1966, the 360,000 libraries, 140,000 clubs, and houses of culture, plus the 11,900 museums in the Soviet Union are all required to engage in constant atheistic propaganda.[14] To achieve this task and to build up a cadre of workers to read the lectures on atheism, to write the newspaper articles or to do the personal counselling with believers, special schools were introduced. These are the so-called schools for Marxism-Leninism. In Belorussia in 1972, 10,000 persons completed the program in scientific atheism. There are also people's universities for atheism and schools for atheist lecturers. At present there are 35,000 People's Universities with nine million persons studying, with most of these universities including a faculty on scientific atheism. Alone in Belorussia there are eighty schools devoted exclusively to the education of atheist lecturers.

Poor Quality of Atheist Program

These statistics notwithstanding, reports about poorly attended lectures and their poor quality appear regularly in the Soviet press. In one not untypical story reported by *Sovetskaia Rossia* a resourceful lecturer was exposed to criticism. Earning his living through honorariums from lectures, he was booked to hold three lectures on the same evening in different locations. He succeeded in signing the register at each place, staying long enough to collect his fee and moving on to the next one, with no one the wiser since no one showed up for the lectures anyway.

The persistent problem with all this atheist propaganda was that although they claimed to teach "scientific atheism," it was not very scientific.[15] The Academy of Sciences had already established a sector for atheism within the institute of philosophy in 1959. As a result, numerous scientific studies were undertaken, notably sociological studies on religiosity by A. I. Klibanov and others but also by party workers so that the results varied in quality.[16] Following the decision of the Central Committee in January 1964, an institute of scientific atheism was established in the Academy of Social Sciences and became responsible for the coordination of all scientific atheist work. Since then, noticeable improvement in research and publications can be observed and there is also some broadening of the scope of research, although ideological restrictions still place restraints on the quality. A major conference in 1974 demonstrated the improved quality of the research and also demonstrated some increase in an interdisciplinary approach.[17]

The continuing problem with atheist propaganda has been the simplistic definition of religion as "anti-scientific world-view, spiritual product of a mixed-up world."[18] It may be true that the churches of the Middle Ages and the Russian Orthodox Church of the nineteenth century were obscurantist and intolerant, but it is unfair to describe the present church that way. As long as Soviet scholars continue to claim that the professed interest of the modern church in such questions as war and peace, in international affairs, and in specific questions about their country's future are merely speculative attempts to appeal to the young people, their own claims to scholarship will not be taken seriously.[19] So far, the Soviet Union has not produced a significant atheist philosopher, the worship of Lenin notwithstanding.

A primary emphasis of Soviet atheism in recent years has been the so-called "individual work with believers." This represents the recognition that the reasons for the persistence of belief are complex. Individual atheist counselors are encouraged to become personally acquainted with believing individuals, to become a personal friend who demonstrates concern for them and whose advice they gradually come to appreciate. Many books and articles have been printed in recent years describing case histories which usually involved sustained effort over a time span of several years.[20] The principles and methodology are obviously borrowed from some Christian personal worker's manual.

The fact that believers fear their young people will become friendly with such a personal worker indicates that this method has been relatively successful. It is a method, however, which is labor-intensive and in spite of all the many atheist seminaries there is still a shortage of dedicated atheist workers, especially of those prepared to live in the villages where religious convictions are still strong. Newspaper articles regularly urge all members of Soviet society to assume responsibility for fellow citizens and to befriend and influence individual believers in order to help them find their way to a full and happy integration into Soviet society.

How Successful Are They?

A total of 600 experts met in Kiev in 1978 to evaluate the achievements over the past fifteen years since the introduction of socialist rituals.[21] Participants were told that in recent years more than eighty percent of those persons that broke with religion did so because they had been influenced by the new rituals. Although the editors of *Nauka i Religia* protested that the socialist rituals had not simply been introduced to replace religious rituals, still they did emphasize that they were a legitimate weapon in the struggle with religion. Substitute rituals were introduced as early as 1923, but the systematic introduction of a wide range of rituals is directly connected to the Khrushchev campaign. The first Wedding Palace was opened in Leningrad in 1958. The Ukraine became the major experimental region. Today there are 400 offices for socialist rituals, 940 special ritual societies, ninety-

four palaces and houses for festive occasions, 8,500 ritual halls, and 500 salons for ritual feasts. In addition the Ukraine has 1,500 vocal collectives or
choirs and 1,150 orchestras available to serve at ritual functions.

Yet in spite of this effort, Soviet criticism continues. A Soviet
ethnographer comparing an Orthodox priest and a Soviet ritualist concluded that the latter lacked the moral authority and the personal contact
with the recipient that the priest had. In addition there were still many religious rituals for which no substitute had been developed. One particular
failure was the inability to devise an appropriate Soviet burial ceremony.
Participants at the Kiev conference also expressed the wish for the creation
of a coordinating center for all Union republics. One critic noted that
perhaps a "ministry for the Soviet cult" will soon be created, similar to the
"ministry for opium," the popular designation for the Council for Religious
Affairs.

State Atheism

That is, in fact, the major factor which explains the massive atheist
program. Soviet atheism is state atheism, it is the official confession of faith
of the majority of Soviet citizens and is sponsored and protected by the state
in the same way that Roman Catholicism was the state religion of Austria in
the eighteeneth century. Austrian Roman Catholic Cardinal König, who
developed this argument at length in a widely publicized newspaper article
in 1975 and thereby touched a tender nerve, has been repeatedly attacked
by no less a personage than Vladimir Kuroedov himself as a falsifier of
Marxist atheism.[22]

Soviet protests, however, remain mere rhetoric, because the evidence
clearly supports Cardinal König's conclusions. Churches are permitted according to the constitution the freedom to practice religious rituals but only
atheism is granted the freedom to propagandize. The Znanie Society, which
began its work in 1947, places major emphasis on atheist propaganda and
the training of atheist cadres. It now has a membership of 2.9 million.[23] In
addition, both party and state apparatus are deeply involved in the atheist
program directly. A Party Central Committee decision in 1964 ordered its
Department for Propaganda and Agitation to direct its atheist program not
only toward party members but toward the entire population. Regional
councils to coordinate scientific atheist propaganda and research were established. Councils for scientific atheism were created in the 4,243 regional
and city executive committees of the party, and even in 390,000 party cells
such councils were established. In the state structure, special commissions

were established which had the task to ensure that Soviet legislation on religion was not being violated. Each local Soviet was ordered to create such a commission where the vice-chairman of the executive committee for the local state administration served as chairman.[24] It is these commissions that keep track of all religious activity on card files and thereby try to restrain its growth.

Estimated figures are unavailable for the amount of money the state has invested in the atheist campaign, but the sum would be astronomic. Christians naturally regard state sponsorship of atheism as unfair, but there is also widespread sentiment in the population generally that state sponsorship is undesirable. Alexander Solzhenitsyn called on the Soviet leaders in 1973 to stop the state subsidies, to allow atheism to compete freely with religion. This, he argued, would permit the entire *agitprop* apparatus "to prove the true strength of their ideological convictions and sincerity." And he went on to ask: "What have you to fear? . . . Are you really so unsure of yourself?"[25]

The abolition of state atheism is unlikely, however. Not only would it require new policy decisions; a large number of laws that imply discrimination against believers would need to be revised. But above all, most observers are convinced that the atheist apparatus would quickly disappear if permitted to compete.

In spite of its lamentable tastelessness, superficiality, and intellectual shortcomings, Soviet atheism has much to offer. That is, to decide to believe in God involves a conscious decision to live with many restrictions and discriminations. On my visit to the Soviet Union in May 1979 a member of our group was handed a short letter which stated: "I am a teacher and a Baptist, and immediately after I was baptized, I was dismissed from school. Ekaterina Alexeevna Morozova, ul. Musorgskogo 11, Apartment 237, Moscow 127490."

What the Evangelicals Offer

In terms of the usual factors for evaluation, such as money, expertise, media access, etc., the evangelicals appear hopelessly at a disadvantage. Father Dmitri Dudko, however, drew attention to other factors that help explain the attractiveness of religion. Atheists, he claimed, base their propaganda on cowardice, that terrible weakness in man. "The Christian faith, however, calls for cross-bearing."[26]

The major propaganda weapon for the evangelicals is the family. The CCECB in a special statute for child-raising parents declared that:

A homemade printing press used by the secret publisher, Khristianin

ABOVE: Meetinghouse of the registered Mennonite church in Alma-Ata, Kazakhstan, 1977.

TOP RIGHT: Meetinghouse of the registered Mennonite church in Novosibirsk.

BOTTOM RIGHT: Some Mennonite preachers in Kazakhstan.

СОТВОРЕНИЕ КАДРОВ

Рассказ о том, как бабка Неонила
К церковникам внучонка заманила

Пойдем-ка, внучек, в божий храм,
Увидишь, как чудесно там.

Картинки это не простые—
Здесь нарисованы святые.

Молись ты боженьке всегда,
Чтоб не стряслась с тобой беда.

И ты служить сумеешь тут.
Угоден богу этот труд.

Беда, коль фанатичные старухи
Внучат в своем воспитывают духе.

Atheist propaganda poster: Cadre Creation—the story of how grandma Neonila enticed her grandson to church.

1. Let's go to God's temple, grandson,
   You'll see how wonderful it is there.

2. Those are no simple pictures;
   Here saints are portrayed.

3. You must always pray to God
   So that no calamity will befall you.

4. And here you can serve;
   Such work is pleasing to God.

How awful, when an old fanatic teaches her grandson this spirit.

The seven Pentecostals, the Peter Vashchenko family and Mrs. Maria Chmykalov with her son, in the American Embassy in Moscow, August 1978.

"Announcement: Today on Wednesday, July 27, 1977, at 7:00 p.m. in the summer rooms of the Jubilee Building there will be a meeting of local residents to consider the question of the anti-social activities of the group of Pentecostals in Stantsia Starotitarovskoe—by order of the executive committee of the Soviet." (Both photos courtesy of Keston College)

CCECB General Secretary Georgi P. Vins. (Photo courtesy of Keston College)

ABOVE: The family of the imprisoned Reform Baptist leader Georgi Vins at the beginning of his term in 1974. (Photo courtesy of Keston College)

BELOW: Interior of the Reform Baptist Church in Kiev which was registered unconditionally in August 1975 while its prominent member Georgi Vins was in prison.

TOP: Six members of the CCECB meeting together in 1976. Front row, left to right: D. V. Miniakov, G. K. Kriuchkov, N. P. Khrapov. Standing: M. I. Khorev, M. T. Shaptala, K. K. Kroeker.

BOTTOM: Members of Council of Prisoners' Relatives in 1979. Seated second from right is President Lidia M. Vins; Secretary Galina Rytikova is standing second from left; the new president following Lidia Vins's departure is A. T. Kozorezova, third from left, standing. (Both photos courtesy Friedensstimme)

CPR activist Galina Rytikova with her six children in the early seventies; she has nine now and the oldest was recently imprisoned for his faith. (Photo courtesy of Keston College)

TOP: CCECB evangelist Iakov Skorniakov with his wife, shortly before imprisonment in 1978.

BOTTOM LEFT: Johan Steffan, leader of the Reform Baptist Church in Issyk, Kazakhstan, began serving his fourth prison setence in 1974. A photo taken secretly in 1979 shows him in a seriously emaciated condition. He wrote to his wife recently, "My conditions cannot become worse than they are." (Photo courtesy of Friedensstimme)

BOTTOM RIGHT: Boris M. Zdorovets in the late seventies after another prison term. An early Reform Baptist leader. (Photo courtesy of Keston College)

TOP: Valentin Naprienko, here shown with his family, was sentenced to three years of strict regimen in August 1979 because he transported religious literature in his automobile. (Photo courtesy Friedensstimme)

BOTTOM LEFT: Boris M. Zdorovets with his wife in 1971 after release from ten years' prison and exile. (Bottom photos courtesy of Keston College)

BOTTOM RIGHT: Close-up of Boris M. Zdorovets, early Reform Baptist leader, most of whose life has been wasted in prison camps.

ABOVE: CCECB member M. I. Khorev (right) with youth evangelist Peter P. Peters (left) and Rostov children's worker Nina Zakharova. Both men are currently in prison.

BELOW: The wife and children of Jakob P. Wolf (Issyk, Kazakhstan), who received a two-year prison sentence in December 1977. (Both photos courtesy of Keston College)

ВОЛЬФ ЯКОВ ПЕТРОВИЧ

семья Шлехт Ивана Готлиповича   семья Янцен Якова Генриховича

ПОМНИТЕ МОИ УЗЫ

ABOVE: A typical photo montage circulated as a prayer reminder among Reform Baptists in the Soviet Union. The words read: "New prisoners for the cause of the gospel. Remember my chains." Photos concern Jakob P. Wolf, the family of I. T. Shlekht, and the family of Jakob G. Jantsen.

BELOW: CCECB member N. G. Baturin with his wife on release from prison in October 1976. (Photo courtesy of Keston College)

317

N. G. Baturin with his family. Baturin, elected acting CCECB secretary in August 1979, was arrested in November 1979. (Photo courtesy of Keston College)

TOP: A group of friends wait in the left foreground for the release of Nina Kravchenko (September 1977) from the prison camp in the background. (Both photos courtesy of Keston College)

BOTTOM: Released prisoner Nina Kravchenko shares a prayer of thanksgiving with her friends outside the prison gates. She had served four years because of her involvement in children's work in her home congregation in Maikop (Krasnodarskii Krai).

Ella Kasper (standing center) reporting to the Reform Baptist church in Taldy Kurgan (Kazakhstan) following her release in 1977 from a three-year prison sentence. She had been in prison simultaneously with her father. (Photo courtesy of Friedensstimme)

"Children are citizens of heaven, for whose life the parents are responsible. If a citizen of heaven perishes because the parents were at fault, the Lord will exact strict punishment, so much so that it would have been better had he not been born."[27] Recent research revealed that eighty percent of the believers gave religious instruction to their children at home.[28] In another study twenty-six percent of the Baptists interviewed had been religious since childhood, twenty-one percent described parental influence as the chief factor in shaping their religiosity.[29] A study of Reform Baptists in Tambov Oblast revealed that forty percent of the membership was between twenty and forty years of age. This was also true of its leaders.[30] Central leadership appeared to consist primarily of persons born before 1910 but 27.5 percent were under forty. At the local leadership level the involvement of the young people was even more striking. In 1961, forty-eight percent of the local leaders were under forty years of age.[31]

Soviet scholars also describe the Mennonites as unique in their special emphasis on the education of children. In Karaganda, Kazakhstan 81.5 percent of the children were taught religion in their homes and 46.3 percent of these were active believers.[32] Only nine percent of the children had joined the Young Pioneer organization. Another study noted that approximately twenty percent of Mennonite membership was under thirty years of age; in the city of Tomsk it was as high as forty-one percent. Generally speaking, more than half of the membership was under fifty. In the Pavlodar Oblast seventy-one percent were under fifty, in Novosibirsk Oblast 77.5 percent were under fifty, while in Tomsk eighty-nine percent were under fifty. "This is one of the major features distinguishing them from other sectarian groupings."[33]

This deep concern that children receive a religious upbringing also comes through when one speaks with AUCECB members locally. Their journal, however, must be more circumspect and contains rather little. In a recent article, "On Being a Christian," the writer stated that "believing parents must convey a knowledge of God to their children, but in this they must not impose their faith on the children, but rely only on faith in God's help and the sufficiency of personal example."[34] Too often, considering the atheist competition, this proved inadequate and parents were relieved to see that their children were attracted to the active youth program offered by the Reform Baptists.

Special activities for children were a key part of the program of the *Initsiativniki.* They conducted Sunday school classes, although they had very little specialized literature for this purpose. When Georgi Vins was put on trial in 1975 a major charge was that he had been actively involved in the preparation and printing of children's literature. A handwritten teacher's manual entitled "The Song of the Shepherd", had been confiscated. This book consisted of individual lessons prepared by F. W. Kasakova with corrections made by Vins. Another book confiscated consisted of religious pictures and was entitled "Paint Them Yourself."[35] Seeing the staggering array of children's literature in North American bookstores, Vins's daughter Natasha announced she would devote herself to translating the best materials so that the CCECB could publish more.

According to Soviet sources, Mennonites are also active in circulating children's educational materials. This German language material has been sent to them by relatives and friends from abroad, and some individuals spend their time making additional handwritten copies.[36] In recent years AUCECB Baptists have again increased their children's activity. This is, however, done at local initiative. The Moscow union is unable to support even one children's specialist. Where this children's work is done, it is carried out under conditions of strict secrecy. Officially, the AUCECB churches do not have Sunday schools.

Parents are specially concerned about the atheist pressure their children experience at school. As a result a tradition has developed whereby the worship service preceding school opening day focuses especially on the children and special prayers are said for them. Enterprising churches, especially Reform Baptists, take the children on a special outing on that weekend. Not only is there much singing and telling of Bible stories, even a treasure hunt in the forest is linked with religious themes. Sometimes as the children follow the signs along the path marked by their teachers, they find themselves following "the pilgrim's progress." Above all, teachers and parents try to communicate to the children that they will not be alone in facing ridicule and abuse in school.[37]

State legislation forbids church membership before age eighteen and also forbids youth circles. In spite of this, Baptists and other evangelicals devote considerable attention to youth activities. In most registered congregations, one worship service a week is a youth service. Although officially described as a regular worship service, there is much more music and singing by the young people, many churches having youth orchestras, and some of the young men preach short sermons. In unregistered congregations youth activity is fostered more explicitly and young people are also encouraged in practical activity. Young people call on the sick and the aged, help in cleaning the church premises, and are usually responsible for decorating the church at feast days. In active churches, whether registered or unregistered, the young people meet each other in large or small groups almost every day. This includes the choir practice, band practice, as well as smaller groups meeting to practice their assignment at the youth service, and often there are also informal Bible studies. Much of this activity is self-initiated and self-organized so that the presbyter cannot be held responsible.

North American evangelicals, like many other religious groupings, have developed and printed a virtual mountain of literature for and about children and young people. In the Soviet Union such literature is extremely scarce. It is scarce not only because the authorities prevent its publication but also because there is a great need for more creative writing and translations. Religious novels for youth and children, religious films, and other similar creative attempts to attract and influence young people must still be regarded by those producing literature for the Soviet Union as luxury items.

The Presbyter Is Responsible

Since there is no central coordinating body for children and youth work, as is true for state atheism, primary responsibility falls on the local presbyter. A recent dramatized account tells the story of an older presbyter in a registered Baptist church whose young people were requesting baptism.[38] They came into his office after the service, asked to speak to him alone, but the church warden, the local spy for the authorities, refused to leave. Whereupon a younger minister suggested to the young people that he would walk them home. On the way they arranged for secret sessions where he would hear their testimonies and examine their knowledge of the faith. The warden managed to overhear one of these sessions at the young minister's house, when they made plans to meet at the lake in the middle of the night for the baptism. The baptism took place because the warden, who had reported this to the authorities, got to the scene of the "crime" ten minutes too late. The role of the warden and the disinclination of the older presbyter to spend a second term in prison finally led to a split with the younger preacher and the young people forming a separate church.

It is a typical story. The brave and zealous young people had less fear of the consequences, but it is unfair to dismiss all registered presbyters as cowards. The task of the presbyter is an onerous one. Except for the large, registered churches in the city, the presbyter works for his living in the factory or on the collective farm like his fellow members and can only devote his free time to church work. That means that after the exhaustions of the day's labor and of standing in line to buy food and other necessities, he is still expected to have the energy and creativity to provide forward-looking leadership. The church's expectations of him are considerable.

Assistant General Secretary Mitskevich described these expectations in a recent article.[39] Above all, he must serve as pastor or shepherd of the flock, which is a high honor but also very difficult. He has a responsibility for each soul; he must be as a father to the church. That means, too, that he must be concerned that the members receive good spiritual food. By means of visitation and conversation he should be personally acquainted with the experiences, illnesses, and suffering of each member. According to Mitskevich, the presbyter must also have the gift of administration. This gift, as he and others such as Karev and Levindanto regularly emphasize,[40] must not lead to dictatorial ruling over the others, but he should be able to rely on assistants and should create an atmosphere of mutual understanding and unity. But as administrator he is responsible to take the initiative on all church activity and should also plan ahead. Mitskevich in particular criticized the tendency to wait until the minute before the start of the service, when the preachers met for pre-service prayer, to find out who would be assigned to preach. Preaching quality would be better if the presbyter had assigned a preaching rota in advance. The Moscow leadership has regularly encouraged an improvement in the quality of the leadership by printing helpful articles in the journal. In 1958 they also sent a handbook for ministers to all the churches, which was replete with practical advice.[41]

Although the evangelicals emphasize the priesthood of all believers, in practice it is not only the Baptist presbyter who has a tendency to dominate his flock. Worship in a typical Pentecostal service is as follows: Following the congregational singing, the presbyter or elder preaches an introductory sermon. During the congregational singing that follows, the elder walks over to one of the preachers and asks him to preach. After this preacher has completed his sermon, there is a call to prayer with everyone praying on his knees. During this time, some of the members speak in tongues. The preacher closes the prayer session. Then follow several more songs, during which the elder, again moved by the Spirit, asks another preacher for the next sermon. The cycle is repeated up to three times.[42]

Mennonites also have an elder (like a bishop) as their leader, plus numerous preachers. Even more so than in Mennonite Brethren circles, the Mennonite elder is accorded great esteem and his word is final at congregational meetings. Mennonites are accustomed to respecting the wisdom of the older men and it is rare to find a younger man in a leadership position. This is a general problem among evangelicals who, because of the lack of theological education, tend to rely on the accumulated wisdom of the older men who will in all likelihood also be more conservative.

A growing number of presbyters in registered city congregations are able to devote full time to their ministry. These receive a salary collected by voluntary donations from the congregation. The presbyter must pay approximately twenty-five percent income tax but his work for the church will not be entered into his working logbook. That means he will not be eligible for a state pension but hopefully his church union will look after him in his old age.[43] Many full-time presbyters are individuals who worked in heavy industry, enabling them to retire at age fifty-five or even fifty and then receive a pension from the state while working for the church.

The Life of a Presbyter

Presbyter Ivan was the leader of a large urban church. Sunday he spent all day in church because it took too long to travel home by bus in between the three services. True, he preached only once on Sunday, since he allowed his assistant to lead one of the services, but he still had to be present because legally he was still responsible. In addition there were three preaching services during the week, each of them two hours long. He had started preaching a series of sermons on the Book of Matthew and that meant extra preparation time because it was equivalent to a Bible study. Once a week he met with the corps of preachers to discuss spiritual concerns of the church. The church council or executive committee also met regularly, and he was present, although legally he had no voice in its decisions. Thanks to the revival at New Year, there were again twenty young people awaiting baptism. He had started weekly classes with them and was trying to revise the material he had used previously, wishing urgently for the book on doctrine he had seen in Moscow.

During the week he had called on the plenipotentiary for the Council for Religious Affairs twice, once to see whether the decision on approving the baptismal candidates could not be speeded up and the other time to obtain permission to undertake slight repairs on the building. Each time the meetings were becoming more strained because the plenipotentiary claimed to be receiving complaints that the noisy singing at the services was disturbing the neighbors. Their active youth group was also presenting programs in neighboring congregations and even in private homes in other villages without his knowledge. So far he had been fined three times this year but the plenipotentiary was threatening other measures. How he wished he could take a break from his duties, get a good rest, and reassess all those little decisions he had been forced to make, small compromises he had agreed to, to give the church more breathing room in other areas. He had not consciously compromised nor cooperated with the state but some of his actions troubled his conscience.

Recently he had started a new activity that was a mixture of blessing and worry. He had told the congregation that on one day of the week he would be available at the church for counseling. This did not work too well until the other ministers who had joined him for the counseling session received the message that the people wanted to see the presbyter alone. Once he was alone with them, they had started unburdening their hearts and often he had been able to help them or at least to pray together with them. But this, too, weighed on him because if the member's secret became known to the authorities, then clearly he alone could have told them. He knew he was suffering from emotional fatigue but didn't know where to turn.

The role of a presbyter in a Reform Baptist church is probably more difficult. Presbyter Ivan Froese of Dzhezkazgan was regularly ordered to appear for questioning at the offices of the city executive committee.[44] The interview was usually conducted by a KGB official. Since 1969 this man had been urging them to register their church but Froese refused because of the conditions involved. The authorities demanded to know everything that was happening at their church but his church brotherhood had determined that the authorities had no right to know about inner-church affairs. Therefore he refused to talk, refused even to say who was the leader of the congregation. The interrogations continued, usually they lasted from five to eight hours, even if he spent the whole time saying nothing. The authorities began offering incentives, suggesting that if he would cooperate they would allow him as a Soviet German to emigrate to West Germany. Froese refused, and one day, after a series of coincidences in which members of his family had been photographed, they were shown a one-hour television program which presented Froese and his family as backward and dull, a family receiving the advantages and privileges of the Soviet state but paying them back with hatred and agitation against the socialist order.

Froese was only twenty-seven when he became presbyter, continuing to work for a living while serving the 200-member congregation in his free time. He had a family of nine children and was very poor. Usually he would arise at 5:00 a.m., and together with some of the older children, go to the fields to stuff several bags full of grass which they had picked with their hands in order to provide fodder for his cow. In the evening and often at night there were always guests coming to see him for spiritual counsel or to discuss affairs of the church. Many of his fellow pastors had spent from three to five years in prison; a growing number of them had been in prison several times. Others were in hiding from the authorities, able to see their family for only fleeting moments every few weeks. That was why, one such person explained, the wife of a presbyter stood with him at the front of the church for the ordination service, why she had to kneel with him and was asked whether she, too, was ready to pay the costs of the ministry. For her that meant assuming the bulk of family responsibilities.

Froese was not the only one regularly urged to cooperate with the authorities. One immigrant tells a somewhat dramatized story of a deacon who was simply asked to inform the authorities on the activities of the pastor and his church.[45] Naturally, he refused, but they said that if he did not do so, they would circulate rumors that the presbyter of his Adventist church was planning to join forces with the Baptists. That would probably mean that the church members would oust him. It was in the deacon's power to preserve the reputation of the presbyter—by reporting he would actually be doing a good deed! When he still refused he was threatened with prison, with false charges of having embezzled money, until finally, literally in a state of shock, the poor man signed the sheet of paper thrust in front of him. Later he was sure it had all been a bad dream because he did not hear from the authorities again, but a half year later they called on him and demanded information. When threats did not work, he was given a drug which loosened his tongue. This deacon's mistake had been that he did not wish to burden his presbyter with additional worry and therefore had not confided in him when the first pressure started. Later he was too ashamed to talk. Few of the church spies, of which there is usually one per congregation whether registered or unregistered, deliberately wish to harm the church. They are people whose weakness has been discovered.

Local Leadership

In most registered congregations there is one presbyter and one or several deacons. Presbyter and deacon are individuals legally registered by the state for their tasks. As a result, the deacons are often presbyters' assistants, engaging in a much broader pastoral activity than is true of deacons elsewhere. Deacons are also ordained, but when a deacon is elected a presbyter, a second ordination service follows. In many churches, the deacons assist the presbyter in visitations with the membership and in generally caring for the spiritual welfare of the church.

The office of evangelist was historically a very vital office in evangelical churches and was therefore held in high esteem. A major reason for the rapid growth in the 1920s was the work of the evangelist who was supported by groups of churches and assigned to specific districts to evangelize. The office of evangelist is not permitted legally since 1929, but it still functions. In registered churches some of the preachers are informally asked to serve as evangelists, which means that they travel to neighboring villages for preaching services to small groups of people which are too small to register. Reform Baptists still place great emphasis on this office by maintaining a special department of evangelism.

In the registered churches the evangelist is often an individual showing promise as a preacher. Weekend evangelistic trips are his apprenticeship and later he may be encouraged to move to another community which is in need of a presbyter. The other preachers are not usually ordained. In a large church, such as the AUCECB church in Novosibirsk with 1,000 members, there is at present a preaching corps of thirty-six persons.[46] All take their turn at preaching, although some are more active than others because they are also deacons, choir leaders, or band leaders.

Recently the word evangelist has once again appeared in *Bratskii Vestnik*. In connection with the question of improving relations with Pentecostals inside the union, both President Andrei Klimenko and the general secretary, Alexei Bychkov, urged the introduction of either assistant senior presbyters or evangelists who would devote their time exclusively to strengthening the unity of the brotherhood. Delegates approved the creation of a department for evangelism and unity at the 1979 All-Union congress.[47]

A little-noted but powerful source of leadership in the local congregation is the executive committee. According to the law, it consists of three persons but may not include the presbyter. The executive committee is responsible for the nonspiritual aspects of congregational life. It negotiates the contract for the building, is responsible for repairs and maintenance and extension or remodeling when these become possible. In most evangelical churches, the non-ordained preachers are elected to the executive committee so that its activities are included in the discussion at the regular meeting of ministers. The AUCECB sought to restrict the powers of this committee in a revised statute approved in December 1979 whereby all spiritual and policy-setting issues became the presbyter's prerogative and the executive committee's responsibility was limited to looking after local administrative matters.

Without discounting the good work these various office holders do, the fact remains that it is the women who have and still contribute the lion's share to the existence of the church. Many of their number went to prison too, but often they were able to keep the church open while the husband was in prison. While Abram Hamm served his sentence (1970-73), his wife invited the congregation to meet in her house in order to show the authorities how ineffectual had been their attempt to hinder church life.[48] In the early years Jacob Zhidkov and others had repeatedly acknowledged the vital role of the women. Maria Orlova, Michael Orlov's wife, was a schoolteacher who had made a futile attempt to become a missionary to India (before the Revolution).[49] She contributed significantly as part of a gifted husband-and-wife team, some feeling that her husband's ministry was not the same after her death.

Yet Soviet evangelicals have tended to apologize for the fact that some of their women do lead. In a major article for presbyters, N. A. Levindanto stated that only one deaconess was referred to in the New Testament (Rom. 16:1). Since there was no reference to ordination, a woman could lead the worship service and preach as did Philip's daughters, but the church ordinances should be conducted by ordained men from neighboring congregations.[50] At the 1979 congress ten of the 525 delegates were women. One of them from Moldavia delivered a lengthy speech on the role of women in the Bible. With great humility she asked the men not to forget to teach the women, including teaching them when to be silent and when to help. Yet she also made a stirring appeal for the creation of the office of deaconess, urging the brothers to help women to serve God. Presiding chairman Ivan Gnida hugged her and apologized profusely for the many times the men had taken the women for granted.[51]

In most Soviet evangelical circles the requirement that the woman wear a head covering (usually a shawl) implies greater subordination than one would expect. Usually the brethren (men) meet separately to make church decisions before sharing them with the entire membership. When visiting in a Russian evangelical home, it is unusual for the wife to participate in the discussion of church affairs. If most Soviet evangelical women do not preach or speak in public, they do pray fervently during the public prayer sessions. In this writer's experience, the content of these prayers was sometimes more edifying than the sermons preached by the men!

The Missing Teachers

Specially trained teachers are a rarity in Soviet evangelical circles. The AUCECB is the only East European evangelical union that is not permitted to maintain its own seminary. Already in 1947 President Jacob Zhidkov had spoken of the need for a theological school, declaring this a vital question which they hoped to consider in the near future and "we believe that the Lord will give us success in this matter."[52] Here his optimism was overextended because even at the present time of writing, a theological school still does not exist. In 1968 permission was received finally to open a theological school by correspondence with a maximum enrollment of 100. Present General Secretary Bychkov first became involved with AUCECB activity by translating and helping prepare course materials. By 1979, 272 persons had graduated from the two-year course. They had studied dogmatics, homiletics, exegetics, bibliology, church history, Evangelical Christian-Baptist history and the constitution.[53] In reporting these results, Alexei Bychkov announced that they were preparing course materials for new disciplines: comparative theology, Christian ethics, and ECB history. As a result of the many proposals introduced at the 1974 congress, courses were also granted in music. In 1976 it became possible to add a third year of instruction, and the authorities now permitted fifty students to register annually. This made it possible to teach all three years of the course of studies simultaneously, thereby increasing the number of participants. In 1979 a special two-year course for church musicians began.[54]

The AUCECB also announced that permission had been received to open a second church on the outskirts of Moscow in a building which will house the new seminary.[55] Since the announcement, numerous delays have arisen, and the seminary still remains a future dream. At most, several guest lecturers beginning with the Baptist Claus Meister of Switzerland have addressed the correspondence students.[56]

The primary problem, even if the state permitted a seminary, is that the AUCECB (like other evangelicals) lack adequately trained teachers. Beginning in 1957, the AUCECB was permitted to send four students to study at Baptist colleges in England. After a considerable time gap, this was resumed in the late sixties so that a total of twenty-seven persons had the opportunity for study abroad before this program was terminated in 1976.[57]

The correspondence course is not really at the level of a theological seminary; many of the courses are based on adaptations from Moody Bible Institute courses. Even those who studied abroad were unable to get theological depth in the two short years of their study, limited as they were by the need to learn a foreign language. Michael Zhidkov, after two years at Spurgeons College, was able to spend an additional year at McMaster University. Of the younger corps of leaders, he is probably the only one approaching the theological qualifications required to teach in a seminary. The Baptist leaders have been unsuccessful so far in obtaining permission to send students to the international Baptist Theological Seminary at Rüschlikon, Switzerland.

The major substitute for a seminary has been *Bratskii Vestnik*. General Secretary Karev and his assistant Mitskevich devoted major effort to filling this journal with high-quality didactic articles. If a local presbyter was fortunate to receive a subscription (it began with 3,000 copies, gradually increasing to 10,000 in 1978) and had built up a file, he would have a useful reference library available. A number of other major contributors to *Bratskii Vestnik* were former graduates of Bible classes that had been held in Moscow and Leningrad from 1924 to 1928.[58]

With the incorporation of the Baltic states and the Western Ukraine into the Soviet Union after the war, the Baptist Union also benefited by gaining access to better-educated clergy in this area. The most outstanding individual was Oswald Tiark, leading minister of the 2,000-member union congregation in Tallinn, Estonia. Tiark had obtained a Master of Theology degree at Columbia University before returning to Estonia to become a pastor.[59] In addition to organizing seminars and correspondence courses for Estonia, he has written Bible commentaries on Mark's Gospel, on Ephesians, and has recently completed the first half of the Book of Romans. This is a major contribution, since a Russian-language commentary on the Bible does not exist, not even in translation. Unfortunately, Tiark, aged 75, cannot anticipate many more productive years and there is an urgent need for persons of his ability and training.

The Reform Baptists have been hampered even more in their access to theological materials. They have, however, been very aggressive in trying to collect valuable articles from old Baptist journals for reprinting and have been influenced by the growing supplies of religious literature that have been brought into the country by tourists and other individuals. Copies of the AUCECB correspondence course material have been obtained in the West, resulting in reproduction for widest circulation. In one instance known to this writer, a dozen Reform Baptist preachers came together regularly, read the instructions for the course on homiletics, and tried to teach each other.

The Soviet Union is the largest and oldest of the communist countries, thereby making it important as a case history for the role of the Christian in Marxist society. Joseph Hromadka, theologian and teacher at the Comenius Faculty in Prague, Czechoslovakia, is still the best-known contributor to the subject. Many of his speeches on the subject of peace were reprinted in *Bratskii Vestnik,* but not his major writings discussing the role of the church under socialism. No person of his quality has emerged in the Soviet Union and there are no articles in *Bratskii Vestnik* that one would recommend reading on this subject. Neither the AUCECB nor the CCECB has produced a Hromadka or even a Joseph Ton, a Romanian Baptist pastor who attempted to deal with the subject from an evangelical perspective.[60] A few AUCECB leaders have attended conferences where this subject was discussed, but their own Soviet situation does not enable them to make a fruitful contribution.

Beating the Odds-Maker

Soviet atheists expect to win the competition for Soviet youth. It is merely a matter of time; the laws of history are on their side. That is their professed conviction.

Like Lenin at the time of the Revolution, they are impatient with the course of history and feel that decisive measures must be undertaken to speed up the process of history. That is why the massive atheist educational program is enforced with such heavy-handed exercises of power. All the advantages are on the side of atheism. The Soviet citizen weighing the options could surely conclude that only a stupid person would opt for religion. ·

And yet, atheist officials constantly complain about the inadequacy of their work, the lack of fervency on the part of their cadres, and are forced to admit that religion is not dead but apparently experiencing a revival. To quite an extent the failure is due to their own making. Soviet citizens speak of atheism as having "torn across our land like a hurricane."[61] In its wake it has left many ruins. The father of one school child was asked to fill out a detailed questionnaire. For the last question concerning his wishes for the school, he wrote the following:

I wish that you would sit down and consider that you are living in the land of the Soviets, in which there exist fundamental laws on freedom of religion and conscience, the right to work and education, to equality and brotherhood. I wish you would not listen to the evil orders of the KGB, that you would understand that children come to school to get an education, but not to have your viewpoints injected into them. Otherwise you are going to disrupt this land if you continue further such actions against Christian children. And all the blood that has been shed for the freedom of this land you will tread underfoot.... Find your way back to the good path and follow it. If you will do that, you will strengthen our land.[62]

The presbyter, the other side of this life-and-death competition for Soviet children and youth, has no education, no access to theological institutions, no library or visual aids and no money. What he has in abundance is state opposition. But what the presbyters have which the atheists appear unable to match is moral charisma. That is why he is still winning even though the odds are stacked so heavily against him.

The key factor that will settle the competition is courage. Atheists lack the courage to attempt a fair competition with the presbyter. Rather,

The atheists use our fear of suffering to stifle our spirit, our free thoughts and feelings. And they in turn frighten us. We must overcome our fear of suffering. Only then will we become really free, active and invincible.[63]

That was Father Dudko's conviction demonstrated in the fearless way he conducted his conversations. That has also been the reason why the Reform Baptists in particular have become a youthful movement. Given this perspective, Dudko was optimistic:

The time for atheistic revelry in Russia has ended. The snowstorms and blizzards have blown away. There will be a religious spring, and everyone is working towards it, believers and atheists alike.[64]

Notes to Chapter 11

1. *Bulletin*, No. 34, p. 8; cf. Nos. 32 and 36.
2. Numerous letters in *Bulletin* No. 54, 1978.
3. See, for example, Bourdeaux, *Faith on Trial*, pp. 153-54.
4. Bourdeaux & Boiter, p. 4 (AS 256).
5. *NiR*, July/71.
6. *Religious Ferment*, p. 126 and 162.
7. In *Informationen und Berichte* (Digeste des Ostens), 3/79, pp. 1-5.
8. *G2W*, December/77 is a special issue entitled "Werde Gottlos" which provides a handy collection of articles and documents in translation plus analysis, p. 166. I have relied heavily on this collection for the following paragraphs.
9. "Legislative Discrimination against Believers in the USSR," *Religious*

Liberty in the Soviet Union, ed. by Michael Bourdeaux *et al.*, 1976, p. 38.

10. Dudko, p. 116.

11. *Nachrichten von den Feldern der Verfolgung*, January/February/79, p. 13. One of several illustrations quoted.

12. *Ibid.*, p. 11. Cf. *Bulletin* No. 52, 1978.

13. *Informationen und Berichte*, p. 4.

14. *G2W*, December/77, p. 164.

15. Academy of Sciences Member A. I. Beletskii gave a lecture in Kiev entitled "Nekotorie zamechanie po povodu ateisticheskoi literaturu poslednikh let" (some remarks about atheist literature in recent years) and found a pattern of uncritical repetition of earlier research that was originally scientifically shaky research. A copy of the speech found its way into Reform Baptist hands, the authorities lending credence to its significance by twice warning about this forgery in newspapers.

16. Bociurkiw, "Soviet Research on Religion and Atheism Since 1945," *RCL*, January-February/74, pp. 11-16.

17. G. S. Lialina, "Religiia i ateizm: problemy istorii i sovremennost'," *VNA*, 17/75, pp. 304-309. Cf. G. L. Andreev, *et al.*, "Piatdesiat let nauchnogo ateizma," *Voprosy Filosofii*, December/67, pp. 37-47, in English translation in *Research Materials*, August/68, pp. 1-5.

18. P. Modesto, "Die religiöse Problematik in der sowjetischen Zeitschrift 'Woprosy Filosofii' (Fragen der Philosophie) Jahrgang 1976," *Religion und Atheismus in der UdSSR*, May/77, p. 2. Modesto in another article, "Sowjetische Belletristik gegen Gott," August/78, remarks that "all cowardice, covetousness, lying, disrespect of humanity, slander, and ignorance is associated with religion," p. 23.

19. B. K. Arsenkin, "Voprosy sovershenstvovaniia ateisticheskogo vospitaniia molodezhi," *VNA*, 22/78, p. 206. Cf. V. I. Garadzha, *Kritika novykh techenii v protestantskoi teologii* (Moscow, Znanie, 1977).

20. For example *Individual'naia rabota s veruiushchimi* (Moscow: "Mysl'," 1974); V. I. Murashova & A. P. Khmel'nitskaia, *Beseda po dusham* (Moscow: Politizdat, 1977); V. E. Titov, *Troitsa* (Moscow: Politizdat, 1978), the latter two are seventy-page booklets suggesting ways of discussing a topic, such as the Trinity, with believers.

21. *NiR*, February/79 analyzed in *Religion and Atheismus in der UdSSR*, May/79, pp. 1-8.

22. Kuroedov dismissed Cardinal König's arguments (published in *Frankfurter Allgemeine Zeitung* (October 16, 1975) as "absurd jungles of fabrication into which even a Cardinal may wander if he is blinded by hostility" ... (*Izvestiia*, January 31, 1976; in English trans. in *RCL*, IV, 2/76, pp. 41-46). Cf. E. I. Lisavtsev, "Sotsialisticheskii printsip svobody i polozhenie tserkvi v SSSR," *VNA*, 22/78, p. 155; *NiR*, 8/78, p. 41.

23. *G2W*, December/77, p. 165, see also pp. 159-171.

24. Kuroedov and Pankratova, p. 168.

25. Solzhenitsyn, *Letter to Soviet Leaders* (London: Index on Censorship, 1974), pp. 48 and 57.

26. Quoted in *Informationen und Berichte*, 4/78, p. 9, from a new Dudko book: *Ein ungeschriebenes Buch—Aufzeichnungen eines russischen Priesters* (Graz/Wien/Köln: Styria-Verlag, 1979).

27. Quoted in Arsenkin, *VNA*, 22/78, p. 202.

28. *Ibid.* citing M. K. Tepliakov, *Problemy ateisticheskogo vospitaniia v praktike partiinoi raboty* (Voronezh, 1972).

29. E. Protasov and D. Ugrinovich, "Issledovanie religioznosti Naseleniia i

ateisticheskoe vospitanie," *Politicheskoe samoobrazovanie*, 11/75, p. 114.

30. A. I. Klibanov, *Religioznoe sektantstvo v proshlom i nastoiashchem* (Moscow: "Nauka," 1973), pp. 224-225.

31. Lialina, *Baptizm*, pp. 54-55. She also claimed that in 1965 only thirteen percent of AUCECB Baptists were under forty, sixty percent over sixty, and only 20.8 percent were men (p. 13).

32. Ipatov, *Kto takie mennonity*, pp. 87-88.

33. Krest'ianinov, p. 177.

34. *BV*, 5/77, pp. 66-67. The article also encouraged to take children for walks, play with them, but not separate them from life around them.

35. *Der Prozess gegen Georgij Wiens, Kiev*, Sonderdruck 11, June 1975, Licht im Osten, Korntal, p. 10. An English translation appeared as appendix to the 2nd ed. of Vins autobiography: *Prisoner of Conscience* (Elgin, Ill.: David C. Cook, 1979), pp. 271-82.

36. A. N. Ipatov, "Mennonity: Proshloe i nastoiashchee," *NiR*, 5/74, p. 41.

37. Umsiedler interviews.

38. Hermann Hartfeld, *Glaube trotz "KGB"* (Uhldingen: Stephanus Verlag, 1976), p. 108f. Before his emigration in 1974 he had been a youth worker in CCECB churches in Central Asia and served two prison sentences. Although the book is a complicated mixture of dramatization and true stories, such incidents as here reported occurred regularly.

39. *BV*, 2/79, pp. 25-32.

40. *BV*, 2/56, p. 19; 5/56, p. 6; 3-4/55, pp. 69-72; 6/57, pp. 8-17.

41. Durasoff, p. 202; a major set of guidelines on "Ordination of Presbyters and Deacons" by D. I. Ponomarchuk appeared in *BV*, 5-6/54, pp. 83-89.

42. Personal communication from Peter Rempel (May 1979). Cf. Pollock, *The Siberian Seven*.

43. At the 1974 congress, Bychkov reported progress in establishing a pension fund for ministers, at least in the RSFSR (author's personal notes).

44. Based on interview in *Newsline West*, September/77 and November/77, and supplemented with Umsiedler data. Froese emigrated to West Germany in 1977.

45. Hartfeld, p. 79f.

46. *BV*, 1/79, p. 79.

47. *BV*, 2/77, p. 74; author's congress notes.

48. Umsiedler interview data.

49. *BV*, 6/46, p. 43. While in Orel Oblast she worked as oblast secretary for the AUCECB, as typist. She also led the choir, the orchestra, and the women's sewing circle. She died May 9, 1947. (*BV*, 3/47, pp. 43-53.)

50. *BV*, 6/57, pp. 16-17.

51. Author's personal notes.

52. *BV*, 1/47, p. 17.

53. *BV*, 1/75, p. 32; Bychkov's report to the 1979 congress. I. V. Bukatyi, G. I. Komendant, and V. P. Fokin were sent abroad (Sweden and Germany) for further study following completion of the two-year course.

54. *BV*, 2/76, p. 71; 5/79, pp. 56 and 64-65. Ten unaffiliated Pentecostals and one Church Mennonite were accepted in 1978. Cf. *EBPS*, November 3, 1978.

55. *EBPS*, July 25, 1978; *KNS*, October 25, 1978.

56. *EBPS*, February 12, 1974. Other lecturers have been Scottish Baptist Andrew McRae (*Baptist Times*, September 15, 1977) and Rüschlikon Seminary President Ballenger (*EBPS*, November 4, 1978).

57. *BV*, 6/63, p. 20; 1/75, p. 32.

58. This included I. I. Motorin who had studied in Poland and Wernigerode.

59. *BV*, 6/74, pp. 63-65. Cf. Bychkov's remarks about not having theologians who know the ancient languages, 1/75, p. 38. This even hinders cooperation with the small project to produce a needed revised translation of the Russian Bible.

60. See his "The Christian Manifesto," *RCL* supplementary paper, January 1976.

61. Dudko, p. 246.

62. *G2W*, December/77, p. 151.

63. Dudko, p. 193.

64. *Ibid.*, p. 183.

Is not my word like fire, says the Lord, and like a hammer
which breaks the rock in pieces?
—*Jeremiah 23:29*

12 Soviet Evangelical Theology: Restitution of Apostolic Christianity

A Biblical Movement

If a tourist to the Soviet Union has a few Bibles in his suitcase, it usually results in an extra-thorough examination of his luggage. Several times Soviet authorities have given me a body frisk and without apology have carefully examined the smallest scraps of paper in my wallet simply because I was bringing a handful of religious literature. You are made to feel like a criminal, a dope smuggler. Bible smuggling is, in fact, still conducted systematically by a large number of East European missions, although the small amounts taken in gifts by individual tourists also constitute a significant amount in total. At present, Reform Baptists are printing the Bible secretly because the state still restricts its official publication and importation so severely. Even at present, Christian prisoners regularly complain that their Bible was either confiscated or they were refused one upon request. All of this shows that the Soviet state has a rather remarkable fear of one book which they like to claim is just a collection of useless myths.

Soviet authorities have a similar fear of the Soviet evangelicals because they are above all a Bible movement. It is their intense emphasis on the Bible as central to their faith which distinguishes them from their Orthodox and Roman Catholic neighbors. The Orthodox and Catholics maintain a high view of the Bible, but they also have a high regard for the accumulated tradition of the church and its theologians. Evangelicals acknowledge the influence of tradition but emphasize it must be judged by Scripture. When Karev reported to the 1966 congress he drew attention to the fact that theological discussion was virtually unknown in their midst. The names of the famous modernistic theologians, such as Harnack and Bultmann were quite unknown and they were even unacquainted with the battle between the old evangelical theologians and representatives of the new theology.[1] When announcing the Bible correspondence course in 1969, Karev noted that "a theological basis is what we have lacked the most."[2]

The evangelical approach was to read the Bible and put into practice its plain and simple message. Karev pointed out that key 19th- and 20th-century evangelists, such as Charles Spurgeon, D. L. Moody, Charles Finney, and Billy Graham had no systematic theological education. Every Christian, he said, can be a theologian, becoming this through constant reading and study of the Bible and other spiritual literature.[3] No formal theological structure developed although individuals were aggressive in arguing alternative interpretations of Scripture passages. The functioning evangelical theology that did develop is quite similar to the standard theology of English-speaking evangelicals. Its specific character has been the result of a variety of adaptations to Slavic conditions and mind-set and also a number of historical influences.

A survey of Soviet evangelical theology by means of the standard theological categories would therefore misrepresent the essential nature and function of Soviet evangelical theology. They are part of the so-called free church or believers' church movement which still places greater value on biblical studies than on systematic theology. In articulating their theology, evangelicals speak about emphases or principles. Soviet evangelicals from both AUCECB and CCECB churches strongly affirm seven historic Baptist principles. These principles are the following:

1. Holy Scripture—the books of the Old and New Testament (canonical) constitute the fundamental confession of faith of Evangelical Christian-Baptists.

2. The church must consist only of regenerated people.

3. The covenants of baptism and the Lord's Supper belong exclusively to regenerated people.

4. Each individual local church functions as an independent unit.

5. All members of each local church enjoy equal rights.

6. Freedom of conscience is assumed for all.

7. It is important to maintain separation of the churches from the state.[4]

Observing how each of these principles has been applied in the Soviet setting helps to identify the unique aspects of Soviet evangelical theology.
Contradictory emphases that do exist simply underline the fact that evangelical interest was in the working of the Spirit rather than a rational understanding of faith.

Roots of Baptist Principles

It is possible to trace direct continuous roots back to the Anabaptists of
the 16th century. For example, the descendants of the Anabaptists, the
Russian Mennonites, had not only stimulated the birth of *Stundism* in the
1860s, a goodly number of Mennonite evangelists and teachers influenced
Baptists and Evangelical Christians through joint publishing activity, joint
evangelism, and cooperation in I. S. Prokhanov's Leningrad Bible school.
The major emphases of Anabaptism had also come down to 20th-century
Soviet evangelicals through other free church denominations, especially the
British and North American Baptists. The latter influence was more immediate and triumphed in the official agreement for the union reached in
1944. Hence it has become customary to speak of Baptist principles.

The most significant Anabaptist influence was their commitment to a
recovery of the life and virtue of apostolic Christianity. Franklin H. Littell,
an influential historian of Anabaptism, has argued that the attempt at a restitution of the true church of apostolic times produced a revolution within
Christian history that "was so thoroughgoing as to be *sui generis*."[5] This is
also the primary factor prompting George H. Williams to speak of the
"Radical Reformation" while others have spoken of the "left wing" of the
Reformation. The Anabaptists, as do 20th-century Soviet evangelicals, accepted the major emphases of the Lutheran Reformation—*sola Scriptura*
and justification by faith alone. But in their ecclesiology they went much
further than Luther did (although Luther's early writings can be quoted in
support of Anabaptist emphases)[6] by calling for a church of the committed
where membership was a voluntary decision by responsible adults
(therefore called believers' church). They rejected any attempt by the state
authorities to interfere in the church, thus being the earliest advocates of a
separation of church and state in the modern era. Since they were immediately persecuted by state authorities, Catholics and Lutherans alike,
they also produced some of the earliest writings calling for liberty of
conscience. The Anabaptists also rejected sacramental notions of
transubstantiation or consubstantiation, arguing instead that the Lord's
Supper was not a means of grace but simply a symbolic remembrance.

The British Baptist movement developed in the early 17th century through the joint influence of Calvinist Puritans and Dutch Mennonites. A later British historian developed the argument that the modern free church was the product of the motherhood of Anabaptism and the fatherhood of Calvinism.[7] Not all historians would agree with his characterization of the mother and the father, but it is clear that new offspring appeared. One of the most important direct influences on the Russian Baptists was the German Baptist Johann C. Oncken. Oncken, born a Lutheran, had received a strong Calvinist influence from Scottish Presbyterians and English Baptists. He was converted in an English Methodist meetinghouse and became a Bible Society agent. After some difficulty, he was finally rebaptized by Rev. Sears of the American Triennial Baptist Convention and was commissioned as their agent. This baptism by total immersion had been introduced by English Baptists around 1641 and had become a major dogma of the American and English Baptists. Oncken's uncompromising emphasis on baptism by immersion, as well as refusal to permit anyone not baptized in this way to participate in communion, produced a very strict exclusivist church order.[8] This emphasis among the Russian Baptists under Dei Mazaev proved to be one of the major hindrances to an early union of evangelicals.

Both Anabaptists and Calvinists had undergone subtle transformations through the influence of the revivalist-holiness movements. Parallel to the Pietist movement on the continent, the Great Awakenings in Britain and North America provided new stimuli for the expansion of the believers' church movement which till then had suffered from minority status, discrimination, and outright persecution. For the Russian evangelicals, these influences came together in the Keswick movement and its most ardent proponent in America, Dwight L. Moody. One scholar pointed out that the Russian journal, *Baptist*, during its four years of publication, printed forty-five articles by foreign writers.[9] Twenty-three of these articles were directly linked with the Keswick movement, which began in England in 1875 with annual conferences for spiritual nourishment, many of the speakers traveling widely. In addition, several dozen Russian emigrés, who had studied at Moody Bible Institute or other institutions influenced by Moody, returned to the Soviet Union after the Revolution. Here they assumed a major role in shaping the unprecedented evangelistic program which caused the Russian evangelicals to grow so rapidly during the twenties.

Besides the emphasis on personal holiness and the strong emphasis on an evangelism fostering dramatic experiences of personal conversion, the

Keswick movement transmitted to the Russian evangelicals a dispensational theology, including premillennialist eschatology.[10] The dispensationalism of the Scofield Reference Bible had also been communicated to the Russians through associates of John N. Darby of the Plymouth Brethren, who played such a vital role in the early birth of the Evangelical Christian movement in the aristocratic salons of St. Petersburg. Dispensationalism understood human history as divided into periods, or dispensations (usually seven), during which God dealt differently with His people. For example, since Christ's resurrection the church was living in the dispensation of grace, drawing its guidelines from the Pauline writings, whereas the ethics of Jesus as summarized in the Sermon on the Mount were applicable to a later dispensation following Christ's second coming and setting up a thousand-year reign. Soviet evangelicals today are mildly dispensational.[11] Their official statements on eschatology are also characterized by restraint.

Russian Orthodox Influence

These external influences from the believers' church movement in Western Europe and America became mixed with influences from their own Slavic milieu, especially from Russian Orthodoxy. A thorough examination of this influence cannot be undertaken here. It is striking to observe, for example, that in the Soviet Union and Romania the evangelicals have experienced dramatic expansion in the 20th century, whereas in other Slavic countries the evangelicals, following initial growth, have remained relatively stagnant. To identify the reasons for this, a thorough study of evangelicals in Eastern Europe needs to be undertaken.[12]

Russian Orthodox influence is particularly apparent in worship. The Russian Orthodox Church has had very few outstanding theologians—it has never emphasized theologizing as became common in the rationalist era of both the Catholics and the Protestants. Orthodoxy is much more a religion of the spirit, where worship or liturgy is central. Russian Germans usually speak of Russians as unsystematic, unable to be orderly in the conduct of their faith, more influenced by their emotions. The apparent lack of concern among Soviet evangelicals that they are affirming doctrinal statements that are rationally contradictory may well be due to this Orthodox milieu. Theology is not as important as worship.

In an Orthodox cathedral, Jesus as the Pantocrator (supreme ruler) looks down on the people from the central cupola. This image of Christ is not that different from the Calvinist image of God as judge. Soviet evangelicals, like their fellow believers in North America, emphasize very personal verbal prayers to Jesus as Savior but the tone is not quite as familiar. When addressing Almighty God, the Soviet evangelical stands to his feet (also at mealtimes, including in a restaurant), or better still, falls on his knees for intense prayer with much repetition of the word *Gospodi* (Lord). Those two positions show their respect for God the all-powerful. After all, school-children stand at attention when the teacher appears and Soviet citizens stand when speaking with representatives from the state authorities. Earlier, the Russian peasant knelt before his lord.

The Orthodox emphasis on the spirit and emotions rather than the mind is also evident in communal prayers. The chorus of whispered prayers at a Baptist service is not unlike the responses of Orthodox worshipers during the liturgy. There is also a long tradition in Orthodoxy affirming the value of shedding tears in repentance and worship. This combined with a Slavic tendency to emotionalism helps to account for the excessive weeping among Soviet evangelicals. An early missionary to Russia complained that Russian evangelicals seemed to feel that a person must make at least one public confession with weeping. "This they call conversion."[13] Conversion occasions I have witnessed took place during the time of congregational prayer where the sinner would call to God for mercy and quickly break down into weeping, unable to finish his prayer. I have heard people question the reality of someone's conversion experience if they were not sufficiently impressed by the remorsefulness of his weeping.

Perhaps the most significant influence from Orthodoxy was the negative stimulus it provided. The resistance to the domination of a hierarchy has virtually as long a history as Russian Orthodoxy itself. The individualism of the sectarians can as legitimately be considered Russian as the claim that to be Russian is to be Orthodox. Soviet evangelicals were very critical of the Eastern church. "What can we say about the church of the East," Ivan Prokhanov once remarked, "whose religion was expressed in the majestic vestments of its bishops, wonderful church music, festive liturgy, but in a language the people could not understand?"[14] Prokhanov went on to declare that "in these churches there is much artistry, but little spiritual life, mystique and aesthetics, but no living fellowship with God, the Father and Son in the Holy Spirit. They feed the people on beauty but don't give them living bread." In addition, the negative image of the illiterate, drunken priest and other abuses provided models the evangelicals wished to avoid.

Experience Teaches Theology

Finally, there was the unmistakable influence of their own deep experiences. The persecution in the 1930s with an intensity unknown since the 16th century and then the ravages of war, having barely recovered from the collapse in the civil war, made everyone expert on suffering. Many passed through periods of weakness and retained a keenly developed sense of having been unfaithful. The feeling that the suffering was also divine judgment because nothing could happen without divine permission is also very strong.

The new evangelical church which emerged after the war had been reduced to a religion of the essentials. How would they be biblicists without Bibles? That is still a problem. These experiences simply underlined for them the primacy of salvation. This is why Christian and atheist observers alike draw attention to the soteriological preoccupation. The persecution and suffering, the implacable opposition of an atheist state, plus a dispensationalist theology produced an unusually strong interest in eschatology. It was an escatology characterized by an escapism. The many prayers urging Christ to come quickly were appeals to cut short their life on earth, which was primarily a vale of tears.

Both ECB unions have actually said very little on the subject of eschatology. None of the Baptist journals in the 1920s carried articles devoted to a detailed discussion of the second coming of Christ. *Bratskii Vestnik* has not devoted a major article to the subject. A possible reason is that the state defines as a crime "the commission of fraudulent actions for the purpose of inciting religious superstition," and Mr. Kuroedov described "the dissemination of rumors about the end of the world" as such a crime.[15] In their correspondence course lessons on dogmatics, the AUCECB warned that in connection with the thousand-year reign of Christ "we must not give way to our human fantasies if they are not based on Holy Scripture."[16] The Bible was brief and unclear on the subject of eschatology, therefore the Baptist leaders urged caution. But in the same breath they went on to say: "We don't have any kind of basis for keeping silence about this blessed period of biblical history."[17]

The confession of faith composed by Oncken for the German Baptists had also been accepted by the Russian Baptists and provided the basis for the first Mennonite Brethren confession of faith. In 1906 both unions (Baptist and Evangelical Christian) submitted confessions of faith to the authorities. They were rather similar, although the Evangelical Christian confession had four additional articles as a result of which there was a stronger emphasis on good works and freedom of conscience.[18] When the union took place in 1944, a formal confession of faith was not adopted but in general the more specific wishes of the Baptists became the basis for union. But it was Evangelical Christians who carried it out and their more relaxed attitude on doctrinal questions irritated the Baptists. Finally, in 1966 the AUCECB adopted a short confession of faith which had been written by Ivan Kargel. This had been adopted by both unions in the 1920s and was also acceptable to the Mennonites.[19]

In the formative years I. V. Kargel (1849-1937) had played a major role in doctrinal questions. I. S. Prokhanov was a prolific writer and poet and the constant reprinting of his writings during the post-war period guaranteed that his influence would continue, but initially his role had been that of activist organizer. Kargel, with whom he cooperated and competed, was the major preacher and exegete for this period.[20] His writings are still reprinted and circulate widely.

After the war Alexander Karev emerged as the theologian and exegete for the AUCECB. He wrote innumerable articles and composed the basic statements of doctrine. A relatively small group of persons assisted in making a contribution in *Bratskii Vestnik* on theological questions.[21] In the 1960s and 1970s, Karev's place as resident teacher and theologian was gradually taken by his assistant, Arthur Mitskevich. One scholar writing on Soviet Baptist theology took the writings of Karev and Mitskevich as representative and official.[22] With the beginning of the theological correspondence course in 1968, the Moscow union prepared course lectures which would help bring a uniform theology into the union. The course on dogmatics has been published recently. It can be regarded as the official statement on AUCECB doctrine. The CCECB also uses it and has expressed no specific objections to it. This textbook, simply called *Dogmatika*, concluded by listing and explaining the seven Baptist principles.[23]

Baptist Principles as Applied in the Soviet Union

1. *Sola Scriptura:* A major complaint which the *Initsiativniki* made was that the 1960 statute claimed to be based on Soviet legislation and was therefore weakly grounded on the Word of God. That statute, as well as all later revisions, affirmed that the Bible was the basis for the ECB confession of faith. But in 1966 the newly adopted statute added that it was also the basis for the "life and activity" of the union.[24] Aside from this rather fundamental critique, the AUCECB regularly emphasized Bible reading, printed Bible surveys, and articles reflecting biblical exegesis.

The *Dogmatika* affirmed biblical inspiration. It rejected the dictation theory of inspiration, as well as a verbal inspiration theory that did not allow for a recognition of the individual writer's memory, intuition, judgment, and character. But it was an affirmation of the Bible as divinely inspired and infallible.[25]

All Russian evangelicals have maintained a very high view of the Bible and there has therefore been no disputation on the nature of biblical authority. As Karev stated, their membership does not know modernism, which, as he claimed, questions many of the truths of Scripture. Still there is growing fear in conservative circles, especially in the Ukraine and in Central Asia, of a creeping modernism that they think is entering through association with the World Council of Churches. A leading American evangelical, W. Elwyn Davies, expressed a similar fear following a trip to the Soviet Union. He told fellow evangelicals that the liberal churchmen (meaning some participants in the WCC) responded to the Russian evangelicals with love and caring, whereas many Western evangelicals, with whom they had much more in common, stood back with criticism and sharp denunciation of the churchmen as Soviet agents.[26]

The *Dogmatika* presents standard evangelical arguments for the doctrines of God, Jesus Christ, and the Holy Spirit. This is also true in anthropology, where there is a heavy emphasis on the doctrine of salvation.

2. *A Church of the Regenerated:* When a person wishes to join an ECB church, he first appears before the presbyter and the church council where the individual must be able to convince his listeners that he has truly experienced salvation. They will be listening whether he repented of his sin, that is, did he recognize his sins, did he resolve to start a new life in Christ, and has this repentance involved his entire being—his intellect, his emotion, and will. Further, they will be looking for a sense of joy, of sin's forgiveness, and indications that he is filled by the Holy Spirit. The *Dogmatika* defines rebirth as "the resurrection of man from his mortal spiritual condition and his birth to a new life."[27] Rebirth is the only road to salvation; it liberates man from his sinful condition and it is demanded by the holiness of God. The *Dogmatika* also warns against false ways of achieving the rebirth. Rebirth cannot be attained through baptism nor through good works.

Rebirth signifies that there has been an inner change in man's condition; evangelicals also speak of justification, which reflects man's changed status before God.[28] Divine grace through the atoning blood of Jesus Christ plus faith in Christ form the basis for justification. Evangelicals also emphasize that a justified person is entitled to sonship or adoption into the family of God.

The second major emphasis in evangelical teaching about salvation is the concern for holy living. As the *Dogmatika* puts it, "justification shows what God did *for us*, but sanctification what God is doing *in us*."[29] As noted earlier, S. P. Fadiukhin and other writers identified three stages of sanctification: (a) Its beginning at the point of rebirth, (b) daily growth in sanctification, and (c) the final, complete sanctification which is reserved for heaven. The *Dogmatika* does not devote a separate section to ethics. In the context of showing evidence of a genuine rebirth and a growth in holy living, the primary positive evidence was to share in the responsibility for evangelism. There were also numerous negative proscriptions. Prohibited practices included dancing, card playing, attending the cinema, smoking, drinking, and sexual immorality. The latter three were considered especially serious.[30]

Maintaining the principle of the "church of the regenerate only" demanded strict discipline. An article by N. A. Levindanto on church discipline was reprinted several times.[31] Here he identified a five-part process, five steps the church should follow: a confrontation with sin; then an admonition; then a specific prohibition; then a trial or probation period for the erring member and if this did not succeed, then the individual would be excommunicated. Should a minister be excommunicated, he would lose forever the right to serve as presbyter should he repent and be restored to faith. This ruling has meant that rather frequently, considering the persecution experiences, a preacher who became unfaithful but was later restored during the revival movement often played an important role as a local preacher but was ineligible for election to church office.

Soviet evangelicals acknowledge a problem with excommunication.[32] S. P. Fadiukhin admitted at the 1966 congress that the union had excommunicated persons due to state pressure.[33] The Reform Baptists had tried to use excommunication as a weapon against the Moscow leadership and also violated acceptable practice thereby. That problem is now less acute, but Alexei Bychkov complained in 1974 that the church still appeared hasty in excommunicating members. During the previous five years, 4,000 persons had been excommunicated.[34] In the city of Volgograd, a foreign visitor reported that couples had been excommunicated for practicing birth control.[35] Very likely the relative inattention to ethics in evangelical theology, relying rather on specific prohibitions, has resulted in a constant struggle with legalism. A group visiting a large church in Siberia asked what were the major concerns that church dealt with at its members' meetings and received the reply that at recent meetings they had struggled with the question whether a Christian should be permitted to wear a ring.

3. *Baptism and the Lord's Supper:* Complaining that no Christian truth underwent such major changes during the history of Christianity as did the understanding of baptism and the Lord's Supper, the *Dogmatika* writers proclaimed that Evangelical Christian Baptists were trying to understand these ordinances as they had been given by Jesus. The writers then proceeded to declare that "bearing the name Baptists . . . we believe that baptism is neither sprinkling nor effusion with water but immersing into the water the entire body of the person baptized."[36] This, they felt, was precisely the way Philip had baptized the Ethiopian eunuch and the way Jesus had been baptized. In addition, immersion was the most vivid way of symbolizing having died to sin and rising to life in Christ.

This emphasis on immersion as the only correct form of baptism distinguishes Soviet evangelicals from their Anabaptist forebears, who were baptized by pouring. The Anabaptists received their name not because of their form of baptism but because they emphasized that only the baptism of a responsible adult was genuine, thus necessitating rebaptism of persons baptized in childhood. By the end of the 19th century American emphasis on immersion had become so intense that a professor of church history at the major Southern Baptist Seminary in Louisville, Kentucky, was forced to resign after demonstrating that immersion became a part of English Baptist practice only after 1641.[37] The Soviet emphasis on the form resulted in sharp conflict with the Mennonites, as was described earlier. Perhaps an additional reason Soviet evangelicals are so insistent that immersion is the only correct form is that even the Orthodox, who practice child baptism, fully immersed the child under water, although effusion has become common there, too, during the Soviet era.

The evangelical attitude toward communion clearly distinguished it from that of the Protestant Reformers and the Catholics. But this third principle had an exclusivist emphasis that resulted in considerable conflict within Soviet evangelical ranks. Even at present, some local churches practice closed communion, closed to all non-members, while others specify that all born-again baptized individuals are welcome to participate. In those cities where many foreign tourists from other confessions visit, guests are welcome to participate.

The present emphasis in conducting the Lord's Supper (held on the first Sunday of the month) focuses much more on reliving the deep pain our Lord suffered. The dramatization of the physical aspect and the highly developed reverence toward the bread and the wine (particularly by the

Mennonites) reminds the critical observer more of consubstantiation than a simple remembrance.

4. *Independence of Local Church:* The New Testament church was located in different cities and towns and the New Testament record indicates that in each town the church was organized independently. The *Dogmatika* also points out that the very influential Apostle Paul did not send orders to churches but appealed to them. The purpose behind this historic free church principle was to prevent the development of a hierarchy. The local church was described in the *Dogmatika* as "the union of born-again people, redeemed by the blood of Christ, living in a specific locality."[38] Still following a New Testament model, the evangelicals noted that the local churches had maintained communication with each other. For the task of spreading the kingdom of God and the necessary education and upbuilding of the members, fraternal links were necessary. This is why church unions were created. The primary task of the church (also stated in the 1966 constitution) was "to worship God and praise his name on earth and to preach the gospel to the whole world."[39]

The independence of the local congregation has been very important in Baptist circles generally, best illustrated in the relative weakness of a Baptist union. In the Soviet scene this principle of local autonomy has been severely tested in the postwar period. The 1929 legislation had guaranteed this principle in law, but following the war state policy changed to encourage centralized control. In spite of its protests to the contrary, the AUCECB during its first fifteen years had clearly usurped extensive powers away from the local churches. Senior presbyters, for example, were appointed by Moscow, sometimes even the local presbyter was appointed by Moscow. The process of statutory revision during the congresses resulted finally in new rules by 1966 which gave local churches the right to elect the senior presbyter. Still, the AUCECB maintains a leadership structure much more authoritative than its counterparts elsewhere.

The CCECB in essence drew attention to the degree in which the AUCECB had been violating the principle of the autonomy of the local church, having gone so far as to dictate a statute which the local churches must obey. In their advice to churches seeking registration, the CCECB advised the local church not to permit any unauthorized person to attend their members' meetings and to insure that all major decisions were taken by the local church. Yet here, too, because of the CCECB's conflict with the authorities and its competition with the AUCECB, it began demanding a loyalty and uniformity from its member congregations that did violence to the autonomy principle. This was the major criticism voiced by Joseph Bondarenko and others against the leadership of Gennadi Kriuchkov.[40]

5. *Equality of All Members in the Church:* This used to be referred to as the "priesthood of all believers," a conscious declaration against hierarchy in the local church and against any human mediator between man and God. The *Dogmatika* noted that presbyter and deacon must be elected by the membership. Their office entrusted them with leadership but not with lordship.[41]

A striking contrast to the emphasis on brotherhood, on mutual responsibility and mutual sharing in the writing of the Anabaptists, is the strong individualism present in principles four and five. It gained its most specific expression in principle six.

6. *Freedom of Conscience for All:* Soviet evangelical understanding of this principle is the same as the classic liberalist individualist understanding. The Soviet state, in contrast, emphasized the freedom of conscience *from* religion. As a persecuted minority when Orthodoxy was the state church, this principle made Soviet evangelicals early activists for religious liberty. But during the Soviet era, this principle was maintained with great difficulty. In fact, the Reform Baptist movement dramatically illustrated the degree to which the AUCECB had begun to accommodate to the restrictions on conscience. During the recent period of normalization the AUCECB and the Orthodox Church have been treated equally by the state while Reform Baptists remained prisoners of conscience. True, state opposition to all religion had not changed, but when it was reported that Brezhnev and Kosygin had invited Orthodox and Baptist leaders to the state reception to celebrate the Great October Revolution, it is appropriate to ask whether the AUCECB was gradually changing into a church-type mentality.[42] At least the years of uncritical support of Soviet foreign policy is in essence similar to the civil religion practiced by sister free churches in North America.

7. *Separation of Church and State:* In the 16th century, this principle had seemed to be the most threatening and elicited extensive suffering. In a radical sense, the principle of separation should necessarily result in suffering—that was the argument of the Apostle Peter.[43] For Russian Baptists the threat eventually became less severe due to the ecclesiology that emerged. According to the *Dogmatika,* churches' activities are exclusively spiritual while as a citizen of his fatherland the believer has his civil rights and responsibilities to the state and powers.[44] The *Dogmatika* also emphasized that the kingdom of God is a spiritual kingdom: "The kingly power of

Christ over the souls of men who have willingly subordinated themselves to the laws of the heavenly kingdom. . . ."[45] Partly this emphasis on a spiritual kingdom was due to their dispensational theology; partly it reflected the changed meaning this principle had undergone following the Stalinist persecutions. A religion focusing exclusively on non-earthly matters could be tolerated by the state. But by 1960 it had become clear that even in purely spiritual matters, the state would not remain neutral.

The Reform Baptists also emphasized that the church had a purely spiritual task. G. K. Kriuchkov had argued at the 1966 unity talks that the Bible required subordination to the state ("Let every soul be subject") but nowhere was the church told to be subject to anything but God.[46] The reformers objected to a situation where a presbyter on Sunday morning pronounced a grand judgment on Judas in his sermon "but on Monday with a peaceful conscience will sit in the office of the plenipotentiary for religious affairs and together with him weave a net for weakening and subduing God's Word."[47] That was a sharply worded statement from the *Orgkomitet*, but when the unity talks were held, it became apparent that the two groups of Baptists differed in their understanding of the nature of separation. Karev felt he was being realistic by declaring that without "ties with the world" they would not have been able to hold a congress or print Bibles. For the reformers such realism was evidence of apostasy.

Doctrinal Wrangling

Aside from the major debate separating Reform Baptists from the All-Union council the conflicts over theology do not deserve the status of a debate. They never had the opportunity to gain experience in the art of theological debate and too often opposing sides found themselves threatened with imprisonment or other punishment which helped sharpen the tone of the conflicts. Primarily, however, the constant tension within Soviet evangelicalism concerns secondary matters of practice.

At the 1974 congress, Michael Zhidkov read a major theological paper on the subject of baptism and the Lord's Supper.[48] This included a short straightforward elaboration of the doctrine but focused much more on questions of order. In some local congregations members had been arguing the merits of immersing the individual once or three times. Should they baptize in the name of Jesus, or in the name of Father, Son, and Holy Spirit? Some were insisting with a passion that a legitimate baptism was possible only in a flowing stream; a lake, swimming pool, or a baptistry was not really an imitation of the way Jesus was baptized. That Zhidkov in this paper gave directive answers to these questions is a further illustration of the wrangling over uniformity of form. Within the Soviet evangelical movement generally, local conflict between the different denominational groupings also appear petty. Churches split over the issue of using grape juice instead of wine at communion or because one side insisted on unleavened biscuits while the other wanted regular bread, whereas still others insisted on holding the bread with a white handkerchief until all had been served.[49]

Much more significant was the conflict in the struggle for purity. Some branches of the Pentecostal movement insisted that only those individuals manifesting the gifts of the Holy Spirit, especially speaking in tongues, were truly born again. This the Baptist union rejected, insisting that there were varieties of gifts of the Spirit, the Apostle Paul having listed others as more significant. The official teaching in the *Dogmatika* on the fruits of the Holy Spirit declared that since the Bible was now available in nearly all languages of the world, the gift of tongues was no longer necessary![50] The tension with the Pentecostals was still unresolved when it became complicated by the charismatic movement which influenced some churches in the Ukraine. The AUCECB has responded very negatively to the charismatics, speaking of them virtually in the same breath as the harmful influence of the Jehovah's Witnesses.[51]

The persistent conflict between AUCECB and CCECB was not supposed to be a conflict over doctrine, rather a struggle for faithfulness. It soon became evident, however, that opposing sides reflected significant difference in viewpoint, including the nature of the unity desired.[52] Once unity discussions came to an end, AUCECB spokesmen started to accuse Reform Baptists of fostering false doctrine. Whether they sincerely felt the reformers were in error doctrinally, or whether this was a tactic to discredit them remains ambiguous. In 1970 A. I. Mitskevich challenged the CCECB viewpoint that only the persecuted church is the true church. In December 1970 the CCECB circulated a major declaration on the question of unity in which they warned all church members that "your salvation is in danger, if you continue to fellowship with AUCECB workers."[53] In the following paragraph they stated: "You cannot be in union with the AUCECB and in union with God at the same time." As the AUCECB understood this, the reformers had introduced a doctrine of a church that saves and a church that does not save, to which the Moscow leadership replied that no church saves, it is Christ who saves.[54] The harsh judgments by the reformers sound disconcerting, but they appear to be trying to distinguish between a church of committed believers not compromising with sin and the so-called nominal church. The former was also the concept of the church supported by the AUCECB.

The question of a doctrine of a suffering church as the only real church is equally difficult to evaluate. Reform Baptists felt that in the Soviet setting the faithful church would necessarily be persecuted and could cite scriptural support which the AUCECB would not challenge. Rather, it became a conflict over emphasis, with Moscow leaders claiming that at least some of the reformers were deliberately seeking persecution, thereby no longer qualifying as "being persecuted for righteousness' sake." In the most recent criticism Moscow leaders claimed the Reform Baptists now demanded a confessional ritual from their members similar to that practiced in Catholicism. Georgi Vins professed ignorance about such an emphasis, when asked to comment, repeating the claim that there are no doctrinal differences between the two unions. Other supporters felt that this change might be explained by jealousy since AUCECB youth, not finding the senior presbyters ready to counsel them, had gone to CCECB presbyters for counseling.[55]

When the union was formed in 1944, it neglected to approve a confession of faith. The Kargel confession was adopted in 1966 as a temporary one. During the past five years the AUCECB has been studying numerous confessions of faith with the purpose of approving a fuller confession of faith at the 1979 congress. The apparent purpose is to produce a uniform belief system, the belief of an Evangelical Christian-Baptist. A. I. Mitskevich gave a progress report at the 1979 congress indicating a proposal was ready and urging widespread adoption, but he also had to report that the presidium was not yet ready to submit it to a vote by the delegates. Leaders indicated privately that denominational differences had not yet been resolved. It was finally printed in 1980 as a provisional draft, and readers were invited to send in their responses.

What Is the Key to Endurance?

A barkeeper once said of a Baptist: "He does not drink; their religion is the best of all; they do not swear and they have peace and love."[56] That observation reflects appreciation and astonishment. Paul Steeves felt that people joined the Baptists because "it provided an easy way to obtain release from an intense burden of felt guilt for human fallibility."[57] Others joined because Baptists offered certainty in the face of death. They offered purposeful living, the compassionate environment of a congregation and the comfort of emotional experiences.

Not only did large numbers of people join, they remained committed members even though there were periods when the less-committed were frightened away. Hans Brandenburg, who knew the movement intimately during the early years of the century, identified five factors which he felt had given the evangelicals the power to endure and to expand.[58] First of all, he detected in the movement a healthy balance of objectivism and subjectivism. It was a Bible movement having an objective basis for its theology. It was deeply subjectivist and individualist in its emphasis on the personal conversion of each member. Putting the matter simply, each preacher knew that in his sermon he must quote the Bible (liberally) and must offer a plea for salvation to his hearers.

It was a missionary movement whose members manifested a strong sense of calling. During the 1920s growth was very rapid and the evangelistic strategy quite simplistic. In the postwar period there has been a development away from the earlier superficial evangelism to an evangelism with more depth which relies heavily on the close relationships between local church members and the proselyte. The evangelicals' sense of mission was strongly influenced by an eschatological awareness that the second coming was imminent. Wilhelm Kahle pointed out that the mobility of many of the early leaders was due to a highly developed sense of the shortness of time, that it did not pay to put down roots in this world.[59] Most of the evangelicals were committed to a "quiet eschatology" which would find them busy evangelizing and suffering.[60] The chiliastic tendency was evident only among small groups of Pentecostals.[61]

Brandenburg also drew attention to the way in which the evangelicals dealt with the so-called scientific attacks of atheism. They ignored them, for they saw no need to argue with science because they had a profound belief in the truth of the message of Jesus. Theirs was a theology of faith.

Similarly, they remained unshakable because of their certainty of the omnipotence of God. They knew that God never lost control of events. Many observers have drawn attention to the triumphalism of the persecuted Reform Baptists. They protested unjust treatment, appealed for redress and for changed legislation, but in their appeals to fellow Christians the dominant theme was much more for prayer support, a concern that God's will would be worked out. This also included praying for their persecutors. Gerhard Fast tells the story of two preachers sent to his cell who immediately set about preaching the gospel. When one of the men was transferred to another section of the prison the other stated: "They probably need the gospel over there."[62]

Soviet evangelicals in varying degrees have also demonstrated the proverbial capacity of the Russian people to suffer. Their 16th-century forebears had taught and experienced that Christians "must expect persecution and exile, for this was the inevitable lot of those who submitted to Christ and would not wrestle for political control."[63] Suffering became a part of worship; it became a bond that united evangelicals in the prison cells and in the various towns where they chanced to meet. Suffering also helped to validate their witness. More so than in most other parts of Europe, they became and remained a church practicing costly discipleship.

The Evangelical Task: Restitution of
Apostolic Christianity

Is there a Soviet evangelical theology? The content of their belief system is part and parcel of general believers' church theology, so-called evangelicalism.[64] It includes Pentecostal and Mennonite concerns only insofar as these are included within evangelicalism. The new nuances that developed might be described as the desired ECB theology. In its expression of personal piety and worship, especially its emotionalism, its Slavic character emerges.

The most striking feature of Soviet evangelical theology is that they have affirmed the goal of restitution of apostolic Christianity more forthrightly and with greater chance of success than more developed believers' churches in Western Europe and North America. The goal of restoring the patterns and principles of a New Testament church had been the major intention and achievement of the Anabaptists. This orientation had shaped their entire theology. I. S. Prokhanov, who did more than any other person to shape the character of the Evangelical Christian movement, reached back a century earlier than the Anabaptist movement to identify with a genuinely Slavic forefather—Jan Hus. Prokhanov drew special attention to the writings of Chelcisky on the separation of church from the state, pinpointing the significance of the Constantinian compromise.[65] Prokhanov's affinity for these fellow Slavic preachers was symbolized by his decision to be ordained in Prague by Czech Baptists but with clergy from the Church of the Unity of Czech Brethren present. This emphasis on a return to New Testament Christianity which he had found in Jan Hus is also expressed in a "resurrection call" which Prokhanov wrote on behalf of the Evangelical Christians. Here he stated that the Evangelical Christian Union "considers itself entrusted with the task of restoring original Christianity on earth in its creative power. . . ."[66]

Alexander Karev repeated a similar goal when he reported on their recent involvement in the ecumenical movement. The mission of their representatives in the ecumenical encounters "must be to witness about the Christianity of apostolic days which has been forgotten in the West."[67] Such a restitution was above all an emphasis on the personal piety and discipleship of the early believers. Karev also hoped to demonstrate the unity of the early church. The example of a union of Russian Baptists and Mennonite Brethren, he told fellow European Baptist secretaries, should prompt them to imitation.[68] The split in Baptist ranks, as well as the continuing threat of the entire evangelical union coming apart, was therefore embarrassing and also painful. Their union, too, consisted of people "remarkable . . . for rightly dividing the word of truth and wrongly dividing themselves."[69]

Like the apostolic church, Russian evangelicals are a church of the poor. They constantly address their appeals to the simplest level of society, and artificial state pressure has guaranteed that their membership will remain lower class and uneducated. This low-class status and the leveling process of their persecution means that their membership probably reveals more potential for costly discipleship than do comparative bodies in North America and Europe. This is particularly true of the aggressive Reform Baptists.

Soviet evangelicals are trying, through their biblicism, to retain the quality of New Testament Christianity. A biblicism which demands of each individual the right to interpret and to study should logically result in a pluralism of interpretation. Yet here the state has been influential in trying to produce conformity. One wonders when the state will recognize that pluralism is a prerequisite for a classless society.

Following New Testament models of Christianity leads to considerable diversity. When General Secretary Bychkov visited North America in 1976 he contrasted the extensive activity of North American Christians in the social sphere with the spiritual emphasis in his own union: "Sometimes the churches in North America look like Martha—not taking much time to sit and reflect at the feet of Jesus, but always working and inviting people to serve on committees, subcommittees, and sub-subcommittees. Some Soviet churches look more like Mary—quiet and reflecting. Continuing contacts will be important in helping both churches to be more like Martha and Mary."[70] Bychkov could not have known that a British student of the Russian churches in an earlier age gave his book the title: *The Way of Martha and the Way of Mary!*[71]

Notes to Chapter 12

1. *BV*, 6/66, p. 17.
2. *BV*, 2/70, p. 33.
3. *BV*, 6/66, p. 20.
4. Reproduced in *Dogmatika*, AUCECB Bible Correspondence Course (Moscow, 1970), pp. 256-281, based on article written by A. I. Mitskevich, *BV*, 1/66, pp. 44-55. Georgi Vins, *Three Generations of Suffering*, p. 103, lists the same seven principles although in different order. When Mitskevich listed the seven principles at the 1963 congress, he omitted the last two on freedom of conscience and separation of church and state, substituting rules for electing local leaders and how they were to conduct themselves (*BV*, 6/63, p. 53). An earlier listing of principles by Robert Vyzu (*BV*, 3-4/56, pp. 55-57) differs considerably. Six American Baptist Conventions presented a statement on Baptist distinctives in 1967: 1) Authority (Christ as Lord, Head of the church, the Scriptures), 2) Christian experience (spiritual rebirth), 3) The church (fellowship of believers, immersion baptism, the Lord's Supper, democratic government, ordained ministry, principle of association of churches), 4) Freedom (individual liberty, church liberty, in relation to state), 5) Mission. (*Watchman Examiner*, 26 January 1967.)
5. Franklin H. Littell, *The Origins of Sectarian Protestantism* (New York: Macmillan, 1952) p. 79.
6. Donald F. Durnbaugh, *The Believers' Church* (London: Macmillan, 1968) pp. 3-4. This volume is a good handy summary of believers' church principles.
7. Peter Taylor Forsyth, quoted in Durnbaugh, p. 21. From Calvinism came the emphasis on the Word, from Anabaptism "the personal and subjective religion of the Spirit."
8. Kahle, p. 66f. Cf. W. Morgan Patterson, *Baptist Successionism: A Critical View* (Valley Forge, Pa.: Judson Press, 1969) p. 28.
9. Steeves, p. 336f. The second half of Steeves' dissertation is devoted to a discussion of Baptist theology.
10. *Ibid.*, p. 444. "The Baptists seem to have simply absorbed dispensational eschatology without thinking about it very much." Cf. C. Norman Kraus, *Dispensationalism in America: Its Rise and Development* (Richmond, Va.: John Knox Press, 1958); Richard Quebedeaux, *The Young Evangelicals*, p. 8.
11. A recent doctoral thesis by Alexander de Chalandeau, "The Theology of the Evangelical Christians-Baptists in the USSR as Reflected in the *Bratskii Vestnik*," (Strassbourg, France, Faculté de Theologie Protestante, 1978) faults *Bratskii Vestnik* for omitting this subject but Chalandeau assumes a stronger dispensational-premillennial position than the evidence warrants.
12. That is an area of research for which there appears to be a lack of vision.
13. Quoted in Kahle, p. 74.
14. *Ibid.*, p. 435.
15. *Izvestiia*, January 31, 1976.
16. *Dogmatika*, p. 250.
17. *Ibid.*
18. Kahle, p. 428.
19. *BV*, 6/66, pp. 16 and 23.
20. Kahle, p. 81f.
21. Chief among them were N. A. Levindanto, I. I. Motorin, K. V. Somov, M. Konoplev, and S. P. Fadiukhin.
22. Chalandeau, p. 60f.
23. The publication was actually done by a German mission using a Moscow

copy which had been printed by spirit duplicator. Hereafter referred to as *Dogmatika*.

24. *BV*, 6/66, p. 50.

25. *Dogmatika*, p. 161f., especially p. 167. Essentially the same argument in I. I. Motorin's article, *BV*, 3-4/55, p. 67.

26. "The Church Is Alive in Russia," *Europe Pulse*, March 1, 1976, p. 6. The Chalandeau dissertation uses similar imprecise suspicions to accuse Alexei Bychkov of modernism.

27. *Dogmatika*, p. 130f.

28. *Ibid.*, p. 139f.

29. *Ibid.*, p. 147.

30. Cf. Steeves, pp. 383-4.

31. *BV*, 3-4/55, pp. 10-24. Cf. 1/56, pp. 50-52. Levindanto's article had first appeared in *Baptist* in 1928.

32. A. I. Mitskevich read a major paper on the subject at the 1969 congress (*BV*, 5/70, pp. 50-57). Cf. 1/71, p. 67.

33. *BV*, 6/66, p. 67.

34. *BV*, 1/75, p. 48. Between 1974 and 1979 a further 4,790 persons were excommunicated.

35. *EBPS*, June 24, 1976.

36. *Dogmatika*, p. 260.

37. Patterson, *Baptist Successionism*, p. 29. I am indebted to Prof. Keith Parker (Rüschlikon) for this source.

38. *Dogmatika*, p. 186. Cf. p. 266.

39. *Ibid.* Cf. pp. 267-268.

40. See, for example, an open unsigned letter to G. K. Kriuchkov (July 1976); a declaration from the Rostov Union of CCECB Churches (August 4, 1976); and Josef Bondarenko writing to Gerhard Hamm (June 1976) (Keston College Files). BL 1/77 denounced these critics, describing the letters as the work of the KGB and the Council for Religious Affairs.

41. *Dogmatika*, pp. 218-219.

42. *BV*, 6/75, p. 49. I have in mind Ernst Troeltsch's church-sect typology. VNA, No. 24 (1980), develops this thesis at length, pp. 14-41. In 1978 Klimenko and Bychkov were again invited.

43. 1 Peter 4:12-19.

44. *Dogmatika*, pp. 276-277.

45. *Ibid.*, p. 53.

46. *AS*, 770, p. 223.

47. *Orgkomitet* statement of August 1963, reprinted by *Khristianin* in *Vestnik istiny* 2/76, p. 4.

48. *BV*, 2/75, p. 52f.

49. Umsiedler Interview data.

50. P. 221.

51. *BV*, 1/75, pp. 26-27.

52. See above, Chapter 8, pp. 233-235.

53. *AS*, 622, p. 24.

54. *BV*, 2/70, p. 65; 1/75, p. 52. Cf. 5/71, pp. 70-71; 6/75, p. 62; 2/76, p. 71.

55. *BV*, 4/78, pp. 44 and 47. Cf. G2WID, April 30, 1979, p. 12. Vins in Paderborn, 29 September 1979. (Author's notes.)

56. Steeves, p. 309.

57. *Ibid.*, pp. 332-333.

58. *The Meek and the Mighty*, pp. 204-205.

59. Kahle, p. 334.

60. Cf. Littell, pp. 128-34. "When the last cup of blood has been shed, they might look for the Day of Victory" (p. 133).

61. See a recent study of chiliasm by A. T. Moskalenko, *Ideologiia i deiatel'nost' khristianskikh sekt* (Novosibirsk, Nauka, 1978), pp. 5-7, 169-219.

62. Brandenburg, pp. 176-177.

63. Littell, p. 107.

64. "The theological system of the Russian Baptists was that of the Reformed Protestants in the West. There was nothing distinctively Russian about it. In this respect, the Baptist movement is seen as a western transplant to Russian soil." (Steeves, p. 446.) On "Evangelicalism" see Wells and Woodridge, *passim*.

65. Kahle, p. 430f.

66. *Ibid.*, p. 460.

67. *BV*, 6/66, p. 26.

68. See my "A Call for Unity Issued by a Russian Baptist Leader," *MQR*, L, 3, 1976, pp. 230-239.

69. Durnbaugh, p. 170.

70. *MCC News Service*, June 4, 1976.

71. Stephen Graham, *The Way of Martha and the Way of Mary* (London: Macmillan, 1916).

Now you must stand by us and help us get well-rooted. In another ten years we will be so strong that not only will we be able to stand without your help—no, then we will come and help you! Our preachers and messengers will come and proclaim the Gospel to you, for here in the West all are asleep. You will awake and God will bless us all.
—*I. S. Prokhanov* in 1928

The modern Christian cannot imagine a full-blooded spiritual life without fellowship with his brothers and sisters in the faith both within the country and abroad. He needs the prayers of God's children wherever they may live, and considers it his responsibility to pray "for all men" (1 Timothy 2:1).
—*Alexei Bychkov, BV 1/78*, p. 25

13 The Foreign Connection: International and Ecumenical

Although a uniquely Russian phenomenon in part, Soviet evangelical beginnings were also stimulated by evangelical missionaries. The influence of foreign evangelicals was more pronounced during the early decades of development. Both Baptists and Evangelical Christians had been members of the Baptist World Alliance since 1905.[1] The Evangelical Christians were closely associated with the Evangelical Alliance and with numerous societies such as the YMCA. Russian Mennonites had developed intimate links with fellow believers in Canada, the United States, and Germany. As noted earlier, Pentecostal beginnings were the result of the work of Ivan Voronaev, a missionary sponsored by the Assemblies of God. Continuing foreign ties were natural, for as evangelicals they were part of a worldwide movement. Their essence was internationalist in contrast to the Russian nationalism of the Orthodox Church.

This changed when Stalin took power. Soon Soviet evangelicals from all denominations found themselves in prison charged with anti-Soviet activity, with spying for a foreign country. Their links with churches abroad were the front behind which they reported Soviet secrets to foreign govern-

ments, so went the charge. Financial aid sent to a Soviet churchman in difficulty served as the evidence to convict him. Until approximately 1935 scattered links with evangelicals abroad were still possible; even a few visits
took place, although the last visit Soviet evangelicals had made to the West
was to attend the Baptist World Alliance Congress in Toronto in 1928.

Soviet evangelicals had become isolated. At the end of the war, many
of their fellow churchmen in the West were unsure whether they still
existed.

Postwar Attempts to Restore Foreign Communication

During World War II J. H. Rushbrooke, who had had considerable
interest in the Russian Baptists earlier in the decade, was the European
secretary for the Baptist World Alliance (BWA). His initial correspondence
following announcement of the creation of the AUCECB was quoted
earlier.[2] As soon as Rushbrooke learned of the new union, he made a great
effort to resume contacts, including visits to the Soviet Union. After a long
interview at the Soviet embassy in London, he sent a letter to Walter O.
Lewis in Washington (then general secretary of the BWA), in which he
complained that it "is really unfair that there should be an interchange of
visits between the Episcopal churches which are not even in full communion with one another, and that nothing of the kind should be taking
place between fellow Baptists who are all included in the Baptist World
Alliance."[3] An exchange of delegations had just taken place between the
Church of England and the Russian Orthodox Church. A few months later,
in August 1945, in a further letter, he stated that "to me, it is more important that I should visit Russia than any other country in Europe." This
was not to be, since Rushbrooke died shortly thereafter.

Aside from visiting the Soviet Union, the Baptist World Alliance
pursued two other goals. In his letter of congratulation to the AUCECB
unity congress, Rushbrooke made a broad offer of assistance:

It is our earnest hope that we may be able to assist our brethren in the
Soviet Union, but at present we have no information regarding their
needs. Our hope is that wherever buildings have been destroyed or
seriously damaged, where there is a shortage of Bibles or other literature,
where there is need to train students for the preaching of the gospel—in
short, wherever Christian and philanthropic work needs restarting after
the disruption and ravages of the war—we may be allowed to help our
brothers and sisters through the period of emergency. Could you write

me on this subject, and give me an idea what damage you have suffered, and in what ways it would be possible for us to help you?[4]

Shortly thereafter, Rushbrooke received a telegram from Moscow which included the curious phrase that the AUCECB "rejoice of distribution to our motherland of all Baptist brotherhood God bless you all and us" (sic).[5] Rushbrooke decided that must mean a "thank you" for their contribution via the Lend-Lease program, but direct assistance proved impossible. By 1947 President Jacob Zhidkov was reporting very specifically that there were many different foreign missions who "work as they say, for Russia, though no one ever entrusted this to them." The AUCECB, he said, was responding to all requests from abroad whether they need material aid: "No, we don't need it."[6] That attitude had already become pronounced in the late twenties. Russian evangelicals were attempting to assert their independence and above all were trying to demonstrate to the authorities that they were not a subversion agency financed by Western capitalists.

These contacts soon came to an end due to the Cold War. An additional factor may have been the continuing concern of the Baptist World Alliance for the state of religious liberty in the Soviet Union. In the spring of 1946 Walter Lewis was quoted in the *Religious News Service* saying that Soviets were turning Bibles into pulp in Estonia and closing Baptist seminaries in the Baltic states. Rushbrooke shared these concerns but did point out to Lewis that "this is the first direct attack on the Soviet government by a leading Baptist."[7] Perhaps this hindered a trip N. A. Levindanto and A. V. Karev had hoped to make to Britain. In any case, the AUCECB broke off all contacts when it refused to attend the Baptist World Alliance Congress in Copenhagen in the summer of 1947.[8]

There were virtually no contacts till 1954. In 1952, Carney Hargroves, then a Baptist pastor in Philadelphia (later elected president of the BWA), visited and a few letters were exchanged with Walter Lewis on the subject of peace. Finally, through participation in peace conferences in Sweden sponsored by the Quakers, R. Townley Lord and other British Baptists obtained an invitation to visit the Soviet Union in June 1954. The invitation stated that the purpose of the visit was "to have personal fellowship with us."[9] *Bratskii Vestnik* also quoted Townley Lord as stating that "we found that Baptists here have full freedom of religious confession and equal rights among the other churches."[10] This technique of quoting foreign churchmen professing to find religious liberty in the Soviet Union became a permanent point of anxiety for the foreign visitors. Some hoped that such positive remarks would be rewarded by some easing of the pressure on Soviet believers; others were misquoted (without the chance of rejoinder); while some foreign leaders made thoughtless remarks due to ignorance.

The Baptist World Alliance Congress in London in 1955 became the first serious test of the new relationship. Soviet Baptists had exerted strong pressure for BWA leaders to attend the World Peace Council in Helsinki, which would help persuade Soviet authorities to permit a Soviet Baptist delegation to come to London for the congress.[11] The one observer that was sent appeared to be sufficient so that eight delegates and two translators appeared in London.[12] The Russians were treated as full members of the BWA and were elected to various committees. Jacob Zhidkov was elected one of eleven vice-presidents.

The next major test consisted of two separate but nearly simultaneous visits to the Soviet Union's chief opponent in the Cold War, the United States of America. Robert Denny, then youth secretary and soon to become general secretary, handled the detailed planning which involved some risks to the American Baptist reputation, since public opinion was strongly anticommunist.[13] Would this trip simply serve as a vehicle of Soviet propaganda? The Soviet Baptist delegation traveled the length and breadth of America, attended numerous Baptist conventions, also met with Mennonites, and in general made a good impression. Alexander Karev, in his turn, reported that "we like the American people ... their feelings of love and joy in meeting were genuine, and above all we feel their strong, friendly handshakes."[14] The second delegation was an ecumenical delegation returning the visit of an American delegation to the Soviet Union.[15]

Now began regular participation of Soviet delegates on international Baptist committees. Zhidkov attended a BWA council session in Toronto in 1957.[16] In 1958 the AUCECB joined the European Baptist Federation, an organization that had been established in 1947.[17] By 1962, young Michael Zhidkov (who until them had held no significant position at home) was elected to the EBF executive committee.[18] When the next World Baptist Congress took place in Rio de Janeiro, five Soviet delegates attended; Zhidkov was reelected as a vice-president, Arthur Mitskevich became a member of the executive committee.[19]

In contrast to the early efforts of Rushbrooke and Lewis to establish links based on clearly articulated goals, by 1960 the active contact involved Soviet initiative and it was the Soviet Baptists who articulated their goals most clearly. The detailed reports on visits to churches always included an emphasis on the vigorous religious activity foreign visitors found, the enjoyment of fellowship and preaching, and that the visitors came away convinced that the Soviet people wanted peace. Following the visit of a Swedish delegation in 1956 (which included Erik Ruden, who became responsible for increased links with the Baptists when he served as European secretary of the BWA), Jacob Zhidkov stated: "We think that the confusion which there might be among believers in Sweden, due to unfriendly rumors about religious life in the USSR, have finally been dissipated and have vanished."[20]

This attempt to use visits as image-builders for Soviet Baptists and for the Soviet state became most pronounced during the period when Soviet Baptists were under the greatest pressure from the Soviet authorities. The number of visits abroad increased dramatically in 1960, whereas Western Baptists did not become aware of the Reform Baptist movement until 1964 and remained poorly informed for a number of years subsequently. They were reassured by the AUCECB that this was an internal matter, not very significant, and that they would be hurting the AUCECB if they discussed it in public.

In 1968 Michael Bourdeaux published the first major history of the split and quoted extensively from *Initsiativniki* documents.[21] One major document from the Council of Prisoners' Relatives listing the persecutions which Baptists had experienced was published by the British *Baptist Times*. In response, Alexander Karev and the new AUCECB president Ilia G. Ivanov addressed a letter to the British Baptist Union urging them to reject the Reformers' claims.[22] Before Bourdeaux's book was scheduled to appear, the Moscow leadership sent an envoy to London in order to counteract the publicity the *Initsiativniki* were receiving, urging British church leaders to support the AUCECB but not to support Bourdeaux, who, the envoy claimed, was siding unfairly with the *Initsiativniki*.[23] Michael Bourdeaux's book was published and helped to make the developing public debate more factual, although British Baptists were publicly very restrained, not really supporting Bourdeaux and his research center until 1974.

The AUCECB developed growing letter correspondence with many churchmen abroad, sent their journal abroad, and in the seventies introduced an English-language information bulletin in order to communicate better the fact that their union was alive and growing.

During this period of international development, BWA leaders, as well as EBF spokesmen, played a passive role in relationships with the Russians. They valued the fellowship. Those who visited the Soviet Union were deeply moved by the piety and intensely warm hospitality. A few individuals, such as Carney Hargroves, Joseph Nordenhaug, and Erik Ruden maintained a continuing interest in the Soviet Union but for the BWA as a whole this was only one part of a very large world fellowship.[24] Virtually no one had the language skills to communicate with the Russians significantly.

AUCECB International Department

When postwar foreign relations were developed, General Secretary Alexander Karev did most of the foreign traveling. Unlike Jacob Zhidkov, he was fluent in German and could read a little bit of English, vital credentials for such activity. Soon a young lady named Klaudia Tyrtova became the regular translator to accompany church delegations, Karev introducing her in 1957 as secretary of the international department.[25]

Such a department came into existence more formally in 1959 when Alexei Stoian and Ilia Orlov returned from their studies in England. None of the various revisions to the AUCECB statute make any reference to such a department before 1979, although the 1966 statute authorized the AUCECB to maintain foreign communications by means of letters and exchange of delegations. Karev announced the existence of this department in his first report given at the 1963 congress but otherwise little has been said about the international department. It still appears somewhat shrouded in secrecy. At the 1974 congress, Alexei Bychkov complimented this small department for the work which it had done and claimed that all its work had been conducted under the leadership of the AUCECB Presidium.[26]

The primary activity of the international department is to facilitate the foreign relations of the AUCECB. It handles the preparatory work for the exchange of delegations, and it provides translators to accompany Soviet delegations abroad and to host foreign delegations. The other activity in which the international department plays a significant role is in mediating relations with state authorities.

Alexei Bychkov reported at the 1974 congress that during the past two years "the international department devoted great effort to the dissemination of objective information in foreign countries on the life and service of our ECB churches."[27] In addition to the foreign trips, they had sent out 3, 300 individual letters and 21,000 fraternal announcements since 1969. This department had also received 16,000 letters from abroad, as well as newspapers and journals.

The department itself at present maintains a staff of eight persons: Alexei Stoian, chairman; Ilia Orlov, vice-chairman; Evgenii Ruzski, Klaudia (Tyrtova) Pillipiuk; Nikolai Zverev; Anatoli Sokolov; Alexander Savel'ev, and Valentina Ryndina. Additional translators are often assigned by this department to travel with delegations.

The background of the chairman, Alexei Stoian, is not very well known. He had been recommended by Ukrainian Senior Presbyter A. L. Andreev in 1957 to study abroad. Stoian had been one of six people who studied in England for two years (1957-59). On his return he immediately became a full-time employee of the AUCECB and his name was now listed regularly as an AUCECB representative at international congresses. In August 1962, for example, Jacob Zhidkov and he were the sole representatives of the AUCECB, when their union was accepted as a member of the World Council of Churches.[28] In this connection *Bratskii Vestnik* for the first time identified him as director of the international department. Stoian is still a young man, probably in his early fifties, with a hearty, abrupt manner.[29]

The most striking thing about Stoian is the questions people ask each other about him. All invitations to foreign churchmen are signed by him. Many public declarations on behalf of peace are signed by the president, the general secretary, and Stoian. He is obviously an important person. Sensitive observers ask each other whether they have ever heard him preach or lead in public prayer. He is usually present in his second floor office at the rear of the church in Moscow, but has anyone ever seen him on the platform with the other ministers? Soviet believers, on the other hand, ask each other whether anyone has ever seen him take communion. In short, he is not fully trusted as a brother. Many Westerners, in particular the staunchly anti-communist Carl McIntyre and Paul Voronaev (son of former Soviet Pentecostal leader Ivan Voronaev) freely attack Stoian as a KGB agent. As evidence Voronaev claims the admission of one Soviet churchman who confessed in the privacy of the car that he was forced to report everything and that Stoian was in fact an officer in the KGB.[30] Little is served in attempting to prove or disprove this charge but it does demonstrate how the international department is an albatross around the neck of the AUCECB.

Ilia M. Orlov, the vice-chairman, is the son of the famous Michael Orlov, who preserved the Evangelical Christian Union from total extinction during the war, who served as vice-president of the union until 1954, and remained on the council until his death in 1961. Michael Orlov's children were able to obtain a good education; Ilia was trained as a dentist. He, too, studied in England (1956-58) and returned to become active in the Moscow church. Young Orlov had inherited the tremendous energy of his father and revealed impressive ability. He has been the leading organist of the church for many years, takes his turn at preaching while maintaining a gruelling schedule in the international department. Not only are there letters to answer and trips to accompany, he is also busy approving articles for publication in the journal and producing the English-language information bulletin. I once heard him translate a sermon into English for a visiting scientist sitting in the balcony, punctuating the translation with additional biblical quotes which improved the sermon. At the same time he and I were conducting a conversation on another subject. He is indeed a very complex person and his loyalties to church and motherland also appear complex. He, too, is widely distrusted and feared for the power he wields, but to my knowledge, he is accepted as a Christian brother.

The other staff have less influence. Klaudia Pillipiuk had been studying to be a teacher. Evgenii Ruzski had studied for a career in journalism, came to faith through a healing experience, and studied two years at the Baptist seminary in Hamburg. He is fluent in both German and English. He, too, demonstrates great intelligence and ability, but his aggressive manner has alienated many. The younger men, Anatoli Sokolov and Nikolai Zverev, joined the department after two years of study in England (1973-75). Alexander Savel'ev has studied in Hamburg. The youngest member of the staff, Valentina Ryndina, speaks English and a little Spanish and has officially represented the AUCECB at international youth conferences. She is a quiet-spoken person. During the past year, Nikolai Zverev became vice-chairman.

The international department has gained international prominence while criticism of this department has grown within the ranks of the union. At the 1966 congress several staff persons, including Orlov, were elected as candidate members of the AUCECB with great difficulty. Orlov was appointed to full council membership in March 1969 but delegates refused to elect him to the council in December 1969, in spite of tremendous pressure.[31] This contrasts rather sharply with the role of the international department of the Russian Orthodox Church. The head of that department was usually a leading churchman and both Metropolitan Nikolai and Metropolitan Nikodim have been appreciated by believers for their pastoral role.[32] Which model, whether Orthodox or Baptist, is more advantageous is a debatable point, but the lower prestige of the Baptists' international department illustrates how much more difficult it is for a believers' church to incorporate a state function within a church function than is true of a historic state church. Criticism became quite pronounced and explicit at the 1979 Congress, delegates challenging the Christian character and behavior of members of this department. Regardless of the criticism from the ranks, the international department remains a necessary institution.

Officially, the international department is simply a subdivision in the AUCECB executive office, and does not have decision-making powers. Yet it is quite apparent to careful observers that the international department maintains *de facto* control of the AUCECB. This is its most disconcerting quality. It means that the actions of the elected AUCECB leadership must always be evaluated on the basis of what they were able to achieve in spite of restrictions, in terms of their ability to establish sufficient room to maneuver. For example, Soviet evangelical involvement in peace work is a prerequisite for continued existence. The fact that a separate department assumes responsibility for some of the less attractive aspects of fostering Soviet policy both inside the union and abroad eases the lot and the conscience of the other leaders. AUCECB leaders cannot acknowledge the powers of the international department in public but for foreign churchmen to maintain ongoing relations with the AUCECB it helps to assess the situation realistically. It may even be argued that such a clear identification of the governmental relationship is preferable to the casual, cozy relationship of North American churches to government leaders at prayer breakfasts.

Ecumenical Relations

The AUCECB was not related to, or involved with, preparations for the formation of the World Council of Churches in 1948, in spite of early relations they had had with such ecumenists as John Mott. On their first visit in England in 1955 the Archbishop of Canterbury spoke to them about joining the WCC and they promised to discuss the matter.[33] Alexander Karev wrote a major article on the ecumenical movement in 1959 which revealed good knowledge of detail and an understanding of its historical background. Karev concluded that not all Christian churches had joined the WCC; Roman Catholics were opposed, only a few Orthodox churches had joined, and the majority of Baptists were not members. Then he went on:

> The greatest insufficiency of the World Council of Churches is its very narrow base as a result of the lack of ecumenical awareness among the masses of believers. In point of fact, the ecumenical enthusiasts are primarily archbishops, bishops, theologians and other church leaders and church organizations, but local churches and the broad level of Christians have not been touched till now in any significant measure by the idea of one universal church and the ideals of the ecumenical movement.[34]

Three years later, *Bratskii Vestnik* announced that Jacob Zhidkov and Alexei Stoian had represented the AUCECB at a meeting of the WCC Central Committee in Paris, where the AUCECB, as well as the Armenian Orthodox Church, the Georgian Orthodox Church, the Evangelical Lutherans of Latvia and of Estonia were accepted into membership. Zhidkov was pictured in a full-page photo with the British Baptist Ernest Payne, who was then vice-chairman of the Central Committee.[35] Zhidkov explained that the WCC represents the voice of the majority of churches in the world and will become the voice of the universal church. As argument for joining he cited Luke 9:50—"He who is not against us is for us"—and expressed the conviction that by joining, the AUCECB would experience much blessing as they cooperated in the great work of building the kingdom of God.

The decision to join did not involve a decision of the AUCECB council or even its presidium; apparently there was no discussion. At the 1966 Congress Karev reviewed the history of the ecumenical movement, noting that some did not participate because of the modernistic theology of many of the leaders. But Karev felt there was no need to fear. It is the task of the Christian to be light and salt in the world, and that, he felt, also means to other Christians. This was not a fusion of churches but simply a fellowship of churches, therefore there was no need to worry. The arguments he gave for participating in the WCC were that this allowed them to participate in actions of Christian love: to help the hungry, those reduced to poverty due to catastrophe, and to serve as bridge-builders between enemies.[36] At the end of the 1963 Congress a general resolution had been read and approved expressing appreciation for the work of the AUCECB. This included the sentence: "The All-Union Congress welcomes the contacts between the AUCECB and the Baptist World Alliance and the entrance of the AUCECB into the World Council of Churches."[37] That made it possible to say that the delegates officially voted for membership, at least *post facto*.

The role of the AUCECB within the World Council of Churches has not been significant. It regularly served as junior partner to the Russian Orthodox Church, voting as a bloc on all decisions. It therefore shared responsibility with the Orthodox in blocking numerous resolutions that might have been critical of the Soviet Union. A significant shift occurred at the World Council Assembly in Nairobi in 1975. A Russian Orthodox layman, Lev Regelson, and Father Gleb Yakunin (banned from exercising his office since 1965) addressed a letter to Philip Potter, WCC general secretary. The letter was printed in *Target*, a daily newspaper for the Assembly. The authors of the letter noted the selective indignation which had characterized WCC pronouncements in recent years, listed various facts of religious persecution in the USSR, and offered a number of suggestions whereby WCC member churches could help. Concern for religious persecution, Yakunin and Regelson argued, "ought to become the central theme of Christian ecumenism!" Both the Russian Orthodox and the Baptist representatives published official replies which were defensive but also included candid acknowledgment of problems. Swiss missiologist Jacques Rossel proposed an amendment to a report on the Helsinki Declaration which specifically requested the USSR to implement the religious liberty clause of the Helsinki Declaration. English Baptist Ernest Payne succeeded in transferring the issue to a committee but the Nairobi Assembly marks a certain turning point after which the World Council has become less accommodating to the fears or even threats of withdrawal of Soviet churchmen.[38]

AUCECB representation at the World Council was never of the same caliber as the representation at the BWA. Whereas the AUCECB president or general secretary traveled to BWA meetings, it was international department spokesmen who were the most regular representatives at WCC commission meetings. In addition to Stoian, Belorussian Senior Presbyter K. S. Veliseichik was a longtime member on the central committee.[39] In recent years, however, General Secretary Alexei Bychkov, a member of the central committee since 1975, has begun to play a more active role in the discussions, prompting some to hope for more serious dialogue between East and West.

For the AUCECB its membership in the WCC has meant growing problems within the union. The more conservative Ukraine and Central Asia have a deep fear of the ecumenical movement as such, a fear that has been fed by Western Fundamentalist radio preachers who regularly identify the World Council with the Babylonian whore which is to lead the church astray in the end times. The pronouncements (printed in *Bratskii Vestnik*) of the WCC on many topics, especially the criticism of American policy in Vietnam and of South African racism, and the affirmation of religious liberty without any comment about religious liberty in the Soviet Union, resulted in local believers deeply distrusting this foreign connection. Foreign evangelicals visiting local churches in the Soviet Union have been asked with increasing frequency to give their views on the World Council of Churches. It is quite apparent that local church members, reliant only on the communiqués printed in *Bratskii Vestnik*, are poorly informed about the range of activities and interests, and the varieties of religious persuasion that are included in the WCC. But the questioners are very uneasy. Churches in Kirgizia once voted to reject WCC membership, but that decision had no weight constitutionally. At the 1979 Congress, spokesmen from Central Asia urged withdrawal, or at least a shift to observer status—stressing that to take no action put local church unity in danger back home. Others at least begged for better-quality representation, since they recognized that the AUCECB has no option but to remain a member.

Initially the WCC had tried to woo the Russian Orthodox Church, but when the latter decided to join, the rapid-moving events caught the World Council by surprise. WCC leaders were well aware that the joining of the Russian Orthodox Church in 1961, followed by six other Soviet denominations in 1962, had major political implications. Paul Anderson, longtime Soviet expert and adviser to the WCC, expressed a concern that the participant WCC churches should acquire a more thorough knowledge of the principles, policies, and procedures of the Soviet government and the Communist Party. And he went on, "In my opinion the expertise here demanded from the World Council leaders is still not very impressive."[40] This has been a continuing problem. In a recent book on the Russians and the WCC, Hans Hebly pointed out:

> In Western church delegations at ecumenical meetings there is an abundant amount of expert knowledge of the Third World. But how many Sovietologists were present at Nairobi? For some people the socialist world is a vague ideal, for others it is a bogeyman, but realistic expertise is scarcely available.[41]

It is hardly any consolation to point out that the Soviet delegates were unable to send any experts on most questions of concern to the World Council, because such experts did not dare associate with Soviet churches.

In another study of the WCC, Hans Hebly quoted numerous statements issued by the WCC which criticized the lack of religious liberty in the Soviet Union. Such statements disappeared from official resolutions once the Russian churches joined.[42] In order not to cause reprisals on member churches in Eastern Europe, World Council spokesmen exercised great reserve in speaking about religious liberties in Eastern Europe. They did, however, send letters of inquiry such as two letters to Ilia Ivanov, AUCECB president, in 1967 and in 1970, asking for a response to specific *Samizdat* appeals.

This apparent failure of the World Council to raise its voice on behalf of suffering Christians in the Soviet Union occasioned growing disquiet among ecumenical leaders. A conference held in St. Polten (Austria) in 1974 recommended greater exchange of information and encouraged the WCC to make statements "designed to diminish the negative effects of human rights situations, especially where the local churches or the regional bodies are prevented from doing so."[43] The Yakunin-Regelson letter was welcomed by many because it finally prompted an airing of viewpoints.[44] Former WCC staff member Albert van den Heuvel declared that "it is impossible to have zones of silence in the area of human rights."[45] The spiritual authority of the WCC was at stake if it did not speak openly.

The publicity in the 1970s on behalf of specific Soviet dissidents had made clear that such publicity did not hurt the person involved but often served to improve his prison conditions or to prevent his arrest. During the trial of Georgi Vins, the leaders of the WCC sent a letter to the Soviet prosecutor requesting permission to send a legal observer. "We have reason to believe," they wrote, "on the basis of information received that the charges against Mr. Vins are made primarily because of his religious convictions and activities."[46] That appeal did not help Vins directly but it did give the WCC a more forthright image and served notice on Soviet churchmen that the WCC could no longer remain silent. As Albert van den Heuvel wrote to Metropolitan Yuvenaly following the Nairobi Assembly:

> Our silence and our defence of the churches has not given any effective defence to the local churches in your country.... Some of us can no longer silence their questions and we cannot keep from taking the sides of those who appeal to us in the name of Christ, or even in the name of humanity....[47]

Repeatedly when Western churchmen have spoken up about restriction of human rights in the Soviet Union, Russian churchmen have attacked them. Here, too, a growing number of churchmen fully agree with Hebly's remark:

> We cannot blame them for their silence, but it seems to be rather unecumenical when they blame others for speaking where they had to remain silent. The other churches should not allow themselves to be sucked into the captivity of the Russian church.[48]

Following this debate the WCC executive committee eventually approved a "church-centered human rights programme," gave it a budget of $80,000

(U.S.) and a full-time staff person, and assigned it the tasks of documentation on human rights, coordination of study projects, and improvement of information exchange. This was intended to lead to the development of "a constructive-critical solidarity."[49] So far, observers are maintaining a healthy skepticism about possible achievements.

Since the Russian churches joined the WCC, the latter has also been less able to develop dialogue with Marxism. Russian churchmen feel there is no need to engage in dialogue; all that is needed is practical cooperation. Practical cooperation has invariably meant conformity to state requirements.[50] There are, however, recent signs of a further development. In March 1979, churches from socialist countries met to share experiences on "Christian witness today," a meeting sponsored by a WCC commission. The participants agreed that there was "a recognition of the church's positive social role after half a century of the new socialist order" and acknowledged "the still unused potential for the churches to evangelize within their present context."[51] The final report is to be published as preparatory material for a WCC world mission conference in 1980.

The AUCECB also joined other international bodies, such as the Christian Peace Conference (CPC), and the Conference of European Churches (CEC), and participated in the Conference of Peace-Loving Forces and similar meetings. Ilia Ivanov and Alexei Stoian were regular representatives at CPC meetings but their role was largely passive. In recent years Alexei Bychkov has been utilizing statements from such international bodies, in particular the Helsinki Agreement, to express appreciation for the guarantees of human rights and religious freedom, thereby indicating that his church notices what the state has signed.[52] In all these activities, however, there has never been a voice raised by Soviet churchmen questioning specific Soviet policies that were unjust. At a regular meeting of the CPC Continuation Committee in September 1975, Professor James Will raised some questions that caused consternation and headlines. All he said was:

> I know that many of the churches in socialist societies have required of yourselves a period of prophetic silence in repentance for your earlier neglect of the proletariat and opposition to their revolution. You also have necessarily followed a strategy of proving your basic loyalty to socialist societies now led by communist governments. But isn't that basic loyalty now sufficiently demonstrated that you may begin to speak prophetically again also at home? . . . I must ask my Russian brethren in

love and goodwill, but also seriously, is it really required that they only praise their society when we all know that nothing like perfect liberation or justice has been achieved there?[53]

Even slight qualifiers suggesting reserve in support of Soviet policy would greatly improve the image of Soviet churchmen.

Relations with Fellow Evangelicals

1. *Baptists.* Relations with world Baptists bodies have become so well developed over against other evangelical bodies that many people have the impression that Soviet evangelicals belong exclusively to the Baptist family. What is the nature and significance of the AUCECB involvement in the Baptist World Alliance and the European Baptist Federation?

Once active membership was resumed in 1955, Moscow sent its members regularly to meetings. Gradually the Soviet members became more acquainted with the overall program, but their contribution has been selective. Bychkov claimed credit for fostering a greater interest in peace and justice.[54] Many of the programs in the sphere of evangelism, education, and relief can only be applied in the Soviet Union with great difficulty and modification. Above all, Soviet Baptist participation was limited by the restrictions on the flow of currency. Unable to donate directly to the BWA or EBF, they have resorted to financing the travels of fellow East European Baptists to committee meetings. When Alexei Bychkov served as president of the European Baptist Federation, he invited the executive committee to Moscow for deliberations and his union paid the travel costs of all the members. Similarly, Soviet churchmen coming to meetings of the BWA, for example, in the United States, spend an additional week or two visiting churches and raising donations for the BWA. An attempt to gain permission for Soviet financial involvement in relief projects in a Third World setting has not succeeded so far.

Committee membership has long been limited to a small group of persons. Jacob Zhidkov served two terms as BWA vice-president. In 1962 his son Michael was elected to the executive committee of the EBF. By 1965, when he was still identified simply as an AUCECB co-worker, he was elected vice-president of the EBF. Only the following year was he ordained as presbyter of the Moscow church and was also elected a member of the AUCECB Presidium. Since 1975 he has been a vice-president of the BWA like his father before him. Zhidkov's role in these committees was largely nominal as was true of many of the other Russian members on committees.

Much more significant was the election of Alexei Bychkov as president of the European Baptist Federation in 1975. For the first time an East European churchmen led this organization, which required much more intimate cooperation between him and the secretary-treasurer, Gerhard Claas, based in Hamburg. In March 1976 the EBF executive committee held an expanded session in Moscow, the first such meeting in Eastern Europe. A second meeting took place in Budapest in September of that year. This experience proved to be very positive, since there was no indication of censorship of activity, although more European Baptists leaders felt obliged to attend a peace conference in Moscow in 1977 in order to demonstrate solidarity with their president.

During the past 25 years of East/West Baptist relations, it is difficult to detect any clear articulation of policy and goals by the international Baptist leaders. A primary reason was the lack of expertise on the Soviet Union. Those few Baptist experts on the Soviet Union that did exist were not sufficiently utilized by the BWA because it lacked funds. As a result, the secretary for Europe was left to his own ingenuity and he was in any case burdened with other tasks throughout Europe. A growing number of official exchanges of delegations served to improve personal relations, and the Western visitors usually reported in the press on their personal impressions. But a more thorough, detailed reporting with recommendations based on lessons learned from previous trips or other information gained did not take place.

International Baptist relations were therefore shaped very much by the interests of the European secretaries. J. H. Rushbrooke had an intense interest in Russia. This strong interest was resumed by the Swedish Baptist Erik Ruden, who held the office during the sixties, and did attempt through personal persuasion to bring about reconciliation between *Initsiativniki* and Moscow. He was succeeded by the British leader, C. Ronald Goulding (1967-74). Goulding had little experience with the Soviet Baptists, except for some students at Spurgeons College where he had served as principal. During his time in office he visited the Soviet Union several times, the most significant being his attendance as the only foreign observer at the 1969 AUCECB Congress.[55] His reporting subsequently helped provide an outside perspective on the congress, although his observations were limited by reliance on translators and the uniqueness of the event. During his time in office, however, Goulding devoted much more energy to the developing conflict between church and state in Romania, where his intercession on behalf of Baptists with state officials brought some improvements.

Goulding was succeeded by the former general secretary of the German Baptist Federation, Gerhard Claas. Claas and his union had a long-standing active interest in the Soviet Union, knew many of the leaders personally, and Claas was able to converse in German with leading persons outside the Moscow circle. Claas, due to his own initiative and the growing experience of the organization, has provided creative leadership with the goal of assisting in normalizing church-state relationships but more so to foster more theological depth in church life. Claas and other Baptist leaders were involved in attempts to assist in the creation of a seminary, by providing guest lectures and library materials. The EBF introduced the Summer Institute of Theological Education whereby East European students could spend two summers of study at the Rüschlikon seminary and complete the remainder of the program by correspondence. The first year of the program was well received, but only one Soviet student from Estonia was present.[56]

BWA and EBF actions have been hampered by their own constitution. According to the constitution of the BWA, the organization may accept an additional Baptist union into membership only if Baptist unions from that country already in the BWA give their approval. For this constitutional reason they were prevented from interfering in the split that took place in the Soviet Union, and prevented from establishing relations with the Reform Baptists directly. But that is a formal argument—the ruling might easily have been broken. Just after the split became irrevocable in 1961, A. I. Mitskevich had himself urged the BWA leaders to interfere by sending its workers with recognized authority to countries where there were divisions.[57] But when even minor references to persecution of the *Initsiativniki* were made at an EBF Congress in 1965, Russian leaders became very upset and threatened to walk out. EBF leaders did not consider themselves in a position to call their bluff and were reduced to wishing other believers would take up the cause of the *Initsiativniki*.

The early failure to hear and understand the *Initsiativniki* appeal damaged the reputation of the BWA. As early as 1963 the *Initsiativniki* had sent a letter to the president and general secretary of the BWA, informing them of the split and that the Moscow leadership had been excommunicated.[58] The *Initsiativniki* also tried to establish contact with William Tolbert, president of the BWA (1965-70), as well as president of Liberia. Tolbert visited the Soviet Union in 1970 and in published remarks greatly disappointed the hopes of the CCECB. *Bratskii Vestnik* reported him as saying: "I would also like to remind this group of Baptists (CCECB) that to go along this road is wrong. Indeed it is wrong to ignore the laws of the country or to permit disobedience, and also to treat the authorities with dis-respect."[59] A more specific statement in support of state policy the au-thorities could scarcely have hoped for. No other Baptist leader has condemned the CCECB leaders as strongly in public. Most of the other BWA leaders were deeply embarrassed by Tolbert's remarks and no doubt embarrassed that Tolbert had not been properly briefed, that he did not even know of the existence of the Reform Baptists before his trip.

But the BWA remains severely hampered to the present in its ability to respond to the Reform Baptists because of the veto powers of the AUCECB. German immigrants from the Soviet Union, some of them hav-ing been charged by Russian congregations before their departure to represent them at the World Baptist Congress in Stockholm in 1975, asked permission to attend the congress. Unofficial talks were held between the Soviet-German leaders and the BWA leaders, and they did manage to meet with AUCECB representatives casually. But the AUCECB demanded in a long telegram that the BWA not recognize the Germans, citing appropriate paragraphs of the BWA constitution.[60] Later *Bratskii Vestnik* reported that the German immigrants had tried to sow discord but their influence had been neutralized.[61]

In response to a request from a fellow Baptist for the dates of formal appeals addressed by the Reform Baptists to the BWA, Ronald Goulding re-plied: "As far as I am able to discover there has been no direct approach from any dissident group made to the Baptist World Alliance or the Eu-ropean Baptist Federation at any time."[62] He did add that in 1965 a docu-ment addressed to the UN and other organizations and also to the BWA "was reported as being sent" but the copy that arrived in London had no address for sending a reply. Another document was received in 1967. In their files the BWA have a copy of the 1960 Letter of Instructions (received through other channels later) and a few other materials in translation but they were generally not well informed on the issue.

They had relied for advice on a man who knew the Soviet Union inti-mately. Adolphs Klaupiks had been general secretary of the Latvian Baptist Union before becoming a refugee during World War II. Later he became the relief secretary for the BWA and beginning with 1961, he made trips to the Soviet Union almost annually.[63] Some of the early *Samizdat* materials were known to him but he decided it was better not to publicize the con-flict. When he published a statement in *Baptist World* in 1968, the em-phasis was that the crisis had been surmounted, no longer was there a drop-off of members to the dissidents and even some of their preachers were returning to the AUCECB. Klaupiks regularly emphasized that the split was an internal Baptist matter; publicity could only do harm.

Klaupiks knew the situation well, probably thought that the wisest policy was to maintain silence and to try to encourage reconciliation through personal visits. But his partisan sentiments were clearly with the AUCECB. Many of those men he had known and loved personally for years. Given the difficult situations in which they lived, his natural response was to be protective. He was also heavily influenced by the personal comments of Moscow leaders who described *Initsiativniki* as extremists, typical of the quarrelsome ways of Baptists in many other countries. These typical factors were certainly present in given incidents, but the overwhelming documentation that was accumulating clearly pointed to systematic violation of religious liberty. The Baptist World Alliance, which prided itself on being a spokesman for religious liberty, found itself muzzled in this case.

Baptist leaders were also not free of the tendency to engage in excessive praise of the genuine piety they encountered. When Andrew MacRae was president of the EBF in 1971 he visited the Soviet Union. On his return, he wrote a long, serialized article on his experience which was full of superlative praise for the AUCECB and included rather ill informed criticism of the CCECB.[64] For him, apparently, the primary criterion for deciding whether there was religious liberty was that he was permitted to preach freely wherever he traveled and no one censored his sermons in advance. He was roundly criticized, including by fellow Baptist leaders, who were embarrassed that their spokesman sounded more like a round-eyed tourist than a well-informed church leader. On a later trip in August 1977 his report was printed in the *European Baptist Press Service* and his superficial knowledge of the situation seemed to persist. He claimed that the number of prisoners might be as low as 25, which was an exaggeration. He stated that Georgi Vins was not a minister and he thought that the fact that he had been asked in an interview quite openly what he thought of the split-away group was proof that this group was not underground.[65] One would expect a Western Baptist leader in such a critical situation to exert a bit more effort to discover the facts or else to keep silent.

Since 1975 world Baptist leaders have been taking a second look at their policies toward the Soviet Union. When they attended the congress in December 1974 and announced their intention to appeal for imprisoned Baptists in an interview with the Council for Religious Affairs, Alexei Bychkov showed approval.[66] BWA Associate Secretary Carl Tiller was becoming uncomfortable with their "seeming inactivity" in key world trouble

spots during the years that they were emphasizing a ministry of reconciliation. How could the BWA become a reconciling force? Did the situation require a member body (with veto rights) or a no member body before the
BWA could intervene? What has happened has been a process whereby
BWA leaders have personally expressed their concern to Soviet authorities
with frankness. Not as a spokesman for the BWA but as secretary of the
British Baptist Union, David Russell, for example, spelled out the concerns
of his membership for the release of Georgi Vins and other prisoners. He
also wrote a letter to the Soviet authorities when the new legislative revisions on cults was announced in 1975, listing all the clauses in the legislation
that still gave him and other Western Christians cause for concern. Such
well-documented letters clearly demonstrated a genuine concern. Other
Baptist leaders, unable to issue formal statements through the World
Alliance, privately urged fellow Baptists to address simple appeals to the Soviet ambassador and in other ways to inform Soviet Baptists of their
concerns.

The BWA relationship to the AUCECB is a strong one and is beginning to have benefit for the AUCECB. Constant negotiations have brought
official promise for a seminary. Klaus Meister of Switzerland was followed
by Isam Ballenger and Andrew MacRae as guest lecturers for the Moscow
correspondence course.[67] Another point of negotiation in which Baptists
were also involved finally paid off when in December 1978 25,000 Bibles
were imported to the Soviet Union, the BWA assuming responsibility for
the funding.[68]

2. *Mennonites.* International Mennonite relations with the Soviet
Union have been much more difficult. Partly this is due to the fact that Soviet authorities felt that Russian Mennonite links with fellow believers
abroad were helping to delay the conversion of Mennonites to atheism.[69]
When official delegated trips became possible, Harold S. Bender, president
of Mennonite World Conference, was immediately ready to try to resume
relations with Russian Mennonites. He met the AUCECB delegation that
came to London in 1955, and another that came to America in 1956, and
then joined a mixed denominational delegation together with David B.
Wiens for a trip to the Soviet Union in November 1956.[70] Travel proved to
be exceedingly complicated and all they managed to do was to meet a few
Mennonite spokesmen who traveled long distances to meet them in a hotel.
Even then, one of the men, Philip Cornies, was held seven hours for questioning before being able to see the visitors. One pleasant aspect of the trip

was the first-class treatment and close Christian fellowship shown by the Russian Baptists.

The Bender-Wiens trip was followed by a series of delegations at approximately two-year intervals.[71] Most of these visits were officially conducted under Intourist sponsorship, whereas others were possible because the Mennonites received an invitation together with a Baptist delegation. Four Soviet Baptists visited the United States by invitation of Mennonite Central Committee (MCC) in May 1964, combining this with attendance at a major American Baptist congress. In response to another invitation issued jointly by MCC (Canada) and the Baptist Federation of Canada, a five-member delegation visited Canada in June 1969. The delegation included one Mennonite, Viktor Kriger. A more direct official exchange of delegates with the AUCECB began in May 1976 when five persons visited North American Mennonites. This was followed by a return visit and an invitation for a delegation representing the Mennonite World Conference to come visit. Usually these delegation exchanges consisted of visiting a variety of churches where delegation members preached sermons. During the day they toured the city. The 1976 delegation exchange was different in that much greater emphasis was placed on attempting dialogue between participants. Seminars with smaller groups of invited participants provided the basis for sharing and mutual influence in a variety of church concerns.[72] A further development of this technique was a major meeting of European Baptist leaders in Moscow in April 1979.[73]

Mennonites saw these official visits as only one aspect of a broad approach to East/West relations. Official Soviet visitors were able to present their perspective to a North American audience, but spokesmen for the *Initsiativniki* or the independent Mennonites (as well as articles by experts) were given a hearing in order to enable North American Mennonites to form a balanced picture. To foster personal contact and mutual enrichment many individuals, as well as several choirs, were encouraged to visit the Soviet Union and to report their experiences. Study tours have also been sponsored.

For the Mennonites, relating to Soviet evangelicals via the AUCECB was only partially satisfactory. Most visitors therefore also attempted to express their concern about the status of the Mennonites (*Kirchliche*), urging the Baptists to be more tolerant, or to help the Mennonites obtain legal recognition. Another point of concern was the inability to visit many of the areas where Mennonites live because these were still closed to foreign travel. There was also discomfort about a deepening relationship to the

AUCECB while remaining unable to develop one with the CCECB.[74]

North American Mennonite relations to Soviet evangelicals has largely been the responsibility of the Mennonite Central Committee, the relief and service agency of the Mennonite and Brethren in Christ churches in Canada and the United States. Following each trip, leaders met to share and evaluate experiences and to plan future steps. For a decade and a half after the Bender-Wiens trip, the general assumption was that it was better to keep silent about the persecution of believers. To say something in public would hurt the believers in the Soviet Union. That they wished to avoid. This argument was expressed most strongly by Mennonite families who had close relatives in the Soviet Union and who urged caution. The traditionally quietist Mennonite should not agitate but rather rely on prayer support and suffer quietly.

As the prisoners' list lengthened (it included many names of obviously Mennonite origin) and other harassments became public knowledge, as Soviet Reform Baptist resistance stiffened and their appeals for public support increased, the attitudes and advice of Mennonite leaders in the West began to change.

The present writer was assigned to work with Michael Bourdeaux in his newly established Centre for the Study of Religion and Communism in 1973. This did not represent blanket endorsement of this organization, but it reflected the conviction that the collection and objective analysis of factual materials on the Soviet situation would help Western Christians to respond more intelligently and would therefore also help Soviet evangelicals in the long run.

The AUCECB leaders initially expressed sharp criticism of this assignment, charging that Bourdeaux was biased toward the *Initsiativniki;* therefore this action must mean that the Mennonites were also siding with the *Initsiativniki* instead of with the AUCECB. Mennonites saw the criticism as an attempt to force Mennonites to be partisan in the AUCECB-CCECB conflict, and refused to bow to the pressure. Eventually relations improved when it became clear that a sympathetic attitude toward both unions was possible.

Mennonite Central Committee has held numerous consultations on East/West questions, seeking to develop a relationship in keeping with Mennonite emphases. That meant the rejection of secret or deceptive tactics such as Bible smuggling. Mennonites hoped for mutual enrichment in the area of biblical study, peace, and service. It was time, they felt, to recognize that American and Soviet citizens had a joint responsibility for the poor of the Third World, since North America and the Soviet Union represented the two big and rich superpowers.

The Mennonite World Conference was first organized in 1925. At that first conference in Basel, Switzerland, one Soviet delegate managed to come as far as the train station on the Swiss boundary but was not permitted into Switzerland. Since then no Soviet Mennonites were permitted to leave the Soviet Union to attend the Mennonite World Conference, even though ten percent of the Mennonite body still lived in the Soviet Union. Some Mennonites were particularly disappointed when, in spite of the many Baptist conferences to which AUCECB leaders were traveling, no delegation was permitted to attend the Mennonite World Conferences in Amsterdam in 1967 and in Curitiba, Brazil, in 1972. Negotiations for the 1978 conference in Kansas were long and complicated, but eventually a six-man delegation from the Soviet Union received a standing ovation when they were introduced. The delegation included one representative of the Mennonites, one from the independent Mennonite Brethren, two Mennonite spokesmen within the AUCECB, plus a translator, and Michael Zhidkov as leader of the delegation. It was a beginning, even though the AUCECB had to serve as the umbrella for the unaffiliated Mennonites.[75]

Both MCC and Mennonite World Conference have made a conscious attempt to regard the Mennonites within the AUCECB as fully part of that union. But North American Mennonites are concerned about the apparent tendency to force Mennonites and Pentecostals to be swallowed up by the Baptists. Mennonite trips to the Soviet Union, like Pentecostal trips, have usually been underplayed in contrast to visits by Baptists. At the 1974 Congress, for example, Mennonite representative Peter Dyck's words of greeting were totally omitted, whereas the Baptist statements were reported in great detail.[76]

Official links with the CCECB have not been possible. At best, a letter of greeting at Christmas was dispatched but failed to be delivered on time due to a misunderstanding. Mennonites have attempted to write articles about the CCECB in order to give their position a hearing and have sought to relate to them via the Soviet immigrants in West Germany. In recent meetings with Council of Religious Affairs representatives, they have appealed for the release of prisoners as did the Baptists. A similar appeal was approved at the annual meeting of Mennonite Central Committee in January 1980, where Georgi Vins was a featured speaker.

3. *Pentecostals.* Foreign Pentecostal links with the AUCECB have

had a similar second-rank status to that of the Mennonites. Official Pentecostal ties to the Soviet Union were initiated in 1967 when Robert Makish became a fraternal representative to Eastern Europe on behalf of the American Assemblies of God. Makish, a former pastor in Wichita, Kansas, began to visit the Soviet Union annually as well as Pentecostal bodies in other East European countries. The visits usually involved preaching with a concern to foster the moderate Pentecostal position characteristic of the Assemblies of God.

Pentecostals within the AUCECB first attended a World Congress of Pentecostals in 1970, the congress taking place in Dallas, Texas.[77] A six-member delegation attended the world congress in London held in 1976, while several attended the subsequent congress in Vancouver, Canada, in 1979.[78] The Pentecostal World Congress, like the Mennonite one, is a gathering for fellowship and inspiration and does not involve an organizational structure to carry on programs. As in the case of attendance at the Mennonite World Conference, delegations to the Pentecostal congresses were always led by an AUCECB leader who was not a Pentecostal.

The AUCECB has also attempted to utilize the support of foreign Pentecostal bodies, particularly that of the American Assemblies of God, in order to put pressure on Soviet Pentecostals to support the AUCECB. Thomas Zimmerman, president of the world body, as well as of the American Assemblies of God, personally visited the Soviet Union in 1974. Percy Brewster, a British pastor and secretary of the world body, paid a similar visit in 1977. It was a period when both the AUCECB and the state were urging local independent congregations to register and Brewster was asked for his advice. In a statement quoted by *Bratskii Vestnik* Brewster stated:

Regardless of where we live, we must be obedient to the laws of our own country. The church should be registered. In England registration is obligatory. I cannot marry a couple unless I am registered.[79]

The statement sounded perfectly natural when applied to the British context which he knew. But it was apparent that both he and his colleague Zimmerman before him were uninformed about the restrictive meaning of registration in the Soviet Union. Although these men also met Pentecostals not in the union and enjoyed fellowship with them, the public message seemed to be that all should join the Moscow union. On another point of conflict with Pentecostals, Robert Makish on a visit in 1976 was quoted as saying that foot washing should not be understood literally; it was expressed symbolically by serving your neighbor.[80] Foreign Pentecostals are not unaware, however, of the second-class status of Pentecostals in the union and would welcome more openness.

The casual nature of Pentecostal relations to Soviet evangelicals is due to the fact that Pentecostals have a less developed organizational structure than do the Baptists. There are, therefore, a large number of Pentecostal individuals who maintain close links with their fellow believers in the Soviet Union, including the AUCECB. Some well-known examples are Steve Durasoff of Oral Roberts University and Earl Poysti, the best loved of all radio preachers to Russia. A number of Pentecostalist missions have also developed active ties.

4. *Other Evangelical Bodies.* The number of evangelical organizations that have been invited to visit the Soviet Union is too extensive to recount here. The AUCECB early developed unique relationships with Slavic-speaking unions of Baptists and Evangelical Christians abroad. For example, the Union of Ukrainian-Russian Baptists led by Oleg Harbuziuk became a supporter of the *Initsiativniki* and the AUCECB attacked them in print for making false charges of nationalist discrimination against Ukrainians.[81] AUCECB relations are much closer with the Slavic Evangelical Baptist Convention, led by Alex Leonovich, and the World Evangelical Christian Fellowship, led by John Sergei.

The Moscow union has also been visited by a number of famous evangelicals. Billy Graham and Oral Roberts visited in 1959 and 1960 respectively, but did not have permission to speak, but when Bill Bright of Campus Crusade visited in 1977 this had changed.[82] Quaker theologian Elton Trueblood, another well-known individual, completed a speaking tour. Since Billy Graham visited Poland in 1978, Soviet Baptists have been negotiating for permission to have him visit their country.

Considering the extensive foreign travel of AUCECB leaders, it was notable that no representative participated at the World Congresses on Evangelism held in Berlin in 1966 and in Lausanne in 1974. This is especially striking when we consider that evangelism is the major practical expression of being an evangelical.[83] Nor does the AUCECB have ties with the National Association of Evangelicals in America or the Evangelical Alliance in Europe. These organizations appear to represent interests which Soviet authorities do not wish to encourage. The fact that the National Association of Evangelicals has regularly issued anti-communist resolutions was a further barrier to relationships. Yet AUCECB representatives have regularly attended the annual meeting of the National Association of Religious Broadcasters. The primary purpose appears to have been to make sure that these religious broadcasters would continue to avoid political references in radio programming to the Soviet Union.

Conclusion: The Balance Sheet

When Alexander Karev died, it was announced that he had made 39 trips abroad in his lifetime. His successor, Alexei Bychkov, during the past ten years, has very likely surpassed that record already. He is only one of the Soviet Baptist leaders who are constantly traveling to different international meetings or making visits to local churches in some foreign country. In 1977 alone, 72 foreign guests from more than 14 countries visited by special invitation of the AUCECB. The AUCECB representatives responded with visits, as well as attending many international conferences. During 1977 an average of four tourists a day visited the Moscow Baptist church, the total of 1,223 recorded foreign guests came from 28 countries. More than 2,000 letters were received from abroad and several thousand were mailed abroad.[84]

What has this all achieved? How much money has been spent? Was it worth the investment?

Such questions are hard to answer but necessary to face. In 1979 some economies on foreign travel were introduced. Bychkov in his report to the presidium emphasized that with each passing year the influence and authority of the AUCECB is growing in the world Baptist brotherhood. Through their initiative, the BWA conducted conferences on theological subjects such as the charismatic movement. AUCECB influence was significant in getting BWA approval of the International Peace Conference held in Moscow in 1977. By AUCECB initiative, a resolution supporting the Helsinki Agreement was approved.[85]

This emphasis on peace resolutions illustrates that the AUCECB was concerned to demonstrate success as a peace-making influence. It can be stated that although they made no major converts to Soviet peace policy, they also helped prevent any serious criticism of Russian foreign policy. Through their influence, the BWA and the WCC did not become leaders of public opinion to force changes toward greater liberty in the Soviet Union. Perhaps more significant than the attempt to prevent publicity for the CCECB, through their many visits abroad they at least managed to present their viewpoint of life in the Soviet Union, and they have won many friends and supporters.

In fact, compared with the Russian Orthodox, Baptist foreign relations are vitally important as a protection against future elimination by the state. The extensive travels have guaranteed them a high visibility that may stand them in good stead when pressure is resumed.

Through their foreign connections they have gained much in knowledge. They have developed experience in ecumenical dialogue which has also led to closer ecumenical links with the Russian Orthodox Church. Where once Orthodox priests were responsible for sending Baptists to prison, they now share annual ecumenical services in the Moscow Baptist church and a Russian Orthodox clergyman shares chairmanship duties with Bychkov on one of the WCC commissions. Through their many travels, some of the leaders have gained a personal vision of world needs.

Whereas North American evangelicals spend large sums of money visiting mission projects around the world, negotiating development projects, and financing the shipping of relief, Soviet evangelicals have been unable to contribute significantly. They have not been involved in world mission, although there is a growing sense of mission responsibility to Soviet society.[86] They have been prevented from contributing their goodwill, energy, and funds for relief work in the Third World. Thus far one cannot speak of any contribution that they have made to theological and biblical studies.

The AUCECB has also been able to utilize its wide contacts abroad in order to strengthen the significance of its union versus other Soviet evangelicals who have no foreign partners. True, they have helped other Soviet evangelicals establish links with fellow believers abroad, but the tendency to absorb other evangelicals makes reliance on the AUCECB somewhat risky. These unaffiliated Soviet evangelicals have, however, received considerable support from an astounding variety of mission organizations.

Notes to Chapter 13

1. I. S. Prokhanov was a vice-president, 1911-28. Kahle, pp. 10-12.
2. See above, chapter 3, pp. 91-92.
3. BWA files, Washington (J. H. Rushbrooke).
4. *Ibid.*
5. *Ibid.*
6. *BV*, 1/47, p. 17.
7. BWA files, Washington (J. H. Rushbrooke).
8. *BV*, 4/47, p. 7. See above, p. 121f.
9. *BV*, 3-4/54, p. 112. Cf. 2/54, pp. 53-57.
10. *BV*, 3-4/54, p. 110.

11. See above, chapter 4, p. 124.

12. They were: Jacob Zhidkov, Alexander Karev, N. A. Levindanto, A. L. Andreev, I. G. Ivanov, A. I. Mitskevich, F. R. Astakhov, and E. N. Raevski (BV 5/55, p. 6). Half the issue was devoted to this trip.

13. Interview with Robert Denny, November 1976, and BWA files (Russia trip, 1956).

14. *BV*, 3-4/56, p. 23. The Russians reported on the trip with great detail. Delegates were: Jacob Zhidkov, Alexander Karev, I. G. Ivanov, N. A. Levindanto, and Klaudia Tyrtova.

15. Baptist members of the delegation were A. L. Andreev and A. N. Karpov (Moscow presbyter and AUCECB member).

16. *BV*, 5/57, p. 52

17. *BV*, 6/63, p. 17. The attendance of Jacob Zhidkov, Alexander Karev, I. G. Ivanov, A. I. Mitskevich, and P. A. Parchevskii at the 1958 meeting was not reported at that time.

18. *BV*, 1/63, p. 72. Zhidkov had just returned from a year of study at McMaster University in Ontario.

19. *BV*, 5-6/60, pp. 6-8. Aside from those two the delegation included Michael Zhidkov, Alexei Stoian, and Klaudia (Tyrtova) Pilipiuk.

20. *BV*, 2/56, p. 41. Swedish Baptists were at least as active as the British and American Baptists in fostering Soviet relations.

21. *Religious Ferment in Russia. Protestant Opposition to Soviet Religious Policy* (London: Macmillan, 1968).

22. *Baptist Times*, December 28, 1967. The letter stated: "People are not persecuted in our country for their religious convictions, but to our deep regret some brethren and sisters have been answerable for nonobservance of the laws on religion and for breach of the public order." The letter ended with the warning "let no rumors confuse you." A similar letter on 28 May 1973 to EBF leaders urged use of the Novosti Press version of Ivan Moiseev's death and discouraged publication of CCECB *Samizdat* (BWA files, London).

23. Keston College files, 1968.

24. Carney Hargroves was BWA president 1970-75; Joseph Nordenhaug was BWA president 1960-65; Erik Ruden, formerly Swedish Baptist Secretary, was EBF secretary till 1967.

25. *BV*, 5/57, p. 52. She had hoped to become a school teacher but has remained on the AUCECB staff till the present.

26. *BV*, 1/75, p. 39.

27. *Ibid.*

28. *BV*, 5-6/62, pp. 18-20.

29. Biographical card file, based on information from numerous sources. My card file is also the major reference for the subsequent biographical sketches.

30. *Miami Beach Views*, June 29, 1965. The story has been repeated frequently in the *Christian Beacon*.

31. *BV*, 3/69, p. 72.

32. Directors of the Patriarchate's International Department were: Metropolitan Nikolai (1945-60); Archbishop, later Metropolitan Nikodim (1960-72); Metropolitan Yuvenali (1972-   ). But it should be remembered that Orthodox hierarchs are not elected by the people.

33. *BV*, 5/55, p. 23. The matter was also raised by Dr. Bell, Bishop of Chichester.

34. *BV*, 2/59, p. 74.

35. *BV*, 5-6/62, pp. 18-20.
36. *BV*, 6/66, p. 26f.
37. *BV*, 6/63, p. 41.
38. For the text of the letter and a brief summary, see David Kelly, "Nairobi: A Door Opened," *RCL*, 4, 1 (Spring/1976), pp. 4-17.
39. See above, chapter 9, for a characterization of Veliseichik.
40. J. A. Hebly, *The Russians and the World Council of Churches* (Belfast-Dublin-Ottawa: Christian Journals Limited, 1978), p. 119.
41. *Ibid.* p. 150.
42. "Religious Liberty, the WCC and the USSR," *Religious Liberty in the Soviet Union*, pp. 10-24.
43. Quoted in *Ibid.*, p. 16. A further sentence was: "In many instances the closer one is to the realities, the less one is able to act."
44. A second, much more substantial letter, dated March 6, 1976, is printed in *Religious Liberty in the Soviet Union*, pp. 40-53.
45. *Ibid.*, p. 16.
46. WCC *News Release*, January 30, 1975. The letter was signed by M. M. Thomas and Pauline M. Webb (Chmn. and Vice Chmn. of the Central Committee) and by General Secretary Philip Potter.
47. Hebly, *The Russians*, p. 172.
48. *Ibid.*, p. 169.
49. *EPS*, July 21, 1979.
50. Hebly, p. 143.
51. *EPS*, April 5, 1979.
52. See, for example, *BV*, 2/77, p. 75; 4/78, p. 40.
53. Unpublished speech kindly supplied by Professor Will.
54. *BV*, 2/77, pp. 39-41.
55. BWA files, London.
56. *EBPS*, June 1, 1979. Cf. *EBPS*, September 27 and December 4, 1978, for more details on the SITE program. Gerhard Claas was elected to succeed Robert Denny as BWA General Secretary, beginning July 1980.
57. *BV*, 5-6/61, p. 35.
58. *AS*, 772, p. 6 (September 19, 1963).
59. *BV*, 5/70, p. 16.
60. BWA files.
61. *BV*, 6/75, p. 54.
62. BWA files, London (November 1973).
63. Adolphs Klaupiks died March 27, 1979.
64. "Christian Life in the Soviet Union," *Life of Faith* beginning May 27, 1972.
65. *EBPS*, September 14, 1977. The CCECB has from the beginning refused to be an underground church.
66. BWA files, London.
67. *EBPS*, July 27, 1977, and November 3, 1978. At the European Baptist Congress in Brighton, England, in July 1979, AUCECB spokesmen presented the building plans of their hoped-for seminary but it remains a future hope in spite of all the publicity.
68. *EBPS*, January 25, 1979.
69. Krestian'inov, p. 56. Visiting delegations were accused of holding secret meetings with Russian Mennonites, bringing card files of addresses along, etc.
70. MCC files, 1956.

71. They were: MCC Exec. Sec. Orie Miller (1958), a four-man tourist group in 1960, a three-man tourist group in 1966, a three-man tourist group in 1968, three men as part of a joint Baptist delegation in 1970, a two-man tourist group in 1974. Usually on the Intourist sponsored trips, the AUCECB sent an interpreter along.

72. Mennonite seminar papers in abbreviated form were printed in *BV*, 2/77, pp. 7-15.

73. *EBPS*, April 25, 1979.

74. MCC files.

75. Delegation members were: Bernhard Sawadsky (Mennonite presbyter in Novosibirsk), Heinrich Goertzen (independent Mennonite Brethren presbyter in Karaganda), Jacob Fast (Presidium member), Traugott Kviring (senior presbyter for Central Asia), Michael Zhidkov (AUCECB vice-president), and Sergei Nikolaev (translator).

76. *BV*, 1/75, p. 66.

77. *BV*, 3/71, pp. 30-32. Delegates were Peter K. Shatrov, G. T. Bulgakov (Gor'ki Oblast), and Valentina Ryndina (translator).

78. They were: Michael Zhidkov, Peter Shatrov, V. S. Glukhovskii (Deputy SP for Ukraine), B. I. Bilas (L'vov Oblast), A. N. Stoian, and Valentina Ryndina. (*BV*, 1/77, pp. 17-20.)

79. *BV*, 6/77, p. 21.

80. *BV*, 6/76, p. 17.

81. *BV*, 2/70, p. 4.

82. *BV*, 4/78, p. 43.

83. Wells and Woodbridge, *The Evangelicals*, p. 312.

84. *BV*, 4/78, pp. 42-43.

85. *Ibid.* pp. 39-41.

86. A new CCECB-related journal entitled *Mission* appeared in *Samizdat* in 1978. It contained news on mission around the world.

Remember those who are in prison, as though you were in prison with them. Remember those who are suffering, as though you were suffering as they are.
—Hebrews 13:3, GNB

We put aside all secret and shameful deeds; we do not act with deceit, nor do we falsify the Word of God. In the full light of truth we live in God's sight and try to commend ourselves to everyone's good conscience.
—2 Corinthians 4:2, GNB

14 "Anti-Soviet Interference": Assessment of East European Mission Societies

He was the owner and operator of a Christian travel agency. He had conducted tours through Eastern Europe many times. This time the border crossing in Czechoslovakia took longer than usual. The suspicious guards finally discovered the secret compartment in the bus containing nearly 3,000 Bibles. Tour leader David Hathaway was arrested and sentenced to two years in prison.[1]

This incident is probably one of the most famous of many similar incidents, many of which remain unreported. The business of Bible-smuggling continues, however, because apparently most of the smuggled Bibles are not discovered. Hathaway, for example, calculated that he had brought 150,000 pieces of literature into Eastern Europe before he was stopped. Smuggling also continued because the appeals for Bibles continue.

The Bible hunger is greater in the Soviet Union than in any other East European country.[2] This is because it is the largest country where evangelicals in particular urgently appeal for the Book that is the basis of their movement. The Soviet Union has also been stricter than other countries in limiting the production and import of Bibles. They have permitted only a very limited amount to be printed or legally imported.[3] Customs officials regularly insist that it is forbidden to bring Bibles as gifts. No published Soviet legislation forbidding Bibles exists, but then, Soviet policy has never been that dependent on legislation.

During the past decade the impact of Bible smuggling and other attempts to import religion have obviously caused the Soviet authorities great concern. In 1974, 200,000 copies of a book with the strange title *Diversion Without Dynamite* was published.[4] A second expanded edition appeared in 1976. This attacked a long list of missions to Eastern Europe and radio stations. By means of religion these were trying "to impair and weaken the moral-political unity of our people, to undermine the power of the world socialist system."[5] Most of the religious centers, the writers claimed, were part of the anti-communist front that was trying to overthrow the Soviet system. But Leonid Brezhnev at the 25th Communist Party Congress had said that:

> In the struggle of two world views there can be no place for neutralism and compromise. Here the highest political vigilance is needed, active, effective and convincing propaganda work, while at the same time rebuffing harmful, ideological diversion.[6]

Westerners appear unsure which propaganda to believe. Is there really an underground church? Should one smuggle Bibles? Do the underground missions help or hinder believers?

Nature of Soviet Charges

Soviet writers tend to regard any expression of criticism as anti-communist. The *Diversion* writers, A. Belov and A. Shilkin, developed a whole series of charges to illustrate that once the possibility of direct overthrow of the communist regime had passed, the opposition began to engage in psychological warfare which became ever more refined. The purpose of the psychological warfare was to change the thinking of Soviet citizens, to cast doubt on the communist world-view. Even détente, purely a tactic for the so-called doctrine of bridge building between imperialist and socialist countries, was intended to contribute to the erosion of socialism. Religion would play a significant role in contemporary psychological warfare because it was the single ideology existing in the Soviet Union which was in opposition to Marxist-Leninist ideology. The introduction of religious literature was an elaborate camouflage for fostering anti-Soviet ideology. They hoped thereby to create disbelief among believers in Soviet legislation on religion and toward the policies of the Communist Party. The religious forces did so by falsifying the real conditions of religion in socialist countries.

These charges have been repeated regularly without any attempt to discuss whether in fact all religion was anti-socialist, whether all clergymen were anti-communist imperialists, etc. In contrast to East Germany, for example, there has been no acknowledgement of the great variety within Christianity in its attitudes toward society. A recent booklet did distinguish between constructive and reactionary religious organizations and individuals who had involved themselves in the negotiations for the Helsinki Agreement. The Vatican had managed to get two of its three major concerns approved in the final Helsinki Declaration, but the writers of this brochure still insisted that the ultimate goal of these progressive Christians who worked for peace was to assure safer living conditions that would permit the church to expand its influence in East European countries. And the expansion of religion, regardless of protests to the contrary, meant opposition to communism.[7]

Western observers, on the other hand, charged that the entire purpose of détente, including the Helsinki Agreement, were tactical maneuvers to facilitate increased communist propaganda in Western countries. *Newsweek's* Moscow correspondent said the Helsinki Agreement "has to be scored heavily as a one-sided Soviet success." George W. Ball called it "a Western defeat."[8] While state authorities were signing friendly agreements with Western powers, Soviet newspapers and books were increasing their verbal attacks on capitalist imperialism and state administrators increased the pressure on religious dissidents. The volume of *Samizdat* listing violations of human rights has expanded dramatically. Is this simply a propaganda contest with both sides engaging in fabricated charge and counter-charge?

A growing number of research centers are helping turn the balance against Soviet propagandistic accusations. Their effectiveness is illustrated by books like *Diversion*, which warn against Western religious propaganda and attempt to include the research centers among the forces of anti-Soviet imperialism. But Soviet critics have not managed to produce persuasive evidence challenging the fundamental veracity of Western scholars, resorting instead to verbal abuse.[9]

Research Centers Provide Facts

Many mission agencies have employed individuals to "research" for them in order to make their work more effective. Only in a few cases was such research of a high quality. It usually focused on the specific program needs of the sponsoring agency. In recent years independent research institutions financed by voluntary donations have emerged, enabling trained scholars to pursue objective research and writing. Most of these scholars have a positive bias toward Christianity, but their research is characterized by adherence to accepted standards of scholarly objectivity.

(a) *Russia Cristiana* (Via Martinengo 16, 20139 Milan, Italy) was one of the first research centers, founded in 1960 near Milan, Italy. The work of such scholars as Pietro Modesto and Giovanni Codevilla are known internationally.[10] Russia Cristiana has developed a highly specialized library on Soviet atheism and has also published extensively on the Lithuanian Catholics. Since its journal (as well as a monthly Information Service) is printed in Italian, it is less widely read than it deserves.

(b) *YMCA Press* (11, rue de la Montagne Sainte-Geneviève, 75005 Paris, France). This Russian Student Christian Movement began in the mid-twenties and with support from the American YMCA became the main publisher of emigré Russian writers such as Nikolai Berdiaev.[11] Its journal *Vestnik RSKhD* continues a tradition of the pre-Revolutionary "fat" journals. Under the editorship of Nikita Struve this journal has become one of the most valued publications for the Orthodox intellectuals in the Soviet Union. Struve regularly published the writings of the Soviet intelligentsia which have been banned in the Soviet Union. For example, the YMCA press printed most of Solzhenitsyn's writings. With his book, *Christians in Contemporary Russia*, Nikita Struve presented one of the most detailed, dispassionate treatments of Russian Orthodoxy in the twentieth century.

(c) *Centre de Recherche et d'Etude des Institutions Religieuses* (1966-69). William C. Fletcher, an American specialist in Soviet studies, received financial support to establish a research center in Geneva, which focused on religion in all of Eastern Europe. He was assisted by a small staff while scholars from other institutions helped to maintain a bibliographical survey which was duplicated for circulation to a small readership.[12] Better known were Fletcher's own writings which appeared during this period in book form as well as two very important collections of essays.[13] These were the results of study conferences which Fletcher had organized. When funding ceased Fletcher became head of Slavic studies at the University of Kansas while one of his associates, Michael Bourdeaux, managed to establish a similar center in London.

(d) *Religion in Communist-Dominated Areas* (475 Riverside Drive, 10027 New York). Paul Anderson had personally witnessed the Russian Revolution while working as secretary of the Russian Student Christian Movement. During the twenties and thirties he became one of the earliest experts on Soviet religion while working closely with the Russian Student Christian Movement in Paris. In 1961 the National Council of Churches in the USA asked him to provide them with a translation service of significant documents on religion in communist-dominated areas. This translation service was highly respected though its circulation remained small and funding difficult. When Anderson retired, the research center reorganized to become independent of the NCC but still closely associated with it. Blahoslav Hruby succeeded Anderson as editor of *Religion in Communist-Dominated Areas* (RCDA). This journal continues to provide English translations of materials from Eastern Europe, although Hruby's editorializing betrays a more emotional anti-communism.

(e) *Keston College* (Heathfield Road, Keston, Kent, England). Michael Bourdeaux together with Soviet experts Sir John Lawrence and Peter Reddaway managed to organize the Centre for the Study of Religion and Communism in 1970. Initially this consisted of Bourdeaux and a secretary, but the institution grew, was renamed Keston College in 1978, and is at present the most significant and respected of the research institutes. Michael Bourdeaux and his colleagues have produced numerous books including translations of Russian *Samizdat*. Bourdeaux's work plus the regular information supplied by his institute have done more than anything else to clarify the situation of evangelicals in the Soviet Union. Their focus is less on history and philosophy than on the present church-state situation. The large research staff maintains files on all religions in the Soviet Union and Eastern Europe. Since 1973 Keston College has produced a quarterly journal, *Religion in Communist Lands,* and a semiweekly *Keston News Service.* Recently telex services were introduced. A sister organization, Society for the Study of Religion under Communism, was organized in 1976 and is based in California, c/o Open Doors. Keston's most valuable service for researchers is the comprehensive bibliography on religious *Samizdat* which appears in the periodical.

(f) *Glaube in der 2ten Welt* (Bergstrasse 6, CH-8702 Zollikon-Zürich). Shortly after the founding of Keston College, Pfarrer Eugen Voss organized a sister institute in Küsnacht (Zürich) Switzerland. Voss produced a journal with the same name, and in 1977 introduced an information service which is more extensive than the British one. It has taken a much more pronounced advocacy stance for human rights in general than is true of Keston College. Since 1978 the journal *Glaube in der 2ten Welt* has focused on special themes such as the issue on atheism cited above.

(g) *Other Institutions.* Keston and G2W cooperated in 1976 with the

Inter-Academical Institute for Missiological and Ecumenical Research (Utrecht, Netherlands) to produce a publication on *Religious Liberty in the Soviet Union* for the World Council of Churches. Dr. Hans Hebly of this institute has written numerous articles and books in Dutch on Soviet religion, two of which have been translated into English.[14] The Evangelical Church of Germany maintains a research department producing the highly responsible *Ostkirchliche Informationen*. The subcommittee on East/West relations for the British Council of Churches sponsored the writing and publication of Trevor Beeson's book *Discretion and Valour* in 1974. It remains the best overall survey on religion in Eastern Europe.

Research Results

Without question, at the close of this decade, Western public opinion has become much more enlightened about religious conditions in Eastern Europe and the Soviet Union. The news services by Keston and G2W are probably the most widely quoted in the secular and religious press. Usually their information will appear a week or two later than the hot news supplied by Western correspondents on the scene, but their reporting invariably contains more background data. Both institutions attempt to confirm their information with more than one source, atheist and religious. In addition, the volume of *Samizdat* materials that has been published or summarized in translation has become so extensive that the "other voice" of the Soviet Union has now received a wide hearing. Soviet charges of falsifying data have therefore been proved to be untrue. Keston's reputation for accuracy probably explains why Belov and Shilkin repeat their attacks on Bourdeaux numerous times throughout the book.

The most significant influence of the research centers is less on public opinion in general than it has been on the church agencies and East European missions who have relied heavily on the research centers for their information. It has influenced the nature of their response to the task they have assigned themselves.

The East European Missions

Mission work to Russia and other East European countries had already started in the 19th century and had significantly influenced the development of Soviet evangelicals.[15] Swedish Lutherans and representatives of the Evangelical Alliance formed a missions committee in 1903 for work in Slavic countries. In 1947 it was renamed the *Slaviska Missionen* and maintains a major East European program at present. It has sponsored evangelization through its own missionaries and literature, as well as the support of Russian preachers and their education. One of its missionaries, Johannes Svensson, translated a Bible dictionary into Russian which was finally published in 1969. The *Deutsche Orient Mission*, founded in 1897 by Johannes Lepsius, supported Walter Jack, a Reformed theologian, in starting a seminary in Astrakhan. The school was closed in 1911 but Jack remained in Russia, working closely in tent evangelization with a Russian Mennonite, Jacob Kroeker, and others. After World War I, these two men found themselves in Germany working among Russian prisoners of war who begged for help in studying the Bible. A Bible school established in Wernigerode in 1920 became the founding date for the mission *Licht im Osten*.[16]

During the 1920s I. S. Prokhanov also attempted to launch an international Evangelical Christian Union whose major task would be the evangelization of Slavic-speaking peoples.[17] An immigrant from Belorussia, Peter Deyneka, traveled throughout America with Prokhanov in 1926 to raise funds for the Bibles that were printed in Leningrad that year. Deyneka made several visits to the Soviet Union and in 1934 formally established the faith mission, Slavic Gospel Association.[18]

After World War II, these three missions, *Slaviska Missionen, Licht im Osten*, and Slavic Gospel Association, attempted to establish contact with believers in the Soviet Union but with great difficulty. Much of their work therefore focused on other East European countries, on Slavic-speaking refugees in Western Europe, while Slavic Gospel Association expanded its ministry with Russian immigrants, even beginning a Russian Bible Institute in Argentina. Gradually these missions were able to establish letter contacts with believers in the Soviet Union and by the mid-fifties were able to dispatch Bibles to the Soviet Union by a variety of means. Some, for example, were mailed to China and then on to the Soviet Union. In the late fifties international tourism to the Soviet Union began, and this became a new opportunity to respond to the tremendous Bible hunger that was apparent. By that time, these missions had also entered into cooperative arrangements with believers in other East European countries, who were able to travel more freely into the Soviet Union than they were.

During the late fifties and early sixties Bible work in Eastern Europe was primarily the domain of individual enterprise. A young Dutchman, who identified himself quite simply as Brother Andrew, made numerous trips to Eastern Europe, attending socialist youth conferences, for example, in order to present a Christian witness there.[19] His ministry, as he described it later, was accompanied by fantastic adventures and miraculous divine leading. Without Brother Andrew making any publicity, concerned anonymous donors regularly supplied him with precisely the amount of money he needed for the next undertaking. Many concerned Christians were engaged in such private mission enterprises, devoting their vacation time and money to such a trip while combining this with other mission work in Western Europe for which they were receiving financial support. Brother Andrew eventually became too well known at border crossings, but he had already organized a small mission entitled Open Doors. Soon this mission and others like it had grown into professionalized organizations.

The largest mission to Eastern Europe, Underground Evangelism, has provided the generic name for all such undertakings. Underground Evangelism began in 1960 after a young Pentecostal missionary, L. Joe Bass, made a trip to Yugoslavia and became concerned about the needs of East European Christians. Bass organized a small mission which he and his wife struggled to keep alive until they had a godsend. In 1965 two missions in Sweden obtained the deportation of Pastor Richard Wurmbrand and his family for a good-sized ransom.[20] Richard Wurmbrand had been in prison as a preacher in Romania. He reported his experiences to the American Senate, took off his shirt to show the scars from torture, and made headlines. Joe Bass persuaded Wurmbrand to join his mission, a shrewd financial move. Within a year the organization became too small for both men and Wurmbrand set up his own work a few blocks away in Glendale, California. Richard Wurmbrand's mission, named Jesus Christ to the Communist World, quickly became Underground Evangelism's major competitor. Both published gruesome pictures of torture, of secret church meetings in the forest or elsewhere underground, plus glaring headlines. Wurmbrand's paper was called *The Voice of the Martyrs.*

Also in 1967, Brother Andrew's story was printed under the headline-catching title *God's Smuggler.* The book has circulated widely and contributed to the dramatic upsurge in interest in East European missions. Richard Wurmbrand became a prolific writer; his best-known book, *Tortured for Christ,* appeared in many languages. Other stars were sponsored by Underground Evangelism. Best known were Haralan Popov (*Tortured for His Faith*) and Sergei Kourdakov (*Forgive Me, Natasha*).

Patterns of Ministry and Organization

Soon a developing pattern of ministry emerged. The primary activity described in the publicity (even if it seldom became the largest budget item) was Bible smuggling. Missions competed in claiming high rates of achievement, but often the high figures included all pieces of literature printed which included small tracts. Bible smuggling began by simply taking a carton or two of Christian literature in an automobile and hoping that the border authorities would not check the luggage. That is still standard procedure in many East European countries, but in the Soviet Union customs officials are more thorough. Mission societies have therefore been forced to become more creative in their methods. *Diversion* prints a picture of the dismantled door panel from an automobile, behind which literature had been hidden. Many other compartments of vehicles are used and the larger missions rely on specially built vehicles. For a while some missions were able to bribe Soviet sailors to take in quantities of literature. Other techniques have primarily publicity value. For many years the Wurmbrand mission has been distributing small plastic bags containing a gospel tract, a stick of chewing gum as greetings from America, and a drinking straw to make the plastic bag buoyant on the water. In one publicity stunt, a single-engine airplane flew across the Bering Strait toward some of the outlying islands belonging to the Soviet Union and dropped these gospel bags into the water.

It is obviously impossible to obtain an accurate assessment of how much literature has been introduced into the Soviet Union by non-legal means. Belov and Shilkin complained that customs officials were finding such contraband every day.[21] On the basis of confidential information supplied to me and some well-informed estimates, I concluded that by 1974 approximately 1.8 million pieces of Bibles, New Testaments, or Gospels have been imported into the Soviet Union by non-legal means.[22] Since then, that amount may well have doubled.

Another program that involved fifteen to twenty percent of the budget was financial support for underground pastors and the families of prisoners. One mission, a spin-off of Underground Evangelism, called Frontline Fellowship, devotes its entire ministry to raising monthly financial support for pastors in Eastern Europe.[23]

Many missions contribute directly or indirectly to radio ministries. That is, their own staff members or associates prepare and present radio programs or their agency underwrites the radio costs. The best-known radio Stations broadcasting gospel programs on shortwave are Trans World Radio (TWR, Monte Carlo), Far Eastern Broadcasting Company (FEBC), and the Voice of the Andes (HCJB Ecuador). For the larger missions, radio broadcasting involves between five and ten percent of the budget. Others, such as Russia for Christ, are devoted almost exclusively to radio work.[24] These three activities (literature, financial support, and radio) constitute the programs of the larger East European missions. The remainder of their funds are devoted to administration, fund-raising, and other ministries in the West. An older mission such as Slavic Gospel Association has also devoted considerable effort to providing resource personnel in children and youth camps but this type of activity is not possible in the Soviet Union.

Both Underground Evangelism and the Wurmbrand mission devote extensive funds to the preparation and showing of films and the distribution of publicity. Both of them argue that this, too, is mission because they are trying to raise the consciousness of Western Christendom to support persecuted believers under communism. The Wurmbrand mission lists four main goals, two of which are "to bring to Christ leftists and communists in the free world, and to warn Christians in the West of the dangers of communism by informing them about the atrocities committed against our brethren in faith in the communist countries."[25] Instead of this latter goal, Underground Evangelism purposed "to strengthen the spiritual life of Christians of the free world."[26]

Underground Evangelism also articulated a fifth purpose: "to assist in the release of Christians in prison for their faith." Several years after David Hathaway was released from prison, he became the head of Christian Prisoners Release International, an independent organization financially underwritten by Underground Evangelism. The organization spent thousands of dollars organizing simultaneous demonstrations on May 8, 1976 in many cities on behalf of Georgi Vins. Since then that organization has been less prominent and its leader was dismissed for morality reasons. Some success was possible in helping Romanian evangelical prisoners.

The East European missions have developed similar structural patterns. Most of them are voluntary societies, therefore interdenominational. The board of directors, usually small and self-perpetuating, makes decisions to be executed by the salaried staff. A larger body of advisers are there primarily to indicate patronage. Underground Evangelism has a policy-making board of directors controlled and directed by Joe Bass, founder and president. A six-member international committee, which is the chief policy-making and budget-setting body, includes only persons directly employed by the organization.[27]

Because in such a ministry the lives of Christians in Eastern Europe could be put in danger by too much publicity, Eastern European missions have surrounded themselves with an aura of secrecy. Of the large missions, the most secretive is probably Open Doors International (Brother Andrew), whose offices are scattered in several villages in Holland, and telephone numbers are hard to obtain. Each mission maintains its operating secrets and will only describe a specific Bible-smuggling technique after it has been exposed. This concern for secrecy is understandable but provides temptation for gross abuse. State law requires minimum financial reporting, and since most missions are voluntary societies, they can afford to report overall expense with little detail.

Another complicating feature in obtaining an overview of East European missions is the fact that they have tended to proliferate at a disturbing pace. A number of ex-Underground Evangelism workers started their own missions.[28] Most of the larger missions opened branch offices in other countries which sometimes resulted in complicated organizational interlinkage. The Wurmbrand missions, for example, have a great degree of local independence, whereas Underground Evangelism International is highly centralized; national branches perform primarily a fund-raising function. Most of the smaller missions involve only one or two persons.[29] The longer-established missions such as *Licht im Osten, Slaviska Missionen,* and Slavic Gospel Association, with budgets hovering around half a million dollars, are direct contact missions. Other missions are non-direct contact missions, which means that they pass their resources on to a second or third agency before it reaches the final recipient. Although Underground Evangelism has a staff totaling 500 persons,[30] it now provides a mixture of direct contact services and indirect aid, but the latter is particularly true in its relationship to the Soviet Union.

Generally speaking, medium-sized and larger missions maintain only a small full-time staff of missionaries plus administrative personnel. Much of the actual program outreach is done through voluntary labor, including the use of couriers during the summer tourist season. The majority of the couriers are college students interested in gaining experience with adventure, very few of them having had East European training or language ability. A continuing weakness in this staff structure has been the superficial preparation and briefing of the couriers. Slavic Gospel Association launched an Institute of Slavic Studies in order to produce more missionaries who would have up to two years of study of Slavic culture and society.[31]

The fund-raising techniques are those common in voluntary societies or faith missions. Open Doors and other medium-sized missions rely on a growing core of regular contributors who receive the organization's regular reports. Underground Evangelism and Wurmbrand have become most prominent because of their fund-raising. The Wurmbrand organization sends a monthly magazine on glossy paper which is distributed free in large quantities. Richard Wurmbrand is constantly on the road, speaking at large fund-raising rallies. The organization also derives income from the sale of the many books and brochures authored by Wurmbrand, his wife and son. Underground Evangelism is the most professional as fund-raiser, having installed its own computer. The address lists are regularly revised in order to limit free distribution of the glossy magazine and other mailings to contributors. Larger contributors receive personalized replies prepared by electronic typewriters. Each national branch of Underground Evangelism has a net of agents who solicit film showings. At these film showings the distributor collects more addresses and takes a collection, being reimbursed himself on a commission basis. Both Underground Evangelism and Wurmbrand find fund-raising and administrative overhead expensive. Underground Evangelism, for example, spent 18.5 percent of its $8.1 million received in 1977 on administration and 15 percent on fund-raising.[32] During the same year Wurmbrand received $5.9 million, of which 21 percent was spent on administration, 21 percent on postage, freight, and publicity.[33] Other administrators of church agencies consider an overhead of more than 30 percent too high. Underground Evangelism officials claim to be introducing more efficiency, but the affluent style of its leadership remains a point of incongruity.

Evaluation of East European Missions

Soviet authorities do not like the East European missions. That probably indicates that they have had considerable success in attaining their goals. East European missions are an obvious factor in helping account for present growth, especially among evangelicals. (I have focused in this chapter on the evangelically oriented missions which dominate the field in any case.) Flattering as the Soviet attack may seem, it cannot be dismissed with equal equanimity by all missions. General criticism of the specific missions included above is no secret to the Soviets; *Izvestiia* recently drew attention to the financial scandal involving Wurmbrand and Underground Evangelism.[34] Instead of rating each mission separately, I propose to discuss a number of issues from the perspective of modern missiology.[35]

1. *A Smuggling Ethic.* In the spring of 1973 the United Bible Society's European Regional Committee made the following resolution:

The committee emphasizes that all support given to the work by UBS member Bible societies is provided through legal channels. The committee wishes to place on record its dissociation from Bible work done by illegal means. Furthermore, the committee dissociates itself from any Scripture distribution linked with political propaganda.[36]

This statement was subsequently quoted with commendation by AUCECB general secretary Alexei Bychkov.[37] He was able to report in 1978 that the United Bible Societies now had a working relationship with them; two representatives attended an EBF seminar in Moscow in March 1979. The first pay-off for this announced policy of importing Bibles by strictly legal means was the 25,000 Bibles that were imported in December 1978.

East European mission leaders understand the UBS declaration as a rejection of their own work and expressed their resentment in public. Underground Evangelism, for example, responded to claims of a Bible breakthrough in 1978 in the Soviet Union by quoting CCECB sources that the latter were unaware of any Bibles brought into the country officially. Underground Evangelism discussed the subject at length and concluded by dismissing the claims about official permission, regular supplies of Bibles, as "religious fairy tales."[38]

Following the importation of 25,000 Bibles in December 1978, the first such official importation since 1945, BWA officials responded with understandable joy but unnecessary hyperbole. General Secretary Robert Denny, for example, advised his members: "Forget what you read about necessity for underground evangelism; we now have opportunity for above-ground evangelism in Eastern Europe."[39] Then he went on to claim that: "There is no need to smuggle Bibles into Eastern Europe . . . our problem is to find money to pay for those that we have permission to import." Had Denny restricted his remarks to Poland or the DDR, which are relatively well supplied with Bibles, his statement would be acceptable, but a total of 405,000 Bibles and New Testaments which have been printed officially or imported legally since the war scarcely begins to meet the demand of at least 50 million believers. What becomes apparent is that both smugglers and legal importers are desperately competing for limited financial resources.

This competition must be kept in mind when examining the ethics of smuggling. Opponents of smuggling argue that smuggling is usually understood as a criminal activity, and when such smugglers are discovered, atheist opponents of the church gain new ammunition for their war against religion. Advocates of smuggling insist that there is a battle in progress between good and evil and that the forces of good must employ all their weapons, including the weapon of deception in order to win. The primary passage of Scripture cited on behalf of smuggling is Acts 5:29: "We must obey God, not men" (GNB).

Bratskii Vestnik may be unable to print this verse on the pages of its journal, but the validity of this injunction is accepted by both smugglers and their opponents. What is meant by obeying God rather than men?

Brother Andrew recently published a book called *The Ethics of Smuggling* in which he used the image of warfare, whereby the enemy naturally obstructs the road (forbids Bibles) and it is the task of a good Christian soldier to overrun the position (bring the Bibles through anyway).[40] Few Christians would argue the emphasis that when it is a simple matter of preaching or not preaching the Word, Christ's Great Commission comes first, at least in the long run. But how does one proceed? Can a Christian tell a lie, use elaborate means of deception in order to achieve a good end? Is God, who is fully in charge of the world, dependent on evil means to do good? To this, Brother Andrew replied that "concealment is not lying, you must be careful to guard the distinction between partial truth and untruth."[41] Then he went on:

> It's not telling a lie if I hide the truth from people who have utterly forfeited the right to know the truth. If I stand at the communist border and have my car loaded with Scriptures, then I am under no obligation whatsoever to tell them the truth, because they are in the service of the Devil.[42]

Brother Andrew claimed that he himself did not tell a lie. Instead, he said that when he traveled through a communist country, "I pray mighty hard that I don't have to tell the truth either, and this way we manage!"[43] Perhaps Brother Andrew is personally able to maintain this fine distinction but the reports about how couriers actually conduct themselves makes the distinction between withholding the truth and lying quite fuzzy.

Richard Wurmbrand, on the other hand, has taken the most forthright stance in favor of smuggling, regularly protesting about the niggling on ethical fine points. To such a person he offers his own brand of logic: "If deceit is wrong, to use a photograph smuggled out through deceit would be wrong too in this case."[44] Wurmbrand's own ethic is expressed in the following sentence: "To keep my own person 'unstained' and not to 'smuggle' Bibles does not apply to this case when a whole people remain

otherwise without the knowledge of Christ."[45] Because the Soviet authorities prevent their own people from having access to the Bible, "they
oblige me to smuggle. The sin is theirs."[46]

Generally speaking, there are very few mission organizations prepared
to follow a policy of complete openness; they feel it is not practicable. In the
end the debate over the ethics of smuggling boils down to the clash
between American pragmatism and a New Testament ethic that proclaims:
"We do not act with deceit" (2 Cor. 4:2, GNB).

The debate about smuggling has pushed into the background an issue
which is at present more vital. How are the existing Bibles distributed? In
the Soviet Union, as elsewhere, the evangelicals have received a dispropor-
tionate number of Bibles. That is understandable, given their biblicism, but
it is also due to the fact that the evangelically oriented East European
missions have been partisan. That, too, is understandable, but a rethinking
of the policy seems called for. Missions claim to lack contact with non-evan-
gelicals but that can be rectified with effort. Broader distribution would also
be achieved if there would be less reliance on linguistically limited couriers
who simply follow a drop-and-run technique, overload their handful of East
European contacts with unwanted Bibles, and do not share in planned distribution.

2. *Dependency.* It has become customary for Western Christians to
bring presents when they visit Eastern Europe. Besides Bibles, this may include small trinkets, cassette recordings, or even tape recorders. Russian
Christians have discovered that a foreign friend can help them to be better
dressed and to enjoy other simple pleasures which are denied to other Soviet citizens who have no foreign contacts. Some sensitive persons on both
sides have begun to wonder whether this is the best way to build relationships. Perhaps it is at least less demeaning than one occasion where an
East European missionary had the address of only one contact who turned
out to be an 80-year-old man sick in bed. But in spite of this, the courier
stuffed $10,000 in local bills under the man's mattress when the rest of the
family momentarily left the room, and by means of sign language tried to
communicate it was a gift from America. The missionary was able to report
that $10,000 had been given to needy Christians behind the Iron Curtain![47]

Such incidents, which are embarrassingly numerous, can be
eliminated by improving the quality of the missionary, but there is a much
more basic problem in the relationship with East European missions to the
Soviet Union. Those missions that are supporting needy pastors financially

usually send the contribution to the individual directly. Sometimes such an individual is in conflict with his own church union because the latter is afraid to stand up to state authorities. In the Soviet Union such an individual can choose between competing unions, either AUCECB or CCECB. But since he can get highly desired Western money from his mission supporters directly, the pastor can afford to ignore the church union and proceed to build his own independent church. That was identified as mistaken mission policy when applied to Africa or India. Now one expects that mission agencies will strive to cooperate with the local church, will consult together on policy so that in the end organized indigenous churches independent of the mother mission would emerge.

A mission such as *Licht im Osten* or Slavic Gospel Association has consciously restricted its goals, seeing itself as facilitator and resource for mission work done by Soviet Christians themselves. Although many other missions claim similar goals, the working policies of both Underground Evangelism and the Wurmbrand mission fit the image of 19th-century mission imperialism.

3. *Leadership Responsibility.* Back in 1945 the editors of *Bratskii Vestnik* acknowledged that they had been unable to establish communication with many of the churches. That has improved since then, but in comparison with the West, Soviet evangelical congregations are quite isolated. The central leadership has not visited every church nor apparently does *Bratskii Vestnik* manage to visit every church. Even so, a guest sermon once a year or eighty pages of religious reading material every second month is rather minimal outside stimulation. The other source of external stimulation is religious radio broadcasting or the visits of foreigners (in the big cities).

During the past five years there has been growing awareness of the fact that the radio broadcasts have been serving a leadership function for Soviet evangelicals. The striking feature in this awareness is the degree to which radio broadcasters themselves underestimated their influence.[48] Evangelical radio broadcasting to the Soviet Union consists primarily of evangelistic preaching and a teaching of those doctrines that can easily be taught on an interdenominational basis. Most radio preachers have avoided the subject of ecclesiology in order not to sound denominational. And yet the most prominent problem among Soviet evangelicals is their argumentation on what it means to be the church. Few of them would like a radio preacher to give them specific advice on whether to join the AUCECB or CCECB, but most of them would appreciate hearing factual presentations on the nature of the conflict as seen from an outside perspective. Even more, Soviet evangelicals have been asking for more information about church history, church doctrine, conflict resolution from a Christian perspective, and a host of other topics where they sense a vacuum. In short, they are expecting radio broadcasters to exercise responsible leadership which means that the quality of radio speakers must be high. Most radio preachers demonstrate great dedication and self-sacrifice but the majority of them are primarily evangelists. There is a search underway for more diversified talent.

Even on the subject of radio evangelism, there has been considerable criticism. Soviet listeners complain that they find a typical evangelical radio sermon incomprehensible because of the heavy reliance on religious clichés. Others are urging a more conscious audience selection. For example, program content and style would be different a) for believers, b) for those persons who were seeking faith, or c) for those who need something to stop them in their tracks and start them thinking.

Aside from the creativity demanded from such diversified programming, such changed programming involves a further problem. The standard image of a Soviet evangelical is someone who likes gospel songs or hymns, observes a sober dress code, and is not culturally hip. Would religious folk music or pop music or a program reviewing the arts from a Christian perspective be an embarrassment to Soviet evangelicals? Would converts from such programs, responding to such images, fit into a local evangelical congregation? Whether these broadcasters will exercise their *de facto* leadership sensitively remains a question.

4. *Political Attitudes.* The Richard Wurmbrand mission is an anticommunist mission. It is as much committed to the overthrow of communism as to helping believers in communist societies. In Richard Wurmbrand's world-view, a Christian must oppose communism, which logically means that Soviet Christians must be anti-communist, perhaps also unpatriotic. Brother Andrew is not as outspokenly political in his rhetoric, but he constantly emphasizes that there is an intense spiritual struggle going on between the spiritual forces of light and darkness, with communism being the force of darkness.[49] The Wurmbrand position confirms the charges Soviet writers such as Belov and Shilkin make that religion is the servant of reactionary capitalism.

In Wurmbrand's world-view, genuine Christians in the Soviet Union can only be those who are suffering. Those who are not apparently suffering such as the AUCECB leadership must obviously be tools of the political police. Wurmbrand is not particularly concerned if his public pronouncements will result in increased pressure on Soviet Christians. That, after all, gives them an opportunity to witness to their faith.[50]

5. *Fund-Raising and Image-Building in the West.* At present there is intense competition between East European organizations as well as competition with faith missions generally for the financial donations from Western Christians. It is a market situation, where the organization which can package its wares most attractively receives the most money. Thus there is an in-built motivation to highlight persecution in the Soviet Union and to dramatize the way the mission is helping. As a general rule, the less a mission publicizes its program and achievements, the more effective its work will be in the long run. That is one problem where a relationship of trust between organization and its constituency of supporters would be very helpful.

The other problem is the black-and-white image that has developed about life in the Soviet Union. Wurmbrand in particular insists that in a battle situation one can have only friends and enemies and therefore one plays into the enemy's hands if one acknowledges complex nuances, draws attention to gray areas. This mentality therefore enables him to falsify data in order to make his point come across more strongly. After all, the communists also falsify the data.

The reason why I am relying so heavily on Wurmbrand for illustrative material is that his writings are predominant in the religious bookstores of America and Europe, which means that the majority of concerned Christians have formed their image of Christians in the Soviet Union through his influence and distortions. Courageous bookstore owners could counter this by giving the more balanced and responsible literature greater prominence on their shelves even if this reduces sales volume.

A further disturbing feature is the Wurmbrand tendency to dismiss all criticism as communist provocation. Regularly his journal prints abusive remarks about other churchmen who have criticized him. Paul Hanson, European Secretary of the Lutheran World Federation, who advised Christians against supporting the mission smugglers, was threatened with slander charges. Robert Denny of the Baptist World Alliance was described as a "church leader unstable in faith." Billy Graham was attacked for claiming full religious freedom in Poland, which is not exactly what Graham said.[51]

6. *Scandal.* Without question, what has brought East European missions into disrepute generally has been their scandalous behavior to each other. Not all the missions charge their competitors with personal aggrandizement, with being duped by the communists, or simply engaging in personal slander. But the conflicts between Underground Evangelism and a number of workers who left that mission to found competing agencies, especially Richard Wurmbrand and Haralan Popov, have circulated widely enough to damage the reputation of other missions.[52] This is most unfortunate. In March 1977 Underground Evangelism and Jesus to the Communist World (Wurmbrand) became involved in a bitter, multi-million-dollar defamation suit.[53]

In September 1976 Richard Wurmbrand's son Michael (age 40), who became general director of the mission, traveled to Switzerland in order to speak to Underground Evangelism Board chairman Hans-Jurg Stückelberger in order to warn him of serious developments within the Underground Evangelism (UE) organization that Wurmbrand felt threatened the work of all missions in Eastern Europe. Michael Wurmbrand informed Stückelberger about information that he had received that UE president L. Joe Bass and his associate Stefan Bankov had taken part in sex orgies; that Bass had raped Bankov's teenage daughter, Filka, and had threatened to import a sharpshooter from Europe to kill her if she did not remain quiet; that Bankov's claims that pastoral work in Bulgaria were falsified; and that Bankov had referred to Joe Bass as a gangster and mafioso. As a result, Bass and Bankov filed defamation suits, seeking undetermined compensatory damages, plus $1.5 million in punitive damages. Richard Wurmbrand, who had retired as general director earlier (but he still dominates the content of the journal), also resigned from the board of his mission, arguing that Christians should not go to court with each other. Michael Wurmbrand and the mission board, however, decided to file a counter-suit in November 1977, also alleging defamation and asking for $4 million in damages.

Actually, responding to criticism by threatening court action had already become established procedure but this time the stakes were higher. In September 1978 Bass published a very striking 14-page booklet entitled "Conspiracy" which reported a "Plan to Destroy Underground Evangelism . . . Involving an Agency of Communist Bulgaria, Its Moscow-Trained Officials and Others." On the basis of a scrap of paper containing some scrawlings by Michael Wurmbrand, Bass developed a conspiracy theory involving a variety of Bulgarian Orthodox officials, some of whom had been trained in Moscow. These, he said, were cooperating with several Bulgarian evangelicals living in California, including Michael Wurmbrand as chief tool of the communists. As Robert Kelly, a UE executive, explained in a cover letter, their organization regretted the necessity of publishing this material, but: "We trust you will recognize, however, that the facts so clearly outlined in these documents would never, and could never, have been revealed except by availing ourselves of the fair and impartial procedures of our American judicial system." Among other things, the documentation claimed that key witnesses, including Filka Bankov, had been brainwashed by Michael Wurmbrand, and at a subsequent legal deposition, Filka Bankov reversed much of her testimony.

Not to be outdone, Michael and Richard Wurmbrand responded in December 1978 with a 78-page booklet entitled "The Evidence Against Joe Bass, Stefan Bankov and Underground Evangelism." On page one was a photocopy of Joe Bass's arrest record of 1959.[54] This book provided a résumé of witnesses' depositions plus photocopies of major depositions including a love letter from David Hathaway to Mrs. Lois Bass, wife of Joe Bass, written on Christian Prisoners Release International stationery, and the transcript of an interview with Filka Bankov by a California journalist. The latter two were filled with salacious tidbits. The booklet also contained photocopies of UE publications, especially photographs, to demonstrate regular falsification of information and the curious tendency to black out the faces of some individuals leading underground activity in order to protect their identity, having printed the full face a month previously. UE responded with its own evidence to show that Wurmbrand printed pictures such as a photo of children in a communist prison which turned out to be a prize photo in a Dutch swimming contest. In January 1979 Bass released "Conspiracy Part II."

As the writer for *Christianity Today* concluded: "Despite their volume, however, the conflicting accounts generate more questions than answers." What the massive documentation has also demonstrated is that regardless whether the specific charges against UE are proven, it is evident that both missions have systematically engaged in dishonest practices, and in their conduct of the case fail to demonstrate the qualities one would expect of Christian leaders who together were responsible for dispensing $13.3 million in 1977.

The final installment to the scandal story was supposed to be a statement released by Underground Evangelism on July 3, 1979, announcing an out-of-court settlement. Both sides had signed a statement declaring their mutual accusations to be "groundless."[55] Major newspapers carried the announcement, since they had started covering the story months earlier, and it sounded as if "these men can now continue their work for Christ unhampered," to quote the UE International Committee statement.

That was not to be the end. Underground Evangelism in circulating the announcement of settlement, added a brief statement that "Mihai Wurmbrand broke the agreement by making oral statements to a religious publication." UE therefore felt free to publish the signed "Acknowledgment" and added a lengthy commentary. In this they claimed that Wurmbrand had acknowledged each of a detailed list of twelve charges "to be untrue," whereas UE had only acknowledged as untrue four items, explaining that since the Wurmbrands had dropped their charges against the "Conspiracy" report and "The Record of Richard Wurmbrand" earlier, the content of these documents had not been disavowed by UE. In response, the International Committee of Jesus to the Communist World issued its own disclaimer on August 22, 1979. Richard Wurmbrand, they said, acted independently without the approval of the board who opposed the terms of settlement.[56] The letter argued that "the question of guilt would have been settled by the voluminous evidence presented to the court by witnesses." An attached personal statement from Richard Wurmbrand explained why the settlement became possible but failed to put the questions to rest. Wurmbrand stated:

> I had declared before the judge that as Christ has taken upon Himself all my sins and declared me just, so I am ready to take upon myself the responsibility of all real or alleged sins which form the contents of this lawsuit, so that peace shall be restored. . . . Let everyone be deemed innocent and every accusatory statement from either side be deemed untrue, and let all the guilt be mine.[57]

The letter went on to indicate that UE had not kept the agreement (hence this letter), noted various communist slanders against his own person, and concluded: "We have Christ on our side and we invite all Christian brethren of like convictions to join us."

Looking at the record, such an invitation remains virtually impossible to accept for Christians who take ethics seriously. The court settlement may help to restore the flow of donations from well-meaning Christians, but it is difficult to see why the damaging "evidence" against both sides which neither side has really withdrawn in the end should now be dismissed as irrelevant. If both sides now acknowledge they were liars before, how can one decide that the joint "Acknowledgement" belongs to the category of truth or must that word also be enclosed in quotation marks? Or are the post-settlement statements from each side the truth? Aside from dismissing the expensive lawsuit, what has changed? Have their mission policies changed? Are not the same discredited leaders still in office? Does not the advice from a growing number of church leaders at the height of the scandal to place a moratorium on giving to either mission still apply?

Human Rights and the Right to Believe

Although the Reform Baptist movement began earlier than the human rights movement, participants in both soon came to be called dissidents, and in addition to human rights, people began speaking about "the right to believe".[58] Generally in Christian theology, the emphasis is not on rights but on duties.[59] The United Nations Declaration of Human Rights did include religious freedom. Freedom of belief was one of Roosevelt's Four Freedoms and has been accepted in several international documents which the Soviet Union also signed.

When the Russian *Samizdat* journal, *Chronicle of Current Events*, began circulating, it regularly included information about religious dissidents, including Baptists.[60] Initially it was only Boris Zdorovets who had developed any personal links with the human rights movement, having become acquainted with dissidents in prison.[61] More recently a handful of Soviet evangelicals have become involved in the human rights movement, notably Peter Vins, son of Georgi.

The most famous Soviet dissident, the physicist Andrei Sakharov, is not a believer, but he has shown himself more non-partisan than many others in taking up the cause of any individual who is experiencing injustice. In 1976 the so-called Sakharov Hearings were held in Copenhagen, Denmark. These were organized by Dansk Europamission, and a lot of recent immigrants, including believers, testified. The hearings were published subsequently; further hearings were attempted in other cities.[62]

Following the signing of the Helsinki Agreement in August 1975, monitoring committees were established in many countries, including the Soviet Union. The Helsinki Monitoring Committee in the Soviet Union was broken up rather viciously by Soviet authorities and Iurii Orlov and Anatoli Shcharanski received lengthy prison sentences. Regional committees also developed, and young Peter Vins was one of the Baptists who joined the Ukrainian committee. Fellow Baptists criticized him for engaging in what they regarded to be political action, but he persisted until he was arrested and given a one-year prison sentence under the anti-parasite laws. In spite of the arrests, by December 10, 1979, there were five Helsinki Monitoring Groups in the Soviet Union (Moscow, Ukraine, Lithuania, Armenia, and Georgia). Two allied groups were formed in Moscow, one focused on the use of psychiatry for political purposes and the other was called the Christian Committee to Defend the Rights of Believers. Still other groups were formed to defend the rights of invalids, of Reform Adventists, and of Roman Catholics. A total of 92 persons were active in these groups, of which 33 are in prison or exile. Further arrests continued in 1980.[63]

When Georgi Vins was interviewed following his arrival in America, he confirmed the testimony of many other prisoners when he stated that "all Western support—supplying information, demonstrations, and prayer—helps a great deal . . . whenever there was support action in the West, I was treated better by warders and prison administrators. When there was no support, conditions immediately became worse."[64] Vins argued for "peaceful demonstrations arising out of Christian principles" and opposed violence.

The AUCECB has carefully dissociated itself from the human rights movement, but in the post-Helsinki period Moscow leaders have not only publicly affirmed the Helsinki Agreement but have also expressed the hope this will lead to improved conditions for their members. Alexei Bychkov has not only referred repeatedly to the guarantee of religious freedom in this agreement as well as in the constitution, he has also drawn attention to the hoped for benefits from the "man and the law" program. In recent years Soviet authorities have been fostering a greater emphasis on legality, have published numerous pamphlets on this theme, and have also shown some willingness to punish violations. Bychkov, for example, cited several instances where local abuses by state authorities were corrected once the union had appealed to the central authorities. Russia and the Soviet Union have never had a strong legal tradition as is true in Germany or England, and it is unlikely that a sense of legality will develop quickly.[65]

Conclusion: What Has Been Achieved?

It is difficult to escape the fact that the Underground Evangelism-Wurmbrand scandal plus earlier lesser scandals have given the missions a bad reputation. It would be most unjust to dismiss all East European missions as dishonest. The independent faith missions struggle with inherent weaknesses that are less apparent in the denominational agencies which are more subject to open reporting, but the East European missions are a vital factor in the Soviet evangelical scene.

Above all, through their efforts large numbers of Bibles and other Christian literature have become available in the Soviet Union and the Bible hunger has eased noticeably. To what extent their financial contribution to individual believers has been helpful and to what extent this has created harmful dependency relationships remains to be seen. There is some evidence that it has contributed to, rather than hindered, the growing factionalism in Reform Baptist ranks. But that observation must also be seen in the perspective that the financial and moral support of the East European missions has provided a sense of international Christian solidarity which the CCECB was unable to find in the BWA.

Major frontier areas for developing mission programming are in the area of radio broadcasting and literature production. Without question, Soviet evangelicals appreciate present programming very much. Their only criticism, when asked, is that they might have more programming, perhaps at more suitable hours and with less jamming. Whereas the BBC and Voice of America were jammed only selectively following the Helsinki Agreement, this was not true of the religious radio stations which continued to be jammed regularly. Some mission societies have introduced creative programming. Brother Dmitrii from FEBC, for example, has been active for many years preparing children and youth programs, interviews, science programs, etc. Radio programs produced by Slavic Gospel Association are also becoming more diversified.

The attempt at conducting mission on the basis of principles conforming to modern missiological thinking is limited primarily to the older, more established missions which are smaller, as well as to the denominational agencies. Generally speaking, however, criticisms given above call for a radical overhaul of present mission activities in the direction of greater mutuality and responsibility and less clamoring for public credit. Such changes will very likely only take place once the goose (gullible Western Christians) stop laying the golden egg. What is needed is an informed Western supporting constituency that has recognized the need for more complexity in describing, understanding, and helping Soviet churches. Western Christians also need to be much more discriminating in selecting missions and specific projects worthy of their support. It is not merely a question of giving money to the agency promising the most fool-proof channel for bringing Bibles to Russia, but rather to support and become involved with those who have demonstrated the appropriate degree of responsibility in exercising a shared leadership function among Soviet evangelicals.[66]

Notes to Chapter 14

1. David Hathaway, *Czechmate* (London: Lakeland, 1974). Cf. Hans Kristian with Dave Hunt, *Mission Possible* (London: Hodder and Stoughton, 1975); Andre Morea, *The Book They Couldn't Ban* (London, Lakeland, 1976).

2. Walter Sawatsky, "Bible Work in Eastern Europe," *RCL* III, 3, pp. 4-10; III, 4, pp. 4-14; and Ole van Luyn, "Bible Work in Eastern Europe," United Bible Societies *Background Paper*, September 1977.

3. A total of 380,000 have been printed since the war, 25,000 Russian Bibles and 8,000 German Bibles were imported. Cf. *Die Bibel in Osteuropa* Evangelischen Bibelwerk Informationssekretariat, Stuttgart, April 1979.

4. A. Belov and A. Shilkin, *Diversiia bez dinamita* (Moscow: Politizdat, 2nd ed. 1976), pp. 183.

5. A. Sediulin, *Zakondatel'stvo o religioznykh kul'takh* (Moscow: Iuridicheskaia literatura, 1974) p. 4.

6. *Ibid.*, p. 5.

7. N. A. Koval'skii, *Religioznye organizatsii i problemy evropeiskoi bezopastnosti i sotrudnichestva* (Moscow: Znanie 1/77), pp. 6f, 27-31.

8. Alfred Friendly, "Cold War to Cold Peace," *Newsweek*, July 21, 1975, p. 6. Cf. August 11, 1975, pp. 6-14.

9. Aside from Belov and Shilkin's book issued in two editions (1974 and 1976), they also wrote the following brochures: *Ideologicheskie diversii imperializma i religiia* (1970), *Religiia v SSSR i burzhuaznye fal'sifikatory* (1970), *Religiia v sovremennoi ideologicheskoi bor'be* (1971). See also *Izvestiia*, March 14, 1979.

10. In addition to the journal *Russia Cristiana* they produced a pictorial on *Samizdat* (Milano, Russia Cristiana, 1974), pp. 207 printed in German as *Samizdat: Chronik eines neuen Lebens in der Sowjetunion* (Koblenz: Pro Fratribus, 1977), pp. 278. The latter includes more recent materials.

11. Paul Anderson, "Reflections on Religion in Russia, 1917-1967" Marshall, ed. *Aspects of Religion*, pp. 11-33.

12. *Research Materials* is available at Keston College.

13. Fletcher wrote: *A Study in Survival: The Church in Russia 1927-1943* (1965); *Nikolai: Portrait of a Dilemma* (1968); *The Russian Orthodox Church Underground 1917-1970* (1973); Fletcher and Stover, eds., *Religion and the Search for New Ideals in the USSR* (1967); Fletcher and Max Hayward, eds., *Religion and the Soviet State: A Dilemma of Power* (1969).

14. *Protestantism in Russia* (Grand Rapids: Wm. B. Eerdmans, 1977); *The Russians and the World Council of Churches* (Belfast: Christian Journals Ltd., 1978).

15. For this early history see the excellent chapter in Kahle, p. 90f.

16. *Dein Reich Komme* Sondernummer, March 1977. Cf. Kahle, p. 94.

17. Kahle, pp. 275-320.

18. Norman B. Rohrer and Peter Deyneka, Jr., *Peter Dynamite: "Twice-Born" Russian* (Grand Rapids: Baker Book House, 1975).

19. *God's Smuggler* by Brother Andrew with John and Elizabeth Sherrill (London: Hodder and Stoughton, 1967).

20. Simon, *Church, State & Opposition*, p. 179. The Norwegian Jewish Mission and the Jewish-Christian Alliance paid $10,000 in ransom money. Cf. Richard Wurmbrand *Tortured for Christ*, p. 48; Mary Drewery, *Richard Wurmbrand: The Man Who Came Back* (London: Hodder and Stoughton, 1974) pp. 118-119.

21. *Diversiia*, p. 8.

22. See my "Bible Work . . . ," pp. 10 & 14.

23. *On the Frontline*, Louisville, Kentucky. Don Kyer is the director.

24. David Benson, *Miracle in Moscow* (Santa Barbara, CA: Miracle Publications Inc. 1973).

25. *Voice of the Martyrs.*

26. *Underground Evangelism.*

27. They are: L. Joe Bass (President), Dr. Gunter Lange (Vice-president), Hayes Lloyd (Director UE New Zealand), Hans-Jurg Stückelberger (Chairman of UE board, Switzerland), Dr. Curtis Nims (USA), W. A. Temlett (Director UE South Africa and Rhodesia). (*Christus dem Osten* März 1980; cf. *This is UE* 1977.)

28. For example, Richard Wurmbrand, Haralan Popov, Ladin Popov.

29. For example, Jim Dimov, Underground Christian Missions, Inc.; Gene Neill, The Voice of Triumph.

30. *This is UE*, 1977. The staff in Europe numbers 150.

31. Begun in 1974 it is based in Wheaton, Ill., producing the publication *Sparks*.

32. UE Condensed World Wide Financial Statement, March 31, 1977. The income has grown dramatically from 1.7 million dollars in 1971 to 3.1 million in 1972, and 6.6 million in 1976. Figures for 1978 and 1979 were not available at the time of writing. Administration and fund-raising costs hovered around 30 to 35 percent. In 1977 UE increased its net worth by $792,958 to a total net worth of $3,795,909. It therefore needs to find more programs to spend its growing surplus.

33. *Voice of the Martyrs*, 11/78. Income in 1975 was 4.1 million; in 1976 it was 5.2 million with 38 percent and 35 percent respectively spent on administration, postage, freight, and publicity.

34. February 14, 1979.

35. E.g., Orlando E. Costas, *The Church and its Mission: A Shattering Critique from the Third World* (Wheaton: Tyndale House, 1974).

36. UBS *Background Paper*, September 1977.

37. *BV*, 1/75, p. 38.

38. *Newsline West*, June 1978. This is a more factual news service for UE branches.

39. *EBPS*, December 4, 1978.

40. *The Ethics of Smuggling* (Wheaton: Tyndale House, 1974), p. 17.

41. *Ibid.*, p. 42.

42. *Ibid.*, p. 43.

43. *Ibid.*, p. 39.

44. "Are Bible Smugglers Deceivers?" 1974 Wurmbrand pamphlet.

45. *Ibid.*

46. *Ibid.*

47. A number of missions, as in this case, purchase East European currency on the black market and smuggle restricted currency. This was strongly criticized by Paul Hanson of the Lutheran World Federation (*EPS*, May 18, 1978).

48. Jane Ellis, "Religious Broadcasting into the Soviet Union," *RCL*, III, 4-5, 1975, pp. 43-48. This was a provisional study that has led to a number of conferences on religious broadcasting. My analysis is based on papers from such conferences.

49. See his recent *Battle for Africa* (Fleming H. Revell Co., 1978).

50. Simon, pp. 180-84.

51. *Voice of the Martyrs*, 1, 2, and 3 for 1979.

52. UE, for example, circulated rather widely a 200-page documentation against Wurmbrand.

53. "West Coast Bible Smugglers: Less Cloak and More Dagger," *Christianity Today*, March 2, 1979, pp. 50-52. The most thorough and balanced coverage of the

story. I am also using documentation supplied by both missions and other personal knowledge of the case.

54. The arrest concerned taking money under false pretenses. Bass agreed to make restitution and the charges were dropped.

55. The joint statement was signed on June 27, 1979, by Myrus Knutson for Jesus to the Communist World, Richard Wurmbrand, Mihai Wurmbrand, L. Joe Bass, Stefan Bankov, and Curtis R. Nims, the latter signing for Underground Evangelism, USA.

56. A photocopy of the "Acknowledgement" dated the following day (June 28, 1979) shows that all six men also signed this statement, which appears to conflict with the August 22, 1979 disclaimer by Hans Martin Braun, General Secretary of the International Committee of the Wurmbrand Mission.

57. The Wurmbrand statement was dated August 6, 1979.

58. This is the title of a Keston College quarterly distributed to contributors.

59. Gustav Wingren, "Human Rights: A Theological Analysis," *Ecumenical Review* XXVII, 2, 1975. "The one who is active, who provides rights, is always God. . . . Nowhere in the Bible do we find references to 'rights' of a personal kind, rights which the individual can demand of society" (p. 124). See also related articles by Burgess Carr, David Jenkins, Julie Barriero, Edward Rogers, and Victoria M. Chandran in the same issue.

60. Available in Russian or English from Khronika Press, New York.

61. *KNS*, July 15, 1976.

62. Marta Harasowska and Orest Olhovych, eds., *The International Sakharov Hearing* (Baltimore-Toronto: Smoloskyp Publishers, 1977).

63. For a summary see G2W 11/78, *passim:* materials from the Commission on Security and Cooperation in Europe (Washington, D.C.) including fact sheets and *Profiles: The Helsinki Monitors* (December 10, 1979).

64. *KNS*, May 2, 1979. Peter Vins, in America since June 1979, has not committed himself to membership in the Baptist church.

65. John S. Reshetar, Jr., "The Search for Law in Soviet Legality," *Problems of Communism* (July-August 1979), pp. 61-64.

66. Mennonite agencies have circulated a helpful pamphlet giving guidelines on how to "Give from the Heart with the Head."

When is the best moment for the church? Right now. The church is powerful when she's on the cross, when she's persecuted. When she has a "guardian," she gets weak.

It's not by accident that I've become daring. The time has come for *doing*. The fields are white for harvest. We need workers.

—*Dmitrii Dudko*

15 Beyond Survival: New Frontiers After 1974

Alexei Bychkov reported in May 1978 that approximately 100,000 persons had been baptized into their union since 1963. That meant an average of 7,150 baptisms per year for a growth rate of 2.4 percent.[1] Total registered membership for the AUCECB is probably around 350,000, the official claim of 565,000 appears to be overstated.[2] Since there were also losses through death, these statistics do point to the fact that a new generation of Russian evangelicals has come to birth. As Soviet sociologist Lialina also acknowledged, the crisis of aging, of death by attrition, had been surmounted.[3]

If Soviet policy toward religion changed after 1974, the major Soviet evangelical union had also changed. CCECB leaders soon after began reprinting their first *Samizdat* documents in order to remind their young people of the reasons for the split. They did so because they felt that fundamentally the situation had not changed, that the AUCECB was still continuing its pact with the world. But objectively speaking, much had changed. Few of the leaders after 1974 were personally tainted by the action of issuing the letter of instruction in 1960. After the 1974 Congress of the AUCECB, there emerged a clear sense of progress. There was a new optimism, and AUCECB leaders told foreign visitors they had never had it so good.

Ernest Payne observed with considerable insight that virtually throughout its entire history, the Russian evangelical movement had been struggling for survival and had been unable to think and plan deliberately for its goals.[4] Now the AUCECB appeared to be moving beyond the survival phase. That raised worrisome questions. Where would the new freedoms lead them? Was the respite from state pressure only temporary? Would their leaders handle the situation wisely or would they blunder? Should they be aggressive or cautious? This was the setting when Alexei Bychkov reported to the church delegates.

The 41st Congress (1974)

It was Alexei Bychkov's first report to delegates from all the churches on the work accomplished during the previous five years. The impression he would make could determine the degree to which delegates would approve his reelection for a full term. He was speaking before 483 voting delegates, approximately 100 guests, and 20 visitors from abroad, 14 of them from non-socialist countries.[5] Most of the foreign visitors were Baptist World Alliance leaders but there were also two Mennonites and one Evangelical Christian present.[6] Once again, as at earlier congresses, the credentials committee reported that seven supporters of the CCECB were attending as guests. Six others (including key members of the CCECB such as I. Ia. Antonov) applied for delegate status but were refused on the grounds that they should have been elected at one of the 59 regional congresses where the All-Union delegates had been elected. Credentials committee chairman S. P. Fadiukhin also reported to the gathered delegates that the CCECB had attempted a demonstration in the street, a claim that later proved to be unfounded. In any case, the Congress was declared legitimately empowered to proceed and Bychkov began a 4½-hour report.[7]

The lengthy report was as fascinating as was the entire Congress, even though the hard wooden benches and the cramped quarters demanded physical endurance for visitors and delegates alike. At 59 regional congresses "Theses from the AUCECB Report" had been discussed by a total of 4,000 delegates, 700 of whom had expressed their personal opinions. The theses had been approved, but delegates had requested more statistical data, wanted more attention drawn to the activities of the senior presbyters, asked for a historical survey of the multinational brotherhood, wanted more details on the life of local churches, wanted to talk about choral singing, and hoped to discuss the possibility and necessity of fellowship with Christians from other confessions. Generally speaking, Bychkov had organized his report around these questions, indicating a sincere desire to respond to delegates' concerns.

General Secretary Bychkov's Report

As one of the best traveled and best informed of their leaders, Alexei Bychkov started with a survey of major events in the Christian world. He drew attention to the fact of greater openness in the Christian world, including some of the optimistic implications of Vatican II. Bychkov summarized the major discussions on the theme "Salvation Today" conducted by the WCC at Bangkok in 1972. Here he affirmed the AUCECB position that salvation comes only through the new birth in Christ and means to follow Christ. He also drew attention to the new charismatic movement which one might have expected he would treat with warmth, considering their own reputation for Pietist spirituality, but he warned against the charismatic's emphasis on spiritual gifts. The Pentecostals in the union were reminded that their agreement in 1945 permitted no glossalalia in the church. Delegates listened with great interest, many taking copious notes.

Bychkov then moved into his actual report, focusing on seven different aspects of their activities. The first aspect was the Moscow links to the local churches. A total of 935 senior presbyters and presbyters had visited the AUCECB and many other persons visited their offices daily. They had also sent the leading brethren to visit more of the churches. Presidium members resident in Moscow had made 175 trips visiting 640 churches. But Bychkov still granted that believers had a legitimate complaint that they were being visited rarely. In fact, "in many churches brothers from the AUCECB have never yet visited."[8]

By summarizing the various meetings of the AUCECB plenum, he quickly indicated what had been their major concerns. In December 1970 the plenum had focused on unity. A year later the primary issue had been a leadership change occasioned by the death of Alexander Karev and S. T. Timchenko. At meetings in July 1972 and December 1973 the plenum listened to numerous papers on the subject of expanding the role of the senior presbyters and presbyters in the spiritual education of church members. By December 1973 the plenum had begun to discuss the issue of unity with the Pentecostals again. A year later they started preparations for the present congress and dispatched special appeals to all Pentecostals, Mennonite Brethren, and CCECB supporters to take part in the preparation and conduct of the regional congresses. Bychkov also reported that the presidium had met separately with Pentecostals and with Mennonites in attempts to improve relations with them.[9]

Bychkov now gave detailed statistics about the Bible correspondence course which after a six-year period had resulted in two graduating classes totaling 179 persons. The presidium was trying to improve the teaching materials and to expand the courses to include comparative theology and Christian ethics. Bychkov also emphasized that the entrance requirements would be stiffer, requiring higher general educational achievement and also requiring a readiness to serve in places determined by the AUCECB.

Publication achievements were still not very substantial, but Bychkov was able to report in triumph that they had printed and, at the opening of the congress, had received 20,000 copies of the New Testament with Psalms. Some German Bibles had also been sent from the DDR and there was an agreement in principle, he claimed, to print the Bible in German, plus a German songbook. *Bratskii Vestnik* had increased its circulation by 1,000 copies, that is, they were now printing 6,000 copies. Bychkov went on to list a number of other publications that were ready for printing, including a pictorial history and a memoir by Alexander Karev. Since the regional congresses had reported many requests for more articles in *Bratskii Vestnik* about unity which had greater theological depth, he promised they would try to comply. He also promised articles discussing differences of opinion on the question of baptism by the Holy Spirit and articles giving historical surveys of their brotherhood.

It was apparent that Bychkov had a personal interest in producing a history of the AUCECB. He devoted lengthy sections to historical anecdotes about their churches in Moldavia, in Latvia and elsewhere. They were beginning to expand their archives and had received the memoirs of V. M. Kovel'kov, Iu. S. Grachev and S. P. Fadiukhin.[10] They had also obtained the personal archives of Jacob Zhidkov, A. V. Pavlov, and Alexander Karev. In a similar historical vein Bychkov reported that in two years' time they would be celebrating the hundredth jubilee of the publication of the Russian Bible. There was presently a project underway including Baptist pastor Oswald Tiark to translate the Bible into modern Estonian. There was an especially great need to translate the Bible into modern Georgian, since they were using a translation from the 12th century. With regret he also reported that "our Russian brotherhood so far does not have theologians who know the ancient languages."[11] They were seriously considering preparing persons who would be able to study the Old and New Testaments from original sources in order for them to make a contribution to a new translation of the Bible into modern Russian that was being attempted in Leningrad.[12] Here Bychkov for the first time drew attention to the United Bible Societies, noting their emphasis on legality and distinguishing them from the work of people like Richard Wurmbrand, Joe Bass, and Haralan Popov.

Bychkov then proceeded to list many of their international activities, beginning by describing their international department briefly. Generally speaking, they had good relations with the president and general secretary of the Baptist World Alliance, although at times some delegates introduced proposals which they did not approve. Bychkov noted that their many visits abroad and the official guests to their country "involve much work, responsibility and tension, but they are necessary for the sake of the growth of mutual understanding and unity between Christians and nations."[13] He added that objective foreign religious workers "correctly evaluate the life and service of our churches."[14] Such workers recognized that:

> One must say that socialism brought material blessings to a great many people in Eastern Europe.... They are happy to find themselves in their country as good patriots, and they strive to do all in their power to be true to their Christian faith and to their Lord and Savior.[15]

Those who did not correctly evaluate their life were individual religious figures who "do not like the socialist system."[16]

In the local churches there had been growth. Thirty thousand members had joined in the past five years. During the same period more than 50 congregations received registration, although 22 village congregations closed down because their older members died or moved. Urbanization was the major factor. But there were also new regions in Siberia and Kazakhstan, where congregations were newly established, but there was a shortage of church workers.

The report on unity was not very extensive, because there was little progress to report. Since 1969 they had appealed four times to the CCECB to resume discussions on reconciliation, but had received no replies. The CCECB continued to issue statements strongly attacking the AUCECB. An outside observer looking carefully at both sides could only conclude that the will for reconciliation was fading, both sides maintaining nonnegotiable conditions. Bychkov read the full text of a letter sent to M. T. Shaptala inviting the CCECB to participate in the preparation for the Congress and went on to state that on November 30 they had received a letter in reply which Bychkov felt unable to read because of its "unbrotherly style."[17] But he tried to answer the four-point CCECB objection to participation. To postpone the Congress as the CCECB suggested was no use, he said, as had already been demonstrated in 1969. But he could announce that in October 1974 the AUCECB Presidium had appealed to the Supreme Court of the USSR to show mercy and leniency towards believers on trial, and he claimed that senior presbyters were reporting that "many brethren were released."[18] To recognize the legality of the CCECB was, however, not within their competence, Bychkov said.

Delegates Want More

In a church setting with so many delegates and guests, genuine discussion would have been difficult in any case. What did follow consisted much more of set speeches; as usual the first ones were by key leaders such as the new Ukrainian senior presbyter, Jacob K. Dukhonchenko, who gave additional statistical information about church life in their regions. Of the 34 persons who managed to speak before time ran out, a significant number devoted themselves to short statistical surveys of church life in their area and to expressions of appreciation for the work of the AUCECB. All other speakers had a similar positive note, but they also attempted in varying degrees to offer constructive criticism. That came in the form of proposals which they knew could not be decided at the moment, but they hoped they could be achieved during the coming five-year period. These speeches could be summarized with the phrase: "Thank you for trying, but we want more."

They were thankful for the Bibles, but they wanted more. They wanted to see Bibles printed in Moldavian, Estonian, Ukrainian, German, and other languages. They were thankful for *Bratskii Vestnik*, although some speakers reported that they scarcely ever saw it, and they earnestly hoped that it would be possible to print more copies in the future. Seminars introduced in conjunction with the presbyter conferences were working well, many delegates reported, but they asked for more of these with broader participation. They were thankful, as Jacob Dukhonchenko from the Ukraine reported, for those who could participate in the correspondence course, but it would be better if more students could participate. Perhaps the most widely repeated request was for more attention to music. There should be more publications of choral materials. They asked for choral director seminars to be included in the seminar activity. They also asked for music courses as part of the correspondence course.

A great many delegates were still concerned about the problem of disunity. Some shared personal experiences of attempting reconciliation with Reform Baptists. Others described how they were attempting to maintain unity with the Pentecostals. The advice that came through repeatedly was that, for more unity, there should be more love.

Delegates voted by flashing their blue delegate cards in the air. But the opportunities to vote were primarily to express unanimous approval for the general secretary's report, for the brief financial report, and for the resolution summarizing the activity that came at the end.[19] There were no specific policy recommendations based on the "discussion" where they could vote. But they managed to vote after all. Each discussion speaker was granted seven minutes to speak. Most speakers were just getting warmed up at the end of this time when the chairman tapped a spoon against a glass of water. If delegates liked what the speaker said, they would shout to him to continue. But if they did not like what the speaker was saying, they would shout, "*Vse, Vse*" (that's all, that's all), until he had to stop. But then there was one closed session where the voting was direct and not necessarily unanimous.

Delegates Elect New President

Before the Congress started several observers remarked that the Moscow leadership was quite anxious about the elections. Seventy-six-year-old President Ilia G. Ivanov was in failing health and had indicated intentions to retire. That meant a new president. There was considerable criticism in conservative ranks of Bychkov—would a "dump Bychkov" movement succeed?

When the Congress started, individuals, apparently from the Moscow congregation, attempted to circulate a letter to all Congress delegates in order to influence the elections.[20] The letter included a list of "the most faithful and committed brethren," whom they proposed in place of "unworthy ministers." The letter proceeded to make highly personal attacks on leading persons in the AUCECB, and although the writers remained anonymous, they revealed some knowledge of the internal politics in the Moscow office. Not only were members of the international department sharply criticized, local staff were accused of personal enrichment in their position. From the writers' point of view, in God's house, "even the cloakroom attendant should be an exceptional person." The delegates paid no direct attention to this letter, but the resultant elections did reveal a further step toward electing a leadership that the membership could trust. An anonymous list of the new council which circulated subsequently had been checked with a plus or minus sign in front of each name to indicate how this critical group evaluated the results. Only six of the twenty-four persons elected received a minus sign.[21] These included the two Pentecostal representatives, so there may well have been denominational prejudice helping to determine the ratings.

Most informed observers considered the election results a fortunate compromise. Whereas many foreign observers had expected to see Michael Zhidkov become president, the more conservative Andrei Klimenko was elected, while Bychkov, who shared Zhidkov's orientation very closely, gained affirmation as general secretary. The new presidium did include four new persons who had all been members of the All-Union Council.[22] Therefore the new presidium was not that different from the old one, but from a longer perspective it was new. Only Arthur Mitskevich from the Old Guard remained. Over a space of two congresses and the emergency elections of 1971, a new leadership of younger men had emerged. In comparison to their fathers, who had been in prison and who remembered the pre-revolutionary days, the new leadership was accustomed to Soviet ways and likely to know how to proceed with considerable boldness.

Growing Pains as Decade Closes

At the end of the decade, 525 delegates gathered in Moscow (December 18-20, 1979) for their latest regular congress. The past five years had been years of growth, said Nikolai Kolesnikov, senior presbyter for Kazakhstan. Statistically speaking, there had been a net gain of only 10,968 since 1974, but 45,734 new members had joined. Of these, 34,154 had joined through baptism but unreported baptisms were higher. There had also been a significant increase in church registrations, 253 having been registered in the past decade. Most of these new registrations occurred after 1974 and represented a total membership of 9,393 persons.[23] Joining an ECB church was no easy matter, since a total of 8,790 persons had been excommunicated during the past decade, although approximately the same number of excommunicants had also been received back into full membership.[24]

But growth is also qualitative and for the AUCECB that too was not entirely painless. The atmosphere at the 1979 Congress mirrored this. The previous congress with foreign guests present had been a cautious attempt to conduct themselves openly, although the leaders managed things with a very firm hand. This time the delegates were in charge. Central Asian delegates objected to the speed with which Alexei Bychkov had rushed through the elections to congress commissions and in approving the rules of procedure. When informed of the discontent, Bychkov interrupted his report to allow delegates to voice their concerns. Sensing that the delegates were eager for long discussion periods, he skipped major parts of his speech in order to accommodate this wish. Other delegates appealed to the congress for solidarity and described in detail the problems they had experienced with local authorities who refused to register a church or stalled on building permits. And the leaders themselves spoke with a frankness about state imposed limitations that inspired confidence.

Alexei Bychkov had impressive achievements to report, even improved structural changes. In May 1979, at a special meeting of presbyters in the large sprawling Russian Federation (RSFSR), a special church administration for the RSFSR had been organized. They had elected a senior presbyter to head the entire region, three deputy senior presbyters and a five-member advisory council. Hereby, Bychkov explained, "Our brotherhood is enabled to care for the churches more efficiently, and the churches receive more spiritual help on questions of purity of evangelical teaching and spiritual nurture of the church members."[25] The new structure paralleled the decentralized arrangement which had been in effect for the Ukraine from the beginning except that the RSFSR was much more difficult to administer for geographic reasons. Bychkov also announced that the handful of churches in Lithuania had been subordinated under the Latvian administration so that there were now ten regional divisions for their union.[26] The subordination of oblast senior presbyters under such senior presbyters for large regions was also detailed in a revised constitution.

Perhaps an even more fundamental change that was happening gradually was the rejuvenation of the corps of preachers that Alexander Karev had called for. Since 1970 a total of 19 new senior presbyters, most of them Bible correspondence graduates, had been elected.[27] During the period 1970-77, 596 presbyters and 420 deacons had been elected or ordained. Only some of these had graduated from the Bible correspondence course, but at least more of the new local leaders had secondary education. By 1979 half of all the senior presbyters and their assistants had completed the Bible correspondence course.

Bychkov attempt a brief assessment of the Bible correspondence course. By 1979 a total of 272 workers had graduated. That indicated that a significant number failed to complete the course. In 1979, for example, ten persons failed the exams and four others did not take the exams due to illness. Bychkov also reported that during the previous five years eight persons had to be eliminated for various reasons. Another problem was that it was a strenuous course of studies with eleven subjects to master and Bychkov urged possible candidates to keep this in mind. Another problem that would be a factor in accepting future students was that "not all graduates of the Bible correspondence course show a readiness to work

where they are especially needed." The leadership could report little about
the proposed theological seminary except to say that the "question remains
in a status of positive consideration." A few select students were studying
abroad, and in future, the presidium had decided, only those candidates
who demonstrated adequate knowledge of the necessary foreign language
would be sent. Higher educational standards applied also to candidates for
the correspondence course.

Delegates in 1974 had clamored for more literature and, in this area
also, Bychkov had achievements to report. A year earlier they had been able
to import 25,000 Bibles and 5,000 concordances, the first official importation since 1945. A day before the congress opened, several of the Moscow
staff arrived with a truckload of Bibles, bringing 20,000 large-size Bibles
from Leningrad where they had been printed. Bychkov indicated that more
Bibles were in the publication plans for the immediate future. They had
also managed to print songbooks and other literature. Their journal, *Bratskii
Vestnik*, of which they had printed only 6,000 copies before 1974, had been
increased step by step to 10,000 copies per issue.

Bratskii Vestnik has appeared every other month with only a few interruptions since 1945. It is invariably eighty pages in length, but its format
has changed somewhat over the years. It has to serve all the didactic and
communicative functions. Issue No. 5 for 1979 is typical. After the usual letter of greeting from the presidium (this time to mark Unity Day), pages 5-
34 were devoted to "Spiritual Articles." These included continued chapters
of short exegetical commentary on the Gospel of Mark, the letter to the
Hebrews, and the Acts of the Apostles, written by O. A. Tiark, A. M.
Bychkov, and P. K. Shatrov respectively. A second section entitled "Christian Unity" reported on the European Baptist Congress held in Brighton,
England. The third section (formerly the first section) was entitled "The
Christian Voice in Defence of Peace." Usually this contained short communiqués and reports on meetings of the Christian Peace Conference; in this
issue it also included a short article on children as war sufferers. This issue
included an article under the more infrequent category: "From the History
of the Evangelical-Baptist Movement." Pages 48-59 were devoted to
"Music and Singing," a section introduced in 1978.

Many readers turn first to the final section "Local News" and read the
earlier didactic articles at leisure. In many churches *Bratskii Vestnik* is read
over the loudspeaker during the half hour before the service begins. The
local news section in this issue reported on the recent plenary meeting of
the AUCECB and the resultant letter to all the churches, congratulated

senior presbyter E. N. Raevskii on his 75th birthday, and then reported local events on the last fourteen pages, including several full-page black and white photographs. These short local entries reported ordinations, retirements, baptisms, church dedications, regional presbyter conferences, and the odd problem.

The journal, like all Soviet publications, cannot be published without state approval. At present an eight-member editorial board consisting of presidium members (with Bychkov as responsible editor) assume final responsibility. The *de facto* full-time editor is Vitali G. Kulikov, whose title is "responsible secretary." His predecessor was I. I. Motorin (1944-71), who had been a trained journalist. Kulikov became "responsible secretary" in the reorganization following Karev's death and Motorin's retirement.[28] Kulikov has some higher education, presumably in literature and poetry, for which he displays an appreciation. He sings and preaches in the Moscow church, also traveling infrequently, but most of the material is sent in by contributors. He also participates as teacher in the correspondence course.

In 1974 Gabriel Pavlenko had received enthusiastic support from fellow delegates when he presented a detailed program to improve the ministry of the "second pulpit"—music and singing. The presidium later appointed a special committee who were given the task to improve the musical repertoire and to undertake measures to deepen the qualification of local musicians.[29] In 1978 *Bratskii Vestnik* introduced a special section on "Music and Singing," which now not only included the publication of new songs (with notation) as formerly, but also a series of theoretical articles and announcements. More attention was devoted to music at the regional seminars for presbyters and other church workers. Shortly before the 1979 Congress the AUCECB announced that a special course of studies in music had been introduced in the correspondence course. This course had been increased to three years and for the 13 choir leaders presently enrolled, there was a special two-year program. A new revision in the constitution also emphasized that both presbyter and choir leader must serve as "spiritual guardian" of the choir.

At the time of the 1963 Congress the AUCECB income had been declining steadily. Total income for 1963 was around 125,000 rubles.[30] By 1974 treasurer A. I. Mitskevich could report an average income of 545,665 rubles per year and he pointed out that income had increased in 1972 and 1973 by 35,000 and 40,000 rubles respectively.[31] At that time the 42-member congregation in Voronezh had the distinction of the highest per member giving, namely three rubles per member. By 1979 income had increased still further, averaging 838,000 rubles per year, seven times what it had been in 1963.[32] Expenses had also increased with nearly a quarter spent on travel and a total contribution over five years of 902,000 rubles to the peace fund. That caused some whispering in the ranks as did also the information that around 470,000 rubles had been spent on the foreign guests. Foreign delegations invited by the AUCECB receive free travel, lodging, food, and pocket money with the union expected to treat them in a grand style that will make a good impression. That is a state-imposed expectation which prevents lodging in homes and more modest meals which would be more natural to the life style of the hosts and many of the visitors. Matthew Mel'nik, chairman of the auditing commission, also reported to the congress that in 1978 his commission had drawn attention to the fact that the international department had overspent its budget by 11,000 rubles and as a result the presidium ordered economies. These became noticeable in a small reduction in the number of foreign trips. Mel'nik also explained that some of the money spent by the international department was used to pay for tickets for delegates from other socialist countries to travel to international meetings which was understood to be a way of supporting the Baptist World Alliance in spite of currency restrictions. Clearly, confidence in the AUCECB had been restored, although there was considerable room for more open reporting and trust building. So far, *Bratskii Vestnik* has never reported any figures from the financial report, although treasurer Mitskevich could be persuaded in 1979 to read his report more slowly so that delegates could copy down the figures and think about them later.

More Changes

Once again, delegates wanted to devote most of the discussion time to a revision of their constitution. It proved to be a fascinating exercise for foreigners who heard things said that had long been taboo. This time E. A. Tarasov, vice-chairman of the Council for Religious Affairs with responsibilities for the non-Orthodox confessions (including the evangelicals), gave a greeting from the chairman, V. A. Kuroedov, and remained seated in a prominent place throughout the congress. That failed to intimidate many of the spokesmen.

The revised constitution introduced six changes.[33] A significant one was a slight addition to paragraph 3 listing "the preaching of the Gospel" as the first task of the union. That phrase had been restored in 1966 as task for the congregations; now it was restored at the highest level as well. A more restrictive change was a more specific wording change from "Mennonite" to "Mennonite Brethren" with an additional clause that the addition of further denominations to the union would be determined by the AUCECB. E. A. Tarasov explained to me in a private meeting that this reflected the wish of the Mennonite Brethren to eliminate the non-immersionist Mennonites from possible membership. Another change now required a two-thirds voting majority, which was an attempt to guarantee the election of council members who were widely trusted and to make it more difficult to elect persons more acceptable to the authorities. To offset a possible denominational problem, a qualifying clause indicated that the council membership in its makeup must be representative of the denominational makeup.

A very major structural change was the introduction of four departments (Evangelism and Christian Unity, Preparation and Qualification of Church Workers and Musicians, International Department, and Publication, Finance, and Management). These departments were to be subordinate to the presidium with the head of each department required to be a member of the AUCECB Council. Not only did that mean the creation of a new department for Evangelism and Christian Unity, which was a bold step, it also meant new leadership for the international department, although few were optimistic this would change the power relationship very much. But delegates hoped that an additional clause in paragraph 13, requiring that all office employees sign a working contract, might eliminate some of the younger staff on the international department that came under such severe criticism from delegates. Others hoped these changes would lead to the introduction of job descriptions, including those for the general secretary.

Two other major changes were directed toward strengthening the role of the senior presbyter and the presbyter locally. New carefully specified procedures for their election were intended to provide built-in guarantees against some of the abuses Andrei Klimenko had complained of as late as 1978. There were cases where church members had excommunicated the presbyter in his absence, or had collected signatures on behalf of his ouster. A year earlier Klimenko criticized the arbitrary and careless behavior of some senior presbyters. In Dnepropetrovsk, for example, the membership in the presbyter council had been changed without calling a conference of presbyters. Some senior presbyters had ordained presbyters in homes without the church present, and in another case a senior presbyter had ordained a presbyter without his wife present and did not even inform her afterward.[34]

A change in the wording order for baptism and church membership occasioned many questions for clarification. Baptism and church membership are no longer synonymous. Ukrainian leader Jacob Dukhonchenko, who led the discussion, pointed out in response to a question, that the law does not prohibit children from attending church; even Vladimir Kuroedov, Chairman of the Council for Religious Affairs, had said so in print in 1978. Maybe, Dukhonchenko went on, local workers needed to grasp more clearly the distinction between attending church and the state prohibition against children being members. After all, the Orthodox Church practices child baptism and that is not against the law. The point was clear; it would now be possible to baptize young people under 18 without breaking the law. Another practical advantage was that this would allow persons to be baptized who are not prepared for job discrimination because their names are on a church membership roll. There was also an additional clause regulating membership transfer (reflecting the new mobility), which no doubt was intended to prevent the embarrassment of an excommunicated member joining another church in another town and even becoming presbyter, as one man reported!

Another sign of progress and promise was buried in an interpretive commentary to paragraph 27. This stated that the presbyter should devote "special attention to the education of young people." When the discussion period started, the first speaker was a young woman from Moscow who read a prepared statement on behalf of 600 young people in the central church and on behalf of those in Kiev. She welcomed the creation of four departments, but appealed for the creation of a youth department for the union. Whether or not this was a signal to other speakers, numerous spokesmen repeated this call for a youth department which could help with the problems unique to young people. Jacob Dukhonchenko responded to these many requests by reminding the delegates of state legislation, advising them to read carefully a recent article in *Nauka i Religiia* (Science and Religion) which summarized what the law permitted. He urged the delegates to accept the open wording of the interpretive commentary and promised that the presidium would request the Council for Religious Affairs to grant permission for such a department. Later, when he addressed the delegates in his capacity as senior presbyter for the Ukraine, he urged each presbyter to take the concerns of his young people to heart. How that was organized was a local matter. The leaders were obviously encouraging local initiative, a stretching at the present limits that might lead to a more favorable answer from the authorities later.

Difficult Elections

Once again the elections were held behind closed doors. A major upset of the top leadership was prevented when the old presidium agreed to present a united front. Alexei Bychkov had to listen to sharp criticism, primarily because delegates felt he was spending too much time abroad. Andrei Klimenko received less criticism, but many delegates considered him too weak and he had obviously aged during his five years in the office of president. The dominant leaders at the congress were Bychkov and Dukhonchenko.

Many new persons were elected because the size of all the committees was increased. Twelve of the 29 on the council were new, but it was still primarily a body consisting of senior presbyters, giving other groupings in the church less of a hearing.[35] Six of the previous candidate members now moved up to full council status.[36] The new list of nine candidates included a number of younger men who will likely move up into major leadership next time.[37] The last of the Old Guard retired and the average age of the new presidium is younger than it has been for decades.[38]

The presidium was increased to eleven members (six of which were new) and three candidate members. Although Klimenko and Bychkov remained president and general secretary respectively, most of the other positions were new and portend changes.[39] Four individuals would now need to move to Moscow (V. E. Logvinenko, I. S. Gnida, N. A. Kolesnikov, and Jacob Fast). All four are widely respected as churchmen of integrity. If there will be any significant changes in Moscow, it will be because these men will be able to insist on it. That also applied to the candidate members to the presidium who will attend many of the meetings, although without the right to vote.

Yet extra closed-door sessions were necessary. Delegates voted in favor of all 30 nominees (although some leaders barely squeaked through) except for one person—Peter K. Shatrov, the Pentecostal delegate. Delegates had voted for four Pentecostal representatives on the council, two candidates and one on the auditing commission, but the Pentecostal delegates who solidly supported Shatrov insisted on a second round of votes.[40] Once again Shatrov failed to be elected and could therefore no longer be a candidate for election to the presidium. The delegates met in another closed session, proposed two alternative presidium members, but left the decision to the Pentecostal delegates. These weighed the alternative of forming a separate union but eventually in mid-January accepted the compromise of having V. S. Glukhovski and D. L. Vozniuk represent their interests on the presidium.

The New Leadership Team

1. *Alexei M. Bychkov—the Leader.* When Bychkov suddenly emerged as a new vice-president in 1969 very little was known about him. Two years later after election to the highest executive office in the union, he introduced himself with a short autobiography.[41] He was born in Klin (just outside Moscow) in 1928, into an Evangelical Christian family. Following graduation from a Moscow institute, he worked for nearly two decades as a building engineer. He was converted at age 21 in 1949 and was baptized in 1954. In the following years he read extensively in the theological library of an old friend. He also studied English for two years in an institute, graduating in 1960. Following this he became a translator for the AUCECB, then was entrusted with preparing lectures on theology for the Bible correspondence course. He started preaching at the Moscow church in 1967, but only in 1969 did he begin to work full time for the All-Union Council, first as assistant to Ivanov. In 1970 he was ordained to the ministry and began his work as general secretary the following year.

Alexander Karev had been widely loved. Alexei Bychkov was not widely known, which increased the difficulty of stepping into Karev's shoes. Karev had already been severely sick in 1968 but held onto his post. Some associates felt that, had Karev not remained in office so long, Bychkov as a representative of the new generation would not have seemed such a surprise. Bychkov has, however, grown in office, and is by now probably as widely respected as Karev was loved. That is the difference in their personalities.

Bychkov's working style is that of an administrator. He is not an outstanding preacher. During the past decade he has shown himself to be a skillful negotiator—that is, remarkably successful in obtaining acceptable compromises. He appears to favor progress by a series of small steps in a complicated process which many of his followers do not understand until after the goals are reached. He is intelligent and a good listener. Whereas Karev saw himself as a pastor to pastors, Bychkov appears more goal-oriented, seeking to deepen the quality of evangelical church life.

2. *Andrei I. Klimenko—the Church's Leader.* Delegates in private expressed satisfaction with the election of Klimenko in 1974. He had been born in 1913 on the Volga River in present-day Kuibyshev. He was already baptized at 15 and began preaching soon thereafter. He had lived in the city of Kuibyshev since 1930 and was elected the leading presbyter in 1949. In 1963 he became senior presbyter for Kuibyshev and nearby oblasts. This

responsibility grew, so that when he became a council member in 1969 and then a vice-president two years later, he was responsible for 13 oblasts in the Volga region.

Technically speaking, as president Klimenko was the leader, serving as chairman at meetings of the council and presidium. For this reason he was officially responsible in the eyes of the authorities for everything done by the AUCECB. That was what made the task so burdensome. The general secretary, as in the state apparatus, has great executive powers, but Klimenko as president has been able to exert a definite leadership role. Klimenko, for example, presented the major report to the annual meetings of the AUCECB plenum on the spiritual state of the churches. By reporting and identifying problems, he helped shape the agenda of the churches. Often he offered very specific advice, virtually directives to all the presbyters and members. Why would the churches follow him?

Klimenko has only eighth-grade education and preaches very simple sermons. This is the chief reason for his popularity. He is a man of the people who feels deeply for the individual church member. At conferences and in local churches his deep concern for the spiritual tone of the churches was very evident. Regularly he offered advice for the presbyters. He emphasized that the church ordinances should be conducted with appropriate respect. He has also gained a reputation as a skillful adviser in local conflict situations. His is a quiet, steadying influence. His chief quality is that they trust him.

3. *Other Leaders.* Jacob K. Dukhonchenko, as the senior presbyter for the Ukraine, is responsible for 46 percent of the entire membership. He is assisted by four deputies and assistants and a 15-member presbyter council. His region is divided into 25 oblasts with a senior presbyter at the head of each. Dukhonchenko is a younger man (late forties) whose initially most striking feature is his girth. A more lasting impression is his personal warmth and a simple faith that expresses itself by inviting the visitor to pause for a moment of prayer before beginning the discussion.

Dukhonchenko, who graduated from an institute as an engineer, initially served as a presbyter in Zaporozh'e before becoming senior presbyter for the Zaporozh'e Oblast in 1968. In a surprise move, Ukrainian delegates elected him to replace N. N. Mel'nikov as senior presbyter for the entire Ukraine at the pre-congress conference in 1974. That meant he would also be elected first vice-president of the AUCECB. Dukhonchenko's popularity continues to increase and he could have been elected president in 1979 had he agreed. Because his power base and residence is in the Ukraine, his role on the presidium has been a secondary one. Although not well educated theologically himself, one of his major concerns is the introduction of more educated and capable leadership. He has also shown concern to provide this leadership with theological study aids.

Dukhonchenko's deputy in Kiev, Ivan S. Gnida, now moves to Moscow to become the assistant general secretary, replacing the retiring A. I. Mitskevich. It is an exact parallel to Mitskevich's own move to Moscow from Kiev in 1956, but Gnida is a very different person. Gnida personifies the well-known Russian character trait—*Chuvstvo* (feeling). Already in 1956 he was working hard to bring the Pentecostals into the congregation in Aleksandriia (Kirovograd Oblast). He became senior presbyter of Kirovograd Oblast in 1967 and was elected to the AUCECB in 1969. A graduate of the Zaporozh'e Pedagogical Institute, he turned 60 in 1980.

The election of V. E. Logvinenko (born 1925) as second vice-president of the AUCECB was followed in the summer of 1980 by his election as full senior presbyter for the RSFSR, replacing or relieving Klimenko of this responsibility. His election was somewhat surprising since till 1979 he had been serving as presbyter of the church in Odessa which is located in the Ukraine. But he is a Russian, of Evangelical Christian background, who enjoys much broader respect than this local base would have suggested. He was elected to the AUCECB in 1974 without a dissenting vote. He received a diploma as building engineer through evening school. Some observers think he can match Dukhonchenko in ability. In particular he appears to have the ability to inspire his colleagues to exercise their gifts, perhaps because he appears content to leave the limelight to others.

His two associates actually have broader leadership experience. Jacob Fast was born in 1929 in Alexanderwohl (Molotschna), experienced some of the resettlements of the German Mennonites, and came to Novosibirsk in 1949. Two years later he was converted and baptized and was ordained a deacon in 1962. By 1964 he was leading the German wing of the congregation, yet working full time as an electric welder. In 1968 he became assistant senior presbyter of Western Siberia (till 1974), but also spent considerable time traveling throughout the Soviet Union to visit the German congregations. First elected to the AUCECB in 1966 to represent the Mennonite Brethren, he was elected to the ten-member presidium in 1974. In fact, his new post as deputy senior presbyter for the RSFSR (which will bring him to Moscow) is also a Mennonite post. He is widely admired and loved and is an excellent preacher although he has not completed theological study.

Peter K. Shatrov (born 1928) was converted in 1946, baptized and became presbyter in a Pentecostal congregation which adhered to the Smorodintsy. In 1956 his group joined the Leningrad ECB church, where he became a preacher. In 1968 Ilia Ivanov brought him to Moscow where he became a full-time "Inspector of the AUCECB," meaning that he was the staff representative for the Pentecostals, as Viktor Kriger had become for the Mennonites. The following year he was elected to the AUCECB and in 1974 to the presidium, having become by then the major Pentecostal spokesman. He lacks the charming manner of some of his associates, but appears capable, and fellow Pentecostals have come to recognize that he has sought to improve their position.

It will be difficult to find a replacement for Nikolai A. Kolesnikov as senior presbyter for Kazakhstan. He is only 48 and projects a youthful vigor, especially in his fiery preaching. Like Logvinenko he began in Odessa where he was converted in 1952, began preaching, and was ordained presbyter in 1961. He completed the first Bible correspondence course and was elected senior presbyter for Kazakhstan in 1971, having served as assistant and *de facto* leader several years previously already. He now assumes the powerful position of AUCECB treasurer.

The new leaders who are to move to Moscow still need to obtain residence permits which is a major difficulty. Andrei Klimenko only managed to obtain an apartment when a church member surrendered his and moved to another city. Moscow is an attractive city which means that leaders already living there will find it difficult to move. Their time as full-time employees of the AUCECB was not entered into their work logbook so they cannot hope for a large state pension were they to return to secular employment. Fortunately, the AUCECB now provides a pension fund. Another factor making regular leadership changes difficult is the natural attraction of the exercise of power.

Yet the membership tends to grow suspicious, the longer an individual remains in high office. From the church members' point of view, based on local experiences, they know that the state officials are constantly trying to force the church leaders to compromise. With each passing year the leaders will need to make many smaller compromises that do not seem important until they have been gradually bent. Such leaders, the members feel, the state would be happy to keep in office longer, whereas if a leader remains firmly loyal to the church, the authorities would exert pressure to have him replaced. This suspicion by the membership places the leaders in a most unenviable position.

New Time of Troubles for the CCECB

If the AUCECB projected growth and confidence, the CCECB could only envision a bleak future. Instead of freeing their general secretary and legalizing the union, the authorities had exchanged Georgi Vins and four Soviet dissidents for two Soviet spies kept in America. This eased the personal physical suffering of Vins and his family, but it was a major blow to the CCECB. Their union had even less chance of getting legal recognition now and another capable leader had been rendered harmless through deportation. The *Samizdat* network continued to function and there were small triumphs of faith to report but the primary news concerned a wave of renewed state repression.

The new CCECB membership elected in 1976 still included 10 persons but not all were at liberty.[42] Ivan Ia. Antonov read the report at a meeting in December 1976, a function that should have been done by Vins or Gennadi Kriuchkov, who was in hiding. In order to strengthen their work they added B. Ia. Schmidt to the council and four candidate members and added Ia. G. Skorniakov to the evangelist department.[43] Missing from these lists were men like S. G. Dubovoi and P. A. Iakimenkov, who had come into conflict with Kriuchkov. By 1979 the *Bulletin* was full of appeals on behalf of three evangelists (Pavel Rytikov, Peter P. Peters, and Ia. G. Skorniakov), all of whom were back in prison. In the summer of 1979 Ivan Ia. Antonov was arrested and a month before he was due to go on pension, he received a two-year sentence under the parasite laws for not being employed. In November another well-known leader, M. I. Khorev, was arrested. K. K. Kreker and D. V. Miniakov complained about increased harassment and expected arrest. In the absence of Vins, the CCECB had elected Nikolai G. Baturin as acting secretary, but he too was arrested on 5 November 1979.[44]

Baturin and an associate had been arrested as they were correcting proofs for the journal *Vestnik Istiny* (Herald of Truth) which had replaced the old *Vestnik Spasenie* (Herald of Salvation), the new one being printed on the secret printing press. The publication department of the CCECB was to suffer more blows in 1979. Already on April 11, 1979, a bookbinding operation in Moldavia had been discovered. They had been preparing 1,330 copies of *Bulletin* No. 60, which they had then given to two brothers, Nikolai and Alexander Chekh, to transport to Moscow. Valentina Naprienko and Georgi Dzhurik were sentenced to three and two years prison respectively while the Chekh brothers lost their automobile and had 20 percent of their wages withheld.[45] Then on 19 January 1980 another printing press was discovered in Staryi Kadaki near Dnepropetrovsk. Four persons were arrested as they were preparing the next issue of *Vestnik Istiny*. Still another printing press in the village of Glivenki (Krasnoder) was discovered on June 18, 1980 and four persons were arrested. These have been serious hindrances to the work but there are other printing presses still operating and no doubt still others will be built.[46]

The apparent easing of the situation through unconditional church registration was also coming to an end. *Bratskii Listok*, the official CCECB journal, in late 1979 printed a number of documents, all of which carried the same general message.[47] The authorities had sent the registered CCECB affiliates forms to fill out in which they were asked to provide information on their activities. The congregation in Vinnitsa, Ukraine, was to supply details not only on total income but also on all expenses, including how much had been paid to the Peace Fund and the fund for preserving architectural monuments. The church in Ordzhonikidze received a list of 17 prohibitions which was a summary of the legislation on cults which they had not promised to obey in all details when they first registered. In response, these churches returned their registration papers and the CCECB warned all the churches to be certain to maintain full independence of their church from the state.

New Frontiers

1. *Clergy Education.* Where the presbyter maintains a good relationship to the senior presbyter and listens to the counsel of brethren elected by the church, where the presbyter pays attention to the needs of the church, "there the work of unity is strengthened and the church grows spiritually and in numbers."[48] Such was the advice which Andrei Klimenko repeatedly gave to local leaders. The leaders were responsible for the spiritual life of the church, but they must not lord it over the members.

During the anti-church campaign of the early sixties, the local church council consisting of laymen was given increased power in order to break the influence of the clergy. The AUCECB itself had been forced to issue a statute that dramatically strengthened the powers of the senior presbyter over against the local clergy but restricted the role of the senior presbyter to a non-preaching supervisor. Now, as pressures on them eased, the Moscow leadership placed heavy emphasis on restoring the spiritual role and influence of both presbyter and senior presbyter. It was especially an emphasis on leadership style. Style of leadership would be crucial for the future of a modern church no longer as ready to accept authoritarianism but looking for spiritual examples who could motivate them. When the seminary would finally open its doors, it would be possible to train a handful of better quality workers, but most leaders would need to rely on available literature to teach themselves.

2. *Church and Society.* Russian evangelical pronouncements on church and society have often resembled a tightrope balancing act. As Alexander Karev reminded his listeners in 1969, all forms of social activity such as caring for orphans, the sick, the aged, and the needy, "have been taken over by the state which is carrying out this grand task fully.... Therefore the church has no need to conduct this function."[49] At the same time, since state officials were also concerned that religious sectarians should not be isolated from society, *Bratskii Vestnik* frequently advised local leaders to involve themselves in local cultural affairs.[50] The Bible proclaims a strong message of Christian responsibility toward society—the Apostle James defining true religion as "to take care of orphans and widows in their suffering and to keep oneself from being corrupted by the world" (Jas. 1:27). These somewhat contradictory concerns meant that Soviet evangelical pronouncements on church and society were difficult to interpret.

Alexander Karev wanted his listeners to be realistic. The Reform Baptists, he said, were trying to fly in the heavens like the eagle but they have not learned how to walk on earth. Once they learned that, the divisions would disappear "and the 13th chapter of Romans will not surprise anyone."[51] He therefore tended to emphasize a Christian's obligation to obey state law. Since then gradual but noticeable changes in the church-state situation have influenced AUCECB utterances about society.

Alexei Bychkov, for example, drew attention to the democratization process which offered hope that local disagreements could be settled in a fashion agreeable to all.[52] He urged the members not to isolate themselves from society but to develop good relations with the people about them, showing them goodwill and love. By gaining local recognition as useful members of society, they could help alleviate the antagonism toward believers. In the latest lengthy statement, Arthur Mitskevich went much further than previously in advocating Christian involvement in society. The task of the Christian was to ease suffering, both physical and spiritual illness. The Christian, he said, "rejoices and cooperates in the construction of each new hospital, sanitorium, kindergarten, and home for the aged."[53]

In his speech to congress delegates, Alexei Bychkov probably spoke as frankly and boldly as any of his colleagues have so far. He pointed out that in socialist society there is no contradiction between work and capital, work is honorable, and such a society struggles for peace. Those were also the principles for a Christian. Bychkov added that "our Christian convictions call us not to ignore inadequacies and the problems of our society, but to bring a positive contribution to overcoming and eliminating them."[54] Further he expressed the hope that further reworking of the Soviet constitution "will concern also the legislation on the activities of religious societies."

With considerable confidence he challenged a major societal misconception which has been systematically fostered by the state:

> in society the opinion dominates, that religion is a vestige of the past. We are called servants of "ideas that have passed." Certain Christians are saddened by the threat of this widespread view, also by the arguments conducted against belief in God in the name of omnipotent science, by the self-reliance of man, and also by the sufferings and injustice reigning in the world. That raises the question among us: "Where is our God?" We answer: "God is my strength and my song; He is my salvation" (Ps. 117:12).[55]

The emphasis on full obedience to the state remains, but AUCECB members (like CCECB members) are concerned when the state demands obedience violating conscience. Mitskevich in a lengthy passage which again repeated the advice from 1 Timothy to pray for all in authority so that they might live a quiet and peaceful life added a few bold qualifications. Romans 13, he said, demanded unconditional obedience to the law "if such laws do not restrict the free exercise of the duties of our Christian faith."[56] Mitskevich also tried to get his readers to realize that it is not only Christians who do good but that the Bible also records illustrations of how the Persian King Cyrus helped Ezra build the temple in Jerusalem. It was still an affirmation of the quietist approach, but did seem to suggest a growing desire for Christians to participate in the large undertakings for social welfare.

There was some hope that Soviet evangelicals might become involved in social service ministries in developing countries, but so far such a cooperative venture under international Baptist or Mennonite auspices has been foiled. But their representatives have participated in many international conferences devoted to justice and development in the Third World. There are indicators that further involvement might be possible together with other East European churches through WCC initiative.

3. *Secularization.* Although less apparent in the Soviet Union than in the West, secularization and affluence have begun to influence Soviet evan-

gelicals. This constitutes both a problem and a challenge. There is a problem of having developed an ingrown cliché language which makes it difficult to communicate to the world about them. There is also the problem of what could be described as Soviet cant—the excessive verbalizing of Marxist ideals while hypocritically pursuing a highly individualized struggle for personal success and affluence.[57] Will Soviet evangelicals be mastered by affluence or will they represent a strata of socially concerned individuals who will take seriously the social idealism of Marxism? A further challenge is to persuade the state to become consciously secular so that the necessary separation of church and state might finally become a reality.

4. *Unity and Structural Change.* During the past five years it was the tense relations with Pentecostals that again became the major unity problem. The leaders held special talks with Pentecostals in Kiev, Moscow, and in Kharkov and regularly advised senior presbyters and presbyters to be fair and non-partisan in their dealings. Klimenko urged the leaders to follow Paul's advice of being all things to all men, to listen and show love according to Christ's method rather than to hurry to give "my views" on points of conflict.[58] The solution to the tension appeared to be a new movement toward autonomous registration which Klimenko fully endorsed. As a union, however, they insisted on strict adherence to the August Agreement but stressed warm relations toward Pentecostals registered autonomously. Ten presbyters from the latter group were enrolled in the Bible correspondence course and some of their churches received copies of *Bratskii Vestnik* and Bibles.[59]

During the same period relations with the Mennonite Brethren had also developed increased tensions. In the Omsk region were many Mennonite Brethren congregations that opposed registration. Others in the union threatened withdrawal because of Moscow's connections with the ecumenical movement. At the 1979 Congress German spokesman Abram Fast had urged a change to observer status. When German delegates met in caucus during the congress, they explained to foreign guests that they anticipated local church splits if they returned home with no change to report.

Andrei Klimenko reported that there were now 53 congregations of German-speaking Mennonites in the union and that a number of Germans had been elected as assistant senior presbyters.[60] Klimenko, however, felt that the work toward unity remained inadequate. Those Mennonite Brethren not in the union were "very poorly acquainted with our confession of faith and statutes."[61] And they also received very limited information by letter from the Mennonite Brethren. Jacob Fast, Traugott Kviring, and Viktor Kriger had visited many churches, "but we consider that such visits should be increased, since at the congress it was said: 'We elect brethren so that they will visit us.' "[62] Beginning in 1978 there was a new breakthrough in the strongly Mennonite Orenburg Oblast. Klimenko and Kriger were able to visit, and *Bratskii Vestnik* reported the existence of at least seven churches.[63] The appointment of a separate senior presbyter is anticipated.

Must the unity formulas of 1944 and 1945 which produced the Union of Evangelical Christians, Baptists, and Pentecostals remain forever? In 1977 leading Pentecostal spokesmen were still proposing a structural change in the union in order to reduce tensions between Pentecostals and Baptists. This appeared to be threatening to the Moscow leadership and they advised that instead of structural change regional senior presbyters and local presbyters should work harder at improving relations between Baptists and Pentecostals. Rather than relying on organizational structures, they hope to maintain unity by relying on personalities.[64]

Some restructuring is, however, underway, and more will be necessary in the future. In May 1979 an administrative system based on the Ukrainian model had been introduced for the RSFSR. Would this be a step forward or backward? It will clearly strengthen church administration in an area that was long neglected because the All-Union Council leaders were preoccupied with national and international issues and could not devote the necessary attention to provincial matters. Since 1978 the northern and eastern areas of the RSFSR have experienced major revivals and a more coordinated administrative structure may help retain the new growth and give it permanence.

In spite of the decision not to restructure the organization in order to please the Pentecostals, the AUCECB decided to engage evangelists and assistant senior presbyters whose primary task was to concentrate on unity between Pentecostals and Baptists. This again demonstrated a reliance on personalities rather than structure. When Peter Shatrov lost the confidence of the delegates, the Pentecostals understood it as an affront. Forming a separate union depended on getting state approval which seemed possible. It also depended on gaining the support of the independent Pentecostals. In the end caution prevailed but a parting of the ways seems a matter of time.

5. *New Confession of Faith.* Since 1966 the AUCECB has been attempting to draft a new confession of faith. In 1977 Bychkov reported that they had collected and translated the statutes and confessions of faith of a

variety of evangelical bodies in Poland, East and West Germany, and America.[65] A new confession of faith was intended to help them articulate their theology. The challenge before them is to attempt an evangelical theology unique to the Soviet context. Will it serve to identify new goals for the future? Will such a confession of faith be able to surmount the denominational rivalries and still not be too watered down? A draft which a number of local congregations had already approved was ready for the 1979 Congress but the leaders did not feel confident to submit it. It was finally printed in draft form in *Bratskii Vestnik* 4/80 with a request to send in comments.

6. *Youth Work.* This is clearly a major frontier for the eighties. The AUCECB remains severely restricted. Leaders are concerned about losing young people to the CCECB, who they feel play on the minds of young people against them. Such criticism, however, achieves little. The leaders, including local presbyters, are challenged with the risk of encouraging and directing the creative energies of the youth while avoiding the wrath of the authorities. Should they restrain the young people through excessive caution, the events of 1961 may be repeated. More of the taboo on youth work was broken at the 1979 Congress. Will the youth department that delegates asked for ever become reality?

7. *A Missionary Challenge.* Soviet evangelicals are a minority group in a population of 260 million people. Recently Soviet scholars claimed that 90 percent of the population is atheistic.[66] The majority of these are by now fully pagan in the sense that they are entirely ignorant of religion. Their atheism was not a deliberate choice after a careful assessment of the claims of Christianity.

Alexander Karev often urged the members to commit themselves to a church seeking to restore New Testament Christianity. That task was also affirmed by Bychkov. The restitution of apostolic Christianity must also include the missionary vision and the activism of the apostolic church. For Soviet evangelicals this poses a major challenge. Many will be watching to see how much time the new department on evangelism and church unity will devote to unity and how much time to evangelism. Will they really send evangelists on tours as in the twenties?

Being faithful to the missionary task requires identification of goals and resources. Increasing numbers of young people are returning to religion, and young people represent a significant percentage of the Soviet population. Successful proselytization among Soviet young people requires younger trained leadership. Will Soviet evangelicals be able to produce such leaders and will the older members trust them? Already in 1974 Bychkov drew attention to the urbanization process. In order to reach the increasing number of urbanites, Soviet evangelicals will need to develop considerable expertise.

Generally speaking, Soviet evangelicals are confronted with the need for better-educated missionaries able to employ flexible approaches for a modern paganized society. Christians elsewhere in the world are following their progress with interest because the Soviets are clearly living in the post-Christian society now also emerging in the West. Soviet evangelicals appear to be embarked on a growth decade—they must be doing something right.

Conclusion: The Dangers of Normalization
Although the AUCECB now finds itself in a situation of normalization where state pressure has eased considerably, both sides affirm that the church-state relationship is an enemy relationship. The state is still committed to the eventual eradication of religion, whereas the church fully expects to remain in existence until the return of its Lord. What is the significance of the *modus vivendi* that has been reached? How will it affect the ideology of the state and the ideology of the church? Will the AUCECB continue to think like a free church? Are there not signs pointing toward a state-church mentality? Soviet sociologists have recently made this claim.

Reform Baptist leaders still emphasize that nothing has changed, that the persecution is as intense as it ever was, and they also charge that the AUCECB continues to be seriously compromised with the state.[67] The Reformers are indeed being persecuted more seriously again, but they are mistaken in claiming that nothing has changed. Change is inevitable. As we have seen, the AUCECB grew from 250,000 in 1963 to around 350,000 by 1980. This resulted in a new membership and also in a new leadership. There were no major changes in orientation, but a series of gradual steps toward a more genuine free church are apparent.

The growth of the evangelicals still represents a threat to the state and it is quite conceivable that new measures might be undertaken to stop the growth. From the evangelicals' perspective, however, a decline in membership would represent a serious threat to their continued existence. In fact, even maintaining the *status quo* would result in a loss of momentum.

Perhaps the greatest danger of the present normalization is the absence of a leadership type that played a vital role throughout the Old and New Testaments. The AUCECB is singularly lacking in prophets—prophets who can enunciate the necessary criticism to prevent them from unthinking accommodation to the state. Will the younger generation include prophetic types and will the AUCECB find a place for them or will they be shunted into dissidence as happened earlier? The CCECB has also lost much of its prophetic influence on the larger union. With Georgi Vins and other leaders permanently eliminated from the Soviet scene, they too are in search of new leadership and vision. Perhaps a prophet with an appropriately moderate style will come forward.

Notes to Chapter 15

1. *BV*, 4/78, p. 46. Using 250,000 as the 1963 base.
2. If each delegate at the 1979 congress represented 500 members, 532 delegates would represent only 266,000 members. Distribution of the 25,000 Bibles suggests 375,000 (1 per 15 members). Many sources speak of 200,000 in the Ukraine.
3. Lialina, pp. 168-70.
4. Payne, *Out of Great Tribulation*, p. 55.
5. *BV*, 1/75, *passim*.
6. They were: Robert Denny (Gen. Sec.), Ronald Goulding (Eur. Sec.), Gerhard Claas (Germany), David Russell (Britain), Knut Wumpelman (Denmark), David Lagergren (Sweden), Josef Gonzalves EBF Pres., (Spain), Andrew McRae (Scotland), and Adolphs Klaupiks (USA) of the Baptist World Alliance; Peter J. Dyck and Walter Sawatsky of Mennonite Central Committee; John Huk (Toronto) of the Evangelical Christians; and Raymond Oppenheim (American chaplain in Moscow).
7. Alvin Arndt, one of the CCECB delegation seeking entry to the congress, insisted there had been no demonstration; Fadiukhin had been misinformed. (Umsiedler Interview data.) My discussion of the congress, unless otherwise indicated, is based on the official report published in *BV*, 1/75 (also printed in English translation as a brochure) and on my own notes as observer.
8. *BV*, 1/75, p. 30.
9. See above, chapter 10, pp. 280-289.
10. V. M. Kovel'kov (1899-) was a longtime Moscow resident and unity commission chairman 1966-69; Iu. S. Grachev (1911-1973), longtime preacher in Kuibyshev died before completing his major history of the union; S. P. Fadiukhin (1905-) was Leningrad pastor and presidium member, 1966-1979.
11. *BV*, 1/75, p. 38.
12. Konstantin Logachev, "Fundamental Problems of Greek and Slavonic Biblical Textology," *Journal of the Moscow Patriarchate* 2/74, pp. 76-80. See also Logachev's articles in *Technical Papers for the Bible Translator*, 3/74, pp. 313-18, and 3/78, pp. 312-16.
13. *BV*, 1/75, p. 41.
14. *Ibid.*, p. 42.
15. *Ibid.* It should be noted that CCECB leaders also have a positive orientation toward socialism.

16. *Ibid.*
17. *Ibid.*, p. 53.
18. A total of 12 were released early; the other 48 were due for release anyway. Cf. *RCL* III, 1-3, 1975, pp. 14-15.
19. Delegates later asked A. I. Mitskevich to repeat the few financial totals he actually had reported: Total income in 1971—523,000 rubles; 1972—558,000; 1973—563,000. For travel they had spent 139,000 rubles per year, and had spent 164,000 for the correspondence course. (Author's congress notes.)
20. Keston files, February 1975. The letter, since it was unsigned, did not appear to exert any influence, but is a useful indication of the attitudes of some persons in the Moscow congregation.
21. I.e., A. M. Bychkov, P. K. Shatrov, V. S. Glukhovski, K. P. Borodinov, S. P. Fadiukhin, and M. P. Chernopiatov.
22. I.e., P. K. Shatrov, Jacob Fast, Jacob K. Dukhonchenko, I. S. Gnida. Reelected were: A. E. Klimenko, A. M. Bychkov, M. Ia. Zhidkov, M. P. Chernopiatov, A. I. Mitskevich, and S. P. Fadiukhin.
23. Between 1974 and 1979, 37 congregations had been closed due to urbanization, affecting 450 members.
24. Statistics given in manuscript copy of the general secretary's report to the Congress. In the following pages I will be relying on it as well as on my own notes as observer. The official report appeared in BV 1-2/80.
25. *BV*, 4/79, pp. 70-72. Andrei Klimenko was elected senior presbyter; V. E. Logvinenko, Jacob Fast, and Peter K. Shatrov were elected deputy senior presbyters. The presbyter council consisted of N. I. Dolmatov (Rostov), M. M. Kon'shin (Volga region), V. A. Mitskevich (Kaluga and Smolensk), V. F. Fedichkin (Moscow region), P. P. Ens (Orenburg presbyter). Candidate members are: V. D. Erisov (Stavropol), Iu. A. Maksimchuk (E. Siberia and Far East) and S. V. Iashin (presbyter in Surazh, near Briansk).
26. They are: RSFSR, Ukraine, Belorussia, Moldavia, Latvia, Estonia, Caucasus, Kazakhstan, Kirgizia, and Central Asia.
27. They were: K. S. Sedlitskii (Moldavia), V. A. Mitskevich (Kalinin), N. Z. Kvirikashvili (Trans Caucasus), A. A. Lysiuk (Chernovitsy), Iu. A. Maksimchuk (ass't SP for E. Siberia and Far East), F. P. Virts (ass't SP for Kazakhstan), V. I. Bukatyi (Belorussia), Ia. E. Tervits (Latvia), K. A. Sipko (Omsk), V. L. Kibenko (Sumy), N. G. Tsuman (Dnepropetrovsk), F. D. Starukhin (Kharkov), A. P. Mamalat (Kirovograd), V. D. Erisov (Stavropol), A. G. Brynza (Zaporozh'e), V. A. Shul'ts (ass't SP for Kazakhstan), T. F. Kviring (Central Asia), A. F. Burlakavov (ass't for Kazakhstan), Sergei I. Nikolaev (North West).
28. *BV*, 1/72, p. 80.
29. *BV*, 4/78, p. 36.
30. AS 770, pp. 125-6.
31. Based on author's personal notes from the congress.
32. Based on author's notes, figures checked with tape recording. Total income for 1974-79 had been 4,189,843 rubles, total expenditures were 3,876,320 rubles.
33. See appendix for copy of revised constitution.
34. *BV*, 4/78, pp. 31-33; 2/77, p. 64.
35. Members were D. M. Andrikevich (Khmel'nitskii), D. L. Vozniuk (Ternopol'), V. F. Vasilenko (Vinnitsa), I. S. Gnida (Deputy SP for Ukraine), V. S. Glukhovski (Deputy SP for Ukraine), Jacob K. Dukhonchenko (Ukraine), Ia. M. Kravchenko (Zhitomir), A. A. Nesteruk (Volhynia), F. E. Starukhin (Kharkov), N. G. Tsuman (Dnepropetrovsk), A. M. Bychkov (Gen. Sec.), K. P. Borodinov (W. Si-

beria), N. I. Dolmatov (Rostov), M. Ia. Zhidkov (Moscow presbyter), A. E. Klimenko (RSFSR and President), V. E. Logvinenko (Deputy SP for RSFSR), V. A. Mitskevich (Kalinin, Tambov, Kaluga, and Riazan), K. A. Sipko (Omsk), Jacob Fast (Deputy SP for RSFSR), I. V. Bukatyi (Belorussia), L. S. Vladyko (Ass't SP for Belorussia), F. P. Virts (ass't SP for Kazakhstan), N. A. Kolesnikov (Kazakhstan), Robert Vyzu (Estonia), T. F. Kviring (Central Asia), N. Z. Kvirikashvili (Trans Caucasus), N. N. Sizov (Kirgizia), K. S. Sedlitski (Moldavia), Ia. E. Tervits (Latvia), and S. F. Karpenko (Donets) and B. I. Bilas (L'vov) who appear to have been added later (BV 1-2/80, p. 56).
    36. They were A. A. Nesteruk, F. P. Virts, V. A. Mitskevich, D. M. Andrikevich, N. G. Tsuman, and Ia. M. Kravchenko.
    37. Candidate members are: L. F. Agafonov (Kishinev pres.), A. G. Brynza (Zaporozh'e), V. N. Vlasenko (Stavropol), V. E. Zenkin (Pen. Dnepropetrovsk), G. I. Komendant (Kiev), A. A. Lysiuk (Chernovitsy), V. I. Petrov (Kursk), P. P. Ens (Orenburg pres.), A. P. Vashchishin (Pen. Rovno). Revision or Auditing Commission members elected are: M. V. Mel'nik (Ass't SP for Ukraine) as chairman, now making him a member of the Presidium; A. P. Mamalat (Kirovograd), M. M. Kon'shin (Volga region), F. P. Lymar (Cherkassy), N. A. Poberei, O. I. Skuratovich (Minsk) and V. A. Shul'ts (Semipalatinsk).
    38. A. I. Mitskevich (Ass't Gen. Sec.), M. P. Chernopiatov (Vice-President), and S. P. Fadiukhin (retired).
    39. Presidium consists of A. I. Klimenko (President), A. M. Bychkov (Gen. Sec.), Jacob K. Dukhonchenko (first Vice-President), V. E. Logvinenko (second Vice-President), Michael Ia. Zhidkov (third Vice-President), D. L. Vozniuk (fourth Vice-President), I. S. Gnida (Ass't Gen. Sec.), N. A. Kolesnikov (Treasurer), Jacob Fast, Robert Vyzu, V. S. Glukhovski. Candidates are T. F. Kviring, Ia. E. Tervits, and a Pentecostal, L. S. Vladyko.
    40. Pentecostals were D. L. Vozniuk, V. S. Glukhovski, A. A. Nesteruk, L. S. Vladyko, B. I. Bilas on the council; V. E. Zenkin and A. P. Vashchishin as candidates.
    41. BV, 2/72, pp. 66-67. The biographical sketches of Bychkov and other leaders that follow are based on my biographical card file.
    42. CCECB members were G. K. Kriuchkov, G. P. Vins, N. G. Baturin, P. V. Rumachik, I. Ia. Antonov, D. V. Miniakov, M. I. Khorev, K. K. Kreker, N. P. Khrapov, and M. T. Shaptala (BL, 1/77).
    43. Candidate members added were N. I. Kabysh, P. A. Artiukh, P. G. Rytikov, and S. N. Misiruk. (Ibid.)
    44. BL, 6/79, Bulletin No. 71 and 66 and 67. Baturin was sentenced to five years.
    45. Trial report in Bulletin No. 72 (1979). Cf. No. 69.
    46. Nachrichten von den Feldern der Verfolgung Jan.-Feb./1980, pp. 3-5; Sept.-Oct./1980, p. 2.
    47. BL, 4-5/79.
    48. BV, 4/78, p. 31.
    49. BV, 2/70, p. 40.
    50. See, for example, BV 2/77, p. 70; 4/78, p. 44; 1/79, pp. 36-40.
    51. Paraphrasing Karev, BV, 2/70, p. 75.
    52. BV, 2/77, pp. 69 and 75.
    53. BV, 1/79, p. 37.
    54. Manuscript copy of General Secretary's report, December 1979, p. 34.
    55. Ibid., p. 36.

56. *BV*, 1/79, p. 40.
57. On this problem in general, see Smith, *The Russians, passim.*
58. *BV*, 4/78, p. 35.
59. *Ibid.*, pp. 49-50.
60. They were F. P. Virts and V. A. Shul'ts in Kazakhstan. In 1978 Traugott F. Kviring became the first full senior presbyter (for Central Asia) from German-Mennonites. *BV*, 2/77, p. 61; 4/78, p. 34.
61. *Ibid.*
62. *Ibid.*
63. *BV*, 1/79, p. 64. The churches were Sorochinsk, Kuterkia, Podol'sk, Suzanova, Kubenki, Pretorii-Karagui, and Donskoi.
64. *BV*, 2/77, p. 64.
65. *Ibid.*, p. 69.
66. *Pravda*, March 30, 1979. Cf my article, "Recent Evangelical Revival in the Soviet Union: Nature and Implications," read at Second World Congress on Soviet and East European Studies, in Garmisch, October 1980.
67. *BL*, 4-5/76. That is Georgi Vins' message since coming to America, although he is careful not to attack personalities.

We have experienced too much which prevents us from believing in Marx, either in the old Marx or the young one, or in the scientific or the utopian one. At its best, communism challenges us to a unity of the body but without the soul—but we want wholeness in its fullness.

—*Orthodox Youth Seminar*
in Soviet Union, 1979

16 The Evangelical in Soviet Society: Some Conclusions

Will Soviet evangelicals succeed in convincing the Soviet state that they have something positive to offer in building Soviet society? At present it is clear that communist officials and Christians are ideological opponents. That will only change when atheism ceases to be a requirement for party membership and state and party are no longer fused. The majority of Soviet evangelicals have demonstrated political loyalty to the satisfaction of Soviet authorities. But so far Soviet evangelicals have said little about their role in Soviet society. Their primary achievement has been to demonstrate that evangelicals can exist, can even flourish at times, in an aggressively Marxist society.

One of the results of the increased Western and ecumenical influences, perhaps also of their own Bible study, will be to move them beyond an apolitical position that is content to maintain its religious ritual. Will they move further in the direction of an uncritical support of the state, or will they perform a prophetic role? Reform Baptists clearly see themselves in a prophetic role, yet their voice appears to be diminishing. Alexei Bychkov's surprisingly bold challenge to the official dogma that religion belongs to the past hints at a prophetic role for the AUCECB that may need to be taken seriously. The challenge is to steer a course that avoids a state-church mentality committed to fostering the national culture and to maintaining political stability, but that also avoids the isolationism of narrow sectarianism.

By limiting this book to the Soviet evangelical movement since World War II, the movement's Soviet character seems more pronounced. Official religious life had virtually ceased during the Stalinist purges of the thirties. After the war there was a new administrative structure for what became very much a new movement after the outbreak of revivals. Most delegates attending the recent All-Union Congress traced their spiritual beginnings to the postwar period, 60 percent of them having been baptized during the revival years. They have had a new history in a Soviet context of rebuilding society. For the evangelicals this brought new working conditions, new problems, but also new zeal.

The most significant fact about their new existence was that the evangelical movement had survived. In their tradition, they had neither hierarchy nor a strong sense of apostolic succession. That had meant that even though their leaders were arrested and many had perished in the camps, there were always others to step into their places. These dared to preach without getting a theological degree first, because educational requirements had never been a prerequisite for preaching. There had been objections to women serving as preachers, but in a time of need it was the women who often maintained a functioning church life. Since communion and even baptism have no sacramental significance for evangelicals, the practice of these ordinances could wait until an ordained minister managed to visit. Much more, they were driven by a sense of the priesthood of all believers. Mother and father were responsible first of all for the most basic cell group of the church—their own family. Even if regular services were impossible, the children were sure to get religious instruction at home. All they needed for that was a Bible, but many had to manage without for a long time. Its absence remained their major problem.

The new conditions had transformed them. Their members had never been wealthy, but their early leaders were either well educated like Prokhanov and Kargel, or were wealthy farmers like Mazaev. The sober lifestyle expected of an evangelical resulted in a work ethic that brought them into the upper-or middle-class peasant bracket. Those classes were forcibly eliminated in the thirties, and when new elites developed in recent decades, religious discrimination guaranteed that evangelicals remained among the lowest of the proletariat. Thanks to this factor, they continue to appeal to the lowest class of Soviet society, whereas in other countries such as Britain or America, each new free church began as a lower class movement but then gained respectability.

The new conditions had transformed their structures. The new union,

Evangelist Josef D. Bondarenko leading service in his church in Riga not long before his arrest in August 1978. While awaiting trial and sentencing to three years, he suffered a heart attack. (Photo courtesy of Keston College)

ABOVE: Widely known Reform Baptist evangelist Josef D. Bondarenko with his family.

TOP RIGHT: Young people contributing to service. Many bring their tape recorders in order to share the program in other towns.

BOTTOM RIGHT: Meeting place of unregistered Reform Baptists near Leningrad (1979). (Photos courtesy of Keston College)

ОТОИЛЛЮСТРАЦИИ

Электросчетчик-подслушиватель был установлен в доме председателя
Совета церквей Г. К. Крючкова по адресу: г. Тула, ул. Агеева, дом 32.
Установлен 26 апреля 74 г. Обнаружен изъят хозяевами 8 июня 74 г.

осчетчик, в который был вмонтирован
шиватель, состоящий из 34 радиодеталей.

Сняты крышки счетчика.

Удален механизм
и электрическая часть
счетчика. Из-за приот-
крытой маскировочной
стенки виден транзисторный передатчик-
подслушиватель.

кировочная пластина удалена.

Лицевая сторона подслушивателя.

Обратная сторона платы подслушивателя.

TOP LEFT: Believers surveying the ruins of their hastily erected church building which the authorities destroyed in Alma-Ata, Kazakhstan (1977). (Photo courtesy of Friedensstimme)

BOTTOM LEFT: Peter Tkachenko in exile 1977. (Photos at left courtesy of Friedensstimme)

ABOVE: Six photographs showing successive dismantling of the electric meter in the home of Gennadi Kriuchkov in April 1974. They discovered a bugging device (American-made!) that had been installed in order to help trace the whereabouts of Kriuchkov. (Photo courtesy of Keston College)

TOP: Rostov church conducts communion in the forest.

BOTTOM: The Rostov Reform Baptist congregation on the way to a meeting in the countryside.

TOP: Rostov Reform Baptists meeting outside (1979) because of continuous harassment.

BOTTOM: Rostov Reform Baptists meeting outside. (Photos on both pages courtesy Friedens-stimme)

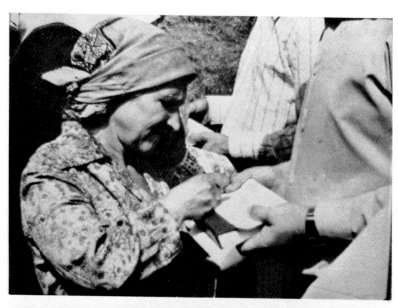

TOP: A member of the Rostov Reform Baptist church signs a document of appeal to the Soviet authorities to cease the harassment and release the workers such as Peter P. Peters. (1979)

BOTTOM: Reform Baptists in Rostov signing documents of appeal to state authorities.

The police attempted to interfere in baptismal services of Reform Baptists in Chernovitsy in 1979, but the baptismal candidates remained in the water till everyone had been baptized. (Photos on both pages courtesy of Friedensstimme)

TOP: Local police captain Valery Kostar in Novaia-Sinchiraia (Moldavia) attempting to break up a baptismal service. (Photo courtesy of Friedensstimme)

BOTTOM: CCECB member Peter Rumachik. By 1979 he had served 11½ years in prison, labor camps, and exile.

TOP: KGB agent Valerii Baraban attempting to break up baptismal service in Novaia-Sinchiraia, Moldavia. (Both photos courtesy of Friedensstimme)

BOTTOM: Reform Baptist baptismal service in Novaia-Sinchiraia, Moldavia, continues despite police attempts to stop it. (Summer 1979)

Ivan Osalskii and Andrei Buratchuk lead a Reform Baptist congregation in Moldavia that is forced to meet outside. (Photos on both pages courtesy of Friedensstimme)

TOP: Increasing numbers of Reform Baptist congregations in Moldavia are forced to meet outside.

BOTTOM: Communion under the trees in Moldavia in the summer of 1979.

TOP: Vasili Kosovan's family living in Novaia-Sinchiraia, Moldavia. (Both photos courtesy of Friedensstimme)

BOTTOM: Vasili Kosovan with a trunkful of paper he was transporting for the secret printing press, Khristianin. (April 1979)

TOP: CCECB member Ivan Antonov with his family before his imprisonment in June 1979.

BOTTOM: A trunkful of paper that Philip Borinskii was transporting for the secret printing press, Khristianin. He was arrested April 9, 1979, and sentenced to three years in prison. (Photo courtesy of Friedensstimme)

Philip Borinskii's family on their knees in prayer for him following his arrest for transporting paper for Khristianin. (Photo courtesy of Friedensstimme)

born in 1944, was never formally approved by the local churches. The new leadership managed to direct church activities without calling a congress of delegates until a major split forced them to nearly 20 years later. By then the leaders had learned an authoritarian leadership style that is still proving difficult to unlearn. The new union was supposed to fuse distinct denominations into one so that the new evangelical simply identified himself as Evangelical Christian Baptist or ECB. But the resultant structural rigidity is regularly challenged.

When church life became possible again after the war, a religious revival swept through the Soviet Union with a force that has not yet been forgotten. Usually there was no visible leadership for the revival and certainly no centralized coordination of it. The requirement for registration placed restraints on this growth, and outright state harassment resulted in waves of revival alternated by waves of repression. In this context Soviet evangelicals first learned their unique techniques for church growth. The week of prayer in the new year became an opportunity for daily evangelistic meetings. Visiting preachers were forbidden by law, and as a result they developed the "greeting" as a new form of proclamation. Financial collections at such services sometimes were used to pay for the evangelist's services indirectly—by paying fines to the local authorities! Sunday school and youth groups were legally forbidden, but birthday parties and choir practices became *de facto* substitutes. Elsewhere the atmosphere of an evangelistic meeting might be inappropriate at a funeral, but for Soviet evangelicals it was a major opportunity to hold an evangelistic rally outdoors with a guarantee that many unbelievers would be present. In spite of the wavelike character of these revivals, their persistence produced a new hope for the conversion of Russia.

The new Soviet evangelicals tried to present a united front. Earlier unity attempts had been complicated by minor theological differences which the evangelicals took so seriously. But the chief difficulties had been due to too many leaders with prickly personalities and to the competition for church members which was jeopardizing their attempts to exercise church discipline. The new union was shaky from the start because its creation violated the principle of congregationalism. Congregationalism was not restored till 1966. A further problem that refuses to go away is the distrust of the leadership because state officials continue to interfere in elections and other church decisions.

In one sense unity has withstood the test of time because the AUCECB still exists today. But it is also evident that not only did the

Reform Baptist split deal the union a powerful blow, the AUCECB is a more unstable union today than it was in 1945. It was a state requirement that all evangelicals should be in one union, therefore the Pentecostals were forced to join in order to be able to exist legally. Perhaps the state specified some of the anti-Pentecostal restrictions expressed in the August Agreement, but the staunch Baptists in the union have also maintained an anti-Pentecostal bias. Perhaps the emphasis on a fusion of the different denominations into one new denomination was too demanding. A unification of different denominational unions, while still maintaining some sense of distinctness, might have proved more successful. As it is, the Pentecostals are seriously considering leaving the AUCECB (they were never welcome in the CCECB) and that will very likely set the Mennonite Brethren to reevaluating their relationship.

Soviet evangelical involvement in society has been restricted to war and peace. From a movement where the majority were pacifist, they were transformed into proud soldiers defending the motherland, who proclaimed that pacifists were untrue to their constitution and to the message of the Bible! Then came another metamorphosis when AUCECB leaders became active in the peace movement. Now they affirmed that "peace is the will of God" but they continued to reject pacifism—the latter remaining a major state prohibition. One wonders what they really believe.

Can their early pacifism be fully suppressed? Is it not the lesson of history that war and violence are futile, that revolution by violence breeds more violence, more injustice and inhumanity? The biblical thrust is deeply pacifistic and the biblical Soviet evangelicals cannot escape this, even if at present they try to appease a bad conscience by separating their personal and public ethics. Living a gospel of peace has frequently proved to be very costly—what will the pacifist message of the Bible cost in the Soviet Union? Will it result in a longer list of prisoners of conscience? Or will constructive alternative service become a possibility finally and permit Soviet evangelicals to demonstrate their love of the motherland in something more constructive than learning to shoot guns and rockets?

In the late fifties, Nikita Khrushchev began to push for a rapid transformation of the Soviet Union from the intermediate stage of socialism to full communism. That meant a major effort to eliminate religion. Officially they were going to use educational methods (*vospitanie*), but the administrative measures (*administrirovanie*) remain in people's memories more vividly. In rapid order, half of the then-existing churches were closed. Secret changes in the legislation on cults made the church life that remained exceedingly difficult. There was little legal protection for the church, since few of the new freedoms permitted after 1944 had been incorporated into the law. As the antireligious propaganda campaign continued its embarrassingly semi-literate attack, a resistance movement developed that eventually forced the state authorities to abandon many aspects of the campaign. The first dissent came from the Baptists, whose skill in communicating with each other through the illegal *Samizdat* channel soon was followed by other religious and also political dissenters. Due in large part to this *Samizdat*, the Western public became aware of what had happened. At present few religious persons are arrested without the Western press reporting it.

The antireligious campaign has been a costly failure. Religion did not disappear. Rather, it is now attracting increased interest in the Soviet population. The Soviet Union suffered a loss of face before its own people, as well as before world opinion, because of its penchant for crude *administrirovanie*. The more recent official claims that state policy guarantees religious freedom but that overzealous local officials sometimes engage in illegality against Christians is an eloquent indication of the still-undeveloped sense of legality in the Soviet Union. Even today it is still unclear who has more power, the Council for Religious Affairs which reports directly to the Council of Ministers, or the KGB. Even *vospitanie* efforts have had limited success. But at least there is promise of better quality propaganda for the future. For church-state relations as they affect the AUCECB there is hope that differences can in future be dealt with in open discussions as Alexei Bychkov affirmed in his recent congress report. For the Reform Baptists the next decade portends renewed pressures and continued polarization between church and state officials.

The Khrushchev campaign was very costly for the evangelicals. Not only were there fines, beatings, meetings broken up by the authorities, closed churches, and imprisoned leaders, the authorities managed to utilize AUCECB leaders to suppress the evangelical activities of their own members. The letter of instruction to senior presbyters sent out in 1960 precipitated a major split that appears to have divided evangelicals permanently. With this letter and through certain subsequent actions, the leadership became compromised in the eyes of the membership. Reformers tried to excommunicate the leaders, thereby reducing excommunication (which should be a loving corrective) to a weapon of power. But the Khrushchev campaign also represented a promise of renewal. As a result of it there was considerable self-purging in evangelical ranks. As the evangelicals enter the eighties, both registered and unregistered evangelicals are now more nearly Bible-oriented than they were before the campaign began. They are also more aware of their legal rights so that now not only the reformers but even AUCECB spokesmen are speaking more frankly.

The Reform Baptist dissent has made a major impact. Support for them peaked in 1966, when they had about 155,000 adherents. At present their leaders claim 2,000 congregations with 100,000 members. If that is a generous estimate as some claim, then their achievements in publication activity are even more impressive. When the leaders were arrested new preachers stepped into the gap, with the result that this growth in the leadership cadres helped to foster the starting of new churches. Often churches started in the new places of exile. The Reformers provided a growing list of heroes of the faith which has stimulated the faith of many throughout the world. This aspect of their witness remains especially appealing to young people—to confess a faith worth going to prison for.

The impact on the AUCECB was more than a temporary loss of membership and an embarrassed leadership. The story of how their union was defended is the story of how a resolute membership gradually forced its powerless leadership to reform the church. By 1966 the union had finally become congregational in polity and successive congresses have continued this trend. At the 1979 congress the leaders were obviously at the mercy of the delegates, who wanted clear indication that their leaders were carrying out delegate wishes.

The story of frustrated reconciliation attempts highlights the practical problems of Christian reconciliation. Reformers began with a strong objection to AUCECB policies which they felt violated the gospel. Their own positive program was a call for sanctification. When the AUCECB made concessions, acknowledged mistakes, and proposed a statement of mutual confession, the Reformers always demanded more. Both sides talked about reconciliation and reunification as a goal, but were they really serious about it? Frustrated reconciliation attempts could not be easily glossed over, for this struggle occurred in the context of a critically watchful state.

At least, the reunification attempts clarified the issues. Both sides had to spell out what sort of separation of church and state they had in mind or saw as practical. They were forced to ask themselves how much they were prepared to pay for a free church. They had to decide what tactics were justified. Reformers believed in confrontation and valor; the registered Baptists often opted for the way of discretion as better in the long view. Both sides affirmed the importance of unity and of purity or sanctification.

Now they were forced to decide which was more important. Essentially the AUCECB argued that unity must be the primary concern, whereas the Reformers thought unity meaningless without purity. Deciding between unity and purity without becoming extremist seems an impossible decision. Observing the leading Reformers in the unity talks raises another problematic question. At what point does an uncompromising faith become sinful pride? Watching the AUCECB leaders in these talks causes one to wonder why staying in office (power retention) should be so important? Would the movement have collapsed had Karev, Zhidkov, and others resigned and permitted new leaders to try to do better? The present new leadership suggests that the state would have had to take seriously the new leaders elected by the will of the membership. The major tragedy in this story is that too often the real attraction of the gospel was missing. Both sides had their legitimate arguments and weaknesses, but the striking thing is that neither side was ready to go the second mile. Is genuine reconciliation really possible without that?

The experience of the other evangelical denominations is instructive. Both Pentecostal and Mennonite Brethren had to subordinate themselves to the Baptists for the union to function. To the degree that they were willing to apply Pentecostal spokesman Panko's advice to follow the humiliating example of Christ (Phil. 2:1-11), they remained happy in the union. Increased restiveness, especially by Pentecostals recently, may mean they have forgotten this advice. But the Baptists claim that they, too, are following this same Christ. Will they come to recognize that a genuine solution to the denominational problem will come only when the Baptists also begin to practice Paul's advice to the Philippians in greater measure? Very likely, Pentecostals will opt for a separate union, denominational multiplication is, after all, also the Western model. But to separate the disagreeing parties is the way of the world; the way of Christ is to create in himself one new man in place of the two, so making peace (Eph. 2:15, RSV).

The question of ecumenism is also complicated by this tension between purism and realism. Evangelicals affirm the desirability of a union of evangelicals. In practice this has meant uniformity on the basis of power rather than a unity fostering pluralism. To attain a more open union is the challenge for church statesmen in the eighties. Abroad, AUCECB representatives are present at innumerable ecumenical gatherings. Hereby they hope to exert some influence for peace in the world. Their foreign visits, which involve describing the freedoms of their own church life and require passing over in silence the many negative facts, has at key points helped to reduce criticism of Soviet violations of religious liberty. Whereas that function appears to be a requirement for foreign travel, the Russian Baptist leaders recognize that these foreign links have become an important lifeline whereby they have been assisted in the importation of literature and have gained friends who will not remain silent, should a new wave of repression start. But the average member, who is often unaware of these realistic advantages, but has heard about the misleading emphases of their spokesmen abroad, is uncomfortable with ecumenism. Since the Western radio preachers denounce the ecumenical movement as the whore of Babylon described in the Book of Revelation, they want no part of it.

Other evangelicals (but also AUCECB member churches) have links with East European missions. Do the missions help the work or are they a hindrance? That question can be answered only by carefully examining the work of each mission individually. But the scandal involving the two big missions, Underground Evangelism and the Wurmbrand mission, has given the whole enterprise a bad reputation. The financial contributions from the missions to the Reform Baptists have contributed to a growing factionalism. Perhaps a more major consideration is the pressing need for a major over-haul of mission activity in the direction of permitting the recipients greater maturity and responsibility, and to practice greater responsibility as missions which can do a good work without immediately needing public credit for it. The challenge before them is to demonstrate a shared leadership function with Soviet evangelicals. Perhaps the radio preachers can begin by offering a more nuanced critique and appreciation of the ecu-menical movement rather than to spout an undifferentiated anti-ecumenism that threatens the unity within the Soviet evangelical move-ment.

From the beginning, the evangelicals were a Bible movement. They emphasized Bible reading and Bible preaching and expected biblical living. That is, they sought to live according to the lifestyle of the apostolic church. Some applied these principles more radically than others in church-state relations. In the early twenties their social involvement included creating Christian communes. Later the persecution caused them to concentrate on the worship of Mary and left the service represented by her sister Martha to sister churches in the West. No doubt differing appreciations of what constitutes a biblical lifestyle will continue, but whether one looks at the Reform Baptists, the independent churches, or the AUCECB affiliates, there is no doubt that they very early became and have remained a church practicing costly discipleship.

Although Bible-centered, Soviet evangelicals have had extremely limited opportunities for serious biblical studies. Perhaps an awareness of the theological illiteracy or naiveté of Soviet evangelicals will prompt the reader to undertake to support some major project of theological education. Maybe he feels that what the Soviet evangelicals need is Hodge's or Strong's systematic theology in a Russian translation. Yet there is a benefit from the biblical simplicity, for without the sophisticated theologizing, they may be reflecting the biblical message more nearly than by restating its message in philosophical-theological categories that one can label evangelical. Should not the urge to help be expressed rather in sharing literature that fosters biblical study such as Bible dictionaries, concordances and commentaries, and literature that helps to contextualize the text (i.e., biblical and church histories, critical studies of Marxism, etc.)?

The speakers at the 1979 All-Union Congress communicated a readiness to enter the next decade with vision. They faced a missionary challenge in many areas and voted to create a department of evangelism and unity. Georgi Vins of the Reform Baptists has also identified evangelism as the continuing major task of his union. His union has always emphasized concentrated work with youth and children. Such activity has increased on an informal basis in the AUCECB in recent years. Perhaps with the strong appeals for a youth department expressed at the last congress, such work may become more systematic in the coming decade. But evangelism and youth work are precisely those areas where Soviet authorities can be expected to be most sensitive, for they still hope to win the youth away from religion. It will require a very sensitive evangelical leadership that can respond positively to the concerns of children and young people without upsetting the authorities unduly. The leaders know that too much restraint on their young people may result in another split in their union and neither they nor the authorities want that.

Atheist scholars predict a new crisis for evangelicals because they will lose the young people to secularism. As long as the presbyter and other believers demonstrate the moral courage and charisma which the atheist evangelist appears to lack, young people will be attracted to the church. The problem emerges as the Christian youth seek to apply the social message of the gospel. Leaders like Bychkov have been urging believers to cooperate with social institutions locally in helping build a more just society. But there are many evangelicals who fear such involvement as a surrender to worldliness. As Soviet society continues to become less ideological, more consumer-oriented, and more influenced by Western culture, it will become increasingly difficult to distinguish what is worldly and what is Christian.

Those are the concerns behind the heavy emphasis on clergy education that one heard at the last AUCECB congress. Alexei Bychkov announced that future students in the correspondence course should be persons with a better-quality secular education, persons who were prepared to work hard at their studies. But they must also be persons willing to be sent to places of need, not simply to provide extra help in the strong central city churches. Alexei Bychkov also announced a major project to translate a New Testament Bible commentary series into Russian. That should help the present untrained clergy improve the quality of the sermons which constitute the main nurture for Christians facing a complicated world.

Reform Baptists still argue that the only way to have a reliable church is to have no relations with state officials, claiming that the AUCECB leaders in Moscow still live with compromise. Some workers in the Moscow offices were sharply criticized at the 1979 congress because their integrity was in doubt. Leadership continues to be a fundamental problem. To outside observers, the quality of leadership in the AUCECB has been improving and the number of senior presbyters distrusted by their membership has decreased. New council and presidium members added in 1979 will improve the leadership image among the members. Perhaps the most able leaders are prevented from serving in elected office due to state constraints, but that, too, seems to be less true than formerly. Leadership for both AUCECB and CCECB churches is more a burden than a joy. The context of decision-making as described in this book is such that few leaders enjoy the full trust of the members or of their colleagues. Reform Baptist leaders have become factionalized because they cannot fully trust each other except in prison. It seemed apparent at the 1979 congress that well-meant efforts by AUCECB leaders were sometimes misconstrued.

Fortunately the New Testament can offer a word of challenge and of comfort for such a time. In his relations with the Corinthian church, the Apostle Paul had been accused of wrong motives, had seen his actions misconstrued, and his words twisted. In reply he asserted that he did not act with deceit and proclaimed as his principle of operation: "In the full light of truth we live in God's sight and try to commend ourselves to everyone's good conscience" (2 Cor. 4:2, GNB). Perhaps the Russian evangelical leaders, like most of us, recognize the desirability of such a principle but still experience it primarily as a distant goal. Yet Paul added an important observation which should also apply when we assess Soviet evangelical leaders: "We who have this spiritual treasure are like common clay pots, in order to show that the supreme power belongs to God, not to us" (2 Corinthians 4:7, GNB).

Alexei Bychkov concluded his latest congress report with boldness and triumph. Socialism and atheism need not be married together, he declared, that was not just the opinion of Christians, but "of many progressive people and movements which are striving for peace and justice." Millions of Christians are living in socialist countries and his own church could bear witness to the fact that "in socialist countries there is adequate place for the activities of the churches." In fact, quoting his predecessor, he affirmed:

The task of the Christian in atheist surroundings consists of showing to atheists the most appealing of the sons of men: Jesus Christ. To reveal him not only by preaching the Gospel but also in one's daily life so that the atheist will come to believe in him, will bow the knee to him, and like the unbelieving Thomas will say: "My Lord and my God" (Jn. 20:28).[1]

The likelihood that state opposition against all believers, including the various evangelical groupings, will be resumed in the not too distant future remains high. At the moment, the Reform Baptists are again experiencing intense pressure, and there are signs that their union has been weakened. Once that union is eliminated, zealous atheistic authorities will see less need to make concessions to the AUCECB. The average evangelical lives with the expectation that, as he puts it, the wind can change any day. But all evangelicals can affirm in triumph with Bychkov that "the present and future church is in the hands of Jesus Christ and delivers us from the dependence on the ideological superstructure of our society." And so they proclaim the enduring affirmation of the Apostle Paul:

We are often troubled, but not crushed; sometimes in doubt, but never in despair; there are many enemies, but we are never without a friend; and though badly hurt at times, we are not destroyed (2 Cor. 4:8-9, GNB).

Note for Chapter 16

1. From the manuscript copy of "Report of the AUCECB to the 42nd All-Union ECB Congress," by Gen. Sec. A. M. Bychkov, Dec. 18-20, 1979, pp. 39 and 43.

Appendix 1

Statute of Unity, October 27, 1944

§ 1

From two unions—the Union of Evangelical Christians and the Union of Baptists—one union for the entire territory of the USSR is established: the Union of Evangelical Christians and Baptists.

§ 2

The leading organ of the Union of Evangelical Christians and Baptists is the All-Union Council of Evangelical Christians and Baptists— AUCEC+B.

§ 3

The following are to be elected from the members of the All-Union Council of Evangelical Christians and Baptists: Chairman, two vice-chairmen (*Tovarishchyi*), secretary and treasurer, who form the presidium of the council.

§ 4

The All-Union Council of Evangelical Christians and Baptists has its seal on which is written "All-Union Council of Evangelical Christians and Baptists" and the words on the inner circle: "One Lord, one faith, one baptism."

§ 5

Evangelical Christians and Baptists existing as separate unions before the amalgamation are now fused into one society. Congregations, existing separately, as congregations either of Evangelical Christians or of Baptists, now enter into one union.

§ 6

Each congregation, entering the Union of Evangelical Christians and Baptists, bears the name: (some specific) Congregation of Evangelical Christians and Baptists.

§ 7

All congregations of Evangelical Christians and Baptists must if possible have ordained presbyters and deacons in accordance with the Word of God: Titus 1:5; Acts 6:1-6; and 1 Tim. 3:1.

§ 8

In each congregation baptism, communion, and marriage are performed by ordained presbyters. In the absence of such, these activities may also be performed by unordained members of congregations, however only by charge of the church.

§ 9

Baptism and marriage, performed with the laying-on of hands, or without laying-on of hands on those baptized and married, has equal force. But to attain full unity in church practice, it is recommended that the performance of marriage and baptism be done with the laying-on of hands, interpreting this action as a form of festive prayer for blessing. Further, in the event of more than two baptismal candidates, the laying-on of hands is performed by raising the hands above the candidates while pronouncing a prayer for them.

§ 10

The Lord's Supper or the breaking of bread may be conducted either by breaking the bread into many little pieces, or else by breaking it into two or three or several larger pieces.

Bread and wine are received by the members of the congregations standing, thereby expressing our reverence for the command to break bread.

Appendix 2

The August Agreement, 1945

The following twelve points were agreed to as a basis of union between the Christians of Evangelical Faith (Pentecostal) and the Union of Evangelical Christians and Baptists. Repeated requests for a revision of the Agreement has not resulted in any changes.

§ 1

The congregations of the Christians of Evangelical Faith unite with congregations of Evangelical Christians and Baptists into one union.

§ 2

The single union has its general executive center in the city of Moscow as well as a single treasury.

§ 3

Representatives of Christians of Evangelical Faith are also included in the headquarters staff.

§ 4

The spiritual workers of the Christians of Evangelical Faith remain in their spiritual calling which they bore before uniting with Evangelical Christians and Baptists, that is, senior presbyters, presbyters, and deacons.

§ 5

Both sides recognize that the fullness of powers from on high, spoken of in Acts 1:8, may be manifested through the sign of other tongues as well as without this sign (Acts 2:4; 8:17, 39; 10:46; 19:6).

§ 6

Both sides recognize, on the basis of Holy Scripture, that diverse tongues are one of the gifts of the Holy Spirit, not given to all but to some (1 Cor. 12:4-11).

This is supported by the words of verse 30 of this chapter: "Do all have the gifts of healing? Do all speak in tongues? Do all interpret?"

§ 7

Both sides recognize that unknown tongues without interpretation is fruitless, concerning which the Apostle Paul explicitly states: 1 Cor. 14:6-9; 1 Cor. 14:28: "If there be no interpreter, then keep silent in the church." Both sides uphold this as a rule given by God, through the Apostle Paul.

§ 8

Considering the word of the Apostle Paul about the fruitlessness of unknown tongues in the absence of an interpreter, both sides agreed to abstain from unknown tongues in general meetings.

§ 9

Recognizing that, along with the operation of the Holy Spirit in the services, there may be manifestations leading to the destruction of the decency and decorum of the service (1 Cor. 14:40), both sides agreed to conduct an educational program against this type of manifestation, remembering that God is not a God of confusion, but of peace (1 Cor. 14:33).

§ 10

In view of the fact that the Evangelical Christians and the Baptists do not practice foot washing, the present agreement recommends that the Christians of Evangelical Faith conduct an educational program designed to achieve a common understanding with the Evangelical Christians and Baptists on this question, aiming toward unity and the uniformity of public worship.

§ 11

Both sides are to utilize all measures, so that among the Evangelical Christians and Baptists on the one hand, and the Christians of Evangelical Faith on the other, the most sincere fraternal and mutual relations will be established for reciprocal joy and blessed joint labor.

§ 12

After signing the present agreement, both sides will announce the unification event to their congregations and will call for a prayer of thanksgiving for the great and praiseworthy matter of unity of all Christians in our country, who have been born again by faith.

(**BV**, 4/57, p. 36)

Appendix 3

Constitution of the ECB Church in the USSR

The following constitution was approved by a congress of delegates on December 19, 1979. The first statute or constitution issued in 1948 was never published. The problematic statute of 1960, as well as the revisions suggested by the *Initsiativniki* in 1961 and the constitution as approved in 1963, are printed in English translation in parallel columns in Michael Bourdeaux, *Religious Ferment in Russia,* pp. 190-210. A major constitutional revision was approved in 1966 which involved considerable renumbering of paragraphs, extensive additions and refinements. At the congress in 1969 and 1979 further amendments were approved. What follows is therefore in essence the constitution of 1966 with the changes of 1969 and 1979 incorporated. Points added in 1969 are printed within square brackets [ ] while additions in 1979 are printed within diagonal brackets / /. Other changes are explained in the footnotes.

CONSTITUTION OF THE UNION OF THE EVANGELICAL
CHRISTIAN-BAPTISTS IN THE USSR

A wise man knows both time and constitution.   —*Ecclesiastes 8:5*

I. General Statutes

§ 1. The ECB Union in the USSR is a voluntary association of churches (congregations and groups) of the Evangelical-Baptist faith, desiring to have fraternal fellowship and to cooperate in the work of God. The ECB Union includes Evangelical Christians[-]Baptists, Christians of Evangelical Faith, and Mennonite / Brethren/. / The addition of other sister evangelical denominations is decided by the All-Union Congress./

§ 2. The foundation for the doctrines, life and activities of the ECB Union is Holy Scripture—the books of the Old and New Testaments (canonical).

§ 3. The ECB Union has the following aims and tasks:
(a) To help to promote in the life and activities of the churches / the preaching of the gospel/, the confession of faith and the principles of Evangelical Christian-Baptists.[1]
(b) To help to promote the unity of the Evangelical Christian-Baptists, Christians of Evangelical Faith and Mennonite / Brethren/[2] who are born again through the Word of God and the Holy Spirit and have received water baptism upon confession of faith (John 17:21-23).
(c) To help maintain the purity of evangelical teaching in ECB churches (Titus 2:17).

II. The Leadership of the ECB Union

Seeking to maintain the unity of the Spirit in the bond of peace.
—*Ephesians 4:3*

§ 4. The supreme organ of the ECB Union is the All-Union Congress of church representatives (Acts 15:6), / which have been elected at oblast, regional, and republican conferences/.

An All-Union ECB congress is called, as a rule, once in three [to five] years.

The norms of representation / and election procedures/, place, and time of the All-Union Congress are determined by the plenum of the All-Union Council of Evangelical Christians and Baptists.

§ 5. The All-Union ECB Congress meets to examine / and decide/ the internal church questions of the Union and of the activities of ECB churches:

(a) Hears and ratifies reports from the AUCECB and its auditing commission;

(b) Reviews, changes, and confirms the statutes of the ECB Union;

(c) Hears and considers papers concerning doctrine and spiritual questions, which arise from the life and activity of the churches;

(d) Elects the leading organs of the Union.

§ 6. For carrying out the resolutions of the All-Union ECB Congress and to conduct, in correspondence with the teachings of Jesus Christ, the activities of the ECB Union in the period between congresses, and also for external representation, the All-Union Congress elects from among its participants by open vote, / but with a majority of no less than two thirds of the delegates,/ the central leading organ of the Union: the All-Union Council of Evangelical Christian-Baptists (AUCECB). / Keeping in mind the representation of the evangelical denominations in the Union,/ the AUCECB is elected from the most experienced and worthy workers of the churches (Acts 6:3; 20:28).

§ 7. The AUCECB elects a presidium from among its members. / Departments subordinate to the AUCECB presidium for carrying out its work are: evangelism and Christian unity; the preparation and qualification of church workers and the leaders of music and singing; international; publishing, finance and management.

Persons responsbile for the work of a department must be members of the AUCECB, approved by the plenum of the AUCECB./

§ 8. The AUCECB plenum meets as necessary, but at least once a year.

§ 9. The AUCECB is responsible for:

(a) Putting into action the tasks of the ECB Union, as stated in Paragraph 3 of this constitution, and to carry out the resolutions of the All-Union Congress of ECB;

(b) Maintaining ties with local churches (congregations and groups) and to conudct these activities in correspondence with Holy Scripture, the constitution, and the decisions of the ECB Congress, both by means of letter correspondence, and also by visiting them;

(c) Helping local churches in inner-church spiritual questions both through senior presbyters and oblast councils of presbyters, as well as directly;

(d) Maintaining contact with churches close to it in faith and with / religious/ unions and organizations in foreign countries[3] through correspondence, sending its representatives to their congresses and conferences, and also inviting foreign spiritual workers to the USSR;

(e) Preparing / and qualifying senior presbyters,/ presbyters, / deacons,/ preachers and choral directors through Bible and choral courses, / conferences for spiritual edification/ and seminars.

(f) Publishing / Bibles,/ journals, and other spiritual literature necessary for ECB churches;

(g) Maintaining a list of churches,[4] presbyters and the number of members belonging to the Union;

(h) Representing the interests of the churches (congregations and groups) belonging to the Union before state organs.

In correspondence with Holy Scripture (Mt. 22:21; Rom. 13:1-5; Titus 3:1, 2) the AUCECB and the churches belonging to the Union respect and observe the laws of the country in those activities not concerned with the inner spiritual life of the believers.

§ 10. The financial means of the ECB Union consist of freewill offerings and income for carrying out the activities of the AUCECB in accordance with budget estimates. The financial resources of the Union are kept on current account in the state bank.

§ 11. The auditing of finances, documents and financial reports of the AUCECB [and the senior presbyters] is carried out by an auditing commission elected in open voting / with no less than a two thirds majority of the delegates/ of the All-Union Congress and consists of seven[5] members. The auditing commission reports the results of its audits to the regular All-Union ECB Congress, and also at plenary sessions of the AUCECB.

§ 12. The AUCECB has a seal and a stamp.

§ 13. The AUCECB has an office under the presidium in the city of Moscow. Only church members may be office workers. / A working contract must be concluded with each of them./

III. Senior Presbyters, Presbyter Councils and Conferences of Workers[6] — Oblast (Regional), Inter-Oblast, Republican

Tend the flock of God that is your charge, not by constraint but willingly, not for shameful gain but eagerly, not as domineering over those in your charge but being examples to the flock.   —1 Peter 5:2, 3

§ 14.

(a) Senior presbyters, / their deputies/ and assistants are recommended by the AUCECB / presidium/ with the approval of the churches in which they are members:

/ Republican and inter-republican (senior presbyters) through their election at republican and inter-republican conferences of church workers; or the approval of senior presbyters at oblast, inter-oblast, regional, or inter-regional conferences by recommendation of republican senior presbyters following the election of these senior presbyters at oblast, inter-oblast, regional and inter-regional conferences of church workers./[7]

/ (b) In the case of irresponsible service of senior presbyters, their deputies or assistants, the AUCECB presidium examines the question of their further service (1 Tim. 5:19) and presents the matter of their reelection at the corresponding conference of workers./

(c) To help senior presbyters, a council of experienced church workers is elected at conferences; the senior presbyter being the chairman of the council.

§ 15. Senior presbyters together with presbyter councils carry out:

(a) The tasks of the Union, stated in Paragraph 3 of this constitituion;

(b) Spiritual help to churches located in the territory which they serve; / help in singing and musical matters by attracting experienced choir directors;/ participate in worship services and in the education of believers in proper relations to their Christian duties;

(c) Participate where possible / in the recommendation/ and election of presbyters and other church workers and in their ordination/ after a probation period of no less than one year from their election by the church, similarly for their dismissal;/

(d) Keep a list of congregations, workers, and the number of church members.

§ 16. Senior presbyters report on their activities to the / corresponding/ conference of church workers[8] and to the AUCECB.

§ 17. The senior presbyter has a seal and a stamp.

§ 18. For deciding questions that arise, as deemed necessary, / the senior presbyter together with/ the presbyter council calls a conference of church workers, in the territory served by him, / but not less than once a year./

IV. Local ECB Churches

I will build my church.—*Matthew 16:18*
And the churches were strengthened in the faith.—*Acts 16:5*

§ 19. Local ECB churches are an association of believers of the Evangelical-Baptist faith, voluntarily united for mutual service to the Lord and for the satisfaction of their spiritual needs.

The tasks of the local ECB churches are:

(a) To preach the gospel (Acts 20:24);

(b) To educate believers to attain holiness, Christian piety, and to observe all that Christ commanded (Mt. 28:20; 1 Tim. 2:1-4);

(c) Develop and strengthen Christian love and unity of believers, in agreement with the high priestly prayer of our Lord (Jn. 17:21-23).

§ 20. For carrying out the tasks specified, the local ECB churches meet for divine worship with preaching of the gospel, prayers, and baptism, communion, marriage, funerals, and other church practices. The worship service is carried out with congregational and choral singing, with musical accompaniment, / declamation,/ etc.

§ 21. The ECB churches meet for worship on Sundays, and also on weekdays at the discretion of the church and on the Christian festivals: Christmas, New Year, Epiphany, Circumcision, Annunication, Easter, Ascension, Trinity, Transfiguration, Harvest Festival, Unity Day / and other church holidays./

§ 22. Communion in local ECB churches (congregations and groups) is observed at the discretion of the church, usually on the first Sunday of each month.

§ 23. ECB churches conduct their worship services in special buildings, provided by the state for their free use, or in properties leased from local organs of power or from individual persons.

§ 24.

(a) Anyone believing in Christ as his personal Savior, having experienced the rebirth through the Word of God and the Holy Spirit, having experienced water baptism on faith and having attained the age of majority,[9] may be a member of a local church.

/ (b) Accepting church members from other congregations is carried out by the church after receiving notification from the church in which he or she was a member./

(c) Each church member takes an active part in the life of the church,

serves the Lord in accordance with his calling, exercises the right to elect
and to be elected for service, bears responsibility before God and the church
for his spiritual condition (1 Pet. 2:5, 9; Gal. 6:1, 2).

§ 25.

(a) Each believer, wishing to receive water baptism on faith,[10] declares
this to the presbyter of the church and / after appropriate spiritual instruc-
tion/ he is examined.

(b) / After the church has decided about satisfying this request,/ the
baptism is performed in natural water or in a baptistry.

§ 26. Each church belonging to the AUCECB union maintains its independence and decides the most major internal church questions at a /
members'/ meeting. The election and reelection of church workers, the accepting and expelling of members, as well as other spiritual questions are
presented / by the presbyter, but managerial and financial matters/ by the
executive committee.

§ 27. For the daily services and conduct of current affairs the church, /
in accord with Holy Scripture (1 Tim. 3:1-12; Titus 1:5-9; Acts 6:3-6),/
elects:

(a) For the presbyterial tasks there is a presbyter / or if necessary
several presbyters, one of/ whom is the chief person, responsible for the
worship service and the spiritual education of church members and for
carrying out the church statutes in the church; as well as deacons and
preachers, who participate instead of a presbyter in conducting worship
services and fulfilling the church statutes.

Other church members as designated by the presbyter / or the person
responsible for the worship service/ may also participate in the preaching
and worship services of the church.

Commentary: / (1) The presbyter may conduct conversations with
deacons, preachers, choir leaders, and church members about the worship service and other spiritual questions, devoting special attention in
this to the education of young believers, and also for the preparation of
recommendations to be approved by decision of the members meeting.

(2) In each congregation baptism, communion, marriage and other
practices are performed, as a rule, by elected ordained presbyters and
upon designation of the presbyter, by other workers. These practices,
including excommunication, can be performed by elected but not yet ordained church workers./[11]

(b) For fulfilling the immediate functions connected with the management and use of the church property, and also for the external representation of the church, there is the executive organ;

(c) For supervising incoming[12] and outgoing funds, and also for the maintenance of the congregation's property, there is an auditing commission of three members;[13]

(d) The presbyter, the executive organ, the auditing commission, and other workers report to the church not less than once a year.

§ 28.

(a) Choristers, their leaders, and also those playing musical instruments are believers.

(b) The spiritual guardian of the choir is the presbyter of the church, and also the choir leader.[14]

§ 29.

(a) The local church's means consist of the freewill offerings of believers, which have been paid into the treasury of the church (2 Cor. 9:7).

(b) The church's funds are spent: On the upkeep of the church premises, on the maintenance of church workers, for transfer to the AU-CECB treasurer, to the treasury of the oblast and to the republican senior presbyter, and for other church needs.

(c) Each church maintains a book for recording income and expenditure.

(d) Each church has an inventory book in which the property of the church is entered—both what is received from the state by contract and what is bought and donated. An audit of the finances and material means is carried out by the auditing commission.

§ 30. The church has its own seal and stamp.

Explanatory Footnotes

1. The order "confession of faith" and "the principles of" were reversed, the 1966 statute putting the principles first.

2. The 1979 revision omitted "and other denominations."

3. Slightly shortened in 1979 to make less definite the distinction between churches and unions close to them in faith and other organizations and unions abroad.

4. Replacing "congregations" with "churches."

5. Changed from three members to five in 1974 to seven in 1979.

6. "Workers" replacing "presbyters," the former being more inclusive.

7. This paragraph was reworded and expanded in order to distinguish between senior presbyters at the republican and inter-republican level from those senior presbyters responsible for smaller areas who are subordinate to republican senior presbyters, having been recommended or nominated by the latter.

8. "Church workers" replaces "presbyters."

9. The order of the latter two conditions is reversed, thereby permitting baptism before the age of 18, but making age of maturity a condition for church membership.

10. Omits phrase "to join the local church," hereby making clear the new distinction between baptism and church membership.

11. This commentary has entirely new content; the earlier commentary stated: "Church ordinances may be performed, upon recommendation of the presbyter and church council, by deacons, members of the church council or preachers of the church."

12. This less precise word replacing "collections" allows funds received privately to be included in the church treasury instead of only money collected inside the church building as the law specifies.

13. The three-member condition earlier appeared at the end of Par. 29 (c).

14. The order is reversed to stress the presbyter's guardianship role.

Appendix 4

AUCECB Council Members and Senior Presbyters

The All-Union Council initially consisted of eight persons, of whom five formed a Presidium. It was increased to 12 in 1945. The role of the five member Presidium was especially strong from 1954-58. The Council was increased to 14 plus two candidates in 1958, but reduced in 1959 to 10 members "in accordance with the law". The existing council was reelected in 1963 (Tatarchenko replacing the deceased Orlov) and five candidates were elected. In 1966 the Council was expanded to 25 members, eight candidates and a 10 member Presidium, delegates electing the Council members and candidates, the Council electing the Presidium from its ranks and the Presidium electing its own officers. In 1969 the Presidium increased to 11 members (until 1971). In 1979 the Council was increased again to 31 members (only 30 were elected), nine candidates. The Presidium was also increased to 11 members with three candidates.

The Revision or Auditing Commission members are included because they are a part of the leadership, membership on the commission usually serving as a stepping stone into the Council. Introduced in 1948, the three members in 1979. Beginning in 1980 the chairman became ex-officio member of the Presidium.

Abbreviations:

°	= present office holder	Pres	= presbyter
SP	= senior presbyter	Cand	= candidate member
Dep	= deputy senior presbyter	Pen	= Pentecostal
Ass't	= assistant senior presbyter	MB	= Mennonite Brethren

Jacob I. Zhidkov (President) 1944-66
Alexander V. Karev (General Secretary) 1944-71
M. I. Goliaev (Vice-President) 1944-54; member 1954-59
M. A. Orlov (Vice-President) 1944-54; member 1954-61
N. A. Levindanto (SP Baltic) member 1944-54; Vice-President 1954-66
A. L. Andreev (SP Ukraine) member 1944-54; Vice-President 1954-65
F. G. Patkovski (Dep Ukraine) member 1944-48; briefly Treasurer 1948
P. I. Malin (Treasurer) 1944-48
°I. G. Ivanov member 1945-48; Treasurer 1948-66; President 1966-74;
    President Emeritus 1974-
K. Latseklis (SP Latvia) 1945
Johannes I. Lipstock (SP Estonia) 1945-59
D. I. Ponomarchuk (Pen, Dep Ukraine, SP Moldavia) 1945-66
A. M. Korps (SP Latvia) 1946-48
A. M. Redlikh (SP Latvia) 1948-53
V. N. Chechnev (SP Belorussia) 1948-58; Cand 1958
P. Ia. Ter-Avanesov (SP Caucasus) Cand 1948-53; member 1953-58;
    Cand 1958-59
Johannes M. Ris (SP Riga region) Cand 1948
F. E. Kuhns (SP Latvia) 1953-59
A. I. Mitskevich (Ass't Gen. Sec.) 1958-59; Presidium 1966-79, also
    Treasurer 1971-79
A. N. Karpov (SP Moscow) 1958-66
I. I. Motorin (Treasurer) member 1958-66; Treasurer 1966-71
E. N. Raevski (SP E. Siberia and Far East) Cand 1958-59; Cand 1963-66;
    Cand 1969-71; member 1971-74
G. G. Ponurko (Pen SP Dnepropetrovsk) Cand 1958-59; Cand 1963-66
K. S. Veliseichik (SP Belorussia) 1959-69
I. Ia. Tatarchenko (Dep Ukraine) 1963-66; Presidium 1966-72
A. M. Sil'dos (SP Latvia) Cand 1963-66; member 1966-69
S. P. Fadiukhin (SP Leningrad) Cand 1963-66; member 1966-69;
    Presidium 1969-79
M. S. Vashchuk (SP Central Asia) Cand 1963-66; member 1966-69
P. K. Egle (SP Latvia) 1966-79
°M. Ia. Zhidkov (Pres. Moscow) Presidium 1966-71; Vice-President 1971-
°Jacob J. Fast (MB, Dep RSFSR) 1966-74; Presidium 1974-
A. N. Kiriukhantsev (SP Leningrad) Presidium 1966
N. N. Mel'nikov (SP Ukraine) Vice-President 1966-74
S. T. Timchenko (Moscow) Vice-President 1966-71
I. Ia. Kaliuzhnyi (Dep Ukraine) 1966-79
°A. E. Klimenko (SP Volga) 1966-71; Vice-President 1971-74; President 1974-
°K. P. Borodinov (SP W. Siberia) 1966-
N. V. Koval'kov (Moscow staff) 1966-69
N. V. Kuz'menko (Pen Dep Ukraine) 1966-69
M. Ia. Rubanenko (SP Krasnodarskii Krai) 1966-68
D. D. Shapovalov (Dep Ukraine) 1966-79

°V. F. Vasilenko (SP Vinnitsa) 1966-
°A. A. Nesteruk (Pen SP Volhynia) 1966-69; Cand 1974-79; member 1979-
P. A. Dzhaniashvili (SP Caucasus) 1966-68
V. T. Mitin (SP Voroshilovgrad) Cand 1966-69
A. A. Arder (Pres. Rakvere Estonia) Cand 1966-69
V. A. Kriger (MB, Moscow staff) Cand 1966-69; member 1969-74
L. F. Tkachenko (Moscow staff) Cand 1966-69
G. T. Bulgakov (SP Upper Volga) Cand 1966-79
°D. M. Andrikevich (SP Khmel'nitski) Cand 1966-69; Cand 1974-79; member 1979-
V. F. Semenov (former Leningrad Pres) Cand 1966-69
I. M. Orlov (Moscow Int. Dept) Cand. 1966-69; member 1969
°Robert Vyzu (SP Estonia) 1969-79; Presidium 1979-
°A. M. Bychkov (Gen. Sec.) Vice-President 1969-71; Gen. Sec. 1971-
°N. I. Dolmatov (SP Rostov) 1969-
°I. S. Gnida (Dep Ukraine) 1969-74; Presidium 1974-79; Ass't Gen. Sec. 1979-
A. D. Savin (SP Krasnodarskii Krai) 1969-74
°V. S. Glukhovski (Pen, Dep Ukraine) 1969-79; Presidium 1979-
M. M. Samotugin (SP Central Asia) 1969-74
P. K. Shatrov (Pen, Moscow staff) Presidium 1969-79
°Jacob K. Dukhonchenko (SP Ukraine) Cand 1969-71; member 1971-74; Vice-President 1974-
S. K. Malanchuk (SP Moldvia) Cand. 1969-74
°D. L. Vozniuk (Pen, SP Ternopol) Cand 1969-74; member 1974-79; 1979-
°L. S. Vladyko (Pen, Dep Belorussia) Cand 1969-74; member Vice-President and Presidium Cand 1979-
°N. A. Kolesnikov (SP Kazakhstan) Cand 1969-74; member 1974-79; Treasurer 1979-
V. I. Lebedev (Moscow staff) Cand 1969-74
M. P. Chernopiatov (SP Tula) Vice-President 1974-79
°N. N. Sizov (SP Kirgizia) 1974-
°T. F. Kviring (SP Central Asia) 1974-79; Cand Presidium 1979-
°V. E. Logvinenko (Dep RSFSR) 1974-79; Vice-President 1979-
°I. V. Bukatyi (SP Belorussia) 1974-79; Presidium 1979-
°F. P. Virts (Dep Kazakhstan) Cand 1974-79; member 1979-
°V. A. Mitskevich (SP South central RSFSR) Cand 1974-79; member 1979-
°N. G. Tsuman (SP Dnepropetrovsk) Cand 1974-79; member 1979-
°Ia. M. Kravchenko (SP Zhitomir) Cand 1974-79; member 1979-
°F. D. Starukhin (SP Kharkov) 1979-
°K. A. Sipko (SP Omsk) 1979-
°N. Z. Kvirikashvili (SP Caucasus) 1979-
°K. S. Sedlitskii (SP Moldavia) Presidium 1979-
°Ia. E. Tervits (SP Latvia) Cand Presidium 1979-
°B. I. Bilas (Pen, SP L'vov) member 1979-
°V. N. Vlasenko (8 SP Stavropoi) Cand 1979-

° A. A. Lysiuk (SP Chernovitsy) Cand 1979-
° V. E. Zenkin (Pen Dnepropetrovsk) Cand 1979-
° A. F. Agafonov (Pres Kishinev) Cand 1979-
° A. G. Brynza (SP Zaporozh'e) Cand 1979-
° P. P. Ens (Pres Orenburg) Cand 1979-
° V. I. Petrov (SP Kursk) Cand 1979-
  G. I. Komendant (SP Kiev) Cand 1979-
  A.P. Vashchishin (Pen, SP Rovno) Cand 1979-

Revision Commission Members:
  V. T. Pelevin (SP Kursk) Chairman 1948-54
  A. I. Mitskevich (Ass't Gen. Sec.) 1948-58; chairman 1959-66
  N. N. Mel'nikov (Dep Ukraine) 1948-66, chairman 1958-59
  F. R. Astakhov (Dep Ukraine) chairman 1954-58; member 1958-66
  B. A. Rusanov (SP North Caucasus) 1958-59
  M. P. Chernopiatov SP Tula) Chairman 1966-74
° M. V. Mel'nik (Ass't Ukraine) 1966-74; Chairman 1974-
  P. G. Radchuk (SP Rovno) 1966-74
  N. N. Sizov (SP Kirgizia) 1969-74
  V. A. Mitskevich (SP South Central RSFSR) 1969-74
  N. Z. Kvirikashvili (SP Caucasus) 1974-79
  K. S. Sedletskii (SP Moldavia) 1974-79
  G. I. Pavlenk (SP Sumy) 1974-77
° A. P. Mamalat (SP Kirovograd) 1979-
° V. A. Shul'ts (Ass't Kazakhstan) 1974-
° F. P. Lymar (SP Cherkassy) 1979-
° M. M. Kon'shin (SP Lower Urals) 1979-
° N. A. Poberei 1979-
° O. I. Skuratovich (SP Minsk) 1979-

AUCECB Senior Presbyters: °are present incumbents; the list is arranged according to the 10 regional divisions presently in effect

1. *RSFSR*
        Andrei E. Klimenko, SP 1979-80
      ° V. E. Logvinenko, Dep 1979-80; SP 1980-
      ° Jacob J. Fast, Dep 1979-
      ° P. K. Shatrov, Dep 1979-

    1.01 *Leningrad and North East* (Kaliningrad added 1976)
    A. S. Chizov 1947-53

NOTE: The organizational division for multi-oblast responsibiliites varied as younger senior presbyters gradually assumed more responsibility and older senior presbyters no longer managed the excessive distances.

A. N. Karpov 1953-54
M. A. Orlov 1954-60
A. N. Kiriukhantsev 1960-66
°S. P. Fadiukhin 1966-

Temporary Subdivisions:
   Kalinin—V.P. Arzhanov 1945-47
      V. F. Semenov 1959 (Ass't)
   Pskov—M. S. Kapustinskii 1945-53
     F. A. Kuprin 1953-59 (Ass't)

     1.02 *North West* (includes Vologda, Murmansk, Arkhangelsk, Karelia, Komi ASSR)
M. A. Sorokin 1967-78
°S. I. Nikolaev 1978-

     1.03 *North Central* (Moscow, Vladimir, Ivanovsk, Iaroslavl, Kostroma)
M. A. Orlov 1945-54
A. N. Karpov 1954-65 also Tula and Kalinin 1963-65
G. P. Lampetov 1966-70 also Kalinin
A. L. Kaiukov 1967-72 for Moscow, Kalinin, Smolensk, Ivanovsk and Iaroslavl
°V. L. Fedichkin 1973-

     1.04 *South Central* (Kalinin, Tambov, Smolensk, Kaluga, Riazan, Voronezh)
I. F. Zharikh 1947-58 for Tambov, Riazan, Voronezh
G. T. Bulgakov 1959-63
I. P. Beliaev 1944-57 for Smolensk, later also Kaluga
V. P. Arzhanov 1945-63 for Kalinin
G. P. Lampetov 1966-70 for Kalinin and North Central
A. L. Kaiukov 1967-72 for Kalinin, Smolensk and North Central
°V. A. Mitskevich 1973-

     1.05 *Belgorod*
I. D. Shavyrin 1945-66
M. P. Chernopiatov 1970-74 (for Belgorod, Kaluga, Riazan, Tula)
°S. A. Kiseliuk 1972-

     1.06 *Kursk*
V. T. Pelevin 1945-57
M. A. Sorokin 1958-64
A. A. Nosarev 1964-68
I. A. Evstratenko 1968-74
°V. I. Petrov 1974-

1.07 *Orel and Briansk*
F. F. Barkholenko 1945-57
°A. N. Krainii 1957-
P. F. Dubinin (Ass't) 1958-61 for Briansk

1.08 *Tula*
N. P. Kiriukhantsev 1945-56 (since 1950 combined with the Volga autonomous republics)
A. N. Karpov 1963-65
°M. P. Chernopiatov 1966- (temporarily also for Belgorod, Kaluga and Riazan)

1.09 *Lower Urals* (Kuibyshev, Penza, Ul'ianovsk, Orenburg, Cheliabinsk)
G. M. Buzynin 1945-63 (also Tatar, Bashkir, Udmurt, Churvash, Mariisk and Mordovian ASSRs)
A. E. Klimenko 1963-75 (gradually increased to 13 oblasts on Upper and Lower Volga and Voronezh)
°M. M. Kon'shin 1975-

1.10 *Upper Volga* (Mariisk, Tatar, Chuvash, Udmurt, Bashkir ASSRs, and Gor'ki Oblast)
T. V. Cheburakhin 1946-50
N. P. Kiriukhantsev 1950-56
S. G. Shchepetov 1956-58
G. M. Buzynin 1958-63
°G. T. Bulgakov 1963- (Also Perm, Penza added in 1976)

1.11 *Lower Volga* (Volgograd. Saratov and Astrakhan after 1957)
V. I. Ermilov 1954-63
S. S. Zhuivan 1957-70
A. E. Klimenko 1970-75
°Ia. Ia. Korzhevski 1975-

1.12 *Rostov*
A. A. Koshelev 1945-53
M. I. Goliaev 1954-60
A. R. Surikov (Ass't) 1956-?
I. A. Evstratenko 1960-65
V. A. Selivanov 1965-66
°N. I. Dolmatov 1966-
V. D. Erisov (Ass't) 1968-74

1.13 *Krasnodarskii Krai*
N. I. Kornaukhov 1944-55
V. I. Andreenko 1956-60
I. E. Egorov 1960-65

M. Ia. Rubanenko 1965-66
P. A. Dzhaniashvili 1966-68
V. P. Krasinski 1968-72
A. D. Savin 1972-78
S. E. Dubovchenko (Ass't) 1972- ?
°V. D. Erisov 1978-

1.14 *Stavropol'skii Krai*
N. I. Kornaukhov 1944-54
R. R. Podgaiskii 1954-65
P. A. Dzhaniashvili 1965-68
A. D. Savin 1968-77
E. E. Morgachev (Ass't) 1972-78
V. D. Erisov 1977-79
°V. N. Vlasenko 1979- (Ass't since 1978)
°N. E. Suchkov (Ass't) 1979-

1.15 *Western Siberia* (Novosibirsk, Tomsk, Omsk, Tiumen,
Kurgan, Cheliabinsk, Kemerovo, Altai region)
F. G. Patkovskii 1944-46
E. P. Starostein 1946 (Novosibirsk and Tomsk)
F. R. Astakhov 1946-52
S. G. Ariskin 1952-62
V. I. Ermelov 1962-63
°K. P. Borodinov 1966-
A. N. Mikhailov (Ass't) 1964-66 (for Kemerovo)
Jacob J. Fast (Ass't 1967-76

1.16 *Eastern Siberia and Far East* (Krasnoiarskii Krai, Irkutsk,
Buriat ASSR, Iakutia, Amur, Khabarovsk, Primorskii Krai, Kamchatka,
Sakhalin)
T. V. Toropov 1946-48 (for Krasnoiarskii Krai)
V. I. Kositsyn 1946- ? (for Khabarovsk region)
°E. N. Raevski 1948- (also Far East after 1957)
°Iu. A. Maksimchuk (Ass't) 1974-79; SP for Far East 1979-

1.17 *Omsk*
°K. A. Sipko 1979-

2. *Ukraine*
Senior Presbyter: A. L. Andreev 1944-66
N. N. Mel'nikov 1966-74 Dep. since 1956
°Jacob K. Dukhonchenko 1974-

Deputy Senior Presbyters:
F. G. Patkovskii 1946-48

D. I. Ponomarchuk 1946-57
A. I. Mitskevich 1948-56
F. R. Astakhov 1962-66
D. D. Shapovalov 1966-69
I. Ia. Tatarchenko 1966-72
N. V. Kuz'menko 1966-68
I. Ia Kaliuzhnyi 1966-79
°I. S. Gnida 1970-
°V. S. Glukhovski 1974-
°M. V. Mel'nik (Ass't) 1974- Served as secretary to Ukrainian
    SP since 1962

2.01 Volhynia
A. A. Agripinin 1945-52
F. O. Pavliuk 1952-62
°A. A. Nesteruk 1962-

2.02 Rovno
M. A. Nichiporuk 1945-60
P. G. Radchuk 1960-77
°N. T. Davidiuk 1977-
°A. P. Vashchishin (Ass't) 1979-

2.03 Zhitomir
V. K. Shchavlinski 1945-57
Ia. P. Grishchenko 1957-66
V. S. Glukhovski 1966-69
°Ia. M. Kravchenko 1970-

2.04 L'vov
S. M. Brichuk 1945-52
V. G. Gritchenko 1952-63
E. A. Mazin 1963-64
G. A. Goroshko 1964-69
V. S. Glukhovski 1969-74 (also Zakarpatia)
°B. I. Bilas 1974-
°P. M. Orlov (Ass't) 1974-

2.05 Ternopol
A. M. Tesliuk 1945-53
G. A. Goroshko (Ass't) 1945-54
A. A. Agripinin 1957-66
°D. L. Vozniuk 1966-

2.06 Khmel'nitskii
G. E. Lukianchuk 1945-47

V. L. Sukhanov 1947-53
E. A. Mazin 1954-63
° D. M. Andrikevich 1963-

2.07 *Zakarpatia*
E. E. Stumpf 1946-47 (P. Semenovich and Kondor Ass't).
M. A. Mocharko 1947-69
V. S. Glukhovski 1969-74
° M. M. Andriushko (Ass't) 1973-

2.08 *Chernovitsy and Ivanovo-Frankovsk*
A. G. Linev 1948-57
Z. N. Golik 1957-66 ?
° A. D. Lysiuk 1976-

2.09 *Vinnitsa*
A. P. Kishchak 1945-50 and 1958-63
P. S. Lisovenko 1950-58
D. D. Shapovalov 1963-65
° V. F. Vasilenko 1965-

2.10 *Kiev*
G. G. Aksenov 1945
F. G. Patkovski 1946
A. I. Mitskevich 1946-56
D. I. Eniukov 1957-63
L. F. Feriupko 1963-67 (Ass't 1948-63)
I. Ia. Kaliuzhnyi 1967-79 (Ass't 1948-55)
° M. V. Mel'nik 1979-
° G. I. Komendant 1979-

2.11 *Cherkassy* (until 1955 part of Kiev)
I. Ia. Kaliuzhnyi 1955-69
G. V. Nikalin (Ass't) 1956-60
D. M. Andrikevich (Ass't) 1960-63
° F. P. Lymar 1969-

2.12 *Chernigov*
A. G. Savenko 1945-57
V. K. Shchavlinskii 1957-63
I. D. Laiko 1963-69
° G. F. Spisovskii 1970-

2.13 *Sumy*
A. F. Dmitriev 1945-54
V. L. Sukhanov 1954-58

P. S. Lisovenko 1958-61 (Ass't since 1947)
A. M. Tesliuk 1961
V. K. Shchavlinskii 1962-63
F. I. Priimenko 1964-69
G. I. Pavlenko 1970-77
°V. L. Kibenko 1977-

2.14 *Poltava*
V. A. Orishechko 1945-53
A. M. Tesliuk 1953-63
N. K. Akritov 1963-70
°M. I. Vlasenko 1971-

2.15 *Kharkov*
D. A. Voinov 1945-53
P. A. Parchevskii 1953-63
N. K. Akritov 1963-64
D. D. Shapovalov 1965-78
°F. E. Starukhin 1978- (Ass't since 1976)

2.16 *Dnepropetrovsk*
N. V. Mel'nik 1945
N. N. Mel'nikov 1946-56
G. G. Ponurko 1957-66
V. M. Galenko 1966-77
°N. G. Tsuman 1977-
°V. E. Zenkin (Ass't) 1979-

2.17 *Donets* (Stalinsk)
V. V. Gaenko 1945-54
B. A. Rusanov 1954-58
A. P. Miroshnichenko (Ass't) 1956-57
I. Ia. Tatarchenko 1958-72
S. P. Fadiukhin (Ass't) 1958-60
°S. F. Karpenko 1972-

2.18 *Voroshilovgrad* (includes Lugansk)
I. P. Sushkov 1945-56
A. V. Gaivoronski 1956-70
P. G. Savchenko (Ass't) 1946
°V. T. Mitin 1970-

2.19 *Kirovograd*
V. L. Sukhanov 1946-53
A. V. Medushevski 1953-61
I. Ia. Kaliuzhnyi 1961-67 (jointly with Cherkassy)
I. S. Gnida 1967-71

N. G. Tsuman 1971-77
°A. P. Mamalat 1977-

2.20 Odessa (Ismail added in 1954)
S. V. Krapivnitski 1945-54
M. S. Lipovoi 1954-62 (had been SP for Ismail since 1946)
A. G. Kvashenko 1962-64 (Ass't since 1956)
N. V. Kuz'menko 1964-68
°A. M. Tsap 1969-

2.21 Kherson and Nikolaev (joint since 1963)
S. F. Tikhii 1945
°K. L. Kolibabchuk 1946-
    Nikolaev only: F. E. Mitriaev 1945-56
          P. K. Rudyi 1956-63

2.22 Zaporozh'e
M. G. Bova 1946
I. E. Isaichenko 1947-61
G. G. Ponurko 1958-62
K. I. Sevashko (Ass't) 1962
F. B. Kislits 1964-68
Jacob K. Dukhonchenko 1968-74
°A. G. Brynza 1975-

2.23 Crimea
A. F. Avgustinovich 1945-54
A. V. Kamyshanski 1954-57
A. P. Miroshnichenko 1957-67
D. N. Petrov 1968-69
°V. S. Meshcheriakov 1970-

3. Belorussia
    Senior Presbyter:
V. N. Chechnev 1945-58
K. S. Veliseichik 1958-76
°I. V. Bukatyi 1976-
    Deputy Senior Presbyters:
I. K. Pan'ko 1946-49
I. G. Shatura 1955-66
N. N. Germanovich 1963-65
A. M. Ketsko 1966-78
°L. S. Vladyko 1966-

3.01 Minsk
D. A. Ivanchenko 1945-57

G. A. Boiko 1957 (had been SP of Pinsk since 1948)
I. G. Shatura 1957-66
A. M. Ketsko 1966-79
° O. I. Skuratovich 1979-

3.02 *Grodno*
° K. I. Sevashko 1945-

3.03 *Brest* (Baranovichi and Pinsk added in 1957)
A. I. Alekseev 1946-49
N. A. Andresiuk 1949-57
I. G. Shatura 1957-63 (SP for Baranovichi since 1945)
N. N. Germanovich 1963-65
S. S. Lutsik (Ass't) 1963-66
U. A. Krivchen 1966-78 ?
° P. A. Mukha 1978-
    Pinsk: Vashkevich 1945-47
            G. A. Boiko 1948-57
° A. L. Sebrukovich (Ass't) 1979-

3.04 *Gomel'* (*Molodechno*)
I. K. Kul'bitskii 1946-54
I. T. Mikhailov 1954-66
A. T. Pashkovskii 1966-78 ?
° P. A. Kazakevich 1979-

3.05 Short Term Subdivisions
Vitebsk-Mogila
    N. E. Tkachev 1953-60
    A. P. Polovikov 1966- ?

Bobruisk
    Ia. M. Anikeenko 1945
Polesskoi
    L. N. Leshchenko 1953-?

4. *Moldavia*
I. G. Ivanov 1944-45
I. T. Slobodchikov 1945-49, then Ass't until 1955
F. R. Astakhov 1952-57
D. I. Ponomarchuk 1957-65
S. K. Malanchuk 1965-73
° K. S. Sedletski 1973-

5. *Latvia* (Senior Presbyter is traditionally called bishop);
    from 1945-66 N. A. Levindanto was SP for the Baltic region

K. Latseklis 1946
A. M. Korps 1946-48
A. M. Redlikh 1949-53
F. E. Khuns 1953-61
N. A. Levindanto 1961-66
P. K. Egle 1966-77
° Ia. E. Tervits 1977-

Lithuania: L. Apanasenok 1945-47
       I. M. Inkenas 1947-54
       P. Zil'berts 1954-63
Since 1979 fully part of Latvian administration

6. *Estonia*
Johannes I. Lipstock 1945-61
N. A. Levindanto 1961-66
A. M. Sil'dos 1964-68 (had been Sec. to SP since 1945)
° Robert Vyzu 1968-
° R. Kiviloo (Ass't) 1970-

7. *Caucasian Republics* (Georiga, Armenia, Azerbaidzhan)
P. Ia. Ter-Avanesov 1944-49
M. S. Dushenko 1949-57
F. R. Astakhov 1957-61
B. A. Rusanov 1961-63
P. A. Dzhaniashvili 1965-68
V. P. Krasinski 1968-74
° N. Z. Kvirikashvili 1974-

8. *Kazakhstan*
P. P. Petrov 1945-47
M. D. Tikhonov 1947-58
M. S. Vashchuk 1958-70
N. A. Kolesnikov 1970-80 (Ass't since 1968)
° F. P. Virts (Ass't) 1974-
° V. A. Shul'ts (Ass't) 1978-
° A. F. Burlakov (Ass't) 1978-
° V. V. Gorelov 1980-

9. *Kirgizia*
V. I. Andreenko 1946-56
N. A. Iadykin 1957-60
M. S. Vashchuk 1960-69
° N. N. Sizov 1969-

10. *Central Asia* (Uzebkistan, Tadzhikistan, later also Turkmenia)
Pikalov 1946
Matveev 1947
A. T. Pen'kov 1947-55
L. M. Karakai 1955-60
M. S. Vashchuk 1960-67
M. M. Samotugin 1967-76
°T. F. Kviring 1977- (Ass't since 1976)
°B. N. Serin (Ass't) 1979-

Appendix 5

CCECB Members and Council of Prisoners' Relatives

1. *Organizing Committee (Orgkomitet)* February 1962-September 1965
   A. F. Prokofiev (arrested May 1962, sentenced to 10 years prison and exile)
   G. K. Kriuchkov
   G. P. Vins
   A. A. Shalashov (died December 1963)
   N. G. Baturin

2. *Council of Churches of Evangelical Christian-Baptists* (CCECB)
   °G. K. Kriuchkov (Tula) President, 1965-
   °G. P. Vins (Kiev) Secretary 1965- (deported to USA April 1979)
   S. G. Dubovoi (Dzhezkazgan, Kazakhstan) 1965-76
   °I. Ia. Antonov (Kirovograd) 1965-
   °N. G. Baturin (Shakhty, Rostov Oblast) 1965- (elected acting secretary June 1979)
   P. A. Iakimenkov (Moscow) 1965-76
   °D. V. Miniakov (Barnaul, now Valga, Estonia) 1965-
   S. T. Golev (Riazan) 1965-76 (deceased)
   A. S. Goncharov (Prokop'evsk, Kemerovo) 1965-69 (retired)
   M. P. Kondrashov (Mozdak, N. Ossetia) 1965-69 (retired)
   M. T. Shaptala (Khartsyzsk, Donets Oblast) temporary leader 1966-69; member 1969-80.
   J. D. Bondarenko (Odessa) 1966-69 temporary member
   I. A. Punk (Zaporozh'e) 1966-69 temporary member
   °P. V. Rumachik (Dedovsk, Moscow Oblast) 1969-

° M. I. Khorev (Kishinev) 1972-
° K. K. Kreker (Novosibirsk) 1972-
° N. P. Khrapov (Tashkent) 1966-, formally a member since 1972
° B. Ia. Schmidt (Slavgorod) 1976-
° N. I. Kabysh (Zheltye vody, Dnepropetrovsk Oblast) Cand 1976-
° P. A. Artiukh (Volkovysk, Grodno, Belorussia) Cand 1976-
° P. G. Rytikov (Krasnodon, Voroshilovgrad Oblast) Cand 1976-
° S. N. Misiruk (Odessa) Cand 1976-

3. *Council of Prisoners' Relatives* (CPR)
    L. K. Govorun (Smolensk) 1964-66
    N. P. Iastrebova (Kharkov) 1964-67
        Rudneva, wife of V. T. (Semipalatinsk) 1964-67
° Lidia M. Vins (Kiev) 1967- Chairman
    N. P. Iakimenkova (Moscow) 1967-76
° A. T. Kozorezova (Omsk) 1967- (elected acting chairman 25 June
    1979)
    K. V. Kozlova (Ioshkar-Ola) 1967- ?
° Galina I. Rytikova (Krasnodon) 1970- Secretary
° A. N. Melashchenko (Seversk, Donets) 1978?-
° A. A. Senkevich (Grodno, Belorussia) 1974-
° V. P. Dombrovskaia (Saki, Crimea) 1978?-
° L. V. Rumachik (Dedovsk, Moscow) 1978?-
° S. A. Iudintseva (Khartsyzsk, Donets) 1978?-
° Z. Ia. Vel'chinskaia (Brest, Belorussia) 1978?-

° = Incumbents, December 1980
? = precise date unknown or approximate

Bibliography

I. Primary Sources

The writings of the Soviet evangelicals constitute the major source for this book. The AUCECB journal *Bratskii Vestnik* became a rich informational treasure when I prepared biographical and geographical index cards on the informational tidbits the journal contains. The book also relies heavily on Reform Baptist *Samizdat* materials, the most complete collection of which is kept at Keston College, London, although my own files are also quite extensive. Much of the *Samizdat* material before 1974 has appeared in the *Arkhiva Samizdata* (Radio Liberty, Munich) with volumes 14, 15, 19, and 27 of the *Sobranie Dokumentov Samizdata* devoted almost exclusively to religious *Samizdat*. Another rich source of information too extensive to cite in detail was the files of clippings from the Soviet and Western press plus other incidental materials in the growing collection at Keston College. Although it was often not possible to cite chapter and verse, the information gained from examining the files of the Baptist World Alliance (Washington and London offices) and the Mennonite Central Committee was of great importance. Perhaps even more valuable was the informtaion gained from systematic interviews that I have been conducting with Soviet German emigrants to West Germany since 1974.

II. Periodicals (cited more than once)

Arkhiv Samizdata (Munich), especially vols. 14, 15, 19 and 27.

Baptist Times (London).
Bratskii Listok (Fraternal Leaflet), CCECB, 1965- .
Bratskii Vestnik (Fraternal Messenger), AUCECB, 1945- .
Bulletin, Council of Prisoners' Relatives, 1970- .
Dein Reich Komme, Licht im Osten (Stuttgart).
Der Bote (Winnipeg, Canada).
Die Gemeinde (Bad Homburg, West Germany).
Ecumenical Press Service.
European Baptist Press Service (Rüschlikon, Switzerland).
Glaube in der 2ten Welt.
Glaube in der 2ten Welt Informationsdienst.
Informationen und Berichte (earlier Digest des Ostens) (Königstein/
    Taunus, West Germany).
Izvestiia.
Keston News Service.
Liudyna i svit (Man and His World, Kiev), 1965-
MCC News Service (Akron, Pennsylvania).
Mennonite Quarterly Review.
Mennonite Reporter (Waterloo, Canada).
Mennonitische Rundschau (Winnipeg, Canada).
Nachrichten von den Feldern der Verfolgung, Missionswerk Friedens-
stimme(Cologne).
Nauka i religiia (Science and Religion), Znanie, 1949- .
Newsline West (Wolfratshausen, West Germany).
Newsweek.
Pravda.
Problems of Communism.
Radio Liberty Research Bulletin (Munich).
Religion in Communist Dominated Areas (New York).
Religion in Communist Lands (Keston, England).
Religion und Atheismus in der UdSSR (Munich).
Sovetskaia rossiia.
Underground Evangelism (Glendale, California).
Vedomosti verkhovnogo soveta RSFSR. Official gazette of Supreme Soviet
    of RSFSR.
Vestnik istiny, CCECB, 1976- .
Vestnik spasenie, CCECB. Irregular, replaced by Vestnik istiny.
Voice of the Martyrs (Wurmbrand Mission, Glendale, California).
Voprosy istorii religii i ateizma (Questions of the History of Religion and
    Atheism) (Moscow).
Voprosy nauchnogo ateizma (Questions of Scientific Atheism), Academy of
    Sciences (Moscow), 1966- .

III. Books

Alexeev, Wassilij and Theofanis Stavrou. *The Great Revival.* Minneapolis: Burgess Press, 1976.

Andrew, Brother. *Battle for Africa.* Fleming H. Revell Co., 1978.

_____ *The Ethics of Smuggling.* Wheaton, Ill.: Tyndale House, 1974.

_____ *God's Smuggler.* London: Hodder and Stoughton, 1967.

Ateizm, religiia, sovremennost'. Leningrad: "Nauka," 1973.

AUCECB. *Proceedings of the All-Union Congress of Evangelical Christians-Baptists 1969.* Moscow.

Bainton, Roland. *The Reformation of the Sixteenth Century.* Boston: Beacon Press, 1952.

Barclay, William. *Daily Study Bible: The Letters to the Galatians and Ephesians.* Edinburgh: The Saint Andrew Press, 1976; rev. ed.

Barzun, Jacques. *Darwin, Marx, Wagner.* New York: Doubleday, 1958.

Belov, A. and A. Shilkin. *Diversiia bez dinamita.* 2nd ed.; Moscow, 1976.

Benson, David. *Miracle in Moscow.* Santa Barbara, Calif.: Miracle Publications Inc., 1973.

Bethell, Nicholas. *The Last Secret.* London, André Deutsch Ltd., 1974.

Die Bibel in Osteuropa. Stuttgart: Evangelisches Bibelwerk Informations-sekretariat, April 1979.

Billington, James H. *The Icon and the Axe.* New York: Alfred A. Knopf, 1968.

Blane, Andrew. "The Relations between the Russian Protestant Sects and the State 1900-1921," Unpublished Ph.D. Dissertation, Duke University, 1964.

Bolshakoff, Serge. *Russian Nonconformity.* Philadelphia: Westminster Press, 1950.

Bourdeaux, Michael. *Faith on Trial in Russia.* London: Hodder and Stoughton, 1971.

_____ *Land of Crosses.* Devon: Augustine Publishing House, Keston Book 12, 1979.

_____ *Opium of the People: The Christian Religion in the USSR.* Indianapolis: The Bobbs-Merrill Co., Inc., 1966.

_____ *Patriarch and Prophet: Persecution in the Russian Orthodox Church Today.* London: Mowbrays, 1975. 2nd ed.

_____ *Religious Ferment in Russia.* London: Macmillan, 1968.

_____ and Xenia Howard-Johnston. *Aida of Leningrad.* London: Mowbrays, 1972.

_____ (ed.), et. al. *Religious Liberty in the Soviet Union.* Keston, Kent: Keston College, 1976.

van Braght, T. *Martyrs Mirror.* 9th ed.; Scottdale, Pa.: Herald Press, 1972.

Brandenburg, Hans. *The Meek and the Mighty*. London and Oxford: Mowbrays, 1976.

Casalis, Georges, *et al. Christliche Friedenskonferenz 1968-1971*. Wuppertal: Jugenddienst Verlag, 1971.

de Chalandeau, Alexander. "The Theology of the Evangelical Christians-Baptists in the USSR as Reflected in the *Bratskii Vestnik*." Strasbourg: Faculté de Theologie Protestante, 1978.

Church and Religion in the USSR. Moscow: Novosti, 1977.

Conquest, Robert. *The Great Terror*. Pelican Book, 1968.

Costas, Orlando E. *The Church and Its Mission: A Shattering Critique from the Third World*. Wheaton, Ill.: Tyndale House, 1974.

Curtiss, John S. *Church and State in Russia 1900-1917*. New York: Columbia University Press, 1940.

_____ *Die Kirche in der Sowjetunion (1917-1956)*. Munich: Isar Verlag, 1957.

Dalton, Herman. *Der Stundismus in Russland*. Gutersloh, 1896.

Deyneka, Peter, Jr., and Anita. *A Song in Siberia*. Elgin, Ill.: David C. Cook, 1977.

Documents of Moscow 1966 All-Union Conference of Evangelical Christian-Baptists. Moscow, 1966.

Dogmatika. AUCECB Bible Correspondence Course. Moscow, 1970.

Drewery, Mary. *Richard Wurmbrand: The Man Who Came Back*. London: Hodder and Stoughton, 1974.

Dudko, Dmitrii. *Our Hope*. Crestwood, N.Y.: St. Vladimir's Seminary Press, 1977.

Dunn, Dennis. *The Catholic Church and the Soviet Government 1939-1949*. New York: Columbia University Press, 1977.

Durasoff, Steve. *The Russian Protestants: Evangelicals in the Soviet Union: 1944-1964*. Rutherford, Madison, Teaneck, Tenn.: Fairleigh Dickinson University Press, 1969.

_____ *Pentecost Behind the Iron Curtain*. 1973.

Durnbaugh, Donald F. *The Believers' Church*. London: Macmillan, 1968.

_____ (ed.). *On Earth Peace*. Elgin, Ill.: The Brethren Press, 1978.

Edie, James M., *et al.* (ed.) *Russian Philosophy*. Chicago: Quadrangle Books, 1965.

Ellis, Jane. *Georgi Vins and His Family*. Keston, Kent: Keston College, 1979.

Esau, Jakob, Sergei T. Golev and Johann Steffen. *Unter dem Schirm des Höchsten*. Wuppertal: R. Brockhaus Verlag, 1979.

Fletcher, William C. *Nikolai, Portrait of a Dilemma*. New York: Macmillan, 1968.

_____ *Religion and Soviet Foreign Policy 1945-1970*. London: Oxford

University Press, 1973.

_____. *The Russian Orthodox Church Underground 1917-1970.* London: Oxford University Press, 1971.

Fedorenko, F. *Sekty ikh vera i dela.* Moscow, 1965.

Feron, Bernard. *Gott in Sowjetrussland.* Essen, 1963.

Fireside, Harvey. *Icon and Swastika.* Cambridge, Mass.: Harvard University Press, 1971.

Francis, E. K. *In Search of Utopia.* Altona, Man.: D. W. Friesen and Sons, 1965.

Gaucher, Roland. *Opposition in the USSR 1917-1967.* New York: Funk and Wagnalls, 1969.

Gazhos, V. F. *Evoliutsia religioznogo sektantstva v Moldavii.* Kishinev, 1975.

Geiger, Max. *Aufklärung und Erweckung.* Zurich: EVZ Verlag, 1963.

Giesinger, Adam. *From Catharine to Khrushchev: The Story of Russia's Germans.* Winnipeg, Man., 1974.

Graham, Stephen. *The Way of Martha and the Way of Mary.* London: Macmillam, 1916.

Grant, Myrna. *Vanya.* Wheaton, Ill.: Creation House, 1974.

Gutsche, Waldemar. *Religion und Evangelium in Sowjetrussland.* Kassel: Oncken Verlag, 1959.

_____. *Westliche Quellen des russischen Stundismus.* Kassel: Oncken, 1959.

Halle, Louis J. *The Cold War as History.* New York: Harper and Row, 1967.

Hamm, Gerhard. *Du hast uns nie verlassen.* Wuppertal: R. Brockhaus Verlag, 1978.

Harris, Rosemary and Xenia Howard-Johnston (eds.). *Christian Appeals from Russia.* London: Hodder and Stoughton, 1968.

Hartfeld, Herman. *Glaube trotz "KGB."* Uhldingen: Stephanus Verlag, 1976.

Harasowska, Marta and Orest Olhovych (eds.). *The International Sakharov Hearing.* Baltimore-Toronto: Smolosky Publishers, 1977.

Hathaway, David. *Czechmate.* London: Lakeland, 1974.

Hayward, Max and W. C. Fletcher (eds.). *Religion and the Soviet State: A Dilemma of Power.* London, 1969.

Hearings before the Commission on Security and Cooperation in Europe, 95th Cong., Vol. II, "Religious Liberty and Minority Rights in the Soviet Union," April 27 and 28, 1977.

Hebly, Hans (J. A.). *Protestants in Russia.* Belfast: Christian Journals Ltd., 1976.

_____. *The Russians and the World Council of Churches.* Belfast-

Dublin-Ottawa: Christian Journals Limited, 1978.

Heier, Edmund. *Religious Schism in the Russian Aristocracy, 1860-1900: Radstockism and Pashkovism.* The Hague: Martinus Nijhoff, 1970.

Hershberger, Guy F. (ed.). *Recovery of the Anabaptist Vision.* Scottdale, Pa.: Herald Press, 1957.

Historical Catalogue of British Bibles. London: Bible House, 1911.

Hollenberger, Walter. *The Pentecostals.* London: SCM Press, 1972.

Individual'naia rabota s veruiushchimi. Moscow: "Mysl'," 1974.

Ipatov, A. N. *Kto takie mennonity.* Alma-Ata, 1977.

——————. *Mennonity (Voprosy formirovaniia i evoliutsii etnokonfessional' noi obshchnosti).* Moscow: "Mysl'," 1978.

Klassen, A. J. and Nelson Springer (eds.). *Mennonite Bibliography, 1631-1961.* 2 vols.; Scottdale, Pa.: Herald Press, 1977.

Kahle, Wilhelm. *Evangelische Christen in Russland und der Sowjetunion.* Wuppertal: Oncken-Verlag, 1978.

Kalendar' evangel'skikh khristian-baptistov 1976.

Kalinicheva, Z. V. *Sotsial'naia sushchnost' baptizma.* Leningrad, 1972,

Klibanov, A. I. *Religioznoe sektantstvo: sovremennost'.* Moscow: Nauka, 1969.

——————. *Istoriia religoznogo sektantstva v rossii.* Moscow, 1965.

——————. *Iz mira religioznogo sektantstva.* Moscow, 1974.

——————. (ed.). *Konkretnie issledovania sovremennykh religioznykh verovanii.* Moscow, 1967.

——————. *Religioznoe sektantstvo v proshlom i nastoiashchem.* Moscow: Nauka, 1973.

—————— and L. N. Mitrokhin, "Raskol v sovremennom baptizme," *Voprosy nauchnogo ateizma,* 3/67.

Kluttig, Robert L. *Geschichte der deutschen Baptisten in Polen von 1858-1945.* Winnipeg, Man., 1973.

Koval'skii, N. A. *Religioznye organizatsii i problemy evropeiskoi bezopastnosti i sotrudnichestva.* Moscow: Znanie 1/77.

Kolarz, Walter. *Religion in the Soviet Union.* London: Macmillan & Co., 1961.

Koltsov, N. V. *Kto takie Piatidesiatniki.* Moscow: Znanie, 1965.

Kommunisticheskaia partiia i sovetskoe pravitel'stvo o religii i tserkvi. Moscow, 1959.

Kraus, C. Norman. *Dispensationalism in America. Its Rise and Development.* Richmond, Va.: John Knox Press, 1958.

Krest'ianinov, V. F. *Mennonity.* Moscow, 1967.

Khristian, Hans, with Dave Hunt. *Mission Possible.* London: Hodder and Stoughton, 1975.

Kuroedov, V. A. *Church and Religion in the USSR.* Moscow, 1979.

_____ and A. S. Pankratov (eds.). *Zakonodatel'stvo o religioznykh kul'takh.* Moscow: Iuridicheskaia literatura, 1971.

Labedz, Leopold (ed.). *Solzhenitsyn: A Documentary Record.* 2nd ed.; London: Penguin, 1974.

Lialina, G. S. *Baptizm: Illiuzii i real'nost'.* Moscow: Politizdat, 1977.

Littell, Frank H. *The Origins of Sectarian Protestantism.* New York: Macmillan, 1952.

Luchterhandt, Otto. *Der Sowjetstaat und die Russisch-Orthodoxe Kirche.* Cologne: Verlag Wissenschaft und Politik, 1976.

_____ (ed.). *Die Religionsgesetzgebung der Sowjetunion.* Berlin: Berlin Verlag, 1978.

Marshall, Richard H., Thomas E. Bird and Andrew Q. Blane (eds.). *Aspects of Religion in the Soviet Union 1917-1967.* Chicago: University of Chicago Press, 1971.

Medvedev, Roy. *Let History Judge: The Origins and Consequences of Stalinism.* New York: Alfred A. Knopf, 1971.

Meissner, Boris. *Die Sowjetunion, die baltischen Staaten und das Völkerrecht.* Cologne, 1956.

Mennonite Encyclopedia. 4 vols.; Scottdale, Pa.: Mennonite Publishing House, 1955-59.

Mennonitisches Lexikon. 4 vols.; Korntal, West Germany: Mennonitischer Geschichtsverein, 1913-67.

Miliukov, Paul. *Outlines of Russian Culture.* Vol. I: *Religion and the Church in Russia.* New York: A. S. Barnes and Co., 1942.

Mitrokhin, L. N. *Baptism.* 2nd ed.; Moscow, 1974.

Morea, Andre. *The Book They Couldn't Ban.* London: Lakeland, 1976.

Moskalenko, A. T. *Ideologiia i deiatel'nost' khristianskikh sekt.* Novosibirsk: Nauka, 1978.

_____ *Piatidesiatniki.* Moscow, 1966.

Murashova, V. I. and A. P. Khmel'nitskaia. *Beseda po dusham.* Moscow: Politizdat, 1977.

Nesdoly, Samuel J. "Evangelical Sectarianism in Russia: A Study of the Stundists, Baptists, Pashkovites, and Evangelical Christians 1855-1917. Unpublished Ph.D. dissertation, Queen's University, 1972.

O religii i tserkvi. Sbornik dokumentov. Moscow: Politizdat, 1965.

O religii i tserkvi. Sbornik vyskazyvanii klassikov marksizma-leninizma, dokumentov KPSS i Sovetskogo gosudarstva. Moscow: Politizdat, 1977. (Contains 1929 law on cults as revised 1975)

Orleanskii, N. *Zakon o religioznykh obedineniiakh. RSFSR.* Moscow, 1930.

Paterson, John. *The Book for Every Land.* 2nd ed.; London, 1858.

Patterson, W. Morgan. *Baptist Successionism: A Critical View.* Valley Forge, Pa.: Judson Press, 1969.

Payne, Ernest A. *Out of Great Tribulation: Baptists in the USSR.* London: Baptist Union of Great Britain and Ireland, 1974.

Pipes, Richard. *The Formation of the Soviet Union.* Boston: Harvard University Press, rev. ed., 1964 by Atheneum.

Pollock, J. C. *The Christians from Siberia.* London: Hodder and Stoughton, 1964.

_____. *The Siberian Seven.* London: Hodder and Stoughton, 1979.

Prisoners of Conscience in the USSR. London: Amnesty International, 1975.

Profiles: The Helsinki Monitors. December 10, 1979.

Putintsev, P. M. *Politicheskaia rol' i taktika sekt.* Moscow, 1935.

Quebedeux, Richard. *The Young Evangelicals.* New York: Harper and Row, 1974.

von Rauch, Georg. *A History of Soviet Russia.* 5th ed.; New York: Praeger Publishers, 1967.

Regel'son, Lev. *Tragediia russkoi tserkvi, 1917-1944.* Paris: YMCA Press, 1977.

Rizhskii, M. I. *Istoriia perevodov biblii v rossii.* Novosibirsk: Nauka, 1978.

Rohrer, Norman B. and Peter Deyneka, Jr. *Peter Dynamite: "Twice-born" Russian.* Grand Rapids, Mich.: Baker Book House, 1975.

Rowe, Michael. "The Pentecostal Movement in the USSR—a Historical and Social Survey." Ph.D. dissertation being completed for Glasgow University.

Rozhkov, Vladimir, *Tserkovnye voprosy v gosudarstvennoi dume.* Rome: Opere Religiose Russe, 1975.

Rudinskii, F. M. *Svoboda sovesti v SSSR.* Moscow: Gosiurizdat, 1961.

Samizdat. Milano: Russia Christiana, 1974.

Sawatsky, Walter. "Prince Alexander N. Golitsyn (1773-1844): Tsarist Minister of Piety." Unpublished Ph.D. dissertation, University of Minnesota, 1976.

Sediulin, A. *Zakonodatel'stvo o religioznykh kul'takh.* Moscow, 1974.

Skovoroda, Grigorii. *Sochineniia v dvukh tomakh.* Moscow: "Mysl'," 1973.

Simon, Gerhard. *Church, State and Opposition in the USSR.* London: C. Hurst and Company, 1974.

_____. *Konstantin Petrovic Pobedonoscev und die Kirchenpolitik des Heiligen Sinod 1880-1905.* "Kirche im Osten," Band 7; Göttingen: Vandenhoeck & Ruprecht, 1969.

Smith, Hedrick. *The Russians.* New York: Times Books, 1976.

Soldatenko, V. Ie. *Piatidesiatniki.* Donetsk, 1972.

Solzhenitsyn, Alexander. *The Gulag Archipelago.* London: Collins, 1974.

_____. *Letter to Soviet leaders.* London: Index on Censorship, 1974.

_____. ed. *From Under the Rubble.* London: Collins and Harvill Press, 1975.

Spinka, Matthew. *The Church and the Russian Revolution.* New York, Macmillan, 1927.

Steeves, Paul. "The Russian Baptist Union, 1917-1935: Evangelical Awakening in Russia." Unpublished Ph.D. dissertation, University of Kansas, 1976.

Stoeffler, F. Ernest. *German Pietism During the Eighteenth Century.* Leiden: E. J. Brill, 1973.

_____. *The Rise of Evangelical Pietism.* Lieden: E. J. Brill, 1965.

Stroyen, W. B. *Communist Russia and the Russian Orthodox Church 1943-1962.* Washington: D.C.: The Catholic University of America Press, 1967.

Struve, Nikita. *Christians in Contemporary Russia.* London: Harvill Press, 1967.

Tepliakov, M. K. *Problemy ateisticheskogo vospitaniia v praktike partiinoi raboty.* Voronezh, 1972.

Titov, V. E. *Troitsa.* Moscow: Politizdat, 1978.

Toews, John B. *Lost Fatherland.* Scottdale, Pa.: Herald Press, 1967.

_____ (ed.). *Selected Documents: The Mennonites in Russia from 1917 to 1930.* Winnipeg, Man.: Christian Press, 1975.

Tökés, Rudolf (ed.). *Dissent in the USSR.* Baltimore: Johns Hopkins University Press, 1975.

Tolstoy, Nikolai. *Victims of Yalta.* London: Hodder and Stoughton, 1978.

Troeltsch, Ernst. *The Social Teaching of the Christian Churches.* New York: Harper Torchbook, 1960.

Vins, Georgi. *Three Generations of Suffering.* London: Hodder and Stoughton, 1976. First printed in America as *Testament from Prison.* Elgin, Ill.: David C. Cook, 1975. A second edition was entitled *Prisoner of Conscience* (1979).

Voprosy nauchnogo ateizma. Vol. XXIV, 1979. Featuring the evolution of Christian sectarianism in the USSR.

Wedel, Walter. *Nur zwanzig Kilometer.* Wuppertal: Brockhaus, 1979.

Wells, David F. and John D. Woodbridge (eds.). *The Evangelicals.* Grand Rapids, Mich.: Baker Book House, rev. ed., 1977.

Williams, George H. *The Radical Reformation.* Philadelphia: The Westminster Press, 1962.

Wurmbrand, Richard. *Tortured for Christ.*

IV. Articles

Anderson, Paul. "Reflections on Religion in Russia, 1917-1967," in Marshall (ed.), *Aspects of Religion*, pp. 11-33.

Andreev, G. L., *et al.* "Piatdesiat let nauchnogo ateizma," *Voprosy Filosofii*, December, 1967, pp. 37-47. In English translation in *Research Materials*, August, 1968, pp. 1-5.

Arsenkin, B. K. "Voprosy sovershenstvovaniia ateisticheskogo vospitaniia molodezhi," *VNA*, 22/78, pp. 199-208.

Avtorkhanov, A. "New Assault on Religion," *Problems of the Peoples of the USSR*, No. 21, Spring 1964, pp. 12-15.

Blane, Andrew. "Church and State in Soviet Russia: The Rise of a New Era," unpublished ms. 1974.

_____. "A Year of Drift," *RCL*, II, 3, 1974.

Bociurkiw, Bohdan R. "Church-State Relations in the USSR," *Survey* (January, 1968); reprinted in Hayward and Fletcher, *Religion and the Soviet State*, pp. 71-104.

_____. "Religion in the USSR after Khrushchev," John W. Strong (ed.), *The Soviet Union under Brezhnev and Kosygin*. New York: Van Nostrand, 1971, pp. 135-155.

_____. "Religious Dissent in the Soviet State," in B. R. Bociurkiw and J. W. Strong (eds.), *Religion and Atheism in the USSR and Eastern Europe*. London: Macmillan, 1975, pp. 58-90.

_____. "The Shaping of Soviet Religious Policy," *Problems of Communism*, May-June, 1973, pp. 37-51.

_____. "Soviet Research on Religion and Atheism Since 1945," *RCL*, January-February, 1974, pp. 11-16.

_____. "The Uniate Church in the Soviet Ukraine: A Case Study in Soviet Church Policy," *Canadian Slavonic Papers*, VII, 1965, pp. 89-113.

Bourdeaux, Michael and Albert Boiter. "Baptists in the Soviet Union 1960-71," *Radio Liberty Research Bulletin*, January 31, 1972.

Bresenden, Evgenii. "The Persecution of Pentecostal Evangelical Christians," in Marta Harasowska and Brest Olhovych (eds.), *The International Sakharov Hearing*. Baltimore-Toronto: Smoloskyp Publishers, 1977, pp. 158-63.

Classen, Virginia, Peter Neufeld and Vern Q. Preheim. "Glimpses of the Mennonites in Russia, 1948-1947." Unpublished research paper based on analysis of letters in *Der Bote*, Bethel College, February, 1957.

Danilov, A. and D. Tabakaru. "Kto takie 'initsiativniki'?" *Kommunist Moldavii*, XII, 1967, p. 70.

Ellis, Jane. "Religious Broadcasting into the Soviet Union," *RCL*, III, 4-5, 1975, pp. 43-48.

Ervin, P. "Mennonity," *Nauka i Religia*, No. 5, 1963, pp. 25-28.

Fletcher, William C. "Protestant Influences on the Outlook of the Soviet Citizen Today," in Fletcher and Strover (eds.), *Religion and the Search for New Ideals in the USSR*. New York: Frederick A. Praeger, 1967.

Fletcher, William C. and Donald A. Lowrie. "Khrushchev's Religious
    Policy, 1959-1964," *Aspects of Religion in the Soviet Union*, 1967.
Grossman, Gregory. "The 'Second Economy' of the USSR," *Problems of
    Communism*, XXVI (September-October, 1977), pp. 25-41.
Hebly, Hans. "Religious Liberty, the WCC and the USSR," *Religious
    Liberty in the Soviet Union*, pp. 10-24.
Iarygin, A. F. "Kharakter sovremennoi baptistskoi propovedi," *Voprosy
    nauchnogo ateizma*, No. 12, 1971, pp. 149-63.
Ipatov, A. N. "Mennonity: Proshloe i nastoiashchee," *NiR*, 5/74, pp. 40-43.
Kahle, Wilhelm. "Die Tränen der Frommen in der Gottesbegegnung: Ein
    Beitrag zur oekumenischer Spiritualität," in Andrew Blane (ed.), *The
    Ecumenical World of Orthodox Civilization*, Vol. III of *Russia and Or-
    thodoxy*. The Hague: Mouton, 1974.
_____. "Fragen der Einheit im Bunde der Evangeliumschristen-
    Baptisten in der Sowjetunion," *Kyrios*, No. 3/4, 1968, pp. 164-79.
Kelly, David. "Nairobi: A Door Opened," *RCL*, IV, 1 (Spring, 1976), pp. 4-17.
Kolosov, A. "Religiia i tserkov v SSSR," *Bolshaia Sovetskaia Entsiklopediia*.
    Moscow, 1947, pp. 1775-90.
Kraus, C. Norman. "Evangelicalism: The Great Coalition," in Kraus (ed.),
    Evangelicalism and Anabaptism. Scottdale, Pa.: Herald Press, 1979,
    pp. 39-61.
Kuroedov, V. A. "Soviet Law and Freedom of Conscience," *Izvestiia*, Jan.
    31, 1976, p. 5.
_____. "Sovetskoe gosudarstva i tserkov," *Moskovskaia Pravda*, Feb. 27,
    1977.
Lawrence, John. "Observations on Religion and Atheism in Soviet Society,"
    RCL, I, 4-5 (July-October, 1973), pp. 20-27.
Lialina, G. S. "Religiia i ateizm: problemy istorii i sovremennost'," *VNA*,
    17/75, pp. 304-309.
Lisavtsev, E. I. "Sotsialisticheskii printsip svobody i polozhenie tserkvi v
    SSSR," *VNA*, 22/78, pp. 147-58.
Logachev, Konstantin. "Fundamental Problems of Greek and Slavonic Bib-
    lical Textology," *Journal of the Moscow Patriarchate*, 2/74, pp. 76-80.
Luchterhandt, Otto. "Die religiöse Gewissensfreiheit im Sowjetstaat,"
    *Berichte des Bundesinstituts für ostwissenschaftliche und interna-
    tionale Studien*. 37 (1976), pp. 1-57; 40 (1976), pp. 4-117.
van Luyn, Ole. "Bible Work in Eastern Europe," United Bible Societies
    Background Paper, September 1977.
Modesto, P. "Die religiöse Problematik in der sowjetischen Zeitschrift
    'Woprosy Filosofii' (Fragen der Philosophie) Jahrgang 1976," *Religion
    und Atheismus in der UdSSR*, May, 1977, pp. 1-11.
_____. "Sowjetische Belletristik gegen Gott," *Religion und Atheismus*

in der UdSSR, August, 1978, pp. 15-23.

Murray, Katharine. "Death of a Baptist Musician," *RCL*, II, 1 (January-February, 1974), 8-10.

_____. "Soviet Seventh-Day Adventists," *RCL*, V, 2 (Summer, 1977), pp. 88-93.

Payne, Ernest A. "The Baptists of the Soviet Union," *Ecumenical Review*, January, 1955, pp. 161-68.

"The Pentecostalist Movement," *Radio Liberty Research*, January 31, 1975, pp. 1-10.

Protasov, E. and D. Ugrinovich. "Issledovanie religioznosti Naseleniia i ateisticheskoe vospitanie," *Politicheskoe samoobrazovanie*, 11/75, pp. 199-216.

Rempel, David G. "Introduction to Russian Mennonite Historiography," *MQR*, 1974, pp. 409-446.

_____. "The Mennonite Commonwealth in Russia," *MQR*, XLVII, 3, 1973 and XLVII, 1, 1974.

Reshetar, John S., Jr. "The Search for Law in Soviet Legality," *Problems of Communism*, July-August, 1979, pp. 61-64.

Rowe, Michael. "Soviet Policy Towards Evangelicals," *RCL*, VII, 1 (Spring, 1979), pp. 4-12.

_____. "Pentecostal Documents from the USSR," *RCL*, January-June, 1975, pp. 16-18.

Sawatsky, Walter. "Baptist Claims about Dramatic Improvement Assessed," *Keston News Service*, May 21, 1976.

_____. "Bible Work in Eastern Europe," *RCL*, III, 3, 4-10.

_____. "A Call for Unity Issued by a Russian Baptist Leader," *MQR*, L, 3, 1976, 230-39.

_____. "Mennonite Congregations in the Soviet Union Today," *Mennonite Life*, March, 1978, pp. 12-26.

_____. "The Reform Baptists Today," *RCL*, VIII, 1, 1980, 28-38.

_____. "Religious Administration and Modernization," in Dennis Dunn (ed.), *Religion and Modernization in the Soviet Union*. Boulder, Col.: Westview Press, 1978, pp. 60-104.

_____. "Secret Soviet Lawbook on Religion," *RCL*, IV, 4 (Winter, 1976), 24-34.

_____. "Union of Soviet Socialist Republics," *Mennonite World Handbook* (Lombard, Ill.), 1978, pp. 63-71.

Sider, Ronald J. "Evangelicalism and the Mennonite Tradition," in C. Norman Kraus (ed.), *Evangelicalism and Anabaptism*, pp. 149-168.

Synan, Vinson. "Theological Boundaries: The Arminian Tradition," in Wells and Woodbridge, pp. 38-57.

Taylor, Pauline B. "Sectarians in Soviet Courts," *The Russian Review*, July,

1965, pp. 278-88.

Timasheff, N. S. "Urbanization, Operation, Anti-Religion and the Decline of Religion in the USSR," *American Slavic and East European Review*, XIV (April, 1955), pp. 234-35.

Toews, John B. "The Origins and Activities of the Mennonite *Selbstschutz* in the Ukraine (1918-1919)," *MQR*, January, 1972, pp. 4-40.

Ton, Josef. "The Christian Manifesto," *RCL*, Supplementary Paper, January, 1976.

Tucker, Robert C. "Party and Church in the Soviet Union—Travel Notes," *The Russian Reivew*, 1959, pp. 285-93.

Waddams, Herbert. "The Church in Soviet Russia," *Soviet Studies*, July, 1953, pp. 8-17.

"West Coast Bible Smugglers: Less Cloak and More Dagger," *Christianity Today*, March 2, 1979, pp. 50-52.

Willetts, Harry. "De-opiating the Masses," *Problems of Communism*, 6/64, pp. 32-41.

Wingren, Gustav. "Human Rights: A Theological Analysis," *Ecumenical Review*, XXVII, 2, 1975, pp. 124-27.

Zacek, Judith Cohen. "The Russian Bible Society and the Russian Orthodox Church," *Church History*, No. 4, 1966, pp. 411-37.

Zlobina, N. S. "Sovremennyi baptizm i ego ideologiia," *Voprosy istorii religii i ateizma*, Vol. IX, 1963, pp. 95-125.

Index

Walter Sawatsky, of Altona, Manitoba, is the Mennonite Central Committee liaison and representative for MCC programs in Europe and responsible for MCC's East/West Research Office in Neuwied, West Germany. He has traveled frequently in the Soviet Union since 1973—for two extended periods as a graduate student in the Canada-USSR Cultural Exchange Program, as a tourist, and as an official church representative.

From 1973 to 1976 he was MCC research scholar at Keston College's Centre for the Study of Religion and Communism at Keston, Kent, England.

Sawatsky holds the PhD and MA degrees from the University of Minnesota, a BA in history from Goshen College, and a diploma in sacred music from Steinbach Bible Institute.

He is a member of the American Association for the Advancement of Slavic Studies, the American Historical Association, and Church and Peace (Germany). His articles have appeared in the international religious and Mennonite press.

Walter and Margaret (Warkentin) Sawatsky are members of Gospel Mennonite Church (EMMC), Winnipeg. They are the parents of Natasha and Alexander.